THE YALE EDITION
of the
GEORGE ELIOT LETTERS

VIII

THE
George Eliot Letters

EDITED BY Gordon S. Haight

Professor Emeritus of English, Yale University

VOLUME VIII
1840–1870

New Haven and London, YALE UNIVERSITY PRESS

1978

Published with assistance from
the Louis Effingham deForest Memorial Fund.

Copyright © 1978 by Yale University.
All rights reserved. This book may not be reproduced, in
whole or in part, in any form (beyond that copying permitted
by Sections 107 and 108 of the U.S. Copyright Law and except
by reviewers for the public press), without written permission
from the publishers.
Library of Congress catalog card number: 52–12063
International standard book number: 0–300–01968–8

Set in Monophoto Baskerville by
Asco Trade Typesetting Limited, Hong Kong.
Printed in the United States of America by
The Vail Ballou Press, Binghamton, N.Y.

Published in Great Britain, Europe, Africa, and Asia (except
Japan) by Yale University Press, Ltd., London. Distributed in
Australia and New Zealand by Book & Film Services,
Artarmon, N.S.W., Australia; and in Japan by Harper & Row,
Publishers, Tokyo Office.

CONTENTS OF VOLUME VIII

PREFACE TO VOLUMES VIII AND IX	vii
ACKNOWLEDGMENTS	xiii
GEORGE ELIOT'S CORRESPONDENTS	xvii

LETTERS 1840–1870

GRIFF AND FOLESHILL	3
THE WESTMINSTER REVIEW	21
21 CAMBRIDGE STREET, HYDE PARK	83
GE IN GERMANY WITH GHL	113
LIVING BY THE PEN	137
ADAM BEDE	219
THE MILL ON THE FLOSS AND *SILAS MARNER*	255
ROMOLA	297
FORTNIGHTLY REVIEW AND *PALL MALL GAZETTE*	325
FELIX HOLT AND *THE SPANISH GYPSY*	371
THORNIE'S DEATH	443

PREFACE TO VOLUMES VIII AND IX

THESE ADDITIONAL VOLUMES of *The George Eliot Letters* are frankly supplementary, every item being linked to the original edition by volume, page, and line number. Many letters of which only fragments could be quoted in the earlier volumes from booksellers' catalogues or other printed sources have now been completed, either by supplying the missing passages among the Addenda in Volume IX or in a few cases by reprinting the whole text.

The largest group of new letters are the forty written to George Combe, the phrenologist, which were found in the voluminous collection of his papers at the National Library of Scotland. Written in the 1850s while George Eliot was editing the *Westminster Review*, they throw fresh light upon those eventful years at Chapman's house in the Strand. Several letters about Chapman's affairs by Combe and others are also included here.

The most startling of the new letters are those George Eliot wrote to Herbert Spencer in 1852, when it was rumored that they were engaged to be married. My search for them began in 1937. Learning from the secretary of the Spencer trustees, Mr. T. W. Hill, that some of his papers had been deposited "at the British Museum and other places," I applied again in 1943 to Dr. Eric Millar, the Keeper of Manuscripts, who again professed ignorance of George Eliot's letters to Spencer. The outbreak of war and Mr. Hill's death delayed further efforts to find them. Then, by serendipity in 1954, while pursuing a quite different matter, I heard from Sir Arthur Keith, the last of the trustees, that about six of George Eliot's letters to Spencer had been "duly deposited in the British Museum." A renewed inquiry brought from Mr. A. T. Collins, who had become Keeper of Manuscripts, a reluctant admission that they were indeed there:

When the offer to deposit was made in 1935, however, two conditions were imposed, and accepted by the Trustees of the British Museum, namely, (1) that the packet should not be opened until the expiry of fifty years and (2) that the fact of the deposit should not be made public. In view of the latter stipulation, I must request you to treat this information as strictly confidential.

Mr. Collins's letter was headed CONFIDENTIAL, underlined in red ink. I should have been less faithful in keeping my promise if he had told me that the packet (Reserve 49) was inscribed: "Not to be opened for fifty years from the present time (August 1935) without the permission of the Trustees of the British Museum," some of whom were my friends. In 1975 Professor

Richard Schoenwald, preparing to write a book on Spencer, was given permission to see these letters, which with several misreadings he published in the *New York Public Library Bulletin.*

Though they scarcely alter the picture of George Eliot as an ardent, generous nature offering herself to an egoist who could love nothing but his own "image," the letters reveal an astonishing intensity of passion.

> I want to know if you can assure me that you will not forsake me, that you will always be with me as much as you can and share your thoughts and feelings with me. If you become attached to some one else, then I must die, but until then I could gather courage to work and make life valuable, if only I had you near me. I do not ask you to sacrifice anything—I would be very good and cheerful and never annoy you. But I find it impossible to contemplate life under any other conditions. If I had your assurance, I could trust that and live upon it. I have struggled—indeed I have—to renounce everything and be entirely unselfish, but I find myself utterly unequal to it. Those who have known me best have always said, that if ever I loved any one thoroughly my whole life must turn upon that feeling, and I find they said truly.

These are not the words of a romantic adolescent, but of a desperately earnest woman thirty-two years old. Spencer rejected her appeal on the ground that George Eliot's lack of beauty made it impossible for him to love her: "Strongly as my judgment prompted, my instincts would not respond." But she "took it all smilingly," he wrote, and they remained friends always. And though he could not love her—or any woman—it was through him (and to his "immense relief") that she came to know George Henry Lewes, on whose love her whole life was to turn.

After they went off to Germany together, George Eliot's affairs were so closely bound with Lewes's that it is impractical to separate their letters. He conducted all the negotiations for publication, foreign reprints, and translations of her novels, often in letters concerned with his own writings. As her fame increased, he undertook more and more of her ordinary correspondence as well. I have therefore included in these volumes all that I have found of Lewes's letters between 1854 and his death in 1878. Letters from his three sons, a little confused at first to find themselves with two "mothers," furnish some intimate sidelights on George Eliot's family life. Thornton, the middle son, was the most voluble, filling his letters with poems, stories, and jokes during his school-days, and after his emigration to Natal, with lengthy accounts of that turbulent region. Space could be spared for only a few of them, but I hope one day to edit a volume of the early letters of Lewes with those of the other members of his family.

Lewes's work as editorial adviser to George Smith on the *Cornhill Magazine* from June 1862 to October 1864, and on the *Pall Mall Gazette* in 1865–66, has left scant record in the letters because most of it was done in personal meetings. But for the *Fortnightly Review*, of which Lewes was the principal planner and author of the Prospectus, his solicitation of articles required correspondence with a brilliant group of writers, among them: Anthony Trollope, who persuaded Lewes to become the first editor, Frederic Harrison, E. S. Beesly, Moncure Conway, T. H. Huxley, George Meredith, Lord Houghton, Lord Amberley, Robert Lytton, Robert Buchanan, and Philip Hamerton. Under the strain of gathering 128 pages of varied and original articles each fortnight, Lewes's health, always precarious, soon failed, and he was compelled to resign the editorship in December 1866. However, he continued to write for the *Fortnightly* from time to time. His articles on Darwin in 1868 led to their interesting correspondence. His relations with Huxley were cordial, if not close. Richard Owen, to whom Lewes had dedicated *Sea-side Studies* in 1858, opposed Darwin's theory of natural selection, clinging to his old belief in design, about which Lewes had long disputed with him; his last letter to Owen is an attempt to assure him that an allusion in a *Fortnightly* article intended no sarcasm. Lewes was now in touch with the younger generation of philosophers and physiologists: G. Croom Robertson, editor of *Mind*, Henry Sidgwick, James Sully, H. C. Bastian, and others, to some of whom George Eliot appealed for guidance in founding the George Henry Lewes Studentship of Physiology in his memory at Cambridge.

During Lewes's connection with these periodicals George Eliot took no active part, though she contributed some slight articles to each of them. Her concern for education appears in her correspondence with Emily Davies about the proposed college for women (Girton), toward which she contributed £50 "from the author of *Romola*," but Mrs. Malleson was unable to stir much enthusiasm in her for a college for working women. Barbara Bodichon tried vainly to enlist her in the campaign for women's rights. As George Eliot told John Morley, she believed that the enfranchising of women was not the solution; "as a fact of mere zoological evolution woman seems to me to have the worse share in existence," and it was "the function of love in the largest sense to mitigate the harshness of all fatalities."

After she became famous many who had scorned the "strong-minded woman living with Lewes" eagerly sought her society. Because of the peculiarity of her position she made it a rule to accept no invitations and to return no calls—a rule she seldom broke. Away from London she occasionally paid brief visits—to Oscar Browning at Eton, to Barbara Bodichon on the Isle of Wight, to W. G. Clark or F. W. H. Myers at Cambridge, to Mark Pattison or Benjamin Jowett at Oxford. George Eliot first met Jowett 1 January 1871, when she was staying with Mrs.

William Cross at St. George's Hill, Weybridge; the following August he sent her a box of game; in October he asked if he might call; and thereafter, almost every year until Lewes died, they went to spend a few days with him at Balliol. Jowett's letters to her are of particular interest.

The Cross family, whom she first met at Rome in 1869, of course occupy an important place in the Leweses' latter years. Mrs. Cross, a hearty, gregarious widow only five years older than George Eliot, lived at Weybridge with the six of her nine children who were not yet married. The Leweses often came to this cheerful household for lunch and a country walk or for longer visits during the Christmas holidays. John, the second son, was a banker in London, and Lewes naturally consulted him for advice about investing the thousands of pounds coming to George Eliot from *Middlemarch*. Many of his letters to "Nephew Johnnie," as they called him, deal with financial matters.

All her life, even in her schooldays, George Eliot attracted the confidences of younger persons, both in private conversation and in letters. Like other novelists, from Samuel Richardson to Virginia Woolf, she would draw them out, and while offering them sympathy, deepen her own knowledge of human nature. Mary Ponsonby came to her with religious doubts; Oscar Browning, with the problem of his dismissal from Eton. Georgiana Burne-Jones, having confided her marital difficulties, could not conceal her chagrin that George Eliot, who had looked so closely into her life, had given no hint of her own intention to marry John Cross. Some of the young women held obviously lesbian feelings toward George Eliot. Few of her letters to them have survived. Cross published extracts from some of those to Mrs. Congreve, who had loved her "lover-wise." For years I pursued the manuscripts, which were left to Mrs. Congreve's niece, Miss Emily Geddes: from Hampstead to Leamington, through convents in Warwickshire and Kent to Folkestone, where in 1953 I failed to persuade Miss Geddes to let me read them. After her death, with the help of Mr. Norman Ouvry, the Public Trustee, I continued the hunt until a search of her papers in the last place of deposit, a bank at Maidstone, forced us to the inevitable conclusion that (as she threatened to do) Miss Geddes had destroyed the letters. Edith Simcox guarded her letters from George Eliot so jealously that neither Charles Lewes nor Cross dared even ask to see them. They were undoubtedly cremated with her. But she left behind an extraordinary "Autobiography of a Shirt Maker," which contains in most vivid detail an account of her relations with the Leweses during their last years. I have quoted extensively from it in Volume IX.

One group of letters I should like even more to see consists of those from Lewes to George Eliot. On the first anniversary of his death she wrote

Preface

in her Journal: "Read his letters and packed them together to be buried with me." There in her tomb in Highgate Cemetery lies the record of that love upon which her whole life turned. There let it lie in peace.

Since the first volumes of this work were published a quarter century ago, George Eliot's letters have received increasing attention. Desirable as it would be, I have not been able to follow their migration from one collector to another; the location given in the headnote must usually remain that where I found and copied the manuscript. I have tried to list previous publications when known but, in other cases, have abandoned the designation "Hitherto unpublished." Among the Addenda will be found, besides the unpublished portions of new manuscripts, numerous changes in tentative datings that require transposing and alteration of headings. The Corrigenda set right a dismaying quantity of mistakes ranging from simple typographical errors, some of the worst of which were truly the printer's fault, to gross examples of my own ignorance. Some that have gone so long unnoticed I was tempted to pass over rather than expose my shame. But having labored for more than forty years to establish a faithful text of George Eliot's letters, I could not omit any correction, however humiliating, and for the many that probably remain I can plead only failing eyesight.

The index incorporates all the corrections as well as the old and new material. Every entry in it has been verified by my dear wife, to whom this book is affectionately rededicated.

ACKNOWLEDGMENTS

Many of those to whom I expressed gratitude in Volume I have continued their help in the completion of this work. Before her death 3 November 1974 Mrs. E. Carrington Ouvry transferred the copyright of unpublished George Eliot and George Henry Lewes manuscripts to her grandson, Mr. Jonathan Ouvry, of 1 The Sanctuary, London S.W.1, who has extended the permission for these volumes. Since most of the manuscripts have now found permanent place in libraries, fewer have been gathered here from private sources.

The National Library of Scotland has made important additions to its great collection by the generous gift of the Blackwood letter books and the purchase of the firm's ledgers, which provide details of the publication of George Eliot's works. The papers of George Combe supply a rich fund of information about the *Westminster Review* during George Eliot's connection with it in the 1850s. For permission to use the new materials I renew my thanks to Mr. James Ritchie, Keeper of Manuscripts, who has been a staunch friend of this edition for more than thirty years. To Mr. Alan Bell, Assistant Keeper of Manuscripts, I am also grateful for constant help in editing them.

At Yale University the George Eliot and George Henry Lewes Collection in the Beinecke Library has grown steadily. My thanks are due to Mr. Herman W. Liebert, Librarian Emeritus, and to Mr. Louis L. Martz, Director, for their zeal in acquiring manuscripts and for permission to publish them. To Mr. Kenneth M. Nesheim, Associate Director, Miss Marjorie G. Wynne, Research Librarian, Mrs. Christa A. Sammons, Mr. Donald G. Gallup, and others of the Beinecke staff, I am grateful for unfailing assistance.

At Princeton University Mr. Alexander P. Clark, Curator of Manuscripts, Mr. Alexander D. Wainwright, Curator of the Morris L. Parrish Collection, and Mr. Robert H. Taylor, whose generosity to scholars matches Mr. Parrish's, have all given their support. I am obliged to Mr. Rodney G. Dennis, Curator of Manuscripts at the Houghton Library, Harvard University, for his cooperation. To Mrs. Lola L. Szladits, Curator of the Henry W. and Albert A. Berg Collection at the New York Public Library, I offer sincere appreciation for permission to publish the many new letters that have been acquired. The British Library (formerly the

British Museum) has provided some of the finest letters in these volumes. My thanks are due to the Trustees for permission to publish them and to Dr. Daniel P. Waley, Keeper of Manuscripts, for making them accessible. Mr. S. H. Barlow, during whose term as Librarian the Nuneaton Public Library greatly increased its George Eliot collection, thoughtfully sent me copies of the new letters as they appeared.

To the authorities of the following institutions I gratefully record permission to publish manuscripts in their libraries: Balliol College, Oxford; Bibliothèque Nationale; Birmingham Reference Library; Bodleian Library; Boston Public Library; Brotherton Library; Bryn Mawr College.

University of California, Berkeley; University of California, Los Angeles; Cambridge University Library; Canberra National Library; Colby College; Colorado College; Columbia University; Cornell University; Coventry City Libraries.

Dartmouth College; Drew University; Fitzwilliam Museum; Folger Library; Frankfurter Goethemuseum; Girton College, Cambridge; Haverford College; Huntington Library and Art Gallery.

University of Illinois; Imperial College of Science, London; Indiana University; University of Iowa; the John Work Garrett Library of the Johns Hopkins University; University of Kansas; Knox College.

Institute of Russian Literature, Academy of Sciences, Leningrad; University College, London; University of London; McGill University; the Bertrand Russell Archives, McMaster University; University of Minnesota; Pierpont Morgan Library.

University of Newcastle; Newnham College, Cambridge; the Fales Collection, New York University; University of North Carolina; Ohio University, Athens.

Historical Society of Pennsylvania; Pennsylvania State University; Carl H. Pforzheimer Library; Royal College of Music, London; the John Rylands Library; the L. W. Smith Collection, Washington's Headquarters, Morristown, New Jersey.

Taylor Institution Library, Oxford; Tennyson Research Centre, Lincoln; University of Texas; Trinity College, Cambridge; University of Virginia; University of Washington; Wellesley College; Dr. Williams's Library, London.

Among private owners of manuscripts I am especially obliged to Mr. Gordon N. Ray, perhaps the most active collector in recent years, who has taken a warm interest in my work from the beginning. Lady Hermione Cobbold and the Hon. David Lytton Cobbold have kindly allowed me to publish both sides of the Leweses' correspondence with the Lyttons. I am grateful to Mr. George Howard for permission to include the letters in

Acknowledgments

his library at Castle Howard. Mrs. Bettina Williams Gojnic, a granddaughter of Herbert Arthur Lewes, permitted me to make copies of her family letters, now in the Nuneaton Public Library. Others to whom I am indebted for letters are: Mr. Percival R. Allen; Miss V. E. C. Balfour-Browne; Mr. Christopher Beauman; Miss Mary Benjamin; Mr. Douglas C. Ewing; Mrs. Maud Hamer; Mr. James L. Harlan, Jr.; Dr. Peter Helps; Mr. Frederick W. Hilles; Mrs. Donald F. Hyde; the Dowager Countess of Iddesleigh; Mrs. Susan Lowndes Marques; Mr. Michael Mason; Mr. Blake Nevius; Mr. Simon Nowell-Smith; Mr. William E. Stockhausen; Miss M. Tait; Dame Rebecca West; and Mrs. Michael Womersley.

Mr. Kenneth A. McKenzie, author of *Edith Simcox and George Eliot*, gave me his transcript of the Simcox Autobiography, in the Bodleian Library, which furnishes the most intimate details of George Eliot's last years. Mr. Walter E. Houghton, editor of *The Wellesley Index to Victorian Periodicals*, supplied helpful information from forthcoming volumes of that indispensable book. Throughout the course of my work on George Eliot I have relied on the advice and friendship of Geoffrey and Kathleen Tillotson. Others who have helped in ways too various to mention are Mrs. Rosemary D. Ashton; the Hon. Betty Askwith; Mr. John Bakeless; Mrs. Marjorie Barclay; Mr. James D. Barry; Marnie, Lady Bassett; Mr. Nicholas Baum; Mrs. Joan Bennett; Mr. Thomas G. Bergin; Mr. Kenneth Blackwell; Mrs. Ann Blainey; Mrs. Vernon N. Bobbitt; Mr. Richard Bowden; Mrs. Charles Boxer; Mrs. P. M. Bradford; Mr. Gerald Brenan, Mrs. Margot Butt.

Mr. Robert A. Colby; Mrs. Elizabeth Adams Daniels; Mr. John R. De Bruyn; Miss Naomi Diamond; Miss Susan Eade; Mr. Joel W. Egerer; Mr. Laurence Elvin; Mr. Edwin Mallard Everett; Mr. Kenneth J. Fielding.

Mrs. Margaret Gaskell; Miss Rosemary Graham; Mr. David Bonnell Green; Mr. Heinrich Henel; Miss Jane Hilton; Mr. Edgar W. Hirshberg; Mr. F. K. Hoyt; Mr. G. Evelyn Hutchinson; Mr. Sidney C. Hutchison.

Mr. E. G. Jacoby; Lady Jeffreys; Mr. E. Dudley H. Johnson; Mrs. Helen E. Jones; Mr. R. T. Jones; Mr. John Pike Judson; Mrs. Alice P. Kaminsky; Mr. Victor Kennett; Mr. Mikhail A. Kraminsky.

Mr. Cecil Lang; Mr. Geoffrey Larken; Miss Marghanita Laski; Mr. John Lehmann; Mr. Laurence Lerner; Mr. J. Lester; Mr. Roger Lonsdale; Mr. Anthony McCobb; Mr. David Masson; Mr. Douglas Matthews; Mr. Frank Miles; Miss Sondra Miley; Mr. William Morse.

Miss Diana Nelson; Miss Judith Oppenheimer; Mr. Richard Ormond; Mr. R. J. Owens; Mr. Frank Paluka; Mr. R. N. Parkinson; Mr. Thomas Pinney; Miss Diana Postlethwaite; Mr. John Preston.

Mr. Vincent Quinn; Mr. F. W. Ratcliffe; Mr. Graham Reynolds; Mrs. John Rintoul; Mr. Edmund T. Silk; Mr. Kenneth Sisam; Mr. Michael Slater; Mrs. Barbara Smalley; Mr. Sidney Smith; Mr. Warren H. Smith; Lord Snow; Miss Dora Steer; Mr. Boris L. Suchkov; Mr. Roger G. Swearingen.

Mr. Fred C. Thomson; Mrs. C. Humphry Trevelyan; Mr. J. R. Tye; Mr. Paul Viallaneix; Mrs. T. Voronova; Mr. Patrick H. Waddington; Mr. Ralph Walker; Mr. Roy Walker; Mr. Peter Walne; Mr. R. K. Webb; Mr. Hermann Weigand; Miss H. M. Young.

GEORGE ELIOT'S CORRESPONDENTS

I, lxi:15   GEORGE COMBE

George Combe (1788–1858), son of an Edinburgh brewer, was educated at the High School there and for two years at the University. He practised law and for a time took charge of the family brewery. After hearing Spurzheim lecture he became an enthusiastic convert to phrenology, which he regarded as the key to every social and philosophical problem. He too began to lecture on the subject and wrote a manual called *Elements of Phrenology* (1824), which made his name widely known. In 1833 he married Cecilia, daughter of the famous actress Sarah Siddons. The £15,000 that she brought him, added to his own fortune after retiring from the business, gave him an annual income of about £1,000, and he spent the rest of his life writing on education and penal reform with phrenology as the guiding principle.

Combe's book, falling by chance into his hands, made an enthusiastic believer of Charles Bray, who had a cast made of his own head and in 1842, soon after meeting GE, had one made of hers, the better to gauge her character from the bumps on her skull. In 1851 when Combe came to visit the Brays, he too examined the head of the learned translator of Strauss and recorded his reading of her propensities in his Journal 29 August. His admiration of her intellect increased during his dealing with her as editor of the *Westminster Review*, which Combe supported in hope of using it as an organ of his views on educational reform. In 1852 GE visited the Combes in Edinburgh, and she was thrice invited to go abroad with them. But in 1854 the revelation that she was living with GHL in Germany forced Combe to admit that phrenology had failed to read her character. He inquired—vainly, of course—whether there was not insanity in GE's family, "for her conduct, with *her* brain, seems to me like morbid mental aberration." All correspondence between them ceased.

I, lxxiii:23   THE EARL OF LYTTON

Edward Robert Bulwer Lytton, first Earl of Lytton (1831–91) was tossed about in childhood by the violent disagreements and separation of his parents Edward and Rosina Bulwer Lytton. After three idle years at

Harrow he was sent to Washington in 1850 as unpaid attaché to his uncle Sir Henry Bulwer, the British Minister there. Other diplomatic appointments followed at Florence, Paris, Vienna, Athens, Constantinople, Madrid, and Lisbon. His early interest in poetry was stimulated by acquaintance with the Brownings in Florence. He published his first volume, *Clytemnestra, the Earl's Return, the Artist, and Other Poems*, under the pseudonym "Owen Meredith" in 1855; it was reviewed by GHL in the *Leader*. His poem "A Great Man" in *All the Year Round* in 1862 stirred GE to write a letter of approval to the anonymous author which has not been found; Lytton's reply is at Yale. GHL had met him while staying with Bulwer Lytton at Knebworth. Their correspondence, beginning with a letter about his poem "Apple of Life" in the *Fortnightly* in 1865, continued until GHL's death. To him Lytton sent the manuscripts of most of his poems for criticism and advice about their publication. His repeated invitations brought GE and GHL to visit them in Vienna in 1870. When the Lyttons were in England they called often at the Priory, and Lytton spent the night with the Leweses at Earlswood Common in 1874. After his appointment as Viceroy of India he wrote them long and amusing letters.

I, lxxv:1   EDITH SIMCOX

Of the many young women in whom GE inspired intense personal affection Edith Jemima Simcox (1844–1901) was surely the most singular. The daughter of a London merchant, she had two elder brothers, both fellows of Queen's College, Oxford. Though little is known of her early life or education, she was—by any standard—learned. She quoted Latin easily, read Plato in Greek, spoke French fluently enough to address meetings of the International Working Men's Association in Paris, and once considered compiling a German-English dictionary. She wrote for *Fraser's*, the *Academy*, the *Nineteenth Century*, and other leading journals articles of extraordinary range and quality. At the same time she led an active life as a reformer, working on the London School Board for compulsory secular education and organizing a commercially successful co-operative of shirt makers, the worst of the sweated trades for women.

Edith's acquaintance with GE began in December 1872, soon after the publication of the last book of *Middlemarch*, which she reviewed brilliantly in the *Academy*. She was soon one of the regular callers at the Priory. Her ardent adoration was shared and encouraged by GHL as an aid in his constant struggle to overcome GE's diffidence. He could hardly have suspected the pathological depth of Edith's obsession revealed in her remarkable journal entitled Autobiography of a Shirt Maker, the MS of which is now in the Bodleian Library. Her notes from October 1877 until GE's death supply the most minutely detailed account of GE and her conversation. Like Elma Stuart, whose correspondence with GE also began in 1872, Edith was one of a number of "spiritual daughters" who were encouraged to call GE "Mother." But in Edith's feeling for her there was a paradoxical lesbian element, which GE ultimately extinguished by the confession that

> she had never all her life cared very much for women—it must seem monstrous to me—I said I had always known it. She went on to say, what I also knew, that she cared for the womanly ideal, sympathised with women and liked for them to come to her in their troubles, but while feeling near to them in one way, she felt far off in another—the friendship and intimacy of men was more to her.[1]

Three days after GE's funeral Edith was at Coventry making inquiries about her idol's life with some intention of writing a biography, which she had to resign when Cross announced his plan. The scores of letters GE had written to her she kept as sacred relics, reread from time to time, but seen by no other eyes. Had they survived they would have formed one of the more extensive groups of GE's correspondence. Though Cross, through Charles Lewes, made a tentative approach toward them, he knew that he could not hope to use them in the *Life*. Edith's name occurs occasionally in GE's letters to others, but (like John Chapman's) is omitted from Cross's index. The Autobiography of a Shirt Maker gives a perhaps more vivid impression of GE's relation with this extraordinary woman. Professor K. A. McKenzie has told her story well in *Edith Simcox and George Eliot*, with an introduction by Gordon S. Haight (Oxford University Press, 1961).

1. Autobiography, 9 March 1880.

LETTERS 1840–1870

Griff and Foleshill

1840–1849 Letters to Martha Jackson, Mary Sibree, and Fanny Houghton.
1846 October 21 GE's "Bücherwurm" letter to Charles Bray.

I, 76:11 GE TO MARTHA JACKSON, GRIFF, 16 DECEMBER 1840

MS: Mr. Gordon N. Ray. *Address:* Miss Martha Jackson | Gobions | near Hertford | Free. *Postmark:* COVENTRY | DE 17 | 1840.

Griff | December 16th 1840.

My dear little cherished sprig of Ivy,

If in the rapid progression of society, women among other attained natural and equal rights should get a seat on the judicial bench and you should be among the recipients of that honourable distinction, bear in mind this instance in your experience of the deceptiveness of circumstantial evidence. I mean the fact that I have allowed week after week to slip away without sending you any indication of my existence, as though I had either become defunct or my affection for you had had a like fate, or, a still blacker inference, that it was never more than a vox et preterea nihil;[1] while spite of all this logical, mathematical and moral proof that your memory if registered by me at all rested on an unturned leaf, I have, I say, written of you, talked of you, eulogized you, scolded you, laughed at you, meditated on you, and a still rarer thing let me tell you, loved, veritably loved you! This very eloquent exordium I hope will establish my innocence as to the main charge you have been inclined to prefer against me, that of faithlessness; but lest you should still harbour a suspicion that I have been too *idle* even to gratify my feelings (a case not uncommon) I must claim the liberty of self-vindication on that head. Jessie can bear me witness that hands head and heart have been fully occupied for the last fortnight, and I must trust to my reputation for veracity to convince you that such has been my case since I received your letter. Our dear Jessie has been making a short and I fear dull séjour with me but I hope to have her again before her return to London if my fitful prospects are not by that time of such a character as to render me *unvisitable*. But I forget my resolution to send you my castigatory animadversions on certain conduct of yours which has outlawed you forever from the community (by no means a happy one I confess) of the susceptible. Would that I knew by what part Mother Nature held you when she plunged you in the insensibility-bestowing stream! I would quickly apprize Cupid and Mr. Field, that they might unitedly lay siege to the pregnable quarter. Seriously, as people say when they bethink themselves that they are talking folly,

1. Plutarch, "Laconic Apothegms," no. 13. *Plutarchi Opera Moralia*, ed. Daniel Wyttenbach, 1795, I, 929.

I cannot help regretting in the language of an acquaintance[2] of ours "That that has not been carried on congruously which was so well begun." I am so strongly biassed to the opinion that the 'rose distilled' is not only earthlier happier than that which withers on the virgin thorn,[3] but that it has higher or rather more humanly available aids to the prelibations[4] and the enjoyment of heavenly bliss, that my trust in the provision of the most suitable conditions for you is not adequate to the making me resigned under the fear that you are not to be united to one who wins opinions so golden as does Mr. Field. After all I am no judge about the matter, an avowal which you will think an abortive attempt at humility after a page full of my dicta concerning it.

I have today, my dear Patty, gone through a little episode in my epic life which when I tell you that it has utterly disqualified me for the enjoyment of a book, notwithstanding the charming security which the snow gives for the continuance of my beloved solitude, you will believe to be a sufficient if not an exonerating reason for my writing extra profitlessly. I have most of the day been bending my gaze on vacancy[4a] in a way that a student of the fine arts might give something to witness, and I give you its last stage only because I expect full occupation to-morrow. I believe I half pledged myself to send you some lines on a quartette of words uttered by you in one of our strolls. I have not fulfilled that pledge but until I do or in case I never should will you accept those I send as a substitute? *Not to be copied*, on the supposition that some of the many wishers for worthless things in this world of wishers should desire to possess the lines. My head is aching as well as silly to-night, so for my credit and conscience sake I will resort to that cheap mode of appearing wise—keeping silence—just as some people have lived on the fame of being rich, never paying a debt because their creditors trusted to their imagined strongboxes. I venture to send my kind remembrances to your happy family though I know them not—'se non come per fama uom s'innammora.'[5] And to you dear Patty I send nothing save the assurance that you already have my warm affection.

Clematis.

2. Miss Franklin?
3. *Midsummer Night's Dream*, I, i, 76–77.
4. Cf. Young, *Night Thoughts*, IX, 2369.
4a. Cf. *Hamlet*, III, iv, 117.
5. Petrarch, "A Cola da Rienzo," *Canzoni sopra Vari Argomenti*, 11. GE's copy of the *Rime*, publicate da A. Buttura, 3 vols. in 1, Paris, 1829, with the signature "Mary Ann Evans" and four stanzas from *Childe Harold*, Canto IV, referring to Petrarch's tomb in pencil on the flyleaf was sold at Sotheby's, 27 June 1923, item 552. The text reads "s'innamora."

I, 81:28 GE TO MARTHA JACKSON,
GRIFF, 4 MARCH 1841

MS: Mr. Gordon N. Ray.

Griff March 4th 1841.

My very dear Ivy

Imagination herself being only a combining faculty and entirely dependent on our much depreciated senses, I am hopeless that she could depict to you my condition and employ for the last three weeks, for right gladly do I believe that you have no materials in your memory wherewith she might construct a type of them. At length an islet of etherial blue seems to be emerging in the midst of my cloudy cope, and under its benign influence I have spirits to make an effort at writing a letter, not dreaming that I shall write one that would be worth the perusal except to a clinging friend, who can be satisfied with bare matter of fact concerning my whereabout, how, and whither. It has been determined for two months or more that our future residence shall be the house on the Foleshill Road formerly inhabited by Dr. Hook[6] and next door to Mr. A. Pears.[7] Thither we hope soon to remove, and thither some time I hope my Patty will come to regain her roses, which I mourn after, provided always she can come with her own heart, otherwise I protest against her reception. I shall be so busily engaged until we are quite settled that I must procure an exemption from all correspondence, for which I promise to contribute a more important quota to her Majesty's Postoffice revenue, if I am spared in health to resume my quill driving. I do hope, my Ivy, that you are looking as a grateful plant should do under the promise of Spring, and that you are able to avail yourself with benefit of facilities for exercise. I beg of you to write *within a week* and tell me how you do and that my muteness has not disgusted you. Indeed, dear, I have gone through some little trials since I last wrote to you, and I should mention that my health has been far from vigourous as well as that I have had persons staying in the house—all this to give you some ground beyond pure charity for attributing my laggard interchange of expressed affection to substantial hindrances.

---

6. Walter Farquhar Hook (1798–1875), Vicar of Holy Trinity, Coventry 1828–37, moved into the house in 1831. Describing it as "on the Leicester Road," he wrote in a letter 13 April 1831: "though in the parish, [it] is in the country; quite rural, with a garden and all." W. R. W. Stephens, *The Life and Letters of Walter Farquhar Hook*, 2 vols., 1878, I, 218. Hook was Vicar of Leeds 1837–59 and Dean of Chichester 1859–75.

7. Abijah Hill Pears. See I, 90, n. 3.

Many thanks for your so kindly wishing to see me at Gobions—it would give me lively pleasure to visit you and see the rest of the Pleiades, one of which is so dear and interesting to me; but I dare not calculate on the indulgence at present. I cordially echo your feeling of comfort in knowing that our little concerns are in the hands of Him who doth all things well. To be so far a Quietist as to receive all with thankfulness is well, but we must stay then in the adoption of the system, and instead of sitting still actively go forward in whatever direction the finger of Providence points. My dear Brother has mentioned you as one whom he admires, and my own dear Father will I know be glad to welcome you again as my visitor, so do come amongst us. I shall have the cosiest hearth in Christendom, as quiet as a summer lake. My Sister wants to see you, and has recently presented us with a little girl,[8] whom we shall be proud to display. I send you as a great sacrifice on the altar of friendship, a pattern L which I have actually cut out of a precious note, so mind you make a good use of it. It is like its executer, very superior, and just my beau idéal. By the bye, I have read Buckland's Treatise on Geology[9] with much pleasure, and I believe Lyell's[1] is good though it differs in Theory, but alas the superficies of the earth are monopolizing my attention. I can neither delve nor soar.

Ever your true and affectionate
Clematis.

I, 115:5 GE TO EDITH HARRIET KITTERMASTER, FOLESHILL, [14? OCTOBER 1841]

MS: Smith College Library.

My dear Miss Kittermaster

Can you come to me next Monday, and stay as long as you feel inclined to immure yourself with such an anchoret as I? I shall be able to take you home whenever you wish, as the carriage will be at my disposal next week.[2] Pray send me an affirmative reply, if possible, that I may be at home, and quite ready to enjoy your society.

I beg to be very kindly remembered to Dr. and Mrs. Kittermaster.

8. Mary Louisa Clarke. See I, 79, n. 2.
9. William Buckland, *Geology and Mineralogy Considered with Reference to Natural Theology*, 2 vols., 1836. A Bridgewater Treatise.
1. Charles Lyell, *The Principles of Geology. Being an Attempt to Explain the Former Changes in the Earth's Surface by Reference to Causes Now in Operation*, 3 vols., 1830–33.
2. Robert Evans was in Derbyshire 19–23 October 1841. (Robert Evans's Journal.)

[*September? 1844*]

I will tell you how I have liked your little book, which I have read many times and gazed at the pictures of its cherub-like hero until I have forgotten that they are only pictures. Thank you very truly for remembering me and my tastes. Continue to do so, and to believe, my dear Miss Kittermaster, that I am

                          Your very sincere Friend
                          Mary Ann Evans.

Foleshill | Thursday Evening

I, 181:1   GE TO MRS. HENRY HOUGHTON, [FOLESHILL, SEPTEMBER? 1844]

MS: Yale.

My dear Fanny,

What could give you the idea that Father was going into Kent *this* week? I hope I did not mislead you. It is next week that he goes but alas! I fear I cannot take more than a day of it for Leamington for I must give one day to Chrissey whom I have not seen for a long, long time, and I have promised to go to Griff as an amende for failing to go thither with Father this morning. I am ashamed to make so much fuss about my visits, but wo is me! life slips away between headaches and eating and chitchat and one does nothing. A lodge in some vast wilderness is the only tempting thing.

I think Wednesday will be the day when I may hope to be with you, but tell Henry not to buy a melon even though he should get it for 6d.

It is very good of you to wish to have me, and I am very grateful for your love—more grateful and humble than my words seem to shew, but the essence of friendship is confidence, which does without fine speeches.

                          Every your affectionate
                          Mary Ann.

**I, 183:18 GE TO MARY SIBREE,
[FOLESHILL, FEBRUARY? 1845]**

MS: Nuneaton Public Library.

My dear Miss Sibree³

I thought of your adding to Miss Hennell's and my happiness by joining us this evening, but I find that other people are coming and that you may consequently be less likely to feel the visit an agreeable one. Will you save me the pleasure of having you until another evening when I shall be under less apprehension of your being "bored"—a condition of which I have so supreme a horror myself that I am always alarmed lest my visitors should incur it.

Thine truly
M. A. E.

**I, 190:26 GE TO MARY SIBREE,
[FOLESHILL, MAY? 1845]**

MS: Nuneaton Public Library.

Dear Mary

Do you still wish to have me tomorrow evening? If so I will be with you at six and stay with you till eight.

Thine
M. A. E.

**I, 195:7 GE TO MARY SIBREE,
[FOLESHILL, JUNE? 1845]**

MS: Nuneaton Public Library.

My dear Mary

I am obliged to go out this afternoon with my Father so we must put off our Faust to another day. I will send you word *when*.

M. A. E.

3. In October 1844 GE began giving German lessons to Mary Sibree. See I, lxxiv.

I, 198:21 GE TO MARY SIBREE, [FOLESHILL, SEPTEMBER 1845]

MS: Nuneaton Public Library.

I am quite alone this week ma chère, and confined to my "small upper room"[4] in more senses than one. Will you not call, since I missed you on Saturday? Can you call on me on your way home to-morrow. Have tea with me, and I will send the man home with you at 7 or when you please.

Yours ever
M. A. E.

I, 208:14 GE TO MARY SIBREE, FOLESHILL, [12 MARCH 1846]

MS: Nuneaton Public Library.

Foleshill | Thursday.

My dear Mary

I obtained your direction from Mrs. Sibree this morning that I might express my regret to you for having failed in sending 'Past and Present.'[5] I did really get the book on the very day I promised to do so, but the next day my amazing faculty of forgetting together with a bad headache made me quite oblivious of the whole affair. This is no excuse, but it is something to be penitent—'Who with repentance is not satisfied is not of heaven, nor earth.'[6] So says Shakespeare, and as I am very sure that you are composed of some of the earth's best mould,[7] I am not afraid that you will withhold your forgiveness. I am so sorry that Mr. Sibree has missed the opportunity of having that thrilling book, while he is at leisure and (I am sorry to hear) an invalid. Pray tell him that it is still at his service when he comes home.

Clifton[8] must look lovely under these smiling skies. I hope you are drinking in all kinds of profit and pleasure, and will remember every thing to tell me when we are tête à tête. You are missing nothing good

---

4. The scene of the Last Supper is "a large upper room." Luke 22:12.
5. By Thomas Carlyle, 1843.
6. *Two Gentlemen of Verona*, v, iv, 79, reads "Who by repentance."
7. Cf. Tobit, 8:6: "Thou madest Adam of the mould of the earth."
8. Mary and John Sibree were staying with Mr. J. Robertson at Widcome Villa, Richmond Hill, Clifton.

except Mr. Macdonald's lectures.⁹ He gave one last evening on Self-educated men, and there is to be a second this evening on the State of society. This is no caviare however, but very simple food, and I dare say you are getting much better where you are. Farewell until you come like a rosy beam of morning to smile on me in my study. In a hurry as usual,

                                    Thine
                                Mary Ann Evans.

I, 223:1 GE TO MRS. JOHN SIBREE, [FOLESHILL, 1846?]

MS: Nuneaton Public Library.

My dear Mrs. Sibree

    May I hope for the pleasure of seeing you and Miss Sibree this afternoon? I shall be alone and very happy if you will bestow a few hours on me.

    Do not trouble yourself to write—a message by the servant will quite answer the purpose.

                               Yours sincerely
                               Mary Ann Evans.

Wednesday

I, 224:6 GE TO CHARLES BRAY, [FOLESHILL, 21 OCTOBER 1846]

MS: Yale. *Endorsed by Mrs. Bray:* Postmark Coventry Oc 22 1846. *Published: TLS,* 12 February 1971, p. 187.

                                Wednesday Evening.

My dear Friend

    When I wrote to Cara I complained that I had no news to tell her—but oh the mutations of this giddy planet! little did I think that ere another week passed away I should be an actress in scenes so novel as those which it has now become a duty of friendship to relate to you. But a truce to prefaces and palpitations. I will plunge at once in medias res.¹

    The other day as I was sitting in my study, Mary came with a rather

---

    9. Archibald MacDonald of Royston lectured at the Mechanics' Institution 11 and 12 March 1846 on "Self Educated Men" and "The Improvement of Society." (*Coventry Herald,* 6 March 1846, p. 1.)

    1. Horace, *Ars Poetica,* line 148.

[*21 October 1846*]

risible cast of expression to deliver to me a card, saying that a gentleman was below requesting to see me. The name on the card ran thus—Professor Bücherwurm, Moderig University. Down I came, not a little elated at the idea that a live professor was in the house, and, as you know I have quite the average quantity of that valuable endowment which spiteful people call assurance, but which I dignify with the name of self possession, you will believe that I neither blushed nor made a nervous giggle in attempting to smile, as is the lot of some unfortunate young ladies who are immersed in youthful bashfulness.

And whom do you think I saw? A tall, gaunt personage with huge cheek bones, dull grey eyes, hair of a very light neutral tint, un grand nez retroussé, and very black teeth. As novel writers say, I give you at once what was the result of a survey carried on by degrees through a long interview. My professor's coat was threadbare enough for that of a first-rate genius, and his linen and skin dirty enough to have belonged to the Emperor Julian.[2] A profound reverence. I begged him to be seated, and this very begrimed professor began in sufficiently good English, 'Madam, you can form no preconception of my design in waiting on you.' I bowed. 'About a fortnight ago I came to London to seek—singular as it may seem to you—a *wife*.' (Surely, thought I, this poor man has escaped from a lunatic asylum, and I looked alternately at the door and the poker, measuring my distance from the two.) 'But,' my professor continued, 'there were certain qualifications which were indispensable to me in the person whom I could receive into that relation. I am a voluminous author —indeed my works already amount to some 20 vols.—my last publication in 5 vols. was a commentary on the book of Tobit. I have also written a long dissertation on the Greek Digamma, a treatise on Buddhism shewing that Christianity is entirely derived from this monstrous oriental superstition, and a very minute inquiry into the date, life and character of Cheops. My chief work, however, and that by which I hope to confer a lasting benefit on mankind is yet on hand. It is a system of metaphysics which I doubt not will supersede the latest products of the German philosophic mind.

'But like most authors who, as our divine Schiller says, live citizens of the age to come,[3] my books are not appreciated in my own country. Now I wish that England should at least have the opportunity of profiting by them, and as I can find no indifferent person who will undertake a translation I am determined if possible to secure a translator in the person

2. Julian, Emperor of Rome 361–363.

3. "Das Jahrhundert | Ist meinem Ideal nicht reif. Ich lebe | Ein Bürger derer welche kommen werden." (*Don Carlos*, III, 10.)

of a wife. I have made the most anxious and extensive inquiries in London after all female translators of German. I find them very abundant, but I require, besides ability to translate, a very decided ugliness of person and a sufficient fortune to supply a poor professor with coffee and tobacco, and an occasional draft of schwarzbier, as well as to contribute to the expenses of publication. After the most toilsome inquiries I have been referred to you, Madam, as presenting the required combination of attributes, and though I am rather disappointed to see that you have no beard, an attribute which I have ever regarded as the most unfailing indication of a strong-minded woman, I confess that in other respects your person at least comes up to my ideal.'

At this the professor bowed and coughed as waiting for my reply. I said that certainly I was taken by surprize, having long given up all hope of such an application as the present, but that I was decidedly pleased with the business-like tone of my suitor, and I thought no woman had been wooed in a more dignified manner since the days of the amazons, who were won with the sword. I thought it possible we might come to terms, always providing that he acceded to my irrevocable conditions. 'For you must know, learned Professor,' I said, 'that I require nothing more in a husband than to save me from the horrific disgrace of spinster-hood and to take me out of England. As negative conditions, my husband must neither expect me to love him nor to mend his clothes, and he must allow me about once in a quarter a sort of conjugal saturnalia in which I may turn the tables upon him, hector and scold and cuff him. At other times I will be a dutiful wife so far as the task of translation is concerned, and I promise to give to the English a lucid idea of your notions respecting Cheops and Tobit etc. As to my want of beard I trust that defect may be remedied, since I doubt not there must be creams and essences which gentlemen whose having in beard is but a younger brother's revenue[4] employ to cherish the too reluctant down, and it is an interesting physiological experiment yet to be tried, whether the feminine lip and chin may not be rendered fertile by this top-dressing.'

So we agreed to refer the matter to my Father. He, considering that it would probably be my last chance, at length consented though the professor peremptorily insisted on the wedding taking place next week, as he could not defer his literary projects for a longer period. My Father theorized a little on the undesirableness of long courtships, in order to reconcile his conscience, and accordingly the arrangements are made. On Wednesday next I become the Professorin and wend my way with my tocher and my

4. *As You Like It*, III, ii, 396.

husband to Germany—never more to appear in this damp atmosphere and dull horizon. So if you wish to utter a last farewell, you must come home before next Wednesday.

I have ordered a magnificent wedding dress just to throw dust into the eyes of the Coventry people, but I have gone to no further expense in the matter of trousseau, as the Professor prefers as a female garb a man's coat, thrown over what are justly called the *petti*coats, so that the dress of a woman of genius may present the same sort of symbolical compromise between the masculine and feminine attire of which we have an example in the breastplate and petticoat of the immortal Joan.

I have requested Sara to be my bridesmaid, but her notions are far too contracted for her to comprehend or sanction a scheme of matrimony so much beyond the views of the present age. But as I know that you, my dear Friend, hold the most enlightened and liberal views of these subjects, and regard all subjection to feeling in such affairs as a weakness, proper to small heads, under 20 inches in circumference, I doubt not you will honour my bridal with your presence.

I, 230:18 GE TO MARY SIBREE, [FOLESHILL, FEBRUARY? 1847]

MS: Nuneaton Public Library.

Dear Mary

Miss Lewis[5] is gone to Leamington, and I shall be quite disengaged this afternoon. Will you ask your brother[6] if it will be convenient to him to come to me? And will you join us when we have done our Greek and have tea with me on your way to chapel?

As tomorrow will be Miss Lewis's last day with me, I must give it entirely to her.

[Signature cut away]

5. Maria Lewis, who conducted a school at Chilvers Coton, visited GE at Foleshill, January and February 1847.

6. John Sibree, Jr., was teaching GE Greek.

I, 233:18 GE TO JOHN SIBREE, JR., FOLESHILL, [1? MAY 1847]

MS: Nuneaton Public Library.

My dear Mr. Sibree

It was owing to my neglect that Mary's letter was put into our bag without having prepaid written on it. You must allow me to make the proper amende by sending the enclosed stamps. Unless you are quite weary of me I shall hope to have a continuation of your last letter soon. But in either case whether you are weary of me or not, I am

Ever your sincere friend
Mary Ann Evans.

Foleshill | Saturday

I, 261:24 GE TO MRS. HENRY HOUGHTON, FOLESHILL, [MAY? 1848]

Text: Lady Charnwood, *An Autograph Collection*, 1929, p. 149.

Foleshill,[7] Tuesday Evening.

My dear Fanny,

Father had rather more sleep last night—this morning he felt very ill, but was not, the doctors said, really worse. He has had a comfortable afternoon and received several visitors. His eyes are looking very bright at this moment. Let yours show a little lustre too—and let us remember that we should make sorry work of it if our wishes could alter the course of things. All good things attend you in your new dwelling.[8]

Your affectionate
Mary Ann.

7. Lady Charnwood reads *Coleshill* and *Mrs. Hinghorn*.
8. Willenhall House, about two miles south of Coventry. (F. White, *Warwickshire*, 1850, p. 495.)

[*July? 1848*]

I, 262:5 GE TO MRS. HENRY HOUGHTON, [FOLESHILL, 26 MAY 1848]

MS: Yale.

Father has decided, unless something should occur to alter the plan, that we shall set out for St. Leonard's on Monday morning. Our direction will be Victoria Hotel | St. Leonard's on Sea.

Forgive any stupidity in my note for I am very poorly this afternoon and it is an exertion to write.

I, 271:14 GE TO MRS. HENRY HOUGHTON, [FOLESHILL, JULY? 1848]

MS: Yale.

My dear Fanny

Father is not apparently worse today than yesterday, but Dr. Powell[9] and Edward have seen him today and they think him worse than he was last week. I am grieved to afflict you by telling you this, but the real cruelty would be to conceal it.

Your affectionate
Mary Ann.

Saturday

I, 271:14 GE TO MRS. HENRY HOUGHTON, [FOLESHILL, JULY? 1848]

MS: Yale.

My dear Fanny

I hardly know what to tell you about Father—he varies so from one hour to another—but I fear his weakness is increasingly trying to him. He has just been a little drive but has found it very fatiguing. I will send for you on Saturday afternoon if possible,

Your affectionate
Mary Ann.

9. See I, 258, n. 7.

I, 278:22   GE TO MRS. HENRY HOUGHTON, [FOLESHILL, FEBRUARY? 1849]

MS: Yale.

My dear Fanny

Father becomes more and more feeble. He can hardly bear me to speak to him and it is with great difficulty that I can prevail on him to take any food. Everything that seems to claim an effort of mind is irritating to him—and this one may well expect from his feebleness and suffering.

Your affectionate
Mary Ann.

I, 313:9   GE TO MRS. HENRY HOUGHTON, GENEVA, 4 OCTOBER [1849]

Text: Typed copy made for Miss Elsie Druce, Yale. *Extracts published:* 1, 313–314.

Plongeon | Thursday October 4th.

My dear Fanny

The blessed compensation there is in all things made your letter doubly precious for having been waited for, and it would have inspired me to write to you again much sooner, but that I have been in uncertainty about settling myself for the winter and I wished to send you my future address. I have finally decided on going to M. D'Albert's. He is a highly respectable artist, a man I am told of *beaucoup d'esprit*, fond of music and possessing a circle of superior friends. His wife is a very pleasing lady-like person with a most kind face. I shall be their only pensionnaire and I am to have a nice apartment with an alcove, that continental device for turning a bedroom into a sittingroom. Everything is to be provided for me except firewood for 150f. i.e. £6 per month. One of the advantages of being in Geneva alone is that people of a really high tone of manners and education receive pensionnaires—the fruit of the revolution I believe, which has reduced many fortunes. The D'Alberts are middle-aged, between 40 and 50, and have two nice boys[1] about 14 or 15. They seem pleased with the idea of having me and are very anxious to accommodate me as far as possible. I am to move to my new home on Tuesday the 9th and my address will then be M. D'Albert Durade, rue des Chanoines, no. 107. I shall not at all regret leaving here, for my only favourite, the Baronne

---

1. Alphonse and Charles.

de Ludwigsdorff will set off for Vienna on Saturday, for the season is beginning to be rather sombre, though the glorious chestnuts here are still worth looking at half the day.

You have heard of some of the people whom I have described in my letters to Rosehill—but I do not think I have mentioned to you Mde. de Ludwigsdorff. She is a very accomplished Englishwoman, who married about 10 years ago an Austrian Baron of large possessions. She has not at all the air of an English person—dark as a Spaniard, with French manners and a perfect Parisian accent. She has been quite a treasure to me for the last month, for something has drawn us together in spite of all the disparities between us and I hardly think that I ever became so quickly attached to anyone before. But alas, she seems to know so little of her future that I am almost afraid our parting on Saturday will be a final one. Her life has been a most interesting one, and I shall always yearn to know how the woof is being spun out.[2]

The society here is less distingué than usual just now. There are two French families whom it is amusing enough to see now and then, but who excite no vivid interest. The dear little old maid Mlle. de Phaisan is quite a good friend to me—extremely prosy and full of tiny details, but really people of that calibre are a comfort to one occasionally, when one has not strength for more stimulating things. She is a sample of those happy souls who ask for nothing but the work of the hour however trivial—who are content to live without knowing whether they effect anything, but who do really effect much good simply by their calm and even maintien. I laugh to hear her say in a tone of remonstrance, "Mde de Ludwigsdorff dit qu'elle s'ennuie quand les soirées sont longue—moi, je ne conçois pas comment on peut s'ennuyer quand on a de l'ouvrage ou des jeux ou de la conversation."

We have had a Scotch family here named Forbes—relatives of the Professor Forbes of Glacier celebrity.[3] They have travelled much in Europe and the East—and by the bye are cousins i.e. the younger generation, to Miss Skene, whose long wild book 'Use and Abuse' Miss Forbes lent me to read.[4] They are very evangelical, but Miss Forbes has a character which renders one's interest in her quite independent of such matters. She has no brilliant powers, but is earnest in feeling and evidently highly valuable in domestic life. She took a great fancy to me—which has transmuted itself into a grave anxiety now that she finds we differ very materially.

2. "Baronne de Ludwigsdorf and Cousin Rosa" appear among GE's notes for possible stories, written on the back of a calendar for 1876. (Yale.)

3. Charles Hay Forbes (1806–59), a brother of James David Forbes (1809–68), who wrote *Travels through the Alps of Savoy . . . with Observations on the Phenomena of Glaciers*, 1843.

4. See I, 308–309, nn. 2 and 3.

They are gone to Rome for the winter, being recommended to go south for Miss Forbes' health. They had been in Spain before coming here.

My health has been very wretched here, partly owing to the unseasonable hours—10 o'clock for breakfast and 6 for dinner, but at present I am better, and I have no doubt that I shall recover my strength when I have a few more bodily comforts. I want to present a very robust appearance to you all in spring. And you dear Fanny, I hope, are getting back again your moderate share of embonpoint. When people who are dressing elegantly and riding about to make calls every day of their life, have been telling me of their troubles—their utter hopelessness of ever finding a vein worth working in their future life, my thoughts have turned towards many whose sufferings are of a more tangible character, and I have really felt all the old commonplaces about equality of human destinies—always excepting those spiritual differences which are apart not only from poverty and riches, but from individual affections.

I have had a second letter from Sara with one from Isaac. Dear Chrissy also has found time and strength to write to me—very precious her letter was, though I wept over it. "Deep abiding grief must be mine" she says and I know well it must be. The mystery of trial! It falls with such avalanche-weight on the head of the meek and patient. I should be much more comfortable in thinking of you if you had some means of transporting yourself now and then to Meriden or anywhere else that your heart would carry you. Can you not manage to use the carriage yet? I am delighted that Mr. Bromley[5] seems to be acting with something like an appreciation of Henry's efforts to serve him. I wish I could do something of more avail for my friends than love them and long for their happiness. You dearest Fanny have a very large share of that very unmarketable benefit. Send me news of yourself as soon as you can without feeling it a tax to do so. The smallest detail is of value to me. To think of you being without a servant a fortnight! You shew too much vigour. Keep some of it latent, remember the Proverb 'The willing horse'[6] etc. Does not Willenhall look beautiful in the autumn? The trees on the knoll opposite your house must have fine effect now. I can hardly see the letters I am framing and am expecting the dinner bell so, dear Fanny, once more believe I love you, and tell Henry I love him for your sake when he is good to you.

Your
Mary Ann.

Love to Robert and Jane[7] whenever you can give it for me.

5. Walter Bromley-Davenport (1788?–1862) of Wootton Hall, near Ellastone, Henry Houghton's employer, was Lord of the Manor of Baginton.

6. "All lay load on a willing horse."

7. Jane Attenborough (1815–81), wife of GE's half-brother Robert Evans.

The Westminster Review

1851 May—Dec. 1853   GE edits the *Westminster* with Chapman.
1851 August 29   GE meets George Combe, the phrenologist.
1852 April 21   GE's relations with Herbert Spencer alarm him.
1852 July   Combe's low opinion of Chapman's business.
1852 July–August   GE at Broadstairs.
1852 July   Spencer rejects GE's love.
1852 October   GE visits the Combes and Harriet Martineau.
1853 February   GE at Meriden with her sister Chrissey.
1853 June 7   Combe's *Prison Discipline* accepted.
1853 October 9   Spencer shown MS of Combe's *Natural Religion*.
1853 October 17   GE moves from 142 Strand to 21 Cambridge St.

I, 351:1 GE TO JOHN CHAPMAN, COVENTRY, 9 JUNE [1851]

MS: Yale. *Endorsed:* Miss Evans. June 9th 1851.

Rosehill | June 9.

Dear Friend

The enclosed letter was all the Post brought this morning. I am sorry it did not come yesterday that we might have talked it over together. As you predicted, James Martineau's answer[8] is the coldest of all—indeed he writes as if he felt some personal pique. His letter, however, reads less disagreeably the second time than the first. We all think that your writing from Rosehill and requesting him to send you an answer here has given him the idea that Mr. Bray has a special pecuniary interest in your project and ⟨that⟩ is therefore likely to have some influence over the Review. But you will know better what he means when you have had an interview with him. Only tell him that contributors are to be well paid and I think he will not refuse to be one of them.

With regard to the secret of the Editorship, it will perhaps be the best plan for you to state, that for the present *you* are to be regarded as the responsible person, but that you employ an Editor in whose literary and general ability you confide. On these practical points, however, you are the best judge.

We seemed quite dull at dinner without you. I hope you found all well and prosperous at home. In haste

Yours faithfully
Marian Evans.

8. Chapman stayed at Rosehill 27 May–9 June 1851. With GE's help he wrote the Prospectus for the *Westminster Review* and sent proofs of it to F. W. Newman, Mill, Hickson, Froude, Martineau, Greg, Sir William Molesworth, Thornton Hunt, Lombe, R. W. Mackay, and W. B. Hodgson. (Chapman's Diary, 4 June 1851.)

I, 351:1 GE TO JOHN CHAPMAN, COVENTRY, 12 JUNE 1851

MS: L. W. Smith Collection, Washington's Headquarters, Morristown, New Jersey. *Endorsed:* Miss Evans. *Excerpts published:* I, 351.

Rosehill, June 12. 1851.

My dear Friend

I am chiefly concerned that you should have appeared to overlook Hickson's interest or have failed in etiquette towards him. If you had asked him for an introduction to J. S. Mill, it was clearly wrong to introduce yourself by letter.[9] I did not suspect the real state of the case. There is no remedy now but to be perfectly open with Hickson, and to drop any proceedings that may appear to him to be premature. Even if this were not "honour bright," which I hope is your first consideration, you know better than I, that any division of interest between you and him would be the most fatal thing for your proprietorship. You must of course not think of answering or of seeking any further communication with him apart from Hickson. I do not remember that you have written to any other old contributor except James Martineau. Your communications with Mr. Lombe are I suppose no secret to Hickson—if they are, pray let them cease to be so, and honestly *consult* him about any steps you may think it necessary to take in the future.

I am quite willing to agree to your proposition about the nominal editorship, or to anything else really for the interest of the Review. On the whole I think with you as to the expediency of your plan. Perhaps it was better to send a written answer to James Martineau. You have done it very well ⟨and more forcibly than⟩ and it will have more force with him than a mere verbal explanation. You had a right to repel his disagreeable insinuation about your "commercial wisdom."

I heartily wish the Prospectus had been longer delayed and thought over before it was sent to any of the don[or]s. The right plan would have been to have written to Hickson telling him your intention to send out a confidential Prospectus and asking his concurrence—then to have let it lie to be thoroughly discussed before printing it. Everything has been too hurried. But you will say "After meat, mustard"—your wisdom comes too late. Still the moral is not useless—*Caution* for the future.

---

9. W. E. Hickson purchased the *Westminster Review* in June 1840 from John Stuart Mill, who continued to write for it. In September 1847 he offered to sell it to Thornton Hunt and GHL, but they could not finance the purchase. See I, 351, n. 4.

29 August 1851

I shall await Combe's letter and your account of Johnson and Co.[10] with interest. I know you will let me have them as soon as you can. I return Hickson's letter. Tell me if I am to return the copy of your answer to Martineau.

Yours faithfully
Marian Evans.

I, 358:23 GE'S DRAFT[1] FOR J. CHAPMAN TO J. MARTINEAU, COVENTRY, 29 AUGUST 1851

MS: Yale. *Endorsed:* Draft of a letter to Mr. Martineau.

August 29, 1851.

My dear Sir

The application to you for an article on Christian Ethics and Modern Civilization was indeed not only by a general sense of your ability to treat such a subject, but more especially by the perusal of those passages in your recent article on the Creed of Christendom,[2] in which you briefly but forcibly exhibit the conviction that the moral teaching of the New Testament is inadequate and partly inapplicable to the needs of the present day, that Jesus himself, on the shewing of the synoptical gospels, was under the influence of serious error, and that the religious theory of Paul was based on the official destiny of Christ and not on his moral character.

The future Editors of the Westminster desire that the article in question should contain an impartial inquiry into the moral spirit and code of the primitive Christians as embodied in the New Testament, conducted on true principles of critical investigation and with entire freedom from conscious or unconscious predisposition to accommodate the phraseology of the Gospels and Epistles to the expression of modern ideas, or to use them with an esoteric meaning. The object of the article should be, not to sustain an argumentum ad hominem against the professor of Christianity by making the term cover as much truth as possible, but to ascertain

---

10. Andrew Johnson. See I, 352, n. 9.

1. Chapman's Diary, 27 August 1851: "I went to Coventry on Saturday and fully discussed the subject [of Martineau's article on "Christian Ethics"] with Miss Evans, after which I noted down the topics and mode of treatment to be adopted in the Article, which she embodied in a sketch for a letter with such modifications as she thought necessary, and from this material I shall write him our views on the subject, but I fear they will not be acceptable."

2. "The Creed of Christendom," *Westminster Review,* 55 (July 1851), 429–453, a review of W. R. Greg's book of that title. GE omits some verb like "prompted" in this sentence.

in all simplicity what the New Testament writers really believed and meant to teach, what was the moral influence of their belief on themselves, and how far a strict conformity to their teaching in the present day would correspond with our modern ideal of individual and social life. The Editors believe that the moral perceptions are greatly confused ⟨and the religious advancement retarded⟩ by the vague reverence for Christ and Christianity which, owing to our national backwardness in critical science, has been countenanced by some of our most candid and recent writers on religious topics; hence their wish that the questions—what are Christian Ethics? and How far are they available for our actual wants and in accordance with our highest conceptions?—should be treated by a mind which to adequate critical knowledge unites thorough directness of purpose and deep sympathy with the onward movements of the age.

An article such as they desire would show that Jesus contributed no new element to ethics, that the emphasis which he gave by his teaching and life to certain true principles was partly counteracted by his misconceptions concerning his own mission and the divine government in general derived from his Jewish culture, and by the false views and expectations which he consequently communicated to his followers, and that the beneficial effect of his character on Christendom has been chiefly due to the substitution of the ideal for the historical. It would discriminate the character of the Pauline development with the moral bearing of its dogmatic elements, from that of the simple Christian school. It would place in strong light the vein of asceticism in the Christian system, leading to such monstrous results in the early centuries of the Church and causing perpetual offences against conscience in simple minds of our own day, its subordination of domestic and social duties to an impractical enthusiasm and the egotistic seeking for 'salvation', its depreciation of the present life [*about 8 words deleted*] especially as regards the culture of the intellect and taste, and its passivity towards political and social abuses—all which had their foundation first in the dualistic theory—the antithesis of God and the world, and next in the expectation of Christ's immediate return. The writer's strictures would extend over many other particulars of Christian theory and practice, for example the creation of doctrinal belief into the condition of fellowship,[3] but the main point would be to shew that the faith and life of the early Christians were entirely based on the idea of the special and the exceptional, whereas the essence of modern advancement is the recognition of the general and invariable, and this must henceforth be the standpoint of an effective religious and moral theory. The article,

---

3. GE has added the last twelve words in pencil.

however, while shewing what Christianity has not done and cannot do for us, should do full justice to the positive side and endeavour clearly to define what we really owe to Christianity as a stage in the religious development of the race.

These few hints will enable you to decide whether the Editors may hope for the valuable aid of your pen on the above subject.

I, 359:7 GEORGE COMBE JOURNAL, COVENTRY, 29 AUGUST—1 SEPTEMBER 1851

MS: National Library of Scotland.

August 29 1851. Coventry. Mr. Bray—Miss Evans

We travelled from Liverpool to Coventry by rail and found Mr. Charles Bray waiting for us at the station, and went with him on a visit to Rosehill, close on the Town. He introduced us to his wife and her sister, the two sisters of the late Mr. Hennel the author of the work against Christianity as a Revelation; and to Miss Evans, the daughter of a farmer. The whole party are superior and interesting persons. Mr. Bray is a Ribbon manufacturer about 40; a Phrenologist and a convert to the natural Laws, with an excellent intellect, bilious, nervous, lymphatic and sanguine temperament, excellent coronal region, but great Comb[ativeness] and Destruc[tiveness] and very deficient Concentrativeness. He is proprietor of the Coventry Herald, which he uses as the organ of the new philosophy and its applications, so far as public opinion will allow him to go.

Miss Evans is the most extraordinary person of the party. She translated Strauss's work "Das Leben Jesu" from the German, including the Hebrew, Greek, and Latin quotations in it, without assistance; and it is said to be admirably executed. She has a very large brain, the anterior lobe is remarkable for length, breadth, and height, the coronal region is large, the front rather predominating; the base is broad at Destruc[tiveness]; but moderate at Aliment[iveness], and the portion behind the ear is rather small in the regions of Comb[ativeness] Amat[iveness] and Philopro[genitiveness]. Love of approb[ation], and Concentrativeness are large. Her temper[ament] is nervous lymphatic. She is rather tall, near 40[4] apparently, pale and in delicate health. She is an excellent musician. She read the Letters of Henry Atkinson on new organs in his and Miss

---

4. GE was not yet 32. After "Philopro." Combe has added in pencil: "This was written from eye-observation. She has gone off as the mistress of Mr. Lewes, a married man with 6 children. July 1854."

Martineau's Book,[5] and we discussed them. She shewed great analytic power and an instinctive soundness of judgment. We had a great deal of conversation on religion, political economy, and political events, and altogether, with the exception perhaps of Lucretia Mott,[6] she appeared to me the ablest woman whom I have seen, and in many respects she excells Lucretia. She is extremely feminine and gentle; and the great strength of her intellect combined with this quality renders her very interesting. Mrs. Bray also is a superior and accomplished woman, extremely modest and unpretending. Her sister plays well on the piano forte and is full of vivacity, with rather a large head, but the anterior lobe is not large.

September 1.

We visited Mr. Bray's ribbon factory, and saw a large apartment filled with looms weaving by steam. We saw a workman weaving a ribbon for the Queen on a Jackard loom, most beautifully flowered and about 5 inches broad. He is the best weaver in Mr. Bray's employment, but very drunken. He has a small brain, a small, but regularly formed, anterior lobe, Individuality, Form, Size, and Weight being predominantly large. His temperament is bilious nervous. He had been off work drinking for 6 days, and received notice that, unless he weave $2\frac{1}{2}$ yards a week, he shall be held as having resigned his employment. This is an example of a small brain with a special combination of certain organs fitting a man for a certain employment, or rather not operating as a disqualification.

I, 360:8 GE TO JOHN CHAPMAN, COVENTRY, 14 SEPTEMBER 1851

Text: Copy by Edmund Gosse, National Library of Scotland. *Extract published,* I, 360.

Rosehill, September 14.

My dear Friend

A trip to Brighton on this perfect autumn day may be a good thing, but lying on the grass is a better.[7] I wonder you will commit yourself to an excursion train. Heaven send you may not return home piecemeal.

---

5. Henry George Atkinson and Harriet Martineau, *Letters on the Laws of Man's Nature and Development,* 1851, pp. 72–89.

6. Lucretia Coffin Mott (1793–1880), abolitionist and champion of women's rights, whom Combe had met in America in 1840, visited him with her husband James Mott at Edinburgh in 1841.

7. Chapman went to Brighton with W. B. Hodgson and Alexander Ireland. (Chapman's Diary, 14 September 1851.) GE was lying on the grass with the Brays at Rosehill.

10 October 1851

Thanks for your note which with its enclosures reached me yesterday. I am glad your conscience does not accuse you about the Hickson business— or rather glad to believe that it has no reason to do so.

Write to [Froude] by all means, and if he declines to choose a subject, we will do it for him.[8]

Yours faithfully
Marian E.

The Combes[9] are coming again on Tuesday! After them Mr. Noel.[1]

I, 368:24 PROSPECTUS FOR THE *WESTMINSTER REVIEW*, 10 OCTOBER 1851

Text: Combe Papers, National Library of Scotland.

MR. JOHN CHAPMAN, having become the Proprietor of the WESTMINSTER REVIEW, invites attention to the enclosed Prospectus.

Mr. CHAPMAN hopes to confirm and extend the influence of the Review, as the chief organ of liberal opinion, by engaging the co-operation of the highest talent and culture; and, being aware that this can be permanently secured only by a regular system of remuneration, he proposes to pay all contributors at the rate of £12 12*s.* per sheet. As, however, he is not in a position with regard to capital to bear the whole weight of the enterprise, in addition to the large payment he has already made for the copyright, he relies on those who, concurring with him in his aims, have the ability to further them pecuniarily, to aid him in carrying on the work with the thoroughness necessary to its adequate success.

The present circulation of the Review is 1000, and if it should merely continue at this rate, without any increase in the number of Advertisements, Mr. CHAPMAN finds that the expenditure necessary to the conducting of the work in the manner he desires, apart from any profit to the Publisher or remuneration for Editorial labour, would exceed the receipts by £500 a year. But he believes that the advantages conferred by the intended mode of management would so increase the circulation, and consequently the value of the work as an advertising medium, that by the end of four years this surplus expenditure would be at least met by the proceeds of sale and advertisements, and that hence the need for assistance from those who are interested in sustaining the Review as an organ of free opinion would be only temporary.

---

8. See I, 359, n. 4. Gosse reads "W.?" for "Froude," and "Rochdale" for "Rosehill."

9. Mr. and Mrs. George Combe returned to Rosehill on the 16th and left for Edinburgh on the 19th.

1. Edward Noel and his children came 23 September and stayed until 10 November 1851. (Mrs. Bray's Diary.)

The arrangement Mr. CHAPMAN would suggest for adoption between himself and the friends who may be willing to aid him, is, that they should advance him such sums as may be convenient to themselves, in the form of loans, to be repaid at the end of four years, in proportion as the circulation of the Review shall have yielded a profit beyond a reasonable indemnification for the labour of management. In the meantime, and so long as such sums shall remain in Mr. CHAPMAN's hands, he engages to supply, for every sum of £20 advanced, a copy of each number of the Review, as it is issued, in lieu of interest. At the end of each year the Accounts will be submitted to every Subscriber who may wish to inspect them.

The required sum of £2000 has already been reduced to £1200 by a donation of £200 a year from EDWARD LOMBE, Esq.
LONDON, 142, STRAND.
Oct. 10*th* 1851

I, 368:24 CHARLES BRAY TO GEORGE COMBE, COVENTRY, 10 OCTOBER 1851

MS: National Library of Scotland. *Endorsed:* 12 ansd.

Coventry, October 10/51.

My dear Mr. Combe,

Dr. Brabant was to give Chapman, towards the Westminster, whatever you gave. Now he can well afford to give *hundreds* if he likes and he has just got off 300 £ which he was to have given towards another literary undertaking, but which will not now be required. Now what I am going to say shall be strictly between ourselves and Miss Evans, to whom I have mentioned it. Have you any objection to receive the subscription of your friends towards enlarging your contribution? If I subscribe it will be because you do, and because our views are to be represented there. ⟨Now⟩ Will you allow me therefore to send my 20 £ to you and you can then write to Chapman and say, that you will, *or* that you think it right, *or* that *circumstances* have enabled you, to give two twenty pounds? I know Dr. Brabant very well, and I assure you that I think it all fair—he is a regular old screw, with more money than he knows what to do with.

Thank you for the newspaper, we shall make use of it.

Mrs. Bray is better. Kind regards to Mrs. Combe, and believe me, my dear Sir,

Very truly yours
Charles Bray.

I, 376:20 JOHN CHAPMAN TO GEORGE COMBE,
LONDON, 26 NOVEMBER 1851

MS: National Library of Scotland. *Endorsed:* London 26 November 1851 | John Chapman.

London | November 26, 1851.

My dear Sir

I am somewhat surprised by your report from Mr. Lombe, as the enclosed note received from him last Saturday seemed to indicate that his annoyance had subsided.

I did *not* draw the £500 from his Bankers, but handed over the Draft to Miss Martineau as soon as possible after the receipt of his definite instructions concerning it.[2] Indeed I never thought of doing anything but returning the Draft, if he listened to my advice. It was payable to Miss Martineau.

On the whole I do not fear any permanent difficulties with Mr. L.; he seems to me fitful and capricious, but I believe he is heartily interested in the Review, and I am persuaded the January number will please him. I believe, at bottom, he is more annoyed that he is not the sole pecuniary support of the Review, than that I have published his name as a Contributor. He did not wish me to adopt the plan of paying the writers of Articles generally, and I incline to think the independent course I have taken has disappointed him, and have some slight reason for believing that he was disposed to be profuse in pecuniary help, himself, and to have a more authoritative voice in the direction of the Review than heretofore. This I think, all my friends would have deemed very undesirable.

I am sorry to say Miss Evans is not very well at present,[3] and Mrs. Chapman has to devote all her time to an invalid Aunt,[4]—while the lady who superintends the housekeeping—Miss Tilley—has gone to Brighton to improve her health, which is far from strong. Mrs. C. and Miss E. desire to unite with me in kind remembrances to Mrs. Combe and yourself, and believe me to remain

Yours very sincerely,
John Chapman.

2. Edward Lombe's draft for Harriet Martineau's abridgement of Comte's *Cours de philosophie positive*. See I, 360, and *George Eliot and John Chapman*, p. 55.

3. Charles Bray wrote to George Combe 6 December 1851: "I am afraid London does not agree with Miss Evans. She is to be with us at Christmas again." (NLS.)

4. Miss Bellamy.

English [margin note]

P.S. I find the Westminster circulates in America to the extent of 3000 copies. I am about to make a strong effort to secure that circulation for the english edition at a reduced price.

I, 377:12 GEORGE COMBE TO JOHN CHAPMAN, EDINBURGH, 28 NOVEMBER 1851

Text: Copy, National Library of Scotland.

Edinburgh 28 November.

John Chapman Esq.
My dear Sir

I am truly sorry to hear of so much bad health in your domestic circle, and hope that it may soon cease. We send our sympathies to the sufferers.[5]

I have received, and now send you, another letter dated 20 November from Mr. Lombe, which please return. I have written to him today that in my opinion he cannot be made liable for the debts of the Review by your announcing "a donation" from him of £200 a year. But, as you have apparently gone too far in making the statement *general* in place of particular, I think that you should write to him calmly, renouncing all claim to £200 a year for general purposes, and that you accept of his gifts for particular articles as he proposes. I have told him that you may have made a mistake, but could have had no intention of either "cheating" or "lieing." These are opprobrious terms, but they are not addressed *to* you.

[*No signature*]

I, 377:12 GEORGE COMBE TO JOHN CHAPMAN, EDINBURGH, 7 DECEMBER 1851

Text: Copy in the hand of Robert Cox, unsigned, National Library of Scotland.

Edinburgh | 7th December 1851.

John Chapman, Esq.
My dear Sir

I have been knocked up by cold at Manchester, and employ Mr. Robert Cox[6] as my amanuensis. I inclose for your perusal a letter dated 8th instant which I have considered it necessary to write to Mr. Lombe. Be so good as

---

5. See I, lix–lx.
6. Robert Cox (1810–72), Combe's nephew, had edited the *Phrenological Journal*, 1841–47.

read it and seal it with a seal different from your own; and send it to the post office without delay.

In announcing the names of the Subscribers to the Review you looked at the matter only from your own point of view, and did not consider how the announcement might affect your supporters. The Review has the reputation of being the organ of infidelity, and at an evening party in Edinburgh last week, a lady called out to Mrs. Combe, "So Mr. Combe has subscribed £20 to the Westminster Review!" This could do *me* no harm; but Mr. Robert Chambers,[7] if he had subscribed, might have been seriously injured by the announcement of his name as the saints are watching every opportunity of convicting him of a leaning to infidelity. My conviction is that several others of my friends have been deterred from coming forward by the announcement of the names. Now, however, that the error has been committed, I advise you before taking any further step in relation to the subscribers, to wait till you see the effect of your letter and mine on Mr. Lombe.

I would again very respectfully recommend to you to use Miss Evans's tact and judgment as an aid to your own. She has certain organs large in her brain which are not so fully developed in yours, and she will judge more correctly of the influence upon other persons of what you write and do, than you will do yourself.

I return the copy of your letter to Mr. Lombe, which I think is quite correct, and called for.

[*No signature*]

II, 7:8 GE TO GEORGE COMBE, LONDON, 27 JANUARY 1852

MS: National Library of Scotland. *Endorsed:* London 27 Jany 1852 | Marian Evans | 10 Feby ansd.

142 Strand | January 27. 1852.

My dear Sir

An important question connected with the bookselling business is so occupying Mr. Chapman, that he finds it impossible to secure an interval for writing to you to-day, and he has therefore requested me to answer for him your letter of Friday last.[8] I cannot regret an opportunity of renewing by letter an intercourse which was so agreeable to me in person.

---

7. Robert Chambers (1802–71), Edinburgh publisher, author of the anonymous *Vestiges of the Natural History of Creation*, 1844.

8. A copy of Combe's letter to Chapman, 23 January 1852, to which GE is replying, is in NLS.

Mr. Chapman has instructed me to say, that he thinks it desirable to have other publications as well as Mr. Ellis's book at the head of your article,[9] and he suggests to you, in addition to the pamphlet of which he has forwarded to you some proof sheets, the reprint of the Reports and Speeches of the National Public School Association and of their opponents, which, if you do not happen to have them by you, he will be happy to supply you with. He will also be glad if it should fall in with your plan to notice the Report of the State of Education in the Sandwich Islands. As to the matter of your article, he is quite sure that he shall best do justice to its subject, and to the interests of the Review, by giving you a *carte blanche*. The arrangements for the April number will render it convenient that your article should not exceed 20 pages in length, but Mr. Chapman would be sorry that you should limit yourself to a sheet. He is anxious to avoid in the next number the error into which he fell in the last—that of excessive bulk, which is as impolitic for the literary as for the financial interests of the Review.

The last communication from Mr. Lombe to Mr. Chapman was a very peremptory demand that the abridgment of Strauss, for which he had advanced £100, should be forthwith completed and placed in his hands, or else that the £100 should be immediately paid in to his banker. I wrote a letter,[1] declining to make the abridgment for immediate publication, on the ground both of Mr. Chapman's interests and my own—interests which I could not think outweighed by the probable advantage to the public—of superseding a complete translation by an abridgment of a work which at present is fitted for the few rather than for the many. I also explained, that I had never understood from Mr. Chapman that the abridgment was expected to be ready for publication before the translation should be sold out, and happily Mr. Chapman had a copy of his correspondence on the subject, which proved that he had been sufficiently explicit to Mr. Lombe in his statement, that until the remaining 350 copies of the translation were either disposed of or paid for by Mr. L., he could not consent to the publication of an abridgment. Mr. Chapman enclosed my letter with one from himself informing Mr. Lombe that the £100 had been paid to his banker. We have heard nothing of the irascible gentleman since, except that he had pointed out the advertisement of the contents of the Westminster

·9. "Secular Education," the opening article of the *Westminster Review*, 58 (July 1852), 1–32, discussed William Ellis, *Education as a Means of Preventing Destitution*; Richard Church, *The Rise and Progress of National Education in England;* and *The First, Second, and Third Annual Reports of Williams's Secular School*.

1. For Edward Lombe's proposal of the abridgement of the Strauss translation, see Chapman's Diary, 18 April 1851. GE's letter to Lombe has not been found.

[24 February 1852]

to Mr. Hickson, who, when he wrote about ten days ago, appeared to be ignorant of the rupture with Mr. Chapman. We think with you, that the "Ethics of Christendom"[2] would not appear to him a suitable investment of his "dollars." The article is certainly very far from being what was hoped for when the application for it was made to James Martineau, and is still farther from being broad enough for its title, but it contains a few valuable ideas which want enforcing and which gain at least as much by the *prestige* as by the style of the writer. It is perhaps that *prestige* which has won such exaggerated praise as that of Froude—that "the article on the 'Ethics' is the wisest word which has been spoken in my hearing for this long time past." In my opinion, the chapter on Christian Eclecticism in Greg's Creed of Christendom is a far wiser word.

I hope Mrs. Combe's health, as well as yours, is better still than when I had the pleasure of seeing her. Pray tell her that it is a happiness to me to think of her and of her kind words to me. Believe me, my dear Sir,

Yours very truly,
Marian Evans.

II, 12:7 GE TO GEORGE COMBE, LONDON, [24 FEBRUARY 1852]

MS: National Library of Scotland. *Endorsed:* London | 24 Feby 1852 | Marian Evans.

142 Strand.

My dear Sir

Yours M.S. was sent to the printer on Saturday, but when we receive it 'in slip' I shall be able to insert the quotations from Montaigne—at least the first, which is remarkably piquant.[3]

I have read your article with great interest and admiration, as I have done everything else proceeding from your pen. I think it will serve at once the cause it advocates and the reputation of the Review. In consequence of your permission, I have rather regretfully suppressed one or two of the less telling quotations from Mr. Ellis's book. My reason for doing so was our great embarassment from want of space for the unexpectedly large amount of matter which it is incumbent on us to insert in the April number. I feel sure that there is no omission which you will consider

---

2. James Martineau, "The Ethics of Christendom," *Westminster Review*, 57 (January 1852), 182–226.

3. No room was found for either quotation, though the article was held over till July.

important, though your selections were all so good that one would have been glad to retain them under other circumstances.

Mr. Bray is with me just now and hearing that I am writing to you he begs me to say to you, that he does not think Mr. Thornton Hunt's difficulties[4] are of his own creating but that they arise from his having worked gratuitously for the Leader for six months,[5] from his having had several long illnesses, and from the living in common with persons over whose expenses he had not the same control as over his own.[6]

The article on Employers and Employed is by Mr. Greg[7]—that on Direct Legislation by Newman.[8] Your idea of an article on the Sandwich Island Report must be considered.

I am glad to tell you that Mr. Chapman's feud with the Booksellers is not on his part a mere struggle for self-interest. He is convinced that he is making a stand against a system of dealing ultimately injurious to the general Book Trade and to the Diffusion of Literature.

I am sorry to write in haste to you, but I am anxious not to lose the post. With kind regards to Mrs. Combe, I am, my dear Sir

Yours very sincerely
Marian Evans.

4. Chapman wrote to Combe, 13 February 1852: "I learn that during the last 2 years Mr. Thornton Hunt has received £650 for his labor for the same interval, as at the rate of £325 a year. He lives in a kind of community with several of his relatives, the result of which is he is now in difficulties; but I cannot help thinking that if a man has £325 a year he ought not to countenance the publication of a circular requesting donations in his behalf because he has been imprudent enough to permit of arrangements which drain him of what I consider an income sufficient to maintain him in comfort." (NLS.)

5. GHL's salary from the *Leader* in 1850 was £28 per month; in 1852 it was reduced to £20. Hunt's was probably on the same scale, but there is no evidence that he worked gratuitously.

6. Hunt lived in the house of his father-in-law John Gliddon, 10 Broadway, Hammersmith. His liaison with Agnes Lewes began in 1849.

7. "The Relation between Employers and Employed," *Westminster Review*, 57 (January 1852), 61–95, by W. R. Greg.

8. "The Latest Continental Theory of Legislation," 143–161, by F. W. Newman.

II, 17:16 GE TO GEORGE COMBE, LONDON, 30 MARCH 1852

MS: National Library of Scotland. *Endorsed:* Marian Evans.

March 30. 1852 | 142 Strand.

My dear Sir

Jeffrey's Life is to be treated in our July number by Mr. Weir,[9] who I believe is well known to you. He proposes to write an article on Scott, Jeffrey, and Chalmers. Mr. Greg contributes an article on another subject.[10] I am not personally acquainted with Weir, but he has been recommended to us as a man of considerable mental power and very diversified attainments. Moreover, he states himself to be familiar with Edinburgh life and Edinburgh literary men. I have no doubt, from the manner in which I have understood him to speak of you, that he will duly value the advantage of being aided by your views and knowledge on the subject of his article.

I am glad to hear that you propose to come to London in May, and that I may therefore hope to have the pleasure of seeing you and Mrs. Combe again. I often think of you, when I want some one to whom I could confess all my difficulties and struggles with my own nature, as the person, among all I have known, who is, as Madame de Stael said of her friend, the most completely 'de son avis'—having a profound faith in his principles and really acting them out.

I am going for a holiday to my friends at Rosehill on Saturday. I am longing to see the budding hedgerows and all the other delights of Spring. With kind regards to Mrs. Combe, I am, my dear Sir,

Yours very truly
Marian Evans.

9. William Weir (1802–58), formerly editor of the *Glasgow Argus*, had been on the staff of the *Daily News* since 1846. His "Lord Jeffrey and the *Edinburgh Review*," in the *Westminster*, 58 (July 1852), 95–110, discussed Lord Cockburn's *Life of Lord Jeffrey* without touching on Scott or Chalmers.

10. "Sir Robert Peel and His Policy," pp. 205–246.

II, 17:16 JOHN CHAPMAN TO GEORGE COMBE, LONDON, 5 APRIL 1852

MS: National Library of Scotland. *Endorsed:* London 5 April 1852 | John Chapman.

London April 5. 1852.

My dear Sir,

I was surprised to learn from Miss Evans your report of the announcement that the 'Westminster' is about to become a very staid and decorous journal, conducted with due regard to the prejudices of the time.[1] I am happy to assure you that there is not one word of truth in the assertion, whatever quarter it may come from. So long as all the articles are determined upon by me, as they are now, with the aid and counsel of Miss Evans, I shall not shrink from the effort to make the work what I conceive it should be—the bold and uncompromising exponent of the most advanced and philosophical views in reference to the various subjects it will discuss. Of course my own convictions as to *what are* philosophical views will not meet with the assent of all liberal thinkers, and it is natural that such men will be disappointed with the Review under *my* controul. But this is *spelling* inevitable from the limitations of the human mind; and all I can promise is that I shall strive to be faithful to my own convictions. I can fully rely upon Miss Evans for the same endeavour, and as our views coincide upon nearly all points both in reference to opinions and duty, I believe her influence will be in the right direction.

I am aware that Miss Martineau is not likely to approve of the Review, —she expressed her disapproval of the Prospectus; but since I cannot regard as verities all the articles of her *last formed* faith, it is not likely that I could allow the Review to endorse them. I suspect that she and those who think with her, on mesmeric matters, are the originators of the rumour you report to us. If she or Dr. Gregory[2] or any *able writer* whom we could rely on as competent to the task, were to offer us a paper embodying the well ascertained result of magnetic investigators it would be welcome, and if we distrusted the impartiality of the observer, his statements could be published in the "Independent Section." Such would be our views in reference to this subject and all other questionable ones,

---

1. No letter from Combe containing this view has been found.

2. William Gregory (1803–58), Professor of Chemistry at Edinburgh, wrote *Letters to a Candid Inquirer on Animal Magnetism*, 1851, and *On the Theory of Imagination, as Explaining the Phenomena of Mesmerism, and on Money Challenges in Clairvoyance*, Edinburgh, 1852. "Some thought him too credulous in regard to animal magnetism and mesmerism. His views have much in common with the recent theory of telepathy." (*DNB*, 1890.)

regarded by themselves,—but such being our views, we should nevertheless not *feel obliged* to put subjects, to us more important, aside in order to give publicity to topics not yet within the domain of science. I shall be happy to be still more explicit, if there is any point you would like me to clear up.

I hope you have received your copy of the Review ere this. I forwarded it through Messrs Maclachlan and Company. You will perceive that my article on the commerce of literature[3] is creating some stir; Longman and Murray wrote to the Times after the appearance of the Times article,[4] which was taken from mine, asking for delay of judgment. Bentley replied[5] (I wrote his letter, but this you must keep a secret,—of course he signed it); then Murray and Parker came out separately. I have sent an answer to Murray, which however is not yet published and my friend Spencer (Social Statics) has written a letter which appears today.[6] So far "The Times." The Leader (i.e. Hunt and Lewes in separate articles)[7] "blows hot and cold"; the Athenæum and Spectator[8] are both on my side, but do not forget the source of their advertisements. The Globe, Herald, Atlas, and Literary Gazette (Longman and Company) are against me, from fear of the Publishers.

I have written to Maclachlan and Company to desire them to supply copies of the Review to your order, charging them to me, with the intention of asking you to present copies to such persons as would be likely to become interested in the work by your doing so.

With kind regards to Mrs. Combe believe me my dear Sir

Yours faithfully

John Chapman.

P.S. There is a very laudatory article in the Daily News on the Review. I have just received a letter from Messrs J. W. Parker and Son to say they have withdrawn from the Association. Bentley preceded them, so I am sure to break it up.

---

3. "The Commerce of Literature," *Westminster Review*, 57 (April 1852), 511–545, Chapman's attack on the booksellers' monopoly.

4. *The Times* had a pleasant article commenting on the affair, 1 April, p. 8d. Longman and Murray sent letters 3 April.

5. Bentley's letter, dated 31 March, appeared 1 April, p. 8d.

6. Spencer's letter, signed "An Author," 5 April, p. 8d, described his experience in publishing [*Social Statics*] a book at 12/, of which the booksellers' charges for discounts, commissions, etc., left him only 7/6 to pay for printing, binding, and profit. For two years' work he could earn perhaps £10. He urged authors to refuse to publish with members of the Booksellers Association.

7. Thornton Hunt wrote "Disorganization among the Booksellers," *Leader*, 3 April 1852, pp. 322–323. GHL, commenting on the *Westminster*, took a more helpful tone in his "Literature," p. 325.

8. "Civil War in the Book Trade," *Spectator*, 3 April 1852, pp. 321–322, a long friendly summary.

II, 17:16 GE TO GEORGE COMBE, COVENTRY, 8 APRIL 1852

MS: National Library of Scotland. *Endorsed:* Rosehill | Miss Evans.

Rosehill, April 8. 1852.

My dear Sir

I rely on your habitually kind construction of me and my actions for having prevented you from putting any wrong interpretation on my slowness in replying to your two last letters—letters which I feel it to have been a real kindness in you to write, and for which I am truly obliged. The reason of my silence has been, as usual, illness. But now that I have fairly sat down to write to you, let me first thank you and Mrs. Combe for your kind invitation, which is the one of all others I should have the most pleasure in accepting. I will allow myself to hope that nothing will happen before October to prevent my spending at least part of that month with you. I have full faith in the promised good to my soul and body.

I am much obliged to you for the "Edinburgh News" containing the notice of Jeffrey's Life by Dr. Samuel Browne.[9] I have carefully compared the estimate of Jeffrey there given with that by Mr. Weir in the Spectator of March 20[1] and I confess I find no essential difference between the two. Dr. S. Browne says: "We feel, notwithstanding all our unfeigned love and admiration, that our brilliant and amazingly successful compatriot and fellow townsman has really created nothing, discovered nothing, invented nothing." Mr. Weir says: "A lively delicate sense of the beautiful, a generous and chivalrous disposition, much benevolence, and a vivid play of fancy, impart a charm to all his observations; but it would be difficult to point out in any of his writings, one original generalized truth" etc. Mr. Weir, too, so cordially recognizes the amiability of Jeffrey's moral and social character, that I must think him free in this instance from the charge of being swayed in his literary judgment by personal considerations—since, from what you say, such considerations must, in his case, have been adverse to Jeffrey. I cannot but regret, however, that our acceptance of Mr. Weir's offer to become the reviewer of Jeffrey's Life for the Westminster, has deprived us of the advantage to be derived from the communication of your knowledge and views on the subject.

Mr. Chapman sends me word that he has written to you on the subject

---

9. *Edinburgh News*, 27 March 1852, p. 8a–c. GE misspells Brown.

1. *Spectator*, 20 March 1852, pp. 275–277.

of one of your letters, which I concluded that you wished me to read to him. I mean the one referring to the conversation in which the Westminster was branded with the imputation of 'trimming' and cowardice. I should have been less surprized if this imputation had been founded on an alleged tameness in the contents of the first number, but it appears to have been given out as if on authority. I can only say for myself, that if, in the management of the Westminster, I found any objects sought after as conditions of success, which would warp the honest effort to secure the best thought and the best writing on the most important topics, I should at once cease to interest myself in it. I say this simply as my testimony to the intended course of the Review. The assertion that "it will not admit even an incidental allusion, if respectful, to such subjects as Mesmerism and Phrenology and that it ignores them altogether as topics of human thought and scientific investigation" is false. But I think you will agree with me that the great majority of 'investigators' of mesmerism are anything but 'scientific.' The reason for excluding that or any other subject of moment from the Review, would be the difficulty of getting it adequately treated. An ordinary pilot will do for plain sailing, but we want clear vision and long experience when we set out on voyages of discovery. It is no small difficulty, in conducting a Review, to secure the right man for each subject, and when you think you have him, he often disappoints you—is not equal to himself, or to your previous conception of his powers. And so it often happens that after very faithful editorial effort, the result is poor. Hence our friends are doing us good service—at least such as you, whose judgment is reliable—in suggesting writers to us. The subject you mention, Mental Physiology, would, I should think, suit admirably for the October number for which no scientific article is yet engaged. I hope you will approve the article on 'Physical Puritanism' in the last number[2] as the onus of its acceptance rests on me. I dare say you will recognize the writer.

I fear I shall have annoyed you with my illegible handwriting this morning. When I write fast I am apt to get rather unconventional in the form of my letters. With kind regards to Mrs. Combe, I remain, my dear Sir,

Yours very truly
Marian Evans.

2. *Westminster Review*, 57 (April 1852), 405–442, by Samuel Brown.

II, 20:5 GE TO HERBERT SPENCER, LONDON, [21 APRIL 1852]

MS: British Museum. *Published: Bulletin of the New York Public Library*, 79 (Spring 1976), 365.

Dear Friend

Not for the "satisfaction of breaking a conventionalism,"[3] but for the sake of hearing Le Prophète[4] and yet more of hearing it with you, I accept your kind proposal. I am not sure that I understand your note, or rather, I am sure that I do not. But prior to all further explanation, or, if you wish, to the exclusion of it, let me assure you that I never imputed to you an ungenerous thought. I felt disappointed rather than "hurt" that you should not have sufficiently divined my character to perceive how remote it is from my habitual state of mind to imagine that any one is falling in love with me.[5] But perhaps I still misapprehend you, so I will run no risk of blundering further. I will only say, that I value your regard very highly, and that the more strictly truthful you are to me, both explicitly and implicitly, the better I like you.

Yours very sincerely
Marian Evans.

142 Strand | Wednesday

3. Apparently a quotation from Spencer's invitation. GE was being seen so frequently with him that he feared people would think them engaged—as indeed happened. See II, 22.

4. Johanna Wagner's first appearance in London was announced for the Royal Italian Opera, Covent Garden, 24 April 1852, in Meyerbeer's *Le Prophète*. But the manager of Her Majesty's Theatre, claiming that she was under contract to appear there, brought an injunction against her and her father Albert Wagner. At the première of Donizetti's *I Martiri* at Covent Garden 20 April Mlle Wagner sat in a box, "and every *lorgnette* was upon the heroine of the mystification," wrote GHL in the *Leader*, 24 April 1852. "Tonight as *Fides* to Mario's *Prophète* she encounters the ordeal of her great fame." (p. 402.) But the injunction prevented her appearance, and *I Martiri* was substituted.

5. In a letter to E. L. Youmans, 3 February 1881, Spencer explained his part in the affair: "My friendship with Miss Evans began in 1851 and soon became very intimate. Having at that time free admission for two, to the Opera, the Theatres, Concerts, etc. and liking her society very much, I was in the habit of frequently taking her; and we were also thrown together in matters concerning the *Westminster Review*. After a time I began to have qualms as to what might result from this constant companionship. Great as was my admiration for her, considered both morally and intellectually, and decided as was my feeling of friendship, I could not perceive in myself any indications of a warmer feeling, and it occurred to me that mischief would possibly follow if our relations continued. Those qualms led me to take a strange step—an absurd step in one sense. I wrote to her indicat-

II, 20:5 GE TO GEORGE COMBE, LONDON, 22 APRIL 1852

MS: National Library of Scotland. *Endorsed:* London | Miss Evans.

142 Strand | April 22. 1852.

My dear Sir

It is time that I should thank you for the two very interesting and valuable letters which I received from you last week. You will see that I have migrated in the interim, and exchanged the pure air and quiet of Rosehill for the smoke and noise of the Strand. I think, however, that I am becoming acclimatized here and that I may hope to be well enough for moderate work, though not up to the pitch of any great undertakings.

We shall be glad if you will finally arrange with Dr. James Coxe[6] that he shall furnish us with an article on Mental Physiology for the October number. It is undesirable, except in special cases, that articles should exceed from 25 to 30 pages in length; but a circular in relation to this

ing, as delicately as I could, my fears. Then afterwards, perceiving how insulting to her was the suggestion that while I felt in no danger of falling in love with her, she was in danger of falling in love with me, I wrote a second letter, apologising for my unintended insult. She took it all smilingly, quite understanding my motive and forgiving my rudeness. The consequence was that our intimacy continued as before. And then, by and by, just that which I had feared might take place, did take place. Her feelings became involved and mine did not. The lack of physical attraction was fatal. Strongly as my judgment prompted, my instincts would not respond.

"It was a most painful affair, continuing through the summer of 52, on through the autumn, and, I think, into the beginning of 53. She was very desponding and I passed the most miserable time that has occurred in my experience; for, hopeless as the relation was, she would not agree that we should cease to see one another. So much did I feel the evil that I had done involuntarily, or rather, against my will, that I hinted at the possibility of marriage, even without positive affection on my part; but this she at once saw would lead to unhappiness. At length it happened that being with Lewes one afternoon when I was on my way to see her, I invited him to go with me (they were already slightly known). He did so. This happened two or three times; and then, on the third or fourth time, when I rose to leave, he said he should stay. From that time he commenced to go alone, and so the relation began—(his estrangement from his wife being then of long standing). When I saw the turn matters were taking it was, of course, an immense relief to me." A note by David Duncan, Spencer's biographer, 24 April 1894, describing the relation with GE, says: "Lewes asked H.S. to take him to see Miss Evans, which he did. When H.S. rose to go, L. remained. Presently L. took to visiting her alone. An attachment grew up between them to H.S. great relief." (Reserve 49, BM.)

6. James Coxe (1811–78), M.D. Edinburgh 1835, had studied at Heidelberg. He wrote the *Report on the Management of the Insane in Scotland,* 1855. (Boase.) The article was not written.

and other practical details is about to be printed, which we will forward to Dr. Coxe. It would be interesting to me, though I do not require it for my satisfaction after having had the guarantee of your judgment, to see a short abstract of the intended article, if it were not asking too much of Dr. Coxe to ⟨supply⟩ request it.

The proper occasion for a discussion of Comte's Philosophy in the Westminster will be the appearance of Miss Martineau's abridged translation, which, I suppose, will be out in the course of a year. I shall be glad to be favoured with your ideas on this subject, and I assure you that you will always find me a willing, if not an adequately intelligent auditor. Mr. Lewes's second and third papers on Comte in the Leader[7] do not promise well, though he is understood to have applied himself very closely to the subject. You have probably seen the review, in the Times, of J. S. Mill—at present the chief English interpreter of Comte.[8] The reviewer has seized some weak points in Mill but is himself floundering among ideas which will presently be obsolete.

The conception of Jeffrey which I have gathered from his Life and Letters corresponds very closely with the character which you attribute to him. The indications of his difficulties as an Editor have a special interest for me. I am struck with one passage in a letter of his to Francis Horner (Vol.II, p. 151) where he says: "it always appeared to me that a considerable diversity was quite compatible with all the consistency that should be required in a work of this description" (the Review,[9] of course) "and that doctrines might very well be maintained in the same number which were *quite irreconcilable with each other*, except in their common tendency to repress servility and diffuse a general spirit of independence in the body of the people." This is allowing latitude with a vengeance, and is quite beyond my editorial creed; still I am glad of any authority to cite which will tend to prove the impossibility of securing perfect harmony in a work dependent on fluctuating contributors.

The agitation in the Bookselling business is being carried on with increasing vivacity. A meeting of Authors, at which Charles Dickens is to preside, will be held here shortly. Some distinguished men, who are unable to attend, will send letters expressive of their concurrence in the

---

7. "Comte's Positive Philosophy" ran in 18 installments in the *Leader* from 3 April to 14 August 1852. The 2d was on 10 April, p. 353; the 3d, 17 April, p. 375.

8. *A System of Logic, Ratiocinative and Inductive*, 1852; *The Times*, 10 April, p. 6d–f, and 12 April, p. 8a–b. "But much that is strange in Mr. Mill's philosophy is accounted for by the positive method adopted from Compte [*sic*]. ... M. Compte is, unhappily, an atheist; and it is a rule of the positive method to ignore the existence of a God."

9. Francis Horner (1778–1817) was one of the first contributors to the *Edinburgh Review*, 1802.

22 April 1852

object of the meeting. Mr. Chapman remarks, in answer to the arguments *contra* stated by you, that though the parallel between the publisher and the patentee may be a just one, the retail booksellers cannot be regarded as *agents* or *employés*, but are simply purchasers, who have made a commodity their own, and have a right to dispose of it at their pleasure. Still he agrees with you that the grand argument for freedom of trade in books is—that it is demonstrably for the interest of the "patentee."

Your mention of a discussion as to the meaning of "originality" renews a desire I have often had to write or to see written a thorough inquiry into that subject and also into the meaning of "genius"—a word equally vague and undetermined in its application. The antithesis of Dr. Combe's[1] reviewer seems to me to be built on confusion. All discovery must be the discovery either of a *fact* or of a *relation*. Now we know that the discovery of facts—even those which have had the most momentous influence on the destinies of mankind—has been often due rather to a happy contingency of external circumstances than to any such wide pre-eminence in the discoverer as would suffice to account for his being such. The discovery of a fact *may* be a consequence of pre-eminent faculties in the discoverer, but is not necessarily so. The discovery of a relation, on the contrary, is strictly and exclusively the consequence of pre-eminent faculties, or *power of origination*.

Thank you very much for the facts about Dr. Gregory's patient. We get impatient of phenomena which do not link on to our previous knowledge, and of which the laws are so latent as to forbid even the formation of a hypothesis concerning them. This and the great mass of loose statement and credulity which surround the whole subject of mesmerism repel many minds from it which are anything but bigoted or unenlightened. But indications of claire-voyance witnessed by a competent observer are of thrilling interest and give me a restless desire to get at more extensive and satisfactory evidence.

Mr. Chapman has requested me to enclose some copies of a letter which appears to him to contain the gist of that vexed and vexing question which is now occupying him. He also begs me to say that if your views on the subject sufficiently coincide with his own to enable you to express your concurrence in a letter which you would authorize him to read at the meeting of Authors,[2] such a proof of your adhesion would, he thinks,

---

1. Combe's brother Dr. Andrew Combe, M.D. (1797–1847), whose *Physiology Applied to . . . Health and . . . Education*, 14th ed., 1852, is reviewed in the *Westminster Review*, 57 (April 1852), 630–31.

2. At 142 Strand, 4 May 1852. A copy by Combe of his long letter to Chapman, 25 April 1852, supporting the effort to break the Booksellers Association's price-fixing, is in NLS (7392, ff. 573–576).

be highly valuable to the cause. He has this morning received a letter from Edinburgh in which he is informed that at least 20 booksellers there are simply *coerced* into compliance with the old system.

I shall be glad to hear from you what is the general opinion in your circle of the "Theory of Population"[3] in the Westminster. Mr. Robert Chambers, who was here the other night, expressed a high opinion of it. I am very ignorant on the subject, but I rather wish to believe the theory than see ground for doing so.

With kindest regards to Mrs. Combe, I am, my dear Sir,

Yours very truly
Marian Evans.

Your article has arrived from Mr. Ellis's[4] this morning.

II, 27:24 GE TO BESSIE RAYNER PARKES, LONDON, [19? MAY? 1852]

MS: Berg Collection, New York Public Library.

Dear Friend,

Alas! I am again engaged—going to the opera—You will renounce me as too tiresome. Cependant—I am ever

Yours faithfully
Marian.

II, 33:22 GE TO GEORGE COMBE, LONDON, 7 JUNE 1852

MS: National Library of Scotland. *Endorsed:* London 7 June 1852 | Miss Evans.

June 7. 1852.

My dear Sir

Many thanks for your letter received this morning. Since I saw you,[5] Mr. Chapman has had a visit from Mr. Bastard,[6] who proposes to pay for

---

3. In "A Theory of Population, Deduced from the General Law of Animal Fertility," *Westminster Review*, 57 (April 1852), 468–501, Herbert Spencer argued that the pressure of population will produce increased intelligence in those who survive—"the select of their generation"—and a reduction of the birth rate until "on the average, each pair brings to maturity but two children." (p. 501.)

4. "Secular Education," in which William Ellis's book is reviewed.

5. Combe's Journal, 5 June 1852, records his talk with GE 3 June about the *Westminster Review*: "Two evils trou-

three articles to be inserted in the Westminster, on subjects specified by himself. One of these subjects is "The hereditary transmission of qualities," and we are anxious to get an article on this subject for the October number. We must therefore defer the article on Mental Physiology to a subsequent number—probably that of April in next year, as we have already engaged a scientific article from Dr. S. Brown for January.[7] Mr. Chapman tells me that Mr. Bastard appeared rather afraid of employing Dr. Brown on his subjects, thinking him rather flighty; still he expressed no decided repugnance. Mr. Chapman and I have thought of another writer who would certainly do as a *pis aller*, but perhaps *you* can mention some one who combines a philosophic mind with the requisite physiological knowledge and some accomplishment as a writer. In haste, I remain my dear Sir,

Very truly yours
Marian Evans.

II, 34:13 GE TO GEORGE COMBE, LONDON, 11 JUNE 1852

MS: National Library of Scotland. *Endorsed:* London 11 June 1852 | Miss Evans.

142 Strand | June 11. 1852.

My dear Sir

We are anxious to have plenty of time for deliberation as to the writer of the article on hereditary disease; hence we desire not to commit ourselves to any one at present, but simply to get as extensive a list as possible of eligible men. Thank you very much for the hints in your letter, and for your kind offer to make further inquiries. We shall be glad of any information you can obtain for us.

No one knows better than yourself what the article in question should be, and the most valuable aid you could give me would be, to sketch a plan which would convey your idea of the mode in which the subject should be treated.

I know that your interest in this matter rests on much higher ground

---

ble it. Mr. Chapman has not capital to carry it on. The loss is £100 a number with its present sales of nearly 1300 copies. 1700 would cover all expenses. Again, she finds it difficult to discover contributors who can write advanced views and do so consistently with each

other. The want of a philosophy is the cause of the latter." (NLS.)

6. See II, 33, n. 8.

7. "The Atomic Theory before Christ and Since," *Westminster Review*, 59 (January 1853), 167–196.

than any personal considerations, and that it would be impertinent in me to apologize for asking you to take this trouble.

I think the objection to Dr. Coxe as a writer would be, not that his style wants clearness or point, but that he lacks the habit of thoroughly organizing his materials—a habit which is the *sine qua non* of effective article writing, as you well know.[8]

I hope you have taken no fresh cold in this cheerless weather and that Mrs. Combe is as well as ever. Pray give my kindest regards to her and believe me, my dear Sir,

Yours very truly
Marian Evans.

II, 37:6 GE TO GEORGE COMBE, [LONDON], 22 JUNE 1852

MS: National Library of Scotland. *Endorsed:* London | Miss Evans | 24 June ansd.

June 22. 1852.

My dear Sir

I have been concerned to hear, through Mr. Bastard, of your severe indisposition. Your letter was welcome as a proof that you are recovering, as well as for other reasons. I assure you that your correspondence would be very valuable to me, even if it were nothing more than the expression of sympathy from such a mind as yours—but it is much more than this— for your suggestions are a help practically. So long therefore as you can spare time and effort to write you will be doing me a real good.

I have read your letter to Mr. Chapman, and have requested him to send you a statement of his position and wants. I need hardly say that he is greatly obliged to you for the effort you are making on his behalf—or rather on behalf of the diffusion of liberal opinion and scientific inquiry. I think better of our forthcoming number now I see the sheets in print. It will certainly be more "readable" than the previous ones.

I am inclined to think that one of the Dr. Browns[9] would be the best

---

8. Philip Gilbert Hamerton in his *Autobiography*, 1897, p. 127, says that in 1852 he wrote two or three papers for the *Westminster Review* "which were declined, and then I wrote to the editor asking if he would be so good as to explain... the reasons for their rejection. His answer came, and was both kind and judicious. 'An article,' he told me, 'ought to be an organic whole, with a prearranged order and proportion amongst its parts. There ought to be a beginning, a middle, and an end.'" The unnamed editor may well have been GE.

9. John Brown and Samuel Brown.

writer on Mr. Bastard's subject for a "Quarterly," but we are deferring decision on all such matters until the July number is off our hands. I am hoping to go to the coast next week, to reinforce myself with some sea breezes. I fear I shall not see you in London before I leave. I remain my dear Sir

Yours very truly
Marian Evans.

II, 39:12 GE TO GEORGE COMBE, LONDON, 29 JUNE 1852

MS: National Library of Scotland. *Endorsed:* London 29 June | 1852 | Miss Evans.

142 Strand | June 29. 1852.

My dear Sir

I assure you that the prospect of paying you a visit in October will make the intervening months pass more agreeably to me. But I do not like to hear such poor news of your health, which promises ill for *your* enjoyment of those months. I hope, however, that your next letter will report more rapid progress.

I thought it best to read to Mr. Chapman those passages in your last letter which referred to his affairs, as I know he wishes to be thoroughly open. I believe he has written to you on the subject,[1] so I need not enter into it further than to say that I think you may rely on his truthfulness.

You said, I believe, that Dr. John Brown had written in the North British. If so, will you be so good as to mention an article by him in that periodical? If he be fixed on as the writer of Mr. Bastard's article, we shall of course be glad that he should have your exposition of that gentleman's views.

With kind regards to Mrs. Combe, I am, my dear Sir,

Yours very truly
Marian Evans.

1. John Chapman to George Combe, 28 June 1852, regretting that he cannot send a statement of the condition of his business without ascertaining what decrease has come from his opposition to the Booksellers Association. (NLS, 7323, ff. 65–66.)

II, 41:15 GE TO GEORGE COMBE, [LONDON], 30 JUNE 1852

MS: National Library of Scotland. *Endorsed:* London 30 June 1852 | Miss Evans.

June 30. 1852.

My dear Sir

I am sure you will notice the frightful typographical errors in the article on German literature and elsewhere in the latter part of the Review.[2] Pray do not impute them to my carelessness. The insertion of the article on Sir Robert Peel[3] was not decided on until a few days before the publication of the Review and the consequence was, the printers were so hurried that I did not see a revise of that article or of the two last sheets of the number.

Pray forgive me for troubling you with this note. You see, I care about your approbation. Believe me, my dear Sir,

Very truly yours
Marian Evans.

I am very much dissatisfied with the article on English Literature and should like your opinion on it. I do not wish to employ the same writer again.[4]

II, 42:24 GE TO HERBERT SPENCER, BROADSTAIRS, [8? JULY 1852]

MS: British Museum. *Published with several misreadings: Bulletin of the New York Public Library,* 79 (Spring 1976), 366–368.

Chandos Cottage. | Thursday.

Dear Friend

No credit to me for my virtues as a refrigerant. I owe them all to a few lumps of ice which I carried away with me from that tremendous glacier of yours. I am glad that Nemesis, lame as she is,[8] has already made you

---

2. Among the glaring errors in the *Westminster Review*, 58 (July 1852), are Woolstoncroft (285), Fennimore Cooper (286), Bocaccio (305), and Monte Christo (313). The German article was probably written by Joseph Neuberg.

3. "Sir Robert Peel and His Policy," 205–246, was by W. R. Greg.

4. It was the work of Ebenezer Syme.

8. Cf. Horace, *Odes,* III, ii, 32, and "Janet's Repentance," ch. 13.

[8? July 1852]   51

feel a little uneasy in my absence, whether from the state of the thermometer or aught else.[9] We will not inquire too curiously whether you long most for my society or for the sea-breezes. If you decided that I was not worth coming to see, it would only be of a piece with that generally exasperating perspicacity of yours which will not allow one to humbug you. (An agreeable quality, let me tell you, that capacity of being humbugged. Don't pique yourself on not possessing it). But seriously and selfishness apart, I should like you to have the enjoyment of this pleasant place. The heat, tempered as it is here by the sea-breezes, is not at all oppressive, and only serves to give one a delicious, voluptuous laziness. There are fresh wild flowers coming out every day—the dear little creeping convolvulus and mignonette and others known to me "by sight, but not by name." And then the sun-set over the plains of wheat and barley, and the sea studded with sails. Do come on Saturday, if you would like it. There is a nice hotel where you can have a bed, and shant I be proud to do hospitalities once more? I think the Boat is better than the Excursion train—in spite of the shorter time of the latter. The heat and dust stretch 3 hours into 6.

I am ashamed to give a report of myself, for I have done nothing but dream away my time since I came. I think of retiring from the world, like old Weller,[1] if my good landlady will accept me as a tenant all the year round. I fancy I should soon be on an equality, in point of sensibility, with the star-fish and sea-egg[2]—perhaps you will wickedly say, I certainly want little of being a *Medusa*.[3] I have had a loathing for books—for all tagging together of sentences since I came, and have liked everything as indefinite as the sounds of an Æolian harp. You see I am sinking fast towards "homogeneity,"[4] and my brain will soon be a mere pulp unless you come to arrest the downward process. I have read Deerbrook,[5] and am surprized at the depths of feeling it reveals. Rose, Blanche and Violet,[6] too—at least the two first volumes—the third I left behind and (damaging fact, either for me or the novel!) I don't care to have it. I have read a

9. Since GE left London 3 July the temperature there had been 78, 89, 85, 81. For her relations with Spencer and his rejection of her love see Haight, *George Eliot*, pp. 111–122, written before her letters to him were available.

1. The elder Sam Weller retired to "an excellent public house near Shooter's Hill, where he is quite reverenced as an oracle." (*Pickwick Papers*, ch. 57.)

2. The sea urchin.

3. The jelly fish; but also the Gorgon, a monster so hideous that men who looked at it were turned to stone.

4. The basic argument of Spencer's theory that all progress is from the homogeneous to the heterogeneous was first expounded in his "The Development Hypothesis." *Leader*, 3 (20 March 1852), 280–281.

5. GE read Harriet Martineau's *Deerbrook*, 3 vols., 1839, in preparation for her visit to Ambleside in October.

6. GHL's second novel, 3 vols., 1848.

good deal of "In Memoriam"⁷—which, believe it or not, has great beauties—though the artificiality of the form is unforgiveable. Froude's much talked of article on Spinoza⁸ too I have read at last, and find it a mere sketch of his life—picturesquely done but with the usual Froudian sentimentality and false veneration. This morning I determined to reform and plunged into Warburton.⁹ Henceforth I mean to live laborious days¹ —that is to say until I have made up my mind to fraternize with the star-fish. In haste,

Ever yours truly
Marian Evans.

I am horrified to see how I have blotted my letter. Grâce—

II, 44:19   MRS. JOHN CHAPMAN TO GEORGE COMBE, LONDON, 14 JULY 1852

MS: National Library of Scotland. *Endorsed:* London 14 July 1852 | Mrs. John Chapman | 20 July ansd. Her own letter shows that Mr. C has no adequate business talent. He must get into a line for which he is fitted before he can succeed.

142 Strand | July 14th 1852.

My dear Sir

We have heard from Mr. Bray that you think Mr. Chapman has many good qualities but that he is not a man of business. As I have been intimately acquainted with him during the whole of his business career I think I can shew you where his faults lie and what is the reason that he has not been successful. You are perhaps aware that he had no business education and when eight years ago he commenced business as a publisher² he scarcely knew the names of Ledger and Daybook. His predecessor's accounts were kept in a most slovenly manner and he soon made great reforms and thoroughly mastered the science of book keeping. He likes every thing to be done well, he must have the best paper and the best printing and for this he pays the highest price, he is apt also to spend both time and money in ornamental covers etc. which are much admired but do not increase the number of copies sold; he says they give him a rep-

---

7. *In Memoriam* was published in May 1850. This is the first reference to Tennyson I have found in GE's papers.

8. J. A. Froude, "The Life of Spinoza," *Oxford and Cambridge Review*, 5 (October 1847), 387–427.

9. William Warburton, *The Divine Legation of Moses Demonstrated on the Principles of a Religious Deist, from the Omission of the Doctrine of a Future State of Rewards and Punishments in the Jewish Dispensation*, 2 vols., 1738–41. GE was beginning to read for her projected *The Idea of a Future Life*.

1. Milton, *Lycidas*, line 72.

2. In January 1844 Chapman bought John Green's business at 121 Newgate Street. See *George Eliot and John Chapman*, p. 3.

utation, which is true, but these expenses leave too narrow a margin for profit; he likes to employ a good printer, one who pays his men well; he likes to pay his assistants well, and has thought that by so doing he would secure their services and cordial cooperation in his plans; he has been singularly unfortunate in his assistants though he takes great pains and care in the selection. Two of them have left in his debt.

In another aspect he has been very unfortunate; he published the life of Channing[3] and under the existing law procured a copyright for it in this country. When the edition was about half sold the decision was given against the legality of the copyright, and the book was republished for 7/ and an abridgement for five. He was obliged to reduce the price to 10/6; the same thing happened with Emerson's Representative Men,[4] from which he might have expected to reap some profit to compensate for the loss on the second series of Emerson's Essays and the Poems.[5] Then in a short time the copyright was made legal and he was subjected to an injunction by Mr. Fellowes[6] for selling one copy of a third edition of a book, in the first edition of which published many years ago Mr. Fellowes had an interest. This cost him £50 and recently Mr. Moxon[7] has subjected him to the same penalty. Mr. Chapman is now convinced that he must go to the cheapest market. The last number of the Westminster is I think equal to the others in appearance but has cost considerably less.

The same thing must be done with other things. He is too generous; when he has gained by a book he feels as if he were bound to make some compensation to the author. When a boy who has been a year in his service asks for an increase of wages he gives it him because he thinks he deserves it, though I believe that a boy with 5/ per week is generally more industrious and punctual than one with ten, and he must learn to curb that generous feeling and look more to his own interest. He has surely gained some experience from the past, he has been trying experiments, when one branch of business seemed failing he tried another. Thus the business is large and complicated, and requires more assistance than a much larger business would if it were confined to one department.

3. *Memoir of William Ellery Channing, with Extracts from his Correspondence and Manuscripts*, Boston, Crosby & Nichols; London, John Chapman, 3 vols., 1848, was reissued in 2 vols., by Routledge, 1850.

4. *Representative Men*, Chapman's Catholic Series, 1844; Routledge, 1850.

5. Emerson's *Poems*, Boston, J. Monroe & Co.; London, Chapman Brothers, 1847; 2d ed. Routledge, 1850. *Essays (Second Series)*, with a Notice by Thomas Carlyle, 1844.

6. Robert Fellowes. See *The Times*, 8 December 1848, p. 7a, and 9 December, p. 3f.

7. In the Vice-Chancellor's Court Moxon applied for an injunction to prevent Chapman's selling *The World's Progress*, published by Putnam, much of it copied from Haydn's *Dictionary of Dates*; Chapman was fined £46.3.10. (*The Times*, 10 February 1852, p. 7a.)

And now for his business qualities: he is methodical and orderly to a *fault*, if such a thing can be; he is industrious beyond any man I ever knew; he generally goes to bed at ten and rises at 5, takes a showerbath and works till breakfast time; he has great energy; often when the assistants have said it was impossible to get a case packed by a certain time, he says it must be possible and by urging and superintending and assisting, the impossible is performed. He always likes to *bottom* every thing and that is his great complaint against his assistants; the first difficulty stops them, but a difficulty only makes him more determined to persevere till it is overcome. He has no habits of procrastination—he does not love business but performs it as a duty.

I could wish very much that he were out of business; if he had the editing of the Westminster Review he would work hard but it would be in a direction that suited him, but then the Westminster is at present a loss rather than a gain. Also we have a good connexion, a considerable stock, all the implements and machinery for carrying on business, and if it is suddenly brought to a close not only shall we lose every thing but our friends will lose also, whereas I hope by going on we might redeem ourselves. When we took to the business the returns were barely 4000 £, they are now or were at Christmas nearly £1200. One great trouble is this large house. The boarding house will nearly pay our expenses but not the rent which is £400, and the rates including water and gas more than another hundred; but I am going into details which are not to the point. My wish is to clear my husband from the imputation of not being a business man, that is, not devoting his energies and talents to his business. He has been long purchasing experience and if he had only the power to do it, I think he is now in a position to win back what he has lost. I hope you will not be annoyed at this long letter. Believe me

Respectfully yours
Susanna Chapman.

II, 45:10 GE TO JOHN CHAPMAN, [BROADSTAIRS, 16 JULY 1852]

MS: Mr. Gordon N. Ray. *Endorsed:* Miss Evans | July 17. 52.

Friday.

Dear Friend

I think Dr. J. Brown will do—I have written today to Geo. Combe to say so and to beg him to conclude the negotiation, so that matter is settled.[8]

8. John Brown refused to write. See II, 48.

With regard to other articles, we only want two, supposing that Martineau writes the one you proposed to him. I dare say your suggestion has been "working in his head like barm,"[9] and that his thoughts have already shaped themselves to some purpose. You said Oxenford[1] wanted to write, but I forget what subject he proposed. If it were a good one, I think you might do worse than close with him. There was Mr. Don, or Dunne,[2] too, whose articles I was to read in the Edinburgh.

Failing Martineau, I think we should get Foxton.[3] A good subject for him would be the Popery of Dissent.

[*The rest of this letter is lacking.*]

II, 45:10 GE TO GEORGE COMBE, BROADSTAIRS, 16 JULY [1852]

MS: National Library of Scotland. *Endorsed:* Miss Evans and J. Brown | 18 July ansd.

Chandos Cottage | Broadstairs | July 16.
My dear Sir

I have read several of Dr. J. Brown's articles, and I think they exhibit considerable depth and earnestness of mind, a refined taste, and very copious and varied information. He seems to me hardly so much a master of the pen as his brother, Dr. Samuel;[4] his style wants a little more of the *labor limæ*;[5] but this a well-managed hint from you will probably induce him to apply. I fancy, the greatest danger with respect to him would be the tendency occasionally rather to exhibit his own information than to instruct the reader and so to produce a striking article, instead of a popular and useful one. But the best guarantee against such a result is your offer to write to him on the subject of Mr. Bastard's article. Since you have kindly undertaken this, I think it would be better for me to leave the negotiation entirely to you and not to write to him myself.

9. Cf. Scott, *Kenilworth*, ch. 34.

1. John Oxenford (1812–77) wrote on Schopenhauer for April 1853. See II, 95.

2. Combe has confused Robert Dunn (1799–1877) with William Bodham Donne (1807–82), author of "The Marquis of Rockingham" in the *Edinburgh Review*, 96 (July 1852), 110–142. See GE to Combe, 25 July [1852].

3. Frederick J. Foxton, whose paper was so bad that it could not be published.

4. John Brown (1810–82), a cousin of Samuel Brown (1817–56), became the more noted author with his *Horæ Subsecivæ* (1858), which contained "Rab and His Friends." Among his articles in the *North British Review* were a review of Ruskin's *Modern Painters*, February 1847; "Dr. Chalmers' Posthumous Works," February 1848; "Vaughan's *Poems*," May 1849; "Locke and Sydenham," November 1849; and "*The Remains of Arthur H. Hallam*," February 1851.

5. Cf. Horace, *Ars Poetica*, line 291.

I am much obliged to you for your opinion on the English article—it coincides entirely with my own. I am concerned to hear that you think so hopelessly of Mr. Chapman's affairs.⁶ The maintenance of his position as a publisher is of importance on other grounds than personal ones.

I am glad to hear of your progress towards health. Pray give my kindest regards to Mrs. Combe and believe me, my dear Sir

Yours very truly
Marian Evans.

II, 46:12 GE TO HERBERT SPENCER, [BROADSTAIRS, 16? JULY 1852]⁷

MS: British Museum. *Published with several misreadings: Bulletin of the New York Public Library,* 79 (Spring 1976), 369–370.

I know this letter will make you very angry with me, but wait a little, and don't say anything to me while you are angry. I promise not to sin any more in the same way.

My ill health is caused by the hopeless wretchedness which weighs upon me. I do not say this to pain you, but because it is the simple truth which you must know in order to understand why I am obliged to seek relief.

I want to know if you can assure me that you will not forsake me, that you will always be with me as much as you can and share your thoughts and feelings with me. If you become attached to some one else,

---

6. According to Chapman the *Westminster Review* sold 2370 copies of the January and April numbers [combined] and 1185 of the July number. (Chapman to Combe, 4 August 1852. NLS.) In his Journal, 6 July 1852, Combe wrote that he found "everything in a very unsatisfactory state. The evil arises from his want of business talent. He was bred a Surgeon, in the midst of studies commenced Bookseller on his own account without previous training to the business; got hold of £4600 of capital belonging to his wife and her Aunt; has applied it inconsiderately, bought the Review when he had no capital to carry it on; entered into a controversy with the other Booksellers, in which he was in the right and beat them, but in which they have taken revenge by ceasing to buy his publications, so that his loss on this head is great; and in short from want of business talent, he has failed in everything, where with that talent he might have succeeded, and he is now insolvent. I see no way of extrication but a bankruptcy, and recommended to him to consult Mr. Bray, which he is to do. The want of business talent will render all temporary assistance ineffectual for good."(NLS.)

7. It is impossible to date this letter with certainty. As I reconstruct the episode Spencer came to Broadstairs on Saturday, 10 July, and after his rejection of her love, GE handed this letter to him. It has no salutation and ends without a period.

19 July 1852

then I must die, but until then I could gather courage to work and make life valuable, if only I had you near me. I do not ask you to sacrifice anything—I would be very good and cheerful and never annoy you. But I find it impossible to contemplate life under any other conditions. If I had your assurance, I could trust that and live upon it. I have struggled—indeed I have—to renounce everything and be entirely unselfish, but I find myself utterly unequal to it. Those who have known me best have always said, that if ever I loved any one thoroughly my whole life must turn upon that feeling, and I find they said truly. You curse the destiny which has made the feeling concentrate itself on you—but if you will only have patience with me you shall not curse it long. You will find that I can be satisfied with very little, if I am delivered from the dread of losing it.

I suppose no woman ever before wrote such a letter as this—but I am not ashamed of it, for I am conscious that in the light of reason and true refinement I am worthy of your respect and tenderness, whatever gross men or vulgar-minded women might think of me

II, 46:12 JOHN CHAPMAN TO GEORGE COMBE, LONDON, 19 JULY 1852

MS: National Library of Scotland. *Endorsed:* London 19th July 1852 | John Chapman.

142 Strand, London | July 19. 1852.

My dear Sir

Quite unknown to me my wife wrote the enclosed letter;[8] she afterwards read it to me and wished to send it to you; I advised her not to do so on the ground that you would consider it biassed testimony and therefore without weight. She then placed it in my hands. On reperusing it to-day I felt that it is written in so just a spirit, and, in the main, is so true in fact that I should not have acted injudiciously in acceding to Mrs. C's wish to send it; and now therefore send it unknown to her. She went to Nottingham today. Though the reasons which induced me to ask her to withold it are still in force, and I feel that I must 'bide my time,' there yet seems no necessity for concealment.

Yours very sincerely,
John Chapman.

8. 14 July 1852.

II, 46:12 CHARLES BRAY TO GEORGE COMBE, COVENTRY, 20 JULY 1852

MS: National Library of Scotland. *Endorsed:* Coventry 20 July 1852 | Charles Bray.

Coventry, July 20/52.

My dear Sir

Excuse my troubling you again. Probably the view you take of Mr. Chapman and his affairs is the correct one, but what I have to say is independent of any difference of opinion on this score. I wish to keep the Westminster in *our* hands—viz: in yours and mine and Miss Evans's et hoc genus omne, and my proposition is, that it be made over to 10 of us, for 100£ each. If in a given time, say two ⟨or⟩ three or 5 years, Mr. Chapman is able to redeem it, let him have the option—if not it would belong to us—and by that time, under present management, and as it is now going on, it would be worth that money. Is this practicable? Mr. C. says that 1000£ would keep him up permanently—if so, all the better for our cause, and the Review could not be in better hands—if not, it will probably keep him up long enough to ensure the success of the Review and we get that for our money. If I were a capitalist I should not mind this risk, because to keep the Review *right* is so important.

I shall be from home for a week, when perhaps you will tell me what you think of my plan. I think the literary men who now write for the Review would gladly take a share in it and perhaps help to keep it up till it became a property. The Quarterly and Edinbro' circulate about 9000 I believe.

I am *very* sorry to hear what you say about your chest. We could ill spare you yet. I am, my dear Sir,

Very Sincerely yours,
Charles Bray.

Will you kindly present my compliments to Mr. Bastard?

II, 47:8 GE TO GEORGE COMBE, BROADSTAIRS, 21 JULY 1852

MS: National Library of Scotland. *Endorsed:* Broadstairs 21 July 1852 | Miss Evans.

Broadstairs | July 21.

My dear Sir

I ought to have told you yesterday that I forwarded your excellent letter to Dr. J. Brown by Monday's post. I hope he will not shrink from the labour necessary to prepare his article for the October number.

You and Mrs. Combe are, I dare say, enjoying nature and quiet as much as I am. London, with its dingy restless life, seems fabulous to me, here among the wild flowers, listening to the plash of the waves.

Mr. Bray tells me he hopes to meet you in London on the 2d of August.[9] I should have liked very much to see both you and him, but I am bent, for my health's sake, on remaining out of London as long as the business of the Review will let me.

With kindest remembrances to Mrs. Combe, I am, my dear Sir,

Yours very truly
Marian Evans.

II, 47:8 GEORGE COMBE TO CHARLES BRAY, CHARLTON, 24 JULY 1852

MS: Draft on verso Bray's letter, 20 July 1852, National Library of Scotland.

Charlton, 24 July 1852 Answered thus:

If a practical scheme can be found for preserving the Review in the hands you mention, I should contribute £100 and ask friends to join in raising £1000 but your scheme is not a practical one. Mr. C. is insolvent in his general business and the Review is still a source of loss, in my opinion of £400 a year. To ⟨take⟩ give Mr. C. £1000 would be simply to cover his general deficiencies perhaps for 2 years, when it would be all lost, and the persons to whom the Review was conveyed would be liable for its debts, and when Mr. Chapman again stood still they would be called on to pay those claims and take the whole concern into their hands.

---

9. The Combes were visiting T. H. Bastard at Charlton, Blandford, Dorset. Writing to Combe 16 July 1852, Bray proposed to meet him "in *Town* or *anywhere* about the 2 August." (NLS.)

If by re-imbursing Mr. C. in the £350 paid by him for the Review, disconnecting it from his general business, and applying the £650 remaining of the £1000 to it, it might be carried on for 2 years, and I should be ready then to allow him to buy it back on refunding the £350 and intermediate loss; but this would leave no remuneration for him and Miss Evans as editors. If they were paid £100 a year each, the loss would be £600, and the £1000 would suffice only for one year. Were the Review taken out of his hands entirely we should lose the advantage of his connection. In short I do not see any way to a practical solution of the difficulty.

II, 50:17 GE TO GEORGE COMBE, BROADSTAIRS, 25 JULY [1852]

MS: National Library of Scotland. *Endorsed:* 1852 | Miss Evans | 27 July ansd. Mr Bastard | agrees to the delay and | I have written to Dr. J. Brown.

Broadstairs | July 25.

My dear Sir

I am heartily sorry that Dr. J. Brown has returned a negative to your proposition, for I have a very favourable impression of his mental character, and I cannot help wishing that Mr. Bastard would consent to defer his article until January, supposing that Dr. Brown would engage to write it within that prolonged period.

Mr. Robert Dunn,[1] whom you mentioned in one of your letters as possibly suited to our purpose in this matter, is, I fear, a dry writer, and does not, so far as I have been able to judge, possess the inestimable advantage of that wide culture which not only gives a charm to an author's presentation of his subject, but also contributes to the breadth and justness of his views. For the rest, Mr. Dunn is a man of considerable intellect and certainly of great professional experience. Whatever may be the decision, it is important that it should be arrived at quickly, as, failing the article on hereditary qualities, we must seek another to supply its place.

I share your disagreement with some parts of the article on the Restoration of Belief (J. Martineau's); indeed, the admission of those theological views into the Westminster is a constant source of dissatisfaction to me. I see nothing for it, however, but that the Review should remain, at least

---

1. Robert Dunn (1799–1877), a surgeon at 15 Norfolk Street, Strand was the author of *A Case of Hemiplegia*, 1850, and *On the Inhalation of Chloroform*, 1851. See GE to John Chapman, [16 July 1852].

[29? July 1852]

for some time to come, a sort of Noah's Ark. On this point I should like to say much more to you.

With kind regards to Mrs. Combe, I am, my dear Sir

Yours very truly
Marian Evans.

II, 50:17 GE TO HERBERT SPENCER, BROADSTAIRS, [29? JULY 1852]

MS: British Museum. *Published with several misreadings: Bulletin of the New York Public Library*, 79 (Spring 1976), 368–369.

Broadstairs | Thursday Evening.

Dear Mr. Spencer[2]

It would be ungenerous in me to allow you to suffer even a slight uneasiness on my account which I am able to remove. I ought at once to tell you, since I can do so with truth, that I am not unhappy. The fact is, all sorrows sink into insignificance before the one great sorrow—my own miserable imperfections, and any outward hap is welcome if it will only serve to rouse my energies and make me less unworthy of my better self. I have good hope that it will be so now, and I wish you to share this hope if it will give you any satisfaction.

If, as you intimated in your last letter, you feel that my friendship is of value to you for its own sake—mind on no other ground—it is yours. Let us, if you will, forget the past, except in so far as it may have brought us to trust in and feel for each other, and let us help to make life beautiful to each other as far as fate and the world will permit us. Whenever you like to come to me again, to see the golden corn before it is reaped,[3] I can promise you such companionship as there is in me, untroubled by painful emotions. I meant to write you a long letter and tell you a great deal about my thoughts and feelings since we parted—but I have been ill for the last three days and everything is an effort to me.

Ever yours faithfully
Marian Evans.

2. Note the sudden formality.

3. In 1852 a cold wet June was followed by two months of extraordinarily fine hot weather. The *Canterbury Journal and Farmers' Gazette* reported 7 August that reaping had become general with the most auspicious weather, wheat, barley, oats, and peas having been cut during the past week. On 14 August it said that the wheat never looked better, being heavy and erect. "Harvest operations have been carried on with great activity in this neighbourhood in the past week."

II, 55:8 GEORGE COMBE JOURNAL, COVENTRY, 10 SEPTEMBER 1852

MS: National Library of Scotland.

Mr. Bray and I discussed Mr. Chapman's affairs fully, and I found a number of discrepancies between the Statement given to me and that given to Mr. Bray, and after hearing every explanation that Mr. Bray could give, I continued to be of opinion that Mr. Chapman is deficient in business talent, in conscientiousness, and in real depth of intellect. He has great ambition, Benevolence, and a sympathy with liberal views, but transcendentally rather than practically. Mr. Bray said that 5 friends have lent him £100 each, and the printer[1] and stationer of the Westminster Review have advanced him £500 on the security of the copy right of it, and that with these sums he will go on. I prophesied that he will need more aid within two years. Mr. Bray hopes he may make a fortune; yet he sees his defects.

II, 59:1 GE TO MRS. HENRY HOUGHTON, LONDON, 2 OCTOBER 1852

MS: Yale.

142 Strand | October 2.

My dear Fanny

Thank you for the nice long letter you wrote me the other day. I hope that by this time Henry is come back with good news about Ireland, for I would rather have you there than in the other hemisphere.

I shall really be glad to know that you have more breathing room both spiritually and physically, than you have at Leamington.

I have had a four days' headache this week but I am well now, and thinking with pleasure of my journey to Edinburgh on Tuesday. I am going to Geo. Combe's for a fortnight and am to pay a visit to Miss Martineau at Ambleside on my way home. I ought to come back refreshed, ought I not? Write to me as soon as you can tell me where you are to go. With love to Henry,

Ever your affectionate sister
Marian Evans.

1. George Woodfall and Son, Printers, Angel Court, Skinner Street, London.

II, 63:14 GE TO JOHN CHAPMAN, AMBLESIDE, 24 OCTOBER 1852

MS: University of London. *Endorsed:* Miss Evans | Oct. 24. 1852.

Ambleside | Sunday Morning.

Dear Friend

The programme is not a bad one, though rather too grave. You are quite right to accept Forster's article.[2] The subject is just the thing now, and I know from Miss Martineau, that he is deeply interested in it and taking pains to collect full information. Miss M. promises that her Irish article[3] shall be of her Number 1 quality. Then the Charity,[4] Chemistry,[5] and Mary Tudor[6] are likely to be good, so that one may set one's heart at rest. If James Martineau declines,[7] *I accept.*

Lewes's letter was to ask me to review Hippolytus for the Leader,[8] and I have written to say *yea.* But *don't tell.* Miss Martineau will write to you soon about Deerbrook and her Irish Letters.[9]

The only drawback to my pleasure here is that I am not at all well. Still I keep up bravely and manage to enjoy. If I had been better, I should have written to you, but I have been so weary at night that I could only go to sleep, and night is the only time I have had for writing.

I go to Coventry on Tuesday. I am thankful to hear that Beatrice[1] is better. Love to Mrs. Chapman.

Ever yours faithfully
Marian Evans.

2. W. E. Forster, "American Slavery, and Emancipation by the Free States," *Westminster Review*, 59 (January 1853), 125–167, discussing *Uncle Tom's Cabin* and other books, strongly urged English support of emancipation.

3. Harriet Martineau, "Condition and Prospects of Ireland," 35–62.

4. W. R. Greg, "Charity, Noxious and Beneficent," 62–88.

5. Samuel Brown, "The Atomic Theory, before Christ and since," 117–196.

6. J. A. Froude, "Mary Tudor," 1–34.

7. James Martineau, "Early Christianity, Its Creed and Heresies," a review of Emmanuel Miller's *Origen*, 1851, and C. C. J. Bunsen's *Hippolytus and His Age*, 1852, *Westminster Review*, 59 (April 1853), 535–584. GE discussed both books in her "Contemporary Literature of England," 59 (January 1853), 263–266.

8. I find no review of this book in the *Leader*.

9. See II, 70, n. 4.

1. Chapman's daughter Clara Beatrice (born 1844) had scarlet fever.

II, 64:12 GE TO GEORGE COMBE, COVENTRY, 29 OCTOBER 1852

MS: National Library of Scotland. *Endorsed:* Rosehill 29 Oct. 1852 | Miss Evans.

Rosehill, Coventry | October 29. 1852.

My dear Sir

I am so in the habit of blending husband and wife together in my correspondence, that I felt as if I were writing both to you and Mrs. Combe in my last letter,[2] and hence I omitted any special message of remembrances to you.

I am sorry to tell you that I did not see Mr. Greg[3] during my stay at Ambleside. He and Miss Martineau are on very friendly terms, but there is not a frequent interchange of visits between them. However, I took care that he should receive your letter and pamphlet, as I dare say you have by this time learned from himself.

Even one who went to see Miss Martineau with a prepossession against her must be won to admiration of her geniality, and energetic efforts for the good of her working neighbours. Her building society, her lectures, and her affectionate interest in the welfare of her servants, who, after being with her several years, are trying to "better themselves" by marriage and emigration, shew a practical goodness quite as rare as her talent for writing. There are so many in the world who have more than all her foibles, without her bright and good qualities, and yet people give her much harder measure than they are willing to grant to those said do-nothings.

I found my friends here quite well and cheerful. Coventry trade is more hopeful than usual, and Mr. Bray's good-natured face is free from any hint of anxiety.

Best love to Mrs. Combe, who perhaps will read this to you by the dining-room fire after breakfast. I think with pleasure of the mornings when I was seated there between you. I hope the screen I used to hold, or something else outward or inward, will now and then remind you both of those same mornings and suggest to you that I may like to hear how you are and what you are doing. Ever, my dear Sir,

Yours truly
Marian Evans.

2. Not found.   3. See II, 66, n. 6.

II, 68:4 GE TO GEORGE COMBE, LONDON, 13 NOVEMBER 1852

MS: National Library of Scotland. *Endorsed:* Miss Evans | 20 Nov. ansd.

142 Strand | November 13. 1852.

My dear Sir

A visitation of my old London companion, the headache, which is still but partially relieved, has prevented me from writing to you for several days, and I must even now ask your indulgence for a letter written under a state of brain of which this foggy London November is the aptest symbol.

On my return here, I found that Mr. Chapman had been in communication with Dr. Hodgson, formerly of Manchester, and now residing at Bonn, with reference to Mr. Bastard's third article for the Westminster—that on the Curriculum of Schools.[4] I believe Dr. Hodgson is known to you, but I have no idea whether you will concur in Mr. Chapman's opinion, that he would be likely to treat the above subject satisfactorily to Mr. Bastard. I will transcribe all that Dr. Hodgson says on the matter in his last letter.

"I shall be very glad to write such an article as you propose; and I think I can do it best in form of a review of a recent work by Professor Pillans on *The Rationale of Discipline*.[5] The main purpose would be, to set the importance of teaching modern languages above that of teaching Classics in schools for the young. I would give the Classics a high place even in education, but I should defer them to a period in the school course later than usual, and by that means, confine them to a smaller number of students, to those, namely, who by their longer stay at school are prepared to profit by them. My views are quite those of Professor Newman. I think, with him, that all the advantages in the way of mental exercise which the Classics give, can be as well derived from French and German, while in addition an acquirement of great, of universal, and of increasing importance is being made. I should range widely enough to take in the class of subjects suitable for schools of the rich as well as of the poor, and endeavour to lay down principles common to both, so as to determine the proper amount of divergence or difference. In essentials, unity; in all else, diversity. What then are the essentials? Here lies the question. I have the order of the article in my head, and some part of it already sketched out."

---

4. W. B. Hodgson, "The School Claims of Language, Ancient and Modern," *Westminster Review*, 60 (October 1853), 450–498.

5. James Pillans, *The Rationale of Discipline, as Exemplified in the High School of Edinburgh*, Edinburgh, 1852, was discussed in Hodgson's article.

I confess that the above extract does not satisfy me as to the probability of Dr. Hodgson's meeting your and Mr. Bastard's views. I do not think you desire an article of which *"the main purpose"* shall be "to set the importance of teaching the modern languages above that of teaching the Classics" though you might agree in regarding that as one point of reformation. However, as the negotiation has gone so far, perhaps the best plan would be for you to state in a note to the Editors of the Westminster the chief heads which Mr. Bastard desires to see insisted on and for Mr. Chapman to forward ⟨them⟩ the note to Dr. Hodgson, in which case, if he declared his dissent from your views, it would be possible, without discourtesy, to withdraw the proposition that he should write the article.

Mr. Greg called on me a few days ago on his way to Paris. He brought his article on Charity. It contains much which is sound and valuable, though perhaps not everything we should have liked. He has headed it "Charitable Malefactors."[6] I remember you objected to this title and preferred another which he suggested but which I have forgotten. I will try to send you the sheets of this article as soon as it is in print.

We are to have an article on Webster[7] in the January number. I should like to know your opinion about his conduct with regard to the Fugitive Slave Law, and whether you believe in the necessity of that compromise. But I have no right to ask for any information in reply to so interrupted and illegible a letter as this. I felt that the matter of Dr. Hodgson and the article on Schools ought not to be deferred, or I would have waited until I was better able to write.

I have not yet procured the pamphlet you speak of. The writer is surely too broad in his statement, when he says there is no authority in *Scripture* for a separate and immortal soul. I think there is none in the Old Testament —certainly not in the Pentateuch—but there are many passages in the New Testament which seem to me to imply the doctrine. However I will get the pamphlet. Mr. Ellis sent me the other day, his new little book.[8] It looks "full of matter"—like everything else of his.

My best love to Mrs. Combe. I hope to hear excellent news of you both. Alas! for the pure air I was breathing with you a month ago. My room here has the light one might expect midway up a chimney, with a little blaze of fire below, and a little glimmer of sky above. Ever, my dear Sir,

           Yours gratefully and truly
            Marian Evans.

---

6. It was changed to "Charity, Noxious and Beneficent," 59 (January 1853), 62–88.

7. "Daniel Webster," 230–263, by Edwin Percy Whipple.

8. William Ellis, *What Am I? Where Am I? . . . By the Author of Outlines of Social Economy*, 1852.

II, 72:15 GE TO GEORGE COMBE, LONDON, 14 DECEMBER 1852

MS: National Library of Scotland. *Endorsed:* London | Miss Evans | 16 Dec. ansd.

142 Strand | December 14. 1852.

My dear Sir

I anticipated several of your criticisms on Mr. Greg's article. Immediately after I had read the MS. we sent him the passage on capital punishments with a request that he would alter it, and he returned it, slightly modified indeed, but still not essentially less objectionable. The passage on Negro Emancipation we have determined, after some correspondence with Mr. Greg, to omit.[9] He is so unused to editorial suggestion or criticism and so unwilling to modify anything when it is once out of his hands, that there is no alternative but to let the article stand in its present unsatisfactory state or to reject it altogether. The whole matter is more vexatious to me than anything which has occurred since we had the management of the Review.

I have *not* read your pamphlet, and should like to do so. I suppose I can get a copy from Simpkin and Marshall?

Mrs. Stirling's[1] sketch of Madame de Sevigné is charmingly done. Pray tell her, with my kind regards, that I have had much pleasure in reading it.

I am overwhelmed with details that must be attended to at once, having accumulated during a two days' absence of mine at Rosehill, where I went to get refreshed. Otherwise I should have written to you more at length.

With kindest regards to Mrs. Combe, I am my dear Sir

Yours very truly
Marian Evans.

It is unnecessary to send me back the proof.

---

9. No reference to capital punishment remains. Some attack on the slave owners is found on p. 83.

1. Anne Charlotte (d. 1875), daughter of Sir Alexander Maitland, 2d Bart., married William Stirling of Castlemilk in 1822. She lived at 44 Melville Street; the Combes, at 45.

II, 74:1 GE TO GEORGE COMBE, LONDON, 21 DECEMBER 1852

MS: National Library of Scotland. *Endorsed:* London 21 Dec. 1852 | Miss Evans | recd 24 Dec. | ansd. 28 Dec.

142 Strand | December 21. 1852.

My dear Sir

I am glad to tell you that by some further efforts since I last wrote to you, we have succeeded in getting rid of the obnoxious paragraphs on capital punishments and prison discipline in Mr. Greg's article.

My mind is painfully preoccupied this morning by a family trouble. My sister's husband—a medical man, not more than forty years of age—died yesterday. My sister is left with six little children, and I am full of anxiety about a future provision for them. I shall be obliged to leave town on Thursday—an unfortunate moment for the Westminster affairs.

With kindest regards to Mrs. Combe, I am ever, my dear Sir,

Yours very truly
Marian Evans.

Geo. Combe Esq.

II, 82:11 GE TO MRS. HENRY HOUGHTON, [LONDON, 17 JANUARY 1853]

MS: Mr. Percival Robert Allen.

Monday Morning.

My dear Fanny

I have been and am very poorly or I should have written to you on Saturday. Thank you for your note with its news and kind words, which were very welcome. I hope to be able to go down to Chrissey for a week by and bye. I wish you would learn from her or ask her to tell me, *when* I should be of the greatest use—whether she would like me to be with her when she is moving?[2]

As I have this prospect, I shall not send a parcel, but wait till I can be my own carrier. When shall you be obliged to leave her? How nice it would be to have a chat with you once more. Best love to all the dear ones.[3] Ever, dear Fanny,

Your affectionate sister
Marian Evans.

2. From Meriden to a small house at Attleborough. See II, 75.

3. Chrissey Clarke and her six children.

II, 82:32 GE TO GEORGE COMBE, LONDON, 22 JANUARY 1853

MS: National Library of Scotland. *Endorsed:* ⟨London 22 Jany 1853 | Miss Evans | & | Wm Glen Moncrieff | on the Soul⟩ Miss Evans | The Bible | 27 Jany ansd.

142 Strand | January 22. 1853.

My dear Sir

It is only as an apology for my long neglect to write to you that I trouble you with another *jérémiade* about my unfortunate health. Since I requested Mr. Bastard to deliver my message to you I have been again quite laid up, and I have at length come to the resolution of seeking a more healthy residence. I must stay here, however, till after the beginning of April, and manage as well as I can in my dim abode, like a potato in a cellar.

I read yesterday the little pamphlet on 'Soul'[4] which you mentioned to me some time ago. I think it is quite valuable, at least as a piece of criticism, though it may perhaps be regarded as one among the many signs of the hopeful fact, that even narrow orthodoxy is beginning to shrink from the doctrine of eternal punishments. For my own part, I was never fond of the plan of availing oneself of the elasticity of the biblical text to make the scriptural writers teach philosophy and to force truth on the believers in inspiration by an *argumentum ad hominem*. I like thoroughly honest critical investigation and could never encourage such a reasoner as our Mr. Moncrieff simply because he wants to make the Bible less mischievous. He appears to be ignorant both of the philosophy of language and the true principles of biblical criticism—he thinks that a theory as to a doctrine can be founded on the merely etymological meaning of a word which has half a dozen derivative meanings, and that there is a *homogeneity* of thought in all the different parts of the Bible in spite of the varieties in their chronology and the other circumstances of their production.[5] As to his argument about the Old Testament, even B[isho]p Warburton long ago proved that the ⟨Mosaic⟩ idea of a future life was not included in the Mosaic system, which was one of purely temporal rewards and punishments. (By the bye, I wonder if you have read a clever work on "*Jesus-Christ et sa doctrine*" by Salvador,[6] a free-thinking Jew, in which the writer attempts to shew that the Mosaic system presented the quintessence of political and social wisdom,

---

4. William Glen Moncrieff, *Soul; or the Hebrew Word Nephesh and the Greek Word Psyche*, [Edinburgh printed], 1852.

5. "Mr Casaubon's theory . . . floated among flexible conjectures no more solid than those etymologies which seemed strong because of likeness in sound, until it was shown that likeness in sound made them impossible." (*Middlemarch*, ch. 48.)

6. Joseph Salvador, *Jésus-Christ et sa doctrine. Histoire de la naissance de l'église et de ses progrès pendant le première siècle*, 2 vols., Paris, 1838.

and that, morally, it was an adumbration of the doctrines contained in "The Constitution of Man."⁷)

As to the New Testament, there are many contradictory texts which have given rise to the *vexata questio* of "the middle state" between death and the resurrection. But surely nothing can be built on the mere word ψυχη which is equally used for the simply *animal* life and, interchangeably with πνευμα for the spiritual existence—the soul. I think Mr. M. has quite failed to explain away the difficulty in Matthew 10.28: "Fear not them that kill the body etc.—a passage utterly meaningless without the antithesis between the life of the body and the life of the soul, which antithesis he has been previously maintaining not to have existed in the minds of the biblical writers. His ultimate argument to which all the rest tends—that the Scriptures teach not the eternal punishment but the annihilation of the wicked—is I think rather difficult of proof to those who are not afraid of any conclusions as to the meaning of the biblical text to which thorough inquiry may lead them. That idea of Plato, of Spinoza, of Goethe, and of many others—that immortality is the destiny of the worthy only,—of those who have sublimated themselves by the pursuit of truth and beauty, is a very fascinating [one], but it seems to me, at least in this stage of my development, which is imperfect enough, to be rather the hallucination of an intense personality than to have any foundation in reason. But it would be far easier to talk of these things to you than to write of them, for they are endless.

I have not yet seen Mrs. Crowe—much to my regret.

I have seen the painful correspondence which has lately been going forward between you and Mr. Chapman—this is a subject on which I cannot dilate.⁸ I will only say, that I think your last letter to Mr. Chapman very kind and judicious—if it be not impertinent in me to express an opinion in the matter.

With my kindest regards to Mrs. Combe I remain, my dear Sir,

Yours very truly
Marian Evans.

7. George Combe, *The Constitution of Man Considered in Relation to Material Objects*, 1828.

8. Combe returned to Chapman the £23.12.6 for his article on "Secular Education" in the *Westminster Review* for July 1852, asking to have it credited against future advertisements of his books. Through Chapman's carelessness, the advertisement was omitted. Combe complained in a letter to Charles Bray, who sent it on to GE to use at her discretion. Chapman, having seen the letter, wrote a long explanation to Combe, 10 January: "In consequence of Miss Evans' absence (through the death of her sister's husband), I had all the proofs and revises of the entire Review to read with the exception of the 2 first articles; some of them entailed great labor and two such serious delay (Greg's was one) in consequence of the necessity

II, 88:1 GE TO GEORGE COMBE, LONDON, 18 FEBRUARY 1853

MS: National Library of Scotland. *Endorsed:* London 18 Feby 1853 | Miss Evans | 10 March ansd.

142 Strand February 18. 1853.

My dear Sir

Your letter of the 27th came to me when I was confined to my bed by a rheumatic attack. Since then I have been into the country to see my sister, and have taken large doses of romping and doll dressing—the very best alteratives for me. I am come back quite well and hardy enough to enjoy the frost and snow. I fear, however, that they do not agree so well with your lungs and Mrs. Combe's as with mine.

Dr. Stamm[1] has been domesticated at Mr. Chapman's for some time. He has the most amiable social qualities, beautiful simplicity and purity of character and considerable attainments; but he is not, I think, destined to have much influence over other men. He would by no means concur in this negative clause; on the contrary he thinks himself a prophet. I ventured

of corresponding with their authors that the printing was thrown very late, making night work essential to get the Review out at anything like the usual time. The printers said that as nearly all the advertisement 'copy' was type, and not M.S., there was little fear of any mistake and that they therefore hoped I should not insist on seeing proof, adding that if I did I must not count on publishing the Review at even a late hour on 'Magazine day.' I consented to forego seeing the proof, and the consequence was I had no means of detecting the blunder—which my assistant had committed, viz., that of inserting the enclosed advertisement of Dr. Combe's books instead of yours."

Chapman's injudicious protest against Combe's reflection on his "business character and management" ended with an offer to return Combe's £23.12.6. (13 January.) This provoked from Combe a detailed 6-page statement of Chapman's faults: (1) publishing in circulars that Edward Lombe was supporting the *Westminster Review* with £200 a year; (2) circulating the names of other supporters without their authority; and (3) omitting Combe's advertisements. But he ended the letter kindly by asking Chapman to take back the money. Chapman wrote humbly on 22 January, confessing his fault, and two days later Combe returned the order. (NLS.)

1. August Theodor Stamm is described by William Hale White, who became Chapman's assistant in October 1852, as "a German boarding in the house who had written a book *Die Religion der That*, [Hamburg, 1852]. It was a materialistic gospel. Expatiating at dinner one day on the baselessness and folly of the belief in immortality, he exclaimed dramatically in his broken English 'I do tink it is a glorious ting to die and have a bad small.' He sent his book to Carlyle, but he heard that Carlyle had given orders to his servant not to take delivery of any more new religions." (Wilfred Stone, *Religion and Art of William Hale White*, Stanford, [1954], p. 51, quoting White's Black Note Book, p. 100.)

to tell him that a translation of a work beginning "*Völker der Erde, hier ist das Buch, nach dem ihr mit Verlangen eure Arme ausstrecht*,"² would be simply "nuts" to our reviewers, but he was evidently incredulous. You will perceive that he has no slight endowment of self-esteem, and this is unchecked by a fine sense of the ludicrous, without which even pure moral enthusiasm is apt to verge on the ridiculous in its manifestations. Still, Dr. Stamm is a charming being, and wins everyone's good will. Perhaps his droll English has something to do with this, and his handsome face still more. His resources are very narrow, and he is determined not to return to Germany until its political condition is more hopeful. Hence he is anxious to obtain some literary occupation in England or America and is working hard to get the mastery of our language. I have not at present access to a copy of Salvador's work, which I read eight years ago, but I will bear in mind your wish to see it.

I thought the last number of the Westminster rather below *par*, but the public seem to have judged otherwise. I must tell you that the 'Contemporary Literature' had not my supervision owing to my being called away to my sister, and I am sorry to see in it certain expressions which are, to say the least, in bad taste. Our programme for the April number is a very rich one. We are trying to get into the plan of having shorter articles and a greater variety of subjects. This was the plan of the Edinburgh in its palmy days, and is, I think, a good one, if exceptions to it are occasionally made in the case of highly important or comprehensive topics. Do you agree with me?

I am deeply interested in the prospect of seeing your work on Natural Religion.³ You promised that I should be one of the few who are to see it before its ultimate publication—a proof of regard which was very pleasant to me.

---

2. *Die Religion der That*, p. 1. Stamm wanted Chapman to publish an English translation of it.

3. *An Inquiry into Natural Religion, Its Foundation, Nature, and Applications*, Edinburgh, printed by Neill & Co. for the Author, 1853. GE's copy in Dr. Williams's Library contains a number of marginal notes in her hand. On p. 48 against "The more favourable the original cerebral constitution of an individual, the higher the cultivation bestowed on his mental faculties," GE wrote: "How do you *judge* that the moral constitution is high? By seeing that he has a form of head which is found in connexion with what is commonly held to be moral. If, having thus determined that he is moral, you make him an authority on morals, you reason in a circle." On p. 53 against a passage saying that the existence of "the Maker of the human body" can only be inferred by perceiving the manifestation of his qualities, GE wrote: "By the hypothesis it is involved that God is a being having '*power*, benevolence and *design*'; that is, it is implied that God is a being having faculties efficiently coordinated. But the having faculties efficiently coordinated is held in the case of the artizan to imply a maker. Then it must be held in the case of God to imply a maker."

My umbrella is come, but I have not seen Mrs. Crowe. She was here one evening last week, during my absence.

When speaking of the Review I forgot to say that I should like to know your opinion of Dr. S. Brown's article on the Atomic Theory.[4] He was extremely irate at certain omissions which my editorial obtuseness or self-sufficiency took upon itself to make. He has a theory as to the influence of Christianity on the development of science which is hinted at throughout the article, but so vaguely, that the result is mere mystification of the reader. I am sorry, however, that he should have been annoyed and chafed. His exuberant faculties, which every one must admire, want the control of a sober, rigorous judgment, so that one is always frightened lest he should fly into an extravagance or even an absurdity.

Mr. Bray and I agree that you are a delightful correspondent. I reconcile myself to the great inequality between your letters and mine by reflecting that "it is more blessed to give than to receive," and that on this principle you certainly have the best of it. Am I not ingenious?

Yes, indeed—I *should* like to renew our conversations by the fire-side at Edinburgh, but I must not so indulge myself this spring. I shall see you and Mrs. Combe in London, though, shall I not? And that will be a compensatory pleasure. Pray tell Mrs. Combe that I hope she is reading "Villette," and will tell me what she thinks of it. I mean to be really industrious now—to write and get money—*not* for myself. Do encourage me, if you can.

With kindest regards to Mrs. Combe, Ever, my dear Sir,

Yours truly
Marian Evans

II, 99:1 GE TO GEORGE COMBE, LONDON, 16 APRIL 1853

MS: National Library of Scotland. *Endorsed:* London | Miss Evans.

142 Strand | April 16. 1853.

My dear Sir

Many thanks for your kind attention in sending me the 'Scotsman.'[5] The reviewer treats us well, but I am sorry that the article on Schopen-

---

4. "The Atomic Theory before Christ and since," *Westminster Review*, 59 (January 1853), 167–196.

5. *The Scotsman* notices the *Westminster Review* 13 April 1853, p. [3b], praising Hodgson's "Educational Institutions in the United States," but attacking Forster's "British Philanthropy and Jamaica Distress" for urging Emancipation but halting at Free Trade. "Altogether the number is a very valuable one, and shows the *Westminster* to have enlisted a corps of writers capable of sustaining and increasing its revived reputation."

hauer,[6] which I think the best in the number, has not apparently attracted his notice. Is not the review of Alexander Smith[7] by Dr. John Brown?

I hope soon to receive what you have promised me—the sheets of your new work,[8] in which I am deeply interested. I hope that when you have put the last touches to this—certainly the most important thing you could do—you will not forget the 'Autobiography' of which we used to talk sometimes. I have met with one or two indications lately of the deep impression produced on some minds by your "Life of Dr. Andrew Combe," and I feel sure that the 'Autobiography' would be equally effective in its way. Here is ample reason for nursing your lungs.

Mrs. Bray writes me word how valuable your sympathy and encouragement are to Mr. Bray in his solitary labours at backward Coventry. He really has managed to sow some good seed there, and some of it has already sprung up.

Do you know Dr. Watts[9] of Manchester? He has been lodging here lately during his examination by the Educational Committee. You see Mr. Cobden told the house the other day that he would be glad if the government would withdraw all its Educational grants and give in exchange repeal of the Taxes on Knowledge. Certainly, a system of secular Education seems to be almost as far off as poor Robert Owen's 'C. of M.'[1] By the bye, have you seen his last Manifesto à propos of the Spirit Rappings?[2] I will enclose it for your and Mrs. Combe's amusement —if indeed you do not think it rather a sad than a laughing matter.

6. "Iconoclasm in German Philosophy," by John Oxenford, *Westminster Review*, 59 (April 1853), 388–407.

7. A long review of Smith's *Poems* in the *Scotsman*, p. [3 e–f], is unsigned.

8. Combe finished *An Inquiry into Natural Religion*, 6 May 1853. "I grieve at the pain it will give to many excellent persons when it is published.... In Edinburgh I should be sent into social banishment were it known." (Charles Gibbon, *The Life of George Combe*, 2 vols., 1878, II, 322.) He never wrote his Autobiography.

9. John Watts (1818–87), educational and social reformer, an early follower of Robert Owen's communistic theories, was born in Coventry, and moved in 1841 to Manchester, where he conducted a boys' school. He was a founder of the Free Library in Manchester, the Lancashire Public School Association, and the People's Provident Assurance Society, which he came to London in 1853 to promote.

1. The letters "C. of M." [Commencement of Millenium] were inscribed on the north end of Harmony Hall, Queenwood, Hampshire, when Charles Bray attended the opening in May 1842. (Bray, *Autobiography*, p. 61.)

2. *Manifesto of Robert Owen to all Governments and Peoples.... 30 March 1853:* "A great moral revolution is about to be effected for the human race, and by an apparent miracle.... through manifestations by invisible but audible powers, purporting to be from departed spirits, and to me especially from President Jefferson, Benjamin Franklin, His Royal Highness the late Duke of Kent, Grace Fletcher, my first and most enlightened disciple, and many members of my own family, Welch and

May will soon be here, and then I hope nothing will prevent your promised journey to London. That will be among my pleasures of the 'Season.'

With kind regards to Mrs. Combe, I am ever, my dear Sir,

Yours very truly
Marian Evans.

What is become of Mr. R. Cox's book on the Sabbath?[3]

II, 103:8 GE TO GEORGE COMBE, LONDON, 7 JUNE 1853

MS: National Library of Scotland. *Endorsed:* London 7 June 1853 | Miss Evans | accepts article on | Prison Discipline.

142 Strand | June 7. 1853.

My dear Sir

I at once communicated to Mr. Chapman the proposition contained in your letter of the 2nd, but I have been unable to send you a definite answer until this morning.

We shall be happy to accept an article from you on Prison Discipline,[4] but we must beg you to allow us the option of deferring its insertion until January, unless public discussion on the question should render it peculiarly seasonable in October, in which case we shall of course be anxious to print it at once.

Hoping soon to have the pleasure of seeing you and Mrs. Combe, I am, my dear Sir,

Yours very truly
Marian Evans.

I write in haste, and must trust to your goodness to excuse the brevity of my answer to your letter.

Scotch." All people are to be made happy once the errors of all religions and all existing governments are removed. The revelations came through an American medium, Mrs. Haydon.

3. See II, 123.
4. "Criminal Legislation and Prison Discipline," heavily edited by GE, was not published in the *Westminster Review* until April 1854.

II, 108:24 GE TO GEORGE COMBE, LONDON, 9 JULY 1853

MS: National Library of Scotland. *Endorsed:* London 9 July | 1853 | Miss Evans.

142 Strand | July 9. 1853.

My dear Sir

I am very grateful to you and Mrs. Combe for your willingness to have me as a travelling companion. Your invitation is so tempting that I have been resisting the reasons *contra*, and that is why I have not written to you until this morning. But I really must renounce the pleasure and be content with a shorter relaxation. I hope to be richer and freer too next year.

You and Mrs. Combe are very kind to me and I have to thank you for many pleasures. Pray add to them that of hearing from you when you are away, and believe me, my dear Sir,

Yours most truly
Marian Evans.

Geo. Combe Esq.

II, 108:24 GHL TO HERBERT SPENCER, LONDON, 9 JULY 1853

MS: University of London.

Saturday, 9 July 1853.

My dear Spencer

Many thanks for the proof of your article on the Universal Postulate.[5] I have read it with immense interest, and think you make out an irresistible case against Hamilton, Hume, Kant & Co.[6]

Ever yours faithfully
G. H. Lewes.

Herbert Spencer Esq.

---

5. *Westminster Review*, 60 (October 1853), 513–550. Spencer wrote to his father 15 June 1853 that it would not go into the July number. "Editorial exigencies have necessitated its postponement till the succeeding number. However, Chapman proposes to put it into type at once, so that I may send proof sheets to each of the leading thinkers forthwith." (David Duncan, *The Life and Letters of Herbert Spencer*, [1908], p. 70.)

6. Spencer declares (p. 530) that "*a belief which is proved, by the inconceivableness of its negation, to invariably exist, is true.* . . . Hence, as being taken for granted in every act of understanding, it must be regarded as the Universal Postulate."

II, 110:14   GHL TO JOHN CHAPMAN,
[LONDON, 16 JULY 1853]

MS: University of California, Los Angeles. *Endorsed:* G. H. Lewes | July 16. 1853.

My dear Sir

You know my opinion respecting length of articles, but you also know (or have forgotten,) my decided refusal to accept any limits to the Developement Hypothesis article[7]—what space the subject naturally and necessarily takes I have more than once declared must be given to it, if it be done at all. But we do not appear to consider the importance of the subject in the same light as you now, after allowing 50 pages to John Knox,[8] want the Dev. Hypo. within 32!

As you do not seem to value the proposed article enough to give it the space in which it can be made effective, n'en parlons plus. I will do it elsewhere.

Yours truly
G. H. Lewes.

II, 110:14   GHL TO JOHN CHAPMAN,
[LONDON, 18 JULY 1853]

MS: University of California, Los Angeles. *Endorsed:* G. H. Lewes | July 18th 1853.

My dear Sir

I confess to having been annoyed by your proposal (though your last removes the annoyance) and for these reasons:—

It was I who indoctrinated you with the advantage and necessity of limiting your contributors, and have—in my own case—always written within the limits—allowing you indeed to cut out and even materially injure my contributions (as in Mad. von Krüdener[9]) although during 10 years contributing to the Edinburgh I never was limited at all and in the British and foreign Review have had even 70 pages when I wanted it.[1] I

---

7. T. H. Bastard commissioned three articles for the *Westminster Review*, one of which was "The Hereditary Transmission of Qualities." The subject had been touched in Spencer's "Theory of Population," (April 1852). GE suggested "Lewes on Lamarck" to Chapman, [24–25 July 1852].

8. J. A. Froude, "John Knox," *Westminster Review*, 60 (July 1853), 1–50.

9. "Julia von Krüdener, as Coquette and Mystic," *Westminster Review*, 57 (January 1852), 161–182, was cut to 20 pages to make room for James Martineau's "The Ethics of Christianity," pp. 182–226, filling 44 pages.

1. GHL's "Shakspeare's Critics: English and Foreign," *Edinburgh Review*, 90 (July 1849), 39–77, was his longest; most of his contributions were less than

still maintain the principle of short articles. But brevity is a relative term, and to limit a paper such as the one I scheme would be to stultify it; therefore from the first I declined to think of limits. It has cost me a great deal of severe thinking, patient research, and even dissection; it is a subject, I conceive, of the very highest importance and I do not intend that it shall suffer from any procrustean tyranny. I mean to write an essay not a volume; if the essay extend beyond the limits which would be advisable in a review under any circumstances, I shall enlarge it with more illustrations and publish it as a volume; but the space it will occupy as an essay or article I do not know.

It will not be ready for the October number in any case. This proposition however I will make. Should the article extend beyond 60 pages (I don't *think* it will reach 50, but it is impossible to say—and my object in this, as in all cases, is brevity for the sake of effect) you are at liberty to decline it, and I will then do something else with it.[2] The only reason I have for wishing any understanding at all about it is that if written for publication in a Review it will be written in the plural editorial form, and written with more uniform brevity of illustration and citation. As it is *historical* as well as expository you can imagine how such a condition would operate—a phrase taking the place of a section in a book.

Ever faithfully yours
G. H. Lewes.

II, 118:5 GE TO GEORGE COMBE, LONDON, 23 SEPTEMBER 1853

MS: National Library of Scotland. *Endorsed:* London 23 Septr 1853 | Miss Evans.

142 Strand | September 23. 1853.

My dear Sir

I am now resolutely seeking what I have long been yearning for—a quiet home of my own in a healthy situation. This, as you are probably aware, is the most favourable season for securing such a home on moderate terms.

Moreover, I have made a business engagement with Mr. Chapman[3] which will oblige me to remain in London throughout the coming quarter.

---

30 pages. His longest article in the *British and Foreign Review* is "The Character and Works of Goethe," 14 (March 1843), 78–135; several others are nearly as long.

2. The article did not appear.
3. To translate Ludwig Feuerbach's *Das Wesen des Christenthums* for Chapman's Quarterly Series.

Thus, you see, circumstances sternly forbid me the pleasure of being with you in October. That it would have been a pleasure I think I need hardly assure you. I am sorry to say that before I received your letter I had, on the strength of your permission, lent *my* copy of your work to a critical friend. I accompanied it with strict injunctions of secrecy and my friend has so rigid a conscientiousness that I am more sure of him than of myself. So Mrs. Combe may set her heart at rest as to any consequences of this make. Of course I shall not err again in the same way. I gave Mr. Chapman your order about the Act of Parliament, which I hope you will duly receive.

With kindest regards to Mrs. Combe, I am, my dear Sir,

Yours very truly
Marian Evans.

II, 119:5 JOHN CHAPMAN TO GEORGE COMBE, LONDON, 3 OCTOBER 1853

MS: National Library of Scotland. *Endorsed:* London | 3 October 1853 | John Chapman.

London October 3. 1853.

Dear Sir

As I explained to you some time ago it is incumbent upon me to secure two gratuitous articles for each number of the Review; I venture therefore to ask whether in proposing the article on Prison Discipline you did so on the assumption that it would be paid for on the usual terms.[4] If such were the case I must of course make my arrangements accordingly with reference to the rest of the papers in the number.

I am glad to say that the current number is selling well. It had a very narrow escape from being all burnt; the type which was still standing was all destroyed.[5] My loss altogether will fortunately not exceed £35. I am dear Sir,

Yours sincerely
John Chapman.

George Combe Esq.

---

4. In his reply drafted on the back of this letter Combe wrote from Edinburgh, 5 October 1853, that he did not contemplate asking "cash down" for the article, but to have the amount placed to his credit to pay for advertisements of his books and for any of Chapman's publications he might order. (NLS.)

5. See II, 118, n. 7.

II, 119:5 JOHN CHAPMAN TO GEORGE COMBE, LONDON, 6 OCTOBER 1853

MS: National Library of Scotland. *Endorsed:* London 6 Oct. 1853 | John Chapman | & | Article on Prison | Discipline.

London 142 Strand | October 6. 1853.

Dear Sir,

My note of enquiry was not intended in the least degree to imply that I should be loth to receive your article if not a gratuitous one, I merely wished to *know* the terms intended for the reason alleged. I had quite counted on the article under any circumstances. The mode of payment which you kindly propose is very welcome to me as it accomodates me while enabling me to be of use to you by means of the advertisements. I shall be glad to send any books you may order.

We think it would be best that you should write the article precisely as shall seem to you best without regard to our editorial views on consistency; we will then put the article in the Independent Section. If you feel disposed to add your name to it, we shall be glad to have it.

Dr. Hodgson was quite uninfluenced respecting the treatment of his article, and no word has passed between us as to the propriety of recognizing phrenology in his paper. No considerations of policy influence me in the least in determining how the Science of Phrenology shall be regarded by the Westminster. If my mind were clearly made up as to the possibility of applying *practically with success* the doctrine of phrenology to prison discipline the review should immediately endorse the recommendation of the system. I am dear Sir

Yours very truly
John Chapman.

Geo. Combe Esq.

II, 119:5 GE TO GEORGE COMBE, COVENTRY, 9 OCTOBER 1853

MS: National Library of Scotland. *Endorsed:* Rosehill 9 Octr 1853 | Miss Evans | & | Herbert Spencer.

Rosehill | October 9. 1853.

My dear Sir

I came here yesterday on my way to my sister's, where I am going to stay a few days. A full answer to your letter received on Friday I must

9 October 1853

defer until my return to London, at the end of this week, but I write now that I may satisfy you at once as to the person whom I have made the depositary of your secret. That person is Mr. Herbert Spencer, the author of "Social Statics," of the article on "Over-Legislation" in the July number of the Westminster, and of "The Universal Postulate" in the current number. He is a person for whose moral as well as intellectual character I have a very high respect and he is under no temptation, either constitutional or circumstantial to speak of your book to any third person.

I hope to write more at length in the course of next week. With kindest regards to Mrs. Combe, I am ever, my dear Sir,

Yours very truly
Marian Evans.

21 Cambridge Street, Hyde Park

1853 October   GE's intimacy with GHL begins.
1853 November 28   GE, "a woman and something less than half an editor."
1853 December   GE's editorship of the *Westminster* ends.
1854 Jan.–March   GE revises Combe's *Prison Discipline* and sees it through the press.
1854 February 26   Declines invitation to travel with the Combes.
1854 March   Combe disputes with Chapman over pamphlet.
1854 June 9   GE declines to visit Combes at Kingston.
1854 June 25   GHL declines Brays' invitation to Coventry.

II, 120:1 GE TO GEORGE COMBE, LONDON, 21 OCTOBER 1853

MS: National Library of Scotland. *Endorsed:* Science and Religion | Miss Evans | 22 Octr ansd.

                21 Cambridge Street | Hyde Park Square | 21 October 1853.
My dear Sir

For the sake of reference, I enclose that part of your letter which contains the questions relative to your book.[6] I have not been sufficiently at liberty to reexamine it since I talked with you, so that I am not able to verify the general impressions on which my replies are founded by particular instances. I think the Introduction might be with advantage *abridged*. Some of the quotations appear to me diffuse and ineffective—for example, the one from the "Cyclopædia of Rel. Denominations" p. xi.[7] I think a *brief* Introduction setting forth, in your own forcible manner, the anomalous condition of the religious world, the practical ignoring of professed beliefs, and the duty of thorough outspeaking, would be *read* and would give an appetite for the *pièces de résistance* in the body of the work; but a long Introduction will either be skipped altogether or will be felt wearisome. I think the effective use of quotation is an important point in the *art* of writing. Given sparingly, quotations serve admirably as a climax or as a corroboration, but when they are long and frequent, they seriously weaken the effect of a book. We lose sight of the writer—he scatters our sympathy among others than himself—and the ideas which he himself advances are not knit together with our impression of his personality.

As to your friend's second query, I think it must refer to an occasional inconsistency in expression. You sometimes use phrases such as "approaching the Throne of God" which are irreconcileable with your opinions elsewhere expressed. But I do not find any difficulty in ascertaining the views you really inculcate. The inconsistency arises probably from a momentary sympathy with views you are describing or alluding to. The 3rd question seems to me quite irrelevant to the desirability of publishing your work. We wish to know the moral and religious views of a thoughtful, experienced and distinguished man, not because we expect him to tell us something new on these subjects, but because he is himself a new fact—a new mind which has gone through the steps of the great problem.

6. Combe's *Relation of Religion to Science* was not published until 1857.
7. *Cyclopaedia of Religious Denominations: Containing Authentic Accounts of the Different Creeds and Systems Prevailing throughout the World. Written by Members of the Respective Bodies*, London and Glasgow, 1853.

I have not solved the enigma (4th). I can see nothing to expose you to ridicule in the said paragraph. I think the stricture number 5. is a very useful caveat, and that, bearing it in mind, you would see many passages in the course of the work through which you would decide to draw your pen. You seem to look too much from an *Edinburgh* point of view for a writer whose reputation is European.

Pray let me know how Mrs. Combe's health is, and yours also, when you write. I am settled in my new lodgings, but I feel uncertain whether what I wish to do in relation to the Westminster will be compatible with this distant residence. Ever, my dear Sir,

Yours very truly
Marian Evans.

II, 125:24 GEORGE COMBE TO GE, EDINBURGH, 17 NOVEMBER 1853

MS: Copy in Combe Letter Book, National Library of Scotland.

Edin[burgh] | 17 November 1853.

My dear Miss Evans

The accompanying article[8] is the text of my lucubration for the Review; which is now far advanced, and will be in your hands by the first of December. I shall have it revised by Rob. Cox and James Coxe M.D. before sending it to you. You and Mr. Chapman may feel quite at ease about rejecting it, if found too phrenological and technical, for I shall print it as a pamphlet and distribute it, if you reject it, and thus my labour will not be lost. I expect this result: so you will not disappoint or annoy me in the least by an adverse decision on the part of the Review.

I have had several letters from Sir James Clark lately. At my suggestion, he is working, and with some prospect of success, towards inducing Lord Palmerston to consult physiologists in his forthcoming prison building and prison discipline, instead of parsons and military officers. Conceive, then, my judgment of the discretion which introduced that long paragraph of conglomerated nonsense from the British Review into the *Leader*,[9] on Phrenology, with approval, and with a piece of fresh nonsense added. The ignorance of the writer of the extracted lines is equalled only by his self-

---

8. On "Prison Discipline."
9. Commenting on "Portrait Painting in History," an article by David Masson in the *British Quarterly Review*, 18 (November 1853), 506–509, GHL ridicules "the science of the thirty-five 'bumps' into which craniology itself has degenerated in too hasty hands," and declares that the size of a head has no relation to intellect. (*Leader*, 12 November 1853, pp. 1095–1096.)

complacency. I do not know *who* is now the Editor of the Leader and, therefore, have no personal reference when I ask him whether there will be more phosphorus in one part of the same man's brain, than in another? and so that his small organ of Causality, for instance, shall have so much phosphorus, as to make him a second Bacon, while his large organ of Self-esteem shall have so little, as to render him a second Moses in meekness?[1] *That* is the *practical* question in deciding on the relative strength of the mental powers of a man. Besides, would not Iron be as good as Phosphorus for the purpose in hand in the Editor's remarks. It is deplorable to see the *Leader's* bending backwards on the science through which only certain and selfconsistent progress in all interests emanating from and resting on the mind of man, can be made.

We are both well and unite in kind regards to you. I remain, My dear Miss Evans

Yours sincerely
Geo. Combe.

II, 127:1 GE TO GEORGE COMBE, LONDON, 20 NOVEMBER 1853

MS: National Library of Scotland. *Endorsed:* London 20 Nov | 1853 | Miss Evans | 22 Nov ansd.

21 Cambridge Street | Hyde Park | November 20. 1853.

My dear Sir

Before I received your letter of the 17th I was about to write to you the (to me) unpleasant information that, owing to an arrangement which has been made for an article on "Strikes,"[2] it will be impossible to insert your article on Prison Discipline in our next number. Mr. Chapman, whom I went to speak to on the subject yesterday, has desired me to tell you that your article shall absolutely be inserted in the April number, as no amount of technicality will be an objection in the Independent Section[3] of the Review. The only remaining consideration, then, is whether the certain and wide circulation which your ideas will have in the Review, will counterbalance the disadvantage of delay. A *pamphlet* by you would of course have an extensive circulation, but perhaps one of a more ex-

---

1. Cf. Numbers 12:3.
2. W. E. Forster, "'Strikes' and 'Lock-outs,'" *Westminster Review*, 61 (January 1854), 119–145.
3. The Independent Section, intended to cover articles for which the editors were unwilling to accept responsibility, was used only for the two first numbers in 1852. Combe's article appeared in the main body of the magazine.

clusive character than that of the Westminster. The "text" you have sent me is admirable, and sets forth very impressively the momentousness of the subject. I left it with Mr. Chapman yesterday.

I spent a very agreeable evening at Sir James Clark's about a fortnight ago. It is always a great pleasure to me to see both him and Lady Clark; he is so direct and sensible, she so graceful and benignant. And I do not forget that I owe their acquaintance to you and Mrs. Combe.

I must tell you in excuse of that passage in the Brit. Quarterly, which is by David Masson, that it is the writing of a *littérateur* who has no pretension to scientific knowledge. I agree with you that it is sufficiently shallow and shows profound ignorance of the "Craniology" which he undertakes to pronounce upon. Can you tell me anything of *Mr. Noble*[4] who has just published a book on Insanity, in which he makes a recantation of phrenology?

I am exceedingly comfortable in my new abode. My landlady[5] is a very motherly, respectable woman and attends very thoroughly to my comfort.

Miss Martineau is in town, enjoying the consciousness of having finished her great work—Comte, and writing away for journals and periodicals. It is delightful to see that a woman can have so much energy and freshness at fifty.

I am glad to know that you and Mrs. Combe are still well. Pray give my kindest regards to Mrs. Combe and believe me, my dear Sir,

Yours very truly
Marian Evans.

II, 127:1 GE TO GEORGE COMBE, LONDON, [25 NOVEMBER 1853]

MS: National Library of Scotland. *Endorsed:* 25 Nov 1853 | Miss Evans | Name of new editor of Review | Huxley | 27 ansd.

21 Cambridge Street | Friday Morning.

My dear Sir

I have mentioned to Mr. Chapman your proposition and inquiry concerning the printing of your article and he will write to you on the subject.

4. Daniel Noble, *Elements of Psychological Medicine. An Introduction to the Practical Study of Insanity, Adapted for Students and Junior Practitioners*, 1853. GE was interested because GHL was preparing to review it in the *Leader*, 10 December 1853, pp. 1192–1193, and 24 December, pp. 1240–1242. Combe is not mentioned in either.

5. Mrs. Pitt.

28 November 1853

I called on Lady Clark the other day but did not find her at home; when I see her I will remember your suggestions.

I believe that I may be justly acquitted of having communicated any opinion of yours concerning Dr. Hodgson's article.[6] I never shew your letters to Mr. Chapman, but merely read to him, or cut off, such portions as refer to his business.

David Masson is not the editor of the Leader, he is only the author of the article in the British Quarterly. Mr. Lewes is still editor of the *literary* department of the Leader.

Thank you for your information about Mr. Noble. His new book is committed to Mr. Huxley,[7] a scientific man who is becoming celebrated in London, and who is to write the scientific department of the Contemporary Literature in the Westminster. It is not probable that I shall have anything to do with the editorship of the Westminster *after* April, if until then.

Pray excuse me if I am incoherent or brusque this morning, for I am not well and am writing on my knee. Ever, my dear Sir

Yours very truly
Marian Evans.

II, 128:21 GE TO GEORGE COMBE, LONDON, 28 NOVEMBER 1853

MS: National Library of Scotland. *Endorsed:* London 28 Nov | 1853 | Miss Evans | Mr. Huxley | described.

21 Cambridge Street | November 28. 1853.

My dear Sir

I have had a sharp bilious attack from which I am still feeling a good deal shattered, but I am quite able to write in answer to your letter just received.

Mr. Huxley is a man of brilliant talents and patient, hard-working

---

6. "The School Claims of Languages, Ancient and Modern," *Westminster Review*, 60 (October 1853), 450–498.

7. Chapman wrote to Thomas Henry Huxley 23 October 1853 asking if he would be disposed to undertake writing the scientific section of the Contemporary Literature articles in the *Westminster Review*. A draft of his reply is written on the back of the letter, accepting the offer and asking, "What's the pay?" Chapman replied 26 October that for a half-sheet of 8 pages for each number he would pay £6.6.0, though he hoped that increased sales would permit him to pay the *Edinburgh* rate of £1.1.0 per page. (MSS: Imperial College of Science, London.) Huxley's brief notice of Noble's *Elements of Psychological Medicine*, *Westminster Review*, 61 (January 1854), 267–268, remarks that Noble has abandoned Phrenology, of which he was formerly a defender.

observation, but who is occasionally tempted to prefer *paradox* and *antagonism* to truth. I do not mean that his conscious and ultimate aim is not truth—for he is a real man of science—but that he is constitutionally liable to deviate from the direct path in the way I mention. You know better than I do that such an organization is not a *teachable* one and that the fact of its being beckoned in one direction may incline it to turn off in another. Moreover, your forwarding the testimonials etc.[8] would need accounting for. If I were sole editor of the Westminster, I would take the responsibility on myself, and ask you to send them through me, but being a woman and something less than half an editor, I do not see how the step you propose could be taken with the naturalness and *bienséance* that could alone favour any good result. I should not like Mr. Huxley to allege against me that my having communicated the fact of his being engaged to write on a certain subject had drawn upon him unsought correspondence, however valuable in my own opinion such correspondence may be.

I think however that if a copy of the "Testimonials" could be spared me for a short time I could make use of it in the sense you desire, if not in relation to Mr. Huxley, certainly in other directions.

Pray excuse any want of clearness or other deficiency in a letter written with a bilious head and believe me, my dear Sir,

Yours very truly
[*no signature*]

II, 132:7 GE TO GEORGE COMBE, LONDON, 12 DECEMBER 1853

MS: National Library of Scotland. *Endorsed:* London 12 Dec 1853 | Miss Evans.

21 Cambridge Street | December 12. 1853.

My dear Sir

I am going to Mr. Chapman's this morning and I will give him all the details concerning the publication of your article, as stated in your

---

8. Probably the "Medical Opinion of the Principle on which the following Pamphlet is based," published in the reprint of Combe's "Criminal Legislation and Prison Discipline." In part it reads: "Having been asked to state our opinion of the annexed pamphlet, we, without being understood to become answerable for the accuracy of all the facts, or the soundness of all the reasoning which it contains, have no hesitation in giving our opinion that the fundamental principle which pervades it [that prison discipline must be based on physiology of the nervous system] is a sound principle." It was signed by Benjamin Brodie, James Clark, Henry Holland, Richard Owen, John Forbes, John Conolly, and William B. Carpenter.

letter of Saturday. Whatever I can do towards getting your wishes accurately understood and fulfilled shall be done. When this number of the Review is out I believe I shall not have anything more to do with the editorship, but I shall be very happy that the reading of your article will come within this quarter's duty.

I am glad indeed to hear even of a slight provision for poor Mr. Simpson's daughters.[9]

With kindest regards to Mrs. Combe, I am, my dear Sir, In haste,
Yours very truly
Marian Evans.

II, 133:1 GE TO GEORGE COMBE, LONDON, 16 DECEMBER 1853

MS: National Library of Scotland. *Endorsed:* Miss Evans | Mr. Chapman agrees.

21 Cambridge Street | December 16.1853.

My dear Sir

I ought to have told you before this that Mr. Chapman thinks your arrangement with regard to the printing of your article an excellent one, and has begged me to say that he entirely accedes to it.

Thank you for sending me the letter from the "Manchester Examiner." Mr. Huxley's article is gone to press without my seeing it,[1] so that I am in ignorance as to the mode in which he has dealt with Noble's book. Mr. Huxley's is not the organization for a critic, but it is difficult to find a man who combines special scientific knowledge with that well-balanced development of the moral and intellectual faculties, which is essential to a profound and fair appreciation of other men's works.

I hope you and Mrs. Combe are not suffering from the severity of the weather. For lungs that can bear it, it is a great improvement on the fogs we have been living in till the last week. Ever, my dear Sir,
Yours very truly
Marian Evans.

I have not seen Sir James Clark for some time.

---

9. James Simpson (1781–1853), advocate and friend of Sir Walter Scott and Combe, died suddenly 3 September. "His services to the cause of [secular] education were recognised by the government granting a pension of £100 a-year to his two unmarried daughters." (Charles Gibbon, *The Life of George Combe*, 2 vols., 1878, II, 324.)

1. But after seeing the MS, GE protested to Chapman against Huxley's attack on the scientific errors in GHL's *Comte*. See II, 132.

II, 134:18 GE TO GEORGE COMBE, LONDON, 23 DECEMBER 1853

MS: National Library of Scotland. *Endorsed:* London 23 Dec. 1853 | Miss Evans.

21 Cambridge St. | December 23. 1853.

My dear Sir

Mr. Chapman has agreed to give me *carte blanche* with regard to your article, so I can now tell you that I will with pleasure undertake the task you do me the honour to trust to me. I am going into the country to see my sister and my friends at Rosehill on the 2nd, and as I shall probably be away a fortnight, it will perhaps be best to defer the sending of the M.S. to town until my return. I shall most likely be here again by the 14th. The proximate cause of my withdrawal from the management of the W.R.—a withdrawal which, so far as its occurrence just now is concerned, is my own act—is Mr. Chapman's want of money.[2] I am on perfectly friendly terms with him.

I dined with Sir James and Lady Clark on Wednesday, and had the additional pleasure of meeting Mr. Helps, whose agreeable writings had prepared me to like him.

I am glad that Mrs. Combe has so pleasant a *distraction* as the Italian Opera.[3] It is the one I like best myself. With kindest regards to her, I am, my dear Sir,

Yours very truly
Marian Evans.

II, 136:21 GE TO GEORGE COMBE, LONDON, 2 JANUARY 1854

MS: National Library of Scotland. *Endorsed:* London 2 Jany 1854 | Miss Evans | 9 Jany ansd.

21 Cambridge Street | January 2. 1854.

My dear Sir

It has just occurred to me that when I last wrote to you, I omitted to answer your question about the Testimonials. Pray pardon this forget-

---

2. It is not clear how much Chapman paid her; possibly her room and board at 142 Strand were included.

3. Caradori made her debut in Bellini's *Norma* in Edinburgh 19 December with Formes, who also sang with her in Donizetti's *Lucrezia Borgia* on the 20th. (*Scotsman,* 21 December 1853, p. 2h.)

fulness. I can truly plead in its excuse a painful pre-occupation of mind. I *did* receive three copies of Testimonials, but—I suppose by an oversight of Longman's—they were all "additional."

I am just going to set off on my journey into Warwickshire[4] almost fearing that I shall be frozen on the way. In ten days I shall probably be at home again, so that I shall be ready to receive your MS.[5] on the 12th. If you wish me to read it before it goes to press, it will be better to send it directly to me, but if *not*, I shall be much obliged if you will send it to Mr. Chapman with a note saying that you wish him to forward the proofs to me.

I am writing in a hurry just before setting out, so I must defer many other things that I should like to say.

With kindest regards to Mrs. Combe, I am ever, my dear Sir,

Yours very truly
Marian Evans.

II, 138:26 GE TO GEORGE COMBE, LONDON, 25 JANUARY 1854

MS: National Library of Scotland. *Endorsed:* London 25 Jany 1854 | Miss Evans.

21 Cambridge Street | January 25. 1854.

My dear Sir

I have been incapacitated for work by a bad headache for the last three days, otherwise I should not so long have delayed asking you the following questions. You say in your last letter that you wish me to send a *proof* of your pamphlet to Sir James Clark and Mr. Perry.[6] Will it not be better for me to correct the proof and supply the headings, to forward this corrected proof to you that you may add or cancel what you please, and then to send a *revise* to Sir James and Mr. Perry? Any suggestions of theirs can still be carried into effect before the sheets are struck off. Again, will it not be desirable to *leave out of the Pamphlet* the list of books which will be prefixed to the article in the Review? I will take care to supply the necessary references, and make the corresponding omissions in the text. I think the first page of the pamphlet will look more dignified on this plan.

4. GE visited Chrissey Clarke at Attleborough 2–7 January 1854 and then stayed with the Brays at Rosehill 7–12. (Mrs. Bray's Diary.)

5. "Criminal Legislation and Prison Discipline."

6. John George Perry (1802–70), surgeon, was Medical Inspector of Prisons 1843–70. (Boase.)

I shall be much obliged if you will send me an answer to these questions by return of post. The pamphlet seems to me on the whole admirable, and as I never do things justice while they are in manuscript, I have no doubt that I shall think much better of it when I read it in print. I fear that numerous *verbal* alterations will be inevitable in the proof. Print is like broad daylight—it shews specks which the twilight of manuscript allows to pass unnoticed. This will cause a little additional expense, which I must beg of you to excuse.

Pray let me know how you are. Better, I hope, on the strength of the milder weather. With kindest regards to Mrs. Combe, I am ever, my dear Sir,

Yours very truly
Marian Evans.

Alas! This greasy paper will annoy you as much as it does me.

II, 142:1 GE TO GEORGE COMBE, LONDON, 7 FEBRUARY 1854

MS: National Library of Scotland. *Endorsed:* London 7 Feby 1854 London | Miss Evans | @ Printing | Pamphlet | 9th Feby wrote John | Chapman @ &c. | Miss Evans | 9th wrote John Chapman @ printing.

21 Cambridge Street | February 7. 1854.

My dear Sir

I have read and posted your letter to Sir James Clark. I think the suggestion it contains an excellent one so far as the *Pamphlet* is concerned. As to the Review, I confess I am in doubt as to the practicability of producing an *effective* article within the allotted space, but I cannot form a decided opinion until I have seen the pamphlet in print. I am sorry to tell you that I have not yet received a proof though it is a fortnight or more since I gave the M.S. to Mr. Chapman, who at once sent it to the printer. In whatever I have to do in the matter, there shall be no delay, but with regard to the speed or tardiness of the printers I am powerless, except so far as begging Mr. Chapman to spur them on, will go.

My doubts as to the possibility of contracting the pamphlet into a *telling* article arise from the fact that almost all the matter is essential to a just and at the same time striking presentation of your views. But if the condensation can be accomplished without doing injustice both to your ideas and your exposition of them, it is certainly desirable that the circulation of the Westminster should be made the means of spreading truths so important.

With kind regards to Mrs. Combe, I remain, my dear Sir,

Yours very truly
Marian Evans.

II, 142:20 JOHN CHAPMAN TO GEORGE COMBE, LONDON, 13 FEBRUARY 1854

MS: National Library of Scotland. *Endorsed:* London 15 Feby 1854 | John Chapman | @ | Prison Discipline | Pamphlet.

London | February 13. 1854.

My dear Sir,

No time has been lost in supplying a proof of your paper to Miss Evans; she has now returned it to me and I shall get a revise quickly.—The paper extends to nearly 100 Westminster Review pages! Miss Evans proposes to make the attempt to cut it down to 32 pages in order to form an article for the Review, but I fear she will find it very laborious and difficult if not impossible so to reduce it and at the same time to preserve its characteristic merits. I have read the whole of it with much pleasure.

Yours very truly
John Chapman.

Geo. Combe, Esq.

II, 142:20 GE TO GEORGE COMBE, LONDON, 22 FEBRUARY 1854

MS: National Library of Scotland. *Endorsed:* London 22 Feby 1854 | Miss Evans.

21 Cambridge Street | February 22. 1854.

My dear Sir

I send you by today's post an entire proof of your pamphlet. I have two more proofs, one of which I will take to Sir J. Clark, and the other to Mr. Perry. When you return yours corrected, I will order half a dozen revises to be struck off and one of these can be sent to Dr. Browne[7] of Dumfries.

7. William Alexander Francis Browne (1805–85), M.D., a distinguished alienist of Dumfries, where he was director of the Crichton Institution, "a lunatic asylum for affluent patients." (Francis Hindes Groome, *Ordnance Gazetteer of Scotland*, 6 vols., 1884–85, *sub* Dumfries.)

As I saw the first proof *in slip*, the printer has filled up the right hand headings with the general title.[8] If you wish this to be replaced by a special heading, please to say so. I shall be much obliged also if, in reading the pamphlet, you will keep in view the idea that the 96 pages have to be abridged to 32, and put a pencil mark where you feel that there is something not essential to the Review edition. I have admonished the printer of the disparity between the type of the italics and the general type in the three last sheets, but he has taken no notice of it.

Thank you for the perusal of the letter to the Manchester Examiner. I have forwarded it to Mr. Bray.

A pleasure I had the other day—that of dining with Mrs. Jameson at Mr. R. Noel's—is indirectly due to you.[9] I was much pleased with her.

Headache and palpitation of the heart have robbed me of half my time lately, so that I am sadly in arrear.

With kindest regards to Mrs. Combe, I am ever, my dear Sir,

Yours truly
Marian Evans.

II, 142:20   JOHN CHAPMAN TO GEORGE COMBE, LONDON, 25 FEBRUARY 1854

MS: National Library of Scotland.

London February 25. 1854.

My dear Sir,

I send you a proof of the Pamphlet by this evening's mail and have sent one to Dr. Browne of Dumfries; also four more to Miss Evans for giving a further supply to Sir James Clarke.

May I ask your opinion as to the possibility of reducing the pamphlet to the dimensions of an Article of 32 pages? I am not sanguine generally with reference to the publication of Pamphlets and especially when addressed only to the thinking few; hence although I should feel it an honor to be the publisher of the one in question, I do not feel that I ought to incur the risk, for as you know I am not warranted unless I feel very

---

8. In the pamphlet the left-hand pages are headed "Criminal Legislation," the right-hand "and the Practice of Prison Discipline." In the *Westminster Review*, 61 (April 1854), 409–445, the left-hand heading is "Criminal Legislation and Prison Discipline"; the right-hand varies on each page.

9. See II, 105. Barbara Bodichon told Edith Simcox that she first met GE at Mrs. Jameson's in 1852 "and thought her very charming and wonderful." (Simcox Autobiography, 5 July 1881.) GE wrote that Bessie Parkes introduced her. (II, 40.)

fully assured of success, in giving myself the chance of gain when accompanied with the risk of loss.

I *believe* my name has been printed on the title page by the printers ⟨contrary⟩ without my order; I say I *believe* because it has only just occurred to me, and I have not the means of being sure, having sent the pamphlet off.

Being out the greater part of yesterday I could not write until now. I am, My dear Sir,

Yours very truly
John Chapman.

II, 142:20 GE TO GEORGE COMBE, LONDON, 26 FEBRUARY 1854

MS: National Library of Scotland. *Endorsed:* London 26 Feby 1854 | Miss Evans.

21 Cambridge Street | February 26. 1854.

My dear Sir

I have requested Mr. Chapman to send a proof to Dr. Browne, and I have this morning taken three more to Sir James Clark. Mr. Perry had his several days ago.

I am concerned at the mistake about the postage, but it was not owing to carelessness, for I took the parcel to the Post Office myself and had it weighed. My own recollection of the regulations was, that all M.S.S. books and pamphlets, weighing not more than a pound, and left open at the ends, were charged 6d. But the man at the Post Office assured me that 3d would be enough, and I trusted to what turns out to have been his superior ignorance. I am still at a loss to understand on what principle the pamphlet was charged 8d since it was left open at the ends.

I ought to have mentioned to you before, that Mr. Chapman suggested the insertion of the titles of the works referred to in the pamphlet, *on a fly leaf* instead of at the head of the first page, and I accepted the suggestion as leaving the least difficulty in case the project of an article for this Review should be given up.

I thoroughly appreciate your kindness and Mrs. Combe's in inviting me to accompany you on your summer excursion. That a thorough and agreeable change like that would do me good I have no doubt, but I am far less confident that my circumstances will allow of my having such an indulgence. I remain, my dear Sir,

Yours very truly
Marian Evans.

George Combe Esq.

II, 143:23 JOHN CHAPMAN TO GEORGE COMBE, LONDON, 28 FEBRUARY 1854

MS: National Library of Scotland. *Endorsed:* London | John Chapman.

London February 28. 1854.

My dear Sir,

I was out this afternoon when your letter arrived, and therefore could not answer it in time for the evening mail. I am very vexed to find that you did not get the proof along with my letter; on enquiry this evening it seems that the youth who took it to the post did not put it in until after 6 when it was "too late," and moreover that by some incomprehensible blundering he did [not] stamp it at all so that you would doubtless be charged double rate, as also would be Dr. Browne. I therefore send you 1/- worth of stamps to pay for the result of the error. Perhaps when next writing to Dr. Browne you would send him the 6d and explain the circumstance. Of course the proofs will have arrived ere this.

Concerning the reduction of the Pamphlet to the limits of an Article:— I am somewhat perplexed; the delay in giving me any assurance that the thing was feasible and would be done, and the doubt which has been intimated as to its practicability have kept me in suspense so long that I found myself running the risk of relying on the Article when in fact it might not be supplied to me so that I was in danger of being an Article short although the time for beginning to print had come. I felt myself compelled to provide for the emergency and therefore, last Friday, agreed for an article to be ready for April in place of yours if yours were not available, but yet with the hope that if at the 11th hour yours were prepared to go in, the Review might admit it without much exceeding its usual bulk.

Your letter of yesterday is the first intimation that I might really expect the article, and now therefore I have made an approximative estimate of the space which will be occupied by the 8 articles already engaged, and I find, I am sorry to say, that with the Contemporary Literature they will exceed the 300 pages which ought to be the size of the Review. Under these circumstances I am constrained to ask whether you could allow of the postponement of the publication of the article until the appearance of the July number? I incline to think that no legislation on the subject will take place in the mean time. I am dear Sir
Yours very sincerely
John Chapman.

II, 143:23 JOHN CHAPMAN TO GEORGE COMBE, LONDON, 1 MARCH 1854

MS: National Library of Scotland.

142 Strand, London | March 1. 1854.

My dear Sir

The *decided* assurance contained in your letter of this morning as to the availableness of your article has determined me to omit one of the articles I had agreed to insert in order to enable me to give place to yours in the April number.

Please therefore to let me have the proof of the Pamphlet as it is to be worked off, so that the type may be afterwards used for the Article. It does not seem to me to look quite the thing that a reprint of an Article from the Westminster should be published separately by another house, and intrinsically, as I said before, the Pamphlet is one which I should be glad to publish; therefore if you have no *decided* reason for preferring Simpkin & Co. perhaps you will order my name to remain on the Pamphlet.[10] But if you have, I beg you will tell me so as frankly as I have spoken on the subject.

How many copies of the Pamphlet will you print?

Yours very sincerely
John Chapman.

II, 144:11 GEORGE COMBE TO JOHN CHAPMAN, EDINBURGH, 2 MARCH 1854

MS: Copy in Combe Letter Book, National Library of Scotland.

Edinburgh 2d March 1854.

John Chapman Esq.
My dear Sir

Your letter of the 28th February reached me only this morning. Before answering it, I must refresh your memory on a few points which you, in thinking of your own interest and convenience, seem to have forgotten.—You expressed a desire that I should furnish you with an article on prison discipline for the January number of the Review: and I

---

10. The title page of the pamphlet reads: London: Simpkin, Marshall and Co. | Edinburgh: Maclachlan and Stewart, 1854.

agreed to place it in your hands on the day named by Miss Evans, 1st December, and on your own terms, as to pecuniary remuneration, or rather non-remuneration.—At the sacrifice of *my* health and convenience, I had the article ready by the day named; and wrote that it was at your command. You wrote to me begging that, *for your convenience*, it might stand over till April.—*I felt* that it was one-sided to leave *me* to labour, at every cost, to keep faith with you, while you coolly consulted your own convenience, and bid me wait; but making every allowance for your necessities, I did not express what I felt, but assented frankly to your proposal.—I was then desired to send the M.S. to London by a certain day in January. I availed myself of the interval in working up my materials into a full exposition of the subject for a pamphlet, and wrote to you offering as much of it as you chose to print for an article in the April number, and you were satisfied with my terms. The M.S. was delivered to Miss Evans *two days before* the day specified for its being sent. If delay in setting it up and sending me a proof ensued, this was no fault of mine. No proof reached me till 23d February nearly 7 weeks after the M.S. was delivered in London. I immediately wrote that I could make it into an article, and desired you to send a proof to be cut down. *You* lost *two posts* in sending it. It reached me on 28th February at 9. a.m. and by one o'clock on the same day, I wrote to you that I had gone over it and reduced it to 35 pages and would reduce it to 32 if you could not afford to give 35.—But after putting me to all this trouble, I then, on the *2d* March, receive a letter from you, dated *28* February, requesting me to postpone its insertion till July!

Now, there has never been a delay of one hour on my part: I have made health, convenience, and every consideration in money, give way to meet your wishes: the whole disappointments have arisen from your own style of managing business: But your style does not suit mine. I have borne as long as my patience would hold out; and now I have done. You may do as you please about inserting or not inserting the article; but it shall not wait till July. The pamphlet shall be published as soon as it can be completed: and here again my interest is sacrificed to your convenience. Had I known that you were to delay sending me a proof till you could not insert the article, I should have printed the pamphlet here, at less expense, in a neater form, and saved Miss Evans a world of trouble.

By this evening's post I shall return to Miss Evans the proof with all my corrections, and the proof cut down for the Review, and you can do precisely as you please in the matter; but you will excuse me for never again subjecting myself to this kind of treatment. I remain, My dear Sir

Yours faithfully

Geo. Combe.

II, 144:11 GEORGE COMBE TO JOHN CHAPMAN, EDINBURGH, 2 MARCH 1854

MS: Copy in Combe Letter Book, National Library of Scotland.

Edinburgh 2 March 1854 | 4 p.m.

John Chapman Esq.
My dear Sir

Your letter to me dated 1 March reached me after mine to you of this date was posted for our *morning* mail. Had it arrived sooner, it would have saved me writing, and your reading that letter. However, I do not regret that it has gone; because I wish you to know that when I make an engagement, I make every possible exertion to fulfil it; and that I expect corresponding treatment from others.

I send you the remaining sheets revised; and to-morrow I shall send the reduced proof to Miss Evans. *Your* proof *to me* was *paid* correctly; but if Dr. Browne's was not, the 1/- worth of stamps sent by you will pay *his* double postage. In no case, could it have paid *both* his and mine. I have written him on the subject.

The reasons why I wish my own publisher's names inserted was that it will save opening a new publishing account; that it will save us all trouble attending to advertising, sales, etc. for they do all that most attentively without my needing to prompt them; and lastly, it will save separate advertisements, for they will add it as a line or two to my other advertisements.

You may order 500 copies of the pamphlet to be thrown off and I wish a complete copy for my own use as soon as it is thrown off.—The top line at present is a sheer waste of paper and type; but it would be expensive to alter it now, otherwise it might be withdrawn from the pamphlet. I shall send a table of contents, and also advertisements to go at the end of it. These and the title page may stand over, till the decision of Sir James Clark is known, unless the Title is already part of the first sheet, in which case it may go to press. I remain, My dear Sir

Yours sincerely
Geo. Combe.

II, 144:11 JOHN CHAPMAN TO GEORGE COMBE, LONDON, 3 MARCH 1854

MS: National Library of Scotland. *Endorsed:* London 3 March 1854. | John Chapman | 5 March ansd.

London 142 Strand | March 3. 1854.

George Combe Esq.
My dear Sir

I have received your two letters of yesterday's date. As you do not regret having sent the one first written I beg to say that its reception by me was needless as a proof that you make every possible exertion to fulfil any engagement you may enter into; for I never doubted your endeavours in this respect, and as the language of the letter is such as I think one gentleman ought not to write to another without larger and better ascertained grounds of complaint than those which I believe you to have in this instance, I trust that the few words I may have to say will induce a conviction on your part that if your letter does not insult me it at least does me a gross injustice.

You say I expressed a desire that you would furnish me with an article on prison discipline; if my memory serves me rightly it would be more correct to say that you enquired whether such an article would be acceptable—adding an expression of your willingness to write it, and that I then *in answer* said I should be glad to have it. But so far from wishing you to write it "at the sacrifice of your health and convenience" was I, that I expressed a readiness to insert the paper chiefly because I believed its publication would give you pleasure. For however important the subject may be in itself, and however ably you might treat it, there were others which at the time seemed to me of *quite equal* if not more pressing urgency.

With reference to your complaint that the publication of your paper was postponed from January to April I can only say that in politely asking your assent to that postponement I was only acting conformably to long recognized editorial custom which *necessarily* accords great freedom and option in the management of a review; and it seems to me that if up to the last day of going to press such freedom were witheld all really efficient editorship would be at an end.

The cause of the delays since January in no respect lies with me, whatever you may think of my "style of doing business"; and I believe they would have been avoided had your communications been made to me directly instead of through a third person—a plan which has evidently resulted in misunderstanding all round. Miss Evans requested proofs *in slip* of the article; slips 1 to 20 were sent to her February 7; 21 to 28 were sent February 8th; 29 to 36 were sent February 9th, and 37 to 46 on February 10th since which time I have been urgent for a decision as to whether the pamphlet could and would be cut down to the dimensions of an article, and your note of (I think) the 27th of February was the first affirmative intimation I could obtain. It is I who have been so long kept in suspense—pledged on the one hand to insert your article if presented in time and if reduced to the prescribed limits, and, while uncertain whether it would be supplied, bound on the other hand to provide an article, at the cost of £20, to go in its place in the event of my not receiving it. This I did at the very latest date at which I dared to run the risk of uncertainty.

After Miss Evans had corrected the slips she returned them and requested a proof *in pages* or pamphlet form—saying she could give no decisive opinion as to the *reduction* of the article until she had it in that form. She received sheets A, B, C, D, and E February 18th and F on the 21st.

Before proceeding further in this matter I wish to have a distinct understanding, if the article be inserted, as to the amount of time which you will be willing shall elapse after the Review is published before the article shall be published as a pamphlet; also, that after what has passed, I cannot consent simply to place the amount of remuneration for the article (£20) to the credit of your account but that I must pay you in cash as I do other contributors. I am, my dear Sir

Yours sincerely,
John Chapman.

II, 144:11 GEORGE COMBE TO GE, EDINBURGH, 3 MARCH 1854

MS: Copy in Combe Letter Book, National Library of Scotland.

Edinburgh | 3 March 1854.

Miss Evans—21 Cambridge Street
My dear Miss Evans

My heart is grieved at the annoyance and trouble I am giving you, but it is in a good cause. Mr. Chapman has agreed to insert the article in the April number and I now send you the Proof, with the Passages to be kept in and omitted to constitute the article, marked by me in pencil on the margins. You will soon judge whether the article will read continuously; and you can have little difficulty in adding a few connecting sentences if necessary.—I presume that you will get a clean proof with all the corrections made. I have made corrections on this proof on pages *62* and *92*, which please transfer to the corrected proof, in so far as that on page 62 is not already there. Page 62 is *not* in it, and is necessary to avoid cavilling.

I have written to Mr. Perry, and you will not wait for him or any of the others longer than *suits Mr. Chapman's convenience.* I shall run all risks rather than incommode him. I shall write also to Sir Jas. Clark explaining how things stand, but this need not interfere with the action of himself and friends, for the *pamphlet* will not be published for a month, and their opinions, if given, can be thrown off with the title page, and table of contents, which I now send. There will also be some advertisements at the end, which I shall send. I have ordered 500 copies of the Pamphlet to be printed. I regret that I cannot give it to Mr. Chapman as publisher, but I have told him so.

With our united kindest regards, I remain, My dear Miss Evans
Sincerely yours and obliged
Geo. Combe.

II, 144:11 GE TO GEORGE COMBE, LONDON, 3 MARCH 1854

MS: National Library of Scotland. *Endorsed:* London 3 March 1854 | Miss Evans.

21 Cambridge Street | March 3. 1854.

My dear Sir

I saw Mr. Perry on Wednesday, and he told me that he found some inaccuracies in the facts of the Pamphlet. He has promised to correct them on his proof and to let me have it that I many transfer them. I will try to get it today and take it to the Strand, since you have sent your proof there.

I beg you will not make me a referee in any matters relating to Mr. Chapman, as I have nothing whatever to do with his affairs. You must allow me to return the stamps which you have enclosed, as I have had no expense with your proofs. I remain, my dear Sir,

Yours very truly
Marian Evans.

II, 144:11 GEORGE COMBE TO JOHN CHAPMAN,
EDINBURGH, 5 MARCH 1854

MS: Copy in Combe Letter Book, National Library of Scotland.

Edinburgh 5th March 1854.

John Chapman Esq.
My dear Sir

I am favoured with your letter of 3d March, and beg to remark that, according to my recollection, I told you that the act abolishing Transportation had been passed; that new prisons must be built, new modes of discipline instituted, and that as the convicts would be liberated after a few years confinement, there would be a public interest excited, as soon as the nature of the act was known. All this information I derived from Mr. Perry, medical inspector of Prisons, before the Act was printed for the public, or its probable effects known; and I communicated it to you and asked you whether you would wish to have an article on the subject in your January number, which would probably anticipate the other Reviews. You said you would be glad to have it. I certainly said that I should be willing to write it; but apparently you thought that I suggested the article to gratify some wish of my own; I, on the other hand, being conscious only of a friendly desire to aid the Review by furnishing an article on a subject of public interest which, it appeared to me, no other person was likely to supply. Your view, I am willing to allow, may have been as natural to you, as my own was to me; and here was a mistake for which neither of us was to blame.

I never hinted a complaint of your postponing the article from January till April, until you proposed again to postpone it till July, and then I could not help saying that I thought that you should have given me the earliest possible notice of your wish to postpone it, to set me at liberty, whereas you allowed me to toil on, and proposed postponement only *after* I wrote that I had finished it. Perhaps you did not know sooner; but no explanation was given me to that effect.

In regard to the delay between the slips and the proof, and the difficulty of reducing the Pamphlet to the size of an article, I was wholly in the dark, until your letter of the 3d March explained the former, and the moment I got a proof I removed the latter.—Miss Evans informed me that her official connection with the Review had ceased on 1st January, but I imagined that she continued to take an interest in its affairs, and that from her knowing more of Phrenology than you professed to do, the arrangement by which she agreed to edit the pamphlet and judge of its suitableness for an article, would be equally beneficial to you and me. When she expressed her difficulty in reducing it, which she did before a proof was sent to me, I said that I could not judge whether I could to it myself, until I got a proof. When one came, I instantly saw that the thing could be done, and did not lose a post in saying so. I may add that when the M.S. was sent to Miss Evans in January I was sleepless and confined to bed for weeks, rising only for a few hours in the evening, otherwise I should have probably saved her the trouble I imposed on her.

You will perceive from this statement that your proposal to delay inserting the article till July came upon me quite by surprise, and that while you assigned the delay in preparing it, as your reason for the postponement, I felt that I was wholly guiltless of that delay, and that on your side alone it had arisen, imagining, as I did, that you and Miss Evans were co-operating in the matter. With these explanations, I leave the matter in your own hands. Insert or reject the article as suits your own convenience. I see no reason for your paying me £20, and do not ask or wish you to do so, because I wrote the article with the desire to aid the Review; but if you are of a different opinion, I leave this to your own decision also.

I remain

II, 144:11 GE TO GEORGE COMBE, LONDON, 9 MARCH 1854

MS: National Library of Scotland. *Endorsed:* London 9 March | 1854 | Miss Evans.

21 Cambridge Street | March 9. 1854.

My dear Sir

I have seen a revise of the pamphlet and have inserted both Mr. Perry's corrections and your own alterations at pp. 62 and 92. One of your verbal alterations I was obliged to cancel as you did not appear to have completed it and I was uncertain about your meaning. It is on p. 33 where you say—"the only way in which the question of sanity or insanity can be decided, is to call in physicians and cerebral physiologists, whose professional duty it has been" etc. You had supplied "Cerebral *physiology*" instead of physiologists, and this would not tally with the continuation of the sentence. I hope there will be no vexatious mistake revealing itself in the pamphlet when it is too late; but the fallibility of human brains is in nothing more obvious than in proof reading. Should you like to see a proof of the *article?*

12 March 1854

I am going to Sir James Clark's this evening, and I hope to hear something propitious to the cause you have at heart. Mr. Perry seems to have some good reasons to urge against one or two of your opinions on points of detail, but the main principles of the pamphlet are independent of these.

I like to think of your making a period of life which with most people —even the most distinguished—is one of mere retrospect, fruitful in active service to the interests of humanity. A beautiful *decline* of life is to me as full of cheering promise as a beautiful opening—of promise that with future generations age in general will be lovely and harmonious.

Alas! I am reminded by contrast of poor Mrs. Crowe's sad story.[9] I can imagine how closely it must affect you and Mrs. Combe who have been her friends so long. With kindest regards to Mrs. Combe, I am my dear Sir,

Ever yours truly
Marian Evans.

George Combe Esq.

II, 146:3 JOHN CHAPMAN TO GEORGE COMBE, LONDON, 12 MARCH 1854

MS: National Library of Scotland. *Endorsed:* London | 12 March 1854 | John Chapman.

London March 12. 1854.

My dear Sir

I send you the first few pages of your article, please return them by next post as they will liberate another sheet for press. What title shall we adopt? The one on the Pamphlet is too long, and "Prison Discipline" seems to me scarcely descriptive of the article.[1] "The Treatment of Criminals" seems to me the text of the article—but perhaps you will fix on a title.

I think 6 weeks should elapse from the first of April, before the Pamphlet is published separately. Will this arrangement meet with your approval? Notwithstanding this early re-publication and the fact that you do not transfer to me the copyright of your article, as is the case with the other contributors to the Review (one[2] only excepted), I should still feel bound to pay you for the article as proposed in my last letter, had not the tenor

---

9. Returning to visit in Edinburgh in February, Mrs. Crowe suffered a mental breakdown and behaved strangely.

1. *The Principles of Criminal Legislation and the Practice of Prison Discipline Investigated* was shortened to "Criminal Legislation and Prison Discipline," *Westminster Review*, 61 (April 1854), 409–445.

2. Chapman returned GE's receipts for her articles. See his letter to her 16 January 1860.

and tone of your reply removed the feelings which dictated that proposal. I shall now be glad conformably with your suggestion to accept the article on the terms originally arranged between us.

There is a parcel lying here (a roll) for you, will you please direct what shall be done with it? I am my dear Sir

Yours sincerely
John Chapman.

II, 149:13 JOHN CHAPMAN TO GEORGE COMBE, LONDON, 8 APRIL 1854

MS: National Library of Scotland. *Endorsed:* London 8 April | 1854 | John Chapman | @ | Pamphlet. | 12 April ansd per book.

London April 8. 1854.

My dear Sir

The pamphlet is being packed and will be sent to the Steamer this afternoon; I trust therefore there may be no delay in your receiving it at the time you count upon.

Your letter of December 10th addressed to Miss Evans contains the conditions on which you proposed that I should publish your article, but it says only with reference to the publication of the pamphlet as one of the conditions;—"and that I shall not put the pamphlet in circulation until after the publication of the Review." But in a letter, written I think while you were staying in Cambridge Terrace[3], you said, I believe, that provided I supplied you with $\frac{1}{2}$ a dozen copies of the article at the time the review containing it should be published, you would be quite content to wait several months for the publication of the pamphlet in a separate form. I cannot however find that letter.

To republish in so short a time as a month after publication affords an injurious precedent. The public counts on the same process with other articles for the sake of which the number would otherwise be bought. The sale of the Review is by no means over in a month after publication, and I should be glad to learn that you allowed 2 months to elapse before issuing the pamphlet.

I enclose the printer's bill as forwarded to me by him; the paper I have also charged you at exact cost. I am my dear Sir

Yours very sincerely
John Chapman.

3. James Combe lived at 3 Cambridge Terrace, Regents Park.

II, 149:13 J. M. MOIR FOR CHAPMAN TO COMBE, LONDON, 13 APRIL 1854

MS: National Library of Scotland. *Endorsed:* London 13 April 1854 | Mr Moir for | John Chapman | @ | Pamphlet.

142, Strand London. | April 13. 1854.

Dear Sir

In reply to yours of yesterday's date[4] I beg to inform you that the 'rule' to which you refer in the first paragraph of your letter is 'local.' I will inquire respecting the missing 80 pages of your M.S. Unless it is in Miss Evan's possession I cannot at present say where it is.

The *item* £7.12.0 is solely for the 'corrections and making up' of *your* Pamphlet.[5] The corrections were very numerous. You are entirely wrong in supposing that the sum "includes not only the completion of" your "Pamphlet, but the expense of adapting it for the Review."

Yours truly
John Chapman
Per J. M. M.

George Combe, Esq.

II, 149:13 JOHN CHAPMAN TO GEORGE COMBE, LONDON, 13 APRIL 1854

MS: National Library of Scotland. *Endorsed:* London | John Chapman | 16th April ansd per book.

London, 142 Strand | April 13. 1854.

My dear Sir

Being obliged to be out this afternoon I asked Mr. Moir—one of my clerks new to the business—to make the enquiries necessary to enable me to answer your letter. I regret to find that, contrary to my intention, he also undertook to answer the letter himself. Being new to the business, he has been I find misled as to the '4 per cent extra copies' about which you write: It is the custom in London, if you ask a printer to deliver the edition of any work he may print, for the printer to send in the exact *nominal*

---

4. Only the first page of this letter survives in copy. (NLS.)

5. In a letter to Combe 30 November 1853 Chapman wrote: "The cost per sheet for pamphlets uniform with the West. Rev. would be, including paper, £3.2.0 for 250 copies and £4.0.0 for 500 copies." (NLS.) Combe's pamphlet filled six-and-a-half sheets.

number printed; any surplus copies which he may have, and which are called "waste," are reserved for a further order upon him.

What is called a "perfect ream" of paper contains 520 sheets, hence, if not a sheet were spoilt, it would yield 520 copies of a pamphlet—one sheet in lenth. Of course there are often some sheets injured. I will get whatever "waste" there may be from the printers. I find there are 6 copies on my premises,—one also was given to Mr. Wilson, and I believe I have a copy in my private room.

You will perhaps remember that before you saw a proof at all, corrections had been made by Miss Evans on the slips; and the delivery of proofs *in slip* is always expensive. The printers make *me* a separate charge of 18/6 for corrections of your article, besides my share of the composition. "Corrections" as charged by printers are always a most unsatisfactory item; they cannot be fairly estimated or checked, and I resign myself to pay for them usually without question;—my only resourse being, if I find them charged, *as it seems to me*, very heavily, to change my printer. I will ask Miss Evans about the missing M.S.

My memory of circumstances is almost invariably associated with *locality*, and I have a strong *impression* connected with Cambridge Terrace, that when there you assured me either personally or by letter to the effect I have already mentioned. I *may* be mistaken altogether. I repeat—I cannot find any such letter. With regard to the time of publishing your pamphlet, I should be sorry to oppose your *wishes* and beg of you therefore to publish it when [it] shall seem to you best and I shall be content.

I am grieved that circumstances, chiefly beyond my controul, have resulted in causing in your mind a considerable amount of dissatisfaction with respect to the publication of your article; but I trust you will derive some gratification from the knowledge that your views on Criminal Legislation have, by means of the Westminster, obtained an immediate and wide circulation on both sides of the Atlantic. I am my dear Sir

Yours very truly
John Chapman.

II, 161:9 GE TO GEORGE COMBE, LONDON, 9 JUNE 1854

MS: National Library of Scotland. *Endorsed:* London 9 June 1854 | Miss Evans.

21 Cambridge Street | June 9. 1854.

My dear Sir

I fear it is not practicable for me to accept your kind invitation to pay you a visit at Kingston. I must wait for the pleasure of seeing you until you come to town.

"Sir Mowbray Mount Edgecombe" is Charles Cole, the brother of Henry Cole (*Felix Summerly*).[6] He is, I fancy, rather a *mauvais sujet*. Mr. Pigott[7] was unwise enough to accept his proffered contributions to the Leader—articles of gossip under the title of "Private and Confidential"— but they turned out to be in such very bad taste, and so offensive from their indiscretion that Mr. P. at length politely declined them, whereupon Mr. C. Cole broke out into very *im*polite manifestations of wrath, though he has been paid for articles which he volunteered as gratuitous. This is one of the agreeable aspects of human nature with which editors are favoured.

One lives with hope that this "winter of our discontent" will be soon "made glorious";[8] else this introduction to summer would be dismal indeed. Horace Walpole's *mot*[9] is this year no joke but a literal fact. The winds have really been *severe* and I have been, like the rest of the world, grumbling with a cold. I am delighted to hear that you and Mrs. Combe are so well. With kindest regards to you both, I am, my dear Sir

Yours truly

Marian Evans.

6. Charles Cole wrote *Apsley House, a Poem,* 1853, and edited *Memorials of Henry V,* 1858, and a guide to Paris, 1867. His "Private and Confidential" articles, written in a bantering, gossipy style, appear in the *Leader,* 5 (1854), 298, 322, 348, 397, 442, and 468. Henry Cole (1808–82), Assistant Keeper in the Public Record Office, was prominent in planning the Great Exhibition, and in 1853 became Joint Secretary of the Science and Art Department at South Kensington. Under the pseudonym Felix Summerly he published 12 vols. of illustrated children's books, 1841–49.

7. In January 1852 E. F. S. Pigott bought out the proprietors of the *Leader* and assumed editorial responsibility.

8. *King Richard III,* I, i, 1–2.

9. "The way to ensure summer in England is to have it framed and glazed in a comfortable room." (Walpole to William Cole, 28 May 1774.)

II, 162:1 GHL TO CHARLES BRAY,
LONDON, [25 JUNE 1854]

MS: Yale.

26 Bedford Place | Kensington | Sunday.

My dear Bray

Miss Evans will have told you why I could not take Coventry in my way.[1] I hope she explained it fully, for I was in too great a hurry (the Donkeys were at the door, saddled and "pawing the impatient air"!) to write to you a full true and particular account. I assure you it went very much against the grain to give up the visit and only my sense of unfairness to Water made me do so.

I am very much set up though not quite free from oppression and singing in my ears.

Remember me kindly to Mrs. Bray and Miss Hennell and Believe me
Ever your unfulfilling
G. H. Lewes.

1. While GE was at Rosehill, GHL had been invited to stop on his way to or from Malvern for the water cure.

GE in Germany with GHL

1854 July 20	GE and GHL leave for Germany together.
1854 August 4	GE proposes article on Mme de Sablé to Chapman.
1854 August 10	GHL meets Ottilie von Goethe at Weimar.
1854 September	Combe horrified at having misread GE's character.
1854 October 15	GE prepared for renunciation by all her friends.
1854 October	Combe discusses liaison with Bray, Chambers, and Chapman.
1854 October 24	GE calls GHL's conduct toward Agnes "irreproachable."
1854 October 28	Bray knew that GE would "devote herself to some *one* other, in preference to all the world."
1854 November 15	Combe asks if there is not insanity in GE's family.
1854 November	GE translating Spinoza in Berlin.
1855 March 11	GE and GHL start for England.

II, 169:1 GE TO JOHN CHAPMAN, WEIMAR, 6 AUGUST 1854

MS: Yale. *Endorsed:* Miss Evans. *Extracts published:* Haight, *George Eliot*, p. 158.

⟨Weimar⟩ 62a Kaufgasse, Weimar | August 6. 1854.

Dear Friend

Your letter made me glad and sorry. It is the immemorial fashion of lady letter-writers to be glad and sorry in the same sentence, and after all, this feminine style is the truest representation of life. I was delighted to see your writing on the back of the letter which the Post-Beamter, like a conscientious man, refused to give me because I had not my passport in my pocket, and when at last I did get it, I opened it with all sorts of grateful, affectionate feelings towards you for having written to me so soon. But I was deeply saddened by what you tell me about yourself. I have always cherished the hope that you would work your way to independence by gradually paying all debts and anything short of that I can never regard as a relief for you.[2] But I think I am able to enter sympathetically into your whole position, and to estimate both your inward and outward difficulties, so you may rely on always having a fair appreciation from one person in the world, as well as a sisterly interest, which is perhaps less worth having. I shall be very anxious to know how things turn out—but I know you will write to me when you can.

On reading your letter, we determined to get Cousin's book[3] and to unite it with several others as a subject for an article *by me* on "French writers on women." Do you approve of this? If so, I will endeavour to send you the MSS. early in September. I happen to have the material at hand to make such an article piquant and fresh, which are perhaps the qualities likely to be most welcome to you. (Tell me what space you want filled). But you must know that this Weimar—this Athens of the North—is in fact a large village rather than a town, and we are laughing at ourselves for having said of this book and the other, "O we can get it at Weimar," the truth being that the Court-Bookseller (Hof-Buchhandler) has a shop

---

2. In 1854 when Chapman was facing bankruptcy Harriet Martineau advanced him £500, taking a mortgage on the *Westminster Review*. But two creditors, her brother James Martineau and W. B. Hodgson, anxious to acquire the *Review* for their own use, attempted to upset the mortgage and "pursued their debtor with (as some men of business among the creditors said) 'a cruelty unequalled in all their experience.' " (Harriet Martineau, *Autobiography*, ed. M. W. Chapman, 2 vols., Boston, 1877, II, 97–98.)

3. Victor Cousin, *Madame de Sablé. Études sur les femmes illustres et la société du XVIIe siècle,* Paris, 1854. Chapman may have proposed the subject to GHL, who was absorbed in his *Life of Goethe.*

with about as commanding a front as Mr. Tupling's in the Strand.⁴ However, he has a good stock of German books, but ⟨goo⟩ *new* French publications, and most old ones, are only to be had by sending to Leipzig or even to Paris. I have ordered Victor Cousin's book, Sainte Beuve's "Douze Portraits de Femmes"⁵ which I know to be charming, and Michelet's "Femmes de la Revolution."⁶ Besides these, we have several books with us which will give me valuable material and suggestions. When we are at Berlin I shall be able to get Kingsley's works, without which an article on them might be like themselves, more imaginative than solid. You know, I have not been an industrious writer, otherwise I might by this time have been adept enough to criticise a man's works not only without having them at hand, but without having seen them.

We have had enjoyment enough compressed into the last fortnight to make a year more than endurable, if it had been sprinkled over that space. Our route has been through Antwerp, Brussels, Namur, Liege, Cologne, up the Rhine to Coblentz and thence to Mainz, to Frankfort, and finally to Weimar, where we arrived on Thursday. We have a charming little lodging here and are enjoying the quiet, which is the more complete that all the *vornehme* people are away at the Baths or elsewhere taking their summer pleasures. We think it likely that we shall stay here two or three months, but what is most likely is not always what comes to pass.

Mr. Robert Noel was our companion—and a very pleasant one—in the steam boat from London to Antwerp, and on our way to Cologne we were joined in the railway carriage by Dr. Brabant, who very kindly exerted himself to procure me an interview with Strauss at Cologne. With these exceptions we have encountered no friends and acquaintances. Strauss looks worn and saddened and gives one the impression of a man for whom life has lost all charm. Yet he has his two children with him, and Dr. Brabant says they are remarkably interesting. I should like to tell you a great deal about our journey and the lovely things we have seen, but your mind is full of other matters, and I should think you will hardly have patience to read even so much as I *have* written. Some day, I hope, you will have as much happiness, and of the same kind, and will let me share it by telling me of it.

Any London news will be welcome, but most of all what relates to yourself. Give my kind remembrances to Mrs. Chapman, if she will accept them, and believe me always

Your faithful and affectionate
Marian Evans.

4. John Tupling, bookseller at 320 Strand, across from Chapman's house.
5. Charles-Augustin Sainte-Beuve, *Douze Portraits de femmes*, Paris, 1852.
6. Jules Michelet, *Les Femmes de la Révolution*, Paris, 1854.

[*11 August 1854*]

I advise you to get a sight of a work by Ewerboeck "Qu'est ce que c'est que la Bible?"[7] It is a résumé of the results of German Biblical criticism by a clever Frenchman—the same who wrote a compendium of Feuerbach's doctrines.

II, 170:29 FRAU OTTILIE VON GOETHE TO GHL, [WEIMAR, 10 AUGUST 1854]

MS: Frankfurter Goethemuseum.

Wollen Sie die Güte haben nach 11 Uhr sich in den Sammlungen meines Schwiegervaters einzustellen, wo Sie Herrn Secretair Schuchardt finden werden, dessen Bekanntschaft Ihnen angenehm sein muss. Alles Uebrige was Ihre Wünsche betrifft, erfahren Sie dort. Da ich bald Weimar verlasse so wünche ich das Sie die Güte haben uns einen Abend aufzusuchen. Ich bitte im Fall Sie verhindert sind zu kommen die Gefälligkeit zu haben es Ueberbringerin zu sagen.

Ergebene
Ottillie v Goethe.

II, 170:29 GHL TO FRAU OTTILIE VON GOETHE, [WEIMAR, 11 AUGUST 1854]

MS: Yale.

My dear Madam
  Ten thousand pardons. The answer was purposely vague because I did not perfectly understand the question—whether it referred to my coming at 11, or to you, in the evening. I meant to do *both*—but *später* was not the word I used.
  I shall not fail to be there at 11; and shall take my chance of finding you at home this evening.

⟨Lewes.⟩
[*signature has been inked over*]

7. [August] Hermann Ewerbeck, *Qu'est-ce que c'est que la religion d'après la nouvelle philosophie allemande*, Paris, 1850, contains (pp. 64–498) a rather free adaptation or translation of Feuerbach's *Das Wesen des Christenthums*. Vol. II, *Qu'est-ce que la Bible*, 1850, deals with Daumer and Ghillany on the Old Testament and Lützelberger and Bruno Bauer on the New Testament. GE's translation of Feuerbach is generally more faithful to the original.

II, 174:26 GEORGE COMBE JOURNAL, LONDON, 15 SEPTEMBER 1854

MS: National Library of Scotland.

John Chapman and the Westminster Review.

Dr. Hodgson writes to me that Mr. Courtauld, John Chapman's friend and patron, has paid him (Dr. H.) Chapman's debt to him £ in full to avoid calling another meeting of creditors, or forcing Chapman into Bankruptcy.

There is truly a great deal more of benevolence than of conscientiousness and discriminative intellect in the world. Mr. Courtauld is sacrificing his money apparently from the best of motives, to uphold Chapman as the organ of advanced opinions, without any perception of the inadequacy of the man to accomplish the end in view. Chapman is deficient in business talent, in conscientiousness, in knowledge, and in sound practical sense; he is a dreamer and a schemer; his leading motives are ambition and the love of the new; and his chief talents are a capacity for plausible talk, rendered easy by large Secretiveness, Love of approbation, and Wonder, acting unrestrained either by Causality or Conscientiousness. Great efforts making to preserve the Westminster Review in his hands; and this, in my opinion, is an error in judgment. He is morally and intellectually incapable of taking the lead in the philosophy, religion, ⟨practical⟩ social economy, and science of the 19th century; and yet this is what he aims at. He must be editor as well as publisher; in short the great oracle of liberal opinions. He will fail again in a few years. He has much good nature, but ill directed.

II, 174:26 JOHN CHAPMAN TO GEORGE COMBE, LONDON, 18 SEPTEMBER 1854

MS: National Library of Scotland. *Endorsed:* London 18 Sept. 1854 | John Chapman. | 24 Sept. returned his statement.

8 King William St. | Strand September 18. 1854.

Dear Sir,

My conversation with you yesterday makes me desire that you should have a thoroughly clear idea of the condition and prospects of the Westminster Review.—I therefore send the enclosed for your perusal and return. ⟨The third page of the letter to Mr. Martineau is what I particularly wish you⟩

The memorandum of data for the formation of an opinion concerning the worth of the W. R. which is on the same sheet of paper as the copy of the letter to Mr. Martineau is what I particularly wish to call your attention to.

I presume I may count upon your assent to the resolution of my creditors to accept a composition of 8/– in the pound on their respective debts? I am dear Sir

Yours very truly
John Chapman.

Geo. Combe Esq.
P.S. Did I understand you to say that Mr. Robert Cox *has* returned from America, or only that he is expected shortly?

II, 174:26 MRS. CHARLES BRAY TO MRS. GEORGE COMBE, COVENTRY, 23 [SEPTEMBER 1854]

MS: National Library of Scotland. *Endorsed:* Coventry 23 Septr 1854 | Mrs Bray @ Miss Evans.

Conventry | 23d Saturday.

My dear Mrs. Combe

We have not heard of anything dreadful happening to Miss Evans and therefore are quite at a loss to know what has "astounded" your friend. She wrote to us from Weimar a few weeks ago[8] in high health and happiness, said she was enjoying the luxury once more of feeling really well and equal to exertion—was writing hard, and for relaxation exceedingly enjoyed the society of the few savan[t]s who flourish at Weimar to whom Mr. Lewis introduced her, and especially rejoiced in the acquaintance of Liszt the musician—the only really inspired man, she says, that she ever saw. You are aware doubtless that she travelled to Weimar under Mr. Lewis's escort, who had been suffering from congestion of brain and required change. At Cologne they met Dr. Brabant, who procured for Marian an interview with Dr. Strauss, which she had long desired. I feel quite sure we should have heard if any mishap had befallen her and therefore, as you say trust that the report is no truer than Mr. Combe's fatal accident at Lucerne.

With our best wishes for your prosperous journey and no increased colds, Believe me

Yours most truly
Caroline Bray.

8. [16 August 1854].

II, 174:26 GHL TO CHARLES AND THORNTON LEWES, WEIMAR, 27 SEPTEMBER 1854

MS: Yale.

Weimar | 27 September 1854.

My dear Boys

I suppose you will be glad to hear from Papsy as he would be glad to hug you! Here I am in the capital of the Grand duchy of Weimar, about which you, Thornie, know something already, I have no doubt—or soon will. It is a very queer little place although called the "Athens of Germany" on account of the great poets who have lived here; one of them, the greatest of all, you know already by the portraits and little bust in our house—I mean *Goethe*. I am writing his Life, which work brought me to Weimar, to seek for materials. Fancy a little quiet town without cabs, omnibuses, very few carts and scarcely a carriage—with no gas lights for the streets, which are lighted (in winter only) by oil lamps, slung across the streets on a cord. These, which are rare, give so little light that when ladies go to the theatre they take a servant with them to carry a lantern.—But though the town is quiet and queer, it it very agreeable as the Park is within five minutes walk of even the most distant parts, and the Park is something like Kensington Gardens with a river running through it, and with rocky paths and winding ways.

As my poor head continues very bad, and prevents my working I walk a great deal; and take little journeys to Jena, Berka, Wartburg, Ilmenau etc.⁹ At Jena I visited the field of battle where Napoleon thrashed the Prussians so terribly. At the Wartburg I saw the room where Luther lived so long, as Squire George; they show his inkstand, chair, footstool, and the spot on the wall made by the Inkstand which Luther through at the devil's head, when the devil came to tempt him. You know the story, don't you? I saw there portraits of Luther, of his mother and father; and a magnificent collection of ancient armour which would have pleased you more than anything else.

The other day the Grand Duke¹ sent word that he should be glad to

---

9. In her Journal GE describes their first visit to Berka, 2 September 1854, to Jena on the 11th, and to Ilmenau on the 20th. GHL is drawing on memories of his visit in 1839 for the details of the battlefield and the Wartburg, which they did not see in 1854.

1. Charles Alexander, Grand Duke of Saxe-Weimar (1818–1901), succeeded his father Charles Frederick 8 July 1853.

see me at his summer palace. As I had never paid a visit to a crowned head before I felt very uncomfortable lest I should not behave myself according to strict *etiquette*. How should you have felt, Charley?—However the Grand Duke at once made me feel at home, and except that I called him "Royal Highness," I did not behave otherwise than I should to any gentleman whom I might visit for the first time. He was very kind to me, and begged me not to hesitate to ask him any service I might desire. He has a just regard for the English. When the Grand Duchess[2] comes to Weimar he is to present me to her.

The last week I have been roaming through the Thuringian forests—splendid forests of solemn pines and brilliant beeches—with wide stretching valleys and mountains of the loveliest aspects. One day I lost my way, taking a wrong path, and had a terrible roundabout before I got right again.[3]

I heard of your accident, dear Thornie, and of the clever way in which you swallowed the tooth—I suppose to give your stomach an extra weapon for all the extra food thrust into it—eh? And you too, dear Charley, I heard of. May I continue to hear good reports of both of you (but no more tooth swallowing) and that you are getting on well with your studies.

Give my kind remembrances to Mr. and Mrs. Pearce[4] and *kiss each other* for me—the only way I know of sending a kiss so far.

Your loving
Pater.

II, 175:24 JOHN CHAPMAN TO GEORGE COMBE, LONDON, 4 OCTOBER 1854

MS: National Library of Scotland. *Endorsed:* London 4 Octr 1854 | John Chapman | @ | Balance of £35.12/. | 6 Oct. ansd per letter | Book copy.

London October 4 1854.

Dear Sir,

Am I to understand that you wish me to regard the balance now at your credit—£35.12.0—as an additional subscription to the West. Rev.

2. Before her marriage Princess Sophia of the Netherlands.

3. At Ilmenau. "From Gabelbach we went on to Kickelhahn, where Goethe's queer little wooden house stands. We wrote our names near one of the windows. The view of hills from this point is very grand. We did exploits on our way home, not knowing the road, and were amused to find ourselves at last at the spot from which we had begun our uphill walk to the Gabelbach." (GE Journal, 22 September 1854.)

4. Mr. and Mrs. Thomas William Pearce conducted the Bayswater Grammar School, 46 Bedford Place, Kensington, where all three Lewes boys were students.

fund, an account of which I shall be called upon to render to the subscribers at the end of 1855?

It is desirable for the sake of obtaining a definite settlement, and for the satisfaction of the other creditors that the balance in question should be so regarded, or else subjected to the composition. I venture to ask the question because I am not sure that I distinctly apprehend the latter portion of your note. I am dear Sir

Yours very sincerely
John Chapman.

Geo. Combe Esq.

P.S. I commissioned Mr. Robert Chambers to say a few words to you concerning Miss Evans, as your enquiry is on a subject about which I do not like to write. Mr. Lewes and Miss Evans certainly went to the Continent together. He went with the avowed object I believe of taking his sons to a continental school and of obtaining material for his life of Goethe.

II, 176:10 CHARLES BRAY TO GEORGE COMBE, NITON, 8 OCTOBER 1854

MS: National Library of Scotland. *Endorsed:* Isle of Wight | 8 Oct. 1854 | Charles Bray.

Niton, I. of Wight[5] Sunday Evening | October 8/54.

My dear Mr. Combe

I have heard that Mr. and Mrs. Lewes have not been man and wife to each other for some years, but I do not see what that has to do with the case before us except to give plausibility and colour to scandal. What I have heard is that Mrs. Lewes after the birth of her 3rd child took one of those strong and unaccountable dislikes to her husband that sometimes does occur under similar circumstances amounting to monomania and that Lewes was most sincerely attached to his wife and greatly distressed by it. Mr. Lewes would naturally appreciate a mind like Miss Evans', and the more, from the want of sympathy from his wife. I know he had a great friendship and respect for her. His health required that he should travel, he had overworked his brain, he had constant ringing in his ears and fear of apoplexy. Dr. Balbirnie,[6] with whom he had been staying at Malvern, told us, that he feared serious injury to the brain. Miss Evans has long been

---

5. The Brays went to the Isle of Wight 1 October and returned to Coventry the 14th. (Mrs. Bray's Diary.)
6. See II, 160, n. 8.

[*15 October 1854*]

wanting to go abroad and Mr. Lewes offered to introduce her to friends of his in Germany and leave her there for 12 months, which is what she wished. This is all I know and all I believe and I do not see anything very serious to disapprove in it—at least I *did* not. I see now all that may and will be said about their going together and I think it would have been much more prudent to have had others of the party. I can see how necessary it was for Lewes to travel and that he should have a friend with him and that Mrs. Lewes, with her family, could not go, but I fear it was asking too much on Miss Evans part, if she sets any store by public opinion or indeed cares for that of many of her friends. She is just the person however to disregard gossip if a friend wanted her *aid* or I think even if she could go abroad.

Nothing that I have yet heard or know will make any difference in my conduct towards her, although I may regret what she has done as imprudent and as laying herself open to evil report. I shall be at home this day week and shall be glad to hear from you. We very much regret Mrs. Combe's and your indisposition. We hope to hear a better account. With the kindest regard from our "trinity in unity" I remain my dear Mr. Combe

Most sincerely yours
Charles Bray.

II, 176:10 GE TO JOHN CHAPMAN, WEIMAR, [15 OCTOBER 1854]

MS: Yale. *Endorsed:* M. Evans. *Mostly published:* Haight, *George Eliot*, pp. 161–163.

62a Kaufgasse, Weimar.

Dear Friend

It was a comfort to have a letter from you. Pray do not be so long again without writing to me. There are two ways in which you may send me the money;[7] either by Bank of England notes sent in halves by separate posts, or through Coutts's who would send it for me to their correspondents at Weimar. The advantage of the *former* plan is, that there would be no delay in it and consequently, no probability, as in the other case, of my being obliged to remain in Weimar longer than another week or ten days.

I am sorry that you are annoyed with questions about me. Do whatever seems likely to free you from such importunities. About my own justification I am entirely indifferent. But there is a report concerning Mr. Lewes which I must beg you to contradict whenever it is mentioned to you. It is, "that he has run away from his wife and family." This is so

7. For her article on Madame de Sablé.

far from being true that he is in constant correspondence with his wife and is providing for her to the best of his power, while no man can be more nervously anxious than he about the future welfare of his children. The letters he has received from Mrs. Lewes since he has been away, as well as those which he has written to her, have confirmed everything he has told me about their past history and proved to me that his conduct as a husband has been in the highest degree noble and self-sacrificing. Since we have been here, circumstances (in which I am not concerned) have led to his determining on a separation,[8] but he has never contemplated withdrawing the most watchful care over his wife and the utmost efforts for his children.

We have been told of a silly story about a "message" sent by me "in a letter to Miss Martineau" which letter has been shown at the Reform Club. It is hardly necessary to tell you that I have had no communication with Miss Martineau, and that if I had, she is one of the last persons to whom I should speak as to a confidante. The phrase "run away" as applied to me is simply amusing—I wonder what I had to run away from. But as applied to Mr. Lewes it is more serious, and I have thought it right to explain to you how utterly false it is. You are in possession of the broad facts of the case, but there are very many particulars which you do *not* know and which are perhaps necessary to set his character and conduct in their true light. Such particulars cannot be given in a letter. He has written to Carlyle and to Robert Chambers, stating as much of the truth as he can without too severely inculpating others. Helps already knew, and his sympathy was a great comfort when he passed through Weimar.

You ask me to tell you what reply you shall give to inquiries. I have nothing to deny or to conceal. I have done nothing with which any person has a right to interfere. I have surely full liberty to travel in Germany, and to travel with Mr. Lewes. No one here seems to find it at all scandalous that we should be together. Mr. Wilson and Mr. Marshall are as friendly and attentive as possible. But I do not wish to take the ground of ignoring what is unconventional in my position. I have counted the cost of the step that I have taken and am prepared to bear, without irritation or bitterness, renunciation by all my friends. I am not mistaken in the person

---

8. Agnes Lewes had borne a son and two daughters by Thornton Hunt, the last (Ethel) on 9 October 1853. Carlyle in a letter to his brother 2 November 1854 wrote: Lewes "has certainly cast away his Wife here,—who indeed deserved it of him, having openly produced those dirty sooty skinned children which have Th. Hunt for father, and being ready with a *third*; Lewes to pay the whole account, even the money part of it!" (NLS.) Carlyle was unaware that the son Edmund was also Hunt's. The news that Agnes was again pregnant may explain the "circumstances" in which GE was not concerned.

to whom I have attached myself. He is worthy of the sacrifice I have incurred, and my only anxiety is that he should be rightly judged.

I don't like writing so much about myself, but I hope I shall be able to avoid entertaining you with such uninteresting matters in future. Perhaps I ought rather to say *melancholy* matters, for all human difficulties are interesting. I assure you yours are most interesting to me, and I am impatient at the very imperfect knowledge of them which a short letter gives me. I suppose James Martineau has won Froude over to his views and purposes.[9] Their hostility will affect the circulation of the Review, I fear. But you have courage and perseverance, at all events, and they are half the battle.

You said nothing about Herbert Spencer's address. I unfortunately told him to write to Berlin, thinking we should be there much earlier than it has turned out.

Mr. Lewes was in doubt whether he should not return to London to refute the report of his having "run away," but his health is so far from being established and he is so unequal to spending a winter of worry and sadness there that he will not do so unless it should prove absolutely necessary. He has given up the Leader.

Do write to me when you can, and believe me always, sincerely

Your obliged friend
Marian Evans.

Has Miss Tilley sailed for Australia?

II, 176:10 JOHN CHAPMAN TO ROBERT CHAMBERS, LONDON, 16 OCTOBER 1854

MS: W. & R. Chambers, Edinburgh. *Extract published:* Haight, *George Eliot*, p. 167.

London October 16. 1854.

My dear Sir,

I am extremely obliged by your kindness respecting the Deed; please to retain it until you hear from me again. I may now venture to assure you that my settlement is all but completed. It has been a terrible trial. The contest with Dr. Hodgson and Mr. Martineau has been very painful to me. I am sorry to hear that you suffer much from Orr & Co's failure. They say he has been living at a fearfully extravagant rate,—I hope this report is not true.

A word about Miss E[vans].—I am very anxious that what I *said* to

---

9. To take over the *Westminster Review*.

you about *her especially*, should be regarded as strictly confidential. I mention this because Mr. Bray connected your name with a rumour about her; and I should be sorry ⟨that⟩ to be thought disposed to disparage her. I only dropped the word I did because I felt that Lewes was not as you imagined almost alone to blame. Still I think him much the most blameworthy in the matter. Now I can only pray, against hope, that he may prove constant to her; otherwise she is *utterly* lost.

She has a noble nature which in good circumstances and under good influences would have shone out.

Yours very sincerely
John Chapman.

II, 176:10 CHARLES BRAY TO GEORGE COMBE, COVENTRY, 18 OCTOBER 1854

MS: National Library of Scotland. *Endorsed:* Rosehill 18 Oct 1854. | Chas. Bray | @ | Miss Evans.

Rosehill October 18/54.

My dear Mr. Combe,

I still think my view of Miss Evans' case the correct one. I saw something of both parties before they left and heard the matter a good deal discussed by them. Dr. Brabant also met them and introduced Marian to Dr. Strauss and seemed to take the same view of the matter as I do. I also heard the report in Town of Miss Martineau's letter and mentioned it to Mr. Chapman, who pronounced it, I forget on what ground, *impossible*.[1] I have written to Miss Evans and hope for an immediate reply, and therefore it will be unnecessary to write to Miss Martineau—indeed with my belief in the matter, I would rather not mix myself in with the scandal part till I have better evidence than the good-natured gossip afloat. You shall hear immediately I can tell you anything.

May I ask you, if you approved of Dr. Hodgson taking his money in full at the expense of the other creditors or rather of another creditor, because I believe that he reports every where that you did? My wife and Miss Hennell are sadly troubled about all this and wish me to say that Miss E's going had not their sanction, because they knew nothing at all about it. I trust you and Mrs. Combe are now quite recovered. We returned from Niton, I. of Wight, on Saturday last. Ever, my dear Sir,

Yours very sincerely
Charles Bray.

1. See Chapman to Combe, 4 October 1854.

II, 180:1 CHARLES BRAY TO GEORGE COMBE, COVENTRY, 24 OCTOBER 1854

MS: National Library of Scotland. *Endorsed:* Coventry 24 Oct. 1854 | Charles Bray | @ | Miss Evans & Mr. | Lewes

Coventry October 24th/54.

My dear Mr. Combe,

The day after I wrote to Miss Evans, I received a letter from her with reference to her monetary affairs. There is a passage or two in it, that our people say I had better send to you. She says "It is possible that you may have heard a report prevalent in London that Mr. Lewes has 'run away from his wife and family.' Since he left England he has been in constant correspondence with his wife; she has all the money due to him in London; and his children are his constant thought and anxiety. His conduct as a husband has been not only irreproachable, but generous and self-sacrificing to a degree far beyond any standard fixed by the world." Of herself she says, "Of course many silly myths are already afloat about me, in addition to the truth, which of itself would be thought matter for scandal. If you hear of anything which I have said, done or *written* in relation to Mr. Lewes beyond the simple fact,[2] do me the justice to believe that it is false. x x x The only influence I should ever dream of exercising over him as to his conduct towards his wife and children is that of stimulating his conscientious care for them, if it needed any stimulant." This would entirely discredit the Miss Martineau story—besides she expressly says that Mr. Chapman and myself are the *only* persons to whom she has ever spoken of her relation to Lewes. There is an article of hers in the last Westminster on French Women, which I think would please you much, as having the "physiological basis." It is very clever and contains the only true and just distinction between the sexes I have ever seen. I am very glad to hear that you are better and that Mrs. Combe is mending. Believe me

Ever yours sincerely,
Charles Bray.

2. Bray here omits: "that I am attached to him and that I am living with him."

II, 180:1 CHARLES BRAY TO GEORGE COMBE, COVENTRY, 28 OCTOBER 1854

MS: National Library of Scotland. *Endorsed:* Coventry 28 October | 1854 | Charles Bray | @ | Miss Evans. | 30th ansd.

Coventry, October 28/54.

My dear Mr. Combe,

I have heard from Miss Evans.³ She says "In answer to your letter, let me first say that I have never written to Miss Martineau or had any communication with her since last November. I do not think her love of detraction would lead her to tell a deliberate falsehood and hence I conclude that the story of my having written to her etc. etc. is a gradually formed myth. The last folly I am likely to commit is that of thrusting my private affairs on others or seeking to make myself conspicious on the ground of them."

I pressed upon her for the sake of herself and friends that she should seperate herself from Lewes, supposing *he* was not immediately to return, according to the plan first settled, and she replies, that his health will not permit it at present, that she is absolutely necessary to him, and she refuses to do what she should consider wrong out of deference to the opinion of the world. She says "I mean this letter for you alone and I beg that you will not *quote* me either in my justification or otherwise. No one has any right to interfere with my conduct—no one is responsible for me; and I beg that you will free yourself from annoyance and enquiries by stating that I am quite too old ⟨enough⟩ for you to be supposed in any way answerable for me. So far as my friends or acquaintances are ⟨concerned⟩ inclined to occupy themselves with my affairs, I am grateful to them and sorry that they should have pain on my account, but I cannot think that their digestion will be much hindered by anything that befals a person about whom they troubled themselves very little while she lived in privacy and loneliness."

So if you please consent to let the matter drop, and people must be allowed to come to their own conclusions as to the right or wrong of her ⟨action⟩ conduct. She also must be allowed to satisfy her own conscience. As a daughter she was the most devoted I ever knew, and she is just as likely to devote herself to some *one* other, in preference to all the world, and without reference either to the regularity or legality of the connection.

3. The letter Bray quotes from, written 23 October 1854 (GE Journal), has not been found.

15 November 1854 129

It would never be other than a *strong sense* of *public* duty to the highest interests that would seperate me from her or her from my friendship. I have known her for years and should always feel that she was better *by one half* than $\frac{99}{100}$ of the people I have ever known.

With the kindest regard from all our circle, whom you must not hold responsible for any thing I write as they know nothing of it, I remain, dear Mr. Combe

Very sincerely yours
Charles Bray.

II, 186:18 GEORGE COMBE TO CHARLES BRAY, EDINBURGH, 15 NOVEMBER 1854

MS: Copy in National Library of Scotland. *Extract published:* Haight, *George Eliot,* p. 166.

Private

Edinburgh 15 November 1854.

My dear Mr. Bray—

An intimate friend of Mr. Lewes's in this city, wrote to him begging of him to contradict the reports of an improper connection with Miss Evans. He gave ample explanations about his wife, denied that Miss E. had written to Miss Martineau; but in regard to the main question, he said that he is not answerable to his correspondent for his conduct. He has written in precisely similar terms, in answer to a similar request, to Mr. Carlyle. The conclusion, then, is irresistible that the reports are too true.—They are spread everywhere, and we now meet them in society. We are deeply mortified and distressed; and I should like to know whether there is insanity in Miss Evans's family; for her conduct, with *her* brain, seems to me like ⟨insanity⟩ morbid mental aberration.

I have no right to dictate to you, but I esteem you too much not to state frankly to you my convictions. T. Hunt, Lewes, and Miss Evans have, in my opinion, by their practical conduct, inflicted a great injury on the cause of religious freedom. "The Leader" has become disagreeable to Mrs. Combe and me as the recorded thinking of minds that can act in such a manner, and when my subscription expires I shall give it up. "The greatest happiness of the greatest number" principle,[4] appears to me to require that the obligations of married life should be honourably

---

4. Jeremy Bentham attributes to Priestley the "sacred truth,—that the greatest happiness of the greatest number is the foundation of morals and legislation." Bentham, *Works*, ed. Sir John Bowring, 11 vols., 1838–43, x, 142.

fulfilled; and an educated woman who, in the face of the world, volunteers to live as a wife, with a man who already has a living wife and children, appears to me to pursue a course and to set an example calculated only to degrade herself and her sex, if she be sane.—If you receive her into your family circle, while present appearances are unexplained, pray consider whether you will do justice to your own female domestic circle, and how other ladies may feel about going into a circle which makes no distinction between those who act thus, and those who preserve their honour unspotted?

I again assure you that it is in deep sorrow that I write these lines, and that love and respect for you and yours, alone prompt me to unburden my mind to you in this manner.

With our united kind regards to you, Mrs. Bray, and Mrs.[5] and Miss Hennell, I remain, My dear Mr. Bray,

Yours very truly
Geo. Combe.

I think that Mr. Lewes was perfectly justified in leaving his own wife, but not in making Miss Evans his mistress.

Chas. Bray Esq.

II, 188:1 CHARLES BRAY TO GEORGE COMBE, COVENTRY, 19 NOVEMBER 1854

MS: National Library of Scotland. *Endorsed:* Chas. Bray @ Miss Evans.

Rosehill November 19/54.

My dear Mr. Combe

Thank you for your kind letter—I quite agree with you in every word. The cause of religious freedom has suffered lately in more ways than one —this scandal—Chapman's failure etc. Still a cause is not to be judged by its professors. Unfortunately those who throw up the religious sanction to marriage, and who despise conventional law, do not always recognize and admit a natural law. We have still got to fight for this recognition. There is much to be said against the *working* of present law; there is a wide field of opinion on the Continent on the subject and I am not prepared to put down every one as *wicked* who may not agree with me upon the subject. We want a good book or article on the subject of marriage and divorce. Could not you write one for the Westminster? *it would do great*

---

5. Mrs. James Hennell, Mrs. Bray's mother, who came with Sara to live with the Brays at Ivy Cottage 15 July 1854. (Mrs. Bray's Diary.)

good just now. Treat it physiologically, phrenologically, morally, socially, practically.

I do not think that Miss Evans would admit that Lewes had a wife now, or has had for some years, and they may both of them intend to fulfil all the conditions that belong *naturally* to the marriage state. Mind I have no wish to defend the part she is taking—only I do not judge her. I don't think she is *mad.* She had organically, all the ⟨str⟩ intellectual strength of a man and ⟨all⟩ in feeling all the peculiar weaknesses of woman. I know she would prefer the close and devoted affection of one mind, to the ordinary and customary attentions of all the world besides i.e. if she were called on to make her choice. In alluding to her friends however before (which I quoted) I must do her the justice to say that she did not mean you or me—but her own relations who have never noticed her—never appreciated her. Perhaps, poor thing, from her own experience, we may still have heard the powerful advocate and expounder of *our* views. Excuse this hasty and ill-expressed note and believe me always

> Very sincerely yours
> Charles Bray.

Mr. T. Hunt does not now edit the Leader. Mr. Whitty[6] does—in a letter received from him today he calls upon me not to believe the things I may hear of him and says hold up till we see personally.

II, 190:1 GE TO JOHN CHAPMAN, BERLIN, 9 DECEMBER 1854

MS: Yale. *Endorsed:* Miss Evans. *Extract published:* Haight, *George Eliot,* p. 174.

62 Dorotheen Strasse, Berlin | December 9. 1854.

Dear Friend

It was agreeable to have some news of you after your long silence, but it would have been still more agreeable if you could have told me that you were in good health.[7] I hope however, that, as life is generally a see-saw of troubles, your bodily discomfort is compensated by greater ease and satisfaction in other respects.

---

6. Edward Michael Whitty (1827–60), who had written Parliamentary summaries for *The Times,* contributed the "Stranger in Parliament" articles in the *Leader.* He began to serve as editor in July 1853, and under Pigott's control was removed in 1854 because of his Roman Catholic bias. See Allan R. Brick, *The Leader: Organ of Radicalism,* (Yale dissertation), 1957, pp. 226–233.

7. "Letter from Mr. Chapman—a chef d'oeuvre of bad taste." (GE Journal, 7 December 1854.)

The information you gave me about Miss B. Smith[8] is quite an unexpected source of painful sympathy. She seemed so secure in the possession of physical strength that I can hardly imagine her an invalid. I heartily wish she may be restored by southern air and get back to England as bright and blooming as ever.

I am much obliged to you for your offer to send me the W. R., but I need not give you that trouble, as there is a copy at the Library here.

Mr. Lewes's health is far from being completely restored; he is frequently, indeed constantly, obliged to rise from his work by a burning sensation in his head. This is particularly trying to one who enjoys work so much as he does, and who is so much in need of its results. With this exception, our life at Berlin is eminently agreeable; we have seen some very pleasant and varied society, partly made up of Mr. Lewes's old friends and partly of new ones. But we enjoy our evenings at home most of all—we read furiously and are trying to get very wise, in spite of Solomon's proverb about the unimprovability of bad materials.[9] I ought to mention, as another exception to happiness, our anxiety about the war,[1] which you must all be feeling terribly. Kossuth's representation of the English position seems in some respects irrefragable, and is no cheerful one.[2] The sympathies of the *people* here seem to be entirely with the Allies. We have been pleased to hear it observed at table that the English despatches and journals are the only ones to be relied on for telling the truth. One would of course prefer that the whole world should tell the truth, but if there must be liars, I suppose we are not to carry our generosity so far as not to wish that somebody else should have the misfortune to be such rather than ourselves. We are having the most variable weather imaginable—no severe cold, but alternate rain, slight frost, and mugginess. I dare say you are no better off in London—the more's the pity.

I hope Mr. Mackay's book[3] will prove a success for you and him—it is a dismal thing to write and publish in vain. But the treatment which books get from periodical critics is really disheartening—the more I read the Athenaeum, the more I feel disgusted with the incompetence and unconscientiousness of the people who have the pretention of guiding the

8. Barbara Leigh Smith, who had been having a love affair with Chapman, fell ill and, with her sister Nanny, was taken by their aunt Julia Smith to Rome for the winter. (*George Eliot and John Chapman*, pp. 88–92, and Hester Burton, *Barbara Bodichon*, [1949], pp. 74–75.)

9. "That which is crooked cannot be made straight." (Ecclesiastes 1:15.)

1. England and France had invaded the Crimea in September 1854 and laid siege to Sebastopol.

2. Speaking at the Polish celebration in London, 26 November 1854. The *Leader* commented (2 December, p. 1128) that Kossuth's speech had "inflicted a heavy blow on the Government."

3. Robert William Mackay, *A Sketch of the Rise and Progress of Christianity*, published by Chapman in 1854.

public. The marvel is that any sensible person can think such reviews any criterion of the value of books. But you do not want to read *Jérémiades* of this sort, for you must be singing them yourself only too often.

I have just asked Mr. Lewes if he can think of anything interesting to tell you, and he replies by quoting a discovery as to the anatomy of *perches* just made by some French anatomist!—I tell you this to show you my utter destitution of news which you would care to hear. This scrap of a letter is to be enclosed in one from Mr. Lewes to Mr. Pigott, so you must not marvel to see it without a post mark.

I wish you all possible success,—including good out of Nazareth *i.e.* desirable theology from Oxford,[4]—to cheer you by your Christmas fires, and am always

Your sincere Friend
Marian Evans.

II, 190:1 GE TO JOHN CHAPMAN, BERLIN, 9 JANUARY 1855

MS: University of Texas. *Endorsed:* Miss Evans. *Partly published:* II, 190.

62 Dorotheen Strasse, Berlin | January 9. 1854.[5]

Dear Friend

Glad to hear from you again, though I was casting no mental reproaches on you for your silence, as I was aware that you must be very busy at the high tide of your editorial affairs.

I still think the "Ideals of Womanhood" a good subject and one I should like to treat, but I have been thinking lately of an article on another subject which I believe I could make interesting and which I could prepare for your next number if you agree with me that it is promising. Meanwhile, if you think well, I will *slowly* prepare the other article for some future number. The subject I now propose is "Woman in Germany"[6] —not simply the modern German woman, who is not a very fertile subject (metaphorically speaking) but woman as she presents herself to us in all the phases of development through which the German race has run from the earliest historic twilight when it was still blended with the Scandinavian race—and its women were prophetesses, through the periods of the Volks wanderung and the romantic and *bürgerlich* life of the Middle Ages up to

---

4. Cf. John 1:46. The "Theology and Philosophy" section of the Contemporary Literature article in the *Westminster Review*, 63 (January 1855), 206–228 was written by Mark Pattison (1813–84), Rector of Lincoln College, Oxford.
5. See II, 191, n. 4.
6. See II, 190, n. 2.

our own day. There is a great deal of picturesque material on this subject and I am just in the midst of it here, so that it would suit me perhaps better than any other just now. What say you?—No, of course, unless you heartily concur—and I shall equally remain etc. etc. as politeness says at the end of letters, meaning Go to the ———. The article would very likely not reach 32 pages, but I should be glad to be allowed that length of tether as it would be a disadvantage to the subject for me to feel cramped.

I am amazed to hear that Dr. Hodgson and company could think of venturing on the attempt to establish a new quarterly.[7] I cannot believe it will be carried through. But if no heresies are allowed in it, it will not be a formidable rival to you. Heresy would have been strength to it. I see the propriety of your objection to sending private matters in Nutt's parcel, and one can always wait for the story of people's misdoings. I am sorry to be obliged to think that Dr. Hodgson has behaved ill.

Mr. Lewes's health has been variable, but I think he is on the whole better. He desires me to send his kind remembrances to you, as indeed he always does, and I always forget to give them. We like our Berlin life immensely—an ugly place it must be to any one who comes to it hipped or solitary or what is worse, with a disagreeable companion. But, to make a very novel quotation—"the mind is its own place"[8] and can make a pretty town even of Berlin. The day seems too short for our happiness and we both of us feel that we have begun life afresh—with new ambition and new powers. I say so much to you, because I know you have a friendly interest in me, and to that extent I am not afraid of incurring the fatality which the Germans seem still to believe in. When any one is spoken of as being very happy, they say "Unberufen"—meaning "Don't talk of it, or their happiness will vanish."

It is distressing to see the multitude of soldiers here—to think of the nation's vitality going to feed 300,000 puppets in uniform. In the streets one's legs are in constant danger from officers' swords, and at tables d'hôte the most noise is always made by officers. Will you be kind enough to let me owe you a 1d stamp and send the enclosed letter to Miss Hennell?

We have just come from hearing "Fidelio," and I write tonight to save the working time in the morning. Pray let no one else see this hasty and unconsidered letter.

Ever yours sincerely
Marian Evans.

---

7. After their failure to get the *Westminster Review* out of Chapman's hands, James Martineau and W. B. Hodgson established the *National Review* in 1855.

8. *Paradise Lost*, i, 254.

In a sentence of my article which was altered, *perspicuity* was printed for *perspicacity*[9] a mistake which would make any one with a nice sense of the language shudder. Verbum sapientibus. Please to put a seal on Miss Hennell's letter. You can read it if you like.

9. "Woman in France: Madame de Sablé," *Westminster Review*, 62 (October 1854), 451: "The quiescence and security of the conjugal relation are doubtless favourable to the manifestation of the highest qualities by persons who have already attained a high standard of culture, but rarely foster a passion sufficient to rouse all the faculties to aid in winning or retaining its beloved object—to convert indolence into activity, indifference into ardent partisanship, dulness into perspicuity."

Living by the Pen

1855 August 7	Carlyle reads proof of GHL's *Goethe*.
1855 November 3	Carlyle thanks GHL for dedication.
1856 January	GHL begins revising *History of Philosophy*.
1856 March 9	Cautions Spencer to ask for "Mrs. Lewes."
1856 May–July	Writing *Sea-side Studies* at Ilfracombe and Tenby.
1856 June	Quarrels with Bohn over Spinoza translation.
1856 September	GE begins "Amos Barton" at Tenby.
1857 March–May	More *Sea-side Studies* at Scilly and Jersey.
1857 May 27	GE becomes "Mrs. Lewes" to all her family.
1857 October 29	*Scenes of Clerical Life* completed in *Blackwood's*.
1857 November 7	GHL to revise *Chemistry of Common Life*.
1858 January 5	*Scenes of Clerical Life* published in 2 vols.
1857 December 13	GHL proposes *The Physiology of Common Life*.
1858 March 1	Blackwood approves 1st vol. of *Adam Bede* MS.
1858 March 27	GE sends Mrs. Bray her photograph.
1858 April 1	Refuses to tell Blackwood plot of *Adam Bede*.
1858 April–August	GE and GHL at Munich and Dresden.
1858 November 3	Blackwood offers £800 for *Adam Bede*, £250 for *The Physiology of Common Life*.
1858 November 20	Advises lessening local dialect in *Adam Bede*.

II, 198:3 CHARLES BRAY TO GEORGE COMBE, COVENTRY, 7 APRIL 1855

MS: National Library of Scotland. *Endorsed:* Coventry 7 April 1855 | Chas. Bray.

Coventry | April 7/55.

My dear Mr. Combe,

I am glad to hear that you and Mrs. Combe have got well through this severe winter.... Miss Evans is at Dover. Mr. Lewes has not joined his wife, *as his wife*; arrangements had been made for an *entire* seperation before he knew Miss Evans and I believe he is in London to complete them. He is also about to publish some large book—and then I believe he is bound for Germany again and Italy. We are all well and desire the kindest remembrances to you and Mrs. Combe.

Do you know W. M. Thackeray? He is to lecture here on the 23rd. I should have been glad to see him, but do not know him.[10]

Believe me my dear Mr. Combe

Ever yours sincerely
Charles Bray.

II, 202:10 GHL TO HENRY CRABB ROBINSON, EAST SHEEN, [14? MAY 1855]

MS: Dr. Williams's Library. *Endorsed:* 1855 | G. H. Lewes | *Life of Göthe.*

7 Clarence Row, | East Sheen, | Surrey.

Dear Sir

I trust the purpose of this note is sufficient apology; for although accident has hitherto prevented my desire to make your personal acquaint-

---

10. Bray had written to Thackeray, inviting him to stay at Rosehill after his lecture. Thackeray replied, 5 April: "I thank you for your hospitable offer, but will ask leave to decline it. I am unwell, and cannot count on myself from one day to another. Under these unlucky circumstances an inn ⟨is⟩ will be the best halting place for the few hours which I shall be able to pass in Coventry." (Yale.) However, he wrote to his mother 22 April 1855: "I am to go and be lionized at Coventry tomorrow—where I am to stay with a man who would take no refusal, and who of course will have a party to meet me." Among the Brays' guests was a young lady [probably Mary Sibree, later Mrs. John Cash], who gave Lady Ritchie an account of the visit: "He usually goes to an inn, hating to be made a lion of, but the Lewes' assured him that the Brays would not lionise him, and so he accepted the invitation." (G. N. Ray, *Thackeray Letters*, III, 437–39, and Lady Ritchie, Biographical Introduction to *The Newcomes*, VIII, xxxv–xxxvii.)

[14? May 1855]

ance, I am sure the name of Goethe is enough to command your interest at once.[11] It is of Goethe I would speak.

For many years I have been employed writing his Biography. Many of his personal friends in Germany have kindly assisted me. You, also, I believe had some personal acquaintance with him in his later years, and I should esteem it a great favor if your inclination and leisure would permit you to furnish me with any personal details. What you have written on Goethe is known to me; at least what appeared years ago in the Monthly Repository. But the biographer sets great store by details which have significance for him, although not perhaps the sort of details which would appear in criticism; and it may be that you could furnish the details which others have forgotten, or not thought significant because they could not forsee the use to be made of them. Believe me, dear Sir

Yours very truly
G. H. Lewes.

H. C. Robinson Esq.

II, 202:10 GHL TO BENJAMIN N. WEBSTER,[1] EAST SHEEN, [JUNE? 1855]

MS: Yale.

7 Clarence Row, | East Sheen, | Surrey.

My dear Webster

Here is the comedy[2] I spoke to you about. If you like the idea, and like to have the part altered for you, I shall be glad of any suggestions from you—certain that your suggestions will benefit the piece.

If you don't take to it yourself—will it not do as it stands for Leigh Murray and Miss Woolgar?[3]

Ever faithfully yours,
G. H. Lewes.

11. Robinson was outraged at this letter "addressing me as 'Dear Sir,' though we have never seen each other" and asking for Göthe anecdotes. "He lives with Miss Evans, and Thornton Hunt with Mrs. Lewes." (*Henry Crabb Robinson on Books and Their Writers*, ed. E. J. Morley, 3 vols., 1938, II, 751.)

1. Benjamin Nottingham Webster (1797–1882), since 1853 manager of the Adelphi.

2. *The Fox Who Got the Grapes*, adapted from *Alexandre chez Apelles* by Bayard and Dupin. GHL finished it at Weimar 7 October 1854. (GE Journal.)

3. Sarah Jane Woolgar (1824–1909) made her debut at the Adelphi in 1843.

II, 209:10 GHL TO BENJAMIN N. WEBSTER, EAST SHEEN, [JULY? 1855]

MS: Yale.

7 Clarence Row East Sheen | Friday.

My dear Webster

Have you read the "Fox who got the grapes"—or *haven't* you?

Do you like it—or *don't* you?

Will it (—if not suitable for you and Madame[4]—) do for Leigh Murray and Miss Woolgar—or won't it? Your Interrogative and ever faithful

G. H. Lewes.

II, 212:27 THOMAS CARLYLE TO GHL, LONDON, 7 AUGUST 1855

MS: Fitzwilliam Museum, Cambridge.

Chelsea, 7 August 1855.

Dear Lewes,—

I go into Suffolk tomorrow, and am likely to be wandering about for some time; so that I find it will only be a bother to you, and delay *without* advantage, to shoot those Proofs after me in my erratic course. I found it an amazing thing to read them in the evening, under the cloud of a quiet pipe in the Garden here: I had, as it were, *nothing* to suggest; and felt that my remarks, had they even been of value, came too late.

The Book goes on rapidly (Printer and all), and promises to be a very good bit of Biography; far, far beyond the kind of stuff that usually bears that name in this country and in others.— I desiderate chiefly a little change of *level* now and then; that you could sit upon some height, and shew us rapidly the contours of the region we are got into, from time to time,—well abhorring to be drowned in details as Viehof and Co. are, or to swim about (not quite drowned, but drowning) in endless lakes of small matters which have become "great" only by being much talked about by fools for the time being.

You missed the *Malefactor's scull* that was on one of the steeples of

---

4. Madame Celeste (1814?–82) had been associated with Webster in management of the Adelphi since 1844.

5. Carlyle was reading proofs of GHL's *Goethe*.

Frankfort; no great matter. I found out, the other year, *who* the proprietor had been (a foolish *radical* about 1600 or so); but have already almost forgotten again, a proof there was not much for you in the story of him.

Slightly more import[an]t for you was another thing I remembered in the reading over of the Proofs, but did not then see how you were to get in: the *"Visitation* of Wetzlar," through *Overhauling* (with an eye to repair) of that "German Court of Chancery," which had been ordered by the Diet, and was just then *beginning*, about the time Goethe went. That was thought a great chime for a young lawyer,—to witness the very *dissection* of Themis. It came as other "Visitations" had done, to *nothing*. If you make an Appendix, there might be some notice taken of this,—though whither to go for summary information I cannot at this moment direct you. My Pfeffel's Abrégé[6] (in Brit. Mus.) which has an Index, could let it lie altogether!—Best speed to you, dear Lewes.

Yours always truly
T. Carlyle.

II, 217:10 GHL TO RICHARD OWEN, EAST SHEEN, [SEPTEMBER 1855]

MS: British Museum.

7 Clarence Row.

My dear Professor

I have persuaded Parker of the desirability of the Magazine's tomahawking you.[7] To assist me in that benevolent process (as an anatomist you can't object to dissection—nor to vivisection!) will you lend me Broderip's two articles in the Quarterly[8] and also the 2nd volume of your Comp[arative] Anat[omy], the volume on Fishes which I have had from the London Library more than once but can't get just now.[9]

You were good enough to say you would let me use the sheets of the Inverteb[rates] for extract in case I wanted to do so. Now the proofs will do very well for me to bind up into a copy; but if you have any duplicates

---

6. Christian Friedrich Pfeffel von Kriegelstein, *Abrégé chronologique de l'histoire et du droit publique d'Allemagne*, 1754.

7. "Professor Owen and the Science of Life," *Fraser's*, 53 (January 1856), 79–92.

8. William John Broderip, "Progress of Comparative Anatomy," *Quarterly Review*, 90 (March 1852), 362–413, and "Generalizations of Comparative Anatomy," 93 (June 1853), 46–83.

9. Richard Owen, *Lectures on the Comparative Anatomy and Physiology of the Invertebrate Animals*, 2 vols., 1843–46.

[*October 1855*]

of revises I need not rob you of another copy. I will tell you when the article is done what extracts are made.

While I am begging I will go on and beg for your Zoological *Sunday* ticket—any Sunday you may have it free?

Ever faithfully yours
G. H. Lewes.

II, 218:1 GHL TO THOMAS HAILES LACY, RICHMOND, 10 OCTOBER 1855

MS: Yale.

8 Park Shot | Richmond | 10 October 1855.

Dear Sir

I have considered your proposition. By the books of the D[ramatic] A[uthors] society I find, *Give a dog an ill name*, is played oftener than I thought. I do not think 12£ would pay for the four pieces;[7] but retaining London right for 3 years of the *Cosy Couple*, I will sell you the 4 pieces for 15£. If this suits you let me know—or send me an agreement and I will sign it.

Yours truly
G. H. Lewes.

II, 221:1 GHL TO THOMAS HAILES LACY, RICHMOND, [OCTOBER 1855]

MS: Yale.

8 Park Shot | Richmond.

Dear Sir

If you apply to Mathews[8] saying you have bought the pieces he will give you the M.S.S. or an order to get them.

As to when I want the cash, why *as soon* as you can let me have it, but you can make it convenient to yourself. So that I get it between this and the end of Novr I shall not grumble.

Yours truly
G. H. Lewes.

---

7. *Lacy's Acting Edition of Plays* etc., 1849–1917, published *Buckstone's Adventures with a Polish Princess, A Cosy Couple, The Game of Speculation,* and *Give a Dog a Bad Name.*

8. Charles James Mathews (1803–78), who produced GHL's plays at the Lyceum.

II, 221:1 GHL TO THEODORE MARTIN, RICHMOND, [2 NOVEMBER 1855]

MS: University of Kansas.

8 Park Shot | Richmond | Saturday.

Dear Martin

Thanks for your delightfully flattering letter.[9] So to have pleased you is success. If you have any faults to find and suggestions to make for my second edition they will be gratefully accepted.

I am going to give you an example by finding serious fault with your very original and striking play.[1] The first act ought to be abolished altogether. The excellence of the writing carries it through, in reading, but on the stage it would be intolerable—long *talk* and no dramatic life. How different the second and third acts, with their deep passionate undercurrent and true dramatic οἶστρος ![2] My advice would be this: *Begin* with your second act, and expand it into two—each scene being an act. The explanation of the family feud, Guido's love, the mysterious passion of Nello, and the fascination exercised over Pia may very well come *after* curiosity has been excited in the persons. See how Shakspeare manages this matter. Othello does not tell the story of his love until we are dying to know all about it. But what robust gentleman in the pit will care for Giacomo and his youthful valour—or for Nello—or for Guido—*before* you have excited curiosity?

As to want of incident it will never be felt when so strong and passionate a story engrosses attention. Besides the very originality of the work will greatly affect an audience. Only you must not in three acts have one weak— like your first. Make the first as good as the others toute proportion gardée and never hesitate as to success.

But then—and here the dramatist's difficulty is over, but the manager's begins—*who* is to play Nello? Unless finely played it will go for nothing. Charles Kean[3]—bad as he is—is the only one "fatal" enough—et encore!

---

9. On GHL's *Goethe*, published in October 1855.

1. *Madonna Pia*, adapted from a one-act play by the Marquis de Belloy produced in Paris in February 1853 under the title *La Malaria*, to which Martin prefixed two acts, embroidering Dante's story of Pia de' Tolomei, murdered by her husband Nello della Pietra. (*Purgatorio*, v, 133–136.) Martin revised Act I, adding to it rather than cutting. The play was never acted.

2. Gad, sting.

3. Charles John Kean (1811?–68) in 1850 took over the management of the Princess's Theatre, which he conducted with great success. In 1852, apparently for some slight in the *Leader* about the acting of his wife Ellen Tree (1805–80), Kean removed GHL from the free list. (*Leader*, 7 February 1852.) GHL made capital of this petty revenge and missed few chances to ridicule Kean's shortcomings.

—Then Mrs. Kean would be an awful Pia! Your wife[4] and Charles Kean (Macready[5] not being available) are the only persons I would trust the piece to. However if it never should be played I think the two acts so fine that they are worth any amount of pains in alteration.

I write crudely and hastily but you will gather my meaning.

Ever faithfully yours
G. H. Lewes.

II, 221:1 THOMAS CARLYLE TO GHL, LONDON, 3 NOVEMBER 1855

MS: Yale.

Chelsea, 3 November 1855.

Dear Lewes,

I am sorry to hear you still complain of health; bad health is a very miserable adjunct to one's burden, though not an uncommon one to poor wretches of this craft! *Festina lentè:* don't work *too much* (which proves always *too little* by and by): that is the one way of procuring some abatement, if abolition of the misery is not possible.

I know your clean finger in *The Leader* weekly as heretofore; one of the few writing fingers of this epoch which are not dog's paws, or cloven hoofs of mere human swine. Pah!—

Furthermore I got the *Goethe* the other night, almost at the same time with your Note. Every night since, in my reading hours, I am dashing athwart it in every direction; *truanting*; for I w[on]t wait a time to read the work with such deliberation as I well see it deserves. My conviction is, we have here got an excellent Biography,—altogether transcendently so, as Biographies are done in this country. Candid, well-informed, clear, free-flowing, it will certainly throw a large flood of light over Goethe's life, with many German things which multitudes in England have been curious about, to little purpose, for a long while. It ought to have a large circulation, if one can predict or anticipate in regard to such matters. On the whole, I say *Euge*, and that heartily,—though dissenting here and there. I ought also to be thankful, and am, for the fine manful words you have seen good to say about my poor self:[6] good words go about too, as

---

4. Helena Saville Faucit (1817–98), known as Helen Faucit, was married to Theodore Martin in 1851.

5. William Charles Macready (1793–1873), having acted for forty years, left the stage in 1851.

6. GHL's *Life and Works of Goethe*, published 30 October 1855, dedicated "To Thomas Carlyle, who first taught England to appreciate Goethe, this work is inscribed, as a memorial of gratitude for intellectual guidance, and of esteem for rare and noble qualities."

well as evil;—and all words go to nothing except they *be* the copies of things:

> Denn geschwärzig sind die Zeiten,
> Und sie sind auch wieder *stumm*.

Ach Gott ja, most dumb indeed;—and we read with pain, in M. Thiers and the like, *femme alors celèbre*, homme alors etc.

I returned from my wanderings, which never went very wide, some three or four weeks ago; and am here in my garret, again, up to the chin in Brandenburg *naval stores*; uncertain whether I shall not sink dead, and be buried under them, one day; but struggling to hope not.

Once more, *Well-done*, and thanks; and let me see you soon.

Yours always truly
T. Carlyle.

II, 223:1 GE TO CHARLES BRAY, RICHMOND, 2 DECEMBER [1855]

MS: Coventry City Libraries.

Richmond | December 2.

Dear Friend

I have just read your kind letter and write now, while I think of it, to ask you to give my kind regards to Mr. Noel[1] and say that if ever his excursions bring him near us again, I shall be very glad to see him.

You know that *you* will be always welcome, and we have such comfortable lodgings and such a charming cook, that I can put you in clover.

I don't think my sister is in any anxiety about me, since we often write to each other, and I am going to see her at Christmas.

Mr. Lewes sends his kind regards. We are both flourishing.

I have just been spilling my ink, and am in a quandary—writing this in the interval of hindrance, while the damage is being remedied.

Ever yours affectionately
Marian.

1. Edward Noel and his children came to Rosehill 12 December 1855, went to Leam the 22d, and returned 4 January 1856. (Mrs. Bray's Diary.)

II, 223:16 GHL TO JOHN STUART BLACKIE, RICHMOND, 19 DECEMBER 1855

MS: Yale.

8 Park Shot | Richmond | 19 December 1855.

My dear Sir

Your letter gave me great pleasure: to be praised by a man of genius is worth endless columns of newspaper laudation. I am the more sensitive to your's because I have long been an admirer of your powers.

I really think your Faust *is* worth retranslating, in spite of the terrible labor which translation of such a work must involve.[2]

Yes, the liaison with the Frau von Stein *did* become more than platonic, as you will see I quietly indicate in one passage;[3] but I was forced to keep that part in a subdued light because the British public would have gone into fits at the open avowal. His letters leave *no* doubt of the fact.

Thanks for the Sonnet.—I was glad to hear of Schöll. What an excellent creature! And Saupe also. Though I speak German so badly that I am amazed Schöll should have entertained any hopes of the book. However the Germans seem delighted. Varnhagen has written to me in the highest terms about it. He has recommended its translation, but before he did so I had already concluded a treaty with Duncker of Berlin who will employ a very competent translator.[4] The book has met with far more success than I ventured to hope—900 copies have been sold in six weeks. But sale is only one kind of test. The approbation of men like yourself is far more valuable. Your good word will have great influence in Edinburgh.

If any suggestions occur to you which would enable me to improve a second edition they would be very gratefully accepted by

Yours very faithfully
G. H. Lewes.

I have been much interested in your pamphlet.[5] But will Auld Reekie be moved?

2. John Stuart Blackie (1809–95), Professor of Greek, Edinburgh, published *Faust... Translated into English Verse*, 1834.

3. *Life and Works of Goethe*, 1855, II, 34.

4. Julius Frese. See II, 307, n. 3.

5. *On the Advancement of Learning in Scotland*, Edinburgh, 1855.

II, 225:1 GHL TO JOHN WILLIAM PARKER, JR., RICHMOND, 12 JANUARY 1856

MS: Mrs. Donald F. Hyde.

8 Park Shot | Richmond | 12 January 1856.

My dear Parker

For some years I have been frequently urged to produce a library edition of the "Biographical History of Philosophy,"[6] and I am now seriously bent on doing so if I can come to an arrangement with your father and yourself. Indeed I am already in negotiation with Clowes about the copyright which I wish to purchase back again, if I can see my way clear.

I should make it essentially a *new* book, and render it more worthy of acceptance in colleges and schools not only by rewriting some sections but by supplying others omitted originally from want of space. Thus the Middle Ages and Modern Philosophy are at present dismissed in a few paragraphs. I propose to treat them as fully, in proportion, as the other sections.[7] Besides the absolutely new material, the whole wants revision, to render it what I should like it to be.

Nevertheless the main features concinnity and cheapness must still be the first aim, and I do not think of the work extending beyond one good 8vo at 10/6. The four volumes, with the new matter, can I think be got into one volume; and it is eminently desirable to keep the price down because the original was so cheap.[8]

The book still continues to sell, and would I believe have a steady sale if rendered more worthy of public acceptance. I never thought of its being adopted at Oxford and Cambridge when I first wrote it.

Will you at once consult your father on the subject because my negotiation with Clowes would be very much determined by your answer. Believe me, My dear Parker

Ever faithfully yours
G. H. Lewes.

J. W. Parker Esq. Junr.

6. GHL's *A Biographical History of Philosophy*, Series I, *Ancient Philosophy*, 2 vols., 1845, and *Series* II, *From Bacon to the Present Day*, 2 vols., 1846, were printed by William Clowes and Sons, Stamford Street, London, and published by Charles Knight and Co., Ludgate Street, who paid GHL £320 for the 4 vols. Another title page was given to the same sheets with G. Cox, 18 King Street, Covent Garden, as publisher, 4 vols. bound in 2, 1852.

7. In the Library edition, "Much enlarged and thoroughly revised," published by John W. Parker and Son, 1857, a section of 45 pages is added, discussing Abelard as an example of scholastic philosophy, Algazzali for a brief glance at the Arabians, and Giordano Bruno as a precursor of Bacon and Spinoza.

8. The first ed. sold for 1/6 per vol.; the 1857 ed. for 16/.

II, 225:1 GHL TO JOHN WILLIAM PARKER, RICHMOND, 17 JANUARY [1856]

MS: Dr. H. T. Radin.

8 Park Shot | Richmond | 17 January.

My dear Sir

In the volume, just out, of "Alison's History of Europe from the fall of Napoleon" there is a long survey of "German Literature during the first half of the 19 Century" which is quite a curiosity of literature, in unparalleled ignorance of the language and literature treated of, and not a little remarkable for its bad writing. It must be exposed. I am going to say a few words in the *Saturday Review*;[9] but the subject requires greater space to be properly treated, and if you think well of the proposition, I will review this chapter for Frazer:[10] under some such title as "The Blunders of Sir Archibald Alison."—

Ever faithfully yours
G. H. Lewes.

Mr. Cook[11] gave me good news of John.[12]

II, 226:25 GHL TO JOHN WILLIAM PARKER, RICHMOND, 19 JANUARY [1856]

MS: Historical Society of Pennsylvania.

8 Park Shot | Richmond | 19 January.

My dear Sir

On Wednesday at 3 I will do myself the pleasure of calling on you to speak about the Hist. of Philosophy.

To my amazement I learned from the publisher that 40,000 copies of the work have been sold from first to last. Only about 150 copies remain in Clowes' hands and a few more in the hands of secondhand booksellers, which were bought at the sale two years ago. Mr. Cox says that his 150 will be sold long before I can produce a new edition; the demand being constant.

---

9. "German Literature in Sir Archibald Alison's History of Europe, Volume 5," *Saturday Review*, 23 February 1856, p. 217.

10. No article on Alison by GHL appears in *Fraser's*.

11. John Douglas Cooke (1808–68) edited the *Saturday Review* from its founding in 1855. GHL began writing for it in February 1856.

12. John William Parker, Jr. (1820–61).

Surely 40,000 copies is quite an unprecedented sale? I did not think half that number had gone. It has given me the greatest confidence; because my new edition will be in all respects a new book—much enlarged in matter and much improved in manner.

Ever faithfully yours
G. H. Lewes.

J. W. Parker Esq

II, 231:6 GHL TO HERBERT SPENCER, RICHMOND, [9 MARCH 1856]

MS: University of London.

8 Park Shot | Richmond | Sunday.

My dear Spencer

And so you have become a hewer of wood and drawer of water?[1] Is that the exodus of philosophy? It explains what in English life has hitherto been an obscurity to me, viz. the venerable old men who occupy themselves breaking stones on the Queen's highway—they are all ex-thinkers, broken down by large discourse of reason, decrepit with scepticism, used up from cerebral excitement. I shall take off my hat to the next I see; and ask him whether he has made any annotations on the Biog. Hist. of Phil. which invaluable work he will of course know by heart.

But now about you. Do you get good wages? Is your *beer* included? Do you cut your fingers, and occasionally hack your toes?—not that cutting *hurts*—at least not me; for I am by no means contemplating letting myself out as an ablebodied labourer. My function in life is to be ornamental.

We were amused by your asking if I had anything to do with the Lion article[2] (which indeed I had—it was written in a hurry to stop a gap for J.C.) because you knew my "weakness" for dancing before lions. Marry

---

1. In the winter of 1856 Spencer retired in search of health to a farm house at Brimsfield, near Painswick, Gloucestershire. "By far the best exercise I have found yet is grubbing up tree-stumps and splitting them into pieces for burning," he wrote. (David Duncan, *The Life and Letters of Herbert Spencer*, [1908], p. 80.)

2. "Lions and Lion Hunting," *Westminster Review*, 65 (January 1856), 205–217. GHL wrote: "We were once embraced by an affectionate young lioness, who put her paws lovingly round our neck, and would have kissed our cheek, had not that symptom of a boldness more than maidenly been at once by us virtuously repressed." (p. 216.)

come up, weakness! You might have called it strength which your unfeline weakness couldn't sympathize with.—There's a young lioness in the Z. Gardens just now more *kissable* than the loveliest Circassian in the Sultan's harem. Perhaps you think *that* a weakness? Do *you* never dance before noodles, and shall not I dance before majestic lions?—

Do not fail to come here, when you lounge to London. We shall most likely have a bed for you, at any rate you can get one near, and then we will have such reminiscences!

As you must not reason, and *à fortiori* not excite yourself over the *Reasoner*, I content myself with enclosing you this cutting from that exhilirating publication. Marian pictures to herself you "entering the arena of public controversy" with Mr. T. Cooper,[3] and discussing the principles of Psychology in presence of the whole society of Secularists. It would be pleasant.

[NB. In case the sagacious Psychologist should not think of it—when you come here if Mr. Lewes should happen to be out, mind you ask for *Mrs*. Lewes!]

I have been cutting up Brodie's Psych. Inquiries in the *Saturday*, which gave me an opportunity of again bringing in your "Principles."[4] I hope the book sells. If it can get a decent *nucleus* of a public it is sure to make its way; all that surrounds the nucleus being as you know a *sell*.

My budget is at an end. Marian too heady to write begs her kindest remembrances.

Ever yours
G. H. Lewes.

---

3. Thomas Cooper (1805–92), Chartist, after many years of avowed freethought, startled his audience by announcing his return to orthodox Christianity. J. G. Holyoake in the *Reasoner*, 2 March 1856, though praising Cooper's courage, commended to his attention "the greatest book of the year on the side of free thought," Spencer's *Principles of Psychology*, and urged him to address himself to refuting Spencer, in whom he would find a foeman worthy of his steel. In a letter to the editor (9 March 1856, p. 75) Cooper wrote: " 'Mr Herbert Spencer,' you hint, 'is a foeman certainly worthy of *my* steel.' Be pleased, my friend, to leave me to my own sense of duty. I do not see that I am bound to fight either Mr. Spencer, whom I never saw—and who, most probably, would deem the challenge arrogant and absurd—or any of the numerous correspondents who have sent me their challenges."

4. In a slashing review of Benjamin Brodie's *Psychological Inquiries*, 3rd ed., 1856, *Saturday Review*, 1 (22 March 1856), pp. 422–423, GHL calls it "indeed, a poor book.... Such being our opinion, we should obviously be doing the book an injustice if we tested it by the standards of Mr. Alexander Bain's *Senses and the Intellect*, or Mr. Herbert Spencer's *Principles of Psychology*."

II, 235:1 GHL TO JOHN BLACKWOOD, RICHMOND, [31? MARCH 1856]

MS: National Library of Scotland.

8 Park Shot | Richmond | Monday.

My dear Sir

By this post I send you Part II of the Tale,[5] which contains *all* that there will be of political allusion in the story. I have got some way in Part III, but send you this second part that you may decide, and, if need be, begin printing. I am uncertain whether what remains will form as much as what is already in your hands, or more, but a hint from you as to whether you would like it lengthened or shortened will determine me to develope or merely sketch certain scenes. Believe me, my dear Sir,

Yours very truly
G. H. Lewes.

John Blackwood, Esq.

II, 236:9 GHL TO JOHN SIBREE, JR., RICHMOND, 2 APRIL [1856]

MS: Indiana University.

8 Park Shot | Richmond | April 2.

My dear Sir

Our friend Miss Evans has spoken of you in such terms that I should be very glad if our mutual interests could establish an arrangement. I have three boys, from the ages of thirteen downwards, whom I should like to place under your care. But I should warn you that my project is to take the two elder boys to Germany in about another year, if my means admit of it, so that it is very *possible* their stay with you would be shorter than would enable you to do full justice to yourself. If however you are not indisposed to take them with that contingency, and if the terms which would remunerate you are such as a literary man, who has to look closely to his expenditure, can afford to pay, it would be gratifying to me to know my boys were in such excellent hands.

---

5. "Metamorphoses: A Tale," appeared in *Blackwood's* in 3 parts, 79 (May–June 1856), 562–578, 676–691, and 80 (July 1856), 61–76. Laid in the 1790s, it is a story of Victor Marras, who becomes a Commisary with power over the aristocrats who once employed him. Robespierre, Desmoulins, and other Revolutionists figure in the plot.

[7 May 1856]

The two eldest are at present at the Bayswater Grammar School.[6] The youngest is at home[7] and is *very* backward, because for some years his health was delicate, and I did not like his being at school. The elder boys are clever, and eager to get on. They are already tolerably grounded in Latin, and French, and have commenced German.

An answer at your earliest convenience will oblige,

Yours very truly
G. H. Lewes.

John Sibree Esq.

II, 238:8   GHL TO JOHN BLACKWOOD, RICHMOND, [7 MAY 1856]

MS: National Library of Scotland.

8 Park Shot | Richmond | Wednesday.

My dear Sir

It is gratifying to find you like the story on rereading. It is but a slight affair, but from the variety of incident may perhaps be amusing. I have however determined on completing it in this third part (which I send by this post) because unless a story has a good backbone of interest and character, the shorter the better. Now the defect of my story, as it seems to me, is the defect of the original play from which I altered it, viz. that neither hero nor heroine have sufficiently marked *character*.[8]

I wanted to do something novel with Victor—something out of the ordinary hero type—a semi-humbug. But *nuances* are not fit for the stage; and require even in a novel more patient development than this character seemed to me to be worth.

I quite agree with you that Nicotte and Goulard are the most interesting and have thrown the burden on their backs.

Ever truly yours
G. H. Lewes.

6. Charles and Thornton Lewes were day pupils at Dr. Pearce's Bayswater Academy.

7. Herbert Lewes was enrolled later. All three boys lived with their mother at 26 Bedford Place, Kensington.

8. William Blackwood in forwarding this instalment from London wrote to John Blackwood, 7 May 1856: "The Metamorphoses (of which I send conclusion by this post, and some more pages of the Athelings) is clever, but it is for a story unsatisfactory rather in the conclusion. The shooting of the Count [80 (July 1856), p. 74] jars upon one's feelings and might be altered, I incline to think," (NLS.) "Metamorphoses: A Tale" was adapted from *A Strange History* by GHL and Charles Mathews, first played at the Lyceum 29 March 1853. The hero of the tale Victor Marras and his old love Adrienne de Chateauneuf are outshone by the wily milkmaid, Nicotte, and her rustic lover Goulard.

II, 252:9 GHL TO JOHN BLACKWOOD, ILFRACOMBE, [19 MAY 1856]

MS: National Library of Scotland.

Ilfracombe | Monday night.

My dear Sir

Only this afternoon, after post time, did my box arrive, thanks to the G. W. Railway which has taken exactly a week to send it!

Your letter, proofs, and the checque arrived in due course. I have found your criticism always so just that I am disposed to accept it even against my own judgement—for on reading the proof[9] this evening I do not feel that the story reads like a play—at least not so much as I thought it would. It is too curt and hurried; indeed I was afraid of getting lengthy and have fallen into the opposite extreme. This it is perhaps which causes your objection—and this *is* an objection. However, as I said before, the story is an unambitious one, and if it amuse the reader its object will be gained. Part I seemed to do this—at least those readers I heard of, and as no one knew the story to be mine, I had their unbiassed opinion.

I have tried to remedy the curtness as far as a few minor sentences would do so, and dispatched the 2nd Part to your brother. I quite agree with you about Lestang giving way too soon—but there again I dreaded prolonging the episode. I have not ventured on altering it.

As you have probably stopped the checque, according to my last note, (though I see it would not have been paid if stolen) I shall not present it till I hear from you.[1] By the way my initials are G. H. not H. J.

I don't know whether you are familiar with this lovely coast? It is an enchanting spot; with hills and valleys to employ painters for a life time, and rock pools to make every naturalist's heart thrill with expectation. I have already been very fortunate—alighting upon some rare species, and on animals I long wanted to put under the microscope. I haven't opened a book yet, and shall do my best to be as idle as possible.

You don't say when you will return to London for a prolonged stay—but I hope it will be in the Autumn, as I shall not leave the seaside till August or the end of July and then I take my two eldest boys to Switzerland,

---

9. Of Part II. John Blackwood wrote to William 3 May 1856: "When you send me proof of Metamorphoses mention Lewes's address." (NLS.)

1. GHL's Literary Receipts list £50 in July 1856 for the three parts. See VII, 374.

27 May 1856 155

so that before the first week in September I shall not be back—yet I should like to spend one evening with you.

Ever faithfully yours
G. H. Lewes.

II, 252:9 GHL TO JOHN WILLIAM PARKER, ILFRACOMBE, 22 MAY [1856]

MS: McGill University, Montreal.

Runnymede Villa | Ilfracombe | 22 May.

Dear Sir

Has not the proposition about the History of Philosophy entirely slipped your memory? You were to let me know before I left town; and Clowes will marvel why he does not hear from me. Pray send me just one word, yes, or no.

I suppose John has returned by this time. If so remember me most kindly to him and believe me, Dear Sir

Yours faithfully
G. H. Lewes.

J. W. Parker Esq.

II, 252:9 GE TO ISAAC PEARSON EVANS, ILFRACOMBE, 27 MAY 1856

MS: British Museum.

Ilfracombe | May 27.56.

My dear Brother

When you send me the cheque for my half year's interest, will you be so good as to deduct £5, and give it to Chrissey towards helping to pay Emily's school bill, as that will save the risk of sending a £5 note by post. It would be very good news to hear that an opportunity had occurred of placing out my money more advantageously.

I am rejoiced to learn from Chrissey that you are once more quite strong again. You must enjoy health doubly after suffering so long from the effects of your sad illness.

I hope this wet May is good for the grass crops, for it is anything but exhilarating to us human plants. [*5 lines cut away*] When you send me the cheque, please to address it to Mr. Chap[ma]n's [8 K]ing William St., Strand where you may always address to me, as a letter is then sure to [*Signature cut away.*]

II, 252:9 HENRY GEORGE BOHN TO GHL, LONDON, 3 JUNE 1856

MS: Yale. *Extract published:* Haight, *George Eliot*, pp. 199–200.

4, 5, & 6, York Street, Covent Garden.
June 3rd 1856.

Dear Sir

I shall be obliged by your sending me a copy of the agreement between us for Spinoza[2] as I do not at present find any signed or unsigned. It is so long ago since we entertained the subject, that I have lost sight of it, indeed given it up till I lately saw your M.S. and reminder. It is only now that I can conveniently send it to press, but before I do so shall be glad to see that we are agreed as to terms.

I presume you mean the printer to modernize the English of the printed volume, as it will want alteration.

If you purpose leaving England in July it will have to tarry till you return.

Yours my Dear Sir | Very faithfully
Henry G. Bohn.

G. H. Lewis Esq.

II, 254:1 HENRY GEORGE BOHN TO GHL, LONDON, 7 JUNE 1856

MS: Yale. *Extract published:* Haight, *George Eliot*, p. 200.

4, 5, & 6, York Street, Covent Garden.
London, June 7th 1856.

Dear Sir,

I think there must be some mistake in your recollection of what was intended between us in the matter of Spinoza. The sum in my mind has

---

2. Before leaving London 8 May 1856 GHL delivered GE's translation of the *Ethics* and the copy Bohn had lent him of the *Tractatus Theologico-Politicus. A Treatise Partly Theological, and Partly Political*, 1689, an anonymous transla-

always been fifty pounds, the same as ⟨Le⟩ Comte,³ but it is so long since the subject was entertained that I had virtually given it up, and the particulars have passed out of my mind. Indeed I had no notice from you that you meant to proceed with it till I saw the materials of the volume on my table. What might be a reasonable speculation two or three years ago may be a very doubtful one now, but supposing the editorship not to be more than 50/-/- and the book to be what was then intended, I do not wish to waive the undertaking on account of delay. If half the volume is to be a mere reprint of the old translation, which I never contemplated, I can see no reason why the cost of editing should be more than ⟨Le⟩ Comte.

I am aware that no signed agreement passed between us, but I always meant there should be one, and believe you have a memorandum in my son's handwriting which I should be glad to see as soon as you can conveniently bring it here.

Yours, Dear sir, faithfully,
Henry G. Bohn.

G. H. Lewis Esq.

II, 254:21 GHL TO HENRY GEORGE BOHN, ILFRACOMBE, 8 JUNE 1856

MS: Yale.

(Copy) Runnymede Villa | Ilfracombe.
June 8th 1856.

Dear Sir

Your letter has greatly surprised me. I send you a literal copy of the memorandum drawn up by your son, and you "think there must be some mistake in my recollection of what was intended between us." Surely you cannot have read my letter with ⟨very⟩ attention?

Then again as to the delay. I spoke frequently to your son about the work being in progress and occasionally even to yourself, long before the m.s. was in your hands.

The reprint of the old translation *was* agreed on by us, and *you* gave me the volume for that purpose. The only difference being that if my Introduction and extracts from the other works occupied too great a space,

tion, with passages marked for inclusion in the volume for Bohn's Philosophical Library.

3. Bohn paid GHL £50 for his *Comte's Philosophy of the Sciences* in the Scientific Library, 1853.

it was not to be printed entire, but some portions of it abridged. As however I deemed it necessary that the work should, if possible, be entire, I have so contrived it.

You forget that the 75£ covers not only cost of editing but the translation of the Ethics, which is entirely new and has never been translated before.

⟨I confess not to understand one passage in your letter where you allude to there being no "signed agreement," as I cannot suppose an honorable man thinks a memorandum less binding than a regular bond.⟩ You may remember that when Spinoza was first entertained and Mr. Kelly was to translate ⟨it, I⟩ the works I asked 50£ for the editing alone; and declined to accept less. Subsequently we talked the matter over, and arranged to get the whole of what was necessary in one volume for 75£; and this is what your son records in his memorandum.

II, 255:21 HENRY GEORGE BOHN TO GHL, LONDON, 13 JUNE 1856

MS: Yale. *Extract published*: Haight, *George Eliot*, p. 200.

4, 5, & 6, York Street, Covent Garden.
London June 13th 1856.

Dear Sir,

With regard to my delay in going to press with your Spinoza, you would under any circumstances have little cause of complaint. After taking more than two years to produce what I had reason to expect in a few months, you bring it me at a time when there is no encouragement to publish it. The book was originally a proposition of your own, to be carried out in conjunction with Mr. Kelly; and as our agreement was never completed, and you had given me no indication of your intention to proceed, I concluded you had abandoned it for the more lucrative pursuit of 'Goethe.' Your letter of a recent date announced your completion of the work, but added that as my hands were probably full, you would like to keep it by you till I was ready. You say you spoke frequently to my son about the work, which he does not recollect; and you certainly did not speak to me about it, unless very lately, which does not alter the case.

I never for a moment dreamt of your reprinting the old translation and therefore could not have agreed to it. I gave you that volume as I should have given you any other on the subject, which I might happen to have in stock to aid your labors, but not to become a substitute for them; and when I see that you have not made a single correction in an antiquated text I have reason to be apprehensive. The notion of abridging it may have been in your own mind, but certainly never entered mine, for I detest abridgments. You say I forget that the 75£ covers not only the cost of editing, but also the translation of the Ethics. I remember that our intention was to have translations both of the Ethics and the Tractatus made by Mr. Kelly and accompanied by an Introduction and notes by yourself; and my impression is that you were to receive 25£ for editing and he the remainder of 50£ for translating. My rule of paying 3/-/- or 3/3/- per sheet of 32 pages for translating and editing is so uniform that it must be something more than ordinarily inviting which would tempt me to swerve from it. But you have my son's memorandum of an intended agreement and I will abide it, although unsigned, as far as it commits me to what you state. You will remember that I have nothing which could bind you to the performance of your part of the contract, which I should have required had it been completed in the usual form. Please to bring the paper with you and we will then enter into a proper agreement, for I should not consent to publish without one. I remain,

Dear Sir, Yours faithfully
Henry G. Bohn.

G. H. Lewis, Esq.

II, 255:21 GHL TO HENRY GEORGE BOHN, ILFRACOMBE, 15 JUNE 1856

MS: Yale. *Extract published:* Haight, *George Eliot,* p. 200.

(Copy)   Runnymede Villa | Ilfracombe.
15 June 1856.

Sir

From the tenor of your insulting letter of the 13th June I presume you are so accustomed to have your own word disbelieved that you have grown reckless in expressing your disbelief of the word of others. As I am not accustomed to have mine doubted, and moreover as I altogether decline to have transactions with a man who shows such wonderful facility in forgetting and such persistency in denying his own written agreement as you show in your letters, I beg you will send back my m.s. and consider the whole business at an end between us. If the m.s. be sent to me at the | Office of the Leader | 352 Strand | I will—on hearing of its safe arrival—send you back the written agreement, and so terminate all matters between us.[4]

Your obedient servant
G. H. L.

II, 255:21 HENRY GEORGE BOHN TO GHL, LONDON, 18 JUNE 1856

MS: Yale.

4, 5, & 6, York Street, Covent Garden.
June 18th 1856.

Sir

My letter was not insulting, or intended to be so, nor am I accustomed to have my word disbelieved by honest men, having never intentionally uttered anything which I could not verify, although knaves would willingly have it otherwise. When you can prove anything to the contrary I will present you with all I have.

If after a delay of two years in producing your volume I have forgotten the particulars of a memorandum drawn up by my son, and of which I have no copy, there is not much to be wondered at, and you have no right to take offence at my wishing to see it. I never proposed to deny an agreement between us, but meant to see it, telling you at the same time that I should conform to it although not signed.

There could be no use whatever in written agreements if they are not to be consulted in case of doubt. As a literary man I should have been glad for the honor of the fraternity that your letter had been couched in more gentlemanly phrase. The manuscript has been sent as you directed, to 352 Strand.

Yours respectfully,
Henry G. Bohn.

G. H. Lewis, Esq.

4. If GHL's letter followed his draft, it is possible that he wanted to break off the Bohn agreement in hope of finding a more profitable one with another publisher. In 1859 he offered the *Ethics* to A. & C. Black, who refused to pay £75 for it. They in turn asked him to write an article on Spinoza for the *Encyclopaedia Britannica*, which he declined to do.

II, 255:21 GHL TO EDWARD F. S. PIGOTT, ILFRACOMBE, [24 JUNE 1856]

MS: Mr. Gordon N. Ray.

Runnymede Villa | Ilfracombe | Thursday.

Dear Pigott

Your charming letter deserves a long one but I have nothing to fill it with except zoology; which will keep! You seem to have enjoyed your trip very much!

I write at once because I don't want to miss you and it is probable I shall unless this makes a change in your plans. We leave this on the 26 for Tenby. Can't you run over there from Falmouth? You can find out our address at the Post Office or the principal Inn at the *bar* of which I will leave it.

Can't say much for my health but hope Tenby and idleness will do some good. I do hope and pray you can run in upon us at Tenby. Meanwhile, Believe me

Ever faithfully
G. H. L.

II, 26:7 GHL TO RICHARD MONCKTON MILNES, RICHMOND, [AUGUST? 1856]

MS: Trinity College, Cambridge.

8 Park Shot, | Richmond | Wednesday.

Dear Milnes

By the parcel Del[iver]y Com[pan]y I return Bormolaski,[5] for the loan of which many thanks. I have copied the letter, which will go among the various documents I have collected on the subject.

In three distinct rummages among my books I have failed to alight on that rare volume of which I spoke to you (Rymer on Tragedy)[6] but it will turn up some day, and when it does I will send it.

---

5. Unidentified. In a note at the end of Part II of "Metamorphoses" GHL, referring to a letter of Marie Antoinette to the Emperor of Austria, says: "This intercepted letter is still extant, and in the possession of Mr Monckton Milnes, M. P., who has a rare collection of Revolutionary documents." (*Blackwood's*, 79 (June 1856), 691.)

6. Thomas Rymer, *A Short View of Tragedy*, 1693 (for 1692). GHL's copy is in Dr. Williams's Library.

162 [*August? 1856*]

Louis Blanc writes to say that *la femme égalité* was the duchess of Orleans, Philippe's wife. Ever, my dear Milnes,

Yours faithfully,
G. H. Lewes.

I felt very much tempted to mention in the Leader that you had a translation of Heine's poems in hand, but refrained lest after all you should *not* publish them, which would be a pity, nay worse than a pity, a *shame*—they are so marvellously good.

II, 263:20 GHL TO GEORGE COMBE, RICHMOND, 17 SEPTEMBER [1856]

MS: National Library of Scotland.

8 Park Shot | Richmond | 17 September.

Dear Sir

Your approbation of my article on Dwarfs and Giants is very flattering.[7] I do not think of reprinting the papers, which are rather suggestions on the subject than final conclusions.

With respect to the method of comparative physiology to which you allude I am profoundly convinced that Gall was on the right track and that he laid the basis of a positive psychology, but my own opportunities have been too limited for me to arrive at much in this direction; and indeed I think our knowledge of the nervous system generally is still too incomplete for more than approximative conclusions. Believe me dear Sir

Yours very truly
G. H. Lewes.

George Combe, Esq.

II, 263:20 GHL TO RICHARD MONCKTON MILNES, RICHMOND, 18 SEPTEMBER [1856]

MS: Trinity College, Cambridge.

8 Park Shot | Richmond | September 18th.

My dear Sir

If the pamphlet can be laid hold of again it shall be posted to you; but I have my doubts.

7. See II, 264, n. 3. Combe's letter is addressed "G.H.L., Esq." care of the Editor of *Fraser*'s. (Yale.)

15 January 1857 163

The writer is a Mr. H. W. Smith.[8] The lady you mention must be Miss Bacon,[9] who not long ago published an insane tirade in Putnam's Monthly Magazine, which I noticed in the Leader[10] at the time. She had nothing to do with this pamphlet I should imagine.

The German "Shakspere ein Mythus" is unknown to me and with my consent shall remain so. There are few things revolutionize my liver more than German writing about Shakspeare.

I hope you got a letter from me written from Tenby in answer to an invite to breakfast, which reached me long after the said breakfast had been digested?

Ever faithfully yours,
G. H. Lewes.

R. M. Milnes Esq.

II, 289:1 JOHN CHAPMAN TO GE, LONDON, 15 JANUARY 1857

MS: Yale.

8 King Wm. St. *W.C.* | January 15. 1857.

Dear Friend,

Of course it is impossible to adopt any scale of remuneration whereby I could graduate the payments to contributors to the W. R. so that each writer may be rewarded according to his (*or her*) merit. Still there are cases where a departure from the rule usually acted on would be so obviously just that I can have no hesitation as to the propriety of treating them as exceptional. Your articles are so uniformly excellent that I desire to express my appreciation of their merit by paying for what you may hereafter contribute at the rate of £12.12.0 per sheet.

While paying you for the article on Young, as per agreement—both as to terms and length, I felt that you were inadequately remunerated; but knowing that the number, being a sheet and a half too long, would be a costly one I acted according to *rule*; now however that I have read your article again with greatly increased delight I shall not feel satisfied

---

8. i.e. William Henry Smith, *Bacon and Shakespeare. An Inquiry Touching Players, Play-houses, and Play-writers in the Days of Elizabeth*, 1857.

9. Delia Salter Bacon (1811–59), founded the Baconian theory with her article "William Shakespeare and His Plays; An Inquiry Concerning Them" in *Putnam's Monthly Magazine*, 7 (January 1856), 1–19.

10. *Leader*, 2 February 1856, p. 112. GHL also noticed her pamphlet *Was Lord Bacon the Author of Shakespeare's Plays?*, 13 September 1856, p. 880.

without sending you the enclosed[1] which therefore when added to the £20 already sent on account of the article will not represent its value but which you will perhaps regard as an assurance of my high estimation of it, and of my hope that you will let the "Westminster" be the medium of publication of whatever Quarterly Review articles you may be able to write.

Yours faithfully
John Chapman.

II, 303:19   GHL TO ADOLF STAHR, RICHMOND, [FEBRUARY 1857]

Text: Quoted by Stahr in a letter to Alwin Stahr, 26 February 1857, *Aus Adolf Stahrs Nachlass, Briefe von Stahr* . . . , ed. Ludwig Geiger, Oldenburg, 1903, p. 190.

We read with delight your second volume of Torso and I have made Monti,[2] the great sculptor, happy by directing his attention to the book. He is writing a history of Sculpture and says that, except Lessing, you are the one German writer on Art he can thoroughly admire.

II, 304:7   CHARLES LEWES TO AGNES LEWES, HOFWYL, 1 MARCH 1857

MS: Yale.

Hofwyl. | March 1st 1857.

Dear Mamma,

It is now nearly two months that I have been writing to you for I began the first rough copy on the 12th January and had filled 5 pages with it; but when copying it out for the second time I found there was a great deal that I ought to scratch out. By the middle of February I had done three pages of the new copy, but as I had written at so many different times it was composed of scarcely any thing more than a quantity of contradictory statements, so I have begun, to day being Sunday, to copy a new letter which is to be completed to day in the time we have either for working or for letterwriting just as we choose.

We had a very happy Newyear here, but as Mrs. Müller was not here

---

1. GE's Journal shows £5 additional for the article on Young. See VII, 359.
2. Rafaelle Monti (1818–81) made the replica of the Parthenon for the Crystal Palace in 1854. GHL had met him in Vienna in 1839. There is no record of his history of sculpture.

1 March 1857

on Christmas day we did not have much fun. However we had plenty of amusement among ourselves, sledging, sliding, skating, and snowballing. It was not considered a very cold winter here, for it was not colder than it has been these 2 or 3 winters in England. Have you had many colds and chilblains at home? How is Mr. Bertie Lewes getting on at school. If he would learn a little to read, write, and cipher I think he might come over here to school, for I don't think he would get ill from the feeding here, as he would not be obliged to take things when he does not want them; and I think he would get on [better] here than at Dr. Pearce's for he would learn the languages here, and would be able to indulge in his favourite sports, such as gardening, fishing, soldiers etc. etc.

For I must tell you that during this week we have been playing at soldiers every day. Mr. May gave us permission to go up into the old soldiers' room (I mean the room where the boys in Dr. de Fellenberg's[3] time kept their soldiers dresses) and have taken possession of everything that was in it. There 5 or 6 drums, one real musket, about a dozen swords, two bayonets, a cannon, and 2 trumpets, and a standard. We soon formed an army with these things, as we found also 3 wooden guns up in the theatre room, which when they had bayonets put on look very well. Each boy is also supplied with a cartouche box, which I forgot to mention above. Yesterday we had a grand march and fired the cannon off a quantity of times. The army was placed so; 1st at the head of all walked the drum major with his baton of office (for there is one) José Guimaraes, then the drummer, Wilhelm Rösslisberger (for there was only one yesterday) then a line of swordsmen Walter Young, Hans v. Waltenwyl, Antonio Vismara, Frank Beaumont; then the standard bearer, Gustav Gerster; then a line of musketeers, Hans Muralt, Edward Fisher, Eugenio Strazza, Your humble Servant; then came the cannon drawn by Adolphe de la Marre, and Emilio Strazza, after the cannon walked the three canonniers, Battista, Laurenzo Amaglio, Alberto Ubrich, who were distinguished from the others by white gaiters (Each of them also carried a sword, and cartouche box). I forgot to mention that Albert Herrinshwand was the general and walked at the side of the soldiers, he had a sword and cartouche box. Mr. Pache the French master was the director over all.

Why was it that *Ann*[4] went away? How are Aunt Susannah,[5] and Grandmamma,[6] and Nursie,[7] and Emily?[8] When is Emily going to be

3. See II, 236, n. 8.
4. The Census return for 1851 lists at 26 Bedford Place Annie Bauce, general servant, aged 24, born at Reading.
5. Widow of GHL's brother Edward Lewes.
6. Mrs. John Willim.
7. Martha Baker, later Mrs. Bell,

married? How is Papa's head? How are you yourself? And the children?⁹ Give my love and kisses to them all and tell Papa to kiss you for me. I wish you would tell me the trick of the magic wand so that I could do it with Thornie or Mrs. Müller, for we play all sorts of games with Mrs. Müller of an evening. I believe there are a good many new boys coming at Easter. We shall have an examination also. I wish some of the boys that are at Dr. Pearce's were coming here. If you know of anybody who wants to send his son or sons abroad, I hope you will remember Hofwyl. In de Fellenberg's time there were always from 15 to 18 English boys, and we are at present 6 though only Thornie and I come direct from England. I wish you would send some little plays that we would be able to get up here when the box is sent. By the bye when will it be sent? Have you any idea what month? I can't think of anything else to say so good bye. And I remain Dear Mamma Your affectionate Son

Charles Lewes.

II, 304:7 THORNTON ARNOTT LEWES TO GHL, HOFWYL, 1 MARCH 1857

MS: Yale.

Hofwyl. March 1. 1857.

Dear Papa,

I hope you are quite well. I should have written to you before, but Charlie told me, not to write as he was writing home, though to Mamma.¹ You will be quite surprised to hear that instead of becoming a filial Taddy, I am a frog! Nothing less; I and that very, little, baby who cried when he got into the bath, when you were here, are their two kings.² I have written as you may have heard a play called "Cathelniean" and I have written a copy of it for you.

Dear Daddy, will you please put in the box above all things, for me, books of Natural History, in particular, if they do not cost too much a history of birds, butterflies and plants. I love natural History above all things, and when I grow up, it is my desire to become a naturalist; and you

listed in the Census return for 1851 as "nurse," aged 36, unmarried, born at Brighton.

8. Possibly Emily Gabrielle Jervis (1826–96), half-sister of Agnes Jervis Lewes. According to Burke, *Landed Gentry*, 1939, she became a nun.

9. Edmund, Rose, and Ethel Lewes, Agnes's children by Thornton Hunt.

1. Agnes Jervis Lewes.

2. Many of Thornton's letters are signed "Rex Ranarum," probably a title adopted from Aesop's *Fables*.

may imagine, there is ample scope afforded here, as I can go all about, by telling one of the masters. Another of the boys from Geneva named Beaumont, has also the same taste, so when we can we go out together. I hope your head is quite well, at any rate, much better. Your Christmas, I suppose, was passed very soon at Mr. Helps', and I hope you enjoyed yourself very much. At Christmas, there were 3 Christmas trees beautifully lighted up, but as the presents for the boys were too heavy to be hung up, they were laid upon the tables. Mrs. Müller gave each of us a sort of Gingerbread with the Berne bear on it in sugar; they are so delicious that you ought to be here at Christmas to eat some. One of the lady bears at Berne has kittened! That is to say got a little cub, but she will not let them be seen yet. We have for a long time since played games in the evening and yesterday evening, Charlie was the King and Mrs. Müller the queen of Portugal, when nearly all the boys were tricked. Perhaps you know, that in De Fellenberg's time the boys were soldiers; now we have got the key of the room where they kept most of the arms etc. but as every boy, nearly, took home his weapons and things, only a few were left; these were, a real gun but with the lock broken, a splendid standard, eight or ten swords, a cannon, cartouche boxes, drums, horns for the officers etc. Yesterday afternoon we had a grand parade, the cannon was loaded and fired nearly twelve times, if not more even; I am the guard of the cannon, being the only cross bowman. Altogether, with the drums beating, for three of us can play the drum, it was a very pretty sight. When there are more boys, so as to render it worth having, Dr. Müller is going to have us also soldiers, most likely. Our captain, was one of the biggest boys named Albert, a Swiss. Give my love to all at home, with many kisses. Tell Ethel when you see her, that I have got a nice picture of three cats for her. There is the old mother who has caught a rat and she has got her kittens by her, and she is going to give them some rat for dinner.

There is at Hofwyl an Italian boy, named Marzorati who knows General Allemandi, as well as Signor Monti; the general is not in town, so, of course we have not been invited though I sent the letter a long while ago. Your letter gave me much pleasure, and I know I am a very naughty boy not to have written before. I don't think I should have written yet, if Dr. Müller had not told us that you scolded us for not writing, but you must not scold me. I do not think I have any thing more to say. So with love to all at home I remain Dear Papa

Tuum Filium carissimo
Ranae Rex.

I have begun Latin again.
P. S. Charlie sends his love.

II, 313:22 GHL TO JOHN BLACKWOOD, ST. MARY'S, [27 MARCH 1857]

MS: National Library of Scotland.

St. Mary's | Scilly Isles | Friday.

My dear Blackwood

The pursuit of zoology under difficulties in March gales has brought me here at last. Weatherbound at Penzance I have been eyeing the sea and sky with wistful glances; and for four days remained with corded boxes and without change of linen, to be tumbled about on the Atlantic at last in rare style. The place however is enchanting; quite surpassing all my expectations; and it promises good material, both Maga-wise and animal-wise. The weather is perfect, or would be if a little warmer.

I'm hurrying with letters to catch the post which only goes out twice a week so having given notice of my whereabouts to the best of editors I break off with

Ever truly yours
G. H. Lewes.

II, 315:1 GHL TO JOHN BLACKWOOD, ST. MARY'S, 12 APRIL 1857

MS: National Library of Scotland.

St. Mary's | Scilly Isles | 12 April 1857.

My dear Blackwood

By this post I despatch the article[3] which I hope you will like. I have such a glorious vivarium here that if I don't get at some good results it will be my fault. The place is charming, and the animals abundant. If one could be bovoid Gunter[4] or Soyer would do. Toujours de la perdrix[5] was found tiresome; toujours du bœuf is apt to pall.

I fear I must give up all hope of seeing a proof, the postal arrangements not allowing time. But you can get your zoological compositor to look at the names; and for the rest the printing is usually so accurate in Maga that my mind is at ease.

Ever faithfully yours
G. H. Lewes.

3. "New Sea-side Studies: The Scilly Isles," *Blackwood's*, 81 (June 1857), 669–685.

4. A famous confectioner at 7 Berke-

II, 325:1 GE TO MRS. HENRY HOUGHTON, ST. MARY'S, 3 MAY 1857

Text: Typed copy made for Miss Elsie Druce, Yale.

St. Mary's, Scilly Isles | May 3rd 1857.

Dear Fanny,

Thank you very fervently for sending me Sarah's letters about Chrissy,[6] which both reached me together, last night. I have suffered a great deal from the long intervals that have elapsed between the letters I have received. Until yours came I had not heard since the 22nd when I received a letter from Isaac written on the 19th saying that Chrissy was worse and in great danger! But I can well understand that both he and Sarah have their hands and minds too full to retain a very vivid recollection of those at a distance. Poor Sarah has had a terrible trial.

You too, dear Fanny have had your special trouble; now, I trust being rapidly alleviated. I am grieved both for Henry's sake and yours that his general health is so delicate.

Thank you for your kind question about my health. I can say nothing good of myself in that respect. For several months I have been very ailing and have found my necessary work difficult. But I hope to get strong again with care and not become a troublesome invalid. My writing prospers, which is a great happiness to me, and opens a brighter prospect than I have ever had in my life before, but everything depends on my health.

I do not understand your allusion to Isaac's having said that he had received no answer from me. I have always answered punctually every letter that required answering. But the postal communication hither and back again is terribly slow—only twice a week.

You have not sent me your address, so that I am reduced to the magnificent vagueness of 'Leamington' as a direction. I hope you are the only Mrs. Henry Houghton there.

Once more, dear Fanny thank you for writing to me and taking some of the load off my heart. It has been a heavy load indeed, but I do not like to write useless words about such things.

With kindest remembrances to Henry, I am always, dear Fanny,

Your affectionate sister
Marian.

ley Square. For GE's comment on "the monotony of beef" at St. Mary's see II, 355.

5. Cf. GHL's *Ranthorpe*, 1847, p. 51.

6. Letters from Mrs. Isaac Evans about the illness of GE's sister Mrs. Clarke. See II, 314.

II, 328:3   THORNTON ARNOTT LEWES TO GHL, HOFWYL, 21 MAY 1857

MS: Yale.

Hofwyl, May 21, 1856[7].

Dear Papa,

I am much obliged to you for the letter you sent me which gave me much pleasure. I have told Mrs. Müller about the magic wand, but I think it will be better to leave it, till you come, as then you can do it with her or one of us. Today we are going to bathe, in the big lake, that is to say those who can swim, though perhaps we shall all go.

Wish Mamma many happy returns[8] for me, and let her provide herself with a present out of it.

I have commenced a collection of flowers, which are pressed and dried. I hope you will come with us on the voyage, though I suppose you do not know yet. You are very popular among the boys, and I heard the *little baby*! say you were "si gentil et drôle." We are getting on very well, as always. I hope your head is well. Give my love to the chicks and kiss them for me, and tell them that we have been to Berne to a place where all the animals and Birds of the Alps are exhibited. There are also two Lämmergeier,[9] of whom no doubt you have often heard, which are alive and the female is sitting on the eggs. There are also a good many animals representing scenes from "Reineke Fuchs," such as his hanging, his killing the hare etc. Also three skating hedgehogs, one of whom has tumbled down. I long for winter to come back and yet I like summer, though I'm sure I don't know which I really like best. Give my love to Nursie when you see her and ask her why she doesn't write to either of us, as we have not had any letters for some time. General Allemandi has never written anything to us, so I suppose he has either forgotten us, or not cared for our company.

José is gone to Brazil, at least I don't know if he has started, but he's been living with an uncle in Paris, and he will not come back any more. There will be a small party of relations all English, the cousin of Guppy and the mother of the two Youngs as well as you are coming. Most likely we are going to Italy to Milan, but that is not sure.

---

7. Thornton did not come to Hofwyl till August 1856.
8. Agnes Jervis Lewes (24 May 1822– 22 December 1902).
9. Vultures.

I have nothing particular to say so with Love to all and plenty of Kisses I remain Dear Pater meus
        Filius affectionatus
         Thorntonius Arnottus Ludovicus
          Ranarum Rex.
Giving under my hand this day.
               May 21. 57

II, 334:1   GE TO JOHN CHAPMAN, GOREY, 27 MAY 1857

MS: Yale. *Extracts published:* Haight, *George Eliot*, pp. 229–230; the printer has dropped the last line on p. 229.

       Rosa Cottage | Gorey, Jersey | May 27. 1857
My dear M.D.[1]
 I do sincerely share in the joy you must be feeling. The sweetest of all success is that which one wins by hard exertion, and I am sure all who know you must admire the persevering energy with which you have worked your way through all difficulties to this new starting point in your life.
 I dare say I am the slowest of all your friends in expressing my sympathy, but I have been waiting because I wanted to tell you at the same time that I had taken a step which I have long been meditating—that of telling my brother and sister that I am married. I wrote for that purpose on Monday, so now I shall not need to trouble you further with the transmission of letters, and you must henceforth remember that I am Mrs. Lewes to all my relatives.
 George tells me to say that he shall send you the article on Suicide[2] in a few days. He too claps his hands and says, "Well done!" to you.
 Such grassy vallies in this delicious island, with sleek cows turning mild faces on us as we pass them! Such shadowy lanes and glimpses of the sea at unexpected openings! Everything that you must long for as you walk hot and dusty and deafened along the Strand. But no—I dare say you are too full of review articles and pathological wisdom to have space for dreamy longings.
 We thought the last number of the Review solid and interesting.

---

1. Chapman took his M.D. degree at St. Andrews 8 May 1857. See *George Eliot and John Chapman*, pp. 93–95, 98.

2. "Suicide in Life and Literature," *Westminster Review*, 68 (July 1857), 52–78.

Wilson's article³ and Herbert Spencer's⁴ seemed to me the most valuable. Literature and Society⁵ is the only one ⟨I read which⟩ I thought poor and unsatisfactory.

All happiness attend you as editor and physician! That is the warm wish of

Your sincere friend
Marian E.

II, 354:14 GHL TO JOHN BLACKWOOD, GOREY, [20 JUNE 1857]

MS: National Library of Scotland.

Jersey, Saturday.

My dear Blackwood

If it is not too late I wish you would insert the following sentence in my paper. At that passage where I am speaking of the paradoxes presented by fishes, find some available place to wedge in this: —

"And although in general Fish are neither vocal nor eloquent, there are many of them capable of uttering sounds: there are Fish that snarl, Fish that grunt, like a pig, and Fish that send forth the cuckoo's note. Aristotle knew this, and Johannes von Müller has recently explained the mechanism whereby it is accomplished." (Müller's *Archiv für Anat.* 1857 p. 269.)

I think the passage will best come in just before the close where I speak of Fishes, bisexual and metamorphic.⁶

Ever faithfully yours
G. H. Lewes.

3. GE was mistaken in attributing "Present State of Theology in Germany," *Westminster Review*, 67 (April 1857), 327–363, to Henry Bristow Wilson. It was by Mark Pattison, and is reprinted in his *Essays*, ed. Henry Nettleship, 2 vols., Oxford, 1889, II, 210–262. In the "Theology and Philosophy" section of the Contemporary Literature article, pp. 558–564 are attributed to Pattison in *The Life and Letters of the Right Honourable Friedrich Max Müller*, ed. by his wife, 2 vols., 1902, I, 195.

4. "Progress: its Law and Cause," pp. 445–485.

5. A rambling article by James Hannay pp. 504–525, purporting to review the *Memoirs of Thomas Moore*.

6. This correction arrived too late for insertion in *Blackwood's*, 82 (July 1857), 1–17, where it would have come on p. 8. GHL inserted a modification of it in *Sea-side Studies,*, 1858, p. 239.

[27 July 1857]

II, 361:21 GHL TO DAVID NUTT, GOREY, 7 JULY 1857

MS: Yale. *Endorsed:* G. H. Lewis | Jersey | July 7.

Rosa Cottage | Jersey | 7th July 1857.

My dear Nutt

Herewith I authorize you to indorse or accept the Brockhaus Bill for me.[7] Please pay the money into my account with the *Union Bank of London*, Charing Cross Branch, 4 Pall Mall East.

I should be very sorry if the German sale could in any way interfere with ours[8] but it is not likely that many Germans would give 30/–. Especially when there was a translation; and as to our market, the German edition may not come in here.

Kind regards to Mrs. Nutt, and tell her there has been no rock hunting this hot weather. I shall be home again on the 24th Inst. In haste

Ever yours
G. H. Lewes.

II, 370:13 GHL TO JOHN BLACKWOOD, RICHMOND, [27 JULY 1857]

MS: National Library of Scotland.

8 Park Shot | Monday.

My dear Blackwood

Yesterday I dined with Prof. Owen[9] and in the evening we had out the Microscope and I laid before him several of my preparations of the nervous system of the Molluscs, with which he seemed greatly interested, and said he should like to take some notice of my discovery, if possible, in the article *Mollusca* he is writing for the Ency. Britannica.[1] I have not a copy of Maga, having cut it up for the revision, but perhaps you would send him a copy of the last number. It will give the book a lift should he mention it.

---

7. Heinrich Brockhaus (1804–74) of Leipzig paid GHL £50 for reprinting his *Goethe* in the Continental series.

8. Nutt had paid GHL £350 for the 1st edition of the book.

9. Richard Owen, Hunterian Professor of the Royal College of Surgeons, lived at Sheen Lodge, Richmond Park, where GHL dined with him 26 July 1857. (GHL Journal.) *Sea-side Studies* was dedicated "To Our Great Anatomist Richard Owen."

1. I find no reference to GHL in Owen's "Mollusca," *Encyclopaedia Britannica*, 8th ed., 1853–60, xv, 319–403.

I observe you advertize a new work by little Smith.[2] I have often been going to ask about him, not having seen him for more than a twelvemonth. I suppose he is roaming about, at Brussels or the Lakes. Has he been writing for you lately? I have not recognized him.

Ever faithfully yours
G. H. Lewes.

II, 382:1 CHARLES LEWES TO AGNES LEWES, HOFWYL, 13 SEPTEMBER 1857

MS: Yale.

Hofwyl, September 13th/57.

Dear Mamma,

Thank you very much for your presents of seeds and books. Your portraits are safely locked up in my cupboard, where the other boys cannot get hold of them. I did not recognise Rosie or Edmund in the least, you I did but the portrait does not do you justice. I think Nursie's portrait is the most like. Thank her very much for the Knife she sent me, and tell her I will write to her next Sunday if possible; for I have now more work than ever as my music lessons, and practising hours are in play-hours joined to this English 2 a week and you will find that a good many free hours are taken away. But on Sunday we have 2 hours on purpose for writing letters or learning our lessons for Monday, which I have to do frequently on Sunday because we are given by all the masters more work to do than any other day in the week. Last Sunday I wrote to Mrs. Owen Jones. Not knowing where my geraniums were I left them in Bertie's box for 2 or 3 days the consequence was that most were spoilt and the verbena was dead. However I have still a good many slips which I think will do for next year. It is nice now that we are in another room without a master for I can work much better without a master than with one.

The winter season is now in so we learn our lessons in the evening instead of the morning. It's good for one thing i.e. we can sit up as long as we like working, but the bad is we are never awakened till nearly $\frac{1}{2}$ past six and I like to be up long before six. Jules, one the boys in our room, generally wakes at $\frac{1}{2}$ past 5 and then he awakens me. Since the holidays nearly 12 boys have

---

2. William Henry Smith, *Thorndale,* 1857. According to the Blackwood Contributors Book, GHL was first introduced to the firm in 1842 by Smith, who contributed frequently to *Blackwood's,* though there is a gap between April 1856 and January 1858.

come as some have come since Papa left. There is an English boy from Milan who speaks English with a strong Italian accent. Tell Papa Mrs. Young is not yet gone but I think she is going in a few days. By the time you get this letter she will be perhaps off, and the boys, I mean her boys, will then have to come regularly to classes, and not stay away sometimes the whole day, other times two or three hours. How does Edmund get on at Dr. Pearce's? Bertie who got a great many friends at Dr. Pearce's I am afraid won't do so well here, for the boys here and at Dr. Pearce's are quite a different set. One good thing is we can fight our battles without fear of being caned. However I think he will get on all right. It is a pity for him that he can't speak a bit of French for then he would be able to make himself understood, but as it is he must always get an interpreter.

We shall soon leave off bathing now for the water is getting dreadfully cold. We shall then have gymnastics. We are going to have a uniform now that there are so many but only for Sunday, because a great many boys have quantities of good clothes that they must wear out. I still sleep with only a sheet over me but I am afraid I'll soon be obliged to put on my blanket. They don't have mattresses here but light featherbeds like at Paris. These are tremendously hot, so hot indeed that in the middle of winter I kicked it off always. I hope you were all satisfied with your presents though I doubt if they [are] much to your taste. I had intended to get something at Bern for Emily but I could not find any thing that I thought she would like. I had a much larger and more beautiful swiss cottage I wanted to send over but Papa said he would not have place in his trunk, so I was obliged to content myself with sending the small ones.

It was a beautiful journey this year. We were a good large party but we managed to get beds enough except one night, just on the borders of Vaud in a pretty little village named Le Plan. From there we saw the glaciers beautifully the next morning as we set out for Aigle. At Chamouny we rested a day wandering about the town and its environs. One party of boys went with the masters to "la mer de glace" whilst the others remained in Chamouny. Salusbury and I mounted to the top of one the alps by Chamouny, not snowy alps, to get to the top of which we had tremendous work, as we often had to scale perpendicular rocks where we could only hold on by shrubs and moss, and if I wasn't a pretty good climber I should have fallen several times. However we managed to get up to the top where we rested some time, we then came down at more than double the rate we went up and several times we slipped on the moss and came tumbling down until stopped by some tree.

I have just finished my third lesson in music and am already further than several boys who have had several lessons more than me. When I come home I hope I'll be able to play a little properly. This morning a woman came with peaches at 15 centimes each the largest and 7 for the small ones. The boys of our room have clubbed together to buy a clock to keep in the schoolroom. Give my love and kisses to all at home and I remain

Your affectionate Son
Charles.

II, 382:1   GHL TO JOHN BLACKWOOD, RICHMOND, 13 SEPTEMBER 1857

MS: National Library of Scotland.

8 Park Shot | Richmond | 13 September 1857.

My dear Blackwood

I have shown Monti all the drawings which will serve as the illustrations of our book, and which will give a specimen of each animal spoken of in the text. His estimate is that for 7 plates 8vo containing 28 figures the whole expence—including printing of a 1,000 copies—would be about 30£—not more perhaps less. Woodcuts would cost at least 3 times that sum. We have arranged that the effect of transparency shall be given to the delicate transparent animals, by drawings of white on a black ground. Woodcuts cannot do this.[3]

I have suggested 8vo for the sake of the plates; but if you think post 8vo would be better, because cheaper, I do not think much difference in expence of plates would accrue—perhaps we must then have 8 plates instead of 7—the number of *figures* running the same, the extra expence of one plate would not be more than 30/- I fancy.

I shall be glad to know how much the printed matter will make, as in revising it I find myself tempted to make large additions, but must restrain myself within limits of a portable and cheap volume.

One of the Aquarium makers[4] told me he was often asked by customers whether the papers in Maga would be reprinted, and he urged me to do so, not knowing that the thing had been already contemplated.

Are you drenched? Do the lanes require ferry boats? Do you swim instead of a walk? We have a deluge here.

Ever yours faithfully
G. H. L.

3. Rafaelle Monti engraved on copper the 7 plates for *Sea-side Studies*, the frontispiece and Plate v having white lines on black ground

4. Harford James Bohn, 45 Essex Street, W.C., who is mentioned in *Sea-side Studies*, p. 174.

II, 385:7 GE TO JOHN CHAPMAN, RICHMOND, 27 SEPTEMBER [1857]

MS: Yale. *Endorsed:* Marian Evans. 1857. *Extract published:* II, 385.

Richmond | September 27.

Dear Friend

I congratulate you on your programme—it is promising.[5]

The Prospectives[6] have arrived. But several other books will be necessary for the article on Newman. I do not possess one of his works, and I must have them all by me—i.e. all the theological ones. I should also have the "Eclipse of Faith," and "Mr. Greyson's Letters"[7] might contribute something.

I shall be too busy till Christmas to write any article for the January number but it will be as well to have the Newman books by me, that I may get the reading done, and the requisite passages marked.

We dined with Mr. and Mrs. Call on Wednesday, and I was very much and agreeably struck with Mr. Call.[8] He has a thoroughly cultured and refined mind—one of the few men one enjoys listening and talking to. That was my impression from a first interview.

Surely you might make use of such a man's pen, in the dearth of superior writers. I can't help thinking he would be worth enlisting as a contributor. It is true, charming men are far from being always charming writers, but I fancy in this case some of that delicate flavour I detect in the conversation would be found in the written word too.

George unites with me in kind remembrances and good wishes à propos of your new establishment which we hear of as in prospect.

Ever yours truly
M. E. Lewes.

5. Chapman planned to keep the office at 8 King William Street for his publishing business and conduct his medical practice from his house at 1 Albion Street, Hyde Park, into which he moved in March 1858.

6. Francis William Newman had been a frequent contributor to the *Prospective Review*, published by Chapman 1845–55. For GE's proposed article on Newman see II, 385.

7. Both books are by Henry Rogers (1806–77).

8. Wathen Mark Wilks Call (1817–90), A.B. Cambridge, 1843, after thirteen years as a clergyman withdrew from the Church in 1856. Chapman accepted GE's recommendation, and Call became one of the steadiest contributors to the *Westminster Review*. See 134 (October 1890), 396–397.

II, 385:19 THORNTON ARNOTT LEWES TO GHL, HOFWYL, 2 OCTOBER 1857

MS: Yale.

Hofwyl 2 October. 1857.

Dear Papa

I hope your head is quite well, and that you had a good passage home. Bertie[9] is getting on very well, and likes the place very much. My botanical season is of course now at an end though there are plenty of butterflies still. In the winter I shall have however plenty of work with my plants. Tomorrow there is some sort of a festival at Bern so we are going there, if the weather is fine. We have therefore not much to do this evening, so I take the opportunity of writing to you. Will you tell Nursie when you see her, not to forget my letter, that is to say if she has received it? I wrote to her September 6th. We feel already the effects of near winter, as the evenings now are very dark. I had last week on Monday and Tuesday, attacks of tooth-ache. The Saturday before, I had had my teeth stopped at Bern, but this old rascal, would ache on and on. At last it plagued me so much, that I determined to have him out, and out he came under the hands of the doctor of Buchsee.[1] . . .

Are you now in London or where are you? Please give me an account of your proceedings, and write as soon as possible as we are very dull without any letters. Give my love to all at home, kiss Miss Lewes[2] for me, as well as Mamma, chicks, etc. Also my love to Nursie, Grandmamma, Mrs. Owen Jones, and tell her I will write to her when she has written to Charlie.

With love and many kisses, I Remain, Dear Papsy

Your affectionate Son
Rex Ranarum.

N.B. Given under my hand this day. October 2, 1857.

9. GHL brought his youngest son Herbert to Hofwyl in August 1857.

1. Münchenbuchsee, a village near Hofwyl.

2. Rose Agnes Lewes (b. 24 October 1851), Agnes Lewes's eldest daughter by Thornton Hunt.

II, 395:8 GHL TO JOHN BLACKWOOD, RICHMOND, [29 OCTOBER 1857]

MS: National Library of Scotland.

8 Park Shot | Richmond | Thursday.

My dear Blackwood

The proof, letter and checque for G. E.[3] arrived this morning. Will you please ask the printer always to send me duplicates of the proofs that I may send them to Owen and other pundits for correction when needful?

About the edition I think you had better wait till the plates are ready, some of which I expect daily, as they will give you an idea of the aspect of the book. If Kingsley could sell 3 editions of Glaucus[4] which had nothing whatever new in it, nothing of his own except the preaching, we ought to be able to get off 1250, but it's a horrid bore having a weight of unsold copies on one's shelf.

I have written a paper on "Phrenology in France"[5] which will make the phrenologists all the more savage because they must see that I am not indisposed to recognize such truth as they really have achieved. If you like to print it, and if you would prefer the personal pronoun instead of the impersonal "we," I can make that alteration in proof. If you don't like it, there's no harm done; so I send it on the chance.

Ever yours faithfully
G. H. Lewes.

II, 399:1 GHL TO JOHN BLACKWOOD, RICHMOND, [3? NOVEMBER 1857]

MS: National Library of Scotland.

8 Park Shot | Tuesday.

My dear Blackwood

With the proofs I send rough proofs of some illustrations: they will of course look much better when they are quite ready, but these are sent to

---

3. See II, 394.
4. Charles Kingsley, *Glaucus, or the Wonders of the Shore*, 1855. Kingsley wrote about this time to F. D. Maurice that he must not bother about what the *Westminster Review* says of him. "The woman who used to insult you there ... is none other than Miss Evans, the infidel esprit fort (who is now G. H. Lewes's concubine) ... (he probably being the co-sinner, for he pretends to know all about the philosophers and don't." (M. F. Thorpe, *Charles Kingsley*, Princeton, 1937, p. 93.) A sharp review

give an idea of their character. Seven of these—two with dark grounds—and five others—will make a very pretty book.

The cost of the whole will I believe be as nearly as possible 30£, a trifle more or less; but I have not heard from Monti since his original estimate was given, and that was necessarily uncertain.

Ever faithfully yours
G. H. Lewes.

II, 399:1 GHL TO WILLIAM S. EMDEN,[6] RICHMOND, 5 NOVEMBER 1857

MS: Coventry Public Library.

8 Park Shot | Richmond | 5 November 57.

Dear Sir

Did you ever see Ravel in *L'Etourneau?*[7] If so you will remember the impression half tragic half comic which his acting of the terror produced, and will probably agree with me that Robson would produce a still greater impression in the part. The difficulty in the subject—love for a married woman—I see a way of eluding.

The piece was done at the Haymarket for Hudson, under the name of the *Irish Post.*[8] But it did not produce much effect, as you may imagine in his hands such a part could not. If the piece would suit you and Robson would like to play the part, I shall be happy to do it.[9]

Meanwhile believe me Dear Sir

Yours very truly
G. H. Lewes.

W. Emden Esq.

of Maurice's *The Old Testament*, 1851, in the *Westminster*, 57 (January 1852), 282–283, which may be by GE, is the only possible "insult."

5. "Phrenology in France," *Blackwood's*, 82 (December 1857), 665–674.

6. W. S. Emden took over joint managership of the Olympic Theatre, of which he was already treasurer, with Frederick Robson. (*Leader*, 20 June 1857.)

7. Pierre Alfred Ravel (1814–57) created the rôle of Felix in *L'Etourneau* by Jean François Alfred Bayard (1796–1853) at the Théâtre du Palais Royal, 7 September 1844.

8. *The Irish Post*, by J. R. Planché, Haymarket, 28 February 1846, for James Hudson (1811–78).

9. On the back of this letter Emden has drafted a reply dated 13 November 1857: "I find that the L'Etourneau has been proposed and partly accepted, but I hope to see Robson on Monday and shall know more about it. If not that, we hope to obtain something else from your pen. Yours E."

II, 399:1 JOHN BLACKWOOD TO GHL, EDINBURGH, 5 NOVEMBER 1857

Text: Copy in Blackwood Letter Book, National Library of Scotland.

Edinburgh November 5th 1857.

My dear Lewes

I have just put your interesting paper on Phrenology[1] into the printing office. The only part where I would seriously object is when you seem to put Phrenology on the same platform as Medicine. I do not think you exactly intend to do so, but any difficulties can be obviated by putting the paper in the form of a letter. Phrenology has not, and never will, discover anything so useful to humanity as an humble black draught or seidlitz powder.

I like the whole of the Illustrations and the charge seems exceedingly moderate. The drawings have a genuine look which is a great thing. The book reads well and I begin to be sanguine. I should like to publish in December but this will depend on your returning the proofs for Press. Do not hurry yourself when you have such a man as Owen to consult and advise with.

Do you know much about Chemistry? I want to find a man who possesses a competent knowledge of science and at the same time writes a pleasant popular style to edit Johnston's Chemistry of Common Life.[2] Poor Johnston's own style was admirably clear and readable and this I have no doubt was the main cause of the wonderful success of the book.

I have once or twice spoken to Lyon Playfair[3] on the subject and he was to have called upon me about it. But as it is a long time ago and he has never come, I consider myself entirely free of him. The impression he made upon me, moreover, was that of not being qualified for the work, "more sound than sense" about him, as we say in Scotland. Of course this is all between ourselves.

Ever yours truly,
Sig[ne]d John Blackwood.

G. H. Lewes, Esq.

1. "Phrenology in France," *Blackwood's*, 82 (December 1857), 665–674.
2. See II, 405, n. 9.
3. Lyon Playfair (1818–98), President of the Chemical Society 1858–59, became Professor of Chemistry at Edinburgh in 1858.

II, 400:13 GHL TO JOHN BLACKWOOD, RICHMOND, [7 NOVEMBER 1857]

MS: National Library of Scotland. *Extract published:* II, 395.

8 Park Shot | Saturday.

My dear Blackwood

Your suggestion about turning the paper on Phrenology into a Letter is very good and obviates all difficulties.

My knowledge of Chemistry is almost exclusively in the direction of Organic Chemistry, but as this is the ground occupied by Johnston[4] I feel able to undertake the editing of his book, so as to bring it up to the present state of Science. Pray observe that I construe the passage in your letter as a suggestion rather than a *proposition* on your part; and it is in that spirit I reply to it. I feel that, if called upon, I could do the work, and say so. But I should not like my name to appear. It is doubtful whether any but a very attractive name would be of much service to a book so popular and so respected; but it is certain that mine, not being that of a chemist, would be of no value whatever.

Having answered explicitly for myself, let me add that if you can alight upon a good man who will do the work well and put his name to it, there will be every reason to place it in his hands.

What number do you propose to print of "Seaside Studies,"? and at what price?

I am sorry to say "Thorndale" does not greatly interest me, in spite of my old regard for the author. Some years ago I dare say I should have read it with pleasure; but the age of doubt and vacillation has passed and I want something solid, or seeming solid whereon to stand and look about me. The book is charmingly written, but I think its structure a mistake. Don't tell him so, however. If the public likes it, he won't believe me; if the public doesn't like it, he will find out the mistake fast enough.

Ever faithfully yours
G. H. Lewes.

4. GHL put his name to *The Chemistry of Common Life*, by James F. W. Johnston. A new edition, revised and brought down to the present time by G. H. Lewes, author of "The Physiology of Common Life" etc., 2 vols., 1859. The revisions consist mostly of additions to the tables of statistics such as the consumption of alcohol, etc., and occasional verbal changes such as *odours* for *smells*.

II, 404:21 GHL TO JOHN BLACKWOOD, RICHMOND, [19 NOVEMBER 1857]

MS: National Library of Scotland.

8 Park Shot | Thursday.

My dear Blackwood

I have brought out my meaning more distinctly towards the close of the article. But I cannot see anything to alter in the passage about Medicine which, *as a science*,[5] is, I assure you, in a state not less chaotic than Phrenology; but gains, and deserves, greater respect than Phrenology because its pretensions are humbler.

As I said before I prefer leaving all publishing arrangements to your experience, necessarily so much better a guide than any opinion of mine. Nevertheless as a *suggestion* I would say let 10/6 rather than 12/– be the price of the book, if that will pay a decent profit.[6] Not being a work which people *must* have, the cheaper it is the greater will be the sale; and 10/6 seems to me as much as any one would like to give.

By the way, the only time on which I published at half-profits, my share was paid in advance. Do you care to risk this much, making an approximative estimate of what the profits would be?

Yours very faithfully
G. H. Lewes.

I can't make out your address at Derby[7] so this must go to Edinburgh.

II, 405:13 JOHN BLACKWOOD TO GHL, EDINBURGH, 28 NOVEMBER 1857

Text: Copy in Blackwood Letter Book, National Library of Scotland.

Edinburgh | November 28/57.

My dear Lewes

That you may fully understand the position of "Sea-Side Studies" I inclose our estimate. The only uncertain points are the advertising and

---

5. In "Phrenology in France" GHL wrote: "Our position may be likened to the position usually held by intelligent men respecting Medicine. That the Pathology and Therapeutics taught and practised in our schools are extremely imperfect, even the professors will cheerfully admit." (*Blackwood's,* 82 [December 1857], 673.)

6. *Sea-side Studies,* 1858, was published at 10/6.

7. Blackwood's father-in-law the Reverend Joseph Blandford lived at Sponden, near Derby.

engravings. The paper and boarding are what we pay and the printing is what we would charge to the book were it entirely our own property. The Corrections and extras being estimated from the expense incurred in the sheets already sent to press. The 10 per cent Commission is fully required to cover the discounts from Saleprice allowed to the wholesalers the loss of interest etc. on the length of time that must elapse before we are paid for the Edition even supposing the sale to be very rapid. I grudge the £50 in advertising but I do not think we can spend less. You are I see sparing no labour or trouble on the Volume and my brother and I wish to give you so much as we possibly can consistently with having ourselves any fair chance of remuneration on the undertaking.

We now beg to offer you £75 for the Edition or if you prefer to wait and take your chance of the result we will pay you two thirds of the clear profits when these arrive.

I am glad you think you can edit and bring down to the present state of Scientific Knowledge the Chemistry of Common Life and I have desired an interleaved copy to be sent you. If on looking over the Book you think you can do what is required I should like you to set about it as soon you find leisure. I imagine that very considerable additions will be desirable but you will be best able to judge. I cannot of course form any accurate idea of the amount of labour you will require to bestow in re-editing the book but at all events I propose to give you one hundred guineas (£105.) if that sum meets with your ideas.

I would have written to you sooner about this had I not hesitated a little as to whether an Editor with a Scientific reputation was not absolutely necessary but having the work really well done is much more essential than the bubble reputation and I have seen so much of your businesslike conscientious mode of writing that I feel quite confident anything you undertake will be well done.

Enclosed I have the pleasure of sending a cheque £10.10. in acknowledgement of your little paper on Phrenology in France. My brother goes up to London next week and hopes to have an opportunity of making your acquaintance.

With regards to G. Eliot

              I am ever yours truly
              John Blackwood.

G. H. Lewes Esq.

II, 405:13 GHL TO JOHN BLACKWOOD, RICHMOND, 30 NOVEMBER [1857]

MS: National Library of Scotland.

8 Park Shot | 30 November.

My dear Blackwood

Your letter—checque—and Johnston arrived this morning. I am so much pleased with the liberality of your proposals and the confidence you express that I can only hope both will meet with the right return.

I have never contemplated any but the slenderest money result from 'Sea-Side Studies,' but as to a poor man every addition to the banker's account is important, I shall be quite pleased to get 75£ for the edition—and not less so to hear you have got as much for your trouble and risk.

Johnston is a task which I shall set about con amore. When I see my way clear I will write to submit my plans. No time shall be lost.

It will give me great pleasure to make the acquaintance of your brother, and I hope his stay will be long enough to allow of his giving us a day among the lingering autumnal tints of Richmond Park.

Ever yours faithfully
G. H. Lewes.

II, 410:7 JOHN BLACKWOOD TO GHL, EDINBURGH, 7 DECEMBER 1857

Text: Copy in Blackwood Letter Book, National Library of Scotland.

Edinburgh | December 7/57.

My dear Lewes

I am very glad to find you entering so keenly into the Editing of Johnston's Chemistry of C. Life and the way in which you propose to handle the book satisfies me that you will do it well.

I quite agree with you that your second plan is the best—viz: to incorporate the corrections and new matter with the text. The other common plan of constantly putting Editor or Brackets breaks the narrative and interrupts the Reader. In your preface you can give some idea of the extent to which the corrections and additions go.

Do not hurry yourself inconveniently as we have stock to go on with for a time but I will write you again as to the time when we think it would be advisable to begin publishing. I think we shall reissue the work in parts.

My brother is at 38 Jermyn Street but I daresay he will drop you a line. He is only in town for a week and I doubt not very busy.

I am delighted to know that George Eliot is going on with spirit and any report of progress will be very acceptable.

I feel quite friendly towards the old clergyman who was so deeply affected by Janets Repentance—oddly enough the next letter I opened after yours was from another old clergyman,[8] a correspondent of my own, who said that "Janets repentance was *exquisite*." This gave me pleasure as the writer is a man of good taste and highly accomplished. My pleasure was shortlived as the next paragraph went on to say, "I must write out my own parochial reminiscences." This gave me a spasm as I more than doubt his power of writing anything like a good story, and I know he will be down upon me with his M.S.

G.E. is too diffident of his own powers and prospects of success. Very few men indeed have more reason to be satisfied as far as the experiment has gone. The following should be a practical Cheerer. When I was away in England my brother got more sanguine than we had been about the Clerical Scenes and increased the impression from 750 to 1000. This will necessitate a change in the sum to be paid to the author for the Edition and I propose that we should pay a further sum of Sixty pounds (£60) when 750 copies are sold.

Ever yours truly
John Blackwood.

G. H. Lewes Esq.

I had nearly forgot to say that I think an Index will be desirable for your book. If you can do it without serious trouble you could do it best yourself but I daresay we could manage it here if you were indisposed. Give my regards to G.E.

II, 413:1 GHL TO JOHN BLACKWOOD, RICHMOND, [13 DECEMBER 1857]

MS: National Library of Scotland.

8 Park Shot | Richmond | Sunday.

My dear Blackwood

Can you *lend* me a copy of Stephens's Book of the Farm,[9] in which I suspect there will be a few details useful for me to know? If you haven't got a cut copy I will go to the Brit. Museum and look at it there.

---

8. Rev. George Carless Swayne. See II, 300, n. 2.

9. See II, 417, n. 2.

[*13 December 1857*]

When I had the pleasure of a visit from your brother I mentioned to him the scheme of a "Physiology of Common Life" which has taken shape in my mind to replace the systematic work on Physiology for which I have been several years making collections. I propose to do for Life what Johnston has done for Chemistry—and to explain popularly yet according to the latest results of science what is known of Hunger and Thirst—Food and Drink—Digestion and Indigestion—Respiration and Suffocation—The Blood and its Circulation—Poisons and Poisonings—The Moral and Physical Qualities We Inherit from Our Parents—Sleep and Dreams—Our Senses and Sensations—etc.

I propose to publish articles in the Magazine on these topics first, and to enlarge and alter them afterwards. In the first article[10]—sent by this post—you will see a specimen. It contains an amount of facts and cases which have never been assembled before in any work that I am acquainted with.

One or two of the topics—such as Digestion—have been touched on by Johnston, but my treatment will be not only more exhaustive than his, but will be strictly physiological, and include the unpleasantness so familiar to many which cluster round the *disturbances* of Digestion.

What do you say to the scheme? If you think we had better publish at once without first appearing in Maga, that also can be done; but there are many advantages in having the work in type, as it were, before beginning the serial publication.

I have been commissioned by my friend Mr. Max Schlesinger[1] of 4 King William St., Strand, to tell you that whenever you publish any work likely to find a sale in Germany, Holland, or Russia, if you will forward him a copy he will notice it in his London Letter, which he contributes to *60* of the principal German papers. His notice will not be a *review*, but will take the form of literary news—in fact it is a splendid advertisement which not only appears in his 60 papers, but is copied by a variety of other journals. He announced my "Life of Goethe" in that way, and I had immediately two offers from publishers for the sale of the German translation—and two for the English reprint. It is of no use sending books not likely to have a foreign sale. But Alison—Johnston—Aytoun—and my book would I think benefit by such advertisement. However, I have explained the matter, and leave it to your judgement.

Ever faithfully yours
G. H. Lewes.

John Blackwood Esq.

10. "Hunger and Thirst," *Blackwood's*, 83 (January 1858), 1–17.

1. See II, 434, n. 4.

II, 414:14 JOHN BLACKWOOD TO GHL, EDINBURGH, [17] DECEMBER 1857

MS: Copy, National Library of Scotland.

Edinburgh December 18. 1857.

My dear Lewes

I have read Hunger and Thirst twice with much interest and I am happy to say that I think the Public will take the series greedily. I would strongly urge you to take out the story of the eating of the Negro Boy. It gives one a turn at the start and my brother who has also read the proof with much pleasure made the same objections to it that I feel. A few sentences descriptive of the horrors of hunger would also ballance better with your introductory sketch of the beneficial effects of the stimulus which by the way is particularly good. Do you not take it too much for granted that a loss of 4/10 on weight from hunger is death to man as well as to animals and do you make sufficient allowance for the fatness or condition of the animal or man at the time the abstinence from food begins? You say nothing of the power of the mind in supporting man under Hunger and Thirst and I suppose nothing definite can be said. In the Black Hole of Calcutta[2] one would be disposed to say that the mental Constitution was an element in carrying a man through.

In the magazine it will be better not to give the series the general Title but it would be a shocking bore if any interloper got a hold of it. Do you think we could take any precaution against this, such as registering the first Paper at Stationers Hall under the Title Phys. of C. Life?

Your preface to Sea-Side Studies arrived today. The index is going on rapidly and a proof will be sent to you when ready. How do the illustrations stand? Shall we order the paper or has the engraver done so? We had better see the plates and paper before they are printed off in case of mistakes.

Ever yours truly,
John Blackwood.

G. H. Lewes Esqr.
Return proof as soon as you can.

---

2. GHL discusses the Black Hole as a physical fact only, quoting a long account from the *Annual Register* of 1758 to show that excessive sweating rather than lack of water caused thirst. Though the officer who survived to write of it sucked sweat from his shirt sleeve, GHL says nothing of the salt and water balance involved in thirst.

[9 January 1858]

II, 414:14 GHL TO JOHN BLACKWOOD, RICHMOND, [19 DECEMBER 1857]

MS: National Library of Scotland.

8 Park Shot | Saturday.

My dear Blackwood

I am truly glad that you like the idea of the series which it will be a real pleasure to me to write. This first part is by no means a fair specimen of the interest that can be thrown into the subject.

I will cut out the negro-eating as you both dislike it; although as a rule I always prefer a *specific* to a *general* statement.³

As to the chance of some one usurping the title, it is really alarming. I think the best way to prevent it—and all vexation—will be for you to advertize in the Magazine—on the back of Johnston and anywhere else where you can do so free of expence the following: *In preparation* | The Physiology of Common life | By G. H. Lewes, | As a companion to Johnston's | Chemistry of Common Life. By giving the title and author in full and by saying it is in *preparation* all equivocation is blocked out. What say you to this?

By the way are you going to publish my Algerine friend's paper?⁴ If not—and if you haven't mislaid it among your heaps of m.s.—I should be glad to have it back. In haste

Ever yours
G. H. Lewes.

Proof herewith.

II, 420:1 GHL TO JOHN BLACKWOOD, RICHMOND, [9 JANUARY 1858]

MS: National Library of Scotland.

8 Park Shot | Saturday.

My dear Blackwood

I have just discovered an unpleasant blunder of mine in Sea-Side Studies in which I attribute an oversight to Dr. Carpenter not committed

---

3. GHL kept the reference to Ugolino, but changed that to the negro boy into a general remark on shipwrecked men who fed on human flesh. (p. 1.)

4. GHL sent Mme Bodichon's article to Blackwood 2 June 1857. See II, 337, n. 8.

by him; as an *erratum* will not properly rectify such a passage, I wish you would have page 293 cancelled, and a new one substituted according to the corrected page enclosed.[5] As the fault is mine I should of course pay for this extra printing.

I will send you the first volume of Johnston shortly.

The subscription to Clerical Scenes is very promising—and thanks to the 'Times' the edition will doubtless go off.[6] G.E. is much pleased thereat.

Ever yours faithfully
G. H. Lewes.

I presume you have received the illustrations before this?

II, 420:1 CHARLES LEWES TO AGNES LEWES, HOFWYL, 10 JANUARY 1858

MS: Yale.

Hofwyl 10th January 1858.

Dear Mamma,

I have not written to you for a long time in expectation of receiving a letter from you. Since September I have received only 2 letters from you and this is the 5th or sixth that I send to *you*. September 27th I wrote Nursie but having received no answer I did not write again. I have asked the postman how it was that so many letters were lost and he said that he did not know. That all letters that came from Bern were sent to Hofwyl without fail, and those that were sent from Hofwyl and that he received went punctually to Bern. He did not know how to account for it, unless there were lost in the railway or on the sea. Bertie received a letter from Lizzie[7] today, in which there was mention of a Christmas present for us three which she supposed we had got already. If it was an order for money the letter was lost. If it was a packet, which I hope it was not, it must also have been lost. As regards sending packages, I hope that if Papa or Grand-

---

5. GHL had written that W. B. Carpenter's argument about the multiplication of polyps as a process of budding was "completely destroyed by the fact that the Polype *also* produces Polypes by the union of ova and spermatozoa, as he is perfectly aware, seeing that he has quoted the descriptions, and even given the figures of Professor Allman, illustrating the fact." In the cancelled p. 293 GHL deletes all the sentence after *spermatazoa* and makes two other verbal changes. George James Allman (1812–98), Irish biologist, was Regius Professor of Natural History at Edinburgh 1855–70.

6. See II, 416–417.

7. Mary Eliza Lee, daughter of Mrs. Willim's cousin and housekeeper Mrs. Mary Lee. She became a teacher at a Unitarian school in Hampstead and later married John Huddy (1815–70).

mamma or anybody else wants to send us any packages, you will prevent them, for it costs much to much. If we want any thing we must buy it in Bern or go without it, and with the money we have received from home and the pocket money we can buy what we want. If Thornie wants books he must wait for them till Papa comes again, and Bertie and I don't want anything but what could be got at Bern. I find that writing cases as good as the English ones can be got in Bern for less money so that if Bertie wants so much a writing case he can get one at Bern. What with the 10 francs I received in the summer and my birthday ten francs, I had at Christmas 20 francs and a few over from pocket money which I never use entirely in the month, I bought for 15 Francs presents for the boys and two of the masters, and Dr. Müller has still got 5 francs for me. Bertie only had 7 francs when he came and that soon went in rabbits with which he soon got disgusted. Thornie at the end of the month has never got a sou for he spends the pocket money on grub. To me it does not matter having lost the present whatever it was, except that I thank Grandmamma very much for her kindness. She is only rather too kind, for the money she sends I'm afraid does not do much good to us boys. However I don't in the least mean she should not at least send Thornie and Bertie (if that was her intention) presents and me also for I can I daresay find some use for the money at some time or other. But now let us drop the money subject.

Thornie received a letter from Mrs. O. Jones the other day in which she told us of the death of her brother Mr. Wild.[8] Mrs. M. has got an aunt of that name, Aunt Julia as she is called. One of her sons Edward Wild is an officer in India. A little time ago he was in the list of the dead, Mrs. M. wore mourning for him as of course did his mother, some time afterwards they received the news that the officer Mr. Wild reported to be dead was still alive. It was at Lucknow he was said to have fallen. Since then no news has been heard respecting him. Mr. and Mrs. M. family all speak English amongst themselves for Mr. Mül[ler]'s family although not English has lived most of the time in India. Aunt Julia's husband was a captain or colonel I don't know which in the Indian army, and now her son is an ensign I think.

During the whole of last week we have been skating. We had a few days ago a pretty heavy fall of snow but on the road and trees a very little more, but on the ice and fields there's still a good deal. We have been making roads on the ice like last year. The Christmas holidays this year were rather dull, for we could not skate nor sledge, but now we are making up for lost time. This year like last year I saw the old year out and the new

8. Edward Wild was reported killed at Lucknow, but the report was false.

one in. All the boys were awoken at twelve o'clock and we began singing. In a few minutes some of the masters came in and the boys from the other bedroom, and then began the fun. Such bolstering, and hollaring, and laughing and singing, we woke every body in the house up. Louis the great Brasilian who Papa knows would not get out of bed. Wir wollen den Louis ein wenig quälen, said Mr. Falckerheimer and so we all set on him. A quantity of featherbeds were thrown on him and I don't know what all. Then Thornie finding it dull went to bed, but was instantly attacked by the others. In a minute poor Thornie's bed was torn off and he went crying into a corner of the room. We then made a procession, then sang some more songs and at a little after 1 o'clock got into bed again. I will tell you for a conclusion that I did not take the disagreeable station of watcher this year as I did last but I slept till 12 o'clock. I hope to hear soon from you and remain

Your affectionate Son
Charles Lewes.

II, 421:17   GHL TO JOHN BLACKWOOD, LONDON, [15 JANUARY 1858]

MS: National Library of Scotland.

8 Park Shot | Friday.

My dear Blackwood

By this post I send you the first part of "Johnston," which I wish you to look over, because although I have advanced with the other parts it is possible you may have some criticisms to make which may alter my course. You will see that labor has not been spared.

I shall not be ready with Food and Drink[9] for this month. The extensive researches it has necessitated, beyond my former collections, will not allow me to come up to time, and as the papers are not serial, I am not disposed to sacrifice any point for the sake of gaining time.

I saw Langford on Wednesday and G.E. is not a little pleased with the news I brought away.[10] It appears L. knows the daughter of Amos Barton![1]

---

9. "Food and Drink, I," *Blackwood's,* 83 (March 1858), 325–343.

10. In her Journal 13 January 1858 GE wrote: "G. went today into the City to see Langford about the 'Clerical Scenes.' 750, including 100 sent to Edinburgh, already disposed of to the libraries and booksellers. Letter from Blackwood the other day saying he should have the pleasure of making me both payments together."

1. See II, 298.

3 February 1858

"Sea-side Studies" is I suppose ready now, as I saw the plates in Paternoster Row. I don't feel quite easy about so large an edition in these bad times; but my hopes rest on the growing taste for Aquaria.

With kind regards to your Brother, Believe me My dear Blackwood

Ever yours faithfully
G. H. Lewes.

II, 432:6 JOHN BLACKWOOD TO GHL, EDINBURGH, 3 FEBRUARY 1858

Text: Copy in Blackwood Letter Book, National Library of Scotland.

Edinburgh February 3/58.

My dear Lewes

I had the pleasure of hearing from Mr. Langford yesterday that in addition to the subscription of which I wrote to you on Saturday, Mudie had taken 200 and would take 500 if we would give the extra percentage. I wrote to give it and would have written to tell you the good news had I not thought it probable you might have heard it at the Row.[2]

I think very little of the subscription to Books unless in the case of a succession of Books similar in character by the same author. Then the subscribers can really form a good estimate as the orders are up from the country, but in most other cases unless there has been a regular clamour about the forthcoming Book the subscription is no index although it is always pleasant to see it large. A month ago we subscribed about 600 of Lord St. Leonards Handy Book[3] and have since sold 15000!

I have the pleasure of enclosing a cheque £75 being payment in full for the first edition of the Sea-Side Studies as agreed. The cancel does not matter. We take such things as the chance of War.

In making the arrangement for your Book and for Clerical Scenes I should have named a date for payment and I had not intended to pay until six months after publication as is usual, but let me know if G.E. wishes or expects payment at once.

Ever yours truly
John Blackwood.

G. H. Lewes, Esq.

2. 1350 copies had been printed. Langford wrote to William Blackwood 21 January 1858 that the book "is not moving as I wish—none of the Row Houses have yet sold their subscribed number." To John Blackwood he wrote 2 February: "there are no new sales of Clerical Life, which I cannot under-

II, 434:11 JOHN BLACKWOOD TO GHL, EDINBURGH, 15 FEBRUARY 1858

Text: Copy in Blackwood Letter Book, National Library of Scotland.

Edinburgh February 15/58.

My dear Lewes

I enclose the proof of Food and Drink which I shall be glad to have back as soon as possible.

I have read this first instalment with much pleasure although being introductory I daresay it is not altogether so interesting as the other two parts. It will be liked. If on going over the proof you think there are any portions which could in the meantime be left out without disadvantage, reserve these for the book, as at present the paper has rather too much the air of a fragment of a systematic work on the subject for a magazine paper. Follow your own opinion about this however. I cannot tell what is necessary for a ground work for the development of your further views so I speak with diffidence. I see you are generally "I." I think, on the whole, it will be better to stick to the mystic "we."[4]

I have no recent intelligence of the Studies or Scenes from London so I suppose Langford has no particular feature to mention.

I was delighted to hear from G.E. that I might so soon hope to see something like a volume of his new Tale. I am very sanguine.

I sent a copy of the Studies to the little Doctor (Simpson)[5] and hear he is going about in raptures about the book. I daresay he will *deliver* himself of a note by and bye.

I am glad you like the appearance of the book so much. It is I think a particularly handsome volume so much so that when I saw it I felt we had been weak in not making the rascally public stump up 12/6 for it.

Always yours truly
John Blackwood.

G. H. Lewes Esq.

stand—so much it has been talked about and so well reviewed everywhere." (NLS.)

3. Lord St. Leonards, *A Handy Book on Property Law*, 1858.

4. GHL accepted the suggestion. In the previous part "I" had been used; it was changed to "we" in reprinting.

5. James Young Simpson. See II, 416, n. 1.

[*17 February 1858*]

II, 435:1   GHL TO SYDNEY WILLIAMS,[6] RICHMOND, [16 FEBRUARY 1858]

MS: Princeton. *Endorsed:* 1858. | G. H. Lewes | Richmond | Feby 16.

8 Park Shot | Richmond.

Dear Sir

Will you be good enough to have the Cyclopædia of Biography[7] bound for me in plain *half calf?*

The accompanying book on the Pflanzenkeim which I was seduced into carrying away the other day turns out quite above me and suitable only to some of your botanical friends. Will you take it back, charging me for the cutting thereof whatever you please?

Yours truly,
G. H. Lewes.

Sydney Williams Esq.

II, 435:1   GHL TO ARTHUR HELPS, RICHMOND, [17 FEBRUARY 1858]

MS: Nuneaton Public Library. *Endorsed:* G. H. Lewes Esqre | Feb. 1858.

8 Park Shot | Richmond | Wednesday.

My dear Helps

I have just finished a careful and delighted reading of 'Oulita,'[8] noticing numberless improving touches, but especially noticing the finish and grace of the poetry. Had you devoted your whole life to the "accomplishment of verse"[9] I do not see how you could have acquired a more exquisite sense of melodic expression and descriptive felicity. Dramatically I should still have many objections to make, even to the writing which is often too *reflective*—by which I mean that one sees the author peering through the eyes of his people, and glancing sarcastically or meditatively on life and manners. This, which is permissible in a poem, will have a distracting effect on the stage. Perhaps however it is my knowledge of the

---

6. Sydney Williams, stationer, 11 Lancaster Place, Strand.

7. *Cyclopædia of Biography; Embracing a Series of Original Memoirs of the Most Distinguished Persons of All Times*, ed. Elihu Rich, R. Griffin and Co., 1854.

8. *Oulita the Serf. A Tragedy*, [anonymous], 1858.

9. Wordsworth, *The Excursion*, I, line 80. GE and GHL had read the whole poem aloud in January 1858. (GE Journal.)

author which makes me detect his echos in the voices of his persons. Note therefore if any one less familiar with your thoughts makes the same objection. Possibly if we *knew* Shakspeare we should have that fault also to add to his numerous errors of excess.

I hope there will be some good criticism evoked by Oulita. Although for the most part, owing to the 'd——d ignorance of the drama' which flourishes in our island, my expectations are but moderate.

I wish I could see you to tell you a delicious story about John Forster. Here is one about Lemaitre the actor.[1] When Atala Duchêne left him in disgust at his ill treatment he presented himself at her mother's. 'N'ayez pas peur' he said to her 'je ne viens pas pour enfoncer ma botte dans votre derrière—je viens vous demander un coin pour pleurer Atala!'— Is not this mixture of brutality and sentiment delicious?

Yes, my book is a great success; it is not only *selling* well, but it has drawn forth from Sir Henry Holland, Simon,[2] Huxley, Carpenter, Harvey,[3] Sharpey[4] and others the warmest recognition of its scientific value; and this considering who is the writer is very surprising. Simon says 'had it been the work of one who had done nothing else all his life, it would be very remarkable.'—Voilà!

Love to all. Let me see you before I flit.

Ever faithfully yours
G. H. Lewes.

II, 435:1 GHL TO THOMAS HENRY HUXLEY, RICHMOND, 19 FEBRUARY [1858]

MS: Imperial College of Science, London.

8 Park Shot | Richmond | Friday 19 February.

My dear Sir

I can honestly say there is no man in England whose favorable opinion on any question of biological science could be so gratifying to me as your's, and you may judge therefore with what pleasure your note was received accompanied as it was by a present I greatly value. Some of the papers were already known to me, others were unobtainable and have been asked for in vain. They will all be valuable to me on any subsequent visit

---

1. See *On Actors and the Art of Acting*, 1875, pp. 73–79, for GHL's account of Frédéric Le Maître (1835–70).

2. John Simon (1816–1904), pathologist, Medical Officer of the Privy Council 1858–71.

3. William Henry Harvey (1811–66), Professor of Botany at Dublin.

4. William Sharpey (1802–80), Professor of Anatomy and Physiology at University College, London.

11 March 1858

to the coast and in the event of a second edition of the 'Studies.' Believe me, my dear Sir,

Yours very truly
G. H. Lewes.

T. H. Huxley Esq.

II, 439:18 JOHN BLACKWOOD TO GHL, EDINBURGH, 11 MARCH 1858

Text: Copy in Blackwood Letter Book, National Library of Scotland. *Extracts published:* II, 439, n. 4.

Edinburgh March 11/58.

My dear Lewes

Tell George Eliot that I think Adam Bede all right, most lifelike and real. I wish to read the MS quietly over again before writing in detail about it and since my return I am so overpowered with business that cannot be postponed that I may not for a little get the *mental* leisure necessary to do justice to a second perusal. For the first reading it did not signify how many things I might have had to think of. I would have hurried through it with eager pleasure. I write this note to allay all anxiety in the part of G.E. as to my appreciation of the merits of this most promising opening of a picture of life. Is there much more written or is it merely blocked out? Tell George Eliot also that I hear to-day Simpkins have 12 more of the 'Clerical Scenes' and I think he may make his mind easy that none of the stock of the book will stick to our shelves.

I have the pleasure of inclosing a cheque £24 in acknowledgement of Food and Drink pt. 1 and I shall write you about pt. 2 with proof in a day or two.

In spite of all injunctions I began Adam Bede on the Railway and felt very savage when the waning light stopped me as we neared the Scottish Border. I picked up a Cab about Hammersmith and got to town in good time after a very pleasant afternoon at Richmond.

Best regards to George Eliot when you see him.

Ever yours truly
John Blackwood.

G. H. Lewes Esq.
P.S. Looking over this note I see I have written the word "hurried" in a way that might be misunderstood. By hurried I mean reading as fast as I can, hurried reading in the ordinary acceptation of the term is impossible with anything of George Eliot's. You cannot skim over his pages.

II, 440:12 GHL TO JOHN BLACKWOOD, RICHMOND, [18 MARCH 1858]

MS: National Library of Scotland.

Richmond | Thursday.

My dear Blackwood

Proof goes by this post. But have you forgotten that I want to see proof of part III,[6] as I shall be en route just at the time it would in ordinary course be ready?

It is cheering to find you approve the series. Blood[7] which comes next will be much more interesting than this of Food; and the History of the discovery of the circulation[8] will, I think, excite some attention. I have made some curious experiments, and some piquant researches on this point.

What weather for your golf! and how it must set *your* circulation into vigorous activity. If we poor literary devils could only golf a little we shouldn't suffer so much from dyspepsia.

Ever truly yours
G. H. Lewes.

II, 440:12 GHL TO JOHN BLACKWOOD, RICHMOND, [21 MARCH 1858]

MS: National Library of Scotland. *Endorsed:* ⟨March 21⟩.

8 Park Shot | Richmond | Sunday.

My dear Blackwood

Johnston is finished at last, and enclosed I send the Preface for you to consider. If you approve, let me have it again and I will copy it into the first volume.

"Golden opinions from all sorts of people"[9] continue to reach me about the "Studies," and among these "all sorts" to my great surprise I find Lord John Russell. If the book sells well it will operate favorably on the "Physiology."

Ever faithfully yours
G. H. Lewes.

---

6. "Food and Drink. Part III," headed the number, *Blackwood's*, 83 (May 1858), 515–525.

7. "Blood," 83 (June 1858), 687–702.

8. "Circulation of the Blood," 84 (August 1858), 148–164.

9. *Macbeth*, I, vii, 33.

II, 441:1 JOHN BLACKWOOD TO GHL, EDINBURGH, 25 MARCH 1858

Text: Copy in Blackwood Letter Book, National Library of Scotland.

Edinburgh | March 25th 1858.

My Dear Lewes

Your preface is capital, really quite a model. I was so much struck with its neatness and clearness that Aytoun, who is a considerable artist at such things, coming into my room, I handed it to him saying, There is a thing that you could not beat in its way.—He quite agreed with me.—I shall be glad to see the whole work when you are ready to send it down.

George Eliot will think that I am forgetting him but I am not. I think a good deal about Adam Bede every day. There being no absolute necessity for hurry in the reperusal, I have thought it better both for him and me to delay until I was a little out of my present turmoil of occupation. Tomorrow night the Magazine will be off my hands for the month, and in a few days I shall be able to write at length about the excellent Adam.

I send you the first number of Tales from the Magazine. I thought of starting the scheme ten years ago and delayed for what reason I do not know. It has been much in my mind during the last fortnight and should be a great success. Let me know what you think.

I shall not forget to send you proof of the next part of "Food" in time. When do you intend to start?

Ever yours truly
(signed) John Blackwood.

G. H. Lewes Esq.
I have no recent information from London about the "Studies" or the "Scenes."

II, 441:1 GE TO MRS. CHARLES BRAY, [RICHMOND], 27 MARCH [1858]

Text: Coventry Herald, 7–8 November 1919, p. 8. *Mostly published:* Haight, *George Eliot,* pp. 254–255.

March 27.

Dear Cara,

Your letter was very sweet to me, coming spontaneously, not a propos of a parcel. The feeling that you and Sara have been and always will be the women I have loved best in the world—the women I have had most reason to love and admire—strengthens instead of fading with time and absence. It is impossible ever to revive the past, and if we could recover the friend from whom we have parted we should perhaps find that we could not recover precisely the old relation. But that doesn't hinder the past from being sacred and belonging to our religion. I have some faith, too, that we should never lose our old fitness for each other, and that our talks together, and looks at each other must always be fuller of mutual understanding than we could find elsewhere.

In this faith I shall venture to recommend to you and Sara, a lady of my acquaintance in whom I have a peculiar interest.[9] She will present herself to you shortly, with a note from my hand, and I believe that for my sake you will receive her with indulgence. I can't say much that is good of her, but I am confident that she will not misconduct herself in your society. She will sit in modest silence, looking ready to enjoy any joke that is passing.

Marian.

II, 442:20 GHL TO JOHN BLACKWOOD, RICHMOND, [27 MARCH 1858]

MS: National Library of Scotland.

8 Park Shot | Richmond | Saturday.

My dear Blackwood

I'm glad you like the preface. The book goes by this post. I suppose it will not be *necessary* for me to see the proofs, so that if you wish to do so you may print while I'm away. Or if you think I had better see proofs they can be sent to Munich. We start on Monday the 5th.

The idea of the Tales from Maga[1] struck me as a most promising one, and the sight of the first number assures me that it will be a *great* success; such capital fiction in so readable a shape! The cover has a railway hideousness which will be attractive, no doubt. The print is delightful.

---

9. A photograph of GE taken by Mayall 26 February 1858, inscribed "To my sisters Cara and Sara." It was given to Cross by Mrs. Bray and Miss Hennell. See Cross to William Blackwood, 20 November 1884. (NLS.) An earlier photograph, of which Chapman had a copy, is mentioned in GE's letter to Sara Hennell [23 November 1857]. Herbert Spencer wrote to Cross 16 March 1881 that Mayall at Brighton had the negative of a photograph of GE "taken some thirty years ago." (Yale.)

1. *Tales from Blackwood,* published in monthly numbers at 6d and in quarterly volumes at 1/6. Vol. I contains "The Glenmutchkin Railway" by W. E. Aytoun, "Napoleon" by J. G. Lockhart, "A Legend of Gibralter" by E. B. Hamley, and four anonymous tales.

1 April 1858

The stories are capital, and the price is just *the* price to tempt railway travellers.

I shall send you a couple of articles before I start and that will make my mind easy for some time.

Ever faithfully yours
G. H. Lewes.

John Blackwood Esq.

II, 446:28 GE TO JOHN BLACKWOOD, RICHMOND, 1 APRIL 1858

MS: National Library of Scotland.

Richmond | April 1. 58.

My dear Sir

I am obliged to you for the cheque for £60—the final payment for the first edition of Clerical Scenes.

Your appreciatory criticism of "Adam Bede" is highly gratifying to me. I am especially pleased that you appear to feel with me about my pet characters—Adam and Dinah.

But I entertain what I think is well-founded objection against telling you in a bare brief manner the course of my story. The soul of art lies in its treatment and not in its subject. If a dramatist were to tell a manager that he had a fine tragedy in preparation, the subject of which was a man with a sore foot on a desert island, it is probable the manager would not feel any very brilliant hopes. Yet the Philoctetes is one of the finest dramas in the world.

It is true my theme is not so meagre as a sore foot, nor am I Sophocles; but the mere skeleton of my story would probably give rise in your mind to objections which would be suggested by the treatment *other* writers have given to the same tragic incidents in the human lot—objections which would lie far away from my treatment. The Heart of Midlothian would probably have been thought highly objectionable if a skeleton of the story had been given by a writer whose reputation did not place him above question. And the same story told by a Balzacian French writer would probably have made a book that no young person could read without injury. Yet what girl of twelve was ever injured by the Heart of Midlothian? Of artistic writing it may be said pre-eminently—"to the pure writer all things are pure."[2]

2. Cf. Titus 1:15.

I am not arguing against your hesitation to publish "Adam Bede" in Maga, but simply stating my reasons for objecting to tell more of the story than I have already told you—namely, that it is partly tragic.

It is natural that you should not have sufficient confidence in me to enter on the publication without more precise foreknowledge though you can certainly not be more solicitous about the moral spirit of what you publish in the Magazine, than I am about the moral spirit of what I write. Under the circumstances, it will perhaps be better definitively to give up the idea of monthly publication, and await the printing of the book in three volumes.

Do not for a moment suppose that I look exclusively from my own point of view and fail to appreciate yours. But the nature of the writer is stronger than all circumstances. I could not write at all under a sense of doubt and distrust.

I shall forward you the amount of another part to-morrow. It is possible the perusal of that may in some degree modify your views. In any case I am always very heartily

Yours, with obligation
George Eliot.

John Blackwood Esq.

II, 446:28   GHL TO JOHN BLACKWOOD, RICHMOND, 1 APRIL [1858]

MS: National Library of Scotland.

8 Park Shot | Richmond | Thursday 1 April.

My dear Blackwood

By this post I dispatch two articles for future use—the best of the series hitherto, I think. The others will be written under the inspiration of the Munich pictures. We start on Tuesday.

Do you observe the "Studies" are quoted in two articles of Frazer this month? One by Kingsley,[3] and the other by Broderip.[4] Owen tells me the

---

3. "My Winter-Garden," *Fraser's*, 57 (April 1858), 408–425. "That one word Life; and specially on all that Mr. Lewes has written so well there of late—for instance—" (p. 413). Here he quotes a long paragraph from *Sea-side Studies*.

4. William John Broderip (1789–1859), "Rambles of a Naturalist," *Fraser's*, 57 (April 1858), 441–458. "We have our Gosse; and our Lewes, he who knows how to draw each change of many-coloured life, from a heaven-born philosopher to a sea-anemone." A footnote calls *Sea-side Studies* a book "wherein sound and recondite information is made as amusing as a fairy tale." (p. 445.)

30 April 1858

latter is so charmed with the book that he is meditating an article for the *Quarterly* on it—that would be luck!

I had got thus far when your letter arrived. No, I do not *know* who the whelp of the Literary Gazette[5] is, although I suspect. At any rate he places himself out of court not only by the obvious animus, but by the deliberate falsification of which he is guilty: it was this which made Owen mention the article to me—otherwise I should not have seen it. The Literary Gazette is printed for private circulation otherwise I should expose the writer. Before the book appeared I heard that there was to be an attack on it—and as the book treads on the corns of some naturalists it is but reasonable to expect they will cry out—with eloquence or abuse as may be.

Ever yours faithfully
G. H. Lewes.

II, 452:20 JOHN BLACKWOOD TO GHL, EDINBURGH, 30 APRIL 1858

Text: Copy in Blackwood Letter Book, National Library of Scotland. *Extract published:* II, 449, n. 8.

Edinburgh April 30/58.

My dear Lewes

I would have written as soon as I heard that you were safely housed in Munich had I not waited until the proof which accompanies this was ready. This first paper on the Blood is technical enough but good, especially in the latter part.

Give my best regards to George Eliot and tell him that he will find me quite ready to meet his wishes by the publication of Adam Bede as a separate work at once. In whatever form the Tale first sees the light I am sure it will be an excellent thing both for the pocket and for the reputation of the author.

I am very anxious to hear how it gets on and shall be delighted to see more of the MS when ready. I would write to G.E. but I am desperately busy, having run myself into a corner for time. This you will readily imagine when I mention that I leave for England tomorrow.

---

5. *Literary Gazette*, 27 March 1858, pp. 295–297, a detailed criticism by a professional zoologist. "It is painful to read a book on so fascinating a subject as marine invertebrate zoology and characterized too by real talent, so disfigured by overweening self-conceit and personal vanity," the critic writes, accusing GHL of inexperience and ignorance. It is difficult to believe that Huxley wrote it, though he was in conflict with Owen at the time.

I hope your hunt for Lodging at Munich has proved a successful one and that this will find you very comfortable in the Luitpold Strasse.

I am not going direct to London, having one or two visits to pay which will occupy me until the 10th of May. Let me hear from you whenever you can and I promise faithfully to give you a spell of London news.

Always yours truly
John Blackwood.

G. H. Lewes Esq.
Address to me here.

II, 452:20 GHL TO JOHN BLACKWOOD, MUNICH, 5 MAY 1858

MS: National Library of Scotland.

15 Luitpold Strasse, Munich | Wednesday 5 May 58.

My dear Blackwood

Herewith goes the proof of "Blood." I agree with you, in rereading it, that it is a little trying to the general reader, especially without the diagrams which would make it more intelligible; but, en revanche, every reader who is at all interested in the subject will find there a mass of interesting matter, such as he cannot easily get elsewhere. The next paper being purely historical[6] will not have the same obstacle to its popularity.

You do not say how the books are selling, so in your promised letter of gossip let *that* form an item. The more widely 'Seaside Studies' is known the greater acceptance will Physiology of C. L. find, and it is as a 'Herald' or 'forerunner' that I regard the book.

We are in very comfortable lodgings here, and dine at the table d'hote like princes for 1/3 each, exclusive of wine. Munich contains enough to occupy us a month in mere "seeing," if we were bent on nothing else; but having our daily work to do we find it difficult to get the art and sights "done." Besides this we have the distraction of friends. The "Life of Goethe" has made so great an impression in Germany that its author finds himself in clover, everyone seeming to vie with everyone else in showing attention.

Some of the people here have world-celebrated names—Liebig, Kaulbach the painter, and Martius[7] the traveller—others, of smaller fame, are even more interesting. Liebig is charming, however, and we get on

---

6. "Circulation of the Blood," 84 (August 1858), 148–164.

7. See II, 455, n. 5.

famously. He is at this moment absorbed in a new process, he has invented, of making mirrors with silver backs, instead of quicksilver. He has gone with me through the whole process, and the result is astounding: when you look in one of his mirrors and place an ordinary German mirror beside it, you seem to be looking at a living face and at a corpse. Liebig has also communicated to me some new discoveries in Agricultural Chemistry; but declares he has given up Physiology *in despair*. Tant mieux! Kaulbach we do not much admire although he is assuredly the greatest of their painters; he has given me a proof of his 'Madhouse' which has a terrible Hogarthian power; and one of his new cartoons strikes us as fine—but on the whole, our impression is that a man of remarkable talent has been ruined by German criticism.

The opera is very bad; the tenor outrageous, and the prima donna utterly German. But the orchestra is first rate, and the stalls only cost 2 francs each! The theatre also is poor so that we have not been there more than once.

E. begs his kind regards and believe me ever yours

G. H. L.

II, 456:22 GHL TO JOHN BLACKWOOD, MUNICH, 15 MAY 1858

MS: National Library of Scotland.

15 Luitpold Strasse, Munich | 15 May 1858.

My dear Blackwood

I wrote to you the other day with the proof so that this morning I need only dispatch the bit of "business" which prompts this letter. Liebig gave a Lecture here, on the Identity of the Physical Forces, which was very popular, owing to its clear exposition of facts only known to the learned. He has given me the Lecture, and communicated to me the 12 new "Letters" which he is preparing for the new edition of his "Chemical Letters." The Lecture he wishes me, if possible, to make known in England; and he has been so very kind that, much as I dislike translating, I have gratified him by the promise that I would translate it for him. My first thought is for Maga.[8] Would you like to have it? Not having been published, even in Germany, and having Liebig's name attached, might be sufficiently attractive for you—but unless you would really *like* to have it, pray don't

---

8. The article did not appear in *Blackwood's*.

on my account entertain the idea. Only tell me. I merely wish to give you the first offer.

I find writing here very difficult so much time is absorbed in seeing and discussing. What with Art on the one hand and Science on the other, my brain is like Buridan's ass[9] between water and hay, uncertain which to attack first; except that that stupid young Edward died before he could make a choice whereas I am more likely to die from choosing too much.

E. sends kind regards, And believe me

Ever yours faithfully
G. H. Lewes.

II, 466:29   GHL TO EDWARD F. S. PIGOTT, MUNICH, 27 JUNE 1858

MS: Yale.

Munich | 27 June 1858.

My dear Pigott

I had been wondering why you the most friendly of correspondents did not answer my letter, and supposed your answer had been lost on the road. The letter just received explains your silence but in a very painful way. After so many years and so much money to have parted altogether with the "Leader" is really a hard case.[1] I should have been pleased to hear that a share had been sold, so as to lighten your burden, but to lose all—! Let me hope at any rate that the terms were favorable.

And now what are you going to do? With talents such as your's, and with so many friends—"everybody likes Pigott"—a distinguished place ought to be won; and perhaps after all the present ill-turn of affairs may be the most fortunate turning point in your life, by calling up all your energies for the struggle. Write to me at Dresden poste restante, and tell me all personal matters which you would tell if we were seated once more round the mahogany at Richmond, just before *Una furtiva lagrima*[2] is to be sung in a style which makes me wild with envy. Many such mahoganys will we sit round!

---

9. Jean Buridan (d. 1358), French philosopher, popularly regarded as author of the sophism used by the schoolmen to demonstrate inability of the will to choose between two equal motives. Edward or Neddy is colloquial for an ass.

1. Early in 1852 Pigott purchased the *Leader* and ran it at great loss until 1858. See Allan R. Brick, *The Leader: Organ of Radicalism*, Yale dissertation, 1957.

2. The tenor romanza in Donizetti's *L'Elisir d'Amore*, Act II.

I have only just returned from Switzerland where I found the boys in splendid condition and very happy. Although every one is *so* kind to us here that we shall leave Munich with regret, the climate is so detestable that we shall leave *it* with joy. We start on the 6th for the Tyrol—Vienna —Prague—and Dresden where we shall abide for some weeks. I will give you an account of our voyage when you have written.

Is Galloway[3] still the publisher? If not, will you ask his successor to send me the *Athenaeum* and *Saturday* poste restante to Dresden regularly after this week? I don't know whether the new proprietor will send me the *Leader*; but if he does not, I shall not care to pay for it, unless you continue writing. The other papers, of course, I pay for. Arrange this with Galloway, or successor, for me.

I have done *very* little writing since I came here, mainly on account of health, but I have done an immense deal of work in the laboratories of Liebig, Bischoff, and Harless, and feel myself greatly benefited by the visit.

Marian begs me to send her very kind regards, and with remembrances to the Owens,[4] Owen Jones, Wilkie, Baynes,[5] etc. Believe me

Ever faithfully yours
G. H. Lewes.

II, 470:1 GHL TO EDWARD F. S. PIGOTT, DRESDEN, 20 JULY 1858

MS: Yale.

5 *B*. Waisenhaus Strasse | Dresden | 20th July 1858.

My dear Pigott

You can imagine the real pleasure it was to both of us to hear that your misfortune had at any rate got a silver lining to its cloud, and that you were seriously devoting your talents to profitable work.[6] You know

3. Alfred Edmund Galloway succeeded Thornton Hunt as publisher of the *Leader* 21 October 1854.

4. Richard Owen lived at Sheen Lodge, Richmond Park, where Pigott and GHL occasionally dined with him. See, e.g., GHL Journal, 7 December 1856.

5. GHL had known Thomas Spencer Baynes (1823–87) at least since July 1852, when he took him to call on Carlyle. See Baynes's account of the evening in the *Athenaeum*, 2 April 1887, pp. 449–450. Wilkie is probably Wilkie Collins.

6. Pigott was contributing to the *Saturday Review* and to the *Continental Review*; GHL saw him at the office of the latter 1 February 1859. (GHL Journal.)

what we both think of you; and how often we have 'lectured' you for not writing more. It is therefore hopeful to see you in full swing.

We left Munich on the 6th and had an exquisite journey through the mountains, valleys, and lakes of the Tyrol—drinking in beauty to the intoxicating point every day. Our voyage down the Danube was marred by bad weather. In Vienna we were three crowded days—only making one visit, and that to the great anatomist *Hyrtl*, whose "injections" are the marvel of Europe. These he showed us very kindly, and we spent a delightful couple of hours with him. From Vienna to Prague—and in that superb city we spent a delicious day. I don't know whether you know Dresden; it is the most elegant and habitable of German cities, and after Munich a paradise. We have the whole suite of rooms forming the 2e étage, our front windows looking on a delicious allée in which nothing but foliage, sky, and promenaders are to be seen, and birds to be heard. For this we pay 18/– a week! But if we lived in a garret the diving gallery would make Dresden a paradise—such pictures! such pictures! such! Oh!!!!

Remember me kindly to Cook[7] and ask him whether he has had a review of Seaside Studies yet—I have been anxiously awaiting the same. Remember me also to Sandars, but excuse my not having written for the C. R.[8] I have written ⟨scarcely at all⟩ nothing but science my ⟨whole⟩ time has been much absorbed in *seeing*, and *experimenting*; varied by headachy incompetence.

Since Galloway has left, the nonarrival of my papers is explained. Would you be good enough to ask Mr. Jones of the S[aturday] R[eview] if he would send me the S. R. *here*, from the *10th July* (which I have not received) till *the 21 August*; placing the same to my account? The Athenæum I can do without but I must see my Saturdays especially now you are there.

Kindest regards to the O[wen] J[ones]'s—and tell Mrs. O. J. that I shall set about her commission at once. Polly will add a word on the other side.

Meanwhile believe me

Ever truly yours
G. H. L.

7. John Douglas Cook (1808?–68) edited the *Saturday Review* 1855–68. A review of GHL's book appeared 11 September 1858, pp. 263–264.

8. Thomas Collett Sandars (1825–94), a regular writer for the *Saturday Review*, was a contemporary of Pigott at Balliol. The *Continental Review* began 3 March 1858 and survived till 30 April 1859. Sandars's name does not appear as editor.

[9 September 1858]

II, 470:1 GE TO EDWARD F. S. PIGOTT, [DRESDEN, 20 JULY 1858]

MS: Yale.

Dear Mr. Pigott

I hope you will not think I am assuming a privilege that belongs only to quite old friends, in asking for a corner to express my sympathy under circumstances that will necessarily modify your life. Not unfavourably, however, I feel convinced. And I have the more right to say so, because I, too, waited long before I began to write steadily as a matter of duty, and I have found that my best happiness was reserved for me in that sort of work. So must yours be, for so much faculty of a specially literary kind as you possess implies the impossibility of thorough satisfaction without some corresponding exercise.

I don't say, then, that I am sorry for what has happened. I only ask you not to be offended at my telling you that I share George's sincere interest in all that concerns you, and am especially glad that your new career keeps you in London, where I hope you will not become too busy to dine with us, chat with us, and sing to us, as of old.

Yours truly,
Marian Lewes.

II, 480:25 GHL TO THOMAS HENRY HUXLEY, RICHMOND, [9 SEPTEMBER 1858]

MS: Imperial College of Science, London.

8 Park Shot | Richmond | Thursday.

My dear Sir

Many thanks for the very acceptable papers,[1] which I found here on my return, and which I have read with great interest. The details I can only accept, having no direct knowledge—except respecting the Hydra, in which you have anticipated what I was going to say. The conclusions are very similar to those I advocated in my book—except as regards the "individual" in which I can by no means agree. I was struck with the

1. "On the Phenomena of Gemmation," *Proceedings of the Royal Institution,* 11 (1854–58), 534–538, and "On the Agamic Reproduction and Morphology of Aphis," *Transactions of the Linnaean Society,* 22 (1858), 193–220, 221–236, were perhaps among the papers Huxley sent. The latter is referred to in *Sea-side Studies,* p. 298, as "yet unpublished." Huxley's letter is at Yale.

similarity of your observations with those of Leuckart in his admirable little book just published.

The publisher has sent me some copies of the translation of the Life of Goethe.[3] As you are so familiar with German I will ask you to accept of one—not having an original to offer. It may be worth its room for reference to dates etc.

Believe me, very dear Sir

Yours very truly
G. H. Lewes

Prof. T. H. Huxley

II, 481:23 WILLIAM BLACKWOOD TO GHL, EDINBURGH, 25 SEPTEMBER 1858

Text: Copy in Blackwood Letter Book, National Library of Scotland.

Edinburgh 25 September 1858.

My dear Lewes

I am sorry to find on inquiry that no reply has yet been sent to Trübner. It has been partly my mistake owing to a confusion arising from my brother's absence of a conversation I had with Mr. Simpson on the subject after his return from London. We will write on Monday and hope no injury will happen from the delay to G.E.'s interests.

The prospectus[4] is highly approved of by us. I send you a proof. We announce the work as preparing for publication in this number of Maga, but reserve the prospectus to a later period—probably on 1st November—we will issue it.

Yours truly
Wm. Blackwood.

G. H. Lewes Esq.

Send us back Trübner's letter if you can lay hands on it. It was not returned to us.

3. *Goethes Leben und Schriften*, tr. Julius Frese, 2 vols., Berlin, 1857.

4. Of *The Physiology of Common Life*.

II, 487:9   JOHN BLACKWOOD TO GHL, EDINBURGH, 6 OCTOBER 1858

Text: Copy in Blackwood Letter Book, National Library of Scotland. *Brief extract published:* II, 488, n. 1.

Edinburgh October 7th 1858.

My Dear Lewes

I have the pleasure of enclosing a cheque £20 in acknowledgment of your excellent little treatise on Animal Heat.[5] It is really very good.

The prospectus of the great work[6] reads most appetisingly; you are quite an artist at the construction of such things. Towards the end of this month my tent will be permanently pitched in Edinburgh. I shall then have calculations made and make the best proposition I can to you for our joint interests in the Physiology of C. Life. My brother and I are in great hopes that it may be a permanently successful book and no efforts shall be wanting on our part to insure that very desirable end. You are doing your part admirably.

George Eliot would I daresay show you what I said of Adam Vol. 2. It is very difficult indeed to judge of a second volume as one does not read it with the eager curiosity with which one opens the first, or the rapid haste with which one rushes on to the finish, as for example had Vols. 2 and 3 been before me I am sure that I would have read them in less time than I took to Vol. 2 by itself. There can be no mistake about the merits however and I am not sure whether I expressed myself sufficiently warmly. But you know that I am not equal to the abandon of expression which distinguishes the large hearted school of Critics.

I am only here for a couple of days and driving through as much as I can. At St. Andrews we had a visit for some days from Stanfield and Roberts,[7] two excellent men as well as great artists, and I expect the former will give you some idea of the ancient city of St. Regulus[8] on the

---

5. *Blackwood's*, 84 (October 1858), 414–430.

6. "No scientific subject can be so important to Man as that of his own life. No knowledge can be so incessantly appealed to by the incidents of every day, as the knowledge of the *processes by which he lives and acts.* . . . It is believed by the Author of the proposed Work that a clear and accurate conception of the chief physiological laws . . . may be impressed upon the mind, and illustrated by memorable facts, *without once* *appealing to anatomical knowledge.* It will be his object to *expound principles* rather than to teach a science . . . and he will endeavour to be intelligible and interesting to all, while reproducing the *latest* discoveries of European investigators, and the results of *original research.*"

7. See I, 248, n. 6.

8. St. Regulus (or St. Rule) founded the church at St. Andrews, to which the relics of St. Andrew were brought in 736.

walls of the Academy next year. You ask whether the excitement of Golf can equal that of Mollusc hunting; I can only say that it transcends anything else that I have tried and all Golfers are of the same opinion. When the game comes to a crisis the boldest hold their breath for a time. I have seen the best of us pale and the voice affected among others gallant Sir Hope Grant[9] a first rate Golfer. Excuse this outbreak and with best regards to G.E.

Believe me

I am yours truly
John Blackwood.

G. H. Lewes Esq.

II, 493:7 JOHN BLACKWOOD TO GHL, EDINBURGH, 3 NOVEMBER 1858

Text: Blackwood Letter Book, National Library of Scotland.

Edinburgh November 3./58.

My dear Lewes

Will you let me know how many parts same as this first the Physiology of C. Life will make. I think you said 12 or 14 but cannot recollect. By all means do the article on Biot's Mélanges.[10]

The third volume of Adam is wonderful. I would write more but I am suffering for the last day or two from a nasty shivering cold accompanied by toothache and inflammation of gums pleasant rather!

The Military Spectator may go to the dust. He is always applying for books and I never even saw his paper.

Always your truly
(signed) John Blackwood.

G. H. Lewes Esqr

9. Sir James Hope Grant (1808–75), a general who distinguished himself in the Sikh wars and during the Indian Mutiny, K.C.B. 1858.

10. See II, 491, n. 7.

II, 497:1 JOHN BLACKWOOD TO GHL, EDINBURGH, 15 NOVEMBER 1858

Text: Blackwood Letter Book, National Library of Scotland.

Edinburgh | November 15/58.

My dear Lewes

We have been making our calculations about the Physiology of Common Life, and on the supposition the work will consist of 18 numbers of about 48 pages like the 1st number, which I now send you, we beg to offer you Two Hundred and Fifty Pounds (£250.) for a first edition of Five Thousand copies. The expenses of advertising and fairly starting this first edition will be so great that supposing 5000 sold there will be only a mere trifle of any profit to us, but our hope and expectation is that the sale will go much beyond that number and the book become a steady property. We therefore propose further that for any numbers we print beyond five thousand we pay you at the rate of Three Pounds (£3) per thousand of each sixpenny number. We base the prospective payments to you on the numbers because we know that the sale in that form will be irregular and the proceeds must first be calculated in that way. Afterwards when the sale in numbers had ceased we would adjust the payments to an equivalent on the volumes.

Should it be thought advisable at any time to alter the size and price of the book, we would make you an offer on the same principle as the second part of our proposition in this letter (viz. the £3. per thousand of each number) by which we wish it to be understood that if you accept our offer we have a permanent interest in the copyright to the extent of two fifths, our calculation being that the £3. per thousand will leave about three fifths of the clear profit to you and two fifths to us or rather more if the book moves fast and the advertising is not necessarily heavy.

We propose to stereotype the book as selling in numbers; the stock would not otherwise be kept square, but when a new and revised edition was called for, we would break up the plates.

I hope this offer will be agreeable to you and independently of all monetary considerations it will give you real pleasure should the book prove, as I trust it will, a great success and a good thing for both author and publisher.

Believe me for self and brother,

Always yours truly
(signed)   John Blackwood.

G. H. Lewes Esqr
I am perfectly delighted with the article on Biot and will write with proof tomorrow or next day. Your style is as bright as the Frenchman's.

II, 502:7 JOHN BLACKWOOD TO GHL, EDINBURGH, 26 NOVEMBER 1858

Text: Copy in Blackwood Letter Book, National Library of Scotland.

Edinburgh November 26/58.

My Dear Lewes

Along with this I send a revise of the first part of the Physiology[1] which Mr. Brown[2] has read and makes one or two suggestions as you will see on the margin.

Your hearty acceptance of our offer gives us much pleasure and the feeling you show will add not a little to our satisfaction, should the book prove a great success, while it increases our anxiety to ensure the same.

Inclosed I have the pleasure of sending a cheque £14.14– in acknowledgement of your delightful little paper on Biot. In regard to the dates of payment to you for the Physiology we propose to pay you one hundred when the first number is published and the rest when it is completed, but if you wish the second payment sooner we will be happy to accommodate you. There is also the pleasant possibility of the sale in numbers going beyond 5000 which would accelerate payments and if it does sell above the 5000 in numbers we would make the payments correspond very much with the date of publication or half yearly.

Let us have the copy back soon for press. Tell G.E. that the sheets arrived safely and are sent to press. I think it is wise to lessen the quantity of the local dialect. We are rather puzzled to get on just at present as "Adam" and "What will He do with it"[3] are printing in the same type and from a want of return of proofs of the last there is about a ton and a half of Type locked up. This difficulty will however be overcome immediately.

Ever yours truly
(signed) John Blackwood.

G. H. Lewes, Esq.

1. *The Physiology of Common Life,* issued in monthly parts at 6d. No. 1 was "Hunger and Thirst."
2. John Crombie Brown, Blackwood proofreader, wrote *The Ethics of George Eliot,* 1879.
3. By Edward Bulwer Lytton, published under the pseudonym Pisistratus Caxton, 4 vols., 1859.

II, 502:7 GHL TO JOHN BLACKWOOD, RICHMOND, [28 NOVEMBER 1858]

MS: National Library of Scotland.

8 Park Shot | Richmond | Sunday.

My dear Blackwood

By this post goes the revise. I don't know who Mr. Brown is, but I am much obliged to him for his useful suggestions—as indeed I shall always be to any one. No matter how much trouble, the nearer we can get to satisfying the wants of the public the better.

Please send me a copy—no matter how rough—as soon as one is fairly ready. I have already two German Publishers wanting the right of translation, and to one of them I wish to send the number as a *specimen*.

Is Alison's Physiology[4] going through the press? Do you think the Professor would let me see his sheets as they are worked off? I shall be glad to have the benefit of them and glad to be able to quote them on occasion.

Ever faithfully yours
G. H. Lewes.

John Blackwood Esq.
I forgot to acknowledge the checque which was enclosed in your note.

II, 505:4 GHL TO THOMAS CARLYLE, RICHMOND, [NOVEMBER? 1858?]

MS: National Library of Scotland.

8 Park Shot | Richmond | Wednesday.

Dear Carlyle

I propose dropping in upon you on Friday evening; but as the distance between us is ten times as inconvenient as it is great, I let you know beforehand in case you may be engaged on that evening, and I have my journey for nothing. If you are to be at home, possibly you need not trouble yourself to write.

Ever faithfully yours,
G. H. Lewes.

---

4. William Pulteney Alison (1790–1859), *Outlines of Physiology and Pathology*, 1833, new ed. 1859.

[15 December 1858]

II, 509:1 GHL TO JOHN BLACKWOOD, RICHMOND, [15 DECEMBER 1858]

MS: National Library of Scotland.

8 Park Shot | Richmond | Wednesday.

My dear Blackwood

By this post I send parts 2 and 3 of copy of the Physiology. The two are sent together because, as they are of unequal length and I know not how to estimate fairly what they will print, I think it best to have the whole set up, and then we can divide properly.

What Mr. Simpson says of the trade expectation is very cheering. If the book succeeds at all it will doubtless succeed well and be a permanent thing.

Thank you for the copy of Alison's Physiology which I carried off the other day from Paternoster Row. I grieve to hear of the afflicted state of the admirable Professor.[5]

Ever faithfully yours
G. H. Lewes.

II, 512:5 GHL TO JOHN BLACKWOOD, RICHMOND, [27 DECEMBER 1858]

MS: National Library of Scotland. *Endorsed:* Mr. Lewes's arrangement will be adopted. Revise will be sent on Thursday.

8 Park Shot | Richmond | Monday.

My dear Blackwood

By this post go the proofs of Parts 2 and 3 of Phys. On reflection I think it eminently desirable to preserve the original divisions; that is to say, to make part 2 include the whole of the 1st section, and begin part 3 with section 2. It is true that part 2 thus becomes longer than the other —and longer than we ought to give for sixpence but *that* will be made up by the shortness of part 3.[6] The advantages are these. There is a completeness given to each number. There is so much argumentation in the early portions of part 2 that unless it be carried off by the details of the close, I fear our unphilosophical subscribers (and we shall have but a poor list

---

5. Two or three times in 1855–56 Alison suffered epileptic fits while lecturing; he resigned his chair as Professor of the Practice of Medicine at Edinburgh and retired.

6. Section 1 of "Food and Drink" ran to 68 pages; Section 2 to 42.

if we only include the philosophical) may find it uninteresting. Finally we get an illustration in the second part and that keeps up the idea of an illustrated work. The only disadvantage is the matter of length. Perpend!

I am just starting for Vernon Hill to spend my usual Christmas week with Helps; but shall be back again on Saturday. Remember me kindly to your brother, and With heartiest wishes—Christmassy and other—Believe me

Ever faithfully yours
G. H. Lewes.

John Blackwood Esq.

Adam Bede

1859 January 3   *Physiology of Common Life*, Part I, published.
1859 February 1   *Adam Bede*, 3 vols., published.
1859 March 9   Mrs. Gaskell admires GE's novels.
1859 April 1   GE thinks Owen not a good subject for article.
1859 April 15   Mme Bodichon sure *Adam Bede* is by Marian.
1859 May   George Meredith walks with GE and GHL.
1859 May 27   Blackwood dines with GE and GHL.
1859 June 30   Secrecy of the pseudonym is abandoned.
1859 August 17   Bessie Parkes writes to GE about *Adam Bede*.
1859 August 18   Thornton Lewes's first letter to new "Mother."
1859 September 11   Bridges explains part in betrayal of pseudonym.
1859 September 30   GE asks Brays to move her photograph.
1859 September 30   Spencer's praise of *Adam Bede* delights GE.
1859 November 21   Herbert Lewes's first letter to GE.

III, 3:19 GHL TO JOHN BLACKWOOD, RICHMOND, 3 JANUARY 1859

MS: Berg Collection, New York Public Library.

8 Park Shot | Richmond | 3 January 59.

My dear Blackwood

I returned yesterday with one eye bunged up and vision imperfect in the other, from cold—(*not* drink, nor fighting) but able nevertheless to read your letter and its enclosure viz. the first instalment (may there be many!) of the Phys. of Common Life.

By this post I send you a paper I have drawn up about a German criminal trial which greatly interested me. If you think it as interesting as I do you will put it in Maga—if not send it me back.[7]

When you see Aytoun pray tell him how much gratified I am by his flattering notice of my Goethe.[8] Quotation is one of the pleasantest testimonies a brother author can pay, when that brother is himself of eminence. May Aytoun's shadow never grow less!

Ever faithfully yours,
G. H. Lewes.

III, 4:6 MRS. EDWARD CLARKE TO ISAAC EVANS, [ATTLEBOROUGH, 6 JANUARY 1859]

MS: British Museum.

My dear Brother,

I should much prefer settling my bills myself—but as you do not approve of it I will send the accounts to you as soon as I can. I send you Emily's[9] school account and am very sorry she cannot go any longer she is very anxious to do something towards maintaining herself. Edward[1] is well, but I am in a constant state of anxiety about him.

---

7. "Falsely Accused: Trial in Nürnberg," *Blackwood's*, 85 (February 1859), 208–222.

8. Aytoun wrote: "His accomplished biographer, Mr. Lewes, has said of these, with equal truth and felicity of expression," followed by a long quotation. (W. E. Aytoun and Theodore Martin, *Poems and Ballads of Goethe,* 1859, p. vi.)

9. Emily Susannah Clarke (1844–1924). GE contributed to her schooling in 1855 and in 1859 paid also for her and her sister Catherine at Miss Eborall's School in Lichfield.

1. Edward Clarke (b. 1838) was working in Birmingham, but emigrated to Australia in 1861.

My cough and breathing are very bad I hope the weather is the cause. I hope Edith[2] is better, and with kindest love and best wishes to all, I am

Your affectionate sister
C. Clarke.

I was *45* Monday[3]—only 2 years younger than my Mother when she died.

III, 14:7 GHL TO JOHN BLACKWOOD, WANDSWORTH, [17 FEBRUARY 1859]

MS: National Library of Scotland.

Holly Lodge, Wimbledon Park | Southfields, Wandsworth | Thursday.
My dear Blackwood

The proof which goes herewith was addressed by one of your clerks to *Richmond*.

I send also "Digestion and Indigestion."[4] The cuts for this I presume you have received as the drawings were given out a long while ago; but Mr. Branston[5] has not shown me a single proof so that I am completely in the dark. "Food and Drink" part III[6] is I presume in the printers hands?

We are beginning now to get a little settled in our new home;[7] but 'tis a horrible business this moving, especially when your books are reckoned by thousands.

G.E. has received a charming letter from Owen, which he thinks you may like to read. You can return it when you have occasion to write.

Ever yours faithfully
G. H. Lewes.

John Blackwood Esq.

2. Edith, eldest daughter of Isaac Evans, later Mrs. William Griffiths.

3. GE's sister Christiana was born 3 January 1814.

4. Ch. 4 of *The Physiology of Common Life*, pp. 190–238, was not published first in *Blackwood's*.

5. Robert E. Branston, engraver, 36 St. Andrew's Hill, E.C.

6. Pp. 151–189.

7. GE and GHL moved to Holly Lodge 11 February 1859.

III, 28:1 GHL TO JOHN CHAPMAN, WANDSWORTH, [1 MARCH 1859]

MS: Yale.

Holly Lodge, Wimbledon Park | Southfields, Wandsworth | Tuesday.
My dear Chapman

I have written to Call to-day with my opinion—I am sorry to say *unfavorable*. With a great deal of good matter, the article wants a certain 'knack' in the writer to make it effective; and only a man of wit could make it amusing.[8]

I was very happy to be able to give to friendship the amount of time and trouble in this matter, the more so as I feel a good deal of sympathy with him. 'Tis no light matter to spend days and nights over an article to get in love with your subject and your execution of it, and then find it unacceptable in headquarters!

Believe me, Ever yours faithfully
G. H. Lewes.

We have already sold 6,000 of the Physiology—and the demand "steady."

III, 31:11 WILLIAM BLACKWOOD TO GHL, EDINBURGH, 9 MARCH 1859

Text: Blackwood Letter Book, National Library of Scotland.

45 George Street, Edinburgh 9. March 1859.
My Dear Lewes

We received yesterday the inclosed letter from Mr. Hargreaves[1] one of poor Johnston's executors. From it you will see that Johnston, short time as he lived after the completion of the Chemistry of Common Life,[2] had corrected a copy which has been only *now* sent to us. This delay is most provoking as from the glance I have given through the annotated copy, Johnston appears to have gone about the work systematically and to have collected many more interesting facts and illustrations for his various chapters which would have added greatly to the interest and éclat of a new edition both from their intrinsic merit and as being the last corrections of the Author.

8. "Call and Chapman having a dispute about an article on Wit and Humour referred it to me. Read the article and wrote to both with the verdict." (GHL Journal, 28 February 1859.)

1. J. G. Hargreaves
2. J. F. W. Johnston, *The Chemistry of Common Life*, 2 vols., in parts, 1853–55.

We send you this corrected copy and will feel obliged if you will look through it and give us your opinion as to whether any of the new matter can be given in an appendix or whether the whole should be reserved for another impression. All that has been done appears to me merely additional explanation and illustration, not correction of statements or opinions, so that we feel we can with perfect good faith reserve it. Nearly the whole of your edition is printed off so that it would be a very heavy sacrifice to cancel it. When we purchased from the executors about three years ago all the author's interest in this and his other works, we specially noticed to them the necessity there would be for corrected editions and how our having to calculate upon this was a matter we had to take into consideration in making our offer. We also inquired generally about the papers Johnston had left. We never thought therefore of applying again to them on the subject when we proposed to you to edit the Chemistry. With the writer of the inclosed we have not had correspondence but with his coexecutor Mr. Shields[3] we settled everything in the most friendly way about the estate and have occasionally corresponded since, so that we can only look upon our not having [had] sooner put into our hands the corrected copy as an unfortunate oversight.

III, 32:1 MRS. E. C. GASKELL TO JOHN BLACKWOOD, MANCHESTER, 9 MARCH [1859]

MS: National Library of Scotland. *Published:* J. A. V. Chapple and A. Pollard, *The Letters of Mrs. Gaskell*, Manchester, [1866], p. 533.

Plymouth Grove | March 9th.

Dear Sir

As you would learn from my letter yesterday I received the copy of "Adam Bede" which you were so kind as to send me quite safely; and I am very much obliged to you for it. I thoroughly admire this writer's works. (I do not call him Mr. Elliott, because I know that such is not his real name.) I was brought up in Warwickshire, and recognize the county in long description of natural scenery. I am thoroughly obliged to you for giving it me; it is a book that it is a real pleasure to have. And if for every article in your Magazine, abusive of me, you will only be so kind as to give me one of the works of the author of "Scenes from Clerical Life," I shall consider myself your debtor. You must have been mistaken, or I must

3. John Shields, of Claypath, Durham.

have explained myself badly, if you thought I believed that Mr. Aytoun wrote the review of C. Bronte.[4] I know the author's name perfectly well.

I do not remember the title of the article I wrote, and which you published long ago, in 1835 or '36 I think.[5] It was in the days of a very kind friend of mine who was then Editor—Professor Wilson. My article was a poem on a character whom I subsequently introduced into "Mary Barton"; and I remember it began

> "In childhood days I do remember me
> Of a dark house behind an old elm tree
> By gloomy streets surrounded" etc. etc.

It was worth very little; but I was very much pleased, and very proud to see it in print. I sent some articles, in prose, afterwards to Blackwood,—but they were, as I now feel, both poor and exaggerated in tone; and they were never inserted.

Once more let me thank you for your kindness. One of Mrs. Poyser's speeches is as good as a fresh blow of sea-air, and yet she is a true person, and no caricature.—But I could go on pointing out touches that delight me till you might think it an impertinence.

Yours very truly
E. C. Gaskell.

III, 33:1 WILLIAM BLACKWOOD TO GHL, EDINBURGH, 12 MARCH 1859

MS: National Library of Scotland. *Endorsed:* From the Major. *Extract published:* III, 33, n. 6.

45 George St. 12 March 1859.

My dear Lewes

Thanks for your note about Johnston's Chemistry. I am glad to find your opinions coincide with our own here that it is better to reserve altogether the author's additions for another impression.

The rest of the article on "Food and Drink" is rather short for the next number of the Physiology and we want 8 pp. more to make it of sufficient bulk. Will you be good enough to let us have them as soon as possible. You have had the proof of Digestion [and] Indigestion for some days I believe. I am glad to tell you the Physiology is selling very satisfactorily. A good feature in the sale is that number 1 is constantly asked for.

---

4. E. S. Dallas was the author of the review, "Currer Bell," *Blackwood's*, 82 (July 1857), 77–94.

5. "Sketches among the Poor. No. 1," 41 (January 1837), 48–50.

John has "Only a Pond."⁶ It will be Sunday reading for him, I have little doubt. He is off to golf, for his Saturday's amusement. Langford writes with his usual philosophical calmness, in the middle of a letter filled with details of little consequence, which has just come, "Mudie has just made up his number of Adam Bede to *1000*. Simpkins have sold their subscribed number and have had 12 today. Everyone is talking of the book." Your allusion to G. E's new tale excites strong interest.

Yours truly
W. Blackwood.

A copy of Mr. Tate's pamphlet⁷ has come to us for G.E. I send it you though I daresay he will not care to see it. John will be in London probably the end of next month or beginning of May.

G. H. Lewes, Esq.

III, 33:1 GHL TO WILLIAM BLACKWOOD, WANDSWORTH, [15 MARCH 1859]

MS: National Library of Scotland. *Endorsed:* /59.

Holly Lodge, Wimbledon Park | Southfields, Wandsworth | Tuesday.
My dear Major

The sight of a letter from Edinburgh always excites the pleasantest ideas in this house, for it is pretty sure to be the harbinger of good news or kindly feeling. "Hommes de relations charmantes—c'est le cas de le dire!" Your news is good—better—best.

Respecting "Food and Drink" however I have a sort of qualm. I thought we had agreed that some parts might be a little longer than others, and that of course implied a latitude the other way. If Part III of Food and Drink be somewhat short, the others were somewhat too long.⁸ It would damage Digestion and Indigestion to tag on 8 pages to Food and Drink—I mean that it would spoil the exposition, and hurt the sale of the particular part. If each number is more or less complete in itself, that is all the respected public cares about—quantity is quite a subordinate matter. So at least I think; but you can decide. Let me know.

The Digestion proof has been delayed because I sent it to a scientific friend for severe revision. I think he must be repeating the experiments he is so slow about it; but I don't "hurry no man's cattle."

6. "Only a Pond," *Blackwood's*, 85 (May 1859), 581–597.

7. Thomas Tate (1807–88), *The Philosophy of Education, or the Principles and Practice of Teaching*, 1854, 3d ed., 1860.

8. *The Physiology of Common Life*, ch. 2, "Food and Drink" was published in three sections of 58, 42, and 39 pp.

G.E. has been made very happy by your news; but like "Oliver Twist" he is for ever "asking for more." He seems to me a sort of obverse of that Roman Emperor who had a slave at his elbow to whisper constantly to him "Remember you are mortal"[9]—*he* wants a friend at his elbow to whisper "You see, George, you really are not a confounded Noodle, and the public *doesn't* think so."

Ever yours faithfully
G. H. Lewes.

III, 36:28 WILLIAM BLACKWOOD TO GHL, EDINBURGH, 18 MARCH 1859

Text: Copy in Blackwood Letter Book, National Library of Scotland.

Edinburgh 18 March 1859.

My dear Lewes

We have printed off No. 4 without *Digestion and Indigestion*. We are not sure however that the public may not grumble at such a thin 6d worth.

Try and keep the parts as near to forty eight (48) pages as possible. There are numerous practical inconveniences, and expense too, attending the variation in size of the numbers, and at the same time I see the unsatisfactoriness to the author in particular of issuing the subjects in so disjointed a form as the taking in of 8 introductory pages of a new subject at the end of an old one merely to make the part of the required number of pages. Still purchasers look so much to quantity as well as quality that Mr. Simpson thinks they won't be satisfied with 40 pp. for their sixpences one month although they get 60 the next. The stupidity of the public in this way is hopeless.

With the original issue of Johnston's Chemistry we looked only to the completeness of the parts and in consequence had to vary the price of each. This we found very troublesome and hurtful to some extent to the sales as the *dealers* said their subscribers grumbled at the variation in price. It would be a considerable convenience to us if you could keep us well ahead in the printing office with *copy*. It would also leave time for considering any difficulty about extent of a number.

Yours faithfully
(signed)   W. Blackwood.

G. H. Lewes Esq.
Inclosed is a letter from Williams and Norgate. We do not concur in Mr. Tauchnitz's opinion that he cannot expect such a success for A.B.

9. Phocylides, *Sententiae*, 109.

in Germany as a less English novel would have and think he ought to give a good deal more than he gave for Clerical Scenes. Let us know what G.E. thinks he ought to have.

III, 38:22   GHL TO EDWARD F. S. PIGOTT, WANDSWORTH, [21 MARCH 1859]

MS: Mr. Gordon N. Ray.

Holly Lodge, Wimbledon Park | Southfields, Wandsworth | Monday.
My dear Pigott

You may imagine how sorry we were on our return to find your card;[1] but how *could* you have been so imprudent, after getting no answer from me to your note?

To make up let us say *next Saturday*—if that will suit you and Redford[2] whom we shall both be very glad to see again. If Saturday will not suit both fix some other day, but please let me know in time that I may not be in town, or have accepted any other engagement.

If you come to *Putney* station leaving Waterloo at 2.15 we will meet you there, and walk over the delicious Wimbledon Common through the Park here. I name Putney because the price is the same and the road is so much prettier. Let me know whether this hour suits, or whether you prefer the *3.15.—*

Mind both of you bring Music and let us make the welkin ring.

Ever yours faithfully
G. H. L.

III, 40:29   JOHN BLACKWOOD TO GHL, EDINBURGH, 30 MARCH 1859

Text: Blackwood Letter Book, National Library of Scotland.

Edinburgh | March 30th/59.
My Dear Lewes

I enclose a letter for G.E. with continued good accounts of Adam. I am curious to know how he likes the Magazine paper. I was so overwhelmed with M.S.S. this month that I had nothing for it but to postpone the Ponds which will not become stale by the delay.

Stereos from the cuts in the Physiology are being taken for Brockhaus

---

1. "We went into town to look after a servant, and order some toggery." (GHL Journal, 19 March 1859.)
2. George Redford. See III, 178.

and duplicates will be done at once from the rest of the cuts. How had we best send these as well as the two copies of the book?

Do you ever see anything of Professor Owen now? I sometimes think of a paper on him and his discoveries. I am afraid you would be too heathenish for me. I was remembered of him today by receiving a sort of Abstract of a lecture of his on the Gorilla[3] one of these confounded monkey tribes so disgustingly like ourselves. I know very little of Owen but what I do I admire very much. Scientific men are so often either too dull or too trifling, but he is entirely free from any of these faults.

ever yours truly,
John Blackwood.

G. H. Lewes Esq.

III, 42:1 GHL TO JOHN BLACKWOOD, WANDSWORTH, 1 APRIL 1859

MS: National Library of Scotland.

Holly Lodge, Southfields | 1 April 1859.

My dear Blackwood

I don't know how far my heathenism might be an objection to my writing an article on Owen and his Discoveries, but I know that my ignorance would be a very formidable objection against such an attempt. Indeed there are *very* few men in England at all competent; the paleontologists are not sufficiently versed in comparative anatomy and the anatomists seldom know enough of paleontology.

Moreover I doubt whether an interesting paper could be written on Owen at the present time; all that would interest the public has been told over and over again—quite recently in the North British and Quarterly Reviews.[4] I so greatly admire and like Owen, that I would rejoice at all honor he might anywhere receive; but I don't think he affords you or me a chance just now, of expressing more than a general admiration.

If you will tell Langford to put himself in communication with Trübner on Brockhaus's affairs (Trübner acts as his agent) I will write to Leipzig today to send them word to that effect.[5] I concluded that "Ponds" had swamped you, by my not getting a proof.

---

3. Richard Owen, *On the Gorilla*, a lecture delivered at the Royal Institution, 4 February 1859.

4. "The British Museum," *Quarterly Review*, 207 (July 1858), 201–224, discussed the difficulties of Owen's supervision of the Natural History department under the Principal Librarian [Panizzi], and urged the formation of a separate institution with Owen as its head.

5. The German translation of *The Physiology of Common Life*, for which Brockhaus paid GHL £50.

Should the "Thunderer"[6] nod and shake Olympus, please remember we don't see that majestic person. I observe the West. Rev. has a long article on "Adam Bede." The more the merrier. Plus on est de fous et plus on rit.[7]

By the way I must tell you of an honor which has come to your physiologist—Victor Carus,[8] a celebrated German Anatomist, has offered to translate the "Physiology" for Brockhaus. *That* will have good effect on our public, when known, meanwhile it is a pleasant tribute.

Ever faithfully yours,
G. H. Lewes.

III, 43:16 JOHN BLACKWOOD TO GHL, EDINBURGH, 6 APRIL 1859

Text: Copy in Blackwood Letter Book, National Library of Scotland.

Edinburgh | April 6/59.

My dear Lewes

I think you are mistaken about Owen as I have frequently observed that people generally have a notion that he has done a great deal but nothing like precise knowledge of what it is. That you are mistaken in thinking yourself unfitted for reviewing his discourses I feel certain. You are quite the sort of man to do the thing. The papers in Quarterlies do not much matter.

By the way when you see him ask if in his present state of existence he will ever be able to review Keith Johnston's Physical Atlas. He said he would do so, some years ago but I fear he will always be too busy.

Let G.E. know that I am told there is to be a most enthusiastic Review of Adam in the North British.[9] I should not wonder if it were by our friend Dr. John Brown, "the worshipper of genius" as we call him.

Ever yours truly
John Blackwood.

G. H. Lewes Esq.

This is a lovely summer day and I grudge consummately not being in the country.

---

6. *The Times*, which reviewed *Adam Bede* 12 April 1859.

7. GHL was less happy after he read this article by John Chapman, 71 (April 1859), 486–512. Having wormed the secret out of Herbert Spencer, Chapman hinted at the author's not being "of the masculine gender." (p. 510.)

8. Julius Viktor Carus (1823–1903).

9. *North British Review*, 30 (April 1859), 502–564. The reviewer was troubled by Hetty, "the dark shadow lying athwart the tale."

III, 50:21   MME EUGENE BODICHON TO GE, [ALGIERS, 15? APRIL 1859]

MS: Yale. *Address:* Mrs. Lewes | Holly Lodge | Wimbledon | Wandsworth. *No postmarks: probably enclosed with another letter.*

My dear Marian

We have bought this house and 12 acres of land for £800 so congratulate me please when I come to see you on the 3d Sunday in June which is my intention as at present advised so keep it clear for me and you need not trouble yourself to write if you are not inclined before that time. We are jollier and jollier every day only I [am] sorry when he says he won't go to England.

Now I read the "Deux freres"[1] and it disagrees with me as much as tother and that reminds me of a book which causes our society to be convulsed and to feel something deep I judge by my sisters letters so I have sent for Adam Bede believing by a passage I read in a review that it must be written by somebody wise and tender as you.

The weather is so beautiful now and the white iris in our garden at sunrise (500 of them) are more beautiful than angels. There you see a long troop—over their heads the blue sea and over and beyond and afar from that the peaks of pure snow or rather rock ice, pure as the white iris, are glowing in rosey light yet the colour of these mountains is purer and more marvellous. Such a delicious melody of colour it is. [*The rest is lacking.*]

III, 51:25   W. BLACKWOOD TO J. H. LANGFORD, EDINBURGH, 16 APRIL 1859

MS: National Library of Scotland.

Edinburgh 16 April/59.

My dear Sir

I have the pleasure to inclose a cheque for two months' salary. The accounts of the demand for Adam Bede are very gratifying, and there can be little doubt but that edition number 2 will be out of print very soon. We have got the type of one volume standing,[2] and have ordered the remainder to be set up again immediately. When the public attention

1. Alphonse Brot, *Les Deux Frères,* Paris, [1859?].   2. Presumably Vol. III.

is once fairly attracted to such a book its sale must be very great. I have not heard of a single person who has read it who has not expressed perfect satisfaction with it. Syme the eminent Surgeon[3] here and Professor Simpson[4] are as warm in their eulogy of it as Theodore Martin, so that we may calculate on every reader who is attracted to the book by the Times still further extending it's reputation.

I had a letter from Mr. Crawley[5] two days ago soliciting an increase of salary. We have always entertained a favourable opinion of his ability and exertions for the business—and understood that he has given you perfect satisfaction. We have therefore raised his salary to £120 a year.

Yours sincerely
W. Blackwood.

Our balance is rather small at Coutts' at present; pay in a little in the beginning of the week.

J. H. Langford, Esq.

III, 60:1 GHL TO JOHN BLACKWOOD, WANDSWORTH, [28 APRIL 1859]

MS: National Library of Scotland.

Holly Lodge | Thursday.

My dear Blackwood

The checque arrived yesterday while I was in town. Many thanks. But you make me uncomfortable about your printers shouting for copy. More than a fortnight ago I sent back the *revise* of *Digestion and Indigestion*, which will appear in May. The two next parts in revise have also been sent to me, and I return one by this post. Is it possible that you have not received *Digestion?* I should be much obliged to Mr. Simpson if he would keep me regularly informed respecting the progress and wants of copy and proofs. *I* won't be behind hand; but I like to retain copy and proofs as late as possible in order that the book may have the benefit of the very *latest* discoveries, or revision. The whole m.s. is done; but is constantly being altered, and added to; and this will be the case as long as there is a chance left.

I am exceedingly happy to find that the book is producing an impres-

---

3. James Syme (1799–1870), Professor of Surgery at Edinburgh University.
4. James Young Simpson (1811–70), Professor of Midwifry at Edinburgh University.
5. Samuel Crawley, long in Blackwoods' employ.

sion among eminent medical men, and that the articles in Maga were much talked of, and have been quoted by the profession. This must affect the general public. If we can secure a reputation sale will inevitably follow.

A letter from Algiers today[6] informs us that "there is a work which seems to have convulsed English society" (of the higher class) and accordingly it has been sent for by our correspondent. She says it is "Adam Bede." Do you know of such a book?

Ever faithfully
G. H. Lewes.

III, 61:19   GHL TO EDWARD F. S. PIGOTT, WANDSWORTH, [6 MAY 1859]

MS: Mr. Gordon N. Ray.

Holly Lodge | Friday.

My dear Pigott

It is unfortunate that you should have delayed your welcome visit until just as we are "on the wing"—*whither* we know not, nor for how *long*—but only a few days,[7] our health being *very* far from satisfactory. *Not* Saturday therefore!

When we return I will ask you and Redford to dédommager us. It is an age since we chatted and chaunted together!

I began to be alarmed about myself the other day, for I fainted dead away suddenly, without *any* premonitory symptom.[8] Whether head or stomach, or both were in fault I know not; but it made me grave.

Capital news from Hofwyl and the best of all news from Edinburgh.

With our kind regards to both, Believe me ever yours

G. H. Lewes.

6. Barbara Bodichon's first letter, [15? April 1859].

7. They took long rambles about Wimbledon and drove to Dulwich, Tooting, Clapham, and Streatham, but were not away from home over night. (GHL Journal.)

8. See III, 61.

III, 68:17 GHL TO EDWARD F. S. PIGOTT, WANDSWORTH, [18 MAY 1859]

MS: Mr. Gordon N. Ray.

Holly Lodge, Wimbledon Park | Southfields Wandsworth | Wednesday.
My dear Pigott

One cause after another has delayed our expedition[9] but as we shall be here next Saturday I hope you and Redford are disengaged on that day and can run down.

As I am very busy I will ask you to come by the *3.15* train from Waterloo to *Putney* (same price as Wandsworth and much pleasanter route), and if you will promise to come by that train I will come and meet you and take you a walk to reach this.[1] If you can't undertake to be *punctual*—this is your route:

On coming up the Putney steps turn sharp round to your *left* and continue down the lane, the 2nd turning on the *right* will bring you to Holly Lodge, which is the last house but three near the Park.[2]

Ever yours truly
G. H. Lewes.

9. To Switzerland, where GE was to stay with the Congreves while GHL visited his sons at Hofwyl.

1. Holly Lodge, now 32 Wimbledon Park Road, marked with a blue plaque recording GE's residence there, is described by my friend Frank Miles as "a flat-chested, undistinguished building, consisting of a twin Victorian construction, with the two front doors side by side in the middle."

2. At Wandsworth GE and GHL saw George Meredith several times. His wife having deserted him, Meredith was living in Chelsea with his young son and often walked down to Wimbledon. GHL met him at Frederic Chapman's and had a pleasant chat with him 26 February 1859. On 6 March: "During my ramble I met George Meredith who strolled with me over Wimbledon Common." On Sunday, 29 May: "George Meredith called as we were setting out for our walk and accompanied us; but we were driven back sooner than usual by a storm. He dined and spent the day with us, producing an impression of considerable weariness on both." On 2 July 1859 GHL notes his reading "To myself 'The Ordeal of Richard Feverel.'" GE noted in her Journal 27 November 1859: "Mr. Meredith brought his little boy to see me—a nice little fellow; and we had a Sunday walk together."

III, 70:5 GHL TO JOHN BLACKWOOD,
[WANDSWORTH, 21 MAY 1859]

MS: Berg Collection, New York Public Library.

Saturday.

My dear Blackwood

Enclosed is a letter from G.E. Observe: the *Putney* station is the pleasantest and quite as near as Wandsworth. On coming up the steps at Putney, turn round to your left, at the corner, by the butcher, and keep straight on, down the lane, till you come to a turning (the 2nd on your right) having a finger post "To Wimbledon Park Road." *This* turning will bring you to Holly Lodge, which is the last villa but three on the left.

We dine at $\frac{1}{2}$ past 5, but as much sooner as you can contrive to come by so much the more welcome will you be. Drop me a line to say what day, in order that no other visitor may be admitted.

Ever yours faithfully,
G. H. L.

III, 73:1 GHL TO JOHN BLACKWOOD,
WANDSWORTH, [24 MAY 1859]

MS: National Library of Scotland.

Holly Lodge | Tuesday evening.

My dear Blackwood

We shall be out tomorrow. Can you make it Thursday instead? If not name any day except Sunday or Monday.

In haste ever yours
G. H. Lewes.

III, 73:21 GHL TO JOHN BLACKWOOD,
WANDSWORTH, [25 MAY 1859]

MS: National Library of Scotland.

Holly Lodge.

My dear Blackwood

Come by all means any time you like.

Yours ever
G. H. Lewes.

III, 73:21 GHL TO JOHN BLACKWOOD, WANDSWORTH, [26 MAY 1859]

MS: National Library of Scotland.

                      Holly Lodge, Wimbledon Park | Thursday.

My dear Blackwood

We shall expect you tomorrow, and a letter for your venerable correspondent[3] will be ready.

E. begs me to add that he accepts the proposition made in your last.

                                              Ever yours
                                                  G. H. L.

III, 90:1 GHL TO JOHN BLACKWOOD, WANDSWORTH, [21 JUNE 1859]

MS: National Library of Scotland.

                                      Holly Lodge | Tuesday.

My dear Blackwood

Your letter has given *great* pleasure. We have friends[4] coming on Thursday; so will you come on *Saturday*—either to lunch or dinner, or both—at your convenience.

                                          In desperate haste
                                                  G. H. L.

III, 104:1 ANNIE LEIGH SMITH TO GE, LONDON [29 JUNE 1859]

MS: Yale.

                                                5 Blandford Square.

My dear George Elliott,

Yesterday I should have sent my picture[5] without a word or a name, afraid as an unacknowledged artist, of being impertinent; today I send it, with pleasure a thousand-fold greater and with thanks unlimited for the

---

3. Probably Professor W. E. Aytoun, whose letter about *Adam Bede* Blackwood sent to GE 25 May 1859.

4. The Brays and Sara Hennell.
5. See III, 107.

[4 July 1859]

glorious satisfaction it is to know *you* as the author of the most inspiring novel of the age.

I can never tell you how glad I am, but I hope you will believe that I am always gratefully yours

Annie Leigh Smith.

III, 107:6 GHL TO CHARLES BRAY, WANDSWORTH, [30 JUNE 1859]

MS: Yale.

Holly Lodge | Thursday.

My dear Bray

We have resolved to keep the secret no longer. In aristocratic and literary circles the conviction has become general—and as thanks (or no thanks) to Spencer all the Garrick Club have his authority for the belief —he having volunteered to tell Pigott that " he knew the authoress and has seen her recently" (Call you *that* keeping a secret solemnly entrusted to you alone?), it is hopeless for us to do anything now. So you may tell any one you please that it is no longer a secret at all; but *avowed.*

Ever yours faithfully,
The husband of
George Eliot.

III, 110:17 GHL TO WILLIAM BLACKWOOD, WANDSWORTH, [4 JULY 1859]

MS: National Library of Scotland.

Holly Lodge | Wandsworth | Monday.

My dear Major

I send another chapter; and the *final* chapter[6] will be sent on Wednesday, if no headache intervenes to delay it.

Sheets E. and F.[7] arrived today, but tell Mr. Simpson that they did *not* arrive before, and that the parcel had no appearance of having been opened.

We hope to be off on Saturday.

Ever yours faithfully
G. H. L.

6. *The Physiology of Common Life*, ch. 12, "The Qualities We Inherit from Our Parents," II, 372–411, and ch. 13, "Life and Death," II, 412–454.
7. II, 65–96.

III, 112:1 GHL TO MME EUGÈNE BODICHON, WANDSWORTH, [5 JULY 1859]

MS: Mr. Gordon N. Ray.

Holly Lodge, Tuesday morning.

My dear Barbara

My mother bids me bind my hair[8]—(no not that, because I'm getting bald) Polly bids me bind myself to the desk, and write a note for her. To hear is to obey—under penalty of a milkjug whirling in the air.—

The purport of said note is this: She wants to write to your sister to thank her for the picture; but as you don't send said picture her letter is unconscionably delayed.

Dispatch. With P's love,

Ever yours faithfully
Sir John Brute.[9]

III, 114:1 GE TO ANNIE LEIGH SMITH, [WANDSWORTH, 8? JULY 1859]

Text: Copy owned by Mr. Douglas C. Ewing.

My dear Miss S

You are the first person in the world, the world as distinguished among my very few intimates, who has said to me—"I am more glad of Adam Bede because it is yours." I tell you that because there are moments in all our lives when we find it a comfort to remember the instances in which we have been able to help another by word or deed. And when such moments come upon you, remember this act of yours in writing me that kind letter at the right season.

And now the picture[1] is come—a charming bit of color for my eye to rest on in the pauses of my writing. I wanted something pretty before me very much, and now I have it.

The picture too turns out to have a symbolism perfectly fitted for my case, for after it came yesterday I had reason to foresee the great need I

---

8. Anne Hunter (1742–1821), *Poems,* 1802, p. 110.

9. Sir John Brute in Vanbrugh's *The Provoked Wife* (1697) was one of Garrick's famous parts.

1. Annie Leigh Smith, Barbara's sister, sent GE "a charming water colour as a tribute of admiration." (GHL Journal, 2 July 1859.)

6 August 1859 239

should have of the Princess Parizade's² cotton wool in my ears, lest certain noises should distract me from going steadily along my way. It is a beautiful story and you could not have given me a happier suggestion. I thank you. You will always be gratefully remembered by

[*signature lacking.*]

III, 120:1 GE TO MME EUGÈNE BODICHON, [WANDSWORTH, 23? JULY 1859]

MS: Berg Collection, New York Public Library. *Written on flap of envelope; no postmark.*

George Eliot presents his compliments to Mde Bodichon and begs to grumble at having to return these caricatures.³ He finds the human race divided into two classes: those who never thought of doing him a pleasure, and those who, on second thoughts, refrain.

III, 128:5 CHARLES DICKENS TO GHL, HIGHAM, 6 AUGUST 1859

Text: The Letters of Charles Dickens, ed. Walter Dexter, 3 vols., 1938, III, 115.

Gad's Hill Place, Higham By Rochester | Kent.
Saturday Sixth August 1859.

My dear Lewes,—

The receipt of your note⁴ has given me real pleasure; but I am afraid I cannot have the greater pleasure yet, of responding to it in person, until I return to town for the winter.

I have not been quite well since we had the great summer heat—a circumstance so unusual with me, that I have been lost in indignant surprise. Being very busy besides I only go to town to the office on the

2. Copy reads "Penizade." The Princess Parizadê, heroine of "The Two Sisters," the last tale in the *Arabian Nights*, "stopped her ears so hard with cotton wool that she was not distracted by the threatening voices and secured the talking bird, the golden water, and the singing tree." (4 vols., 1825, IV, 359.)

3. One caricature not returned shows Liggins biting his pen and with a cat on each shoulder; it is entitled: "Popular idea of George Elliott, in the act of composing 'Adam Bede.'" (Yale.) For Joseph Liggins, the impostor who claimed to be the author of *Adam Bede*, see III, 21 and 110.

4. Not found. GE had been reading aloud *A Tale of Two Cities* and some early chapters of *The Mill on the Floss*. (GHL Journal.)

days when my presence there is necessary, and immediately return to work here. Thus, I do not think that I should be able to get to Wandsworth, until I go into winter quarters at Tavistock House.

But I will not fail, you may be sure, to propose myself when the opportunity is nearest to my reach and in the meantime I hope you and George Eliot will hold me in your kind remembrances.

Faithfully yours always
Charles Dickens.

P.S. I have a horrible and unnatural desire upon me to see Liggins, whom, I am proud to remember I contemptuously rejected.

III, 133:26 GHL TO JOHN BLACKWOOD, WANDSWORTH, 17 AUGUST [1859]

MS: Berg Collection, New York Public Library. *Extract published: John Blackwood,* p. 56.

Holly Lodge | Southfields, Wandsworth | August 17th.

My dear Blackwood

The proof I return to .Edinburgh, as the shortest route.

Owen[5] I will ponder on; and Nature's Seaweeds—with the materials from Bradbury[6]—may turn out a practicable article. It is true I know as little as possible about seaweeds, for one who has had so much to do with them. But what then? Is a reviewer called upon to know anything? doesn't he know everything in virtue of his egotism? If facts fail him, is there not the moral consciousness out of the depths of which he can construct immense wisdom? "Base is the slave who *knows*"![7]

Your picture of your daily life is suggestive of pleasant hours; but I see you don't turn the dogs to account. Four dogs! my dear fellow, how *can* four dogs be without attraction? I would rather hear Mrs. Blackwood's opinion on that point, not believing in your ability to edit a dog. Perhaps the dull dogs have wearied you with too many contributions to make you appreciate justly the genus dog. When you have seen Pug your mind will be more expanded, your sensibilities heightened. Till then believe me

Ever your canine
G. H. Lewes

5. Blackwood first broached the possibility of an article on Richard Owen 30 March 1859, and returned to it several times.

6. See III, 145, n. 8.

7. Cf. *Henry V*, II, i, 100: "Base is the slave that pays."

17 August 1859

III, 133:26 BESSIE RAYNER PARKES TO GE, LOWESTOFT, 17 AUGUST 1859

MS: Yale. *Extracts published:* III, 134.

Lowestoft. August 17. 1859.

My very dear Friend

How many days since Barbara told me that the Famous Unknown was my Marian have I been intending to write to her; and how often have I been been so overwhelmed with each days correspondence as to feel the writing of a letter to my Friend next to an impossibility.

This is the true reason why everything like private correspondence drops more and more out of my hand, and must do so until my work is so far organised that I can retreat from the incessant labor it imposes in this particular direction. I am doubly anxious that *you* should understand this, since our personal opportunities of intercourse are at present so few and far between.

Dearest Marian, remembering as I do, day after day, in which you used to say with a sort of dispair, "I have no creative power" it is with an amused delight that I see you take all England by storm as you have done.

On me, much as I like Adam Bede, the other stories made a profounder impression. In particular Janets Repentance but all the three seemed to me masterpieces when I read them a year ago; full of a quaint touching beauty that I have never seen surpassed.

I am up here for 3 or 4 days with Lady Monson,[8] more on business than pleasure, as she is closely concerned in the Princes St. work.[9] She begs I will give her *thanks* to the Authoress of Adam Bede. I daresay you know who Lady M. is; a very clear-headed stronghearted woman, whom I hope you will some day know personally.

I am going on to Norwich, on business; then to my parents at Deal. By the bye Mama was so intensely delighted at Mrs. Poysers tongue; laughed till she cried; you know my Mothers hearty nature, and how keenly she relishes wit and humour.

I think I have given you our new address since we left Savile Row; 17 Wimpole St. Cavendish Sq. Office letters are opened, unless you put "private" outside; then they are forwarded.

8. See II, 84, n. 7.
9. The office of the *Englishwoman's Journal*, which Bessie edited, at 14A Prince's St., Cavendish Square.

Give my kind regard to Mr. Lewes. I find Lady M. enjoying his seaside book immensely, she reads bits out to me with great gusto. Ever dear,

> Your loving
> Bessie.

III, 133:26 THORNTON ARNOTT LEWES TO GE, HOFWYL, 18 AUGUST 1859

MS: Yale. *Fragments published:* Paterson, p. 73.

> Hofwyl the 18th August 1859.

Dear Mother,[1]

For the first time do I seize the pen to begin a correspondence which is to be lasting, and which affords me much pleasure, and answer your letter to Charlie. We received your letter at St. Moriz in the canton of the Grisons, some three hours walk from Italy. You can imagine how glad we were to get it, as being the first from you. It put a touch to our happiness on the journey.

As I suppose you will like to hear something about the journey, I will give you a short description of it. . . .

I am much obliged to you for your 10 frs. and also for the book of butterflies. In my next I will send you an impression of some butterflies, but can not this time because I am not yet in order from the confusion of the journey. Tell ⟨Papa⟩ Father that the old brute of a Dr. Stamm has been convicted of stealing silver spoons, and will therefore of course never return. If you happen to have many letters, stamps from foreign countries, I shall be very glad if you send me them for my collection.

I have nothing more to say. So with kind love and kisses to Papa and yourself, I remain, Dear Mother,

> Your affectionate Son
> Thornton Arnott Lewes.

Charlie and I both like A. B. very much. When you receive a letter from me, if at the bottom of the envelope there is a p.M. = pro Matre, it is for you, if not, it is for Father.

1. GHL came to Hofwyl 13 July 1859 and told his sons about Agnes. This is Thornton's first letter to his new "Mother." See III, 115–116.

III, 151:1 GHL TO EDWARD F. S. PIGOTT, WEYMOUTH, [11 SEPTEMBER 1859]

MS: Mr. Gordon N. Ray.

39 East Street | Weymouth | Sunday.

My dear Pigott

Your letter has been forwarded here. By not getting an answer you will I hope have concluded that we were away. But we shall leave this on Friday morning and although it is uncertain whether we shall loiter on the way or proceed home at once, it is certain we shall be home next week. Now on Saturday the 24th you will still be in town, won't you? If so, suppose you ⟨and George⟩ come and meet Fred Chapman (of Chapman and Hall) whom I intend asking down one day—and let *that* be the day?

Is Wilkie Collins in town? If he is, ask him whether he will accompany you—both George Eliot and myself will be very glad to see him once more.[2]

Let me know in time to ask Fred Chapman. If you write *after* Thursday morning address to Wandsworth. In haste

Ever yours
G. H. Lewes.

Wilkie will not mind the informality of this invitation I hope. He must hate writing letters as much as I do.

III, 151:1 J. H. BRIDGES[3] TO GE, PARIS, 11 SEPTEMBER [1859]

MS: Yale.

Hôtel des Américains Rue Quatre Vents Paris | September 11th.

My dear Mrs. Lewes,

I see from the English papers that the authorship of Adam Bede is no longer a secret. Will you let me trouble you with two words on a subject of which perhaps you are long ago wearied?

I gather from the Congreves that you are not without an impression that Dr. Chapman communicated his belief on the subject to me, and I to him. In justice to both of us let me state the truth of the matter.

---

2. George Redford (see III, 178, n. 7), Pigott, and Wilkie Collins came to Wandsworth 24 September 1859. The last two had dined with them at Richmond 10 November 1858.

3. See III, 238, n. 6.

Whilst Adam Bede was the topic of conversation in Albion Street[4] I frequently heard Dr. and Mrs. Chapman express to one another their conviction that they knew the author. It was also evident from Dr. Chapman's article[5] that he did not think it was written by a man, but by a woman. Now as he professed to have considerable acquaintance with the author and frequently expressed his conviction that there was but one person who could have written it, I certainly ⟨came to the conviction coupling their written⟩ did couple these remarks with others that he had made at other times with reference to you—and as I happened to have heard that you had lived in the Midland Counties, I arrived altogether at an inference which I communicated to the Congreves, just for what it was worth. Dr. Chapman had told me nothing whatever.

It is therefore clear that neither has Dr. Chapman violated your confidence nor I his. Though I am quite unable to share in the views about anonymous writing expressed in a letter of 'George Eliot's' to the Times, I attach great importance to this explanation and the more so because I gathered from certain remarks of Dr. Chapman, as well as from some of yours, that there was already some misunderstanding, of what nature I know not. It would excessively grieve me to have been the means of increasing this.

I would much rather have filled this letter with explanations of my gratitude to yourself for your beautiful creation. Having lived all my life among the English peasantry, and spent months of childhood inside farmhouses, I as well as my sister were really delighted to find an existence hitherto quite neglected as unromantic and unpoetic thoroughly understood and portrayed by so true a painter. On the higher qualities of the book I shall not take the liberty of expressing any judgment.

I do not apologize for this letter as I am sure you will have the justice to see that it was desirable. I very much regret to hear from the Congreves that you think of leaving Wandsworth. Believe me,

Sincerely yours
J. H. Bridges.

4. Bridges, at this time a medical student, lived with the Chapmans at 1 Albion Street.

5. "Adam Bede," *Westminster Review*, 71 (April 1859), 486–512.

III, 169:16 GHL TO CHARLES BRAY, WANDSWORTH, [30 SEPTEMBER 1859]

MS: Yale.

Holly Lodge | Friday.

My dear Bray

Your Mr. Bracebridge seems to me a shuffler as well as a fool. I don't believe a word the man says; and I think a miserable vanity is at the bottom of his efforts. I have written him a stinger; and brought him to four distinct questions.

Marian begs me to say that in friendship to her she wishes you would remove her portrait from the dining room and place it in your bedroom.

She is horribly worried, and will leave England altogether I think if fools obtrude themselves more upon her.

Ever yours
G. H. L.

III, 169:16 HERBERT SPENCER TO GE, DERBY, 30 SEPTEMBER 1859

MS: British Museum.

17 Wilmot Street, Derby, | 30 September 59.

Dear Friend

At length I have read Adam Bede—finished it last night in considerable alarm at the probable consequences of having read a volume and a half in the day: consequences however which were not so bad as I expected.

It *was* true that when I got it at Derby immediately on its publication, I was obliged to speedily relinquish it by a state which forbad reading. It *was* true that while in town I made many fruitless efforts to get a copy. It *was* true that on my return to Derby I was delayed in getting a copy until just when the conclusion of the article on Geology[6] had brought on an attack of giddiness, which greatly alarmed me. And it *is* true that since that time I have until now had no opportunity of getting hold of it.

And now that I have read it what am I to say. That I have read it with laughter and tears and without criticism. Knowing as you do how

---

6. "Illogical Geology," *Universal Review* (July 1859), was dictated at Derby in June 1859. (David Duncan, *The Life and Letters of Herbert Spencer*, [1908], pp. 95, 581.)

constitutionally I am given to fault finding, you will understand what this means. That I who am so little given to enthusiastic admiration, should not know how adequately to say how much I admire, will give you some idea of my feeling respecting it. It comes up to my ideal of a work of art—possesses *all* the requisite qualities in due balance; which is more than I can say of any fiction I ever read. But especially I am delighted with its thorough genuineness. Every bit of dialogue gives one the impression of its having been actually spoken; and all the little details of event and description have that kinship to the scene which ⟨give one⟩ produce the impression of being an eye-witness. I find too that its beauties are much more numerous than can be taken in at a first reading. Various passages which I have re-read this morning delight me more even than they did at first. And then let me not forget the moral effect. I feel greatly the better for having read it; and can scarcely imagine any one reading it without having their sympathies widened and their better resolves strengthened. Not only in the interests of literature but in the interests of progress I hope that we shall have many more such books from you.[7]

I have been much annoyed by the misunderstanding that has recently been disclosed.[8] I should feel it as a serious misfortune if anything were to dissolve our friendship. That I had given any reasons for such suspicions as those you and Lewes entertained I was quite unaware. When in town I had been to see you as often as I thought you would like, though not so often as I should have liked myself; and I did not know that my manner had altered. Taking for granted however that you are more likely to be good judges on that point than I am, I may name what seems a probable explanation. During the last 18 months I have been ⟨more than usual⟩ much away from town; and from that and perhaps other causes we have seen less of each other than usual. Now I always find that after much absence I contract a certain awkward restraint in behaviour towards friends, which it takes some little time to rub off; and perhaps when, after such absence, I see them but seldom and for a short time, it does

---

7. As a member of the Committee of the London Library Spencer is said to have opposed the inclusion of novels— "except, of course, those of George Eliot."

8. Spencer had been intrusted with the secret of GE's pseudonym, which John Chapman, puzzled at her refusal to write for the *Westminster Review*, wormed out of him. (See Spencer, *Autobiography*, II, 38.) When Spencer came to dine with GE and GHL, 5 November 1858, he "brought the unpleasant news that Dr. Chapman had asked him point blank if I wrote the Clerical Scenes. I wrote at once to the latter to check further gossip on the subject." (GE Journal, 5 November 1858.) After the publication of *Adam Bede* in February 1859, the coolness increased. For GHL's account in his Journal, 24 March 1859, see III, 49, n. 6.

not get rubbed off at all. This is the only cause I can conceive for the change of behaviour of which I was unconscious.

Yours as ever | very sincerely
Herbert Spencer.

III, 170:5 GE TO HERBERT SPENCER, WANDSWORTH, 2 OCTOBER 1859

MS: British Museum. *Published: Bulletin of the New York Public Library*, 79 (Spring 1976), 370–371.

Holly Lodge, South Fields | Wandsworth | October 2. 59.

Dear Friend

Your words about 'Adam Bede' are very precious, and they came opportunely, for I have been much worried of late. To have written a book that can move people as they say they are moved by 'Adam Bede' *ought* to be happiness enough for me—ought to make me strong against minor personal griefs. But I have a new proof of the predominance of an egoistic sensitiveness in me, in the power these minor griefs retain over me.

Yet I *did* feel very happy this morning, in spite of previous depression, when I came to that part of your letter where you say you felt the better for reading my book. It will always be one of the things I shall think of when I want to gather courage.

I have often accounted to myself for the change I imagined in your manner towards me by the supposition that I had made myself disagreeable in some way. I should not have trusted my own inferences, because I know I am rather morbid in such matters; but George, who is not apt to err in the same way, had a similar impression, and long ago, at Richmond, we used to try and recal some possible offence on my part.

Never mind: it is enough that you are not conscious of any change in feeling.

Ever yours sincerely
Marian Evans Lewes.

Herbert Spencer Esq.

III, 170:5 MRS. CHARLES BRAY TO GE, COVENTRY, [2 OCTOBER 1859]

MS: Berg Collection, New York Public Library.

Dearest Marian

I must express how much pain it gives us that you should have to suffer from these petty annoyances. It is so grievous that works like yours should bring anything to you but pure good. I suppose it is in the nature of things that such annoyances should cluster about a great fame as the toadstools grow at the foot of the oak and the shining ones of the earth always get crucified somehow. People who have no difficulty in believing in the miracle of genius some hundred years ago, make every effort to escape believing in it when it is before their eyes and seek some common vulgar solution of it suited better to their own mode of thought; and I hardly think anything will effectually drive the Liggins nightmare out of some people's brain but the production of other works from your pen which will certainly prove to the dullest that the inspiration has but one source. I feel intensely the provoking, shuffling tones of Mr. B's letters. He is irritated by Mr. Lewes's censure which he does not evidently feel was deserved, and meets it, not in a manly, but in a small spiteful way. I am very sorry that we have unavoidably been the means of these absurdities coming to your knowledge. I cannot bear to think of their pestering you.

We have removed your dear picture and it will be nearer to us in our bedroom than in the dining room. Dear Marian, I hear your voice and see your sympathising smile every time now that I take up Adam Bede, and cannot at all account now for the Liggins incubus having blinded us from seeing you in every line, every thought, as it certainly did. I now see us really to read the book for the first time. You do not want praise—you must be tired of that, but I think it would please you to hear some things as we do, of the *good* the book does in unexpected quarters, such as a young minister we know saying that it has "awakened him to a higher life" and one fast fancy man being convinced of sin by it.

I owe Mr. Lewes a great amount of delight from the Physiology.

Yours ever
C. B.

III, 183:7 JOHN BLACKWOOD TO GHL, EDINBURGH, 14 OCTOBER 1859

Text: Copy in Blackwood Letter Book, National Library of Scotland.

Edinburgh October 14/59.

My dear Lewes

I am happy to tell you that the prospects of the Physiology are very satisfactory. Mr. Simpson did not think it worth while to make any Statement as at Midsummer, and it was not, as a volume has not been published and no results could have been shewn.

The Sales are something like 4000 at least in numbers and about 1800 of the volume are disposed of. We made the price of the volume 6/– as it looked worth that. This makes the profit on the sale in volumes greater in proportion than in numbers and of course we will give you your full Share of the benefit when we see what is the Sale in numbers and volumes.

What are you about for the Magazine? When I went into my library to look for the nature printed volume[9] I found a Balaklava of chairs and tables carried from the drawing room and the bookcases matted up. So that I could lay hands on nothing but J. Lausay. Bradbury will give another copy if you think you would go at that subject at present.

A friend of mine Mr. Patterson has got the Press Newspaper[10] and I suppose enters on his labours almost immediately. He is a very able, well informed man and a good writer. He is also a real good worthy fellow as you could wish to know. I think you might give him a hand with advantage occasionally and I should be glad if you could. Should I give him a note to you or would you adopt the simple process of calling at the Press office where he is to be found although he has not fairly taken possession yet? I know he is anxious to make your acquaintance.

I remain in the country until the end of the month and am only in town for a few days.

Always yours truly
John Blackwood.

G. H. Lewes Esqre

9. Henry Bradbury, *The Nature-Printed Seaweeds*, 1859.

10. Robert Hogarth Patterson (1821–86), editor and later proprietor of the *Press*, 1859–65. GHL called on him 22 November, had a pleasant chat, and agreed (against his original intention) to review a book for him occasionally. (GHL Journal.) No review is listed in his Literary Receipts.

III, 188:27 EMILY SUSANNAH CLARKE TO GE, LICHFIELD, 20 OCTOBER [1859]

MS: Yale.

Lichfield | October 20th.

My dear Aunt Pollie,

Miss Eborall bought me a dress, and also a pair of boots for dancing. Thank you very much for them dear Aunty.

I have read "Adam Bede" and like it so much I am going to read it again soon, Miss Jebb is reading it now. We have twenty boarders now so that the house is quite full. I like dancing very much and am trying to get on with it. The Queen passed through Lichfield last Monday. The train went so fast that we did not see much of her. Aunt Sarah[1] has been to see us again since I saw you, she brought Nelly[2] with her.

My Uncle Henry Clarke has a little boy, I am so glad. He has had several and they have all died.

Katie joins me in love to you and Uncle, I remain

Your affectionate niece
Emily S. Clarke.

III, 188:27 GE TO ELIZA EBORALL, WANDSWORTH, 21 OCTOBER 1859

MS: Princeton.

Holly Lodge | October 21. 59.

My dear Miss Eborall[3]

The only plan I can recommend to your friend Mrs. Boyd is to forward her translations to the editor of "Blackwood," taking care to retain a copy, as the editor's box for rejected contributions is an abyss from which no manuscript returns.

The editor, who is no other than Mr. John Blackwood himself, is sure not to leave an offered contribution without such an examination as will satisfy him whether it will suit his purpose or not, but I must warn your

---

1. Mrs. Isaac Pearson Evans.
2. Elinor Mary Evans.
3. Eliza Eborall conducted the Lombard House School at Lichfield, where GE's nieces were pupils. See vii, 356.

GE "was much comforted by the sight of them, looking happy, and apparently under excellent care" when she and GHL called to see them, 31 August 1859. (GE Journal.)

[22 October 1859]

friend that she must not be surprized if, supposing the conclusion a negative one, she should receive no communication informing her of the fact. The editor is in the habit of letting silence do the work of refusal.

If the tales are such as will suit his purpose, they will be inserted just as readily coming from an unknown person, as if their contributor were introduced by a friend. Some of the most successful things in "Blackwood" have been presented in this way; and on the other hand, no introduction will be influential in the absence of essential suitability to the Magazine.

I have long made up my mind not to introduce any contributor again, finding that intrinsic qualities in the offered contribution are the only requisite and decisive advantages.

Pray don't apologize for asking me anything. I am very glad to answer any questions, though today, I answer them under some pressure of haste, since your friend's time is limited. Ever, dear Miss Eborall,
Yours very sincerely
Marian Evans Lewes.

III, 188:27 GHL TO EDWARD F. S. PIGOTT, [WANDSWORTH, 22 OCTOBER 1859]

MS: Mr. Gordon N. Ray.

Das Singende Deutschland | Album.
Leipzig: Philip Reclam Junr.[4]

My dear Pigott

Voilà ton affaire. We jog on much as before—annoyances and pleasaunces. I suppose you have seen that that gentleman Newby tries to deceive the public with a Sequel to Adam Bede? If you could put some brief paragraph in the D[aily] N[ews] which would be copied in the other papers, stating on authority, that the work is not by the author of Adam Bede and hinting that such counterfeits are very immoral, it would do good.

Yes we must have an orgie soon. Old Spencer is back again and must join us.[5]

Ever yours faithfully
G. H. L.

Polly is at work or would send a message.

4. GHL's fooling may glance at the paragraph he asks Pigott to insert about Newby. (*Daily News*, 31 October 1859, p. 3.)

5. "The day before yesterday Herbert Spencer dined with us, and there was talk—for the last time, I hope,—about my books. We have made a

III, 212:11 HERBERT LEWES TO GHL AND GE, HOFWYL, 21 NOVEMBER 1859

MS: Nuneaton Public Library.

November the ⟨19⟩ ⟨20⟩ 21 1859.

Dear father

I wrote a letter not very long ago to ask you if I could leaf of ⟨En⟩ Music but has you have not answered me I thought the letter had not reached you. I do not want to learn music any more I could get on better alone, I should practis more then I do I have not learnt much with the master who gives me lessons I dersay you think I aught to still have lessons but I shall not learn well with him I learn much better alone. Befor I had lessons of music I was allways practising but now I have lessons I ⟨do not⟩ only practis 2 × a weak. I got on very well before I had lessons. And I shall get on now better if I have no lessons. Sunday the 20 we had a very fine consert there were meny pieces played. There was some music with 8 hands that was very pretty. The boys who played are Charles Walter Guppy and Frank Townsend. There was a small bit of a play, played by *Dubois* and Vallette it was in french. They did it very well and made every one lafe. We began at 7 o'clock and ended at halfpast nine. *Dubois* and Vallette are two French boys Dubois you did not see when you came here, but Vallette you did. The school is increesing and we have got 57 boys. The two Chapmans[6] have left and the boys are very glad for they did not like them. There is snow on the ground, and the boys go out sledging, I do not like sledging much but I like skating very much indeed. I hope you will get this letter and write to me soon.

I have nothing more to say to you I remain your Loving Son

Herbert Arthur Lewes.

Write soon ⟨give my love to Mother⟩

November ⟨19⟩ 21st 1859.

Dear Mother

I have not written a letter to you for some time but now I will write you a small one. I have been wating for some time for a letter from father

---

resolution that we will allow no more talk in our own house on the subject. I find it destructive of that repose and simplicity of mind which is the only healthy state in relation to one's books: it has the same effect as talking of one's religion, or one's feelings and duties towards one's father, mother, or husband." (GE Journal, 25 October 1859.)

6. James and William, sons of Frederic Chapman (1823–95), the publisher.

I wrote him one but I have not received one from him. Dear Mother I orfan think of you when I take out my knife to cut any thing.[7] I long to come to England again, it is 3 jearys that I have not seen England.[8] The books that father gave me I have read many stories out of them. I like them pretty well.

I have not got any more news to tell you. I remain your Loving Son
Herbert Arthur Lewes.

write soon

III, 222:1 GHL TO ÉMILE MONTÉGUT, WANDSWORTH, 1 DECEMBER 1859

Text: *Revue de littérature comparée*, 49 (September 1975), 77.

Holly Lodge, Southfields
Wandsworth, Surrey, 1 December 1859.

My dear Sir

Knowing your admiration of "Adam Bede"—on which you wrote so exquisite an article—I am tempted to renew our long interrupted correspondence, to ask you if among your literary acquaintances you know of any one who would be competent to translate it properly, and willing to undertake the task. George Eliot is Mrs. Lewes—so you see I have an interest in the matter. We have already had several applications but it is of consequence to get a good translator, and I think you would be very likely to know of one. A work which has had greater success than Bulwer or Thackeray have ever achieved, and which in less than nine months has sold 10,000 copies, must surely be a good commercial speculation for a French publisher; and if a good translator could be found we are willing to sell the right of translation for 1,000 francs.

I have not seen Carlyle since he [left for] Scotland; but Pigott [we had] with us the other day and we talked of you and the Revue des Deux Mondes. I suppose you know he has sold the "Leader,"—is now one of the editors of the "Daily News."

When fate brings me to Paris, I shall hope to [see you]. If you [come to] London, [don't] forget me.

Ever faithfully yours
G. H. Lewes.

7. The present from GE delivered by GHL 26 August 1859.

8. Bertie left England 24 August 1857.

III, 238:1 GHL TO JOHN BLACKWOOD, WANDSWORTH, 27 DECEMBER 1859

MS: Berg Collection, New York Public Library. *Brief extract published: John Blackwood*, p. 52.

Holly Lodge | 27 December 1859.

My dear Blackwood

A dismal Christmas and a miserable New Year to you! May Maga perish; and Maggie *not* "repay perusal"! Voilà!

I suppose you got Mrs. Lewes's letter[9] addressed to the Cavendish? She is now in deep water (and deep feeling) and is sailing away at a steady rate.

On the fly leaf I send you a translation of Karl Vogt's[1] opinion of the "Seaside Studies" for use when wanted.

Mrs. Lewes begs me to add that, thanks to you, she is now enjoying Prof. Wilson's glorious rhapsodies on Homer in tempting type.[2]

With our kind remembrances to the Major believe me

Ever faithfully yours,
G. H. Lewes.

John Blackwood, Esq.

III, 239:6 GHL TO EDWARD F. S. PIGOTT, WANDSWORTH, [1860?]

MS: University of California Los Angeles.

Holly Lodge | Wednesday.

My dear Pigott

I have many times threatened to make a descent upon you, and as I *must* go to St. John's Wood[3] on Saturday, I will look in on you at chop time if you are not otherwise engaged on that day.

Ever yours faithfully
G. H. Lewes.

9. 20 December 1859. See III, 236.

1. Karl Vogt (1817–95), German naturalist, exiled for political reasons, became Professor of Zoology at Geneva. He translated Chambers's *Vestiges* into German, 1851.

2. John Wilson, *Homer and His Translators and the Greek Drama*, crown 8vo, Edinburgh, 1860.

3. Pigott lived at 28 South Bank, Regents Park.

The Mill on the Floss and *Silas Marner*

1860 January 16   Chapman wants to reprint GE's articles.
1860 March 20   Thornie troubled to explain "Mother" and "Mamma."
1860 March 23   GHL warns Bray against statements about GE.
1860 April 1–28   GE and GHL at Rome.
1860 April 4   *The Mill on the Floss*, 3 vols., published.
1860 April 14   Bulwer Lytton criticizes *The Mill on the Floss*.
1860 August 15   Charles Lewes appointed to Post Office.
1860 September 11   Thornie leaves Hofwyl for Edinburgh.
1860 December 17   GE and GHL move to 16 Blandford Square.
1861 March 21   GE recalls debt of gratitude to Mrs. Bray.
1861 March 28   Blackwood buys Laurence portrait of GE.
1861 April 7   GHL dines and sleeps at Waltham Cross.
1861 May 5   GHL describes their second Italian journey.
1861 July 5   GHL on Tom Trollope's *La Beata*.
1861 July 6   GHL takes A. Trollope to see Carlyle.
1861 September 25   GE corrects her novels for 1-vol. edition.
1861 November 18   Alexandre Dumas raves about *Adam Bede*.

III, 250:6 JOHN CHAPMAN TO GE, LONDON, 16 JANUARY 1860

MS: University of London.

1 Albion St., Hyde Park | 16 January 1860.

Dear Mrs. Lewes

Have you any objection to my republication of the five articles which you contributed to the Westminster Review?[4] I am aware that I gave you back the receipts which conveyed to me the entire copyrights in the articles, and therefore only ask your acquiescence in my republication of them with the understanding and agreement on my part that after paying the expenses of paper, printing, binding, advertizing and commission on publishing from the proceeds of sale I should divide the profit with you. The articles make altogether about 150 Westminster pages,[5] and would not extend therefore beyond a small post 8vo volume which however I should have much pleasure in issuing. It would reflect equal credit on you and on the Westminster—No, not *equal* credit for of course it would be chiefly yours; and though the Volume would be small, I hope and believe you would derive some substantial advantage from its publication.

You will not take it as a compliment, but of course I do, that T. C. Sandars and W. B. Donne separately ascribed the article on "Christian Revivals"[6] to you!

Hoping you are both[7] well, I am

Yours sincerely
John Chapman.

4. "Memoirs of the Court of Austria" (April 1855), "Evangelical Teaching: Dr. Cumming" (October 1855), "German Wit: Heinrich Heine" (January 1856), "The Natural History of German Life" (July 1856), and "Worldliness and Other-Worldliness: the Poet Young" (January 1857) are probably the five Chapman refers to. GE contributed three other articles: "The Progress of the Intellect" (January 1851), "Woman in France: Mme de Sablé" (October 1854), and "Silly Novels by Lady Novelists" (October 1856).

5. Closer to 160 pages.

6. "Christian Revivals," 73 (January 1860), 167–217, by Chapman himself, was reprinted as a pamphlet in 1860. (BM.)

7. GHL Journal, 18 January 1860: "Chapman last night wrote a cool request to be allowed to republish Marian's articles from the Review, and offering her half profits. Squashed that idea." GHL's letter has not been found.

III, 253:6 GHL TO EDWARD F. S. PIGOTT, WANDSWORTH, [26 JANUARY 1860]

MS: Mr. Gordon N. Ray.

Holly Lodge | Southfields | Wandsworth | Thursday.
My dear Pigott
Fred Chapman (of Chapman and Hall) is coming to dine here on Saturday and I have asked Wilkie. Will you and Redford, or you alone if he is not to be had, join them? *Music of course.* Dinner on *table* at ½ past 5. Train from Waterloo 4.15.

Let me know *at once* whether you can come and if he can too.[7a]

Ever yours faithfully
G. H. Lewes.

III, 269:6 GHL TO THEODORE MARTIN, WANDSWORTH, 2 MARCH 1860

MS: University of California Los Angeles.

Holly Lodge, Wimbledon Park, Wandsworth | 2 March 1860.
My dear Martin
The hurry and bother of preparation for our trip to Italy will prevent my reading all the Translation of Horace[8] you were good enough to send me; but I have read many of the odes with great admiration, though qualified by the deep sense I have,—as you yourself have—of the impossibility of the thing ever being quite successful. I feel inclined to say of you as Francis the First—or some other monarch said of his archer—"Sir I compliment you on splendid talents for missing."

I observed one favorable sign, that whenever my remembrance of the original is dim you seem proportionately to excel; whence I conclude it is the rhythm of the original which interferes in the other cases and does not perhaps allow me to be quite just to you.

Recal me to the remembrance of your dear wife and believe me

Ever faithfully yours
G. H. Lewes.

Theodore Martin Esq.

7a. "January 28. Mr. Pigott, Mr. Redford, and Mr. F. Chapman dined with us and we had a musical evening, Mrs. Congreve and Miss Bury joining us after dinner." (GE Journal.)

8. Martin's *The Odes of Horace Translated into English Verse*, 1860.

III, 273:23 GHL TO EDWARD F. S. PIGOTT,
WANDSWORTH, [15 MARCH 1860]

MS: Mr. Gordon N. Ray.

Holly Lodge | Thursday.

My dear Pigott

We are off next week. Please write to Langford about the "Mill" and he will do what you wish.[9] Polly begs me to send her kindest remembrances. In haste

Ever yours
G. H. L.

III, 277:21 THORNTON ARNOTT LEWES TO GHL,
HOFWYL, 20 MARCH 1860

MS: Yale. *Extracts published:* Haight, *George Eliot*, pp. 329–330.

Hofwyl 20 March 1860.

Dear Father

We received your letter last night, and were very glad to get it, though you ought to have written to me and not to Charles, as I wrote a long while ago. I should prefer by far being confirmed here; there is such a small difference between English and Swiss theology, that even Empson's parents, whose Ideas are so strict that he may not play on Sunday, will be confirmed, but as you prefer our not being confirmed, I suppose it is hopeless to wish for it. Our box has *not* come, in spite of my diligence in looking for it every evening when the letters come; so I suppose it is lost, and with it my precious Schamyl. I hope you will write to Leipzig, if you sent it to Mr. Brockhaus and ask him if he has sent it or not. We have therefore not read the Cornhill magazine.[10]

There is a difficulty now, as Empson is going away at August, and not at Easter, as he has seen Mamma, and knows her, he will of course see that Mother is not she, so that we have agreed, viz: Charles and I, that we had better tell him, enjoining at the same time secrecy, as at any rate, he would know it 3 or four months later, when he goes home. Mother will have therefore when we present him to say "How d'ye do"! etc. etc.

9. About a review copy for the *Daily News?*

10. GHL's "Studies in Animal Life" ran in the *Cornhill* from January to June 1860.

And we only wait for your permission to tell him. You will therefore, please, answer this letter, directly you get it, as the sooner the better.

I am going on stuffing famously and have already given 4 or 5 fine ones away. I shall not give you any when you come, as it would be difficult for you to take them with you, but when I am in England, I shall fill the house with stuffed sparrows, Crows and chaffinch. . . .

I am glad that Nursie[1] will keep house for you, she will have a nice time of it, give her my love, and tell her that though I am so idle in writing, I will send her some little present by you.

You have told Mamma, that you had told us, didn't you? In ⟨your⟩ her last letter there were one or two sentences, from which Charles and I concluded you had.

I have several Entwürfe, for immense poetical works, which I shall most likely carry out in my room, with a cup of coffee, in the summer evenings.

I have nothing more to say, so I remain, Dear Father

Your rascally pup
Rex Ranarum.

Answer the letter directly you get it. | Amen!

III, 280:1 GHL TO CHARLES BRAY, WANDSWORTH, [23 MARCH 1860]

MS: Yale.

Holly Lodge | Friday.

My dear Bray

We start tomorrow morning and hope to be in Rome by Palm Sunday.

Knowing your real regard for Marian there is one point on [which] I wish to speak. You know how Gossip Report—liar that she is—busies herself with every one who has the misfortune of being famous; and you may imagine how eagerly people cite "friends of many years" as the authorities, for their legends. Unhappily friends—when biographical— have as little chance apparently of being accurate, as the merest strangers; yet who would question their authority, when the fact stated seems simple and patent? When George Combe, for instance, cited you as the authority[2] for saying that Marian was "self-educated" and a "farmer's" daughter the facts were simple—and the authority seemed indisputable. Again it has come to our knowledge that you have said that Marian, when young,

1. Martha Baker, Mrs. Bell.   2. See III, 169.

was "a regular boy," and joined in all boyish games—and *this* was adduced as a *reason* why she could paint the psychology of boys so wonderfully as she has done in her new novel! I should have thought that any one who knew her as a woman would see that so timid a creature was little likely to have been a tomboy—at any rate the fact that she "had been" one, was quite new to her. These points are trivial, but I mention them as *samples* of the liability to error, which even the oldest friends fall into; and it is only necessary I am sure to hint that unless she is to be gratified by seeing them in print, and hearing them in the reported gossip of the day, her friends should carefully abstain from any *biographical* statements—of which they have not clear and immediate knowledge.

I am sure you will not misunderstand this appeal. It is open to every one to mention likings and dislikings, and personal details of which they have unequivocal knowledge; but biographical statements are different; and when they are made, those who made them must expect that their authority will be cited, and that the reports will finally reach the ears of the unhappy subject.

Ever faithfully yours
G. H. Lewes.

III, 289:3 SIR EDWARD LYTTON TO JOHN BLACKWORTH, KNEBWORTH, 14 [APRIL] 1860

MS: National Library of Scotland. *Brief extract published:* III, 314, n. 1.

Kneb[wor]th 14 1860.

My dear Sir

I have just finished the Mill on the Floss and can assure you of my very high opinion of its many beauties. That rare and minute knowledge of the female heart which struck me so forcibly in A. Bede is here brought out with more variety, and in more richness of humour. All the Dodson sisters are wonderful. I feel it a great relief to get rid of the Provincial Dialect, and the language of Dialogue in the rural characters is extremely natural without vulgarity and full of point and playfulness. The only criticism I should here make is that here and there is a little unconscious imitation of Dickens; not more so perhaps than so fascinating and popular a genius as his would inevitably cause in persons writing somewhat after him and resorting to somewhat the same classes of Society for characters. Putting that aside, the general style is admirable.

In the 1st Volume as to construction and position I did not see a fault.

Tom and Maggie as children are most beautifully drawn. Towards the latter part of the 2nd Volume I began to fear that there might be the same fault (as *I* think it) which I found in Ad. Bede. viz.: the want of clear perception and close study of what I call 'position' in Narrative. There is position in Narrative as well as Drama, and it can never be neglected without more or less injury to the story. In fact it comprises much of what the antient Critics meant by "the Becoming." No character should be placed in a position that does not become the conceptions already formed of that character, and it is in vain to reply that there is no violation of the Natural in such a position. The Natural that belongs to the Individual Character *is* violated. There is nothing for instance of the "unbecoming" or "false position" in the beating of Thersites; it becomes him to be beat. But if Achilles had kicked Agammenon for taking away Briseis it might be quite natural in Achilles to do so, but it would have been "unbecoming" so far as Agammenon was concerned, and it would have been difficult afterwards to respect him as the King of Men.

Now when Tom and Maggie go to meet Phillip, Maggie is put into a false position as regards the previous description of her hasty generous impulsive character to stand by and listen with so little interruption to her brother's coarse abuse of Phillip, and her natural fear must have been felt that Phillip would think she had brought Tom there, and it was a sort of treachery, and her inevitable impulse would have been to burst out with profound sympathy for Phillip. She is brought here as it is, for no sufficient cause in the plot, merely to witness her lover's humiliation and the situation is untrue to the courage of her character. Hence she loses somewhat in interest after that scene. But this is unimportant compared to the error, as I think, of her whole position towards Stephen. It may be quite natural that she should take that liking to him, but it is a position at variance with all that had before been Heroic about her. The *indulgence* of such a sentiment for the affianced of a friend under whose roof she was, was a treachery and a meanness according to the Ethics of Art, and nothing can afterwards lift the character into the same hold on us. The refusal to marry Stephen fails to do so. This brings me to another view of a fault in the same direction. In studying plot or incident the very remarkable writer does not eno[ugh] weigh what is Agreeable or Disagreeable. Now the Disagreeable should be carefully avoided. You may have the painful, the terrible, the horrible, even; but the *disagreeable* should be shunned. For instance, it is a disagreeable and unworthy position for Phillip to treat so lightly *the blows* his father had received from the *father* of the woman he wants to marry, and Phillip sinks in dignity on acc[oun]t of it. Lastly—the Tragic should be prepared for and seem to come step by step as if unavoidable. But that is not the case here.

One feels from the time that Maggie's father *dies* in consequence of his meeting with Phillip's father that the end cannot be happy, but the steps that lead towards an end so gloomy are not sufficiently marked and solemn and when the Drowning comes at last, it fails accordingly in the pathos and terror it would otherwise excite; there has not been even sufficient care taken to make that final reconciliation in death of brother and sister as touching as it should be. Tom indeed has been by that time set so far apart from his sister that he can't be jerked back into the old boyish love of a sudden, and we don't see *why* he should be drowned at all. These are to my mind defects that belong to the same class of defects as those in Ad. Bede but they are not so marked, and these defects did not prevent or even injure the great popularity of Adam Bede. Neither will they in this case. I even doubt whether they will be visible to most readers. Where such defects really tell (even supposing I am right, which I may not be) is 10 or 20 years hence in the *duration* of a work. They scarcely touch its first sale or the author's immediate reputation.

I have been more lengthy in dwelling on faults real or supposed, because I measure the author by a very high standard. I know no female author with such grasp of character, such deep cuts into secret recesses of the heart, such ease and power of language, such charming combination of unaffected pathos and delicate affluent humour. And on the whole I like the Book even better than Adam Bede—which is indeed saying a great deal.

Yours
E. B. L.

III, 289:3 GE TO FRANÇOIS D'ALBERT-DURADE, ROME, 17 APRIL 1860

Text: Cross, New Edition, pp. 310–311.

I think you have made rapid progress with the translation,[3] seeing that you can only use fringes of time for it. It is a very sweet thought to me that the work may be a source of some pleasure to you and Maman (I am very glad to be assured that I may still say "Maman," for that is the name by which she has always gone in my silent memory).[4] It will interest

3. Of *Adam Bede*, begun in February 1860. D'Albert wrote 19 March 1860 that he had finished half the book in a literal translation, and that he and Mme D'Albert were spending three or four hours every evening correcting and refining the style. (Yale.)

4. "Pour vous, chère Madame, nous vous nommons encore Minie quand nous parlons de vous, moi et ma femme, qui est trés affligée de ce que dans vos lettres vous ne l'appelez plus Maman." (19 March 1860.)

you, perhaps, to know that it is translated into Hungarian, and the first volume is fairly rendered into German—possibly the second also by this time.

You see I am counting on your and Maman's interest in everything that belongs to me. I do not write about Rome: you have read much better things on that subject than I can tell you. But no one can tell you about myself, unless *I* take upon me that agreeable labour.

What a delight it would be to take the old walks in Geneva once more! But I fear there are many changes that would check the current of my memory. And the change from the old to the new is always painful to us who are getting old and living more and more in the past. Tell Maman I enter now into her conservative feelings, which I used inwardly to disapprove in my revolutionary mood—the mood I was in when you knew me.

You will forgive me for writing hastily and briefly, and will understand that temporary preoccupation with the wonderful place I am in is not *indifference* to other things. With affectionate regards to Maman, I am always yours, with sincere and faithful friendship.

III, 293:22 GHL TO HIS SONS, NAPLES, 6 MAY 1860

MS: Yale.

Naples Sunday 6 May 1860.

My dear Pups

We left Rome on Sunday last and have been vastly enjoying the lovely weather and incomparable scenery of this place. To see Naples and die—is the proverb. We are seeing Naples, but have no immediate intention of dying either hair or whiskers, for all the proverbs in Europe. It is in vain to hope to squeeze into a letter all or half that we have seen at Rome and this place; but I will just jot down a few items and leave your vivid imaginations to fill the picture.

While at Rome we visited Frascati, and ascended, by the aid of jogging donkeys, to *Tusculum*[5]—or rather to the ruins of that ancient and famous site, which Roman History and Horace have doubtless made familiar to you. It is a lovely spot, with an exquisite view of the campagna, and all the hills—Mount Algidus, Soracte, Monte Cavo, the Alban hills, Castel

---

5. This excursion with a quite unreliable guide is described in GHL's Journal 23 April 1860.

6 May 1860 265

Gandolfo etc. From thence we saw the Lake Regillus. On another day we went to Tivoli,[6] famous for its beautiful waterfalls, its Temple of the Sybil, and its scenery. The morning was lovely when we started but we had not traversed much of the Campagna before it grew threatening and cloudy, and on reaching Tivoli (through a beautiful grove of olive trees) down came the rain, which had been coming down almost daily all the time we were at Rome—and down it poured while we explored the valley and gazed at the waterfalls. But disagreeable as the rain made the expedition, there was so much beauty, that we enjoyed it on the whole very much.

Here at Naples we have visited Pozzuoli, Baiae, Cumae, Misenum, Posilippo, and Pompeii. The day at the last named place was one I shall never forget. Imagine the delight of finding yourself in the long silent streets of the ancient city so recently dug up—the very marks of the Roman chariots on the pavement being still as they were worn away nearly 1800 years ago—and the signs on the shop fronts reminding you of today. Everywhere at the end of each street you see the rich hills around, and the deep blue sky above. The houses, Temples, Forum, and Theatres, are many of them in excellent preservation, the paintings and arabesques on the walls being often well preserved and very graceful. All the utensils and objects have been removed into the Naples Museum, where we have examined them with intense interest, but they would have added greatly to the effect if they could with safety have been left where found. For example in the baker's shop they found a loaf with his name printed on it, an oven, yeast, etc. But these must be seen at Naples now.

Tomorrow we start for Salerno, Paestum, Amalfi, and Sorrento, and shall start for Florence on Tuesday week, so you must address your letters to Florence, Poste Restante.

I hope, dear Charlie, you have not forgotten to let your hair grow, and that we shall find you blooming. And you too, Bertie, must present yourself to your mother in splendid condition. As for Thornie—but I have a special postscript to address to him in answer to his last letter.

Well Thornie! in the first place I have to "pick a crow with you" about that gun story. I was sorry to find that you did not appreciate what I said about its not being *right*, and only replied to what I added as a secondary reason, about its not being *prudent*. I thought that the mere *mention* of its not being right would have sufficed. You must bear in mind that so long as you are an inmate of Dr. Müller's house, so long you must conform to his rules and wishes, and any attempt to evade or violate them is morally wrong. For observe, suppose an accident *should* happen—of course you

6. GHL Journal 26 April 1860.

intend to be very careful, but accidents constantly happen even with men—and then consider what an injury you would have inflicted on Dr. Müller, merely, because it was at his school that a boy was shot! Dr. Müller would really have been blameless, but the responsibility would nevertheless be borne by him, and people would say he ought to have taken care that no gun was kept by boys.

Enough of this unpleasant topic, and now for stamps.[7] Enclosed you will find a *complete* set of Neapolitan stamps which I got at the post office (one of them stamps this letter) but you misled me about the Roman stamp of uno soldo. I inquired at the Post and they had only $\frac{1}{2}$ baj. or 2 quattrini which I had already sent you. The one you say was received by a boy must have come from one of the Roman states, as uno soldo is not Roman, but means a sou or bajoso. If I can pick up any of the stamps you mention be sure I shall.

I am surprised to hear that the books have not arrived yet. I would advise you Thornie to drop a line to Dr. E. Brockhaus, Leipsig saying that Trübner undertook to forward it to him for Hofwyl in March last, and asking him if he has addressed it on to Bern, and to whom.

And now dear boys it is time to dress for dinner, but as I have pretty well exhausted my budget I can afford to end this. Your mother sends showers of kisses—she is very well—but I am only so, so. God bless you my dear boys

Ever your loving
Pater.

III, 293:22 THORNTON LEWES TO GHL AND GE, HOFWYL, 16 MAY 1860

MS: Yale.

Hofwyl the 16. May. 1860.

Dear Father and Mother!

We received your letter last night, and I am very much obliged for the neapolitan stamps, of which the 50 Grani was not in the school before, the others I had but not new. I hope you will have got me some of Sicily, Parma, Tuscany, and Modena. It is very strange about the red 1 soldo of Rome. It is of Rome for I examined it particularly last night. Perhaps it is an old one.

---

7. Thornton's interest in stamps produced his only published work. See III, 463, n. 1.

16 May 1860

About the gun, which picks and tickles *the* crow, when I hit him, as you will not give me a powder one, will you give me a cap and ball one, which Dr. Müller allows, (though, bye the bye, I don't know why, as it is almost as easy to shoot a man with it as with a powder gun), it costs rather more it is true, viz. about 50 frs in Germany, here they cost 90. Now if you like to give me one, the uncle of the 3 Brasilians, the Serra's (do you remember them) is comeing over in June, from Dresden, and if you give your consent, they will write to him to bring one with him, which you will pay, this will save you also the postage.

When you come, you will well understand why I want a gun. I do not like to pay, 20, 30–50 cts for a bird, which I myself could shoot for nothing, as it takes all my pocket money, and if I do not take the birds the peasants and hunters send me, they won't send me any more.

Mamma[8] says that Grandmamma is very uncomfortable from not having received her quarterly allowance from Mrs. Webber,[9] who has died, and has therefore not even thought of sending me my birthday tin. Can I ask Dr. Müller for it on your account, and you will settle accounts with Grandmamma afterwards.

When will you arrive at Hofwyl, and where will Mother stay? I am very glad to hear you have led such a happy life in Italy, and we envy you very much. Ah! well, the time may come, when Mr. and Mrs. Thornton Lewes have fat pups at Hofwyl and go over to Italy "to ride in the path you rode in," and leave poor old Pater at home thinking how unkind his son is, not to take him with him.

Today is the birthday of the best master we have, such a kind and clever man, Dr. Nauck. He came at Easter and he is by far the favourite of the boys. I gave him the stamps of Naples which I had in my collection, and which I took out to put in the new ones you sent me, as he is making a collection for a friend in Germany. He showed me how to stuff with tow instead of peat, and I gave him today a nicely stuffed *red backed shrike* "Lanius collurio" as a birthday present, with which he was much pleased.

We have also got a new drilling and fencing master. Mr. Nauck who

8. Agnes Jervis Lewes.
9. Susanna Webber, widow, died 22 March 1860 at 4 Gracechurch St., London, formerly of Devonport. Frances Webber, widow, died 29 April 1860 at the Rectory House, Runnington, Somerset, formerly of 27 Marchant St., Paddington, had a son John Webber, wine merchant. GHL's elder brother Edgar James Lewes worked in Oporto, Portugal 1825–30 for the Offley, Forrester, wine merchants. In a letter to Mrs. Willim 26 August 1826 he refers to a Mr. Webber, whom he was to see in London. I cannot yet explain which Mrs. Webber is meant. Frances Webber's will does not mention Mrs. Willim.

understands phrenology, felt my head, and told me my character, it is this:

Muth (ziemlich)	Eitelkeit (stark)
Religiosität (schwach)	Gutmütligkeit (entschieden)
Scharfsinn (sehr stark)	Mordsinn (schwach)
Dichtersinn (entschieden)	Zahlensinn (stark)
Nachahmungsinn (gut)	Beständigkeit (stark)

I have nothing more to say so, with awful, tremendous, terrible, cartloads[1] of kisses for Mother,

I remain, Dear Father and Mother

Your affectionate Son
Thornton Arnott Lewes.

III, 326:13 GHL TO WILLIAM BLACKWOOD, WANDSWORTH, [20? JULY? 1860]

MS: National Library of Scotland.

Holly Lodge | Friday.

My dear Major

I have just been warned that the *American* reprint of the Physiology (by Messrs. Appleton[3] of New York) is announced in "La Bibliographie de France" as for sale in Paris where it has no more *right* to be sold than in London; and it is urged upon me that we ought, as a matter of principle, to resist this. Qu'en dites vous?

The letters you enclosed were of the usual order of foolishness and one's admirers so seldom "rise above the rank of an idiot" as Carlyle says!

I have been so busy that my second visit to the Row has still to come off.

Mrs. Lewes begs me to add her kind regards and believe me

Ever faithfully yours
G. H. Lewes.

1. The last 4 words are underlined progressively 2, 3, 4, and 5 times.

3. Appleton had offered £300 for early sheets of *The Mill on the Floss* (see III, 268), but there is no record of any arrangement with GHL for the *Physiology*, which they reprinted in New York in 1860.

III, 330:7 ANTHONY TROLLOPE TO GHL, WALTHAM CROSS, 9 AUGUST 1860

MS: Yale. *Published: The Letters of Anthony Trollope,* ed. B. A. Booth, 1951, p. 68.

My dear Lewes.

I hear that C. L. Lewes was at the head of the Poll at that Civil Service examination, and I suppose I may congratulate him in being a Queens servant. I hope I shall soon shake hands with him over his desk at the Post office.[5]

Do not let him begin life with any ideas that his profession is inferior to others. Men may live as vegetables, or again as dead sticks, in the Civil Service. But so they may, and so many do, in the church and as lawyers. But in the Civil Service nowadays, exertion will give a man a decent gentleman's income not late in life, if it be accompanied by intellects not below par. I do not know that more can be said of any profession except that in others there are great prizes. To compensate this the Civil Service allows a man, who has in him the capacity for getting prizes, to look for them elsewhere. A government clerk, who is not wedded to pleasure, may follow any pursuit without detriment to his public utility. One such man in our days edits the Edinbro, a great gun in his own way; another has written the best poem of these days; a third supplies all our theatres with their new plays; and a fourth plies a small literary trade as a poor novelist.[6] We boast also of artists, philosophers, newspaper politicians, and what not.

Do not therefore let him think that six hours a day at the shop is to be the Be all and End all of his life.

Yours always
Anthony Trollope.

Waltham
August 9. 1860.

5. Trollope wrote to GHL 20 July 1860: "When I asked for the nomination I did not wish to tell you, and put his name down—G—at a shot. If, as the chances are, it be not G. let me have a line saying what it is." Corrected by GHL, he wrote again 23 July: "I have written to have the name altered from George to Charles." (Yale.)

6. Henry Reeve (1813–95), Clerk of Appeal to the Privy Council in 1837 and Registrar 1843–87, edited the *Edinburgh Review* 1855–95. Matthew Arnold (1822–88), Inspector of Schools since 1851; Tom Taylor (1817–80), Secretary to the Board of Health since 1854, wrote *Our American Cousin* (1858) and many other plays; Trollope may be referring to "Sohrab and Rustum" or "The Scholar-Gipsy." He himself is the "poor novelist."

III, 331:21 ANTHONY TROLLOPE TO GHL, LONDON, 14 AUGUST 1860

MS: Yale. *Published: The Letters of Anthony Trollope*, ed. B. A. Booth, 1951, p. 69.

Post Office
August 14 | 1860.

My dear Lewes.

There are two men just appointed to the Secretarys office, your son being one. The man who first comes to duty stands senior. Let your son present himself at once to Mr. Parkhurst[7]—at whose table I am now writing. If he then wants a few days leave of absence he can get it, but it may [give] him one step in seniority.

I hear that he passed quite a first rate examination. He got the full numbers for general intelligence which is *very* unusual.

Very faithfully yours
Anthony Trollope.

III, 345:1 THORNTON ARNOTT LEWES TO GHL, HOFWYL, 11 SEPTEMBER 1860

MS: Yale.

Hofwyl September 11. 1860.

Dearest Father

Last night I received your letter, and answer it now at 7 o'clock a.m., so that you may get my answer soon. I will tell Dr. Müller about the clothes, and will go to Berne about them one of these days. Must the trowsers and waistcoat be black or only very dark brown?

I hope you will soon be settled as the sooner I am off, the better; I have no lessons, but walk about, catch moths, write letters etc. the whole day. I hope I shall be able to start by the 20th, as I suppose in a fortnight you will have been quite settled.[8] When did you begin moving? I am glad to hear that Charles is getting on well. Give my love to Nursie, I hope she will always live with us. I hope you will soon settle where I am to live at Edinburgh, I do not care who was there before me, and were they Kings of England, so long as it is comfortable. I am already, (in imagination) an

---

7. Rodie Parkhurst, Chief Clerk in the Secretary's Office, General Post Office.

8. GHL and GE moved to 10 Harewood Square, N.W.1 24 September 1860.

11 September 1860

Edinburgh student, kicking up rows, and attacking the peelers, the most poetic part of students life. I am very glad there is a Garibaldi there, I hope he is a good fellow, if so, I shall fraternize with him with a vengeance, and who knows if I don't run away some day with him to Sicily, and make the world ring with the glory of my name, so that when in future any one asks, who were the three liberators of Sicily? the answer will be Garibaldi, Türr[9] and Thornton Lewes. (Ein würdiges Kleeblatt!)

You did not translate Goethe's life into Polish and Hungarian, did you? Better translate it into Latin or Greek.

About my journey: I hardly think we agree on that for you will want me to sleep at Bâle first night, Mülhausen, the second, Belfort, third, Paris fourth, I suppose; not a bit. I travel as fast as steam can carry me. Here is my Programme. We will say I start the 20, well and good. The first night I sleep at Paris, on the 21 I pay a visit to Mrs. Brown, to whom I have to carry a *load* of photographs and sleep in the evening at Boulogne. I take the first steamer, (if it is tolerable weather, but I prefer waiting if there is a storm, like when we came) and arrive at London as fast as possible on the 22. Do you approve this way of travelling? It will cost less than the other, anyhow. And as to company, I don't want that, so all the Hofwyl boys may remain at work, I don't wish to take them with me. About my stuffed birds, you need not fear, I have got no more, they are all given away a long while ago. All my stuffing apparatus is packed up in a box, a foot long. And all my unnecessary books have been given away. Shall I take Adam Bede, or give it to Mrs. Charles Müller? I have read it, and can always read it again when I want in England. I have given Scenes of clerical life to Dr. Müller's sister, a great friend of mine, with whom I used, two years ago, to rid her garden of snails, which we killed afterwards in hot water; a nice amusement for a liberator of Sicily. I hope Mother is all right today, I send her another hundred kisses back, and Bertie says ditto to Mr. Burke.

I have nothing more to say, i.e. what I have still got, I shall say when I arrive home. So good bye, Dear Father

Ever your affectionate Son
Thornton Lewes.

P.S. How long shall I remain at home? Please answer me as soon as you get this letter.

9. Stephen Türr, (b. 1825), a Hungarian general serving under Garibaldi.

III, 352:1 GHL TO FREDERIC CHAPMAN, LONDON, [28 SEPTEMBER 1860]

MS: University of California Los Angeles.

193. Piccadilly. London. W.[1]

Dear Chapman

My new address is 10 Harewood Square, Regent's Park, N.W. where I shall be glad to receive those 2 boxes of cigars you have set aside for me and glad to see you after my return from Edinburgh, whither I go on Monday.[2]

Yours truly
G. H. Lewes.

III, 353:1 GHL TO RICHARD BENTLEY, WANDSWORTH, [2 OCTOBER 1860]

MS: University of Illinois.

Private

Holly Lodge | Tuesday.

My dear Sir

Yesterday I saw Dr. Schmitz, and in talking with him about the Mommsen I learned that his editing is to be confined to writing the preface, and that he is under no responsibility as to the accuracy of the translation.[3] Remembering our conversation on this very point, I would beg to suggest that, unless you have already engaged someone else to see to the translation, it would be eminently desirable to engage Dr. Schmitz to do that *thoroughly*. There are two things and only two which can prevent the book having an enormous sale—the first is inaccuracy and the second inelegance or want of force and attractiveness in the style. For the second you must have a *writer* (not a common article, by any means, as you know); but for the first there can be no difficulty. Believe me,

Ever truly yours
G. H. Lewes.

R. Bentley Esq.

1. Written on stationery with the printed heading of Chapman's office.
2. GHL arrived in Edinburgh with Thornton 1 October 1860 to put him under Dr. Leonhard Schmitz in the High School.
3. Theodor Mommsen, *Römische Geschichte*, 4 vols., Berlin, 1854–56, was translated for Bentley by William P. Dickson, 1862–75 with a preface by Leonhard Schmitz.

III, 360:1 GHL TO JOHN BLACKWOOD, LONDON, [26 NOVEMBER 1860]

MS: Berg Collection, New York Public Library.

10 Harewood Square | Monday.

My dear Blackwood

By this post goes the article on 'Uncivilized Man'—with one of the volumes for extract.[4] The paper is short—let me hope 'sweet' also.—When I proposed it I thought the books (which I hadn't read) would have furnished better details. But so few men have eyes to see!

Mrs. Lewes, who has been very low and poorly is better again and at work. She is writing magnificently and as usual can't be made to believe that it is worth reading! It was pleasant to see the 'Mill' in the two charming volumes.[5]

Our kind regards to the Major.

Ever yours truly
G. H. L.

The greatest of German physiologists[6] (whom I *don't* know) has just sent me a book of his—which shows that the 'Physiology' is held of some account abroad.

III, 361:23 GHL TO JOHN BLACKWOOD, LONDON, [1 DECEMBER 1860]

MS: National Library of Scotland.

10 Harewood Square | Saturday.

My dear Blackwood

I return the proof at once because I see at page 5 an extract has dropped out, or has not been set up. In my m.s. there is a reference to the passage. Another reason why I do not retain it is that I cannot extend the article without weakening it. The details at my command were few, and I used all that were interesting.

---

4. Johann Georg Kohl, *Kitchi-Gami; Wanderings round Lake Superior,* tr. Sir F. C. L. Wraxall, 1860, one of four books noticed in "Uncivilised Man," *Blackwood's* 89 (January 1861), 27–41.

5. *The Mill on the Floss,* A New Edition, 2 vols., 1860.

6. Rudolf Virchow, *Cellular Pathology, as Based upon Physiological and Pathological Histology,* tr. Frank Chance, 1860. GHL's copy in Dr. Williams's Library is inscribed on the flyleaf "With the compts of the Author and of the Translator."

Considering the number taken by the Libraries of the 3 volume edition, we do not think the subscription to the 'Mill' by any means bad.

Don't you think it would be advisable to have the Phys[iology] for Schools[7] out ready for the new year—that schools might begin upon it then?

Yours in haste
G. H. L.

Will you please send Kohl to my cub?[8]

III, 369:1 GHL TO RICHARD BENTLEY, WANDSWORTH, [1860?]

MS: University of Illinois.

Holly Lodge | Tuesday.

My dear Sir

It is twenty years since I was in Heidelberg and then only for two days so that there is no information I can give you about the place. Nor do I think *I* know any of the Literati or Professors there, although they probably know of me through the Life of Goethe—and although you cannot need any introduction I shall be glad if my name can be of any service to you.

Ever faithfully yours
G. H. Lewes.

R. Bentley Esq.

III, 376:1 GHL TO JOHN BLACKWOOD, LONDON, [2 FEBRUARY 1861]

MS: National Library of Scotland.

16, Blandford Square, | **N.W.**

My dear Blackwood

Your checque with the news about 'Adam' catches us just as we are starting for Dorking for three or four days holiday.[9] We have both been ailing, and hope a breath of fresh air will set us up.

---

7. When he saw Blackwood in Edinburgh, early in October 1860, GHL proposed an abridgement of Johnston's *Physiology for Schools*, which he finished 5 November. His Journal, 6 December 1860, notes Blackwood's dislike of the book and GHL's decision to abandon it. See III, 363.

8. GHL thought that *Kitchi-Gami* might interest Thornton.

9. See III, 375.

Though I am sorry to lose so piquant a title, I agree in what you say and will find some other.[1] In haste

Ever yours faithfully
G. H. L.

III, 382:11 GHL TO ARTHUR HELPS, LONDON, 21 FEBRUARY 1861

MS: Nuneaton Public Library. *Published: Correspondence of Sir Arthur Helps,* ed. E. A. Helps., 1917, pp. 243–244.

16, Blandford Square, | N.W.
21 February 61.

My dear Helps

The gods were not propitious to me yesterday and would not let me see you. I came to congratulate you (if you *wished* it) on the completion of your arduous and important book[2]; though I have some doubts whether it ought to be all congratulation for I think you will sadly miss the companion of so many years. One never likes to say finis. In spite of the trouble and vexation I dare say you already begin to feel a void left. Nor am I at all sure that your readers compound for the idea of not having more such volumes, or the poor reflection that at any rate the work is complete. The only satisfactory reflection is that we shall have *other* works,—and the more because they won't be so expensive of time as this was.

I hope you are in tolerable strength and spirits. I don't ask you to write and say so, knowing your faint fondness for letters.—By the way, if ever you don't want a solitary dinner and don't want the bore of a club, please drop in here at $\frac{1}{2}$ past 5 and take what you find; or come in for an hour some evening when you feel sociable and not too tired to talk. We are always at home; and there is *no one*, literally no one, whom we both see with such pleasure.—On the other hand if you don't like moving after the fatigue of the day we won't reproach you for *not* coming.

I long for these dreary months to be over, and pant for Italy once more. I was with Carlyle the other day—grimmer than ever.[3]

Yours faithfully
G. H. Lewes.

1. GHL's next article in *Blackwood's* was called "Recent Natural History Books," 89 (March 1861), 334–351.

2. *The Spanish Conquest in America and its Relation to the History of Slavery,* 4 vols., 1855–61 succeeded his anonymous *The Conquerors of the New World and Their Bondsmen,* 2 vols., 1848–52.

3. A letter from Carlyle to GHL 16 January 1861 was sold at Sotheby's 2 June 1919, item 107.

III, 394:6 GE TO MRS. CHARLES BRAY,
LONDON, 28 MARCH 1861

MS: National Library of Scotland, transferred from the Edinburgh Public Library. *Extract published:* Haight, *George Eliot,* p. 459.

16 Blandford Square | March 28. 61.

Dear Cara

I have not been well enough to write to you earlier, and I am not sure that I am quite well enough yet to say just what I mean and feel—the most difficult and rarely achieved task of "speech-dividing man."

It is perhaps well to exchange a written word now and then, for it is not in my nature to believe in any love that makes no sign. But I know that is a shallow-hearted irreligious disposition, and no words, or deeds either, have any value apart from the faith—the trust in our friend's goodness—that interprets them.

I suppose I must lose my memory altogether before I could forget all the tenderness, forbearance, and generous belief that made the unvarying character of your friendship towards me when we used to be a great deal together. I think I was not insensible to these things at any time, but experience deepens our insight into the past, and we feel we never understood or appreciated it thoroughly while it was the present. I should think it quite a chief blessing if that past which lives invisibly, though it has gone away from our outward daily existence, could have some sort of worthy worship in the present. I hardly know what other word to use but *worship*; for there is no such thing as a return, or a making amends for deficiencies. We can only feel that very great and good things have been given to us, and that they ought to be hallowed for ever more in our speech and actions. So that if ever you can let me be in any way a sharer and helper in trouble as far as our parted lives and duties make that possible, you will be adding something more to what you have already given of trust and kindness.

Mr. Lewes read aloud to me the "Hidden Fires,"[4] and I asked him particularly for his criticism. I said, "What should you say if that paper had been sent to you as an editor?" His answer was: "I should say that the writer had a turn for essay and reflective writing, and I should advise her to expand the introductory part." I think he has a wonderfully correct and rapid estimate of writing, and for that reason I venture to send you his

---

4. "Hidden Fires," *The Welcome Guest,* Part XVII (March 1861), 515–518, signed J. S. Linwood (a pseudonym of Caroline Bray?).

opinion. But I think the Welcome Guest ought to have paid you before this. The rule is to pay on publication, for periodical writing; though the rule is not always observed.

Tell Sara, if she has any questions to note—to ask them, and I will answer. My portrait is still in Mr. Lawrence's hands, Mr. Blackwood being under the sad trouble of expecting the death of his brother, Major Blackwood, so that his coming to town is likely to be deferred. We hear from those who know Mr. Lawrence well that his conduct in this matter is not an isolated instance.[5] Farewell.

Ever yours
Marian.

III, 396:21 GHL TO JOHN BLACKWOOD, LONDON, 2 APRIL 1861

MS: National Library of Scotland.

16, Blandford Square, | N.W.
Tuesday 2 April 61.

My dear Blackwood

Your two letters with their checques have just arrived and I intend saving this post to acknowledge their arrival.

The trifle I had "in hand" was an experiment of which you must judge—viz. the turning of an old unacted piece of mine into a lively story. As just such an experiment was the fortunate commencement of a connec-

---

5. For Samuel Laurence's portrait of GE see III, 343, 401–402. In a letter to the *Athenaeum*, 12 November 1881, p. 637, Laurence wrote: "Mr. Lewes gave me no commission. Miss Evans readily consented to sit to me *at my request*. When the drawing (the only one I have done) was completed, I had her leave to exhibit it. But this leave was withdrawn in a note *she* wrote me, stating that upon consideration, Mr. Lewes had shown her sufficient reasons why it should not be exhibited. Then, thirdly, Mr. Lewes did not refuse to take the drawing. He pressed me over and over again to give it to him, as he said he had all along expected me to do. This I altogether declined.

"A few weeks after I told Mr. Lewes I should not give him the drawing, the late Mr. John Blackwood bought it of me, and it hung in his private room—not in 'the back parlour of Mr. Blackwood's shop,' as Mr. Gosse says—till the day of his death, with other likenesses of authors he much esteemed, and is now in the possession of his widow. I have not seen it since." It was sold by his daughter Mrs. Gerald Porter at Sotheby's, 8 April 1914, item 667. Its present whereabouts is unknown. A preliminary study for it kept by Laurence, later signed by him and misdated 1857, was sold at Sotheby's 27 June 1923, item 640, and is now at Girton College, Cambridge.

tion with you,[6] which has been most agreeable and profitable, I was seduced into repeating it, the more so because I have long since cut the theatre and its affairs. I don't know what you will think of the story.[7] It seems amusing and lively to me; but it *may* smack too decidedly of its origin; so don't be under any misgiving about returning it, if you don't take to it.

Murray advertizes De Chaillu's book for April. As before hinted, I should like to review it, since it will be full of natural history stories.[8] I'm afraid if we go to Italy I shall not be industrious enough to write; but be assured that if I write at all, it will be for you.

I can sympathize with your swelled cheek. Some three or four years ago I was a martyr to it and it always indicates an anarchical condition of Schleswig Holstein, as you remark.

Mrs. Lewes will write, I suppose tomorrow, meanwhile she bids me send her kind regards. I think we go to the Prophète tonight—that is if Langford has a box.[9]

Ever yours
G. H. Lewes.

III, 405:15 GE TO JOHN BLACKWOOD, LONDON, [15? APRIL 1861]

MS: National Library of Scotland.

16, Blandford Square, | N.W.

My dear Sir

It was a double satisfaction to see your handwriting as a sign that nothing was hindering you from returning to work—the best of visible comforters.

I shall be very happy on all accounts if I am able to send you promising news of my progress. I am not at all confident: but I shall do the best my brain and strength will let me do. And there is always the pleasant background to my work, that I shall find nothing but help and agreement (in all fundamental matters of feeling) in you. This makes a great difference in authorship—in mine especially, with my tendency to suffer disproportionately from all discords.

We had not heard of Mudie's new demand for 500, and I am particularly glad to know of the prudent limitation as to printing.

6. GHL's first article in *Blackwood's* was "Lesurques; or the Victim of Judicial Error," 53 (January 1843), 24–32, adapted from the play *Le Courier de Lyon.*

7. "Mrs. Beauchamp's Vengeance." See III, 406, n. 4.
8. See III, 406, n. 5, and III, 430.
9. See III, 397, n. 9.

Since we have a second time the evil chance of missing you on your Spring visit to London, I hope something will demand an extra visit from you before another May. Pray give my kind remembrances to Mr. W. Blackwood and believe me.

Always yours truly
M. E. Lewes.

John Blackwood, Esq.

III, 401:1 ANTHONY TROLLOPE TO GHL, WALTHAM CROSS, 7 APRIL 1861

MS: Yale. *Published: The Letters of Anthony Trollope,* ed. B. A. Booth, 1951, pp. 88–89.

Waltham Cross. | April 7. 1861.

My dear Lewes.

I must consider your letter as in some degree special, and give it a special answer.

You take me too closely au pied de la lettre as touching husbands and lovers.[1] As to myself personally, I have daily to wonder at the continued run of domestic and worldly happiness which has been granted me;—to wonder at it as well as to be thankful for it. I do so, fearing that my day, also, of misery must come;—for we are told by so many teachers of all doctrines that pain of some sort is mans lot. But no pain or misery has as yet come to me since the day I married; and if any man should speak well of the married state, I should do so.

But I deny that I have done other. There is a sweet young blushing joy about the first acknowledged reciprocal love, which is like the bouquet of the first glass of wine from the bottle—It goes when it has been tasted. But for all that who will compare the momentary aroma with the lasting joys of the still flowing bowl? May the bowl still flow for both of us, and leave no touch of headache.

When do you go Alpwards? and what do you do before that. I shall be here from Sunday 14th to Friday (morning) 19th but with no one in the house but wife and boys. Again from Monday 23rd, to Sunday 28th and then shall have friends, who will like to meet you. Can you name a day for either period? Of course a man who comes here sleeps here.

Yours always
Anthony Trollope.

1. GHL had perhaps commented on the love affairs in Trollope's *Framley Parsonage,* which had concluded in the *Cornhill* for April 1861.

III, 405:15 THORNTON LEWES TO GE, EDINBURGH, 14 APRIL 1861

MS: Yale.

1. Duncan Street | Newington | Edinburgh. | April 14. 1861.
Dear Mother,

I am very sorry that you did not enjoy your trip to Hastings very much, but of course you will like your voyage to Italy all the better. I should like *uncommonly* to go with you as far as Switzerland and then stick at Hofwyl till you came back, as I eschew Italy, as a land where there is no water to be got to drink, no butterflies to be caught, no plants to be found, nothing but straight roads 6 miles long to walk on, nothing but dust to eat (when walking, that is to say), etc. etc. etc.

I am extremely obliged for your birthday present, but it will be more convenient, if you send down the tin as I can get it here at a much cheaper rate than you can, as a quantity of shops give a reduction of 2 pence in the shilling. But if you send it, for goodness sake do not send the coloured edition, as it is very badly coloured and costs a good deal. Take the edition published in Bohn's illustrated Library!

Thank Father extremely for the 16/. and inform him, that it would be a most difficult thing to tell him how I had enjoyed myself at Dundee, considering that I start for it on Tuesday the 23rd inst. I will give you however an eight page description of it when I return, when I know your address in Italy. Our Session ends at the end of July. Please tell me the route you intend taking, and please Mother dear, look after stamps when you are in Italy, as I will not trouble Pater with them this year, as he bought just the wrong ones last year, though perhaps I did not express clearly what I wanted and what I did not want. If you go through *Parma* and *Modena*, please get me *all the stamps*, there are not more than 5 of each, and if you go to Sicily, and if there are *different ones there from the Neapolitan*, send as many as you like. And please put, when you are at Rome stamps of $\frac{1}{2}$, 1, 2, 3 baj on the letters to me.

You heard of course that Major Blackwood is dead. I did not know it, till yesterday when I went to call on Mr. Simpson, to ask how the Major was, and he then told me that he had died on Wednesday or Monday[2] I forget which.

Silas Marner is splendid. I like it extremely, preferring it to Adam Bede or the "Scenes." And when I had come to the last page I almost got angry

---

2. Major William Blackwood died Monday, 8 April 1861.

at there being no more of it. There is a very good article on it in the Saturday Review of yesterday.³

How is Charlie getting on? Thumping I suppose all day long. Pat him on the back and tell him from me that he is a "good little boy" for delivering my message to Empson, who wrote me a very nice letter on Thursday, in which he says he supposes Master Charles must have stolen his first letter to me, at the post-office, to prevent my getting it. I, of course, decidedly coincide with his opinion. Pater is out about my not writing in cos as 'ow he (Empson) had not sent any stamps, for otherwise I should be sadly off for correspondance.

I am writing to Grandmamma today. You will of course go to see Bertie when coming back from Italy. How long is he to remain at Hofwyl? Yesterday I kept my birthday and Mrs. Robertson gave me a grand dinner and a bottle of sherry, and I invited 3 friends of mine, and Mr. Robertson's two sisters were there and the whole company enjoyed themselves very much, and I was not least in that respect. I got 3 birthday presents viz: 2 portraits, and a pot of homemade marmalade, the latter given me by a Mrs. Gregor a great friend of mine, with whom I enjoy the title of son.

Having nothing more to say, I remain, Dear Mother

Your affectionate Son
Thornie.

III, 407:1 GHL TO JOHN BLACKWOOD, [LONDON, 16 APRIL 1861]

MS: National Library of Scotland. *Endorsed:* April 16/61.

Tuesday.

My dear Blackwood

Thanks for the checque; but you have been hasty in sending me the whole of the 20£ from Holland⁴ since you have an account *against* me for binding of m.s.s. of Mill and Silas—as well as for some other things. But as you have sent the checque, that account must be settled in future.

I have just returned from a visit to Anthony Trollope⁵—an honest hearty fellow—and the sight of the sunshine in the country makes London doubly odious.

Ever faithfully yours
G. H. Lewes.

3. "Silas Marner, the Weaver of Raveloe," *Saturday Review*, 34 (6 April 1861), 361–362.
4. *Silas Marner de Wever van Raveloe,*
tr. Mevr. van Westrheene, Amsterdam, P. N. van Kampen, 1861.
5. "Went down to Waltham to dine

III, 411:31   GHL TO CHARLES LEE LEWES,
FLORENCE, 5 MAY 1861

MS: Yale. *Published:* III, 411–412, with many omissions and revisions.

Florence Sunday 5 May 1861.
My dear Boy

It did the hearts of the tired Mutter and Pater good, last evening, shortly after reaching the hotel, to get your long and pleasant letter. We had swallowed some tea, and said deux mots to a thin beefsteak, not by any means juicy, when, as I learned the post would be open for an hour, I trotted out in the rain, and quickly came back bearing letters from "the boy," and from Blackwood—that from the latter containing the best of news about 'Silas' namely that the "Row" is buying furiously, that every one speaks admiringly, and that the edition is 7,500 copies, or was on the 24th last month.

I presume that on Monday after writing to us you received the darling Mutter's long letter which she wrote at Nice, while I enjoyed a sick headache. Therefore from *that* point shall be resumed the history of our very long, very delightful, and very expensive journey here. Writing to you brought us up to the hour of table d'hôte. After that we went to the French theatre, and saw *Le Père Prodigue* which was prodige-ux! We came away disgusted at the end of the third act; disgusted with the piece, and with the audience which did not rise against it in protest.[6]

On Friday we started by vetturino (one always says by vetturino, though why one should go by coachman and not by coach is not clear) for Mentone which we reached at noon. The carriage was as comfortable and elegant as a private carriage in England and the horses good. The road was a succession of pictures, winding up the mountain passes, with the snowy Apennines as a grand line on one horizon, and the Mediterranean, "deeply darkly beautifully blue"[7] on the other; through groves of olives, and orchards of orange trees and lemon trees bearing their golden fruit; the day being transcendant, bright, warm yet not sultry, and with no dust. At Mentone we had half a day of delicious rambling among the orchards of oranges,

and sleep at Trollope's. He has a charming house and grounds, and I like him very much, so wholesome and straightforward a man. Mrs. Trollope did not make any decided impression on me, one way or the other." (GHL Journal, 15 April 1861.)

6. "Certainly any amount of prudery is better than the license of French Literature. We left after the end of the 3d act, disgusted with the audience for not rising to protest against such desecration of honest feelings." (GHL Journal, 25 April 1861.)

7. Robert Southey, *Madoc in Wales*, I, 5, reads "darkly, deeply."

sitting "under the shade of melancholy boughs,"[8] reading our books, and planning to have a lovely place of our own, some day, wherein Pater would rear his own peas, his own pears, and his own frogs—leaving filius to do the hard work of digging etc. We dined at 6, and—as usual—were in bed by ½ past 7.

Saturday we had another exquisite day, but much longer en route. We stayed two hours to lunch and repose at San Remo where we saw palm trees in blossom, a thing I once saw in Kew Conservatory, but never before in the open air. But palms here are abundant. The aloe is on this coast a common hedge weed; and the cactus grows freely in many places. We reached Oneglia, an uninteresting place at ½ past 4—dined and went to bed early, as a step to getting wealthy and wise.

Sunday the route to Savona was less beautiful, but even less means much beauty; the day also was cloudy, though mild. Monday we got to Genoa by 2 o'clock having stopped to lunch en route. We were so enraptured with Genoa last year that I feared lest a second visit should be a disappointment. But a "thing of beauty is a joy for ever, its loveliness increaseth"[9] (as I remark to Mutter respecting my own beauty) and our stay at Genoa was again intoxicating (*not* alcoholic). At the hotel where we stayed there was Garibaldi's Col. Peard[1]—his "Englishman" of whom you doubtless often heard. We had been very much struck by his appearance before we learned who he was, and *after* learning it we saw him no more. At Genoa, where we stayed Monday and Tuesday, we went to the opera and heard Verdi's *Attila* bawled with great vigour. The "scourge of god"[2] was represented by a basso with the shortest arms and the most obtrusive stomach, I ever saw, doch war es immer nicht der Held![3] The Mutter conceived a violent passion for him. The tenor labored under a deficiency of voice and a redness of nose. The prima donna was a vigorous little fat jewess, not bad at all.

Mutter sternly resisted Genoese velvets, and Genoese bracelets, so that we bought nothing at Genoa but a few volumes of Italian lit[erature] and history.[4] On Wednesday, May 1 when we *ought* to have been here had we

8. *As You Like It*, II, vii, 111.
9. Keats, *Endymion*, I, 1.
1. John Whitehead Peard (1811–80) went with Garibaldi on the Sicilian expedition in 1860, was made a colonel and decorated for his service by Victor Emmanuel. "At the table d'hôte we were much struck by the fine massive energetic head of an Englishman with a huge iron grey beard." (GHL Journal, 29 April 1861.)

2. Attila was called "the Scourge of God."
3. Goethe, *Maximen und Reflexionen*, 47, ed. Max Hecker, Weimar, 1907, p. 8.
4. "Bought a novel on Savonarola, and Varchi's *Istorie Fiorentine*." (GHL Journal, 30 April 1861.) Benedetto Varchi's *Storia Fiorentina*, 5 vols., Milan, 1803–04, with GE's pencil markings is at Yale. Another edition, 3 vols., 1853, is among GE's books in Dr. Williams's

not taken this delicious but lengthy route, we started again with our vetturino, through a lovely country, still coasting the Mediterranean, remember that! staying at a charming place (Camogli) to lunch, and reaching Sestri at 5, in time to enjoy a ramble by sunset after dinner, and to get to bed well tired. Next day we got to Spezia which is very beautiful—I mean the bay and Carrara marble mountains which rise on one side of it. We were here in time for a delicious ramble along the sands; and we did not quit till ½ past 12 the next day, when we started on a much less interesting route to Pietra Santa; and yesterday got thence to Pisa, where we stayed four hours, and for the third time were thrilled by the marvels of the place.

During the last part of the journey Mutter has not been quite well, and yesterday was positively ill. But today she seems only languid, tired and with a slight cold. It is cold and raining so we have not been out today, and are languidly vegetating in the hotel,[5] rather unsettled as to our future settlement. We are too expensively lodged at present, but tomorrow I shall look about. Meanwhile address poste restante—and *prepay;* as *we* shall do in future; for I find that letters not prepaid are charged double. I have scarcely left room for the Mutter's p.s. so will only say God bless you, my dearest boy.

Ever your loving
Pater.

III, 430:1 THORNTON ARNOTT LEWES TO GE, EDINBURGH, 25 JUNE 1861

MS: Yale.

2[6] Duncan Street, | Newington, | Edinburgh | 25 June. 1861.
Dear Mother,

As I received a letter this morning from Pater, informing me that you were alive and kicking I hasten to assume the pen to *un*dress myself to you. I am in the first place extremely obliged to every body for every thing i.e. to you and Pater for the stamps etc. which you sent from Italy. In the second place I am very glad that you enjoyed yourselves so much, though doubtless if your heads had not troubled you, you would have enjoyed yourselves much more. When I received Patris epistolam from Italy, I was enjoying

Library. GHL may have confused Varchi with Giovanni Villani's *Istorie Fiorentine*, 2 vols., Milan, 1859–61, also in Dr. Williams's Library.

5. Hotel de l'Europe.

6. George Robertson's address is changed from 1 to 2 Duncan Street in the Edinburgh directories for 1862; George Dick is listed at 1.

the temporary honours of the Duxship, temporary because honours in this fleeting vorld don't last long, and therefore Pater's growl about my not writing de meis litterarum studiis c'est-à-dire mes études littéraires came very mal-à-propos. The reason for my not writing about my lessons was, because I had other things to say, and as lessons are the dullest things, *to write about*, not to learn, I only mention them, when I have nothing else to say, whereas last time I sent Pater a terse, vigourous, funny, punning, amusing, interesting, English, French, German, Italian and Latin epistle.

I am very much obliged to Pater for allowing a trip to the Highlands of Scotland, but I am a true Swiss, attacked ever since I came here with an incurable disease commonly known under the name of nostalgia or under the more poetical one of Heimweh, and consequently there is nothing I should like half so much as to go to Switzerland for a fortnight with Empson, who I suppose will not go before the 27 or 28 July. Please, Pater et Mater, take this matter into your favourable consideration, I should like *so* much to see Switzerland once more. Vidi la Svizzera e poi muori!

I am going to dine this evening with Mr. Blackwood, and shall see your portrait, which he says looks rather sad; but I will give you my opinion in my next.

I suppose you don't know that Mr. Howard (the great concert man here) has opened what he calls an operetta house,[7] and Miss Julia St. George is the directress (I suppose you never saw her), well I knew her again the instant I saw her, though I had not seen her I should think for 6 or 7 years.

How long did you stop at Hofwyl? 2 or three days, I suppose.[8] Dr. Müller sent me a beautiful letter the other day from which I quote the following:

Von allen unsern Schülern bist du wohl so ziemlich der einzige, der nicht in dieser Sprache geboren, sich das Deutsche *ganz* zu eigen gemacht, was allerdings keine Kleinigkeit ist etc.

I suppose neither of you are coming down to the Examination, which takes place on the 24 and 25 July. I am said to be quite sure of the *Club prize* (the best of the lot,) though I should prefer the Dux's medal) consisting as Mr. Robertson says of almost a library, some 8 or ten splendid volumes. The competitors are to be examined in Latin, Greek, French, German, English and Mathematics in a fortnight or so.

7. William Howard's Operetta House in the Waterloo Rooms was first advertised in the *Scotsman*, 11 May 1861. He is described as "sole lesee and musical director"; Miss Julia St. George as "directress." The season opened 24 May 1861.

8. Returning from Italy, GE and GHL stopped overnight at Berne 11 June 1861, saw Bertie at Hofwyl, and walked with him on the morning of the 12th before going to Paris. (GHL Journal.)

My stamps are flourishing, 550. Butterflies ditto though I have made no new acquisition. In the shooting line I am such a crack shot, that I hardly ever fire at a bird sitting. I shoot swallows almost easier than anything else, but as it is a great pity to shoot the poor beasts I have given it up, so I have only shot 5 of them.

I suppose you have seen the glorious books published by Routledge at 1/ each, viz: British Butterflies, British Birds eggs, Common objects of the seashore, of the country, and the microscope etc.[9] They are the cheapest books ever published. Blackwood says that 8000 copies of Silas Marner have been sold, the more the merrier.

I was in a *very* good humour yesterday, so one of my friends, who always puns and quizzes when he gets the chance, said: Ah! ha! I know why you are so elated today. Where were you fencing this morning? Now it happened that in the morning I had been fencing in Dr. Schmitz's garden with one of his boarders and had seen Dora, which fact had been communicated to the other fellow, who always asks me when I see Dora, whether she *squeedged* my hand or not?

I express great sorrow at not having written to thank Grandmamma, but I hope you will do it when you see her and I will do it soon by letter. Tell Charlie I shall write to him soon. Is Walter Young living close to you? Tell Charles to tell Empson to answer my letter.

> Here ends my tail, that with affection wags
> From want of stuff not want of time it flags!

Ever your affectionate Son
Thornton Arnott Lewes.

Messrs. R. and Schmitz send kind regards.

Rex Ranarum.

III, 435:16 GHL TO THOMAS ADOLPHUS TROLLOPE, LONDON, 5 JULY 1861

MS: The Johns Hopkins University.

16 Blandford Square N.W. | 5 July 1861.

My dear Trollope

We have now read 'La Beata'[2] and must tell you how charmed we have been with it. Nina herself is perfectly exquisite and *individual*; and her story

---

9. W. S. Coleman, *British Butterflies*, and J. C. Atkinson, *British Birds' Eggs and Nests* in Books for the Country series; J. G. Wood, *Common Objects of the Sea Shore*.

2. See III, 435, n. 3.

5 July 1861

is full of poetry and pathos. Also one feels a breath from the Val d'Arno rustling amid the pages; and a sense of Florentine life, such as one rarely gets out of books. The critical objection I should make to it, apart from minor points, is that often you spoil the artistic effect by quitting the artistic attitude, and adopting a critical antagonistic attitude—by which I mean that instead of painting the thing *objectively*, you present it critically, with an *eye to the opinions* likely to be formed by certain readers. Thus, instead of relying on the simple presentation of the fact of Nina's *innocence*, you *call up* the objection you desire to *anticipate*, by side glances at the worldly and 'knowing' readers' opinions. In a word I feel as if you were not engrossed by your subject, but were sufficiently aloof from it to contemplate it as a spectator—which is an error in art. Many of the remarks are delicately felt and finely written. The whole book comes from a noble nature, and so it impresses the reader.

But I may tell you what Mrs. Carlyle said last night which will in some sense corroborate what I have said. In her opinion you would have done better to make two books of it—one the love story, and one a description of Florentine life. (She admires the book very much, I should add.) Now although I cannot by any means agree with that criticism of hers, I fancy the origin of it was some such feeling as I have endeavoured to indicate in saying you are often critical where you should be simply objective.

We had a pleasant journey home over the St. Gotthard, and found our boy very well and happy at Hofwyl, and our bigger boy *ditto*, awaiting us here. Polly is very well, and as you may imagine, talks daily of Florence and our delightful trip—our closer acquaintance with you and yours being among the most delightful of our reminiscences.

Yesterday Anthony dined with us, and as he had never seen Carlyle, he was glad to go down with us to tea at Chelsea. Carlyle had read, and *agreed* with the West Indian book,[3] and the two got on very well together; both Carlyle and Mrs. Carlyle liking Anthony—and I suppose it was reciprocal, though I didn't see him afterwards to hear what he thought. He had to run away to catch his train.

He told us of the sad news of Mrs. Browning's death. Poor Browning! that was my first, and remains my constant reflection. When people love each other, and have lived together any time, they ought to die together. For myself I should not care in the least ⟨who⟩ about dying;—the dreadful thing to me would be to live after losing, if I ever should lose the one who has made life for me. Of course you who all knew and valued her will feel the loss, but I can't think of anybody's grief but his.

3. Anthony Trollope, *The West Indies and the Spanish Main*, 1859. He shared Carlyle's opinion of the Negro as vain and lazy.

The next page must be left for Polly's postscript, so I shall only send my kindest regards and wishes to Mrs. Trollope, and the biggest of kisses to la cantatrice.[4]

Ever faithfully yours
G. H. Lewes.

III, 451:1 GHL TO FRANCIS ESPINASSE, LONDON, 27 AUGUST 1861

MS: Yale.

16, Blandford Square, | N.W.
27 August 61.

My dear Sir

I have pencilled on the margin the trifling corrections you have asked for.

The work[5] seems to promise great things.

Yours in haste and pain
G. H. Lewes.

F. Espinasse, Esq.

III, 451:1 GE TO MME EUGÈNE BODICHON, [LONDON, 3? SEPTEMBER 1861]

MS: Yale. *Envelope:* Mrs. Bodichon No. 5.

Dear Barbara

Mary Lee[6] is here. Should you like—or are you able to come and see her now, or will you mention some other time at which you would like her to come for that purpose?

Ever yours
M. E. L.

---

4. Beatrice Trollope, who sang for GE and GHL at Florence.

5. Perhaps part of the MS of his *The Life and Times of François-Marie Arouet, calling himself Voltaire*, 1866. This letter is the only evidence found of GHL's relations with Espinasse, whose *Literary Recollections and Sketches*, 1893 provides one of the fullest accounts of GHL's life.

6. Mrs. Lee was a relation of GHL's mother Mrs. John Willim, with whom she lived for many years. See III, 455.

III, 452:5 GE TO JOHN BLACKWOOD,
MALVERN, 12 SEPTEMBER 1861

MS: National Library of Scotland. *Published: TLS,* 10 March 1972, p. 281.

Malvern[7] | September 12. 1861.

My dear Sir

Your letter enclosing the cheque for £600 reached me here this morning. You will have heard from Mr. William Blackwood that there were reasons for not sending me the order for £1000, as you proposed.[8] Many thanks for your promptness, and a sincere Amen to your wishes for our mutual future. I can desire nothing more satisfactory to myself than that our relations should continue as long as my writing life.

And now, for the new edition of my books. Mr. Lewes's suggestion is, that a 6/. edition might be published in moderate numbers, which, if stereotyped, might be reproduced on thinner paper as the 2/6 edition—one set of types thus serving for two editions. You, of course, will weigh the merits of this suggestion against those of any other plan you may have in your mind.

Meanwhile, reconsideration has changed my views as to the retention of copyrights, and made me wish to consult you on a question which has arisen. As we have no young children and as our responsibilities for others lie in the present rather than in the distant future, I feel that the profits ⟨of my works⟩ henceforth to be gained on my four published books will be less valuable to me spread over the long term of copyright, than in the form of an immediate sum calculated in due proportion to the probable amount of those profits. And I should like to know from you whether you consider that it would be for the advantage of your firm to give me such a sum for my copyrights as it would be for my advantage to receive at this early stage of their existence.

We came here about a week ago to initiate a trial of the water-cure for Mr. Lewes, and it is a comfort to be able to say that he is already considerably strengthened, if not by hydropathy, at least by the bracing air and abundant exercise we get on the hills. We shall return to town by the middle or end of next week, so that all letters had better be addressed to us at Blandford Square. I am to tell you that Mr. Lewes has an article already written for you, but it requires some modification, which he will give it as soon as we get home again. We mean to carry on Dr. Gully's[9] processes of

7. Written on GE's printed stationery with the address cancelled.

8. See III, 453.

9. James Manby Gully (1808–83),

packing, sitz bath etc. in London, for after all, they are extremely simple, and might be attained without paying so many guineas for them as Malvern systems demand. Thornton is coming from Switzerland in another week or ten days, so that we must be at home to receive him and be with him till he starts for Edinburgh again.

You can't possibly think more of the "great work"[1] than I do, or than Mr. Lewes does. He thinks hopefully; I think doubtfully. On the whole I should recommend to your attention the supplementary beatitude "Blessed is he that expecteth nothing" etc—if it were not that I *never* expect anything, but don't find myself beatified in consequence. All work will go on better when I can once be easier about Mr. Lewes's health. I congratulate you on being obliged to stay in the country.

I may venture to send through you, or through this letter, my kind regards to Mr. William Blackwood and thanks for his explanation about the order.

Mr. Lewes unites with me in all kind remembrances.

Ever yours truly
Marian Evans Lewes.

John Blackwood Esq.

III, 455:1 GE TO JOHN BLACKWOOD, LONDON, 25 SEPTEMBER 1861

MS: National Library of Scotland. *Published:* TLS, 10 March 1972, p. 281.

16, Blandford Square, | N.W.
September 25. 61.

My dear Sir

Thanks for the precious cheque, which has just been safely deposited in Mr. Lewes's pocket on its way to the bank.

He begs me to tell you that he made the requisite alterations in the proof, and sent it on yesterday. He is in better working order now, and I hope there will be no drawback on the improvement which has very decidedly begun.

We have our noisy hopeful, Thornie—"Sturm und Drang" as one of our friends has christened him—just come home from Switzerland, which will cause the parental meditations a few days of distraction—happily not of an unhealthy kind.

M.D. Edinburgh, 1829, author of *The Water Cure in Chronic Disease*, 1846, was also a Spiritualist, and testified to D. D. Home's floating about the room during a seance. See *The Spiritual Magazine*, 2 (1861), 63–66, and Mrs. D. D. Home, *The Gift of D. D. Home*, 1890, p. 136.

1. *Romola*.

25 September 1861 291

I have read carefully all through "Adam Bede" and "The Mill" and have marked all the *errata* I have discovered.[2] I hope the new editions will be carefully printed after these corrected copies, which I shall presently send. I have also marked in the Clerical Scenes some corrections which Mr. Lewes noted when he last read them. But I cannot read these and Silas Marner through, as I have done the other two books—I find this reading excite me too much and carry me away from the present. I am very glad, however, that I have given the needful time to "Adam" and "The Mill," for there were several mistakes which affected the sense in an important manner. It has moved me a good deal—reading the books again after a long interval, but it has done me good, for I can say a full Amen to everything I have written. I shall await your letter about the new editions and then send the corrected copies.

I am glad to hear of your sanitary measures. To a certain extent one must adopt the creed attributed to Mr. Buckle[3]—

> "I believe in all the gases
> As the means to raise the masses."

I find myself considerably depressed by the gases on close London days, I know. But perhaps one of the best sanitary influences is the laughing gas you get in the form of your friends' fun.

It would be a great pleasure to me to add to the already agreeable acquaintance I have with Mr. White[4] through his writings by some personal knowledge of him.

We are having frequent rain here. I hope you are more fortunate, and have moisture in no other form than that of white morning mists, soon dispersed by sunshine.

Ever yours truly
Marian E. Lewes.

John Blackwood Esq.

2. This careful reading renders the 6/ edition important in establishing the text of GE's novels. She used the "Eighth Edition" (i.e. the 5th impression of the 2nd ed.) of *Adam Bede*, 2 vols., 1860, endorsed by Blackwood's manager George Simpson "Corrected by Author Nov. 1861"; and "A New Edition" of *The Mill on the Floss*, 2 vols., 1860, endorsed "Received from Author as copy for Reprint in 3/6d form." *Silas Marner*, 1861, was endorsed "With Author's Corrections, Nov. 1861." *Scenes of Clerical Life*, "Third Edition," 2 vols., 1860, was endorsed "1000 copies by 24th March [1863]."

3. Proof of some doggerel verses entitled "Buckle's Belief" in the George Eliot Collection, Coventry City Libraries, begins: "This is the Creed, let no man chuckle, | Of the great thinker Henry Buckle.—| 'I believe in Fire and Water, | And in Fate, dame Nature's daughter.'" In 1858 GE lent the first vol. of his *History of Civilization in England* to Charles Bray, who may have written the "Creed."

4. The Rev. James White (1803–62), an old friend of John Blackwood and an occasional contributor to *Blackwood's*.

III, 459:25 GE TO JOHN BLACKWOOD, LONDON, 17 OCTOBER 1861

MS: National Library of Scotland. *Published: TLS,* 10 March 1972, p. 281.

16, Blandford Square, | N.W.
October 17. 61.

My dear Sir

I have been considering the offer contained in your last letter, and the result is, that I do not think it advisable for me to part with my copyrights. I can quite understand that it would not answer, as a business speculation, to advance on a prospective benefit, a sum which it would be wise in me to accept.[5] The inducement on my part to entertain the idea was not any immediate want of money, but the possibility that my copyrights might be worth a sum which, in addition to what I already possess, would have given us a secure income, that might have enabled Mr. Lewes to give the larger proportion of his time to an important work which he has long been meditating.[6] But now, dismissing this episodic idea, we had better lose no time in arranging about the terms for the cheaper editions.

I have not read the last number of the Chronicles of Carlingford, not having much time for extra reading, but I read the previous number, and thought the scene between the Rector and his deaf mother delightful.[7]

I hope you in Scotland are sharing our pleasant weather.

Ever yours truly
M. E. Lewes.

III, 465:3 GE TO JOHN BLACKWOOD, LONDON, 18 NOVEMBER 1861

MS: National Library of Scotland. *Published: TLS,* 10 March 1972, p. 282.

16, Blandford Square, | N.W.
November 18. 61.

My dear Sir

Your explanatory letter to Mr. Lewes leaves, I think, nothing more to be discussed about this long-agitated business of the new editions. I agree with

---

5. See III, 458, n. 1.

6. GHL planned to write a history of science, of which his *Aristotle: A Chapter from the History of Science, Including Analyses of Aristotle's Scientific Writings,* 1864, was the first part.

7. GE's acknowledgement that she had read "The Rector," part of Mrs. Oliphant's *Chronicles of Carlingford* in *Blackwood's* 90 (September 1861) con-

18 November 1861 293

you that the £4. saved on the paper will be best applied in improving the binding. We can hardly expect a very large sale of the 6s/. editions, so it will be wisest to proceed on the basis of modest hopes in the printing. Let us understand, then, that I ⟨expect⟩ accept the proposition of £60 per thousand for all the four books in their 6s/. edition i.e. if you at length decide on fixing "Silas" at that price.

You will perhaps be interested and amused, as I was, to hear that one of the most ardent among the admirers of "Adam Bede" is—Alexandre Dumas, the elder![8] Count Arrivabene[9] brought us that information from Naples yesterday. Dumas declaimed about it, after his peculiar fashion, with the book in his hand, translating here and there, especially from Hetty's journey—and pronouncing the book to be the greatest novel of the age. After this I will never venture to predict who will like or dislike my books. But imagine what I escaped: by some means or other it was reported by telegraph that we were coming to Naples, and Dumas was preparing to announce my arrival in an article. I shudder at the thought. Pray appreciate the picture of my frightened self accosted by that journalistic whirlwind. It was too piquant a bit of gossip for me to resist telling it you, though I am plunged in the glooms of sick headache.

Mr. Lewes has finished his article on Hamlet and Othello, and will despatch it tomorrow. It is really important that there should be some truthful writing about Fechter's Othello.[1] I think the performance positively injurious to the half-cultivated people who make up the mass of his audiences. That a tragedy like that, should produce a series of small titters in its moments of highest pathos, is an outrage on Shakespeare and is demoralizing to the titterers. I could perceive that most of the elegantly dressed people around me were totally unacquainted with the play and were being introduced to Shakspeare by Fechter. They were in a state of utter obfuscation.

Ever yours truly
M. E. Lewes.

tradicts her later insistence to Sara Hennell, 23 April [1862] that she had not read the stories.

8. Alexandre Dumas *père* (1802–70), drifting about the Mediterranean in his yacht *Emma*, attached himself to Garibaldi, who appointed him to the nominal post of Director of the Museum at Naples. He held court briefly in one of the royal palaces, where this reading of *Adam Bede* took place.

9. Carlo Arrivabene Valenti Gonzaga (1824–74), Italian patriot, fled to London in 1852, where he supported himself by teaching languages. After becoming a British citizen in 1859, he returned to Italy as correspondent for the *Daily News*. In 1860 he followed Garibaldi from Sicily to Naples; captured at the battle of Volturno, he was imprisoned until freed by British intervention. He called on GE and GHL Sunday, 17 November 1861. (GE Journal.)

1. GE saw Fechter's Hamlet with approval 26 July 1861, but his Othello

III, 474:9 THORNTON ARNOTT LEWES TO GHL,
EDINBURGH, 22 DECEMBER 1861

MS: Yale. *Partly published:* Haight, *George Eliot,* p. 363.

   2. Duncan Street | Newington | Edinburgh | December 22d 1861.
Dearest Pater,

Many thanks for the cheque. I do not know how you interpret my letter in an offhand way, for I did not pen it with that intention. In answer to your saying that I should have saved up; pray päterchen how much can I save out of 1/ per week, considering that I have to buy my lunch usually as it is by far too much trouble to come home every day at this time of year.

Dr. Schmitz has none of the commentaries on Aristotle that you mentioned, nothing but the plain text. He is off to London tomorrow morning, on his way to Rome where he intends to spend the Christmas holidays.

I do not know whether I told you last letter that I was Dux for the first quarter, i.e. from October to Christmas? It therefore looks as if I am to be Dux for the other three quarters, and though the High school medal is not worth much compared with passing 1st in the Civil Service examination, still I suppose you won't object to have my name printed in big letters on the board in our classroom, and to have a gold medal to keep (which bye the bye, being good gold can always easily be pawned!!!)

Tomorrow at 9.45 a.m. I am off to Blackwoods so you may look out for game. Dr. Schmitz is coming, I think, to pay you a visit when he is in London.

I am now going to tell you something about which you must *reinen Mund halten*, that is to say, it is not necessary to mention it in any letter to Mr. R. On Friday night I went to the theatre, having won a shilling from Mrs. R. by a bet. I came out at a quarter to 11, and was home by 10 minutes past. I found the gate and door locked, and nobody opened though I rang four times. I knew that Mr. R. was still up, as his light was burning. I therefore, went round to the end of the street, jumped into the lane which goes at the back of our garden, got on the wall, and walked to my window, which not being bolted, I easily pushed up, and I then got in. I went to bed. Got up the next morning and went into town at 10 o'clock, nobody being up. I came back at 2, and then went to Mr. R. and asked

11 November she heartily disliked. Her opinion is echoed in GHL's "Fechter in Hamlet and Othello, *"Blackwood's,* 90 (December 1861), 744–54: "I think his Hamlet is one of the very best, and his Othello one of the very worst I have ever seen."

22 December 1861 295

why I had been locked out. He said because I was beyond the hour, (which was not true, for we rarely are in, when we go to the theatre before 11¼, Mr. R. himself did not come back till 12½ only 2 nights ago), and that if it happened again he would report every case to you. I said he was at liberty to do so, but that if I was turned from the door at a reasonable hour again, I should leave the house. His reply was that I could leave it then, if I chose. I then left the room, went into my own and began to work. Suddenly the door opens and in stalks R. saying that he would report this case also to you, if I did not give him a written apology for coming late. My answer was "So you can!"

This put him in an awful rage, so, calling me an insolent dog, he made his shoeleather acquainted with my posterity. You need not ask me what I did; I did what you would have done in my place—knocked him down (This is what his face is like today, a dark red mark under the eye, 2 spots above this mark, and two bruises on the forehead.) I of course left the house, as he told me to, and proceeded to Dr. Schmitz's to ask his advice, because I did not think it possible that R. would take me back after flooring him. So I spent the night at the Drs. In the evening R. came, not knowing that I was there, and Dr. Schmitz showed him so ably how wrong he had been, that he wrote me a full apology, which of course I willingly accepted, and came back here this morning. When he saw [me] he shook hands and said that he was very sorry for it, but that he hoped it would be buried in oblivion and forgotten, and that we should go on as formerly. And so we are all right again. You will of course not speak about it to him, as it is forgiven and forgotten.

This is all the news I have to tell you, so with love to Mutter and Charlie, I remain

Your affectionate Son
Thornton Lewes.

P.S. Charles will no doubt be desirous of knowing whether I got any blows, so you can inform him that I got one on the cheek, which cut it slightly internally. That is all, as Sayers said to Heenan,[2] when he split the latter's eye open. Dr. Schmitz said to me after having seen Mr. R., "Lewes, you have given him a terrible pummelling, he has got a black eye!"

2. See III, 289, n. 2.

Romola

1862 April 1   Lytton thanks GE for letter on his poem.
1862 May 21   GE's agreement with Smith Elder for *Romola*.
1862 June 2   Tom Trollope reads proof of *Romola*, Part I.
1862 June 28   A. Trollope praises *Romola*.
1863 January   GHL advises Mrs. Bray about publishing.
1863 September 30   Mme Bodichon gives Thornie letters for Natal.
1863 November 5   GE and GHL move to the Priory, 21 North Bank.
1863 November 24   Charles's 21st birthday party.
1864 March 15   Robert Evans II read *Adam Bede* on deathbed.
1864 April   GHL's *Aristotle* published.
1864 May 3   "Brother Jacob" GE's gift to George Smith.
1864 May–June   GE and GHL in Italy with Burton.
1864 June 29   GE's first sitting to Burton for portrait.

IV, 28:6 ROBERT LYTTON TO GE, [VIENNA, APRIL? 1862]

MS: Yale.

The writer of some anonymous verses (entitled 'A Great man') which appeared some months ago in a number of "All the Year Round,"[3] has just received from the office of that Periodical an envelope containing some words for which he is anxious to express to "George Elliot," not only the sincerity of his thanks, but something also of the peculiar sensations with which those words have been read by him.

The silence which surrounds anonymous publication (especially the publication of anonymous verses in periodicals wherein such verses are but so much stuff to stop gaps with) is so echoless and impalpable that to those who speak in it, it may well appear inanimate; and thus, losing the sense of responsibility in the sense of solitude, they feel (at least this writer has felt) like children who sing and shout at random when they think themselves alone. Any voice, therefore, that breaks this silence, in response to such random invasion of it, cannot but be, however kindly and welcoming its character, strange and startling in the effect of it; and the words of George Elliot have indeed in the present instance occasioned "a stirring"—nay, a flutter, of the heart. He who writes this letter yet recalls how, once, when he was a peticoated child, in what appeared to be the solitude of a certain shrubbery, he was detected in the performance of certain devotional ceremonies of an altogether childish audacity, the occasion thereof being the 'Baptism' (or some such formal act of consecration and admission into a child's idea of the general kinship of Nature) of a newly born beetle. He remembers that the child was in no wise disconcerted, in this serious occupation, by that sense of Heavenly witness which children feel, without fearing it; but to this day he vividly recalls the consternation and embarrassment with which he unexpectedly found himself under the enquiring eye of a friendly governess, who was to him at that time a high object of veneration.

Very like what that child then felt, is what the man now feels, on finding that unknown and invisible Everybody (which amounts to Nobody) suddenly replaced by the well known and honoured presence of one who is the object, not of childish, but mature admiration.

It is probable that the Letter of George Elliot has been lying for some

3. *All the Year Round*, 25 January 1862, pp. 421–422. The poem in 27 5-line stanzas defined the great man as "Nature's friend," who, though mortal, can work miracles, serving "a greatness not his own." If this letter refers to one that GE wrote to the author, it has not been found.

months at the office of "All the Year Round," as the writer has only quite recently received it; and the feelings with which that letter has been read are not older than those with which this letter is written.

Some such explanation of a reply so tardy to a greeting so welcome and so valued, seems necessary, since it has been said by a great authority that emotions are like oysters and should be enjoyed fresh, as they will not bear keeping. Apology must also be offered for the length of this letter. If a passerby should drop a pebble down a well, it behoves the water there to render back such echoes as may at least prove that it *is* a well, not a shallow puddle, and that the depths of it have been reached and stirred. If this conviction does not justify, it is hoped that it may at least excuse, the garrulity of thanks for a pleasure deeply felt.

IV, 33:28 ANTHONY TROLLOPE TO GHL, WALTHAM CROSS, 15 MAY 1862

MS: Yale. *Published: The Letters of Anthony Trollope*, ed. B. A. Booth, 1951, p. 114.

Waltham House, | Waltham Cross.
15 May. 1862.

My dear Lewes.

I know my letter will grieve you, but still I think I had better write it. They tell me at the Post Office that your son is not doing well. Nothing is said against his character,—i.e. against his character as to conduct or good feeling; but they say that he utterly fails in making himself useful. "He is careless and very slow; and will not exert himself." That is the report made to me, and I am moreover told that this has been so strongly felt that for this reason he has been sent back to the Missing letter branch. I learn that his name has been taken off the list of candidates for the next step above him.

I fear that you will think me harsh to write in this way. But I am only doing as I would be done by. I believe his defect to be this,—that he is more au fait in French or German than he is in English, and that he is awkward and slow in the use of his own language. If he wishes to remain in the office I would strongly counsel you to put him in the way of writing English quickly. I need not tell you how such lessons are to be learned. The Secretary's office at the G.P.O. is a very good office for a young man, if he can get his promotion in his turn. But it is anything but a good office, if a man is to be continually passed over. You should make him work at English in his after hours.

Very faithfully yours
Anthony Trollope.

IV, 38:1 GE AND GHL WITH SMITH ELDER & CO., AGREEMENT FOR *ROMOLA*, LONDON 21 MAY 1862

MS: National Library of Scotland. The copyist, uncertain about how GE wished her name given, left a blank, which she filled in with "Marian Evans" before she and GHL signed.

It is agreed between Mrs. Marian Evans Lewes and George Henry Lewes Esq. and Messrs. Smith Elder & Co.

That Mrs. Lewes shall write a novel of sufficient length to fill 384 pages of "the Cornhill Magazine" and deliver the Manuscript to Smith Elder & Co. in twelve monthly portions.

That Smith Elder & Co. are to have the copyright of the Novel (for Great Britain and the Continent) both for publication in "the Cornhill Magazine" and for publication in separate form for a period of six years after the appearance of the last part in the Magazine, and the right of disposing of early sheets for America.

After the expiration of the six years the copyright is to revert to Mrs. Lewes, but Smith Elder & Co. are to continue to sell the copies they may then have, and may reprint and sell the Book during the whole term of copyright in any one form they may determine on.

Smith Elder & Co. are to pay Mrs. Lewes for such copyright as is secured to them by this agreement £583.6.8 (five hundred and eighty three pounds six shillings and eight pence) on delivery of each portion of the Manuscript, and such copyright is to be formally transferred to Smith Elder & Co. should they at any time require it.

London | May 21st 1862

Marian Evans Lewes.
G. H. Lewes.

IV, 39:9 GE TO MME EUGÈNE BODICHON, LONDON, [26 MAY 1862]

MS: Berg Collection, New York Public Library.

16 Blandford Sq. | Monday Morning.

Dearest Barbara

I hope I am not mistaken this morning in saying, Welcome to Blandford Square! The sight of you will be a brightening of Spring.

I want to have you with us to-morrow (Tuesday) evening. Do come, if you can. We expect two or three people—men not altogether insignificant, whom you might like to see.[4] If you can join us at eight o'clock we shall like the evening very much better. But I should like to kiss you before then, if you can come in for two or three minutes.

Ever yours
M. E. Lewes.

IV, 40:11 GHL TO THOMAS ADOLPHUS TROLLOPE, LONDON, 2 JUNE [1862]

MS: Morgan Library.

16, Blandford Square, | **N. W.**
2 June.

My dear Trollope

Enclosed is the proof[5] you were good enough to say you would correct. When am I to return the compliment?

I have finished Marietta. Its picture of Italian life is extremely vivid and interesting; but it is a long way behind La Beata[6] in interest of story.

I have finished 1 volume of Anthony's 'America,'[7] and am immensely pleased with it—so much so, that I hope to do something towards counteracting the nasty notice in the *Saturday*.[8]

Ever yours faithfully
G. H. Lewes.

4. Thomas Adolphus Trollope, just arrived from Florence, called 23 May: "Long chat with him and engaged him for Tuesday—wrote off to Anthony, Helps, Burton, and Scharf to ask them for the same day." 27 May: "At dinner Helps, Tom Trollope, and Burton. In the evening Miss [Isa] Blagden, Redford, and Pigott. Very pleasant. Kept it up till 12." (GHL Journal.)

5. Probably of the first instalment of *Romola* through ch. 5, *Cornhill*, 6 (July 1862), 1–43, which contains many Italian phrases.

6. T. A. Trollope, *Marietta: a Novel*, 2 vols., 1862, and *La Beata: a Tuscan Romeo and Juliet*, 2 vols., 1861.

7. Anthony Trollope, *North America*, 2 vols., published in May 1861.

8. *Saturday Review*, 13 (31 May 1862), 625–626, called Trollope's *North America* "most terribly wind-baggy," "as thin-spun, tedious, mooning a journal of travel as has been offered to the public for a long time." In "Our Survey of Literature, Science, and Art," *Cornhill*, 6 (July 1862), 105–107, after a sharp attack on the *Saturday Review* for its journalistic ethics, GHL devoted three pages to fair, though not uncritical, comment on the book.

IV, 44:1 GHL TO CHARLES BOLTON, LONDON, 13 JUNE [1862]

MS: Marylebone District Library, London.

16 Blandford Sq. 13 June.

Dear Sir,

In reply to your letter of application for permission to dramatize 'Silas Marner' Mrs. Lewes begs me to say that although she does not think her story suitable for stage representation, yet if you think otherwise, she would be unwilling to stand in your way by any opposition on her part.[9]

Yours truly
G. H. Lewes.

IV, 46:1 ANTHONY TROLLOPE TO GE, WALTHAM CROSS, 28 JUNE 1862

MS: Yale. *Published: The Letters of Anthony Trollope,* ed. B. A. Booth, 1951, pp. 115–116.

Waltham Cross | June 28. 1862.

My dear Mrs. Lewes.

I have just read the first number of Romola and I cannot refrain from congratulating you. If you can, or have, kept it up so to the end you will have done a great work. Adam Bede, Mrs. Poyser, and Marner have been very dear to me; but excellent as they are, I am now compelled to see that you can soar above even their heads. The descriptions of Florence,—little bits of Florence down to a door nail, and great facts of Florence up to the very fury of life among those full living nobles,—are wonderful in their energy and in their accuracy. The character of Romola is artistically beautiful,—a picture exceeded by none that I know of any girl in any novel. It is the perfection of pen painting;—and you have been nobly aided by your artist. I take it for granted that it is Leighton. The father also of Romola is excellent.

---

9. I have found no further reference to Bolton or his dramatization. An anonymous play derived from *Silas Marner* called *Effie's Angel* was produced at Sheffield, 4 September 1871. In 1876 William Schwenck Gilbert used the novel for his *Dan'l Druce, Blacksmith*, in which Johnston Forbes-Robertson made his first success. GHL and GE took Emily Clarke to see it: "In the evening private box at the Haymarket to see *Dan'l Druce*, a piece partly founded on 'Silas Marner.' Wretched stuff, poorly acted." (GHL Journal, 27 September 1876.)

Do not fire too much over the heads of your readers. You have to write to tens of thousands, and not to single thousands. I say this, not because I would have you alter ought of your purpose. That were not worth your while, even though the great numbers should find your words too hard. But because you may make your full purpose compatible with their taste.

I wonder at the toil you must have endured in getting up your work, —wonder and envy. But I shall never envy your success, or the great appreciation of what you have done that will certainly come,—probably today, but if not, then tomorrow.

Yours very heartily
Anthony Trollope.

IV, 47:3   GHL TO MR. AND MRS. W. M. W. CALL,[1] LONDON, 5 JULY 1862

Text: Mathilde Blind, *George Eliot*, 1883, p. 149.

My main object in persuading her to consent to serial publication, was not the unheard-of magnificence of the offer, but the advantage to such a work of being read slowly and deliberately, instead of being galloped through in three volumes. I think it quite unique, and so will the public when it gets over the first feeling of surprise and disappointment at the book not being English, and like its predecessor.

IV, 52:12   RICHARD MONCKTON MILNES TO GHL, LONDON, 22 AUGUST [1862]

MS: Yale.

Dear Lewes,

I am rather over-clubbed, but shall be very glad to put down my name for this new one,[2] and I can see later whether it would be of any use to me or I to it. I am,

Yours very truly
Richard M. Milnes.

Pall Mall.
August 22d.

1. Mr. and Mrs. Call are identified as recipients of this letter in his article "George Eliot: Her Life and Writings," *Westminster Review*, 116 (July 1881), 154–198, p. 176.

2. See IV, 66, for GE's account of the

26 September 1862

IV, 60:3 GHL TO THOMAS ADOLPHUS TROLLOPE, LONDON, 26 SEPTEMBER 1862

MS: University of California Los Angeles.

16 Blandford Square | 26 September 1862.

My dear Trollope

There were four distinct pleasures given by your letter last night. First there was the sight of the familiar hand itself the mere *fact* of a letter from the Villino Trollope. Next there was the welcome news about la raminga.[3] When she appears in public I have no doubt Froude and Blackwood will *see* their mistake. Thirdly there was the very cheering news of your dear wife's health, which may God preserve! Fourthly there was your cheering word about 'Romola.' Then and at all times would it have been delightful to her to know that you and your wife admired the book, but my wife happened to be at that particular period in an extra state of *dumps* owing to the visit of a "friend" who had expressed his want of interest in the characters, and general appreciation of the book only as an "immense feat"—a racer carrying a hundredweight.[4]

Mr. Smith, the publisher, who has most cause to be sensitive (after the author) is in high spirits about the book, and I have never had but one opinion on the subject.

I am truly glad that you are hard at work at *my* book. Glad because I shall rejoice in the work being done; and glad for you because I know how delightful it is to have a serious bit of work in hand.

We have been for a little "outing" by the seaside,[5] but alas! there is not the faintest chance of our getting southwards *this* year; though we both "languish for the purple seas."[6]

I had written thus far when an interruption came in the shape of a German Physiologist who brought a letter from one of the greatest of the teutons, so I had to show him my preparations, give him lunch, and a cigar

first meeting of this club, to which no one was to be admitted who was not "'Thorough' in the sense of being free from the suspicion of temporizing and professing opinions on official grounds." The scheme "went to pieces before it was finished." (IV, 78.)

3. The wanderer, Trollope's novel *Giulio Malatesta*, 3 vols., 1863. Both J. A. Froude, editor of *Fraser's*, and Blackwood had refused to serialize it. Published by Chapman & Hall, the BM copy is dated 26 May 1863.

4. "Yesterday a letter came from Mr. T. Trollope full of encouragement for me. Ebenezer!" (GE Journal, 26 September 1862.) The "friend" was perhaps Herbert Spencer?

5. At the Beach Hotel, Littlehampton, on the Sussex coast, 5–22 September.

6. Tennyson, "You Ask Me Why," line 4.

and talk an "infinite deal of—something."⁷ But his visit entirely scattered my ideas; and as Polly proposes to finish this, with a few lines, I shall leave her to say anything I may have omitted, except my love to your wife and Bice.

Ever truly yours
G. H. Lewes.

IV, 60:3 GE TO THOMAS ADOLPHUS TROLLOPE. LONDON, 26 SEPTEMBER 1862

MS: University of California Los Angeles (on the same sheet as GHL's letter).

Dear Mr. Trollope

I do not gather from your letter whether Mrs. Trollope is come back to you or not.⁸ Wherever she may be, please offer her my best love, and tell her I care a great deal about any kind thoughts there may be in her mind towards me; and about any pleasure what I can do may ever give her.—For many reasons I should like to be writing at Florence instead of in London. One reason is, that there are constantly questions rising in my work which I should like to consult *you* about still oftener than the libraries. I feel painfully, that with the utmost care I am able to give, I must make horrible mistakes. But there is one grand reason for keeping at home, that outweighs every disadvantage, it is the absolute necessity to me of an even, quiet life when I am writing. You are not a little enviable in having your nice home on the spot where all the materials for your work are around you. I hope you are very happy in it, for it is a work greatly worth labour.

Will you give a message from me to Miss Blagden?—and tell her that I felt her kindness in remembering that little wish of mine to have the photograph of Mrs. Storey's children⁹ and in taking trouble to gratify it. I liked the fact of her remembering me quite as much as I liked the pretty photograph. I hope her health is better now than when she was near us in London, and that she has found a new house to her taste.¹

7. *Merchant of Venice*, I, i, 114.

8. In July 1862 Theodosia Garrow Trollope had contracted tuberculosis and gone to the Italian Lakes with her daughter Beatrice.

9. William Wetmore Story (1819–95), American sculptor and author, married in 1843 Emelyn Eldredge of Boston. They had lived in Italy since 1856. For the photograph of their two boys see Robert Browning to Isa Blagden, 19 June 1862, in *Dearest Isa*, ed. E. C. McAleer, Austin, 1951, p. 107.

1. After Mrs. Browning's death Isa Blagden left Florence with Browning and his son 1 August 1861 and stayed in England during the winter. Her new house in Florence was the Villa Giglioni.

24 November 1862   *Surely a Chapter title in Romola ?*   307

I imagine you <u>under the Loggia</u> smoking those excellent cigars of which George still speaks with fervour, and talking to your changing groups of visitors. I shall think myself very happy if I ever sit under that Loggia again with "Romola" in the distance fairly ended, so as not at least to have degraded a great subject. If fasting and a knotted cord would help one, anxiety might be stilled a little at the expense of one's body.

I suppose you will have Mr. and Mrs. Anthony Trollope with you soon. Surely October must be the most delicious of all months for Italy! Both our visits were made in the spring, and I long for another to be made in autumn; yet when next spring comes the temptation to take our holiday in Italy may be too strong for us to wait till the next September.

Beatrice will not forget us, I hope, for we often recall her to our minds. Please call a kiss or two, that you next give her, mine instead of yours.

M. E. L.

IV, 63:18 GE TO BESSIE RAYNER PARKES, LONDON, 24 NOVEMBER 1862

MS: Dame Rebecca West.

16, Blandford Square, | N. W.
November 24. 62.

Dear Friend

Thanks for the precious books. They are just what I wanted—showing me the practical aspect of the Catholic Church in England[2] in these times, and telling me many details that I care to know. I keep the Dunn's Catalogue,[3] because I have marked some books in it that I want to have.

I hope you are keeping well so that you may brave the January voyage[4] without fear of being too much shaken.

God bless you. Ever yours with affectionate remembrance

M. E. Lewes.

I have forgotten your number in Wimpole Street so I shall take the books to the office in Langham Place.[5]

2. Miss Parkes's interest in the Roman Catholic Church, stirred by her friendship with Adelaide Procter, led to her conversion in 1864.

3. The *Post Office London Directory* for 1861 lists two booksellers: John Dunn, 1 Skinner St., Snowhill E.C., and Joseph Dunn, 191 Upper St., Islington N.

4. To Algiers to visit Barbara Bodichon. But Emily Davies wrote in a letter to Barbara 28 December 1862 that Bessie's family were afraid to let her go alone. (Girton College.)

5. The office of the *English Woman's Journal*. Mr. and Mrs. Joseph Parkes lived at 17 Wimpole Street, Cavendish Square.

IV, 70:5 GHL TO WATHEN MARK WILKS CALL, [LONDON], 18 DECEMBER 1862

Text: "George Eliot: Her Life and Writings," *Westminster Review*, 60 (July 1881), 176.

Marian lives entirely in the fifteenth century, and is much cheered every now and then by hearing indirectly how her book is appreciated by the higher class of minds, and some of the highest; though it is not, and cannot be, popular. In Florence we hear they are wild with delight and surprise at such a work being executed by a foreigner, as if an Italian had ever done anything of the kind.[6]

IV, 74:31 GHL TO MRS. CHARLES BRAY, LONDON, [JANUARY ? 1863]

MS: Yale.

16, Blandford Square, | **N.W.**

My dear Mrs. Bray

Polly wishes me to answer your note because I can do so more explicitly.

From abundant general and from certain special experiences I should say that you could do nothing so misjudged as to let those, or any publishers, have your work[7] on half profits. When I tell you that publishers' accounts *without any cheating*, i.e. without any thing not allowed in the trade, have been *known* to show a loss of 40£ while in fact the profit has been 75£—when I add that I know of a schoolbook which has sold five editions of 5,000 copies each—and yet these 25,000 copies have not yet returned one penny of "half profits"—you will see at once the illusory nature of the arrangement. If you were a young author only anxious to get into print, and hoping to make a name which for subsequent work would secure money, the half profits might be very well. As it is I can only say keep your m.s. till you find someone willing either to pay you a sum of money for the copyright, or so much per copy sold after a specified number to cover first expences.

---

6. Call adds that Manzoni's *I Promessi Sposi* had been "not altogether without success," but that GHL's "jet of affectionate indignation is justified by the essential correctness of his implicit denial of Italian priority."

7. *The British Empire: a Sketch of the Geography, Growth, Natural and Political Features of the United Kingdom, its Colonies and Dependencies* was published by Longman in November 1863.

20 May 1863

If you wish it there are three first rate publishers to whom I could take you and it will be very hard if I cannot get a sum of money from them for a work which in the Row has been thought worth "half profits." Should you think proper to commission me to act for you I should be glad if you would tell me whether you wish to sell the copyright (and for what sum) or only an edition (and for what sum).

I am scribbling this while Polly is waiting to go out. She begs me send her love. Believe me,

Yours faithfully
G. H. Lewes.

IV, 84:14   GE TO SMITH ELDER & CO., LONDON, 7 MAY 1863

MS: National Library of Scotland.

London May 7th. 1863.

Received of Messrs Smith Elder & Co. seven thousand pounds being the amount payable to me by them in accordance with the terms of an agreement for the publication of "Romola" dated May 21st. 1862

Marian E. Lewes.

IV, 86:22   GHL TO GEORG KESTNER, LONDON, 20 MAY 1863

MS: Yale. *Endorsed:* Dieser an mich gerichte Brief ist mir von Mr. Hermann Kindt zugesandt am 17 Mai 1863. G. Kestner.

16 Blandford Square | London | 20th May 1863.

My dear Sir

Mr. Kindt has kindly offered to be the medium of my gratitude, as he has already been the medium of your friendliness. The portraits of your mother and father,[8] and your brother, were most acceptable presents: Lotte[9] being especially charming in that larger lithography, and I shall place her on my walls beside the "Old Jupiter"[1] who so well knew how

---

8. Georg Kestner, Secretary of the Hanoverian Legation at Wetzlar.
9. Charlotte Buff Kestner, whose love affair with Goethe at Wetzlar before her marriage formed the fabric of *Werther.*

1. Goethe, aged 79, engraved by Radclyffe from a portrait by J. K. Stieler (1828), is the frontispiece of GHL's *Life and Works of Goethe,* 1855, Vol. II.

to appreciate her. On looking into that sweet face one cannot help imagining how different would have been the current of his life, had he known and loved her before your father—assuredly very different would have been the influence of such a woman, from that of the Frau von Stein[2] or the Vulpius.[3] But as in that case *you* would not have been, perhaps you prefer the historical to the imaginative fact! and as in that case also *we* should not have 'Werther,' we also may be content. Had Goethe been happily married we might have wanted his greatest work! Ainsi tout est pour le mieux dans ce meilleur des mondes.[4]

I hope that my wanderings may some day bring me near Hanover, in which case I shall gratify myself by personally expressing to you what cannot be adequately expressed by letter. Meanwhile Believe, my dear Sir,

Your much obliged
G. H. Lewes.

IV, 86:22 GE TO MME EUGÈNE BODICHON, [LONDON, 7 JUNE 1863]

MS: Berg Collection, New York Public Library.

½ past 5 o'clock.

Dear Barbara

Your note, which I suppose was put into the letter-box at our door, has only just been brought up to me. I am vexed, because you will have been waiting and wondering at my rudeness in sending no answer. I could be with you to-morrow at the time you mention, if that would suit you.

Thanks many for the folio of sketches which I have been running through by myself, before enjoying them in a more leisurely way with George.

I hope you have been conjecturing that there must have been some mistake to account for my silence to your note.

Ever yours
M. E. L.

2. Charlotte Albertina Ernestine von Schardt, Baroness von Stein (1742–1827), wife of the Grand Duke of Weimar's Master of the Horse. Goethe's long liaison with her began in 1776.

3. Christiane Vulpius (1765–1816), whom Goethe married in 1806, had borne his son August in 1789.

4. Voltaire, *Candide*, ch. 1.

IV, 91:9 ANTHONY TROLLOPE TO GE,
WALTHAM CROSS, 10 JULY 1863

MS: Princeton. *Published: The Letters of Anthony Trollope*, ed. B. A. Booth, 1951, pp. 135–136.

Waltham House, | Waltham Cross.
July 10. 1863.

My dear Mrs. Lewes

Not for your sake but for my own I must write you one line to thank you for your present.[5] I will say nothing further of the book but this;—that were you now departing from us, as I trust you may not till you have added many another leaf to your wreath,—you might go satisfied that you had written that which would live after you.

I will get up to you as soon as I possibly can,—but you are regularly out (with a wise regularity) at the hour at which mortals call.

Yours most sincerely
Anthony Trollope.

You will know what I mean when I say that Romola will live after you. It will be given to but very few latter day novels to have any such life. The very gifts which are most sure to secure present success are for the most part antagonistic to permanent vitality.

IV, 102:11 GHL TO ROBERT CHAMBERS, JR.,[1]
LONDON, 21 AUGUST 1863

MS: W. and R. Chambers Ltd, Edinburgh.

16 Blandford Square | 21 August 63.

My dear Sir

Look at this signature—do you remember me? If not, as I remember you well enough, and was much disappointed at your not keeping time at Verulam House, I plunge at once into business.

Mr. Stodart, of Drumelzier, with whom you were,[2] tells me you know

---

5. *Romola*, 3 vols., 1863, was offered for sale by C. A. Stonehill Ltd., New York, List 22, March 1945, as the copy presented to Trollope, "who has inscribed it 'Given to Anthony Trollope by George Elliot [sic].'" I have not seen the inscription.

1. Robert Chambers, Jr. (1833–88), eldest son of GHL's old friend the author of *Vestiges of Natural Creation*, whom GHL had often visited at Verulam House, Gray's Inn Square.

2. Young Chambers spent a year with Mr. Stoddart of Drumelzier Haugh,

his cousin James of Hillhead. I am thinking of sending one, or perhaps two, of my boys to him to learn farming, but before doing so I should be glad to hear from you what sort of man he is, and what his family is like? I mean how many are there in family—male and female—and are they pleasant as well as upright? Much depends upon the sort of home the boys would have and *this* you can probably guess at from your experience. Drumelzier himself has given up taking pupils. How did you like your life with him?

Are they sour and calvinistic or calvinistic and sweet?

Ever faithfully yours
G. H. Lewes.

Ro^t Chambers Junr. Edinh.

IV, 108:1 GHL TO MME EUGÈNE BODICHON, [LONDON, 30 SEPTEMBER 1863]

MS: Yale.

Wednesday.

My dear Barbara

Have you written the letters to Natal? If so will you please send me the *names and addresses* of your correspondents for Thornie?

The Duke of Newcastle[3] has given him a letter to the Governor[4] and one or two other friends have given letters; so he will be well provided. He starts on Monday; but the luggage goes on *Friday*.

Polly is a little better and sends her love. Kind regards to the Doctor.

Ever your faithful
G. H. Lewes.

Peebles, and describes him in a doggerel poem "The Natives of Drumelzier," privately printed, which Miss Sondra Miley kindly found for me in the Chambers archives.

3. Henry Pelham Fiennes Pelham Clinton, 5th Duke of Newcastle (1811–64), Colonial Secretary 1859–64.

4. John Scott (1814–98), Lieutenant Governor of Natal 1856–64.

IV, 108:1 SIR EDWARD BULWER LYTTON TO GHL, KNEBWORTH, 1 OCTOBER 1863

MS: Yale.

K. October 1, 1863.

My dear Sir,

I know no one at Natal, not even the Governor's name, but enclose a note for him whoever he be also one for Mr. Birch, Col. Off., whom you or your son should try and see. He is private secretary to C. Fortescue[5] (the Secretary of the office) and may be serviceable.

Yours
E. B. L.

IV, 110:7 ANTHONY TROLLOPE TO GE, WALTHAM CROSS, 18 OCTOBER 1863

MS: University of Virginia. *Published: The Letters of Anthony Trollope*, ed. B. A. Booth, 1951, pp. 138–139.

Waltham House, | Waltham Cross.
October 18. 1863.

My dear Mrs Lewes.

Will you accept a copy of Rachel Ray, a little story which I have just published in two volumes. I have desired Chapman to send it you.

You know that my novels are not sensational. In Rachel Ray I have attempted to confine myself absolutely to the commonest details of commonplace life among the most ordinary people, allowing myself no incident that would be even remarkable in every day life. I have shorn my fiction of all romance.

I do not know what you who have dared to handle great names and historic times will think of this. But you must not suppose that I think the little people are equal as subjects to the great names. Do you, who can do it, go on. I know you will not be deterred by the criticisms of people who cannot understand. Neither should you be deterred by internal criticism. That which you have in your flask you are bound to pour forth.

Yours always most truly
Anthony Trollope.

5. Chichester Samuel Parkinson-Fortescue (1823–98), Undersecretary for Colonies 1857–65.

IV, 114:1 GE TO MRS. FRANK R. MALLESON
LONDON, 15 NOVEMBER 1863

MS: Yale.

The Priory, | North Bank, | Regents Park.
November 15. 1863.

Dear Mrs. Malleson[5a]

We expect to have a few pleasant people with us on the evening of the 24th. Will you make one of them? We shall be all the happier if you will.

Ever yours sincerely
M. E. Lewes.

Mrs. F. R. Malleson.

IV, 114:16 GE TO MARY MARSHALL,
LONDON, 15 NOVEMBER 1863

MS: Taylor Institution, Oxford.

The Priory, | North Bank, | Regents Park.
November 15. 1863.

Dear Miss Marshall

We hope to have a few nice people to spend the evening with us on the 24th, when Charlie comes of age. Do come to us if you can: Mr. Lewes thinks, as I do, that yours is a comfortable presence, making life seem easier.

We are nearly settled now, wanting only a few articles that linger at the maker's. But you may imagine that the business or removal was not made more agreeable by my having a fierce cold the week before, drawing after it a comet's tail of cough and small miseries, from which I am not yet free.

Pray tell me that you will come on the 24th at 8 o'clock.

Ever yours truly
M. E. Lewes.

5a. For Elizabeth Whitehead Malleson see IV, 125, n. 3. She and her sister Emily Whitehead were among the guests on 24 November. (GHL Journal.)

IV, 114:16 ANTHONY TROLLOPE TO GHL,
WALTHAM CROSS, 16 NOVEMBER 1863

MS: Yale.

Waltham House, | Waltham Cross.

My dear Lewes.
    I think I can be with you on the 24th. I will do my very best.
                                        Yours always
                                        Anthony Trollope.
November 16. 1863.

IV, 121:10 ANTHONY TROLLOPE TO GHL,
WALTHAM CROSS, 13 DECEMBER 1863

MS: Yale. *Published: The Letters of Anthony Trollope,* ed. B. A. Booth, 1951, p. 141.

Waltham House, | Waltham Cross.
                                        December 13. 1863.

My dear Lewes.
    On returning home I have found your life of Goethe, for which, I presume, I have to thank you. I do thank you heartily. I must get your name in it some day. I shame to say I never read the former edition. I have already been at work at this, and am charmed with it. Alas, me—for 11 years I learned Latin and Greek—nothing else—and know it now, you, who understand our English schooling, will know how superficially. Of German of course I know nothing. Shall I hereafter have an action against my pastors and masters?
                              Yours dear Lewes, always yours
                                      Anthony Trollope.
How excellent is your outside got up.[6] Calico—we call it cloth when we want to be grand,—has thereon achieved its greatest biblical triumph.

6. The second ed. of GHL's *The Life of Goethe*, 1864, was bound in brown cloth, front and back covers beveled and with triple gold frame; spine with gold rules top and bottom, title in gold on ornamental leather label.

IV, 130:24   GHL TO ENEAS SWEETLAND DALLAS, LONDON, [24 JANUARY 1864]

MS: Huntington Library.

The Priory, | 21⁷ **North Bank,** | **Regents Park.**
Sunday

My dear Dallas

I have arranged with Browning for next Saturday, the 30th.⁸ I hope you have kept yourself disengaged and can come. Dinner ½ past 5 *for 6*. I name this early hour because we shall have half a dozen men in the evening, and to have a good talk we must begin betimes.

Our⁹ Kind regards to your Wife.

Ever yours
G. H. Lewes.

IV, 138:24   MRS. ROBERT EVANS TO GE, DERBY, 15 MARCH [1864]

MS: Yale.

Stanley Lodge | March 15th.

My dear Mrs. Lewis

For your kind and soothing letter I must thank you. Unfortunately I cannot find words to express half the gratitude I feel for such an affectionate remembrance of my dear husband.²

The parting has indeed been a great one and every day it appears greater; in the present season especially, every flower that blooms (he was such an admirer of nature) reminds me so strongly of my loss. You will I am sure be gratified to hear that his end was very peaceful, submitting most patiently to the will of God—his disease was that terrible one of Cancer in the Stomach.

I must tell you that the last Book he looked at was "Adam Bede," he had expressed a wish that I should fetch it and read "Dinah's Prayer and Sermon" and when I had done so I was called from the room—and he said "Give me the Book, I shall like to read it again." When I returned

---

7. The numerals have been added to the printed heading.

8. "We had Browning, Dallas, and Burton to dine with us and in the evening a gentlemen's party." (GE Journal, 30 January 1864.)

9. "Our" has been added.

2. GE's half-brother died at Stanley Common, Derby, 29 January 1864. For GE's letter see IV, 133.

he had gone to sleep with the Book in his hand, he was never able to hold another.

I am sure you will forgive me this intrusion and believe me ever with every wish for your happiness

Yours very sincerely
Jane Evans.

IV, 139:7 ANTHONY TROLLOPE TO GHL, WALTHAM CROSS, 21 MARCH 1864

MS: Yale. *Published: The Letters of Anthony Trollope,* ed. B. A. Booth, 1951, p. 150.

Waltham House, | Waltham Cross.
March 21. 1864.

My dear Lewes.

On Sunday I got your Aristotle and went at it at once. It is wonderfully and deliciously lucid. Indeed I know no one so lucid—and at the same time so graphic—as you are. Your Goethe was charming to me as combining those two qualifications.

I shall get to you before long. I went to see Carlyle last week. Oh, heavens;—what a mixture of wisdom and folly flows from him!

Yours always,
A. T.

I have told George Smith to send to your wife the Small House at Allington.[3] Ask her to receive it from me with my kindest regards.

IV, 147:1 GE TO BESSIE RAYNER PARKES, LONDON, [29 APRIL 1864]

MS: Princeton.

The Priory | N. Bank | Friday.

Dear Bessie

I enclose an official letter.[4] It needs no explanation save perhaps this—that the person accepting the commission will not only be paid

---

3. Trollope's novel, concluded in the *Cornhill* for April 1864, was issued in 2 vols. by Smith Elder & Co. MS reads *of.*

4. In sending this note to a Mr. Russell 13 March 1887 Bessie wrote: "The enclosed note is from George Elliot to me, and was written in 1864. It concerns a question of sending a lady to report on the Female Wards of Broadmoor Prison. I was unable to undertake it." (Princeton.)

handsomely for *writing* but will also have the expenses of journeying paid for.

Please send an answer as soon as you can. In twilight and hurry

Yours ever
Marian.

IV, 149:13 GEORGE SMITH TO GE, LONDON, 3 MAY 1864

MS: Yale.

45, Pall Mall, S.W.
May 3rd 1864.

My dear Madam

It was only yesterday that I clearly understood from Mr. Lewes that I was to regard "Brother Jacob" as a present from you.[5] I can hardly tell you how much I was touched and gratified by your kindness. The gift is a princely one in value, and it comes to me at a time when it is even more than ordinarily valuable; but you will I am sure understand me, when I say, that it is not chiefly on that account that I am pleased at receiving such a present from you. I hope that I may regard it as an indication of your satisfaction with the manner in which our business relations have been conducted as well as of your feeling of personal kindness towards myself. And I value your good opinion so highly that such an expression of it is deeply gratifying to me.

Wishing you and Mr. Lewes perfect enjoyment of your trip I remain My dear Madam

Your very faithful and obliged
G. Smith.

Mrs. Lewes.

5. See IV, 157, n. 4. After its publication Smith returned the MS, now at Yale.

IV, 153:1 GE TO GRACE AND AMELIA LEE,[6]
[LUCERNE?, 13? JUNE 1864]

MS: Dartmouth.

I hope we shall find you well and happy, after our long absence. We shall be very glad to see you and home and Ben[7] again.

> Always your sincere friend
> M. E. Lewes.

IV, 158:1 ANTHONY TROLLOPE TO GHL,
WALTHAM CROSS, 26 JUNE 1864

MS: Yale. *Published:* The Letters of Anthony Trollope, ed. B. A. Booth, 1951, pp. 154–55.

Waltham House, | Waltham Cross.
June 26. 1864.

My dear Lewes.

There never was better criticism than that on Greek tragic art in the two first pages of your chapter—called Iphigenia,[8]—and I make you my compliments. I had felt it all before, but could not have expressed it. Of course I speak of the Greek, not of the German which is to me a book altogether sealed. But not so true are you to truth in your rhapsody as to dead bones. "But—dead bones for dead bones—," etc. page 287.[9] You know you are only warming an idea. The history of mans mind must have in it more of poetry than the history of man's body,—even though we throw you in the elephant's.

> Yours ever
> Anthony Trollope.

I tried to see you the other day. Heavens, what pens and ink you do keep in your dining room!!! My kindest regards to your wife. I will if it be possible see you before long.

---

6. Grace A. Lee (b. 1826 at Stonehouse, Devon) had been cook at the Priory since 1861, and her sister Amelia Lee (b. 1833 at Fowey, Cornwall), housemaid.

7. GHL's bulldog.

8. *The Life of Goethe*, 2d ed., 1864, pp. 262–273.

9. "But—dead bones for dead bones—there is as much poetry in the study of an elephant's skull, as in the study of those skeletons of the past—history and classics. All depends upon the mind of the student; to one man a few old bones will awaken thoughts of the great organic processes of nature, thoughts

[*16? July 1864*]

IV, 160:11   GE TO EDWARD F. S. PIGOTT, LONDON, [16? JULY 1864]

MS: University of California Los Angeles.

The Priory, | 21. North Bank, | Regents Park.
Saturday.

My dear Mr. Pigott

Thank you for remembering me and sending me the Débats.

I was glad to see Renan's articles,[1] for I happen to be especially interested in M. Aurelius. Always

Yours most truly
M. E. Lewes.

E. S. Pigott Esq.

IV, 160:11   GE TO MME EUGÈNE BODICHON, LONDON, 12 AUGUST 1864

MS: Berg Collection, New York Public Library. *Brief extract published:* Haight, *George Eliot*, p. 377.

The Priory, | 21. North Bank, | Regents Park.
August 12. 64.

Dearest Barbara

I am glad to think of you in your "cottage near a wood" under these fine skies. But it *was* a pity that we didn't see you that Sunday, and that you didn't see the Orang. She is more touching and amiable than the little chimpanzee at the Crystal Palace, but not so clever and dramatic. Chim has a great piece of heavy drapery in his cage, with which he drapes himself in a magnificent mysterious manner, as if he were trying to find his way to an art that would express his very big thoughts.

About dear Bessie, I will try to think that all will come right.[2] On these matters we outsiders can never judge otherwise than blunderingly. Relations that seem to us full of promise are the preparation of misery, and vice versa. That stanza you quote would serve as a motto for half the history of my life: what pain I have had from the ills that have never befallen me!

as far-reaching and sublime as those which the fragments of the past awaken in the historical mind." (p. 287.)

1. Renan's articles in the *Journal des Débats*, reviewed *Essai sur Marc-Aurèle,* *d'après les monuments épigraphiques,* par Noël Desvergers, 8 and 9 July 1864.

2. The prospect of her marriage to Samuel Blackwell. See [10 January 1865].

29 August 1864

Apropos of that interesting subject, self, I have been having my likeness taken "positively for the last time" or rather by the last person, namely by Mr. F. W. Burton.[3] George saw it for the first time the other day, and was in raptures with it, whereupon Mr. Burton told him it was *his* (George's). I don't know myself whether it is good or not.

George has been very poorly—Dr. Brinton[4] says solely from feebleness —and he looks thinner and thinner. He *is* so good. You are one of those who guess how good he is. God bless you, Barbara, if only for that.

Ever yours
Marian.

IV, 161:16 THORNTON ARNOTT LEWES TO GHL, DURBAN, 29 AUGUST 1864

MS: Yale.

Durban, | 29 August | 1864.

Dear Pater,

Your guess as to my not writing before, being caused by my absence up country was perfectly correct, and as I have now got down again, I answer all yours, which have come in the meanwhile at once. I begin with your 3 February letter, which I got just before I started. I am sorry to say that I can't send a number of the Blunderbuss, as the Captain[5] begged so hard for all the numbers, to get them bound that I could not refuse. However you can imagine what they were like.

I can't understand Colston's having sent in the bill for 'Forged stamps'[6] to you, as Pemberton had taken it over into his own hands, as we had settled everything long before I left and he was to pay the bill. What an amiable beast Ben must be. If you have his portrait[7] taken mind and send

3. GE gave Burton the first sitting 29 June 1864. After GHL saw it, Mme Bodichon was sent to look at it in October 1864 and Mrs. Congreve in January 1865. On 22 July 1865, more than a year after the work began, GE wrote in her Journal, "Sat for my portrait, I suppose for the last time." The drawing was first shown at the Royal Academy in 1867. When it was given to the National Portrait Gallery in 1883, Burton wrote: "The portrait was drawn in 1865, in July, as I find by a diary of the time." An earlier study in red and black chalks was purchased in 1972 by the Princeton University Library.

4. William Brinton, M.D. (1823–67), whom GHL and GE had both consulted since 1861, specialized in treating diseases of the stomach.

5. Of the *Damietta*.

6. By Thornton Lewes and Edward L. Pemberton, published by Colston & Son, 36 pp., Edinburgh, 1863. See III, 463, n. 1. Pemberton was editor of the *Philatelical Journal*, 1872, the *Stamp Collector's Handbook*, 1874, etc.

7. For photographs of Ben the bull-

me a copy. Apropos of portraits, Charlie's, which you enclosed, was carried up with the letter in my coat pocket to the Transvaal, much to the edification thereof, for on taking it out one day lo! and behold, the letter was *just* legible and the portrait——!! So if he does not mind sending me another, which shall not be crushed, I shall be much obliged. Your trip to Scotland and to Italy must indeed have been pleasant for you, particularly the latter, though I should probably have preferred the former. I can imagine Bertie driving about Maggie, which beast I picture to myself as a brown Shetland pony.[8] Am I right? Whenever that young man feels inclined to come out here, he can come; he need not wait for my turning to farming, for I am going in for trading of which more anon, and as land is rapidly rising, out here, the sooner he gets a farm the better. I never was in Glasgow, but know it by reputation.

And so the Captain[9] has "hopped the Living"? I thought he was going to live forever, and I half suspect somebody has been soaping the stairs. However "requiescat in pace." I hope Grandmamma is all right and that Nursie has got over her late attack. And so Charlie is engaged! Well, as I owe him a letter, I think this will be a good opportunity for writing to him. . . .

And so the hedgehog is dead. As I before observed Requiescat in pace. I hope you performed a funeral service over his bristles, consisting of the "Dead March in Saul," and winding up with the pathetic air "Down among the dead men." Poor Peter! never again will he dirty Grace's table's legs by rubbing himself against them.

Much love to everybody, not forgetting the servants and Ben.

Your affectionate son
Thornton Lewes.

P.S. I shall write to Miss Dodd by next mail. I always make impressions (one way or the other) on female's hearts and Miss Dodd was always remarkably fond of me. No fear of *my* marrying. I am to be the bachelor as Charlie is not, that's clear, and I made up my mind to it a long while ago. Ta-ta. If you write by every mail a four page letter, and I write by every 3rd mail a twelve page one, I think that will be about fair.

---

dog and of Charles see Haight, *George Eliot,* facing p. 364.

8. GE and GHL visited Herbert in Scotland 8 April 1864. See IV, 144.

9. Captain John Willim, GHL's stepfather, died 9 February 1864.

IV, 162:1 GHL TO SARA SOPHIA HENNELL, LONDON, 5 SEPTEMBER 1864

MS: Yale.

The Priory, | 21. North Bank, | Regents Park.
5 September 64.

My dear Miss Hennell

Polly and I are meditating an outing somewhere on account of my health principally and as Harrowgate possesses Chalybeate Springs (which I need) we rather incline to go there. Will you, if you can, answer these questions:

I. Are there plenty of decent lodgings to be had, or must we stay in an hotel?

II. Does the place present a crowded crinolism?

III. Are there pretty walks *away* from the visitors promenades?

IV. Is it very expensive?

V. Is it from what you know of our habits and tastes a place to attract us?

Some of these questions I dare say you can answer and oblige

Yours very truly
G. H. Lewes.

IV, 166:18 THORNTON ARNOTT LEWES TO GHL, DURBAN, 7 OCTOBER 1864

MS: Yale.

Durban 7 October | 1864.

Dear Pater,

I have got a letter to answer, and am short of news, so that I can't favour you with a long epistle. My next I shall write three months hence, when I come back from my *second* trip up country. I am not going up alone as originally intended, but a fellow passenger per "Damietta," is coming with me as my partner. His name is Cronin, and his Father is a homeopathic Doctor[1] in the south of London. We have been running about busily to get credit, for the last fortnight, and we start about the 16 October, just a year since we left England. We are going up to the Transvaal and you may

---

1. Edward Cronin, M.D., 10 Claremont Place, Brixton Road, S.

expect a long and interesting letter when I come back. I hope you will see it in the same light that I do that if I write every 3 months a 12 page letter, and you write every month a 4 pager, that our reciprocity is mutual and equal! So that henceforth I may expect a letter every mail.

Many happy returns of Mutter and Charlie's birthdays. Love to Grandmamma, Mamma,[2] Nursie etc. etc.

Your affectionate Son
Thornton Lewes.

2. Agnes Lewes.

Fortnightly Review and *Pall Mall Gazette*

1865 January 13   GHL outlines plan for the *Fortnightly*.
1865 January   GE and GHL spend 10 days in Paris.
1865 February   GHL engaged as consultant for *Pall Mall Gazette*.
1865 March   GHL writes Prospectus for *Fortnightly*.
1865 May 15   *Fortnightly* 1st number published.
1865 June   GE studies comparative philology.
1865 August   Thornie joins in war against Basutos.
1865 Aug.–Sept. GE and GHL in France.
1865 December   GHL asks Lord Houghton to review Swinburne.
1866 January 1   GHL revises *History of Philosophy*.
1866 February 11 GHL demolishes Bray's theory of Force.
1866 February 12 GHL on reviewing Horne's *Prometheus*.
1866 February 14 Thornie's campaign at Plattberg.

IV, 171:20 ANTHONY TROLLOPE TO GHL, WALTHAM CROSS, 24 DECEMBER 1864

MS: Yale. *Published: The Letters of Anthony Trollope,* ed. B. A. Booth, 1951, pp. 160–161.

Waltham House, | Waltham Cross.
24 December 1864.

My dear Lewes.

I cannot deny that I am disappointed and grieved by your letter; but you are not to suppose that I shall either find fault with you or argue with you. I know well how these things go, and do not think that a man is open to censure because he changes his views.[3] I am not one of those who suppose that a mans mind should be subject to no hestitations,—to no vacillating influences. Men who are strong enough never to be so subject are distasteful to me. Haud ignarus dubitationis, dubitantibus succurrere disco.[4] So much I say, to quell any fear that you may have that I should condemn you,—believing that you would not willingly be condemned by one who regards you as well as I do.

But having said this I must go on to declare that I greatly regret your defection. I have felt the necessity of the aid of some one who would know what he was about in arranging the work of such a venture as we propose; and I have also felt,—more strongly perhaps than I can explain to you,—that to make the affairs comfortable to myself the person selected for the above described purpose should be one with whom I could hold close friendly intercourse. I do not care to put myself at the beck of any one whom I do not know, or whom, when known, I may not like.

I would recommend you, for your own sake, to come to the meeting on Thursday. It would, I think, be better that you should state your own withdrawal, than that I should do so for you. As to that, however, you can make up your mind and let me know your intention.

Yours always faithfully
Anthony Trollope.

Give all kind remembrances of the season to your wife. I feel that I ought to congratulate her upon your decision.

3. About acting as editor of the *Fortnightly.* See IV, 172.

4. Cf. *Aeneid,* I, 630.

IV, 172:7 GE TO MRS. FRANK R. MALLESON,
LONDON, 25 DECEMBER 1864

MS: Yale.

The Priory, | 21. North Bank, | Regents Park.
Christmas Day 1864.

Dear Mrs. Malleson

Yesterday, as I was cutting some ivy in our frost-nipped garden, I thought of you—how you had brought me beautiful plants to cheer me as prettiest signs of your good will towards me, for these Christmases past. Then I thought, "Ah, she is gone too far now, for me to hope that she can show me her face again, which was quite as pleasant to look at as the flowers." And precisely when I came in from my ivy-cutting, I saw a plant—a beautiful one, standing on the slab in the hall. Of course I knew *you* had sent it before I saw the initials.

I have given you that history of my thoughts that you may understand better how welcome your remembrance was. Thank you, dear Mrs. Malleson, Perhaps nothing but a more intimate peep into my desponding nature—a peep not desirable—could let you know fully how much good such attentions as yours have always been to me—how much *help* they afford me.

I wish I knew Mr. Malleson well enough to send my kind regards to him,[4a] as Mr. Lewes sends his to you. Perhaps some day I shall see you again. Till then, I am

Always yours most truly
Marian E. Lewes.

IV, 175:4 GHL TO MRS. FREDERICK LEHMANN,
LONDON, [9 JANUARY 1865]

MS: Yale.

The Priory, | 21. North Bank, | Regents Park.
Very charming Woman

As I was putting the key in my garden door I found your two sweet cavaliers with your tempting invitation. I would say *yes* at once, though

---

4a. Mr. and Mrs. Frank Malleson came to the Priory in the evening 25 January 1862. (GHL Journal.)

against rules, but I just now accepted a business engagement[5] for Wednesday *or* Friday; and as the business is to be transacted at dinner and with literary men, if Wednesday is fixed I shall not have strength to come to you afterwards. If Friday is fixed I will come or "perish in the attempt."

We are just about starting for Paris, i.e. after Friday if Friday is my day, on Thursday if Wednesday.[6] But we shall be back by the end of the month *quite certain* and Mrs. Lewes begs me to say that not only is she greatly pleased that you should send her such a pretty message but that she will be very happy indeed to see you any afternoon you may find yourself in these parts. Sunday we are *always* at home all day.

A happy new year to you and yours and may the Gods favor me for Wednesday.

Yours faithfully
G. H. Lewes.

IV, 175:4 GE TO MME EUGENE BODICHON, [LONDON, 10 JANUARY 1865]

MS: Berg Collection, New York Public Library.

Dearest Barbara

Your Christmas Day's letter was very welcome. On that day, perhaps while you were writing, Bessie called to utter her good wishes, and on my asking her if anything dreadful was going to happen to her soon, she expressed her concern that her marriage had been spoken of by any one as an event in any way decided on. She feels it necessary to have such *égards* for her aged parents, that she trembles at any positive report about herself, as long as their minds are not thoroughly settled and reconciled in relation to anything she meditates doing. She says she is exceedingly well in health.

We have had a very cheering Christmas, but [*page torn off*] that you have enjoye[d your r]eading. About your dear Vandals I fear there is nothing more impartial to be had than old Jordanes[7] and *Procopius*.[1] There are translations of Procopius both in English and French. I have lately been much interested in the observations about the Berbers in Dozy's *Histoire des Arabes en Espagne*,[2] and the elements their patriotic tendencies contributed

---

5. To discuss his taking the editorship of the *Fortnightly Review* or acting as consultant to the *Pall Mall Gazette*.

6. After waiting two days for the weather to improve, they left for Paris Sunday, 16 January 1865, and returned the 25th. (GHL Journal.)

7. Jordanes, 6th-century historian, *De Origine actibus Getarum*, 551.

1. Procopius, *History of the Vandal War*, 532–546.

2. Reinhart Pieter Anne Dozy, *Histoire des Musulmans d'Espagne, . . . (711–1100)*, 4 vols., Leyden, 1861.

to the Musulman movement. The worst of it is, his remarks are too brief. He cites a striking point or two from a book which I daresay you know, Daumas' *La grande Kabylie*[3]—for example that the name of a marabout appealed to by a man when the sword is hanging over him will save his life, whereas the name of God is not strong enough to produce the same effect! [*page torn off*]

The season here is horrible: it is impossible for a sensitive person to be happy in this biting east wind, with tiny hard hailstones falling every other hour. The weather seems to get into the very core of me and to make itself felt more than all blessings. Strong people who can be busy clothing the naked and feeding the hungry may feel brave and hopeful, but self-conscious self-contemplative creatures like me must sit in shivering despondency.

I really felt that you were enjoying your life when I read your last letter [*page torn off*]

IV, 176:23 GHL TO HENRY DANBY SEYMOUR,[4] [LONDON,] 13 JANUARY 1865

Text: Printed letter enclosed in letter to Lord Houghton, 6 February 1865, Trinity College, Cambridge.

[*Private and Confidential.*]

13th January, 1865.

My Dear Seymour,

Allow me to submit to you and our friends a brief statement of my conception of the proposed Review. It is needless to enter upon the details; the principles are the most important, and they alone can justify the scheme:—

It is clear that important political changes, both at home and abroad, are slowly but inevitably approaching. Any periodical which can acquire commanding influence with the intellectual classes will have a great part to play. We must first aim at influence—a large circulation will follow. To gain this two things are necessary: we must address ourselves to *various interests;* and we must secure the best services of the best writers.

Besides the many political and social topics which will constantly solicit attention, there are the topics specially interesting to the LITERARY, PHILOSOPHICAL, ARTISTIC, FINANCIAL, MANUFACTURING, MILITARY, and

---

3. Melchior Joseph Eugène Daumas, *La grande Kabylie*, Paris, 1857, I, 366–367.

4. Henry Danby Seymour (1820–77), M.P. for Poole, one of the founders of the *Fortnightly Review*.

SPORTING classes, which we should keep steadily in view, making ourselves, as far as possible, the well-informed and authoritative organ of each class. I do not mean that we should rival the Sporting Magazine or the Banker's Magazine; but that our treatment of subjects interesting to Sportsmen and Bankers should be such as would attract these classes while giving variety to our pages. The publication once a fortnight, and our wide connection, should enable us to do this.

The spirit of the Review ought to secure excellence as well as variety. Keeping ourselves untrammelled by the limitations of a party, or a sect, we shall give expression to every idea which justifies itself by its tendency towards Progress and is consistent with Order—in conformity with the poet's estimate of our country, as one
"Where freedom broadens slowly down[5]
From precedent to precedent."

The writers will be asked to express their own opinions, not the opinions of the editor. At present it is notorious that most of the able writers contribute to several journals of different parties, and are rarely, if ever, allowed to express their most cherished convictions with perfect sincerity, because they have to maintain "consistency." I propose to remove all such editorial restraints. The responsibility of selecting the writer and the subject is all the editor should assume; that done, he should throw all the responsibility of each article on its writer. By this the Review would gain greatly in force and authority, and would never be called upon to answer for a consistency to which it avowedly made no claim. By this also no one contributor would be implicated in what was written by another. The example of *La Revue des Deux Mondes* shows with what admirable success diversity in opinions may co-exist with a general policy. Unless we had the intention of becoming the organ of a party it would be unwise, in losing the intensive force of limitation, not to avail ourselves to the utmost of the extensive force of a large and liberal range.

Such latitude of course demands that the articles shall be signed. There are many obvious advantages in keeping certain political communications anonymous; but in most other cases—especially where the personality of the writer or the individuality of his views gives a relief to his contribution— the signature should appear. It will be an earnest of sincerity. It will give authority to praise and dignity to attack. It will give the writer freedom to a sense of serious responsibility, without which freedom is apt to become anarchy. It will lessen the insolent asperity and the culpable carelessness of criticism. In avowing that the opinions expressed are truly nothing but the

5. GHL misquotes Tennyson's "You Ask Me Why." This line should read "freedom slowly broadens down."

opinions of an individual, to be valued as such, it will remove the false prestige which too often belongs to judgments that would be disregarded were the judges known.

I am aware of all the objections that have been often urged against the practice of signing articles. It is unnecessary for me to answer them here; the fact that I think it an essential part of our scheme shows that I think its advantages greatly outweigh its disadvantages. Let me simply add that it will be a great temptation to many important writers who would otherwise refuse their aid.

In allowing great latitude of opinion and great diversity of opinion, the only difficulty will be in fixing the limits beyond which it would be fatal to pass. If I rightly understand the temper of the public we address it is one which, while yearning for greater freedom of discussion, would never tolerate a negative or aggressive spirit in reference to the fundamental principles of Government and Religion. Our motto, Progress and Order, must inspire us. We have no *ism*, Theological or Political, to advocate. But we shall claim for Theology, Philosophy, and Science their perfect *independence*, each pursuing its own serious course. In the Church, and out of it, there is the agitation of a deep unrest which is daily becoming wider, and which is exasperated by the want of freedom; serious discussion on such questions must arise, and we cannot disregard them. Our course is plain:— *we must take no side;* we must espouse no party; we must open our pages to various opinions, vigilant only as to their agreement with our motto—Progress and Order.

Believe me, my dear Seymour,

Yours very truly,
George Henry Lewes.

H. Danby Seymour, Esq., M.P.

IV, 177:10 GHL TO LORD HOUGHTON, LONDON, 6 FEBRUARY 1865

MS: Trinity College, Cambridge.

The Priory, | 21. North Bank, | Regency Park.
6 February 65.

My dear Lord Houghton

If you like the idea of the enclosed—as I hope you will—perhaps you will give me half an hour some *afternoon,* to talk it over with you? Believe me,

Yours very truly
G. H. Lewes.

IV, 179:1 GE TO MME EUGÈNE BODICHON,
LONDON, 27 FEBRUARY 1865

MS: Berg Collection, New York Public Library.

21 North Bank | February 27. 1865.

Dearest Barbara

Your letter, just received, has comforted me greatly. We did go to Paris, but did not go to the Hotel de Saxe, which perhaps was the reason that I lost the chance you had given me of hearing from you there. Not having had the Paris letter, I felt it long since I had had some assurance of your being at least well in health and able to enjoy some of the good things Fate has granted you. Your letter this morning is just what I wanted.

Gertrude and Charlie will be delighted with the <u>Burnous</u>—and I will duly deliver your message. They are to be married on the 20th, and we shall be glad now when the epoch has come—if one can really be glad at the lapse of time irrecoverable. We have loved Gertrude better and better as we have seen more of her, and we both feel that we could have desired no better lot for Charlie.

George and I enjoyed our ten days at Paris, making the most of our time in theatre-going and sight-seeing. I have lost my old dislike of Paris—but, it must be confessed that the Paris of today is another Paris than the one I used to detest. What a delight it is to think of the precious Gothic remains being restored with Violet le Duc's perfection of knowledge and taste![6] We reserved seeing St. Denis until we can go in better weather—and Sèvres and St. Cloud and Fontainebleau, and all the other summer places.

I see you have had your article on Pottery printed—seen that fact, but not the article. I like to think of you as "thätig" in all sorts of ways: it is the best remedy for one's own ills, and helps a little to remedy other people's. Mr. Theodore Martin[7] was telling us yesterday how he is changing the face of a neighbourhood in Hampshire, by building cottages, and a dining-room, and establishing a co-operative store, for the workmen engaged in new

---

6. Eugène Emmanuel Viollet-le-Duc (1814–79) had restored the Sainte-Chapelle and Notre Dame de Paris as well as Amiens, Laon, and St. Denis.

7. It was not Martin, but Arthur Helps. Having found china clay at Vernon Hill, his estate near Bishop's Waltham, Hampshire, Helps "built a large house, *i.e.* dormitory with an eating-room and recreation-room, a chapel and school for his workmen." But the House of Commons refused an act for the short railway to carry the clay from the pits to Botley Station, and Helps lost some £13,000 in the speculation. See C. B. Johnson, *William Bodham Donne and His Friends*, [1905], p. 310, and *Hampshire Notes and Queries*, 6 (1892), 66. In 1865 Martin bought Bryntysilio, near Llangollen, North Wales.

pottery or terra-cotta works there. I should have envied him, if I allowed myself to envy anyone, in a world where each has dire need of his share.

Will the doctor come with you to England this year, I wonder? And Nannie?[8] I heard good news of her from some friend or other a little while ago. I hope it was not false. It would do me good to know that she was once more able to walk about and find the hours something more than hours of endurance. O sadness—that a sweet clear-eyed woman striving after all that is beautiful and best, should be taken away for so many precious years, from the active influences of the world.

George is pretty well now, and expects soon to be very busy about the new Fortnightly Review, which I think I mentioned to you. I am so so: dyspeptic and dismal occasionally, and had I been a Hebrew prophet near the time of the captivity I should doubtless have written Lamentations. Dyspepsia determines a great deal of literary production.

A carpenter, putting up brackets, wants me. You see, I am scribbling in a hurry—because I want to let you know at once how pleased I was to hear of you.

Ever dear, Your true and affectionate

M. E. L.

IV, 184:17 GHL TO THOMAS ADOLPHUS TROLLOPE, LONDON, 20 MARCH [1865]

Text: T. A. Trollope, *What I Remember*, 2d ed., 2 vols., 1887, II, 312–313, misdated 1864.

The Priory, | 21. North Bank, | Regents Park.
20 March.

My eldest boy, who spends his honeymoon in Florence (is not that sugaring jam tart?), brings you this greeting from your silent but affectionate friends. Tell him all particulars about yourselves, and he will transmit them in his letters to us. First and foremost about the health of your wife,[9] and how this bitter winter has treated her. Next about Bice, and then about yourself.

We rejoice in the prospect of your *History of Florence*, and I am casting about, hoping to find somebody to review it worthily for the *Fortnightly Review*. By the way, would not you or your wife help me there also! Propose your subjects!

8. Barbara's sister Anne Leigh Smith.
9. Theodosia Garrow Trollope died 13 April 1865.

I hope you will like our daughter. She is a noble creature; and Charles is a lucky dog (his father's luck) to get such a wife.

We have been and are in a poor state of health, but manage to scramble on. Charles will tell you all there is to tell. With our love to your dear wife and Bice,

Believe me, ever faithfully yours,

G. H. Lewes.

IV, 185:1 GHL: PROSPECTUS FOR *FORTNIGHTLY*, MARCH 1865

Text: Trinity College, Cambridge.

THE FORTNIGHTLY REVIEW.

It has often been regretted that England has no journal similar to the *Revue des Deux Mondes*, treating of subjects which interest cultivated and thoughtful readers, and published at intervals which are neither too distant for influence on the passing questions, nor too brief for deliberation.

The FORTNIGHTLY REVIEW will be established to meet this demand. It will address the cultivated readers of all classes by its treatment of topics specially interesting to each; and it is hoped that the latitude which will be given to the expression of individual opinion may render it acceptable to a very various public. As one means of securing the best aid of the best writers on questions of LITERATURE, ART, SCIENCE, PHILOSOPHY, FINANCE, and POLITICS generally, we propose to remove all those restrictions of party and of editorial "consistency" which in other journals hamper the full and free expression of opinion; and we shall ask each writer to express his own views and sentiments with all the force of sincerity. He will never be required to express the views of an Editor or of a Party. He will not be asked to repress opinions or sentiments because they are distasteful to an Editor, or inconsistent with what may have formerly appeared in the REVIEW. He will be asked to say what he really thinks and really feels; to say it on his own responsibility, and to leave its appreciation to the public.

In discussing questions that have an agitating influence, and admit diversity of aspects—questions upon which men feel deeply and think variously—two courses are open to an effective journal: either to become the organ of a Party, and to maintain a vigilant consistency which will secure the intensive force gained by limitation; or to withdraw itself from all such limitations, and rely on the extensive force to be gained from a wide and liberal range. The latter course will be ours. Every Party has its organ. The FORTNIGHTLY REVIEW will seek its public amid all parties.

It must not be understood from this that the REVIEW is without its purpose, or without a consistency of its own; but the consistency will be one of tendency, not of doctrine; and the purpose will be that of aiding Progress in all directions. The REVIEW will be liberal, and its liberalism so thorough as to include great diversity of individual opinion within its catholic unity of purpose. This is avowedly an experiment. National culture and public improvement really take place through very various means, and under very different guidance. Men never altogether think alike, even when they act in unison. In the FORTNIGHTLY REVIEW we shall endeavour to further the cause of Progress by illumination from many minds. We shall encourage, rather than repress, diversity of opinion, satisfied if we can secure the higher uniformity which results from the constant presence of sincerity and talent.

We do not disguise from ourselves the difficulties of our task. Even with the best aid from contributors, we shall at first have to contend against the impatience of readers at the advocacy of opinions which they disapprove. Some will complain that our liberalism is too lax; others that it is too stringent. And, indeed, to adjust the limits beyond which even our desire for the free expression of opinion will not permit our contributors to pass, will be a serious difficulty. We must rely on the tact and sympathy of our contributors, and on the candid construction of our readers. The *Revue des Deux Mondes* has proved with what admirable success a Journal may admit the utmost diversity of opinion. Nor can we doubt that an English public would be tolerant of equal diversity, justified by equal talent.

The FORTNIGHTLY REVIEW will be published on the 1st and 15th of every month. Price Two Shillings. The first Number will appear May 1.[1]

CHAPMAN & HALL, 193, PICCADILLY.

IV, 185:1   GHL TO LORD HOUGHTON, LONDON, [25 MARCH 1865]

MS: Trinity College, Cambridge.

21 North Bank | Saturday.

Dear Lord Houghton

Editorial cares make it impossible for me to give up a morning just now even to come to your delightful breakfasts.

Here is our prospectus. Won't you aid us with something? Is there no subject you would like to treat, no book you would like to criticise?

1. The first number appeared 15 May 1865.

4 May 1865

    Mrs. Lewes is *always* at home on Sunday afternoons, and generally on other afternoons.

    Believe me,

Yours very truly,
G. H. Lewes.

Lord Houghton

IV, 187:9   GHL TO LORD HOUGHTON, LONDON, [MARCH? 1865]

MS: Trinity College, Cambridge.

The Priory, | 21. North Bank, | Regents Park.

My dear Lord Houghton

    I shall be very happy to accept your kind invitation for Sunday the 12th.

Ever yours truly,
G. H. Lewes.

IV, 191:24   GE TO JOHN BLACKWOOD, LONDON, 4 MAY 1865

MS: National Library of Scotland. *Endorsed:* 330 A.B. sold 78 Clerical. *Published:* *TLS*, 10 March 1972, p. 282.

The Priory, | 21. North Bank, | Regents Park.

May 4. 65.

My dear Sir

    I congratulate you more on being at Strathtyrum than on the prospect of coming to London, though I shall be happy to see you when you *are* condemned to streets instead of sea-shore and mountains.

    I see from Mr. Simpson's account that in February 1864, in accordance with the intention you had mentioned to me, there were reprinted 500 of the 1 volume edition of the Clerical Scenes with Silas Marner, and 1000 of the 1 volume edition of Adam Bede, for which you will remember that I have not received any payment.[2] Probably further reprints of the 6/– edition will not be required, and Mr. Lewes thinks that it will be well to defer a cheaper edition until I have published another book.

    As you will imagine, he is very busy just now with the approaching first number of the Fortnightly Review, and the problem, well known to you,

---

2. The 6/ edition. See IV, 137.

of reconciling uncalculated length of articles with calculated amount of space.

Believe me,

> Always yours truly
> Marian E. Lewes.

John Blackwood Esq.

IV, 191:24   GHL TO EDWARD SPENCER BEESLY, LONDON, [9? MAY 1865]

MS: Yale.

The Fortnightly Review, | Office—193, Piccadilly.
Tuesday.

My dear Beesley

Your Catiline is first-rate. I have taken the liberty of entitling it "An Apology for Catiline"—as you first named it to me—because *that* is an attractive title, and yours is *not*.³ You will have proofs shortly, but I fear there will be no possibility of my printing it in No. 1. so that your being too busy for No. 2 will not matter. Only as soon as you *have* a gap of leisure pray let us have the benefit!

> Yours ever
> G. H. L.

IV, 191:24   GHL TO FREDERIC HARRISON, LONDON, [10 MAY 1865]

MS: Cornell University Library.

The Fortnightly Review, | Office— 193, Piccadilly.
Wednesday night.

My dear Harrison

I must tell you how admirable I think your paper⁴—high in tone, close in reasoning, unanswerable I think, and certain to be very effective and perhaps to create a row. I wish it had not been so long. I would then have put it first—but it has the second place of honor (the last)—and you see makes 21 pages even in the smaller type.

3. Beesly's article appeared in the *Fortnightly*, 1 (1 June 1865), 167–184, entitled "Catiline as a Party Leader."

4. "The Iron-Masters' Trade-Union," *Fortnightly Review*, 1 (15 May 1865), 96–116.

[12 May 1865]

When shall we have the second paper?[5]—By the way some one told me (I forget who) that you had written or were about to write a paper on St. Bernard—might we hope for that?

I propose with your permission to call your article "The Strike and the Lock Out"—as a more generally attractive title. If you object of course I have nothing to say.[6]

Meanwhile many thanks. If the Review can but get papers like yours its success is assured. Beesly has also sent a first-rate paper on Catiline.

Ever yours truly
G. H. Lewes.

If there are any persons to whom you would like the Review to be sent pray let me have their addresses.

IV, 193:1 GHL TO MONCURE DANIEL CONWAY, LONDON, [12 MAY 1865]

MS: Columbia University.

The Fortnightly Review, | **Office— 193, Piccadilly.**
Friday.

My dear Sir

I have not a copy of the proof at hand but the Review will reach you tomorrow. I have ordered the copies to be sent as you directed. The Initials are correct in the Review. I suppose our clerk made the mistake in sending out advertisement.[7]

The editor of the Pall Mall Gazette asked me if I could name any one whom I thought would write him a series of papers on American Statesmen —personal and graphic—each of about a column and a half in length. I mentioned you. If you like to write this series perhaps you will at once communicate with the editor, as I am leaving town. He wishes Johnston, Seward, Stanton, Chase, Sumner etc. if you know them well enough to describe them, as I have no doubt you do. Obviously these articles must have a certain personal stamp and not be like the general comments which have appeared in newspapers. If you were to write "President Johnston" as a

---

5. "The Limits of Political Economy," 1 (15 June 1865), 356–376. He did not write on St. Bernard.

6. Harrison like Beesly preferred his own title.

7. "Personal Recollections of the President," *Fortnightly*, 1 (15 May 1865), 665, by M. D. Conway. In the advertisements his name was given as M. W. Conway.

first paper, and send it on, mentioning my name, I have little doubt it would lead to a taking series. In haste

Ever yours truly
G. H. Lewes.

Rev. M. D. Conway

IV, 194:15 ANTHONY TROLLOPE TO GHL, GLASGOW, 30 MAY 1865

MS: Yale. *Published: The Letters of Anthony Trollope*, ed. B. A. Booth, 1951, pp. 165–166.

Glasgow 30 May 1865.

My dear Lewes.

As to putting Belton E. first in No. 3,[8] do just as you please. I have a strong opinion against putting the novel always first as it indicates an idea that it is our staple;—which indicates the further idea that the remainder is padding. Were I Editor I think I should always give the novel a distinctive place just before the Chronique.[9] But that is a matter of small, or no, moment.

My revises were returned 4 days since,—and the non return up to then was not my fault. Indeed I had not asked for revises. But they were sent, and sent without the original proofs, and were therefore useless. I wrote for the original sheets and then returned the revises.

Touching the signing[1] I have been so driven by official work that I have not put a pen to it. But I will. I am not *at all* anxious as to the number in which it may appear. Indeed it would be too late now for the third. Fourth or fifth will do as well. I shall be with you in about a week.

Who is to do your chronique? If you are in a difficulty *I will attempt it.* Only, could not the pages be less pressed? It is closer than we at first intended. Poor Billy![2] Why did he give up?

I have got, just got, No. 2 and have only read your article.[3] It is beautiful, but, oh, so cruel. You are as hard almost as Carlyle;—without the salve which one has for Carlyle's blows, in the feeling that they are all struck in

---

8. Only 4 of the 15 parts of Trollope's *The Belton Estate* headed numbers of the *Fortnightly:* 5, 6, 11, and 15.

9. "Public Affairs" in each number of the *Fortnightly* was unsigned.

1. "On Anonymous Literature," *Fortnightly*, 1 (1 July 1865), 491–498.

2. Booth speculates that William Howard Russell (1820–1907) had written "Public Affairs" for the 1st number.

3. "The Principles of Success in Literature (Ch. 2): The Principle of Vision," *Fortnightly*, 1 (1 June 1865), 185–196. GHL classifies writers of genius, of talent, and imitators.

the dark, and may probably, after all, not be deserved. But it is very beautiful. Your style leaves nothing to be desired.

Enjoying myself! revising a post office with 300 men, the work and wages of all of whom are to be fixed on one's own responsibility! Come and try it, and then go back to the delicious ease and perfect freedom of your Editors chair!

Yours always
Anthony Trollope.

IV, 194:15 GE TO NIKOLAUS TRÜBNER, LONDON, [JUNE ? 1865]

MS: Marylebone Public Library, London. *Envelope:* N. Trubner Esq. *Endorsed:* George Eliott.

The Priory, | 21. North Bank, | Regents Park.
Sunday Morning.

My dear Sir

I return,[4] with many thanks, three of the books you kindly lent me à propos of comparative grammar. The little Catechism I remember you recommended to my especial care and I am therefore anxious that it should be in your hands again.

I retain at present Clark's Comp[arative] Gram[mar] and Baudry's little grammar. Schleicher's is an admirable survey and makes me desire to see others of his works.

Thank you also for Miss Cobbe's volume.

Yours very truly
M. E. Lewes.

4. Probably by GHL, who often called Sunday mornings on Trübner at 29 Upper Hamilton Terrace, near the Priory. Among the books were Frédéric Baudry, *Grammaire comparée*, Paris, 1863; August Schleicher, *Compendium der vergleichenden Grammatik der indogermanischen Sprechen*, 2 vols., Weimar, 1861–62; and Frances Power Cobbe, *Broken Lights*, 1864, or *Studies, New and Old*, 1865, both published by Trübner.

IV, 194:15 ANTHONY TROLLOPE TO GHL, GLASGOW, 1 JUNE 1865

MS: Yale. *Published: The Letters of Anthony Trollope*, ed. B. A. Booth, 1951, pp. 166–167.

Waltham House, | **Waltham Cross.**
Glasgow | June 1. 1865.

My dear Lewes.

Beesly's paper on Catiline is admirable. It is written by a man leaning on his pen with delight, which leaning always gives a life to the work. But he writes too much like an advocate with a side to defend, to be perfectly convincing. I still believe that Cicero was more of a patriot than Catiline. That both were false and both cruel is to be assumed,—for they were Romans of that false and cruel time that began with Sulla and ended when there was no longer spirit enough in Rome either for falsehood or cruelty. That Cicero was constitutionally a coward,—though he knew how to die,—and Catiline a man of nerve was little to the credit or discredit of either,—as little as having strong arms or long legs. Had Beesly been more historic and less enthusiastic he would have told us that Cicero, who was so loud against Verres was at any rate honest in his own province,—(a very rare virtue) and that he sought nothing from his countrymen at home beyond the objects of a fierce ambition, and was therefore entitled to deal heavily with a demagogue.

That he did,—is as I have said a matter of course because he was a Roman; and equally a matter of course that he did successfully, because he was gifted with the use of words. I however, am myself so given to rebellion in politics that I am delighted to see and hear any Catiline defended, and any Cicero attacked.

I am glad you have no difficulty about the chronique.

Yours ever
A. T.

Tom immersed in a lawsuit with a Russian—(in Florence!) which is like to keep him there all the summer,—as to the sale or non sale of his house!!!

IV, 194:15 THORNTON ARNOTT LEWES TO GHL, SAND SPRINT, 12 JUNE–12 AUGUST 1865

MS: Yale.

Tent Hotel | Sand Sprint | June 12th 1865.

Dear Pater,

As I did not write by last mail, at least not thinking that any letter left here by it; for I am never sure when letters written here leave Durban, I take up the pen now having nothing else particularly to do, although I don't know how I shall fill one page, much less four. Life has been so monotonous lately that I have nothing of importance.

Our trading is finally settled. Two of the Creditors take over our estate paying 10/– in the £; which was very good of them, not that they will lose by it, but still times are so bad here that it is a wonder they consented to burden themselves with the risk. Although it is a considerable *sell*, to be bankrupt, or what in reality comes to the same thing, after only carrying on business 6 months, but seeing that the largest firm in Natal will probably not pay 1/– in the £, and very few of the large failures which have taken place lately pay more than 5/– we may think a good deal of ourselves for paying as much as we do. However though we don't lose anything (perhaps rather the opposite) in the opinion of the Natalians, I can't get credit to start on another trip, to redeem the failure of the first. If Bertie comes out, we should start about April next. If not, I shall have to take a situation, somewhere, and wait till I can lay buy 2–300£, which will take at least 5 years and then I can think of starting again.

I have for the last week been *working* here, as Kafir storekeeper and general Bottlewasher etc. at £7 per month, with board, lodging, washing and grog free, and I like it very much. The only drawback is, that I have to go down to Maritzburg to hand over our oxen etc. and by that time this Hotel will be sold by Auction, and the chances are against my getting the berth from the new occupier, however I shall try and if I get it, shall be comfortably established till Bertie arrives or not as the case may be. If I don't get it, I have not the slightest idea what I shall do with myself, however I suppose something will turn up.

By the bye, Pater, your collywobbles being always mutinous did you ever try Homeopathy? If you feel inclined to try it, Cronin's brother and father who live at Brixton are both Homeopathic doctors the latter a celebrated one. Cronin himself, left me 6 weeks ago here, to look after the oxen, whilst he went down to Durban to get a situation, which he has got, so that the firm of Lewes and Cronin (established 1864) is a thing of the past.

I have not lifted a gun to my shoulder for an age, except yesterday when I shot two plovers; from the simple fact that I have sold both mine for oxen during the trip and the oxen have departed this life. Of my other favourite pursuits, butterfly hunting is at a discount, there are very few here, and many of them English. Durban and the coast generally boasts an infinite number of beauties, amongst others that famous fellow the Deathshead, and whenever I happen to be staying in Durban I shall make some impressions for Burckhardt, who is a great collector. I suppose if I send home one or two, they will be duly admired, so will send some. I am sorry to say that as yet I have not got my April letters, excepting one from Mamma; so that I have no accounts of the *two* important weddings of the month, for I daresay you do not know that Luise Burckhardt is married; i.e. was to be married in April, and Gustav's letter not having arrived, I am in a state of blissful ignorance. The happy man is a professor Bachofen; to think of her rejecting a Lewes to marry an *oven*; the pun is near enough for the obtuse (to puns) intellects of foreigners, so of course I have made any amount of them to Gustav, hoping that the *Loaves* will be *well baked*. However! sing Hallelujah and be joyful.

July 1, 1865.

I have just taken up this letter, which I had written so far on the 12th, and which I should have concluded before, but I have not had time, so many things have occupied my time. I had been busy riding about country on horses not up to my weight (I am 180 lbs.) in order to collect the four miserable horses (I call them miserable because they made me so) which we had traded, and was sent about like the bad penny, of which we read, from one man to another, having to pass the night in Kaffir Kraals, half eaten up by Kaffir lice (as big as *grubs*, white with a dark streak down the back), and had at last got them all together, when on the morning of Tuesday the 27th June I was awakened by the news that the Basuto Kaffirs, who live on the west boundary of the Colony, and therefore close to Sand Sprint, were down the Berg and over the border in tremendous force, and were at that time attacking the nearest house to us, about a mile and a quarter off, and which we can see distinctly. The Zulu Kaffirs, who live close to us, were all bolting as fast as they could, but the Basutos told them that they only came to fight the Boers, and not the English or Kaffirs, so they came back quietly to their Kraals. Soon down came an old woman whom they had turned out of her house and plundered it. Report after report of the Basutos' misdeeds, including the murder of 6 Boers, one a plucky young fellow of my acquaintance; and some Kaffirs and Hottentots. Then down came my two Kaffir boys April and Willsir informing me that every one of my troop of cattle was gone, and that they had nearly been killed themselves. One of their companions was assagaied. Well, you may imagine that I felt extremely *grateful* to the Basutos for stealing the cattle! They decamped with some thousand head of cattle, sheep etc. etc. and 150 horses. We immediately sent in a messenger to Ladismith the nearest town, for the Natal Frontier Guard, and they came the next day. Of course by this, the news is all over the country, and by tomorrow we hope to have 2,000 men here to start for Basuto land, to wreck vengeance on their heads. Of course I volunteer, and hope to have the pleasure of potting a few Basutos before I have done with them.

Who would have thought, that by my coming out here, instead of going to Poland, I should have fallen from the frying pan into the fire, and instead of fighting an enemy I hate, I should have to fight one I despise. However it is clear to me that fighting is my destiny, and go where I will I shall come in for it, so with all my heart I am going now into Basuto war.[5] I shall give you all the news when I can, but I don't suppose I shall be able to write often; this letter can't start yet, so I shall fill it up later on.

August 12, 1865. | Ladismith.

It is two months since I broke off this letter, and as I am just leaving this town, for the farm of a friend named Robson. To begin where I left off, viz: 1 July, On the 2nd of July I joined the Natal Frontier Guard, a cavalry corps, I took one of the 4 horses, which had caused so much mischief, and was supplied by the Corps with short Enfield rifle, sabre and ammunition. At 4 o'clock on the morning of the third, the Bugle sounded 'To horse,' and in half an hour we were wending our way up the Drakensberg. We numbered about 25 fighting men, having left 3 with the Commissariat waggon and were soon joined by as many Dutchmen, and the two parties proceeded on together. We soon arrived at the scene of the murder of the Boers, and there we found the murdered Kafir servants of the Boers, and a Coolie who was with the waggons at the time. The Boers had been buried by a party from Harrismith, or rather had had some branches and earth strewn over them, and their legs were sticking through. We crossed the boundary and drove along through the Free State, following up the Basuto spoor. Here and there we came upon feathers strewing the veldt, where the Basutos had destroyed the feather beds. We got by nightfall to the top of another Drakensberg pass, and were within a short distance of a large body of Kaffirs. Lucky for them that we did not know it, or we would have walked into them. It was only found out next morning, when too late. Our patrol came upon the dead bodies of two Basutos, who had been wounded in the attack on the house near us, and who had been

5. To resist the advance of the Boers the Basuto in 1868 accepted the protection of Great Britain.

abandoned by their comrades. The same day we went down the Berg by this second pass, and found the Weenen Cavalry, encamped at the foot; they welcomed us with three cheers, and we soon fraternised. Our encampment was formed in the deep bed of a dry brook or sprint as they are called here, and a whole sheep stewed in Dutch fashion in butter, revived our courage, for we had been living the day before and this one, on one or two weevilly and musty biscuits. We remained in Camp 9 days; 2 hours-sentrygo every night, occasional parades, sword exercise etc., cleaning bits and stirrups, with singing in the evening was all we had to do, so we played the intellectual game of whist all day. I composed a Frontier Guard Song for the occasion, which though very mediocre, was welcomed with great applause. At the end of the nine days we rode into Ladismith, and were disbanded pro tem, with orders to hold ourselves in [*The rest of this letter is lacking.*]

IV, 196:12 GE TO MME EUGÈNE BODICHON, LONDON, [23 JUNE 1865]

MS: Berg Collection, New York Public Library.

The Priory, | 21. North Bank, | Regents Park.
Friday.

Dearest Barbara
 Welcome home! Will you come on Sunday at ½ past 2?[6]
 Till then,

Yours ever lovingly
M. E. L.

IV, 196:12 GHL TO LORD HOUGHTON, LONDON, [26 JUNE 1865]

MS: Trinity College, Cambridge.

The Priory, | 21 North Bank, | Regents Park.
Monday.

My dear Lord Houghton
 I have sent on the letter.
 Respecting breakfast on Wednesday, Virtue sternly shouts No; and Vice seductively whispers Yes. Of course the vulgar loudness of Virtue

6. Barbara came with Dr. Bodichon Sunday, 25 June 1865. (GE Journal.)

can't expect to carry the point. I side with Vice—and will leave the consequences to your conscience.

Yours very faithfully,
G. H. Lewes.

IV, 196:12   GHL TO J. BAILEY, LONDON, [28? JUNE? 1865]

MS: Yale.

The Priory, | 21. North Bank, | Regents Park.
Wednesday.

Dear Sir

I *hope* to be able to join your dinner on the 15 of July, but as there is a contingent possibility of my not being in town that week, I can only accept your kind invitation under that proviso.

Yours truly
G. H. Lewes.

Mr. J. Bailey

IV, 196:12   GHL TO MONCURE DANIEL CONWAY, LONDON, [28 JUNE 1865]

MS: Yale. *Endorsed:* "Modern Times."

The Fortnightly Review, | Office— 193, Piccadilly.
Wednesday.

My dear Sir

Your paper[7] is intensely interesting and I should be glad of more from the same mint. If the Note[8] can be engraved in time I will have it copied; if not, your description will do and I will return you the curious original. Proof will reach you I hope tomorrow.

Yours faithfully
G. H. Lewes.

Revd. M. D. Conway

---

7. "Modern Times, New York," *Fortnightly*, 1 (1 July 1865), 421–434, describes Conway's visit in 1857 to Modern Times (now Islip), New York, founded as a utopian free-love commune. The standard of value was the time required for labor and the disagreeableness of the work. The colony embarked for South America when the Civil War began.

8. A note of the colony's currency, "Five Hours in Professional Services or 80 Pounds of Corn," reproduced on p. 424.

IV, 196:12 GHL TO JOHN BLACKWOOD, LONDON, [3 JULY 1865]

MS: National Library of Scotland.

The Priory, | 21. North Bank, | Regents Park.
Monday.

My dear Blackwood

Mr. Kebbel wishes to forward you a contribution under cover of an introduction from me, although you doubtless know him already as one of the few staunch conservatives and a contributor to the Quarterly;[9] but, since he wishes the formal business of introduction to be gone through I am only too happy to be the introducer.

Ever yours truly
G. H. Lewes.

John Blackwood Esq.

IV, 197:21 GE TO MME EUGÈNE BODICHON, LONDON, [27 JULY 1865]

MS: Berg Collection, New York Public Library.

The Priory, | 21. North Bank, | Regents Park.
Thursday.

Dearest Barbara

Do not come to me to-morrow, because Gertrude will be with me and after her, I expect Mrs. P. Taylor. The time I should be most likely to be alone would be Saturday at $\frac{1}{2}$ past 1. Can you come and lunch with me?

On second thoughts, perhaps Mrs. P. Taylor may write to say she can't come. In that case I will let you know, if you would like to come tomorrow evening about $\frac{1}{2}$ past 8. But don't come unless I write.

Ever yours,
Marian.

---

9. GHL published Thomas Edward Kebbel's "English Love of Latin Poetry" in the *Fortnightly*, 1 (15 July 1865), 605–611. He had published two articles in the *Quarterly*. But his first article in *Blackwood's* was in September 1887.

[3 August 1865]

IV, 199:7 GHL TO THOMAS ADOLPHUS TROLLOPE, LONDON, [31 JULY 1865]

MS: Morgan Library.

The Priory, | 21. North Bank, | Regents Park.
Monday.

My dear Trollope

We were vexed to find that we had missed you and still more that you had not left your address which however I got from Chapman yesterday. Now we must have a glimpse of you in your brief stay but as you are of course much engaged we wish you to fix the day and hour. On Wednesday we have a party but I don't suppose you would care to come to that. Will you lunch at 1.30 or dine at 6.30 with us on Thursday? ⟨or if⟩ Choose the hour *most* convenient to you. Or if neither will do will you come and lunch on Sunday?

Ever yours
G. H. Lewes.

IV, 200:18 GE TO MME EUGÈNE BODICHON, LONDON, [3 AUGUST 1865]

MS: Berg Collection, New York Public Library.

The Priory, | 21. North Bank, | Regents Park.
Thursday.

Dear Barbara

You did not come again, but the picture[1] came. We are both very much pleased with it and grateful to the soul and the hand that produced it for us. It is deliciously fresh and airy and happy. It is settled now that we go for a month's holiday in Normandy and Brittany starting next Thursday. So I am reading Villemarqué[2] and setting my mind towards Celtic legends, that I may people the land with great shadows when there are no solid Bretons in sight.

Yesterday the two Trollopes[3] dined with us and we had a good deal

1. A watercolor landscape, now owned by Mrs. Peter Cash, GHL's great-granddaughter.
2. Théodore Claude Henri de la Villemarqué, *Contes populaires des anciens Bretons*, 2 vols., Paris, 1842, and *La Légende celtique en Irlande, en Cambrie, et en Bretagne*, St.-Brieuc, 1864.
3. "Mr. A. Trollope and his brother dined with us—the first time we have

of pleasant talk, or rather shouting. Also I sat for the last time for my portrait, and Mr. Burton was disappointed to find that you had left town before he had been able to call on you and see certain oil sketches. I gave him your address that he might write to you.

Let me know how you get on.

Ever yours
M. E. Lewes.

IV, 201:6   GHL TO ROBERT LYTTON, LONDON, 13 SEPTEMBER [1865]

MS: Lady Hermione Cobbold.

The Fortnightly Review, | Office— 193, Piccadilly.
Wednesday 13 September.

My dear Lytton

I was away scouring Brittainy when your letter and proof[4] came so that my locum tenens could do nothing but follow my instructions and print your poem according to proof. It is so fine a poem that I should have been glad to have used the pumice stone of which Horace speaks[5] here and there; though I perfectly understand how if it was recently written your ear may be too wedded to the old song to be able to alter it or see where it was alterable.

Don't let it be your last contribution. Prose or verse "my great revenge hath stomach for it all."[6] We are a great success, but the Fortnightly uses up material so much faster than good material can be had to replace it that my anxieties are many and serious.

What do you think of little Amberley's paper?[7] His name was against him but the tone was so good that I thought it right to print—and by the way the tories howl I conclude they have been hurt!

I must tell you that my mother who is 76 is constantly quoting your poem to me; having been vastly taken with it. What the press gang have said I don't know for I never look to see what they may have to say.

Ever yours truly
G. H. Lewes.

Rob. Lytton Esq.

seen Mr. T. Trollope since his wife's death, which happened in March last." (GE Journal, 2 August 1865.) Theodosia Garrow Trollope (1825–13 April 1865).

4. "The Apple of Life," *Fortnightly*, 2 (1 September 1865), 184–192.

5. *Ars Poetica*, line 304.

6. *Othello*, v, ii, 74–75.

7. "Liberals, Conservatives, and the Church," *Fortnightly*, 2 (1 September 1865), 161–168.

IV, 204:28 THORNTON ARNOTT LEWES TO GHL, LADISMITH, 22 SEPTEMBER 1865

MS: Yale.

Ladismith, | September 22. 1865.

Dear Pater,

Yours of the 15th July, has just turned up, along with 2 first numbers of the Fortnightly, for which I am much obliged. My other letters, will by this time have arrived giving you all the details "the latest news from 'Our own Correspondent.'"

Respecting Bertie, he is knocked on the head (morally) for some time to come, as there will be no trading to be done for a good time, now. The War between the Free State and the Basutos must first be over, even supposing there is no war between Natal and the Basutos, of which there is a strong possibility. In fact this country is so fearfully unsettled, that it is hard enough for the present inhabitants to get anything to do, and therefore not at all the time for new arrivals. When the time seems fit I will write you full details.

Of course, I should go on with the trading for a couple of years or so at least till Bertie could manage perfectly independently for himself, and I would be at Durban ready to receive him, whenever he might come. Of course, you would let me know in what ship he would start and when. Wherever I might be in Natal, I should not take long to get to Durban in case of his arrival.

I start today or tomorrow to join the Free State Boers against the Basutos, as I hear, there is a Commando (consisting of all the armed men of a district) just over the Natal boundary. Percy Whitehead, to whom I brought out a letter of introduction from his sister Mrs. Malleson,[8] has just come down from the seat of war, where he has been distinguishing himself. I came into town yesterday, from the farm where I have been stopping, on purpose to see him and make arrangements to go back with him, but unfortunately he has gone to Maritzburg. I hope soon to have a little wild fighting to describe, but the Basutos are such cowards, they run very soon. I should think 2,000 Basutos have been killed and wounded (at least) during the war, and not more than 50 Boers, if as many, so you see the danger is not very great. I will write and give you all the news, with descriptions of Commando life etc. whenever I have an opportunity, but don't be frightened if you don't hear for two or three months. Since last I wrote I have been doing nothing, staying on the farm, painting a waggon,

8. See IV, 125, n. 3.

papering rooms etc. mild work of this kind. I have just recovered 13 oxen of those stolen, the Kaffir chiefs having sent down some of the stolen cattle. So these go towards paying the debts of the firm.

I am glad to hear Charlie is so happy, how do you find the house without him? But I suppose you see a good deal of him. I hope the Fortnightly pays *you* well, whatever it may do as regards the publishers.

This letter is a short one, for there is nothing to be said at all, vegetation is so like in all parts of the world, that when I tell you, I have been vegetating for the last 2 months, you know as much about me as I do myself. I forgot to say that by volunteering for the Free State I obtain a right to a farm in that country and to a share of the booty, which I am afraid won't be enormous. I wish everything was comfortably settled, the state of disturbance here, is so uncomfortable; one can't make up one's mind to settle down quietly to anything, as at any moment, one may be called out to fight Basutos or Zulus.

Luise Burckhardt was married on the 4th of April, and as she went to Italy for her honeymoon, Charlie and she must have been pretty close to each other, at Milan, Florence or somewhere thereabouts.

My latest literary intelligence, is that I have composed a song in 23 verses for the Natal Frontier Guard, likewise various bad jokes, of which I insert one for your special amusement. What is the most wonderful British hybrid? The Bull-ass (Bullace)!!! I call that "*Plum* a falla."

With much love to everybody,

Your affectionate Son
Thornton Lewes.

IV, 205:27 GHL TO LORD AMBERLEY,[9] LONDON, 14 OCTOBER 1865

MS: The Bertrand Russell Archives, McMaster University. *Published: The Amberley Papers*, 2 vols., 1937, I, 432–433.

The Priory, | 21. North Bank, | Regents Park.

14 October 65.

My Lord

The paper on Young England, according to my conception of it, could only be written effectively by a young man, because it should set

---

9. John Russell, Viscount Amberley (1842–76), married in 1864 Katharine Louisa Stanley, daughter of the second Baron Stanley of Alderley. They were the parents of Bertrand Arthur William Russell, third Earl Russell (1872–1970).

forth what the young men really think, and not what their seniors think they think, or think they ought to think. It is a subject which demands above all things sincerity, and with the courage to speak plainly the talent to speak effectively: two qualities which I recognized in your lordship, and which led me to hope that you might undertake the task.

The young men of our day have their own views of political social and religious questions—views in advance of and sometimes divergent from those of their seniors—adumbrating an ideal which may or may not be practicable but which at any rate must be the guide for them. It is important for them and for the public to know *what* it is they aim at—what *are* the serious hopes and convictions which animate them.

I presume that you are sufficiently acquainted with the views of your own contemporaries—especially of your own class—certainly of your own personal convictions; and I cannot but think that you would fix public attention by a statement of your mental attitude, should your leisure and inclination permit it.

At the risk of appearing intrusive I have thus recurred to the subject which I will now leave to your lordship's consideration

And remain | My Lord

Your lordship's obedient servant
G. H. Lewes.

The Rt. Honble Viscount Amberley

IV, 207:19 GE TO ISA CRAIG, LONDON, 1 NOVEMBER 1865

MS: Yale.

The Priory, | 21. North Bank, | Regents Park.
November 1. 65.

My dear Miss Craig

Bon voyage to your Argosy![1] How you must work to get through Editorship and Secretaryship too.

We shall be glad to see Mr. Call on board your good ship. He is a highly accomplished man, who from self-diffidence and want of "go" has

---

Amberley did not write the article on Young England that GHL was proposing for the *Fortnightly*.

1. Isa Craig (1831–1903), Secretary of the National Association for the Promotion of Social Science, was for a short time editor of the *Argosy. A Magazine for the Fireside and the Journey*, founded in 1865.

never had a good share of opportunity. He was a clergyman and on some subjects is unusually instructed.

You know we are always glad to see you.

Ever yours sincerely
M. E. Lewes.

IV, 207:19 GHL TO SIR JOHN BOWRING, LONDON, [3 NOVEMBER 1865]

MS: Yale.

The Fortnightly Review, | Office—193, Piccadilly.
Friday.

My dear Sir John

The m.s. you send[2] has much interest but is a little unshapely. Considering the importance of the subject and the attention it will attract I think it would be well worth your while to expend some trouble in re-writing it from beginning to end, shaping it into a more effective whole, and throwing in, if possible, more personal touches. The anecdotes are certain to be largely quoted. If you can let me have it on Wednesday next it will be in time for you to see proofs.

Pray do not take any notice of what our chroniqueur may have said.[3] What is wanted is *your* view of Palmerston, and not an accommodation of your view to that of others. I believe that if you choose to take the requisite pains with the article it will make a sensation.

Ever yours faithfully
G. H. Lewes.

Sir John Bowring

2. "Recollections of Lord Palmerston," *Fortnightly*, 3 (15 November 1865), 1–11.

3. Palmerston's death 18 October was commented on in the "Public Affairs" article, 2 (1 November 1865), 756–763.

IV, 207:19 GE TO MARY MARSHALL,
LONDON, [7 NOVEMBER 1865]

MS: Mr. Gerald Bullett.

The Priory, | 21. North Bank, | Regents Park.
Tuesday Evening.

Dear Miss Marshall

I think this note will reach you in time to prevent the vexation of our missing each other again. Tomorrow we go to lunch with Mr. Lewes's mother, and, for a wonder, shall not be at home after 1 o'clock. I hope you will be able to come the next day, or at any rate, very soon.

Sara hinted to me that you had been suffering in health. I hope that is all over now. *We* have been perfect wretches—fit for a lazaretto. But now we are emerging from our dyspeptic miseries. I think most people have been ill lately except a few hardened creatures who have no sympathies with their kind. Do come soon.

Ever yours affectionately
M. E. Lewes.

IV, 209:7 GE TO SARA SOPHIA HENNELL,
LONDON, [19 NOVEMBER 1865]

MS: Yale. *Endorsed:* Nov. 19.

The Priory, | 21. North Bank, | Regents Park.
Sunday Morning.

Dear Sara

I shall be at home on Wednesday,[4] and shall be very glad to have you. We lunch at ½ past 1.

Ever yours
M. E. L.

4. Sara Hennell lunched and dined at the Priory Wednesday 22 November 1865. (GE Journal.)

IV, 209:7 GHL TO LORD HOUGHTON, LONDON, [DECEMBER 1865]

MS: Trinity College, Cambridge. *Endorsed:* To review Swinburne's 'Chastelard.'

The Fortnightly Review. | Office—193, Piccadilly.
Friday.

My dear Lord Houghton

Will not your friendship for Swinburne and good will to the Fortnightly prevail over your scruples, and induce you to review 'Chastelard' for us?[5] We are a great success; but it is in the direction of Literature that we are weakest, therefore I want your aid. Don't say no! Believe me,

Yours very faithfully
G. H. Lewes.

If you refuse I shall have to do it myself—a loss both to the Review and to Swinburne.[6]

IV, 212:21 GHL TO MONCURE DANIEL CONWAY, LONDON, [DECEMBER 1865]

MS: Columbia University.

The Fortnightly Review, | Office— 193, Piccadilly.
Thursday.

My dear Sir

By all means fill up the 16th page; but if you add *more* than the half page, strike out an equivalent number of lines.[7]

I am going out of town for two or three weeks so please address to the office.

Yours truly
G. H. Lewes.

I shall be glad of the other paper[8] you mention.

---

5. Swinburne's *Chastelard*, published toward the end of November 1865, was reviewed by Lord Houghton in the *Fortnightly*, 4 (15 April 1866), 533–543.

6. According to Theodore Watts in the review of Swinburne's *Atalanta in Calydon* by J. Leicester Warren, *Fortnightly*, 1 (15 May 1865), 75–80, GHL added lines 15–16 on p. 75 describing Swinburne as "a minor poet." See *Athenaeum*, 30 November 1895, p. 755.

7. Conway's "America, France, and England," *Fortnightly*, 3 (1 January 1866), 442–459, is the only one of his papers that filled 16 pages.

8. "The American 'Radicals' and Their English Censors," *Fortnightly*, 3 (1 February 1866), 705–720.

IV, 214:16 GHL TO THOMAS ADOLPHUS TROLLOPE, LONDON, 1 JANUARY 1866

Text: T. A. Trollope, *What I Remember*, 2d ed., 2 vols., 1887, II, 316.

The Priory, | 21. North Bank, | Regents Park.
January 1. 1866.

My dear Trollope

A happy New Year to you and Bice!...[9]

And when am I to receive those articles from you, which you projected? I suppose other work keeps you ever on the stretch. But so active a man must needs 'fulfil himself in many ways.'[1]

We have been ailing constantly without being ill, but our work gets on somehow or other. Polly is miserable over a new novel, and I am happy over the very hard work of a new edition of my *History of Philosophy*, which will almost be a new book, so great are the changes and additions. Polly sends her love to you and Bice.

Yours very faithfully
G. H. Lewes.

IV, 215:6 GHL TO LORD HOUGHTON, LONDON, [8 JANUARY 1866]

MS: Trinity College, Cambridge. *Endorsed:* For article on 'Buxton's Ideas.'

The Fortnightly Review, | Office— 193, Piccadilly.
Monday.

My dear Lord Houghton

I should very much like an article *on* Buxton's Ideas[2] from you. A brief review of the book by Trollope[3] appears among the short notices of the number now at press; but that need not in any way interfere with your article which I conclude will be a discussion rather than an exposition.

You have not given up Swinburne[4] I hope?

Ever yours truly,
G. H. Lewes

---

9. Trollope adds: "[After speaking of some literary business matters, the letter goes on:—]."

1. Tennyson, "Morte d'Arthur," line 241.

2. Charles Buxton, *The Ideas of the Day on Policy*, 1865.

3. Anthony Trollope's review is among Notices of New Books in the *Fortnightly*, 3 (15 January 1866), 650–652.

4. Lord Houghton wrote "Mr. Swin-

IV, 220:22 GE TO MME EUGÈNE BODICHON,
LONDON, 15 JANUARY 1866

MS: Berg Collection, New York Public Library.

21 North Bank | January 15. 1866.

My dear Barbara

My not writing is due rather to the want of health, which robs me of energy for things that are not peremptory, than to want of time. One can always find time to scribble a letter, if the spaces between work are not filled with malaise. George and I have both been more suffering than usual,[5] but we are always grumblers, so there is no use in dwelling on what is so far from exceptional. *Your* illness is much more of a case to inquire about. Why did you not tell me what was the matter with you?—Palpitation—or what else? And are you well again? I am terribly afraid that you are worrying yourself about the unchangeable—looking for fowls' milk or some other impossibility—when half the great lesson of life is to adapt one's soul to the irremediable.

Confess, and be healed by adopting the prescriptions you have had over and over again. There are no other. Certain human natures, and certain periods of life for some natures, have limits as immovable as the Jura. You may say that one can't help feeling anguish, and that is true enough. But the anguish is fed by false hope, as fire is fed by fuel. However, I will not go on preaching across France and the Mediterranean: perhaps by this time you are bright again, well in health and able to paint.

Life is very interesting to us in spite of disordered mucous membranes. Great subjects become greater to us, and for that reason smaller ones lose their power of tormenting. As soon as Bertie is gone to his farming again, we shall migrate to Tunbridge Wells for a fortnight and try the effect of the purer air to take our daily walks in. George gets thinner and thinner, and the less there is of him, as with the Sybil's papers, the more precious he becomes.

Poor Mr. Neuberg had a sad accident in driving his little carriage, about six weeks ago. His sister was pitched out and had a contusion of the head which has caused a prolonged state of feebleness. He says it made

burne's *Chastelard*," *Fortnightly*, 4 (15 April 1866), 533–543, but nothing on Buxton.

5. "For the last fortnight I have been unusually disabled by ill health. . . . George is also sadly ailing—thinner and thinner, and less able to digest even the plainest food." (GE Journal, 20 January 1866.)

him feel twenty years older. But she is recovering without having incurred erisypelas, which was the great dread.

I have been delighted to know of Bessie's final decision against the marriage. She seems bright and happy, and courageous in the hope of working with her pen so as to eke out her income.

You remembered the beautiful-eyed, clever, amiable Lord Edward Seymour?[6] Did you see the account of his death—after amputation of a leg, made necessary by a gunshot? I was grieved by his death. He was not one of the ordinary young Liberals, who echo the catchwords of a party. He had genuine opinions, and strove after their precise expression.

When you write again, remember to tell me particularly about the progress of Nannie's health. I want to hear that she is thoroughly restored to all the enjoyments of life—that she can walk, ride, paint, and be active in the many valuable ways her nature prompts. Yesterday, Mr. Hamerton, whose books and (bad) pictures you are acquainted with, came to be introduced to me.[7] He is a very unaffected man, but not of transparent porcelain, rather of good honest earthenware. He really writes well, but I have been told by others as well as you that his pictures are a painful *non sequitur* to all his able theorizing. "So vast is art, so narrow human wit."[8]

We were much interested by your account of all you gathered about Courbet, and after reading your letter I was less sceptical as to Proudhon's conception of his genius. Apropos of Proudhon, in the Revue Contemporaine,[1] there are four interesting papers by Sainte Beuve, giving a sketch

6. Lord Edward Percy Seymour (1841–20 December 1865), died at Yellapoor, India after being bitten by a bear he was shooting. (*The Times*, 20 January 1866, p. 9b.)

7. Philip Gilbert Hamerton (1834–94), art critic and essayist, details in his *Autobiography*, 1897, p. 160, an earlier meeting with GE at 142 Strand, probably in 1853. R. W. Mackay told him that Miss Evans was "a very accomplished lady and played remarkably well on the piano.... She was at Mr. Chapman's little conversazione and performed for us. I remember being well pleased with the music and thinking that she was one of the best amateurs I had heard, but I cannot remember what she played, nor anything about her talk, which would probably be a series of little private conversations with people that she already knew." Perhaps GE was "the editor" who in declining two or three papers he submitted to the *Westminster Review* explained that "An article ought to be an organic whole, with a pre-arranged order and proportion among its parts. There ought to be a beginning, a middle, and an end." (p. 127.) At the Priory 14 January 1866 Hamerton found fault with GE's remaining seated and talking to only one person at a time, but on his next visit she invited him to sit beside her. Hamerton wrote to his wife: "Nous avons parlé d'art, de littérature et d'elle-même. Elle m'a dit que personne n'avait eu plus d'inquiétudes et de souffrances dans le travail qu'elle, et que le peu qu'elle fait coûte énormément." (pp. 343–345.)

8. Pope, *Essay on Criticism*, I, 61.

1. "Proudhon étudié dans ses cor-

of Proudhon from his correspondence which was unusually copious and representative of the man. If the last 4 Numbers of the Revue Cont[emporain]e come in your way, read them.

Always, dear Barbara

Your faithfully affectionate
Marian.

IV, 221:9 GHL TO THOMAS HENRY HUXLEY, LONDON, [19 JANUARY 1866]

MS: Imperial College of Science, London.

The Fortnightly Review, | Office— 193, Piccadilly.

Dear Huxley

The gorilla came was refused admittance told I was busy—persisted and said he came about a matter concerning Prof. Huxley—was *then* admitted—produced his impression—and carried off my ready assent to the republication a month hence. M. Barbier also came and received permission of course.[2]

My mother (aged 75[3]) is delighted with your sermon[4] and foresees a change in Religion coming.

We are going out of town for 2 or 3 weeks after that we hope you will have a Sunday to give us.

Yours truly
G. H. Lewes.

IV, 232:15 GHL TO THOMAS ADOLPHUS TROLLOPE, LONDON, [8? FEBRUARY 1866]

Text: T. A. Trollope, *What I Remember*, 2d ed., 2 vols., 1887, II, 313–314.

My dear Trollope

Thank Signor —— for the offer of his paper, and express to him my regret that in the present crowded state of the *Review* I cannot find a place

respondences intimes," *Revue Contemporaine*, 47 (31 October 1865), 577–611; 48 (15 November–15 December), 63–100, 209–251, 459–496, signed by Sainte-Beuve.

2. Neither the gorilla nor Barbier has been identified.

3. Mrs. John Willim, born 21 May 1787, was 78.

4. "On the Advisableness of Improving Natural Knowledge," *Fortnightly*, 3 (15 January 1866), 626–637, one of Huxley's Lay Sermons, delivered at St. Martin's Hall 7 January 1866.

[*February 1866*]

for it. Don't you however run away with the idea that I don't want *your* contributions on the same ground! The fact is ——'s paper is too wordy and heavy and not of sufficient interest for our publication; and as I have a great many well on hand, I am forced to be particular. Originally my fear was lest we should not get contributors enough. That fear has long vanished. But *good* contributions are always scarce; so don't you fail me!

We have been at Tunbridge Wells for a fortnight's holiday![5] I was forced to 'cave in,' as the Yankees say—regularly beat. I am not very flourishing now, but I can go into harness again. Polly has been, and alas! still is, anything but in a satisfactory state. But she is gestating, and gestation with her is always perturbing. I wish the book were done with all my heart.

I don't think I ever told you how very much your *History of Florence* interested me. I am shockingly ignorant of the subject, and not at all competent to speak, except as one of the public; but you made the political life of the people clear to me. I only regretted here and there a newspaper style which was not historic. Oscar Browning has sent me his review,[6] but I have not read it yet. It is at the printer's. Polly sends her love.

Ever faithfully yours,
G. H. L.

IV, 232:15 GHL TO CHARLES BRAY, LONDON, [FEBRUARY 1866]

MS: Yale.

The Priory, | 21. North Bank, | Regents Park.

My dear Mr. Bray

Your discovery is a very old friend with a new face—and the new face one not presentable in scientific circles. I have no time if I had the desire for discussion of the various hazy conceptions and misconceptions of your pamphlet,[7] but with regard to the new face on 'the discovery' which is to

---

5. From 23 January to 6 February 1866.

6. "Trollope's *History of Florence,*" *Fortnightly,* 4 (15 February 1866), 70–86.

7. Bray sent GHL his pamphlet *On Force, Its Mental and Moral Correlatives; and on That Which Is Supposed to Underlie All Phenomena; with Speculations on Spiritualism, and Other Abnormal Conditions of Mind,* 1866, which argues that thought and electricity are the same force in different forms or modes of manifestation; emanation from all brains, the result of conscious and unconscious cerebration, puts mediums en rapport with other minds. This was the work of which William Maccall's review began: "Fitly art thou called Bray, my worthy friend!" (Bray, *Autobiography,* p. 101.)

bridge over physics and metaphysics, let me point out this glaring logical error.

Mental force you first declare to be force 'conditioned' by the brain. You then suppose this force can exist apart from its conditions—floating free of brains like a bird in the air. Now the a.b.c of logic affirms that this force when no longer conditioned will no longer present the qualities it presented when conditioned—i.e. the force which became mental under cerebral conditions will cease to be mental when those conditions on which its mentality depends are removed, it will assume its 'unconditioned' state. Ergo the idea of emanation of mental states to form a thought atmosphere, is tantamount to the emanation of *spectral brains spectrally active*—which for those who believe in spirits and rappers may be acceptable enough, but for those who are to follow the methods of science is an 'unpresentable' idea.

Stripped of this illogical notion of a thought atmosphere away from the conditions of thought, your hypothesis is the old materialistic hypothesis clouded with the term of many meanings 'Force.'

In a word while I sympathize with the pleasure you must have felt in weaving these speculations, I cannot but regret that you should have wasted money in printing anything so crude, and am quite sure you will get no man of science to pay the slightest attention to it.

Yours faithfully
G. H. Lewes.

IV, 232:15 ROBERT LYTTON TO GHL, SINTRA, 11 FEBRUARY 1866

MS: Yale.

Cintra. 11 February 1866.

My dear Lewes

I am ashamed of having left so long unanswered your very kind letter of some months ago about my verses in the Fortnightly. The cause of my silence, however, is so bad a one, that it constitutes a very good excuse. I have for some months past been suffering from a strange diminution of sight almost amounting to total blindness of one eye, which the oculists have attributed to congestion of the nerve of the retina. It came on suddenly with the appearance of a small circular cloud about the size of a sixpence between the right eye and all objects,—black by day and blood red by night. For many months I have in consequence of this been under Doctor's

11 February 1866 363

orders to abstain altogether from either reading or writing. But I am now conscious of rapid progress towards complete recovery, and have already regained almost the full strength of the eye affected. I hasten to apologize, and account for these tardy thanks for your welcome letter.

I assure you my dear Lewes that I am exceedingly flattered by your wish for further contributions from me to the F[ortnightly]. It is impossible for me to overstate the peculiar interest which, for a host of reasons, I feel in the success of your hitherto *most* successful undertaking. To contribute however feebly towards the existence of the Fortnightly I should have worked con amore: and I may mention that when my sight was first attacked I was about the preparation of some historical sketches, in prose, as well as some reflections on the elements of Tragedy and a paper upon Mr. Hare's electoral theory, in the hope that I might be able to make them available for the F. But the Doctors still enjoin upon me abstinence from brain work of any kind for some time to come, and the little which I *can* do in that way I am constrained to confine to the completion of a new book of verse which has been dawdling at the end of my pen for more than six years, and which for many reasons I am anxious to complete if possible by next Autumn. I cannot therefore—for the present at any rate—attempt to prove my good will in the way I should wish—by Contributions.

I wish to heavens I could enjoy the privilege of more frequent intercourse with you, and if I could move just now I would make a journey on the chance of seeing you at the end of it. You will not understand, and I don't think I could explain, if I tried to do so, the strength of this wish: but there has been much in my mind of late, that shapes itself more and more into strong yearnings for reference to your opinion. I shall certainly be here till latish into the Autumn months of this year. I daresay you will be passing a holiday somewhere abroad between this and then. How I wish I could tempt you to pass it, while we are yet here, at Cintra which is one of the loveliest spots I have yet seen in Europe! If yourself and Mrs. Lewes were travelling without your little ones, and would be our guests, we could put you up at our Villa here: and anyhow as I shall during the whole of the summer be in charge of the Mission at Lisbon, I should have the means of making myself serviceable to you if you came this way.

I should take it as exceedingly kind of you if you could at any time spare ten minutes to mark and send me those corrections of the 'Apple of Life' which your absence from England prevented your making on the text of those verses. I may print the verses again; and should be grateful for the benefit of your suggestions for the improvement of them. My wife is in ecstacies with your paper on Comte,[1] which has deeply interested and delighted us both. When I was in Holland, years ago, I found there a large colony of his *religious* disciples and *taxpayers*.

Ever faithfully yours
R. Lytton.

IV, 233:11 GHL TO RICHARD HENGIST HORNE, LONDON, 12 FEBRUARY 1866

MS: University of Iowa. *Envelope:* R. H. Horne Esq. | ⟨Blue Mountain | Victoria⟩ | McGuires Cottages | Robe Street | St. Kilda | Australia. *Postmark:* LONDON NW | X | FE 15 | 66; KYNETON | AP 14 | 66; STREATHAM | AP 17 | 66 | VICTORIA; MELBOURNE | A | APX 18 | 66. *Extract published: Books at Iowa*, No. 18 (April 1973), p. 24.

The Fortnightly Review, | Office— 193, Piccadilly.
12 February 1866.

My dear Horne

You must have strangely interpreted any thing Mary Gillies could have written to have twisted it into a statement that I declined to *admit* a review of Prometheus.[2] No review was ever proposed to me. No one has ever mentioned the poem to me by word or letter except Dr. Schmitz and Mary Gillies; and when Dr. Schmitz mentioned it to me he said you were very anxious about its reception. Therefore I told him as I told Mary Gillies that I could not notice it because I did not choose to give you pain and I could not write of it so as to give you pleasure. But in order that you might not suffer from my fastidiousness, I sent the poem to a distinguished contributor whom I knew to be a very warm admirer of 'Orion',[3] and asked him to write either an article or a critical notice. He sent me word that he had tried to like it but couldn't, and excused himself from speaking of it. Since then I have thought it best to leave the poem alone and I still think so. This seems the general impression since I observe no notices of it in the journals.

You may imagine that it is not pleasant to have to say these things. But we all stumble at times; we have all our failures; and you have had your share of successes.

1. "Auguste Comte," *Fortnightly*, 3 (1 January 1866), 385–410.

2. GHL had known Horne since 1840 and, though he had lived in Australia since 1852, heard about him from Gertrude Lewes and Mary Gillies. Leonhard Schmitz saw his *Prometheus,* the *Fire-bringer* through the press in Edinburgh, 1864.

3. *Orion. An Epic Poem in Three Books*, 1843, was extravagantly praised by Elizabeth Barrett, Douglas Jerrold, Edgar Allan Poe, and other contemporary critics.

Your friends will be none the less delighted to welcome you back in England, because this poem has made no stir.[4] But you will find most of us strangely altered!

As for me I am a shadow of what I was—dyspeptic and feeble; but I rub on from day to day, resolved to wear out rather than rust out. My eldest boy, as you know is married to Gertrude Hill. My second is trading and volunteering in Natal. My last is a farmer equipping himself for colonial life. As to my wife, whom you don't know in the flesh, she is a Mediæval Saint with a grand genius. That's my budget!

Ever yours,
G. H. Lewes.

IV, 233:11 GHL TO ROBERT LYTTON, LONDON, 23 FEBRUARY 1866

MS: Lady Hermione Cobbold.

The Fortnightly Review, | Office— 193, Piccadilly.
February 23rd 1866.

My dear Lytton

You can hardly imagine how pleased I was to get that letter from you containing an account of yourself which was a great relief. I had heard from Vienna that you had entirely lost the sight of one eye and that fears were entertained for the other. The shock this was, and the deep pity it excited you cannot guess; and now your letter comes to reassure us that the calamity has been enormously exaggerated and that you have only had an alarm. When I tell you that some years ago Greek type and midnight metaphysics brought on a somewhat similar terror to me—and that for weeks I was forced to abstain altogether from reading or writing, you will understand that over and above my old personal regard for you there was a cause for sympathy in your affliction. As Mr. Winkle passionately urged the drowning Pickwick to save himself for his (Winkle's) sake[5] so I urge you to be careful for my sake—and your wife's—whom I hope some day to know—all the more because she has been interested in the account of Comte.

As a part of this request to save yourself it would be ordinary logic to beg you at once to set to work on an article for the Review. But I have a higher logic which can reconcile your interests with my own, namely—to

---

4. Horne returned from Australia in September 1869.

5. *Pickwick Papers*, ch. 30.

get some of the poems that you are about to publish in a volume, and let them have a rehearsal in our pages before appearing in the volume. What say you to this?

I should be glad if the Fates would carry me anywhere in your direction partly because I should like to see Cintra and Portugal generally—and partly because I gather from your letter that you would like to unbosom yourself on some points to a sympathetic friend. It has been my lot in life to be a large receptacle of confidences—and I like it. Probably it's because I like it that it comes to me. But at present I know not what my movements may be. We talk of Spain, of the East, of Sicily, of many places.

As to our "little ones" which you hypothetically repudiate as travelling companions, know that they are all centered in a bulldog—but such a bulldog—such a synthesis of love and ugliness, and gentleness, and spoiled-childishness!—and with him (to my sorrow) we never travel. Our eldest (boy, not bulldog!) is married and settled comfortably; the second is shooting tigers and Basutos in Natal; the third is a farmer in Warwickshire—so you see we are alone in the nest and can fly away without other hindrances than editing and novel-writing. Mrs. Lewes is hard at work on a book and will not move until it is finished. I am rewriting a great deal of the History of Philosophy for the 3rd edition, and I shan't move if my health will allow me to remain until that is finished. After that we shall take wing.

I send you the "Apple of Life" on the margin of which I have scribbled one or two impertinent cavils. I like the poem better every time I read it; and my mother (75) is constantly quoting it. So great and genuine a faculty as you have ought to find its proper element in which to work, but your external conditions seem to me to have been unfavorable hitherto. May your marriage[6] be a new birth and poetry the natural consequence.

Ever yours truly
G. H. L.

IV, 233:11 THORNTON ARNOTT LEWES TO GHL, ROUXVILLE, 24 FEBRUARY 1866

MS: Yale.

Rouxville A village on the Orange River, Free State February 24, 1866.
Dear Pater and every body else

---

6. Robert Lytton married 4 October 1864 Edith, daughter of the Hon. Edward Ernest Villiers.

24 February 1866 367

After waiting and waiting and waiting since writing the inclosed account of the battle of Plattberg for something important and decisive to tell you about, I resolved today to write what I can although the something decisive has not yet happened. Still the various items will I have no doubt swell the pages and make a good little epistle.

In the first place as I wrote to you from Natal in October last I started on the 1st Nov. for the Free State, where I have been ever since. There have been some accounts of the Basuto war in some of the English newspapers, so I daresay you have seen some of them, and made yourself au fait with the facts of this important struggle. However as my name has not been mentioned yet in any official dispatches, you will have learned nothing from the papers of my wonderful doings in the war. I presume you have a map of S. Africa before you, if not get Hall's (it is good; published, I think by E. Stamford, Charing Cross) and can follow my movements.

On the 8th Nov. I left Harrismith with 4 or 5 Volunteers and some 16 deserters from the Cape Mounted Rifles, who were stationed in Natal under the Drakensberg for Bethlehem in waggons. Two days "trek" brought us to this village, where I got from the magistrate, to whom I had a letter of Introduction, a fine horse, which I was to deliver to the owner at the great Camp or Lager. From Bethlehem, believing said Lager to be near Winburg, the 5 volunteers and myself rode on to Winburg having to keep a sharp lookout for enemies. After a hard days ride of 12 hours we got there, and upon stating our desires were provided by the landdrost or Magistrate, with a tent, 200 lbs. of meal, coffee, sugar, a slaughter ox etc. etc. On the third day, an express having arrived from the President, the Magistrate desired one of us to show the bearer the road. Having by this learned that the Camp was about 4 hours ride from Bethlehem, and that by coming to Winburg, we had been riding out of our road, I offered to take the dispatch through. The offer was accepted and escorted by three men, a German, an Irishman and an American Pole, I rode back to Sandriver. From here I got an Escort of 2 men to Retiefs Nek where a small Commando of 100 men lay. The Captain of these had to supply me with a fresh horse and at midnight with two companions I started again. Tramp, tramp, on through the dark till day-light showed us the Boer Lager.

I delivered my dispatch and joined the deserters in their tent for a day or two. After looking round, and seeing no prospect of getting a horse and gun, to serve as a Cavalry man, I joined the Artillery and was attached to the 12th Howitzer, familiarly called "The Mountain Deer" as No. 6 or powder monkey. On the 1st December I first smelt powder when we drove Molappo from his mountain, Killing some 12 or 13 Kaffirs, without any casualty on our side. On the 5th we started for Plattberg, and on the 6th had my first proper battle, as described elsewhere. Leaving the artillery on the 8th, I stayed with two young fellows Sanger and Raaff, who were in the camp with a load of goods, and whose acquaintance I had made. The Boers having been cowed by the day at Plattberg were awfully afraid of the Kaffirs and nothing was to be done, so when Sanger and Raaff went into Bloemfontein on the 22nd Dec. I accepted Raaff's offer to come and stay at his house there. There I spent Christmas day, and the 4 following days, and then on the 30th left Bloemfontein for Reddersburg in Raaff's trap. From Reddersburg I trudged on foot to Smithfield, and as I was entering that town, I met four of Webster's volunteers, with whom I at once proceeded to join their camp in Basuto Land.

On Wednesday evening Jan. 3rd I arrived there, and found the corps to consist of 40–50 English and 150 native allies, so-called Fingoes, formerly inhabitants of Natal, but driven out thence before the English took possession by the Zulus whom they much resemble. Towards the end of January after our men along with a Boer Commando had stormed a strong position on a mountain inhabited by a chief called Makwai, though without being able to take the cattle placed there, with a loss of one German shot through the head and one wounded in the arm (both belonging to the Boer camp, not to the Volunteers) the corps retired to Rouxville, whence this is dated. By the bye, I was not at Makwaisberg, not yet having gun and horse. From Rouxville, Webster went to Bloemfontein to confer with the President and returned a few days since, having obtained the necessary supplies, and permission for all English belonging to the Boer Lager, who like, to join him. We shall thus have 3–400 men in a week or so and then we shall walk into the Basutos. All the cattle, horses, etc. we capture, is to be divided amongst us, and every member of the corps receives at the end of the war a farm of 5,000 acres, on *condition of occupation for 3 years*.

Clothes have just arrived and we are all dressed in brown moleskin suits check shirts and leather caps, hence our familiar name "The Leathercaps." In a week we hope to be among the enemy or rather among his cattle, for booty is our main object; fighting is only to be done when we must.

When we make a haul I will at once drop a line, but posts are irregular and correspondents too lazy though they have not much to do I must confess. Wars and rumours of wars must stand as my excuse.

We have been staying here in Rouxville, a deserted village for nearly a month, sending out a waggon every 2nd or 3rd day for a load of peaches and wood from the neighbouring farms. I have been quartered with 5,

[April? 1866]

and then 3 others, till at last the 3 went also, and I had the house all to myself. Now there are 4 new arrivals in the house. I mess by myself and am become a great cook; if you could see my beefsteak pies and peach pies, and taste my bread, I think you would say they are not bad for a bachelor. Unfortunately we are almost eaten up by flies, and the beefsteak pies have become suspicious in my eyes since my discovering in my last, half a dozen fat ——, well, flies in the larva state!.

The page is done and the contents of my brain likewise, so till my next, Goodbye. When something important happens you shall hear; in the meanwhile don't be uneasy, the Basutos have not yet cast a bullet for me.

Love to everybody from your affectionate

Thornton Lewes.

IV, 235:1   GE TO ISA CRAIG, LONDON, [APRIL? 1866]

MS: Colby College.

The Priory, | 21. North Bank, | Regents Park.
Wednesday Evening.

My dear Miss Craig

It happens, for a wonder, that we are going out to-morrow evening, and I cannot bear to let you come in vain. So I send you this word. Perhaps you can change or rather *ex*change the evening for another.

We agree that the new cover[7] is an improvement. Certainly the first was hideous—yet Mr. Lewes heard a publisher admiring it. Have you not found that there is always some one who will pick out one's mistakes for laudation?

Always yours
M. E. Lewes.

7. Of the *Argosy*, which Isa Craig edited. See 1 November 1865.

IV, 239:1 GHL TO LORD AMBERLEY,
LONDON, [12 APRIL 1866]

MS: The Bertrand Russell Archives, McMaster University.

The Priory, | 21 North Bank, | Regents Park.
⟨Wedn⟩ Thursday.

My dear Lord

It will give me great pleasure to see you again, and Saturday next between 3 and 4 will be perfectly convenient to me.[8]

Meanwhile, believe me,

Yours obediently
G. H. Lewes.

The Right Honble Viscount Amberley

8. Lord Amberley called on GHL Saturday, 14 April 1866. In her Diary Lady Amberley reported: "It seems to have been a pleasant visit as Lewes was agreeable and talked a good deal. He is a very ugly man—pimpled face. He had a bull dog in the room. He talked to A. about work and said he had once made a rule not to work more than 4 hours a day and thought it of great importance to do all work before luncheon. He talked of Miss Evans as his wife and said she had such an appetite for reading, that she was too discursive, but she had grt. energy and believed she wd. even undertake to begin Sanscrit then. She had a bad headache which was the reason A. did not see her. He asked A. if he wd. write again for the Fortnightly but A. said not at present; (however some day he means to write a sort of continuation to his first art. in the Fortly." (*The Amberley Papers*, ed. Bertrand and Patricia Russell, 2 vols., 1937, I, 484–485.) The first article was "Liberals, Conservatives, and the Church," 2 (1 September 1865), 161–168.

Felix Holt and *The Spanish Gypsy*

1866 April 25	GE accepts £5000 for *Felix Holt*.
1866 June 7—	
August 3	GE and GHL on the Continent.
1866 June 20	Bulwer Lytton comments on *Felix Holt*.
1866 August 3	A. Trollope thanks GE for *Felix Holt*.
1866 September 4	GE writes to Melusina Peirce.
1866 November 9	GHL resigns editorship of *Fortnightly*.
1866 December 9	Bertie leaves to join Thornie in Natal.
1866 December 22	GE accepts £1000 for her 5 novels for 5 years.
1867 May 14	GE writes to Morley about Female Enfranchisement.
1867 May 29	GHL writes text for *Female Characters of Goethe*.
1867 August	*History of Philosophy*, 3d edition published.
1867 Aug.–Sept.	GE and GHL in Germany.
1867 October 4	Owen hurt by GHL's reference to him in article.
1867 November 19	Emily Davies discusses Ladies College with GE.
1868 April–Nov.	GHL's *Fortnightly* articles on Darwin lead to correspondence.
1868 March 4	GE gives £50 to College "from the author of *Romola*."
1868 March 25	*The Spanish Gypsy* published.
1868 July 31	GE's nephew Edward Clarke writes to her.
1868 October 12	Lewes boys fail to trade blankets for ivory; Thornie has serious spinal disease.
1868 November 3	GE fails to interest Benzon in the College.
1868 November 18	Darwin proposes GHL for the Linnean Society.

IV, 240:6 GHL TO JOHN BLACKWOOD, LONDON, 18 APRIL 1866

MS: National Library of Scotland.

The Priory, | 21. North Bank, | Regents Park.
18 April 1866.

My dear Blackwood

Mrs. Lewes is finishing the novel which has been so long delayed by the state of her health, and will in all probability be ready to publish it by the end of May. She wishes it to appear all at once, and the printing to be so far advanced that the last sheets may be set up as soon as written. It is therefore necessary that the question of publication should be settled forthwith, and she would not like to make any arrangement until she had heard your views on the matter, if you are disposed to make her an offer for the *entire right for 5 years*; without your seeing the m.s. which would involve too much delay.

It is a novel of English Provincial Life just after the passing of the Reform Bill in '32. I need not say that the political tone is as *dramatic* and *impartial* as her tone has been in all her writings, and that the fact of the story moving amid political scenes which form its background will only render it more interesting to *all* parties.

Let me hear from you as soon as you conveniently can and believe me

Yours very truly
G. H. Lewes.

John Blackwood Esq.

IV, 244:13 GHL TO JOHN BLACKWOOD, LONDON, [25 APRIL 1866]

MS: National Library of Scotland.

The Priory, | 21. North Bank, | Regents Park.
Wednesday.

My dear Blackwood

In enclosing the formal acceptance of your offer let me tell you what a cordial your letter was to the drooping spirits of Mrs. Lewes, who as you know never believes there is any good in her books until somebody she can rely on (I count for nothing!) tells her so. Your first letter gave her a glass of moral champagne. The letter of this morning repeats the dose. You convince her that you have entered into the spirit of her book. When the lawyer[9] whom she consulted (and who was evidently almost as much struck by her mastery of the law of Real Property as by anything else) told me he thought it would have a greater success than any of her previous books, she concluded *that* to be mere friendly politeness, though she knows he is an enthusiastic admirer. But you have (for a moment) given her confidence.

Isn't it altogether a most *original* book? so unlike novels?—Though the drama of the 3rd volume, will, unless I am a bad prophet, lay hold of even those frivolous readers who care only for story.

It is a great pity that it isn't quite ready for publication just in the thick of the reform discussion so many good quotable 'bits' would be furnished to M.P's.[10] However the subject will not grow cold. She expects to be entirely finished by the end of May; so as to appear at the beginning of June.— Would it be too late to insert a slip into Maga this month announcing it for June—*with* the title?

I am suffering from one of my bilious attacks which makes correspondence and everything else laborious—so if this is a little incoherent you know the cause.

Ever yours faithfully
G. H. Lewes.

Your telegram arrived three hours *after* your letter. The old story!

IV, 252:13 GHL TO EDWARD F. S. PIGOTT, LONDON, [APRIL? 1866?]

MS: Mr. Gordon N. Ray.

Dear Pigott

I *dare* not breakfast with you on account of my delicate stomach not permitting irregularities of any kind just now. But I will come in at 10.30 and chat to any amount.

Ever yours
G. H. L.

9. Frederic Harrison.
10. Gladstone's bill reducing the £10 voting qualification to £7 for householders in the boroughs was introduced in March 1866 and defeated in committee in June.

IV, 259:1   GHL TO JOHN DENNIS, LONDON, 10 MAY 1866

MS: Yale.

The Fortnightly Review, | Office— 193, Piccadilly.
10 May 1866.

My dear Dennis[1]

If any expression of my belief in your scrupulous conscientiousness and punctuality in discharge of all duties devolving on you can be of assistance to you as a candidate for the editorship of the periodical you speak of I shall be happy to give it. I set my face against testimonials in general, because they are commonly insincere, and are mostly written without any knowledge of the qualifications of the candidate. But I have had you assisting me in the 'Fortnightly Review' so long and with such entire satisfaction that I do not hesitate to express my belief in your doing well whatever you undertake. Let me recal the fact that when you were appointed subeditor of the Review, it was with the distinct understanding that unless I found you thoroughly efficient the engagement was to terminate at once. So satisfied have I been that I should greatly regret losing your services, though of course I would not for a moment stand in the way of your taking a more advantageous position.

Ever yours truly
G. H. Lewes.

John Dennis Esq.

IV, 267:25   THORNTON ARNOTT LEWES TO GHL, LADISMITH, 2 JUNE 1866

MS: Yale.

Ladismith | June 2. 1866.

Private Business
Dear Pater,

The beginning of your letter of the 7th puzzled me immensely till on finishing it, I discovered the enclosures of F.I.D.[2] and Cronin's letters, which disgusted me immensely.

---

1. John Dennis, sub-editor of the *Fortnightly* since March 1865. See IV, 185, n. 9. He took a place with the *Reader*, which ceased publication 26 July 1866.

2. F. I. Dickinson, money lender in Durban.

The way I got into debt of 20£, not £22 (2 pounds were Cronin's accounts) was this. I intended to start up country in the beginning of September, but owing to Cronin's joining me, to weather, dilatoriness of the waggonmaker etc. we did not start till the end of October, and as I had to stay in Durban during the time Hotel expenses were unavoidable. As to Cronin's statement that he *"incautiously* made a bill in my favour" that is all bosh, if he had not made the bill, for our combined debts, *he* would not have been able to go, any more than I, though certainly his was a smaller amount. To prevent the endorsers of the two Bills from suffering more loss than possible at the moment, I sent down my watch and chain to Cronin to sell and repay them, but I believe the watch never reached him.

Cronin's letter was written on the 2nd of September before he had seen me, before he had understood how it was that I had not been quicker in coming down owing to non receipt of his letters, and as to his statement about my running myself into debt etc. he had heard the report that I was "*spree*"ing it at Sandsprint (of course a pure fiction). Notwithstanding his letter is as you say an impertinence, both to you and to me, and I shall not forget it when I see him again. . . .

I turn to the more pleasant part of my letter. . . . The Free State war with the Basutos being now ended, by the Basutos giving up the best fourth of their country, the Govt. of the F. State has determined to protect itself from future wars by giving 3 rows of places averaging 3000 acres each along the new boundary line to men who are willing to occupy them on military tenure. . . . Now I, am one of those who have the preference in getting a farm, being as Art. 15 1 says "a white person who has done actual burgher or commando service during the present war." And this farm I must occupy. . . . If you send out Bertie to me, we will go partners, he putting in the cash with which you will fit him out, and I putting in my farm, pledging myself to stick thereto for the term of 3 years. [*A detailed list of the cost of house, waggon, stock, oxen, etc. totaling £400 and for Bertie's guns and clothes.*]

Since my last letter with the description of the battle of Plattberg I only made one patrol, and though 23 of the enemy were killed, there was no fighting. . . . Peace was concluded about the middle of April, the 15th I think, and we went back to Bloemfontein. I returned slowly to Natal, sometimes on foot, sometimes on horseback, and astonished the natives who had heard that I was killed. . . . During my journey I went in for a month's schoolmastering at a Boer's on the road. My intention was not to go down to Natal till I had got the title deeds of my farm, but afterwards I thought it would be better to go down and get my letters, to hear what your ideas were, in the meantime. However as to schoolmastering, I tried it for a week . . . but the hopeless stupidity of Boer children . . . was such that I was not sorry, when the Boer's daughter, a girl of about 16, gave me "cheek," to make that an excuse and "hook it." ... If Bertie is to come out, you had better despatch him at once. ...

This is I think all I have to say, so with love to every one I remain, Dear Pater

Your affectionate Son
Thornton Lewes.

IV, 267:25 ROBERT LYTTON TO GHL, LISBON, 3 JUNE 1866

MS: Yale.

B[ritish] Legation, Lisbon 3 June 1866.

My dear Lewes

I wished, and was about, to write to you ages ago: but a pressure of official business on the departure of my chief,[3] obliged me to postpone doing so; and meanwhile, all those little things which frustrate the fulfilment of great ones, having been daily thrusting themselves between my heart and my pen, and postponing the pleasure of recording my great and warm thanks for your most kind letter.

All your valuable ⟨corrections⟩ suggestions for the improvement of the verses I have ⟨availed myself⟩ gratefully adopted, and I hope with good result. I wish that my new book of verse, contributions from which you invite for the Fortnightly, could furnish any thing suitable. But there are very few of its contents that are at all fitted for separate publication, and those few I had already sent to Dickens for All the Year Round before the receipt of your letter.

I have indeed a thousand motives for strongly wishing to see you, and wishing to see very much more of you, than I have any chance of doing: but I don't know that I have any special counsel to ask, or confidence to make: none, at least, which even your good will could, I think, encourage me to find the means of making, if I should have the pleasure of meeting you during the visit which I hope to be able to make to England this winter, but which, I already foresee must be hurried and desultory. My desire is rather that "of the moth for the star":[4] or to put it less poetically, of a young frog to get to the water in spring. An instinctive wishing that I could sometimes sun myself in your fullness of knowledge and freedom from

---

3. William Philip Molyneux, 4th Earl of Sefton (1835–97), headed a special mission to Portugal 17 April 1865–9 June 1866.

4. Shelley, "One Word Is Too Often Profaned," stanza 2.

prejudice, and test the temper of certain instincts in myself by the edge of your keen conclusive intellect. By the way do you really find aesthetic truth and beauty in the realism of those 'London Idyls' of Mr. Buchanan,[5] which you have been publishing in the Fortnightly? They are very antagonistic to all my instincts about art.

I shall be at Cintra all the summer, and wish, indeed, there might be any chance of something bringing you this way: and the bulldog too: if he would not eat up one of my best friends here—a very accomplisht Raven, who has a taste for books—verse especially—and literally devoured the whole Inferno of Dante the other day.

I rejoice to see that "George Eliot's" new book is already advertised. I think Romola among the masterpieces of fiction, and, with all due reverence for Adam Bede and the incomparable Mrs Poinsett [sic] that work appears to me to be the author's highest and broadest. Ever, my dear Lewes,

Very faithfully yours
R. Lytton.

IV, 276:17 SIR EDWARD LYTTON TO JOHN BLACKWOOD, LONDON, 20 JUNE 1866

MS: National Library of Scotland.

H of P June 20 1866.

My dear Sir

You found me reading Felix Holt in a critical moment of Political Party, and I did not stop till I had finished it. This is the best testimony to the highest merit of the Novel qua a Novel, viz. Interest.

Besides that merit, the Book has the higher order of "saleable value"— the interest is of intellectual quality. Beyond the question of interest, it has the excellence of good writing: Composition, parts of which are of very high rank—bits of poetic description and bits of quiet irony, are first-rate specimens of diction.

On the other hand, the work has to my mind faults;—faults of Construction, which confuse faults of Character and faults in the conception of Human Nature.—But it is idle to dwell on these, 1st because they are not likely to affect the run of the Book with the Public, 2ndly because my

---

5. Robert Buchanan, "A London Poem," *Fortnightly*, 4 (15 February 1866), 65–69, e.g., "You're a kind woman, Nan! ay kind and true! | God will be good to faithful folk like you!"

estimate of the persons who review books and are called Critics is so low that I doubt if any one of them can discover the faults which would be obvious to a man who had studied art or knew the ABC of Criticism.—Therefore you and the author may rest quite satisfied.

Yours most truly
E. B. L.

IV, 281:25 GHL TO JOHN BLACKWOOD, SCHWALBACH, 30 JUNE 1866

MS: Berg Collection, New York Public Library.

Schwalbach 30th June 1866.

My dear Blackwood

I have asked Mrs. Lewes to let me answer your pleasant letter[6] because I wished to give you a 'bit' I overheard as we crossed to Calais. Seated beside me on the deck was a nice elderly lady (English) before whom stood a superb crinoline (also British) imparting her views on things in general and at last sliding into literature. The following is verbatim:

Crinoline: Have you read 'Armadale' yet?

E. L. Not yet.

C. It's very clever! Such well drawn characters! I like Wilkie Collins.

E. L. I see we are to have a book by Adam Bede soon.

Crinoline, impressively, Yes, but I'm sorry she's gone into *that*!

E. L. gently, What, the radical?

C. Yes, I don't think politics good in novels.

E. L. Nor I. But she has such a beautiful mind I feel quite confident of her whatever she may take up.

Crinoline apparently not sharing this sentiment or by a specific levity of mind wafted to other subjects, I lost my interest in the conversation.

It was with great difficulty I got sight of the Times review,[7] for although the paper is taken in at the hotel, the particular half sheet had been taken away. However I went to a salon de lecture and read it ⟨feeling⟩ and am entirely of your way of thinking respecting it—a poor performance but a good puff. The stupid allusion to the trial scene he ought to have been warned off by the very fact that the similarity, if similarity there be, exists

---

6. 8 June 1866.

7. *The Times*, 26 June 1866, p. 6, by E. S. Dallas, filled three full columns, beginning: "Hitherto Miss Austen has had the honour of the first place among our lady novelists, but a greater than she has now arisen."

between F. H. and Reade's *last* novel[8]—now it would be too impudent for an author to borrow an incident from a work so very recent. As you surmised she had never seen the work she is supposed to have taken her suggestion from. Reading the *Times* once more convinced me of the wisdom of her practice *not* to read criticisms favorable or unfavorable. This she has—with very rare exceptions—steadily adhered to since Adam Bede. I read them, when they fall in my way and tell her about them; and that is enough. The best testimony is the sale. If there is a large body of readers there is certain to be among them readers to whom the book speaks, and the influence of what she writes is secured.

The weather here continues magnificent—hot, but not too hot, with an occasional shower to relieve the air and brighten the green. Our daily explorations of the country round about only increase our delight in the place, and if climate, idleness, good living, and the waters can help us to flesh we shall come back obese. We leave this on the 5 or 6th for Schlangenbad, where it is possible that we may stay ten days or a fortnight and then take a flying look at the gaieties of Wiesbaden. I dare say you will not have occasion to write again just at present, but a letter addressed to Bonn by the 21st or Aix la Chapelle by the 23rd (I mean reaching those towns on those dates) would perhaps convey some agreeable intelligence and certainly be very welcome because it is in your hand.

Mrs. Lewes in giving me the post of secretary on this occasion begs me to thank you particularly for the interesting details of your letter. She values Bulwer's expression of opinion all the more as she happens to know that he is sincere in his expression about other writers.

I know Oliphant and once hoped to have him as a colleague in the Fortnightly. Morley also I know slightly and like what I have seen of him.

Our routine here is this: we rise at 6 or a little before and after tub and apology for toilet step out on to the promenade (at the foot of the hotel) drink the sparkling and delightful water, listen to the band, and walk about till 8. Breakfast, book and cigar, occupies till $9\frac{1}{2}$. Then we go out into one of the several woods or to some point de vue—sometimes taking a book with us—but oftener not—and walk, and sit, and muse and talk while "Idlesse in her dreaming mood"[9] lets the hours roll noiselessly by till 1. Then another glass of water and siesta till dinner. We always dine alone in our apartment having a strong disinclination for table d'hôtes and the people met thereat. After dinner at 3, coffee, cigar, and a nap prepares me

---

8. Charles Reade, *Griffith Gaunt, or Jealousy*, 3 vols., 1866.

9. James Thomson, *The Castle of Indolence*, i, v.

for the promenade (and more music and more water) at 6–8. Here we observe the swells and crinolines—not a word have we spoken to one of them as yet, a charming deprivation we owe to dining alone. When the music ceases we ramble in the evening sunlight till tea and bed beckon us home. 'Thus runs the round of life from hour to hour.'[1]

Ever yours faithfully
G. H. L.

IV, 294:8 ANTHONY TROLLOPE TO GE, WALTHAM CROSS, 3 AUGUST 1866

MS: Princeton. *Published: The Letters of Anthony Trollope*, ed. B. A. Booth, 1951, p. 186.

Waltham House, | Waltham Cross.
August 3 1866.

My dear Mrs Lewes.

I must welcome you home with a word of thanks for Felix Holt which I received from Mr. Blackwood as a present from you.

I hope you are gratified by the reception which it has obtained. I know how disdainful you are of ordinary eulogium,—being perhaps led on to be somewhat more so than your own nature would make you by the severity of G.H.L. But in spite of him and his severity, and of your own disdain whether natural or acquired, the unrivalled success of Felix Holt must have touched you. For, as far as I can make an estimate of such things, I think its success is unrivalled.

For myself I think it has more elaborated thought in it, and that it is in that way a greater work, than anything you have done before. With the character of Mr. Lyon I am perfectly satisfied, loving all his words dearly. Felix is very great as the result of an admirably conceived plan of a character. With Esther I feel sometimes inclined to quarrel because she seems to doubt, after she knows that she loves the man. Mrs. Transome is excellent and great. Mrs. Holt is very good,—though not equal to Mrs. Poyser as being perhaps less like what I have seen with these eyes of the flesh and heard with these ears. As to story Adam Bede is still my favorite. For picturesque word painting Romola stands first. To me the great glory of Felix Holt is the fulness of thought which has been bestowed on it.

My kindest regards to the Master. If he wants any of the new batch of

---

1. Tennyson, "Circumstances," line 9.

8000 cigars which I have just got over from Cuba let him tell me at once how many. I called on Thursday and heard from cook some feeble excuse about the weather. The summer winds had detained you!!!

Yours always most heartily
Anthony Trollope.

IV. 299:5 GHL TO RICHARD HENGIST HORNE, LONDON, 10 AUGUST 1866

MS: University of Iowa.

The Fortnightly Review, | Office— 193, Piccadilly.
10 August 1866.

My dear Horne

I was glad to get your letter with its assurance that you no longer held me guilty of the lèse friendship, Dr. Schmitz had carelessly led you to credit. We have but just returned from our two months tour through Belgium Holland and the Rhine provinces, and have come back all the better. Mrs. Lewes not only needed a change of air and occupation but also wished to avoid the deluge of criticism and talk consequent on her new novel so as soon as the last proof was corrected we packed up. She has the wise practice of never reading what is written about her, but she cannot prevent people talking about their own impressions and about the 'press'; so we always get out of the way when a new book appears.

Our journey was pleasant enough in spite of the war; but the weather was British in its badness. Now I return to a vast array of arrears—a hideous pile of m.s.s and proofs!—editorial indigestion, which makes me think, as I have repeatedly thought of late, that I *must* give up the Review. I only keep on at the entreaty of the proprietors, but I grudge the sacrifice of time and yearn for my freedom again.

Charles has given me his portrait to send you. I wish I had one of myself to send—but you will see in this the traces of your old friend. Gertrude's letter enclosed.[2]

Ever yours faithfully,
G. H. Lewes.

2. Mrs. Charles Lee Lewes's long letter to Horne 27 July 1866, written from Laverock Bank House, near Edinburgh, where she had taken Mary Gillies for her health. (University of Iowa.) Horne had lived with the Gillies sisters, who brought Gertrude up from childhood. See IV, 156.

IV, 310:10 GE TO MRS. CHARLES S. PEIRCE, LONDON, 14 SEPTEMBER 1866

MS: Yale.

The Priory, | 21. North Bank, | Regents Park.
September 14. 66.

My dear Madam
　I do not usually answer letters unless they demand an answer, finding the days too short for much correspondence; but I am so deeply touched by your words of tenderness and by the details you tell me about yourself, that I cannot keep total silence towards you.[3]
　My consciousness is not of the triumphant kind your generous joy on my behalf leads you to imagine. Exultation is a dream before achievement, and rarely comes after. What comes after, is rather the sense that the work has been produced within one, like offspring, developing and growing by some force of which one's own life has only served as a vehicle, and that what is left of oneself is only a poor husk. Besides, the vision of something that life might be and that one's own ignorance and incompleteness have hindered it from being, presses more and more as time advances. The only problem for us, the only hope, is to try and unite the utmost activity with the utmost resignation. Does this seem melancholy? I think it is less melancholy than any sort of self-flattery.
　I want to tell you not to fancy yourself old because you are thirty, or to regret that you have not yet written anything. It is a misfortune to many that they begin to write when they are young and give out all that is genuine and peculiar in them when it can be no better than trashy, unripe fruit. There is nothing more dreary than the life of a writer who has early exhausted himself.
　I enter into those young struggles of yours to get knowledge, into the longing you feel to do something more than domestic duties while yet you are held fast by womanly necessities for neatness and household perfection as well as by the lack of bodily strength. Something of all that I have gone through myself. I have never known perfect health, and I have known what it was to have close ties making me feel the wants of others as my own and to have very little money by which these wants could be met. Before that,

---

3. Harriet Melusina Fay Peirce (1836–1923) wrote many articles in the *Atlantic Monthly* and a book on *Co-operative Housekeeping*, 1884. See *Lamb's Biographical Dictionary of the United States*, vi, 200. Her letter to GE has not been found.

I was too proud and ambitious to write: I did not believe that I could do anything fine, and I did not choose to do anything of that mediocre sort which I despised when it was done by others. I began, however, by a sort of writing which had no great glory belonging to it, but which I felt certain I could do faithfully and well. This resolve to work at what did not gratify my ambition, and to care only that I worked faithfully, was equivalent to the old phrase—"using the means of grace."[4] Not long after that, I wrote fiction which has been thought a great deal of—but the satisfaction I have got out of it has not been exactly that of ambition. When we are young we say, "I should be proud if I could do that." Having done it, one finds oneself the reverse of proud.

I will say no more about myself except that you must not imagine my position to be at all like Romola's. I have the best of husbands, the most sympathetic of companions; indeed, I have more than my share of love in a world where so many are pining for it. Mr. Lewes, who cares supremely for science, is interested in what you say of your husband's labours;[5] and he is so delighted when anything good or pretty comes to me that I think he is more grateful to you than I am for your generous, affectionate words. Yet I too am not insensible, but shall remain always

Yours in grateful memory
M. E. Lewes.

IV, 312:8 GHL TO FREDERIC CHAPMAN, LONDON, 27 SEPTEMBER [1866]

MS: The Johns Hopkins University. *Endorsed:* "Mr. Dryden of Flairs—"

The Priory, | 21. North Bank, | Regents Park.
Wednesday 27 September.

My dear Chapman

Mrs. Macquoid,[6] the bearer of this, is the author of *Hester Kirton* and one or two other novels which have had fair success. She has just finished

---

4. *The Book of Common Prayer* (General Thanksgiving, Morning Prayer) uses the phrase to refer to the sacraments. John Wesley broadened the definition to include outward signs, words, or actions by which God conveyed grace to men. (*Works*, 1872, v, 187.) GE's use is characteristically secular.

5. Charles Sanders Peirce (1839–1914), scientist, philosopher, founder of pragmatism, was on the staff of the United States Coast Survey, making researches on the theory of gravity. He lectured at Harvard on the philosophy of science, 1864–65, and on philosophy, 1869–70. He married Melusina Fay in 1862 and divorced her in 1883.

6. Katharine Sarah (Mrs. Thomas R.) Macquoid published *Hester Kirton* and *By the Sea*, both in 1864. The novel

[November 1866] 385

another, and asks my advice about a publisher. Am I wrong in telling her that the house in Piccadilly, not far from 193, is the one she ought to go to?

Yours ever
G. H. Lewes.

IV, 313:1 GE TO [?], LONDON, 23 OCTOBER 1866

MS: Yale.

The Priory, | 21. North Bank, | Regents Park.
October 23. 66.

Dear Madam

I thank you sincerely for your kindness in sending me a review which you believed would give me pleasure. I never read reviews of my books, but Mr. Lewes reads them for me, and he has told me of the superior intelligence shown by my German critic.

I remain, my dear Madam,

Yours gratefully
M. E. Lewes.

IV, 314:6 GE TO FREDERICK LEHMANN, LONDON, [NOVEMBER 1866]

Text: R. C. Lehmann, *Memories of Half a Century*, 1908, p. 133.

The Priory, | North Bank, | Regents Park.

Dear Mr. Lehmann,

Friday the 16th will suit us perfectly.

I will forgive you for disappointing me as to Wednesday, since I got the compensation of knowing that there still exist personages so romantic as Wandering Minstrels.[7]

referred to here was issued by Sampson, Low as *Elinor Dryden's Probation*, 3 vols., 1867.

7. Frederick Lehmann wrote: "In the winter of 1866 my wife and family were at Pau, while I was alone in London. George Eliot was a very fair pianist, not gifted, but enthusiastic, and extremely painstaking. During a great part of that winter I used to go to her every Monday evening at her house in North Bank, Regent's Park, always taking my violin with me. We played together every piano and violin sonata of Mozart and Beethoven.... Our audience consisted of George Lewes only, and he used to groan with delight whenever we were rather successful in playing some beautiful passage." (*Memories of Half a Century*, p. 132.)

George continues so far better as to be able to write a sheaf of philosophy[8] every morning, and we feel that it will be very agreeable to listen to your violin in the evening.

Very truly yours,
M. E. Lewes.

IV, 314:6 GHL TO JOHN STUART BLACKIE, LONDON, 5 NOVEMBER 1866

MS: National Library of Scotland.

The Fortnightly Review, | Office— 193, Piccadilly.
5 November 1866.

My dear Sir

Thank you very much for the 'Homer'[9] which I cut open eagerly, dipping as I cut, and which I intend *feasting* on as soon as my health and leisure permit—alas! that will be some time hence, for I am going South as soon as my new edition is out to recruit my feeble body. I am forced to relinquish the Review and indeed find it difficult to get through with my new edition. So you see I am not yet *up* to such a book as yours, from which I expect great things.

Yours very truly
G. H. Lewes.

Prof. Blackie

IV, 314:6 GHL TO LORD AMBERLEY, LONDON, [6 NOVEMBER 1866][1]

MS: The Bertrand Russell Archives, McMaster University.

The Priory, | 21. North Bank, | Regents Park.
Tuesday.

My dear Lord

I am truly pleased that the last number of the Review which will appear under my rule should be strengthened by so admirable and well timed a

---

8. *The History of Philosophy from Thales to Comte,* 2 vols., 1867, the 3d edition of GHL's *Biographical History of Philosophy.*

9. His *Homer and the Iliad,* 4 vols., Edinburgh, 1866, a translation into English verse with commentary and notes.

1. Lady Amberley notes this letter in her Diary, 7 November 1866. (*The Amberley Papers,* 2 vols., 1937, I, 529.)

paper as that you have sent, a proof of which will reach you shortly. My health forbids me to continue as editor, but the Review being a child of my own, I am of course interested in its success and hope to see it flourish after my reign.

Believe me, my dear Lord,

Yours very truly
G. H. Lewes.

Rt. Honble Viscount Amberley.

IV, 314:6 ANTHONY TROLLOPE TO GHL, LONDON, 9 NOVEMBER 1866

MS: Yale. *Published: The Letters of Anthony Trollope,* ed. B. A. Booth, 1951, pp. 189–191.

Athenæum Club, | Pall Mall S.W.
November 9. 1866.

My dear Lewes.

I wrote to you last night an official letter at the request of the Committee;[2] but I cannot let you part from us without saying with more of personal feeling than I could put into that letter how sorry I am that it should be so. I hate the breaking of pleasant relations, and am distrustful as to new relations. I have felt however for some time that it must be so; and that you would not hang on to us much longer. I have felt also that your time was too valuable to be frittered away in reading MSS, and in writing civil,—or even uncivil—notes.

Only two propositions as to the editing are before us. 1st to ask Mr. John Morley[3] to undertake it. 2d that I should do it for 6 months, without Salary, keeping Mr. Dennis with perhaps a somewhat encreased Salary. No doubt a permanent arrangement will be best, and the second plan has little in it of advantage either for me or for the Review. But it is supported by the desire which many of us have to keep the employment for Mr. Dennis as long as it can be kept; and also by a feeling that we hardly know enough of Mr. Morley. This latter may be overcome by better information; and I shall be very glad if you will tell me your opinion. Do you think that Mr. Morley is competent for the work? And do you believe that his opinions as

2. Trollope, Frederic Chapman, Henry Danby Seymour, and other supporters of the *Fortnightly*. See *The Wellesley Index to Victorian Periodicals*, ed. W. E. Houghton, II (1972), pp. 173–177.

Trollope's letter of 8 November 1866 accepting GHL's resignation as editor of the *Fortnightly* has not been found.

3. John Morley (1838–1923) edited the *Fortnightly* 1867–82.

to politics and literature are of a nature to support those views which we have endeavoured to maintain? If I found that the Review had drifted into the hands of a literary hack who simply followed out his task without any honesty of purpose, I should wash my hands of it.

When you want a new pair of boots it is pretty nearly enough for you to know that you are going to a good bootmaker. But this going to an Editor is a very different thing. A man may be a most accomplished Editor,—able at all periodical-editing work,—and yet to you or to me so antipathetic as to make it impossible that the two should work together. You will understand what I mean when I say that should I find I don't like the nose on our new Editors face, I must simply drop the Review; and that therefore I cannot but be very anxious. Let me know what you think about Morley.

Give my kindest regards to your wife.

Yours always
Anthony Trollope.

Address Waltham Cross. I am to see Mr. Morley on Tuesday.

IV, 314:6 GHL TO MONCURE DANIEL CONWAY, LONDON [17 NOVEMBER 1866]

MS: Yale.

The Fortnightly Review, | Office—193, Piccadilly.

Saturday.

My dear Sir

I am very glad indeed to hear that in the exercise of my editorial powers I could fall in with your views.[4] Respecting my successor he is not yet appointed; but I have no doubt that you will receive the same hospitality from him as from

Yours truly
G. H. Lewes.

M. D. Conway Esq.

4. Conway's "Russia and America," *Fortnightly*, 6 (November 1866), 659–665. Thomas Carlyle wrote to his brother John, 6 January 1867, that the *Fortnightly* "has become a *Monthly,* under the old title [beginning in November 1866], and Lewes is quite out of it;—poor Lewes, I hear, is dangerously ill of liver, face of him quite shrunk away etc., a dreary bit of news in its sort." (NLS.)

[1 December 1866]

IV, 314:6 GHL TO LORD AMBERLEY, LONDON, [18? NOVEMBER 1866]

MS: The Bertrand Russell Archives, McMaster University.

The Fortnightly Review, | Office— 193, Piccadilly.
Sunday.

My dear Lord

Your article[5] seems to me even better on a second than on a first reading; but I observe with dismay that it is twice as long as our usual limit, and as I think the effect would be greatly diminished by dividing the paper into two, I have gone over it with a view of reducing it in one or two less important passages. These I have marked with a pencil on the accompanying proof. If you agree with me that they can be omitted without injury, I will disregard the length to which the paper will even then extend and publish it all at once. But as we have only 128 pages in each number obviously 41 cannot be given to a single article without sacrificing variety in the review. I should wish you to be guided in this matter solely by your own preference either for one article (abridged) or for two. Believe me, my dear Lord,

Your lordship's faithful servant
G. H. Lewes.

Lord Amberley M.P.[6]

IV, 315:22 GHL TO RICHARD BENTLEY, LONDON, [1 DECEMBER 1866]

MS: University of Illinois.

The Priory, | 21. North Bank, | Regents Park.
Saturday.

My dear Sir

As you are kind enough to send me a copy of Mommsen[7] may I beg you to let it be addressed as above, and not to the Review Office, my editorship

---

5. "The Church of England as a Religious Body" appeared in the *Fortnightly Review* in two parts, 6 (December 1866), 769–789, and 7 (February 1867), 197–216.

6. Amberley was M.P. for Nottingham 1866–68.

7. Theodor Mommsen, *The History of Rome*, tr. by W. P. Dickson with a preface by Leonhard Schmitz, Bentley, 1862–75.

having ceased—or rather ceasing with this number which is already out of my hands.

               Yours truly
               G. H. Lewes.

R. Bentley Esq.

IV, 317:1 THORNTON ARNOTT LEWES TO GHL, DURBAN, 9 DECEMBER 1866

MS: Yale.

              Durban | December 9. 1866.

Dear Pater,

 At last, as the day for the departure of the mail steamer arrives, I resume the long-still-standing pen, to describe to you what has been done by your two young Africanders, since the arrival of the youngest of this latter.

 Oh! Pater, wherefore didst thou not pay more attention to the day of the departure of mail steamers. All *three* of your letters, one of the 13th August, one of a later date and one of the 7th September, arrived by the same mail steamer that brought Bertie. Hence, not expecting that well grown youth, I was deep in the mysteries of coffee planting at Verulam, 23 miles hence, with my friends the Remnants. On the Friday after the arrival of the mail, which was on a Tuesday, Remnant looking over the list of passengers noticed among others: Mr. H. Lewes. He immediately asked me what my brother's initial was, and when I said H.; he said: Then he has arrived. Next day, I footed it down to Durban and found Bertie installed at the Sanderson's, so it was all right. On the following Wednesday we went in the Omnibus to P. Maritzburg, where we bought horses, and on Sunday the 4th November, we started for the Transvaal Republic.

 I must tell you that the Free State Govt. has broken its promises, and *done* all the Volunteers out of the farms, to which according to Law, they were entitled. This alone would have been enough to make me discontented with the Free State, and as several people recommended the Wakkerstroom district of the Transvaal, as being very like Basutoland in climate, distance from Natal etc. we resolved to go up and see for ourselves.

 Just a week after we left Maritzburg, we arrived at the town of Wakkerstroom, or to use its longer name Marthinus Wesselstroom, the capital of the district, intending to start from there, and ride all over the country, till we came to a farm, which would suit us in every respect. It so happened that the magistrate from Mooi River Dorp, the capital of the Transvaal, a Dr. Otto, was down at Wakkerstroom on business, and hearing that we wanted a farm, he said he thought he could suit us, as he had several he wanted to sell. Next day accordingly we rode out to see one of the farms, the one which we thought would most likely be the best, and we had no sooner ridden over it than we closed the bargain! The price was £100 *cash*, and herewith follows a description of the farm.

It is between 3–4,000 acres in size, on the eastern slope of the Drakensberg, about 30 miles from Natal, 50 from the Free State, 25 from Zululand and 60 from the country of the powerful tribe of Amaswazi Kaffirs. Horsesickness, the scourge of Natal is unknown, it is splendid sheep veldt, good for cattle and for agriculture: of Water, there is abundance, both springs and sprints or streams; there is firewood and *timber, coal*, game, in the shape of small bucks, paamos, or wild turkeys, partridges, quail etc, and last but not least a magnificent waterfall, about 200 feet high, falling into a magnificent ravine with a forest on one side, and several magnificent caves, which shall be more fully described when we are better acquainted with them. We are within two hours rides of the Vaal River flats, which are covered with game. Elands and Buffalos are to be had not very far off, and the scenery around is very fine. Now what do you think of that?

The reason we got the farm so cheap was because we had the cash, which is uncommonly scarse. The other half of the farm, Dr. Otto sold two years ago for £200 in goods, and he has not yet been paid, so that he willingly took half the price for our half, cash. The whole farm you must understand, was about 8,000 acres, and we have one half of it.

After making this investment we at once returned to Maritzburg, where we arrived after an absence of 3 weeks, in which time we had ridden 450 miles. We have just completed our purchases down here, in the shape of waggon, oxen, provisions, plough, tools etc etc, and start for the farm about Thursday the 13th. Sheep we get in the Free State, as they are there about half the price they are here, and we cannot get them or the cows till the other £140 comes out. You said: "Bertie will give you £50, which is a present from your Grandmamma," but Bertie knew nothing about it; he said, that Grandmamma would send out £50 to me at Christmas; so I suppose you forgot to give it him.

However, although not having the sheep and cows at once is in some respect a drawback, as we shall be without milk, butter and cheese for a couple of months, in some respects it is an advantage, as we can go heart and soul into ploughing and building with[out] any stock to bother us in the meanwhile. We take pitsaws up with us so we shall saw all our own timber and drive a good trade in it besides. The Free State is a good market for our wheat, as we get always from £2–3 per 196 lbs for it there, and it is close by. In Maritzburg wheat is much cheaper, and having to take it all that distance (200 miles) would not pay.

The next you hear from us, will be dated "The Farm," what name we shall give it we do not yet know. If the Zulu name for our waterfall is pretty, we shall call the farm after it—if not we must think out a name.[8] Progress will be duly reported, as to how I am knee deep in mud, making bricks by the thousand, while Bertie is ploughing acres, and I hope a couple of years will see us prosperous men, the farm daily increasing in value and beauty. Henceforth address our letters

T. Lewes, Newcastle Natal

Newcastle is only about 30 miles from us and postal communications across the border are unsatisfactory. We shall send a Kafir to Newcastle on the arrival of every mail. So till next mail, goodbye. Love to every body; the family letter will now come regularly since the former smouse, warrior of the Free State, and general vagabond has settled down into that important member of the Transvaal population, who is vulgarly known as

Your affectionate Son
Thornton A. Lewes.

Bertie having gone out for a walk, endorses my sentiments and sends lots of love. He seems tolerably pleased with South Africa, and very much so with the farm. He is rather *raw* yet, but thanks to his country life, not much so, so he already begins to pass for an old Colonist.

Your Thornton.

When we are settled, a photographic friend from Newcastle will pay us a visit, and then we will send views of the farm, the fall, and our noble selves.

IV, 324:1   GE TO JOHN BLACKWOOD,
LONDON, 22 DECEMBER 1866

MS: National Library of Scotland. *Published: TLS,* 10 March 1972, p. 282.

The Priory, | 21. North Bank, | Regents Park.
December 22. 1866.

My dear Sir

I was glad to have your letter this morning, for I was thinking of writing to tell you that we had determined on setting out for the South of France next Thursday. Mr. Lewes's increasing debility, causing him more

8. They named the farm "The Fall of the Assagai."

and more frequent interruptions to the possibility of writing, has made me urge him to leave his work unfinished and let it await his return. This, I feel sure is the only wise course.

I am much obliged to you for sending me the estimate of expenses as a basis of judgment.⁹

I accept your offer of one thousand pounds (£1000) for my interest in Adam Bede, the Mill on the Floss, Felix Holt, Silas Marner, and the Scenes of Clerical Life, during ten years, with a conditional five hundred pounds (£500), over and above the one thousand, at the end of five years, in case of success according to your estimate.

I propose that, if convenient to you, the £1000 should be paid in two instalments together with the two remaining instalments of the sum agreed upon for the five years' interest in Felix Holt.

The estimate for Romola, as you observe, will be best made when the time for its publication has arrived. If a change in our relations with America should open any new prospects, I feel confidence that you would take these into consideration on my behalf as well as your own. As to Brother Jacob and the Lifted Veil, I abide by your opinion.

That two shilling series of Chapman and Hall is among those that make me shudder by the vitiating ugliness of the outside. Even if the profit were considerable, I should feel it a purgatory to see my books published in such a form. A bright colour is certainly desirable, and I should be glad if a cover for the sixpenny series could be chosen with as much taste as the cover of the two-volumed Felix.

Macmillan, talking with Mr. Lewes the other day, said, "If I were to see Blackwood, I would advise him to publish each tale of the Scenes of Clerical Life separately as a shilling volume." Apparently he is one of the special admirers of the "Scenes."

We have had three days of unbroken fog.

Always yours sincerely
M. E. Lewes.

John Blackwood Esq.

9. See IV, 321–323.

IV, 329:9 GHL TO ANTONIN ROCHE,[10]
[LONDON, 1867]

MS: Mr. Gordon N. Ray.

The Priory, | 21, North Bank, | Regents Park.
My dear M. Roche
 On the other page I have indicated extracts which you can choose from. It has not been an easy task to find them for I had but a hazy idea of their purpose.
 Respecting Moxon nothing can be done except writing to Tennyson and asking *his* permission.[11] Browning's I fancy you could get from Chapman & Hall who publish all his poems.
 Kind regards to Mad. Roche.

Ever yours truly
G. H. Lewes.

 Life of Goethe 2d edition
p. 106 "Gottfried von Berlichingen surnamed of the Iron Hand."
 to p. 111 close of the page "can remember."
p. 380 (Goethe and Schiller) "There are few nobler"
 to p. 383 "Kant and the Grecian Sages"—

 G. Eliot. *Mill on the Floss*
Vol. I p. 215 (chap. XII) "In order to see" to p. 222 end of first paragraph "insolvent."
 Romola
From the Epilogue vol. III p. 288 "The other two figures"—to the close of p. 292.
 Felix Holt. Description of England in the opening chapter of vol. I.
 I'm sorry to say I can't lend the books; but you will find them at Mudie's or the London Library.

---

10. Antonin Roche (b. 1813), founder and Director of the Educational Institute of London, where he taught aristocratic young people literature, astronomy, geography, and history, and did much to make French literature known in England. His *English Prose and Poetry, Select Pieces from the Best Authors, for Reading, Composition, and Translation,* 1867, uses the description of St. Ogg's, p. 231; the Legend of St. Ogg's, p. 232; Romola, p. 233; Goethe and Schiller, p. 236.

11. Since 1832 Edward Moxon & Co. had published Tennyson's poems.

IV, 338:1 GHL TO GEORGE SMITH,
BIARRITZ, 26 JANUARY 1867

MS: National Library of Scotland.

Biarritz, in a storm, 26 January 1867.

My dear Smith

You must not suppose that I mean to inflict on you, busy man that you are, the bore of a reply, but I know you will be glad to hear how we are going on, so I seize the occasion of the enclosed memorandum for Sharpe[1] to tell you of our doings. First as to health. After a week of this delicious solitude we were both in the most promising condition; so much so as to project a splendid extension of our Spanish journey without fear of its results. But at the end of a week of summer weather came the snow and frost—a trifle compared with what you have had, but sufficiently severe and continuous to undo a great deal of what the fine weather had done for us. However the warmth and sunshine has returned (though last night and this morning a terrific storm has varied the soft summery weather) and our hopes have risen again.

We only stayed three days in Paris and were glad to quit its excitements, a dinner party and a breakfast at which we met Renan and other distinguished 'parties' added to the Parisian strain.—Renan by the way is not the least of an apostle—but very amiable, and has an indescribable air of a Belgian priest crossed with a dissenting minister. The person we most admired in Paris was the duchesse de Colonna,[2] who is, we hear, a very remarkable sculptor and is assuredly a charming and distinky woman.— We went once to the Théâtre Lyrique but it was to see *Rigoletto*. I was afraid of anything but music.

We stayed a night at Orleans and three days at Bordeaux. Then to Bayonne which was a charming change and for the first time gave us a sense of being in a land of poetry and a climate which made existence pleasurable. Biarritz, where we have been the rest of the time with the exception of two days at Pau, surpasses all expectation. Indeed until the Brownings spoke of it to us we had no conception of its being so beautiful a place. The coast is wild, broad, and grand, with rocks and huge boulders torn away and flung about by the stormy sea which is here grander than I ever saw it before—the waves have such a sweep and the surf is so heavy. To the south runs the varied line of the Pyrenees which lift their snowy peaks into the clearest of skies, and show their bulk purple in the most glorious of sunsets. Had it not

1. See II, 43, n. 2.   2. See IV, 328, n. 9.

been for the sudden change in temperature I should doubtless have been quite restored by this time.

We start tomorrow for Spain. Our first resting place will be St. Sebastian; thence to Saragossa, Lerida, and Barcelona—and there we shall decide whether or not we are to execute our tempting project.

The P.M.G. has been a great delight when it has come—but about one paper in three reaches us, from some cause or other. I hope Spanish p.o's will be more regular.

Mrs. Lewes declares her intention of adding a postscript, so I will say goodbye and leave the stage to her. Kind regards to Greenwood.[3]

Yours ever

G. H. Lewes.

IV, 338:1 GE TO GEORGE SMITH, BIARRITZ, [26 JANUARY 1867]

MS: National Library of Scotland. On same sheet with GHL's letter.

My dear Sir

Since I last wrote to you, a few days before our departure, I have come a long way with my beautiful travelling bag. To imagine what a convenience it is to me, you must have been a lady without a perfect thing of that sort for the greater part of your life, but of all its uses I think the best is that it continually occasions in me the pleasant feeling that I owe it to your kindness.

I had thought of sending to you some letters which my friend Mrs. Bodichon wrote to me during her journey through Spain in November and December, that you might judge whether you would like to print them in the Pall Mall. But I may just as well reserve them till our return, as there is no matter in them which will not keep. They are graphic and simple, and they give a real individual impression, saying nothing that is said in the guide books, and correcting many false views that people get from travellers who go to second or third rate inns, on the one hand, and from writers whose chief object is to make much out of little. Au reste, they are brief, and would shrink into very small space of print. However, when we get back you shall read them, if you will take that trouble.

Mr. Lewes looks a little better, but the month has done little towards

---

3. Frederick Greenwood succeeded GHL as editor of the *Cornhill*. See v, 449, n. 7.

[18 March 1867]

making him either more robust or less thin. We are at least well off in having set out early enough to save him from the terrible cold of which we have had a comparatively mild sample here. What sad things we read about everywhere, but last night and today there have been storms so tremendous on this Atlantic coast, that I keep thinking of shipwrecks.

I hope you keep well under all your heavy work and anxieties. We rejoiced to see the announcement, at last, that the new premises were to be entered on. May they lead to excellent conclusions!

Ever yours sincerely
Marian E. Lewes.

IV, 351:1 GHL TO JOHN BLACKWOOD, LONDON, [18 MARCH 1867]

MS: National Library of Scotland.

The Priory, | 21. North Bank, | Regents Park.

My dear Blackwood

A Hungarian Professor writes me word that he has translated the *Physiology of Common Life* and found a publisher but wants my permission (which of course is gladly given) he also wants to preface it with an account of my works and has not got the *Sea-side Studies.* Would you kindly order a copy to be sent through a Leipzig bookseller to him through L. Csáthy Company | Debreczin, Hungary. His name is Prof. Ladislaus Dapsy.

Another request! When I was in Paris I met Renan who was very anxious to see the article I wrote in Maga about his Essais[4] some years ago; would you send him the number (I think it was in 1858 or 59, the article was called "Another Pleasant French Book," and was a review of the Essais de Critique) address |

M. Ernest Renan | 29 rue Vanneau | Paris.

These bitter winds! This horrid snow! This horrid slush! To come from sunny Spain where even in February we were forced to sit in the shade, and find oneself in the glacial climate of England is enough to undo much of the good of the journey; but I hope we have laid in sufficient strength to withstand even that—especially as I must now be hard at work on my History.

---

4. Ernest Renan, *Essais de morale et de critique*, Paris, 1859, was reviewed in *Blackwood's*, 86 (December 1859), 669–680.

Mrs. Lewes is writing to you so I shall presume all the necessary details will be given or will have been given by her.

Ever yours faithfully
G. H. Lewes.

John Blackwood Esq.

IV, 360:18 GHL TO MRS. ROBERT LYTTON, LONDON, [MAY 1867]

MS: Lady Hermione Cobbold.

The Priory, | 21. North Bank, | Regents Park.
Sunday.

My dear Mrs. Lytton

Your letter was a surprise and a pain to me. I had no conception that Robert was contemplating an operation—not a serious one I hope?

A thought strikes me—was his note to me written under the idea that he was the *kind* of animal I should be likely to operate on, and did he need my vivisecting curiosity?

But to be serious, if while he is an invalid he would like me to come over and chat with him only let me know.

Meanwhile believe me, Dear Mrs. Lytton

Yours very faithfully
G. H. Lewes.

IV, 360:18 GHL TO LADY AMBERLEY, LONDON, [2 MAY 1867]

MS: The Bertrand Russell Archives, McMaster University.

The Priory, | 21. North Bank, | Regents Park.
Thursday.

My dear Lady Amberley

I will present myself on Tuesday at $\frac{1}{4}$ to 8 "or perish in the Attempt"![5] Believe me

Your most obedient
G. H. Lewes.

5. For GHL's account of the dinner see IV, 361.

[8 May 1867]   399

IV, 362:1 GHL TO LORD AMBERLEY,
LONDON, [6 MAY 1867]

MS: The Bertrand Russell Archives, McMaster University.

The Priory, | 21. North Bank, | Regents Park.
Monday.

Dear Lord Amberley

Herewith I send the other volumes of Wilson's Works which Lady Amberley said you would perhaps like to see.[6]

I was sorry to hear of your suffering from a sore throat which is a depressing ailment. I hope tomorrow to find you well again.

Yours faithfully,
G. H. Lewes.

IV, 362:1 GHL TO LADY AMBERLEY,
LONDON, [8 MAY 1867]

MS: University of Washington. *Published: The Amberley Papers*, 2 vols., 1937, II, 28.

The Priory, | 21. North Bank, | Regents Park.
Wednesday.

Dear Lady Amberley

I find I promised what could not be performed—the 'Hindu Drama'[7] not having yet been republished. But in the hope that you may find something to interest you in Wilson's account of Hindu Fiction I send these volumes.

Your charming sister[8] got me on my weak (or strong?) point last night, and I fear I was dreadfully egotistical, (L'amour est l'égoisme à deux); but if any one *will* mention my Madonna to me, why "their blood be on their own head!"

---

6. Lady Amberley's Diary, Sunday 5 May: "A. and I went to hear Congreve lecture at Sussex Hall—Bouverie St. Fleet Str. at 11 on Positivism. Lewes was there and introduced me to his wife, an ugly large woman." (*The Amberley Papers*, II, 33.)

7. Horace Hayman Wilson, *Selected Specimens of the Theatre of the Hindus,* tr. from the original Sanscrit, Calcutta, 3 vols., 1827, 1835.

8. The Countess of Airlie. In her Diary Lady Amberley wrote: "The correct etiquette about Lewes and George Eliot appears to have been somewhat undecided. In the following letter Lewes apologizes for mentioning her." But GHL's Journal shows that she misunderstood. See IV, 361.

That was a most felicitous *mot* of yours in defence of my position that 'class *against* class was better than class *over* class'—it would *tell* in the House. Believe me

Your very obedient and faithful philosopher
G. H. Lewes.

IV, 364:9   GHL TO THE EDITOR, *ATHENAEUM*, LONDON, 13 MAY 1867

Text: Athenaeum, 18 May 1867, p. 663.

ENGLISH AUTHORS IN AMERICA.

The Priory, May 13, 1867.

Permit me to add one more to the many illustrations you have already made public of the extraordinary pretensions of some American publishers.

Messrs. Hurd & Houghton, of New York, desired to reprint the new edition of my 'History of Philosophy,' which is on the eve of appearing.[9] Glad as I should have been to see my work in the hands of a firm so honourably known in England, I felt that Messrs Appleton, of New York, had, in courtesy, a prior claim, on the ground of their having reprinted the previous edition in 1857. Accordingly I wrote to them, through their London agent, stating that I considered they had a claim to the first offer, and stating further, that the new edition was substantially a new book. (As this is an important element in the present case, allow me to add, that the edition of 1857 was in one volume 8vo., published at 16s., whereas the new edition is in two volumes 8vo., published at 30s.; and the work is so considerably altered and enlarged that a new title has been affixed to it, for the purpose of marking it off from its predecessors.)[1]

Questions of courtesy, are, however, but ill understood by some people, and by Messrs. Appleton so ill understood that they did not even answer my letter. After waiting more than three months for an answer, I asked a friend to see their London agent on the subject, and thus I learned that Messrs. Appleton—*risum teneatis, amici?*[2]—"considered they had a right to publish all future editions of my work without payment," because ten years ago they had given the magnificent sum of 25*l.* to secure themselves against rivals for the second edition.

---

9. GHL finished rewriting *The Biographical History of Philosophy* on his 50th birthday, 18 April 1867, and finished the new Prolegomena 7 May.

1. The word *Biographical* was dropped from the title: *The History of Philosophy from Thales to Comte*, 2 vols., Longman, 1867.

2. Horace, *Ars Poetica*, line 5.

[? *May 1867*]

The extravagance of this pretension is seen by comparing it with that of an English publisher who, although his payment is twenty times that of the American publisher, never claims a right over any edition beyond the one purchased, much less over all future editions; and even when the entire copyright is purchased, although that gives him the right to issue reprint after reprint, there is no English publisher who does not pay, and often liberally pay, the author for all new matter, all extra labour which successive editions may involve.[3] If Messrs. Appleton chose to reprint the work which—in the American sense—they purchased in 1857, I, for one, should raise no objection to their doing so; but their claim to reprint another work of greater pretension, except as an act of literary piracy, is one which may be left to the judgment of all impartial persons. The absence of any law on the subject, except the unwritten law, which regulates the conduct of men of honour, gives Messrs. Appleton full power to act as they think proper; and what they think proper may be gathered from this one example.

GEORGE HENRY LEWES.

IV, 364:9 GHL TO MRS. FREDERICK LEHMANN, LONDON, [? MAY 1867]

MS: Yale. *Published:* R. C. Lehmann, *Memories of Half a Century*, 1908, pp. 134–135 date 1864; the paper is watermarked 1866.

The Priory, | 21. North Bank, | Regents Park.
Wednesday.

Sweet little Woman!

The extremely youthful George will certainly break through his rule (for what are rules good but to be broken?) and present himself arrayed in great splendour (i.e. tail coat and waxed whiskers) on Tuesday next. But oh! how little impression his pothooks and signature must have made on your insensible soul that you should mistake them for his better two-thirds! I wrote to you—"alone I did it!"[4]—Polly having installed me in the office of general secretary—with instructions to give her hearty love and wish to see you which of course I forgot.

Come up on Sunday if you can—if not, any other afternoon after 4.[5]

Ever yours faithfully
G. H. Lewes.

3. John W. Parker published the 1857 ed. On 28 May 1867 Longman wrote GHL that he would pay £250 instead of £150 for the new edition. (GHL Diary.)

4. *Coriolanus*, v, vi, 114.

IV, 364:9 GE TO JOHN MORLEY,
LONDON, 14 MAY 1867

MS: L. W. Smith Collection, Washington's Headquarters, Morristown, New Jersey. *Extracts published:* IV, 364–365.

The Priory, | 21. North Bank, | Regents Park.
May 14. 67.

My dear Mr. ⟨Morley⟩[6]

Thanks for your kind practical remembrance. Your attitude in relation to Female Enfranchisement[7] seems to be very nearly mine. If I were called on to act in the matter, I would certainly not oppose any plan which held out any reasonable promise of tending to establish as far as possible an equivalence of advantages for the two sexes, as to education and the possibilities of free development. I fear you may have misunderstood something I said the other evening[8] about nature. I never meant to urge the "intention of Nature" argument, which is to me a pitiable fallacy. I mean that as a fact of mere zoological evolution, woman seems to me to have the worse share in existence. But for that very reason I would the more contend that in the moral evolution we have "an art which does mend nature"—an art which "itself is nature."[9] It is the function of love in the largest sense, to mitigate the harshness of all fatalities. And in the thorough recognition of that worse share, I think there is a basis for a sublimer resignation in woman and a more regenerating tenderness in man.

However, I repeat that I do not trust very confidently to my own impressions on this subject. The peculiarities of my own lot may have caused me to have idiosyncrasies rather than an average judgment. The one conviction on the matter which I hold with some tenacity is, that through all transitions the goal towards which we are proceeding is a more clearly discerned distinctness of function (allowing always for exceptional cases of individual organization) with as near an approach to equivalence of good for woman and for man as can be secured by the effort of growing moral force to lighten the pressure of hard non-moral

---

5. The Lehmanns came "in the evening" Saturday, 11 May 1867, and again on Sunday the 19th. (GHL Journal.)

6. Morley sent this letter to George Lillie Craik, 2 February 1873, saying: "I have only one letter of George Eliot's—but I cheerfully beg you to accept it.

I have crossed my name over; it is a nice letter, and I am pleased that you or any one you care to please should have it." (L. W. Smith Collection.)

7. See IV, 364, n. 9.

8. See IV, 364, n. 1.

9. *The Winter's Tale,* IV, iv, 95–96.

[29 May 1867]

outward conditions. It is rather superfluous, perhaps injudicious, to plunge into such deeps as these in a hasty note, but it is difficult to resist the desired to botch imperfect talk with a little imperfect writing.

The "Spectator" article[1] is a grandiose specimen of what a journalist can do when *not* "stating his thoughts in a manner below his capacity"—for misrepresentation and wriggling.

Alas, for the inarticulateness you mention. One would like to know, for consolation, what it was exactly that St. Paul referred to in saying that his speech was "contemptible."[2]

Always yours sincerely
M. E. Lewes.

By the way, it was *not* Mr. Capes[3] who wrote the article on Blank Verse.

IV, 366:1 GHL TO NIKOLAUS TRÜBNER, LONDON, [29 MAY 1867]

MS: Yale. *Endorsed:* 29/V 67 | London | G. H. Lewes.

The Priory, | 21. North Bank, | Regents Park.
29 May 1867.

Dear Sir

Herewith I send you the Letterpress to Kaulbach[4] which I hope will meet with your approval. In composing it I have steadily borne in view the needs of an English (and for the most part uninstructed) public—and have therefore supplied precisely that kind of information which I found by *experiment* necessary. I showed the plates to several people—men and women who knew little or nothing of Goethe—and *directed by their inquiries* —I constructed the commentary.

It is therefore something wholly different from what I should have written for a German public or a public familiar with Goethe's works. I have added translations to the German passages, because otherwise the quotations would not have been illustrative.

---

1. See IV, 365, n. 2a.
2. II Corinthians, 10:10.
3. J. A. Symonds wrote the article on "Blank Verse," *Cornhill*, 15 (May 1867), 620–640. John Moore Capes (1812–89) in the same number (pp. 410–419) wrote "Music the Expression of Character."

4. *Goethes Frauengestalten*, by Wilhelm Kaulbach, published at Munich with text by Adolf Stahr, was reissued in London by Trübner, as *Female Characters of Goethe. From the original drawings of W. Kaulbach.* With explanatory text by G. H. Lewes. Trübner paid him £100.

Please acknowledge the receipt of this. And let me have Proofs at your convenience. Believe me

Yours truly
G. H. Lewes.

IV, 368:1   GHL TO LORD HOUGHTON, LONDON, 20 JUNE [1867]

MS: Trinity College, Cambridge.

The Priory, | 21. North Bank, | Regents Park.
20th June.

My dear Lord

I will be with you on Saturday at ½ past 9 and you shall induct me to the zoophytic breakfast room.

I miss several old friends among the 'Selections'.[5] But that is generally the case. Cobbett[6] used to say "When I am asked what course of study a young man should pursue I reply *Let him read all I have written.*" A naïve expression of the true authorial state of mind, and one which has its justification after all, for it is only by reading a great deal of one writer that we get thoroughly acquainted with him.

Ever yours faithfully,
G. H. Lewes.

IV, 376:1   GE TO MRS. THEODORE MARTIN, LONDON, 20 JULY 1867

MS: University of California Los Angeles.

The Priory, | 21. North Bank, | Regents Park.
July 20. 67.

My dear Mrs. Martin

I believe that you often take pity on sufferers, so I want to tell you that an ingenious friend of ours has invented an invalid's bed[7] which facilitates the turning and lifting of the patient in all needful directions, without any handling of the body, which is often a cause of so much pain.

---

5. *A Selection from the Works of Lord Houghton,* 1867, a revision of his earlier *Selections from the Poetical Works of R. M. Milnes,* 1863.

6. William Cobbett (1792–1835), radical essayist and politician.

7. Herbert Spencer after his father's death invented an invalid's bed. Wishing it to be sold as cheaply as possible, he did not patent it. He describes it in *An Autobiography,* 2 vols., 1904, II, 147–148, illustrated with 16 engravings in Appendix D, reprinted from the *British Medical Journal,* 27 July 1867.

28 July 1867 405

Unhappily it cannot be made at present under £10 or £12, so that poor people could only get it as a loan or present. I am anxious that benevolent friends should know of its existence, in case of their desiring to confer such a relief on any bedridden creature.

I was indebted to you and Mr. Martin for a great deal of pleasure the other evening from your kindness first, and after that for the sight of many pretty things.

Mr. Lewes is very ailing still. I hope that you and Mr. Martin will not only get robust yourselves but find him so on your return. Always
Sincerely yours
M. E. Lewes.
I should be able to get all particulars about the bed if you needed them.

IV, 379:11 GE TO MRS. FREDERICK LEHMANN,
LONDON, 28 JULY 1867

MS: W. & R. Chambers Ltd., Edinburgh.

The Priory | 21. North Bank | Regents Park.
July 28. 67.

My dear Friend

Your letter was a relief from many painful thoughts about you, and I am especially glad that you waited to tell me what the Doctors said, so that you could give me a plan of your movements for the next two months. I like to be able to imagine where you are, and what sort of prospect is before you. We have seen little of each other, but then that little was under circumstances which interested me more than very lengthy intercourse with other people has often done.[8] And these long separations from your home and husband are just the trouble into which I can best enter, of all troubles in the world. And so I bear you in mind very tenderly.

We too, are going away tomorrow evening—to North Germany. At present, we do not say that we shall go farther than Dresden, but we shall let ourselves be determined by future [inclina]tions. We expect to be at [home] again by the end of September.

I am the most insubstantial of friends to you at present, but when I come back, I hope I may put my hand in yours and kiss you—and then we will talk a little together.

George joins me in love to you and your husband, and I am always
Yours affectionately,
M. E. Lewes.

8. See IV, 336–337.

IV, 379:11 GHL TO ROBERT LYTTON, LONDON, [28 JULY 1867]

MS: Lady Hermione Cobbold.

The Priory, | 21. North Bank, | Regents Park.
Sunday.

My dear Lytton

Sir Henry Holland has ordered me abroad before I thought of going and I shall not therefore be able to come and have another bedside chat with you as I had proposed. I start tomorrow for the firwoods of Ilmenau, but whither our wanderings will lead us I don't know. My minister of the interior is troublesome. If you should happen know of a gentleman willing to exchange his liver for mine let me know!

Kind remembrances to Mrs. Lytton

Ever faithfully yours
G. H. L.

IV, 389:1 GE TO MME EUGÈNE BODICHON, LONDON, [OCTOBER? 1867]

MS: Berg Collection, New York Public Library.

My dear Barbara

I am grieved to hear of your being ill. I send you the only books George can lay his hand on that he can spare just now—that are not too grave or bulky.

I hope the shock of that danger will have done Nannie no harm.

But you will be able to come to say goodby, I trust, before you go quite away. In any case, I am yours

with faithful affection
Marian.

IV, 390:1 GHL TO RICHARD OWEN,
LONDON, 4 OCTOBER 1867

MS: Yale.

The Priory, | 21. North Bank, | Regents Park.
4 October 1867.

My dear Owen

I hope I am wrong in my uncomfortable notion that you have interpreted a phrase or two of mine into a covert allusion of contempt or sarcasm against your sincerely respected self. That we differ profoundly respecting Design and the Creator is an old story—*that* difference never yet has disturbed our harmony—but what is new is the suspicion (it is not more) that you interpret my language as covertly attacking you, and above all as imputing 'infirmity' to you.

If you had cast your eyes over the Prolegomena to my 3rd ed.[9] (to which reference is made in the article on the Reign of Law) you would have seen that by '*Infirmity*' I designated a native tendency (distinguished from the '*necessities* of thought') into which all philosophers are eminently liable to fall and into which *most* have fallen, viz. the tendency to give objective reality to subjective forms. The term 'Infirmity' has not a shadow of reproach or contempt in it as thus used by me. It merely marks a tendency against which we have to guard ourselves. And with regard to the *application* you will see that I applied it to "philosophers from Plato downwards"—and although you are the one most associated with the doctrine of vertebral-type plan in England, I assure you I was *not* specially alluding to you, and certainly never should have thought of a covert sarcasm.

I wanted to say this—and only this—in reference to your paper in Frazer.[1] I may be and hope I am—altogether mistaken. I only don't want our old friendship to be crossed by a misunderstanding. By a difference in opinion it won't be.

Ever yours truly
G. H. Lewes.

Richard Owen Esq.

---

9. GHL, *History of Philosophy*, 3d ed., 1867, pp. xv–xxxvi.

1. In an article on the Duke of Argyll's *The Reign of Law* GHL spoke of Owen's theory that a vertebral type existed before animals were created.

"Science discovers only the law of causation. By a well-known infirmity we transform this into a *nisus formativus*, and the law becomes a plan." (*Fortnightly*, 8 [July 1867], 106.) Owen retorted with an article in *Fraser's*, 76 (October 1867),

IV, 393:24 GHL TO CHARLES KENT,[2] LONDON, [24 OCTOBER 1867]

MS: Huntington Library. *Envelope:* Charles Kent | 1 Campden Grove | Kensington | W. *Postmark:* LONDON N.W | 2 | OC 24 | 67.

The Priory, | 21. North Bank, | Regents Park.
Thursday.

My dear Sir

Although I never attend public dinners yet I must make an exception to honor Dickens; I shall therefore have much pleasure in joining the Stewards. I presume you will let me know the time we assemble.

Ever yours truly
G. H. Lewes.

Charles Kent Esq.

IV, 399:6 GE TO EMILY DAVIES,[3] LONDON, 16 NOVEMBER 1867

MS: Girton College. *Envelope:* Miss Davies | 17 Cunningham Place | N.W. *Postmark:* ST. JOHNS WOOD. SO | N.W | NO 16 | 67 | *Partly published:* IV, 399.

The Priory, | 21. North Bank, | Regents Park.
November 16. 67.

Dear Madam

In a letter which I received yesterday from Mrs. Bodichon, she assures me that you would like to call on me for the sake of some conversation on the desirable project of founding a College for Women.

I shall be very happy to see you on Tuesday at 4 o'clock if that time will be convenient to you.

I remain, dear Madam

Yours sincerely
M. E. Lewes.

531–533, "On the Argument of 'Infirmity' in Mr. Lewes's Review of *The Reign of Law*," defending his acceptance of the concept of Design. "God works by means."

2. William Charles Mark Kent (1823–1902) served as secretary for the farewell dinner given Dickens at Freemason's Hall, 2 November 1867, before his departure for the United States. GHL's name is on the long list.

3. (Sarah) Emily Davies (1830–1921), one of the founders of Girton College, Cambridge, of which she was Mistress 1873–75.

IV, 400:26 EMILY DAVIES TO MME BODICHON,
LONDON, 20 NOVEMBER 1867

MS: Girton College, Cambridge. *Envelope:* Miss Davies | 17 Cunningham Place | N.W. *Postmark:* ST. JOHNS WOOD. SO | NO 20 | 67.

17 Cunningham Place. N.W.
November 20th 1867.

My dear Mrs. Bodichon

I went to see Mrs. Lewes yesterday, and we had a long and most interesting talk about the College. The first thing she touched upon was the religious question, on which we very quickly came to an understanding. I told her my idea was that if we kept on the same platform as Cambridge, we should share any changes which might be made as public opinion changes, and that we could not have a better security for liberality. She quite agreed and repeated it all afterwards to Mr. Lewes who also agreed. They thought it desirable however that a sentence should be inserted in the Programme about prayers, by way of showing that we do not intend to have a Chapel or Chaplain. She thought it most desirable that we should attach ourselves to Cambridge and get their Degrees if possible, but at the same time approved of the proviso that the exam[inatio]ns should not be compulsory. She also strongly approves of having women only as resident authorities, and thought that people who recommended a man and his wife could not have much knowledge of life. It was delightful to find her taking such a warm interest in the whole thing. She said she thought the higher education of women was *the* thing about which there could be no doubt.

I told Mrs. Lewes what Emily Blackwell[4] had proposed to you, about your £1000, namely to withdraw the condition about Miss Blackwell, and to substitute two, first that the £1000 should not be paid till the whole £30,000 had been received, and second that a promise should be made to provide for teaching hygiene. The first condition we both thought very good. The second is more difficult. Miss E. Blackwell told me that she should think it a sufficient security if the Committee would pass the enclosed Resolution. I doubt very much however whether they would, and Mrs. Lewes thinks that they ought not. She says that the principles of

---

4. Emily Blackwell (1826–1910), younger sister of Elizabeth Blackwell (1821–1910), the first woman physician. They were joint authors of *Medicine as a Profession for Women*, New York, 1860, and *Address on the Medical Education of Women*, New York, 1864. Mme Bodichon wanted Elizabeth to hold a professorship of hygiene at Girton College.

Hygiene are so few and so simple that anybody could learn them from a book like Combe,[5] without a teacher, and that the sanitary influence of the College must depend upon the resident authorities. Of course she holds as strongly as anybody the necessity of obedience to the laws of health, especially for women. The only question is about the means. She thinks that it is by the formation of habits in the College, not by direct teaching.

After we had been talking about this for some time, she fetched Mr. Lewes, who took exactly the same view. He thought it desirable to have some teaching of the laws of life, but that, he said, would come under Zoology. They both said we *could not* have a Professor of Hygiene, and that the reason people make themselves ill is that they wilfully do what they know to be unhealthy. Mr. Lewes thought the only thing we could do would be to insert a sentence in the Programme, to the effect that we do not mean to infringe the laws of health, and Mrs. Lewes suggested that it might be brought in among the duties of the resident authorities. I think I see my way to putting in a sentence of this sort, in the last paragraph but one.

I am anxious that it should be *possible* to accept your £1000 at the outset, because this is the only way, as you will not be on the Committee,[6] that you can be counted among the founders of the College. If you wait to see whether we do things in a proper manner, we shall not be able to reckon you among the believing few, who walk by faith and not by sight. It is quite clear to me that if the thing is to be done at all, there must be, not only faith in the idea, but trust in the people who are to carry it out. I have no doubt at all now that we shall do it. It is only a question of a little sooner or later and a more or less beautiful building, and so on. But you know how much pleasure it would give me to feel to be doing it *with* you, who have believed in this idea from the very first. . . . [*About two pages omitted.*]

I will not trouble you with a longer letter. Miss Blackwell gave a pretty good account of you. It is something to be getting on, however slowly.

The bit of blue was a little darker than the Cambridge blue.[7]

Ever y[ou]rs affec[tionate]ly,
Emily Davies.

---

5. Andrew Combe, *The Principles of Physiology Applied to the Preservation of Health and to the Improvement of Physical and Mental Education*, 1834, went through its 15th edition in 1860.

6. Mme Bodichon made one of the largest contributions to the fund in August 1867, but her name was kept off the committee because it was so conspicuously connected with the Women's Rights movement. She agreed 22 November to give the £1000 conditionally. "I will follow your advice, so you can say it is to meet £29,000. I do still think something special must be done about hygiene, but I have decided to leave it to your influence and mine over you!" (Barbara Stephen, *Emily Davies and Girton College*, 1927, p. 163.)

7. A sample for the gown?

IV, 401:27 GE TO EMILY DAVIES, LONDON, [29 NOVEMBER 1867]

MS: Girton College. *Envelope:* Miss Davies | 17 Cunningham Place | N.W. *Postmark:* ST JOHNS WOOD. SO | N.W | NO 29 | 67.

The Priory, | 21. North Bank, | Regents | Park.
Friday.

My dear Miss Davies

Can you come to me on Monday at 4 o'clock? I will expect you then unless I hear from you to the contrary.

Yours very truly
M. E. Lewes.

The Prospectus seems to me decidedly improved. I should vote for 50,000.[8]

IV, 410:15 GHL TO GEORGE SMITH, LONDON, 25 DECEMBER 1867

MS: National Library of Scotland.

The Priory, | 21. North Bank, | Regents Park.
Christmas Day 1867.

Dear Smith

Health and happiness for you and yours! is the prayer offered up at the Priory.

It is not *impossible* that we may see you this afternoon, if you are not at Brighton, or not absorbed in hospitalities, but I don't mean to be anticipated, so I send my 'Merry Christmas' d'avance.

I am making a rash and rapid flight to Germany on Friday—anxious to see whether the German anatomists have made any bricks that will suit my purpose. I am on the track of a great discovery!

I shall be back by the 12 January. Mrs. Lewes remains at home. She bids me say all manner of sweet things.

Ever yours faithfully
G. H. Lewes.

---

8. The original Prospectus for the College suggested £30,000 as the initial sum to be raised.

IV, 416:15 GHL TO MONCURE DANIEL CONWAY,
LONDON, 10 JANUARY 1868

MS: McGill University Library.

The Priory, | 21. North Bank, | Regents Park.
10 January 68.

My dear Sir

Your letter was awaiting me on my return from abroad. Mayall of Regent St. has photos of me both large and small (I have not one by me or I would ask your friend's[9] acceptance of it) but Mrs. Lewes has steadily refused to be photographed.

Yours very truly
G. H. Lewes.

M. D. Conway.

IV, 421:1 GHL TO HENRY CHARLTON BASTIAN,
LONDON, [FEBRUARY? 1868]

MS: Nuneaton Public Library.

The Priory, | 21. North Bank, | Regents Park.
Wednesday.

My dear Sir,

The very remarkable paper[1] you were kind enough to send me has been very instructive, and some day I will ask you to lend me Bouchard's memoir,[2] if you possess it.

I have many doubts respecting Waller's idea of the nutritive centres of nerve fibres.[3] His facts are indisputable, and his idea for a long while misled me on a wild goose chase after the homologies of the spinal and posterior horns; but I have seen too many contradictory and destructive

---

9. See IV, 413, n. 1.

1. Henry Charlton Bastian (1837–1915), *On a Case of Concussion-lesion*, 1867. GHL's copy is in Dr. Williams's Library.

2. Charles Bouchard, *Des Dégénerations secondaires de la moelle épinière*, Paris, 1866.

3. Augustus Volney Waller (1816–70), M.D. Paris, 1840; Professor of Physiology at Birmingham, 1858–60.

"His demonstration of the cilio-spinal centre in the spinal cord and of the vaso-constrictor action of the sympathetic has withstood the test of time, while his name will long be associated with the degeneration method of studying the paths of nerve impulses, for he invented it." (*DNB.*) GHL does not mention Waller's work in *The Physiology of Common Life*.

facts to hold that explanation now. In the special case you have brought forward I do not think the explanation acceptable because I have very many times separated the fibres from those supposed centres of nutrition (by section and hemisection of the cord, and removal of the brain) yet after several weeks the cord has exhibited no degeneration when hardened in chromic acid. On the other hand I did once observe what I *now* (enlightened by you) comprehend to have been a secondary degeneration in the cord of a mole whom I stunned by a blow on the back part of the head. Query: Is not the cause of the degeneration *primarily* an exhaustion of Neurility owing to the excess of stimulus (shock) destroying the molecular structure of the nerve, and *secondarily* a consequent influence on the capillaries?

Yours very faithfully,
G. H. Lewes.

H. C. Bastian, Esq., M.D.

IV, 421:1 GHL TO CHARLES ROBERT DARWIN, LONDON, 2 MARCH 1868

MS: Cambridge University Library.

The Priory, | 21 North Bank, | Regents Park.
2nd March 68.

My dear Sir

I understand that you did not disapprove the little notice I wrote of your last book in the Pall Mall Gazette,[4] and as I am now engaged in a more elaborate consideration of it for the Fortnightly Review I venture to appeal to your greater experience to enlighten me on a morphological detail of interest. Are there not some animals with nails, or hooks, at the tips of the tail?[5] I have an indistinct remembrance of such a thing, but cannot feel sure whether it exists out of my fancy—or in *what* animal. The suggestion arose in my mind when considering the analogical position of nails, claws, hooks, beaks and horns—always at extremities and never anywhere else.

4. "Darwin on Domestication and Variation," *Pall Mall Gazette*, 10, 15, and 17 February 1868, pp. 555, 636–637, and 652, reviewing *The Variation of Animals and Plants under Domestication*, 2 vols., 1868. The day the first article appeared Darwin wrote to J. D. Hooker: "If by any chance you should hear who wrote the article in the *Pall Mall*, do please tell me; it is some one who writes capitally, and who knows the subject." (*Life and Letters of Charles Darwin*, ed. Francis Darwin, 3 vols., 1887, III, 76.)

5. Darwin answered this question in his notes sent to GHL 7 August 1868. See *More Letters of Charles Darwin*, ed. Francis Darwin, 2 vols., 1903, I, 307–308.

While I am troubling you let me also ask in what way you understand Natural Selection to have determined the modification of leaves into flowers? Is there any advantage to the plant in having petals rather than leaves and variously colored petals rather than green? While I think every unbiassed naturalist whose rational organs are not 'rudimentary' must admit your principle, I am disposed to think that many organic details are the simple consequences of organic combination and are quite irrespective of advantage.

Apologizing for trespassing on your valuable time but glad of the opportunity of expressing my gratitude to you, Believe me

Yours very truly
G. H. Lewes.

Charles Darwin Esq.

IV, 421:1 GE TO EMILY DAVIES, LONDON, 4 MARCH 1868

MS: Girton College. *Envelope:* Miss Davies | 17 Cunningham Place | N.W. *Postmark:* LONDON N.W | 2 | MA 4 | 68.

The Priory, | 21. North Bank, | Regents Park.
March 4. 68.

My dear Miss Davies

Whenever it will not be a bad example to set down subscriptions of £50 for the Ladies' College, Mr. Lewes begs that you will enter that sum on the list as coming from "the author of Adam Bede," or of "Romola"— whichever title you may prefer.[6]

We wish to give our adhesion to the good work: but are afraid of promising more money to an object which many rich people are likely to further, lest we should narrow our means of helping in cases known only to ourselves.

Always yours sincerely
M. E. Lewes.

Miss Davies

6. It was entered as "the author of *Romola*."

IV, 423:11 GE TO WILLIAM BLACKWOOD, LONDON, 15 MARCH 1868

MS: Yale.

The Priory, | 21. North Bank, | Regents Park.
March 15. 68.

My dear Sir

I am delighted to get the fresh proof this morning, and the assurance that I need not be fidgetty about occupying type.[7]

I shall be busy at the coast in preparing M.S. as well as in correcting proofs, for I want to get the whole poem in print as soon as I can. Perhaps I shall be able to release the press from the burthen before the end of May, for I do not find myself able to alter anything greatly when I have once written it under strong feelings.

What can be the occasion of such festivities at Edinburgh[7a] in this Lenten time? Perhaps I ought to know, but I have been leading an owl's life lately.

We are going to South Devonshire, and I dare say that I shall have to send to you after we have settled on our abode. Always

Yours sincerely
M. E. Lewes.

IV, 431:23 GE TO CARL ADOLF BUCHHEIM,[8] LONDON, 21 APRIL 1868

MS: Princeton. *Envelope:* Dr. Buchheim | 47 Leamington Rd Villas | W. *Postmark:* LONDON N.W | 4 | AP 21 | 68.

The Priory, | 21. North Bank, | Regents Park.
21 April 68.

The author of "The Mill on the Floss" (Mrs. G. H. Lewes) presents her compliments to Dr. Buchheim and accords him full permission to extract from that work any passage which he deems suitable for his selections.

---

7. For *The Spanish Gypsy*.
7a. See II, 393, n. 1.
8. Carl Adolf Buchheim (1828–1900), Professor at the University of London 1865–70, was German tutor to the Prince of Wales. His *Materials for German Prose Composition, or Selections from Modern English Writers*, 1868, included (pp. 182–185) the final paragraphs of *The Mill on the Floss* as well as (pp. 41–43) "Goethe at the Age of Twenty" from GHL's *Goethe*.

IV, 432:24 GHL TO HENRY CHARLTON BASTIAN, LONDON, [24 APRIL 1868]

MS: Nuneaton Public Library.

The Priory, | 21. North Bank, | Regents Park.
Friday.

My dear Sir

I have read your admirable memoir[9] with as much interest as is compatible with comprehensive ignorance of the subject—especially interested in the part relating to the nervous system. The paper came just in time to give me a quotation for my second article on Darwin.[1]

I don't know how to explain it by any other hypothesis than stupidity but I have ignobly failed in my attempts to make a solution of your Damara[2] and Benzine. At first I thought the cause might be in the lost virtue of the Benzine I had which was very old so I bought some fresh, and yet after a fortnight's immersion the gum failed to melt.

Further I have weighed my bibromate of potasi and ammonia according to your suggestions—and one per cent gives me a solution suspiciously dark—much darker indeed than any I have ever thought of using. I was right was I not in weighing 20 grs to a four ounce bottle of water?

Forgive my bothering you with such small details.

Ever yours,
G. H. Lewes.

IV, 449:15 GE TO GEORGE SMITH, BONN, 1 JUNE 1868

MS: National Library of Scotland.

Bonn, June 1. 1868.

My dear Sir

Mr. Lewes wrote a few words on a card last night, introducing to you Dr. Perry, with whom I had the pleasure of talking a little on the subject

---

9. *On the Anatomy and Physiology of the Nematoids*, reprinted from *Philosophical Transactions*, 1866.

1. "Mr. Darwin's Hypotheses, Part II," *Fortnightly*, 9 (June 1868), 611–628. GHL's quotation from Bastian is on p. 624, n. 1.

2. A resin, dammara, used in varnishes. Bastian lunched at the Priory 19 April 1868 and looked over GHL's preparations. (GHL Journal.)

24 July 1868

of German Education.³ I add a few words before our early departure this morning, to say, that Dr. Perry's long experience as an educator and his close acquaintance with German life have given him rare advantages for the observation of German Schools, of which it is especially desirable for us English to get some accurate knowledge just now. But on this general question I need say nothing to you, who have the best opportunities for knowing the important place it holds in our best minds at home. Dr. Perry, I believe, is personally known to various friends of yours, and is probably already somewhat known to you through his interesting evidence given before the Commission of Inquiry into our Universities.

Hastily, at 6 o'clock. a.m.

Sincerely yours
M. E. Lewes.

George Smith Esq.

IV, 450:15 GE TO [ROBERT HOGARTH PATTERSON],⁴ LONDON, 24 JULY 1868

MS: Princeton.

The Priory, | 21. North Bank, | Regents Park.
July 24. 68.

My dear Sir

I hope that you have conjecturally attributed my silence to its true cause, namely, my absence from home. Before the Spanish Gypsy appeared we set out for Germany and have been spending eight weeks, or more, chiefly in the Black Forest. My thanks reach you laggingly, but they are not the less sincere. I assure you that I value very highly the expression of your sympathy, and shall reckon it among the things that have cheered and helped me.

Sincerely yours
M. E. Lewes.

---

3. Spending the evening with E. F. W. Pflüger, GE and GHL "found there Dr. and Mrs. Perry and a Mr. Drummond." (GHL Journal, 31 May 1868.)

4. Robert Hogarth Patterson (1821–36) wrote John Blackwood that he got a copy of *The Spanish Gypsy* from the *Globe* office. "It seems to me to dwarf all other Poems that were ever written.... George Elliot will write more poems for certain—the success of this one is sure to be so great. But she will not write another that will rival this." (*MS:* Yale.) Blackwood sent the letter to GHL 19 June 1868.

IV, 460:15 GHL TO CHARLES ROBERT DARWIN, LONDON, 26 JULY 1868

MS: Cambridge University Library.

The Priory, | 21. North Bank, | Regents Park.
July 26th 1868.

My dear Mr. Darwin

On my return from Germany yesterday I found your letter of the 6 June[5] awaiting me with its pleasant intimations of approval.

Yes, I certainly do intend to treat of Pangenesis,[6] and without any evasion, as the most remarkable hypothesis yet put forth on that mystery; but I cannot yet determine whether I shall have room for it in the Review, or shall be forced to leave it for the volume I have in contemplation—"Chapters on Darwin." The fact is that greatly as I was interested in your book and the subject, I was with difficulty persuaded to write on it for the Review, having discharged my first feelings in the Pall Mall. I was unwilling to set aside the work on which I was engaged, but once having done this and taken up your book, the subject grew and grew, till after telling the editor I must write two, then three articles, I finally declared it necessary to write four or five, and make a book out of this nucleus!

After three articles were written I had to go abroad[7] (I found all young scientific Germany Darwinian) and have come back again with the hope of getting the articles at least speedily finished—the book may then proceed leisurely.

I have said all this with a purpose—now that you know whither I am tending, you may perhaps give me the benefit of your objections. I do not mean that you should occupy your time in discussion or dissertation (you have other work to do) but if you could note on the margin any passages to which you demur, any facts you dispute, any inaccuracies you may detect,

---

5. Not found.

6. Darwin's theory that the body cells secrete atoms or "gemmules" deposited in the reproductive organs to record and embody growth patterns. GHL's discussion of Pangenesis in the 4th article, "Mr. Darwin's Hypotheses," *Fortnightly*, 10 (1 November 1868), 503–509, pointed out that it was "wholly constructed out of suppositions, each and all of which may be erroneous.... The objection is that if every part of the cell gives off its gemmules, the reproduction of the whole cell ... is just as incomprehensible as the reproduction of the whole organism ... ; the gemmule is only the old germ or egg in a new guise."

7. GHL went to Germany 26 May and returned 23 July 1868.

or any obscurities worth clearing up, it would greatly benefit my book. Meanwhile believe me

Yours very faithfully
G. H. Lewes.

Have you a carte de visite you could spare? I have never seen you in the flesh, though I have several times met your brother.[8]

IV, 463:7 CHARLES ROBERT DARWIN TO GHL, FRESHWATER, 28 JULY [1868]

MS: Cambridge University Library. Only the signature is in Darwin's hand.

⟨**Down. | Bromley. | Kent. S.E.**⟩
Freshwater I. of Wight | July 28.

My dear Mr. Lewes

I need not say that I have been much pleased by your note. The friendless value friends, and Pangenesis has but few, though deserving I feel sure some good friends. Hooker seems to think that the whole view is almost self-obvious, but I cannot agree to this, for it is now about 28 years since I began to try to tie together the various forms of generations, the repairs of injuries, inheritance etc. and succeeded only about two years ago.

You will see that I am away from home:[9] my health failed about a month ago, so that I could do nothing, and I came here for absolute idleness. Nevertheless I sent this morning to my servant at Down in the hope that he would be able to find the Fortnightly Review. If he succeeds I shall enjoy slowly beginning to read all the articles again and will make any notes which may occur to me, but as I do not suppose I shall read for more than $\frac{1}{2}$ an hour a day I shall be very slow. I fear moreover that we differ so fundamentally on one important point that my remarks will be of no use to you, and I do not think I shall have many on any other point to make.

I am delighted to hear that you intend publishing the articles as a

---

8. Erasmus Alvey Darwin (1804–81).
9. The Darwins took Dumbola Lodge, one of Mrs. Julia Cameron's little houses at Freshwater for six weeks. (Henrietta Litchfield, ed., *Emma Darwin. A Century of Family Letters*, 2 vols., 1915, II, 190.)

separate book; whilst reading them I thought over and over again what a pity it was that they should be almost lost in a periodical.[1]

When I return home in about a month's time I will not forget to send you a photograph, and I should be very much obliged if you would send me yours, as it is always very satisfactory to have an image of one's correspondent in one's mind. Believe me

Yours very faithfully
Charles Darwin.

IV, 464:25 GHL TO CHARLES ROBERT DARWIN, LONDON, 30 JULY 1868

MS: Cambridge University Library.

The Priory, | 21. North Bank, | Regents Park.
30 July 68.

My dear Mr. Darwin

It quite distresses me to think of your forced idleness and I reproach myself for having inconsiderately asked you to bother yourself over my papers. Pray consider my request withdrawn—at any rate so far withdrawn as not to involve a moment's interruption of your idleness or of any other work. Since it must be a long while before my work can be prepared, even after the articles are finished, there is no necessity for you to fix any time for marginalia.

When I was in Freiburg Dr. Weismann[2]—one of the hopes of zoology—delivered an Eintritt's Vorrede on your views, which excited great sensation. I was not present at it, but he told me the line he was going to adopt and shortly we shall have it in print. Poor fellow! he nearly lost his sight with microscopic excesses—What asses we are, we who ought to know and *do* know (for others) the penalties of overwork! Believe me

Very sincerely yours
G. H. Lewes.

---

1. GHL incorporated parts of his articles in *The Physical Basis of Mind*, 1877, pp. 79–136. In the interval he was even more strongly convinced that "we shall have to seek our explanation by enlarging the idea of Natural Selection, subordinating it to the laws of Organic Affinity." (p. 111.)

2. August Weismann (1843–1914), German zoologist, noted for his germ-plasm theory denying the inheritability of acquired characteristics, became professor at Freiburg im Breisgau in 1867. His inaugural address was *Über die Berechtigung der Darwin'schen Theorie*, Leipzig, 1868.

IV, 464:25 EDWARD CLARKE[3] TO GE, AUCKLAND, 31 JULY 1868

MS: Yale.

Parnell, Auckland | July 31st 1868.

My dear Aunt

I was very much pleased to receive your letter dated May 7th and trust to be able to keep up a correspondence, for nothing gives me greater pleasure than to hear from Old England, and I long to visit it again, I arrived in the Australian Colonies in 1861, put up with many hardships and with very little success until I arrived in Auckland in November 1864. An engagement was obtained for me upon the staff of the New Zealander, as shorthand reporter, which I held till the newspaper became defunct. I had one other engagement previous to my present occupation.

I married in 1865, the daughter of a respectable settler who holds a good position in society, and a man of considerable property. My wife's maiden name was Ellen Nicholls, (a Cornish family)—she makes me a good wife, the only falt she has, is a quick temper, very high spirited and a great screw, but a first-class housekeeper, her health has greatly improved, and we are both very comfortable.

My engagements at the present time are very numerous—being connected with the Daily Southern Cross as shorthand reporter and subeditor (pro tem). I am employed preparing a new work for the Press entitled the Miners Guide and Pocket Companion with Plans of the Gold Fields, price 10/6. this is my first attempt to write a book, and from the great number of orders for copies that have been received I feel sure that with regard to the pecuniary return, it will be a success. Captain Hutton, the Government Geologist, has undertaken the revising of my work previous to its going to press. I will send you a copy when published. I intend to produce another and larger edition towards the close of the year, which will include the newly opened Gold Fields, which are not yet developed. I find it very difficult to obtain first class litterature in Auckland, the chief expense of the work, has been the high price I have had to pay for Scientific Books—in my letter to Dr. Kittermaster[4] I requested him to procure the following works for me, which cannot be procured in New Zealand (viz.) Dr. Ure's, Dictionary of Science, Arts, Mining, etc. (1868), Käustel on Mining and Machinery used in quartz crushing

3. Edward Clarke Jr. (b. 1838), eldest son of GE's sister Chrissey.

4. James Kittermaster M.D. (1790?–1877) of Meriden.

mills (1867 or 8), J. A. Phillips on Mining and Metallurgy (1868) the above works are published by E. and A, Spon, London, not knowing your address I could not write to you, but said in my letter that perhaps you would undertake to procure the books, being in London and connected with publishers could obtain them at a reduction upon the retail price. I shall remit the cost upon receipt of the books.

I have repeatedly made inquiries about my relatives both at Griffe and elsewhere but have never heard from any of them; Emily promised to answer as many letters as I could write, I have sent her one each month it is now some months since I heard from her; she has never replied to my invitation to come out here. I offered to pay £50 towards her outfit. Mr. Buchanan[5] of Nuneaton informed me that for the present Emily did not wish to accept my offer, she was very comfortable at Miss Crockett's, Lichfield. I do not like her being a dependent upon any one whilst I have the means to make her comfortable. I understand she is very clever, and does not wish to be away from her books, she thinks that we have no intellectual society out here—if this is her excuse, she is very much mistaken —for my friend Mrs. Edward Rumsey, the Great Architect's wife, is a match for any one, and will, if you are in conversation, soon see what extent of knowledge you possess, Mrs. R—— has visited most of the Continental cities and is a thorough linguist. She would just suit you, it is a pleasure to be in her society. I have had 15 months training, so can speak from experience. I do not attend regularly, but have given satisfaction during the time I have had her three sons under my tuition. I have had to study to gain my present position, but I do not regret the many sleepless nights that I have passed over books and papers upon scientific subjects— Captain Hutton and Dr. Maunsell[6] have greatly assisted me. I have a series of articles to write upon the Great Question of Education in New Zealand which has been much neglected, in fact the poor are left without any means of educating their children. I do remember the time when you visited my poor Mother at Attleborough.[7] I did not know your address, otherwise I should have sent a photograph, will shortly send one of myself and wife. My hair is turning grey in many places, and I am only 30, it must be anxiety and hard study that has caused it to do so. I detest low society, and am never so happy as when shut up in my study, or in one of the Libraries. I very seldom read a novel (but I have read most of yours); in fact my time is fully occupied. I shall order your Long Poem. Mr. Wayte, the only pub-

5. Charles Buchanan, attorney, Nuneaton.
6. Robert Maunsell (1810–94), LL.D. Trinity College, Dublin, was Vicar of St. Mary's and Archdeacon of Auckland 1865–82.
7. In December 1853.

31 July 1868 423

lisher in Auckland is bringing out my work—it will be bound in cloth.

Dr. Kittermaster often writes to me,—his letters are a great comfort to me. Mr. Buchanan is a regular correspondent. Miss Smith, Mrs. B's. sister is very ill—so is Mr. Greenway of Attleborough Hall—I have met a Mr. Kirk formerly of Coventry who knew Grandpapa—he is Curator at the Museum and an active member of the Provincial Council. I have made inquiries about my brother Charley, the last I heard of him was that he held an engagement in Sydney. I believe he arrived in New South Wales immediately after I left for Auckland—he has never written to me, but I have addressed a letter to Sydney for him. From what Dr. Kittermaster said in his last letter, I think Charley must be in England—the words of the Doctor are "Charlie was with us last week, he was at Meriden. He promised to write but have not heard from him—my best wishes are for his welfare. My sincere regards to him." I cannot understand this extract, and what puzzles me more is that Mr. Buchanan who is a constant correspondent of the Doctor writes for information about my brother.

A very rich gold field has been discovered in the Waicatto about 120 miles from Auckland—even promises to excel the Thames Quartz reefs, which are said to be the richest yet discovered in the world. One Claim (Hunts) has produced 20,000 ounces of gold, another 3,000, several 1,000 and upwards all within twelve months. I am interested in several Claims. I purchased a share in one of the old Claims for £40—now it is worth £600—in another I have cleared £90 from my purchase. I am now interested in several good Claims yielding on an average of 8 ounces to the ton of quartz. There are more than 20,000 miners at the Thames alone. Shortland the principal township a year ago was a large peach grove—now a large flourishing town, with banks and public buildings, the town extends upwards of 4 miles along the sea shore, the principal reefs are near the beach, the hills are very steep and lofty, one in particular is 10,000 feet above the level of the sea, and Claims all the way up to the top. Good Machinery for crushing the quartz is much wanted. The Gold bearing range of hills, from the sea remind you of an enormous rabbit warren, the drivers and miners moving in and out, often remind me of old times when I used to watch the rabbits in Packington Park.

Sir George Bowen[8] is very much liked—he is very popular—he has a very difficult task to perform with the natives, now that we are to have another war—fighting has commenced about 100 miles from Auckland, —they threaten the Thames, and only wait for the Thames tribes to join them. I feel sure that they will protect the diggers, who pay them for their

8. Sir George Ferguson Bowen (1821–99), Governor of New Zealand 1867–72.

Miners Rights, and the native is too fond of the Rum bottle and money to quarrel with the Miner, they have received upwards of £10,000 this year as rent for the Gold Field at the Thames and Tapu[9] Creek. The New Zealand native[1] is far superior in every respect to the lower class of Europeans, and his honour is unimpeachable. I have always found them a kind, straightforward people if fairly dealt with—but the Government has treated them shamefully.

It is a source of grief to the members of the Church of England to hear that it is being mutilated at home[2]—what is now being done in the Imperial Parliament at home, may be compared to a wedge driven into a log after the first stroke of the axe, it will eventually split up and finally fall to pieces by repeated blows. Without a State Church the English Constitution cannot stand—it is also a disgrace to Christians of all denominations to see men tampering with religion, for without the Established Church is supported by Governmental aid, we shall be in danger of persecution and bloodshed as in Queen Mary's reign. The *Jew*, who is at the head of the English Government, is aware of the calamity, and wishes to prevent it—after the great Novelist's[3] conduct in the House can we do otherwise than respect his sect—and dispise our own. Gladstone, is held in abhorrence in New Zealand, since he introduced his bill for the disendowment of the established church in Ireland. Fennianism has died out in New Zealand. Several persons who have been arrested are to be liberated.

We have had a very gay season. Lady Bowen mixes with all classes of society—she seems to be void of pride—and is already beloved by all. Sir George Bowen said, that the Queen could not have been received in a more brilliant style. He mixed with the natives without a guard—has gained their confidence even more than Sir George Grey[4] who had upwards of 12 wives and concubines, all natives of high caste. Sir George Grey was shamefully treated by the people of Auckland—poor man—he had many trials to contend with during his administration. The Colonial Government is composed of illiberal and for the most part illiterate men.

Please write again when you can find time—for your letters will be always welcome.—Nelly unites in love. Believe me to be Dear Aunt

Your affectionate Nephew
Edward Clarke.

P.S. Please excuse errors—for I am very tired, and have been writing all day, and have now to prepare the leading article for the Cross.

9. Taupo.
1. The Maori.
2. Gladstone's effort to disestablish the Irish Church.
3. Disraeli became Prime Minister in February 1868.
4. Sir George Grey (1812–98), Governor, 1861–67.

7 August [1868]   425

IV, 467:18   GE TO JOHN BLOCKLEY,[5]
LONDON, 6 AUGUST 1868

MS: Princeton.

The Priory, | 21. North Bank, | Regents Park.
August 6. 68.

Mrs. G. H. Lewes (George Eliot) presents her compliments to Mr. J. Blockley and begs to inform him that the songs in the "Spanish Gypsy" are about to be disposed of to a publisher who will purchase the sole right to issue them in a musical form.

IV, 467:18   CHARLES ROBERT DARWIN TO GHL,
FRESHWATER, 7 AUGUST [1868]

MS: Cambridge University Library.

Dumbola Lodge | Freshwater | Isle of Wight | August 7.

My dear Mr. Lewes

I have found very little to say, as you will soon discover; and the little is very badly said.[6]—I have not noticed what I admire, but I must be permitted to say that on the second reading I have admired the whole, *even much more* than I did the first time.

The articles strike me as *quite* excellent, and I hope they will be republished; but I fear that they will be too deep for many readers.

If I have anything to remark on any future article, I will write. Accept my cordial thanks for the kind and honouring way in which you allude to my work,[7] and for the great pleasure which I have derived from reading the whole.

---

5. John Blockley is listed in the *Post Office London Directory* for 1869 as professor of music, 2 Park Road, Haverstock Hill, N.W., and music publisher, 3 Argyll St., Oxford Street.

6. His comments are found in a draft dated 7 August 1868 published in *More Letters of Charles Darwin*, ed. Francis Darwin, 2 vols., 1903, I, 306–308. GHL gave the original notes to Elma Stuart. See VI, 322.

7. For example, "Mr. Darwin has the incomparable merit of having enlarged our conception of the conditions of existence so as to embrace *all* the factors which conduce to the result. In his luminous principle of the Struggle for Existence, and Natural Selection which such a struggle determines, we have the key to most of the problems presented by the diversities of organisms; and the Law of Adaptation, rightly conceived, furnishes the key to all organic change." (*Fortnightly*, 10 [1 July 1868], 65–66.)

Pray think a little over the verbal distinction of the action of the medium in causing variability and in leading to the persistence of the best adapted forms.[8] This surely is an important distinction; and it drives me half mad to see them brought all under one expression.

Yours very sincerely
C. Darwin.

IV, 469:1 GHL TO CHARLES ROBERT DARWIN, LONDON, 8 AUGUST 1868

MS: Cambridge University Library.

The Priory, | 21 North Bank, | Regents Park.
8th August 1868.

Dear Mr. Darwin

You can understand how deeply gratified I am by your approval, which is all the more pleasant because I have the best reasons for supposing that the articles have not been much liked by the public of the Review—the editor is urgent that they should close! I am also indebted to you for your notes and hope I may be allowed to use them in the Reprint.

As to my absurdly obscure sentence—which I see now to *be* obscure—it was meant to express a very plain position, namely that from very different starting points a similar result might be reached.[9] A pus cell or a blood corpuscle has a *genesis* wholly distinct from the forms indistingu[ish]ably similar which are produced in a viscid substance by slow imbibition—here a difference of genesis and an identity of form are demonstrable. In animal identities a like difference of origin (genesis) is conceivable.

I am not defending my phrase which will be abolished—only hinting that I *had* an idea to express.

You have no doubt seen it but if not may be interested in Kowalefsky's Memoir on the Development of Amphioxus in the St. Petersburg Academy Memoirs (tome XI, no. 4).[1] It has made me restless with desire to find

---

8. GHL distinguished between an "External or Cosmical Medium" and an "Internal or Organic Medium," which is unaffected by most changes in the external. (p. 64.)

9. "Mr. Darwin's Hypotheses," *Fortnightly*, 10 (July 1868), p. 498: "The action of the Medium on the Organism is assuredly a potent factor which Biology cannot ignore: but the Organism itself is a factor, and according to its nature the influence of the Medium is defined."

1. Aleksandr Onufrievich Kovalevsky (1840–1901), Russian zoologist and embryologist, advanced the first acceptable theory of line of descent from invertebrates to vertebrates.

[*18? August 1868*] 427

myself somewhere on the Mediterranean coast with a supply of embryos! His observations are all in favor of your view and against mine.—which is not pleasant (for me). Believe me

Yours very sincerely
G. H. Lewes.

Charles Darwin Esq.

IV, 471:1 GE TO EMILY DAVIES, LONDON, [18? AUGUST 1868]

MS: Girton College. *Envelope:* Miss Davies | 17 Cunningham Place | N.W. *Postmark:* LONDON N.W | 2 | AU 18 | 68.

The Priory, | 21. North Bank, | Regents Park.
Tuesday.

My dear Miss Davies

Your paper[2] seems to me excellent, and I go heartily along with it. Mr. Lewes read it before I did, and he said at once that you had made a mistake in giving them long quotations. They lengthen the paper so as to put it out of the question for publication in a magazine, and even for the purpose of reading aloud he thinks you would make the whole thing more effective by summarizing (briefly) the testimony contained in the extracts.

I think he is right. Long quotations always break the current which should carry the reader or hearer along. It is part of good artistic contrivance to get rid of them if possible. Still, I see clearly how valuable the evidence of those official males is, and the necessity of somehow or other giving emphasis to that evidence. Perhaps on reconsideration you will see some mode of statement possible, that will be at once brief and impressive.

I had made up my mind to return your paper yesterday, but was hindered by a mistake as to an engagement. I hope I did not keep it so long as to affect any intention of yours.

Always sincerely yours
M. E. Lewes.

2. See IV, 468, n. 8.

IV, 473:18 GE TO MME EUGÈNE BODICHON, LONDON, [SEPTEMBER 1868]

MS: Berg Collection, New York Public Library.

The Priory, | 21. North Bank, | Regents Park.
Saturday.

My dear Barbara

The picture looks glorious this morning, now there is a better light in the room, and it will be the cause of many happy thoughts to me about many things—beginning with your sweet friendship. Also, the plums were nice yesterday, and I am looking forward to the figs and peaches. Grace[3] begged me to look at her herbs this morning—your bunches which she hung up proudly.

O dear, I know only one thing in the world better than being loved and petted—and that is, loving others perfectly, without guile and without one mite of bitterness.

You see, my thanks consist in trying to let you know how much delight your goodness gives me. I see many, many things in the picture this morning, which I did not see yesterday, and I dare say I shall see more to-morrow.

Ever thine
Marian.

IV, 473:18 GE TO EMILY DAVIES, LONDON, 10 SEPTEMBER [1868]

MS: Girton College. *Envelope:* Miss Davies | 17 Cunningham Place | N.W. *Postmark: illegible.*

The Priory, | 21. North Bank, | Regents Park.
September 10.

My dear Miss Davies

About your paper, Mr. Lewes recommends that your Brother[4] should write to the Editor of the Cornhill[5]—or to Mr. G. Smith, if he knows him—stating that you have such a paper in readiness, and begging a direct answer as to whether it can be inserted by November.

For personal reasons Mr. Lewes can have no communication with the

---

3. Grace Lee, GE's cook.
4. John Llewellyn Davies (1826–1916), liberal reformer, Rector of Christ Church, Marylebone, 1856–89.
5. Edward Dutton Cook (1829–83).

Cornhill people, but if you fail with them, he will be happy to send your paper to Mr. Trollope.[6]

A young physician,[7] an Oxford man of scientific bent, who came to see us on Sunday spoke of Miss Becker's paper[8] as "brilliant," and thought it likely to do good. This, for your consolation.

I am rather a wretch, just now, or I would have returned your "Student's Mag."[9]

We go to Leeds on Monday.

In haste, ever yours
M. E. Lewes.

IV, 477:1   GHL TO EDWARD, LORD LYTTON, LONDON, [OCTOBER 1868]

MS: Lady Hermione Cobbold.

The Priory, | 21. North Bank, | Regents Park.
Monday.

My dear Lord Lytton

The remarkable play[1] you were good enough to send me was all the more welcome because hygienic conditions prevent my risking a visit to the theatre, (although the enthusiasm of some of my friends tempted me in that direction) and because it brought the twofold advantage of letting me see Macready, and *not* see Bandmann, in the part of Vyvyan. The advantages of stage representation to a work constructed for the stage are doubtless immense—but there is also a terrible drawback in the dense

---

6. Anthony Trollope was editor of *St. Paul's Magazine.* Emily Davies's "Some Account of a Proposed New College for Women" was published in the *Contemporary Review,* 9 (December 1868), 540–559.

7. Thomas Clifford Allbutt. See IV, 471, n. 7. GHL had met him at Oxford, but he was a Cambridge graduate.

8. Lydia Ernestine Becker (1827–90), women's suffragist, contributed a paper on "Some Supposed Differences in the Minds of Men and Women" to the British Association at Norwich in 1868.

9. *The London Student,* 1 (June 1868), with Emily Davies's article "Special Systems of Education for Women," pp. 131–142. "That the greatest of female novelists should have taken the precaution to assume a masculine *nom de plume* for the express purpose of securing their work against being measured by a class standard, is significant of the feeling entertained by women." (p. 136.)

1. Bulwer Lytton's *The Rightful Heir,* produced at the Lyceum 3 October 1868 with the leading role of Captain Vyvyan played by a German actor named Bandmann, described as "noisy in speech and vehement in gesture." (*Athenaeum,* 10 October 1868, pp. 470–471.) It was rewritten by Lytton from his earlier version, *The Sea Captain, or, the Birth-right,* produced at the Haymarket 31 October 1839 with Macready as the captain, there called Norman.

stupidity of actors, few of whom nowadays have the faintest notion of a verse and still fewer of a natural expression. I am not sure therefore that I did not enjoy the reading of your play even more than I should have enjoyed the performance. At any rate, with all due deference to magnificent critics who having never written plays themselves are in a position of lofty superiority to those who have, I affirm that the Rightful Heir would have made the reputation of a lesser man. You must pay the penalty (a glorious penalty) of former successes!

Yours very truly
G. H. Lewes.

IV, 477:1 ANTHONY TROLLOPE TO GHL, WALTHAM CROSS, 3 OCTOBER 1868

MS: Yale. *Published: The Letters of Anthony Trollope*, ed. B. A. Booth, 1951, pp. 230–231.

Waltham House, | Waltham Cross.
October 3. 1868.

Dear Lewes.

Thanks. The paper[2] has not come to me, but has no doubt gone to the office. I will order a proof to be sent to you as soon as I get there. I have no doubt all good smokers will express their lasting gratitude in some substantial form;—a pyramid of cigar ashes—or a mausoleum for, long-delayed, future use, constructed of old pipe stems and tobacco stoppers. I will call up and discuss it when I have read it.

In regard to the Spanish Gypsy my regret is that the poet departed in portions of her work from the dramatic form. The departure would seem to imply,—which is certainly not the case,—that she had lacked power to say all her story in that which is certainly the most efficacious and I think the most perfect form of expression. I think too that the strictly dramatic portions of the poem are stronger than those in which she recedes to narrative,—as would be naturally the case.

Fedalma, Zarca and Juan are perfect. Sylva, no doubt intentionally, is so much inferior as a creature to these, that the character, and words attributed to the character, are less striking.

Yours always
A. T.

2. "The Dangers and Delights of Tobacco," *St. Paul's*, 3 (November 1868), 172–184. Trollope edited the magazine from October 1867 to June 1870.

IV, 478:18 GE TO MRS. WATHEN MARK WILKS CALL, LONDON, [12? OCTOBER 1868]

MS: Berg Collection, New York Public Library.

The Priory, | 21. North Bank, | Regents Park.
Monday morning.

My dear Mrs. Call

I wish I could thank you and Mr. Call for the precious gift which Mr. Lewes brought home from you the other day, so as to represent all I feel about it. That can hardly be—for I should have to explain many inward conditions of mine which make me peculiarly susceptible to such marks of kindness. I must be satisfied with telling you that I enjoy not only the possession of the gift; I enjoy also the feeling of gratitude towards two friends who have had me in their minds as worthy of their regard.

We are going "on the tramp" again for a week or so. Always, with keen memory

Yours affectionately
M. E. Lewes.

IV, 478:18 THORNTON ARNOTT LEWES TO GHL, WAKKERSTROOM, 12 OCTOBER 1868

MS: Yale.

Fall of the Assagai Nr Wakkerstroom | October 12. 1868.

Dear Pater

You will doubtless be surprised at not having heard from either of us before, as I promised to write when we came back from our buffalo hunt in the Amaswazi country, but when we came back we heard on the road of a speculation, which had all the elements of success and which if carried out, would have made writing unnecessary. You would have seen me walk into the Priory to communicate viva voce, what this letter must now do. This speculation was as follows: When we went in hunting we took as waggon driver and companion interpreter etc. a young Dutchman named Christian Duprez. In the hunting veldt, we dropped across an old Kaffir of his, who had just come from the country of a friend of his, a chief named Maguta, who having lots of ivory and no blankets wanted to exchange the former for the latter, and had told this Kaffir (Zwartland by name) to go to the white man's country and get some man to fetch blankets to exchange for his ivory at the rate of 1 blanket (value 12/-) for 1 elephant tusk (value from £15 to 50). We of course jumped at the opportunity; directly we got home on the 5th of July, I rode down to Ladismith to see about getting the requisite blankets, and when I had got them, we went down in the waggon and fetched them. Then on the 9th of September we started, taking Zwartland for guide. Everything went well, till we got to the Amaswazi capital, where we first heard that 3 months before somebody had gone in to Maguta's for ivory; this rather frightened us, but Kaffirs are such horrid liars, that we only half believed it, and pushed onto the next Kraal, where we heard that the white man had gone to hunt, and that his waggon was standing this side of the first big river, the Umcomogazi. This reassured us. Bertie and Christian Zwartland and another of our Kaffirs and 3 that we hired at the Kraal, started each with a bundle of blankets for Maguta's leaving me to take charge of the waggon. We could not take the waggon any further or we should have lost the oxen by the tsetse or poisonous fly. Guess my disgust and astonishment upon seeing them, after 5 days absence return *with* the blankets! They had gone onto the Umcomogazi, where they found the waggon of the white men, who turned out to be 2 young fellows from Natal, who, we knew, were aware of the existence of the ivory, and had been aware of it for the last 3 years, without ever making any attempt to get it. Now curiously enough they had slipped away out of Natal without even their nearest neighbours, even their very brother knowing that they were gone, so quiet had they kept it, so that our intense astonishment upon finding the men, we believed snug at home, on ahead of us may easier be fancied than described.

The consequence is that instead of having money in our pockets, to enable me to go to England as we had intended, *why*, I will tell you farther on, we are on our last legs. Our hunting trip was a failure, we had heavy expenses, and the buffalo skins we got fetched literally nothing, and the consequences of the trip: 9 days trekking with the oxen through a country without a mouthful of grass, were that a lot of our oxen died from exhaustion. Not daunted by this, having the ivory in view we scraped together every head of cattle we could muster, sold them at a fearful sacrifice: oxen that had cost us £6.10, and £5, for £3 each etc. etc. merely to raise the wind, and to enable us to get sufficient credit, so that by paying part cash and getting the remainder on credit, we obtained the necessary blankets, beads etc. necessary for the Kaffirs and our outfit for ourselves. Besides this, there was our driver Christian who had told us about the ivory, and to whom we were going to give a share, which we changed to giving him £15 per month, as he is poor, has a wife and family to keep and preferred a small certainty to a large uncertainty, although

12 October 1868 433

the chances were every way in favour of success. So that what with Kaffirs we hired etc. etc. our expenses have been very heavy. We therefore write now to ask you to *lend* us £200, for one year. It is not that our debts amount to that, about £120 or £130 would cover them, but to enable us once more to start, cash in hand, we should like a surplus.

The fact is this: Zwartland has gone to Maguta's to tell him that he has behaved very badly, sending him to fetch white men, and then trading his ivory away with other people, that we shall be in again in the beginning of May (the elephant country where Maguta lives is uninhabitable by white men from November to May owing to the fever) and that he is to keep all the ivory his hunters shoot for us. We have also hired Kaffir hunters to shoot elephants for us during the summer, supplying them with guns, powder, bullets and caps, so that when we go in again, we shall find a lot of ivory ready for us.

Our plan is therefore to start again from here on the 20th of April, get to Magutas, trade what ivory he has, collect what our hunters have got, hire a lot more, about 20 Kaffir hunters, and stay in ourselves shooting elephants and hippopotomuses till August, when the grass between Maguta's and our farm will be good and the oxen be able to trek.

One lives and learns. We should have done this now, only we were too late in the season and these Natal men have got all the hunting Kaffirs for the season. However next year we shall take good care to be in before them. In the first place we are much nearer, in the second they don't know that we know anything about the ivory.

You will now understand what we want the balance of the £200 for, to get blankets, powder, lead, guns, and provisions for the 4 months. If therefore you can oblige us with the loan we shall be very much obliged indeed, as it will be a great help, and we will repay it when we come back from our great trip next year.

So much for that: the next I am sorry to say is again a demand for money but of such vital importance that I do not hesitate in applying to you. I had hoped to have been able to come home to England with the proceeds of the trip but "l'homme propose et Dieu dispose." The fact is this, that with this stone in the kidney and other internal complications, for there is something serious besides the stone, I am gradually wasting away. I eat almost nothing, nothing but delicacies tempt me, and those we can't afford. I can't do a stroke of work of any sort, I can hardly stoop to touch the ground, I can't sit up for half an hour, all I can do is lie down, then get up and walk about for half an hour, then lie down again. Every evening about sundown when the paroxysms come on, I can hardly turn myself over, and if I want to sit up, I must push myself up with my hands, from my shoulder blades downwards I am powerless; and I have a sort of shooting compression of the chest, which makes breathing difficult, and makes me shout with pain. And as this lasts usually for 2 to 3 hours, and sometimes there is more or less pain all night long, so that I get no sleep, and sometimes I have slight attacks in the day time—you can fancy that my life is not a pleasant one. In fact if I were 50 instead of 24, I should have quietly walked some fine day over our waterfall; but while there is youth there is hope; and I hope and trust that a trip to England, to consult one or two of the best doctors may do me good; the change and sea voyage would probably do me good, but at any rate I should like to know from the best medical authorities, whether any thing can be done for me, whether I am to remain a cripple all my life, in short, what my future is to be. I know this trip, seeing physicians etc, perhaps undergoing some operation will cost a great deal of money, but—que voulez vous. It is my last chance in life, and you are the only person I can apply to, so I don't hesitate to make the application. Bertie, who would write but that he is laid up with rheumatic toothache (all his teeth are rotting away as Lintol predicted) is entirely of the same opinion as myself, for I am no earthly good on the farm as I am, I only take a deal of waiting on.

Hoping to hear from you at once, with love to Mutter, Grandmamma and everybody else, I remain, Dear Pater[3]

Your affectionate Son
Thornton A. Lewes.

IV, 478:18 GE TO EMILY DAVIES, LONDON, 13 OCTOBER 1868

MS: Girton College. *Envelope:* Miss Davies | 17 Cunningham Place | N.W.

The Priory, | 21. North Bank, | Regents Park.
October 13. 68.

My dear Miss Davies

I am ashamed of keeping your "London Student" any longer. So I send it, though I had waited to do so till I could put a little prayer to you to come and see me for an hour. But I have been ailing lately, and so we make use of these delicious autumnal days to walk into the country. This week I dare not say that we shall be at home any afternoon, but do try and come next week if you are not too full of other good works.

Ever yours sincerely
M. E. Lewes.

3. "Letter from Thornie made me very miserable. Went into the city to send him £250." (GHL Diary, 6 January 1869.)

IV, 479:6 GE TO HENRY CROMPTON,
LONDON, 17 OCTOBER [1868]

MS: Berg Collection, New York Public Library.

The Priory, | 21. North Bank, | Regents Park.
17 October.

Dear Mr. Crompton
 Thanks for your remembrance of me. I would gladly accept your kind offer,[4] if I were not obliged to economize my strength. But I have already the prospect of one séance in hot air and gas light for next week, and I dare not venture on a second.
                                                         Yours always sincerely
                                                              M. E. Lewes.

Harry Crompton, Esq.

IV, 483:1 GE TO EMILY DAVIES,
LONDON, 3 NOVEMBER 1868

MS: Girton College. *Envelope:* Miss Davies | 17 Cunningham Place | N.W. *Postmark:* LONDON N.W | Z | NOV 4 | 68.

The Priory, | 21. North Bank, | Regents Park.
November 3. 1868.

My dear Miss Davies
 I have promised some friends of mine—Mr. and Mrs. Benzon, 10 Palace Gardens, Kensington—that they shall have a Prospectus of the Women's College. They are very rich, and I have been exhorting them to consider whether they ought not to give some of their wealth to the College.[5]
 May I beg of you to send them a Prospectus?
                                                         Ever yours sincerely
                                                              M. E. Lewes.

4. Perhaps to go with him to a lecture at the Postivist Society, of which he was an ardent supporter.

5. GE's appeal seems to have been unsuccessful.

IV, 487:23 GHL TO CHARLES ROBERT DARWIN, LONDON, 12 NOVEMBER 1868

MS: Cambridge University Library.

The Priory, | 21. North Bank, | Regents Park.
12 November 1868.

My dear Mr. Darwin

It was a serious disappointment to me to find on my return home last night that you should have chosen the Sunday we were away for giving me that opportunity I have long desired but could not hope for of seeing you in the flesh. Are you still in town—or likely to be—and may I call on you some day? I promise to be very moderate in my indulgence, knowing that your health does not permit of social excitement. But to see you for half an hour will suffice for Memory, and as the best part of our existence is subjective

> "One crowded hour of glorious life
> Is worth an age without a name."[6]

I presume you have seen Weismann's Inaugural Address? If not I will post it to you. Haeckel has just sent me his new work.[7]

Faithfully yours
G. H. Lewes.

IV, 487:23 CHARLES ROBERT DARWIN TO GHL, LONDON, [13 NOVEMBER 1868]

MS: Cambridge University Library.

6. Queen Anne St. | Friday 9° P.M.

My dear Mr. Lewes

Your note to Down has just reached me.—I am sure I have quite as strong a wish to see you, as you can have to see me.—I have to call on Sir C. Lyell tomorrow morning and sit with him at breakfast at $9\frac{1}{2}$ and shall try and stay only $\frac{3}{4}$ of hour; and then, as I think you will excuse so

---

6. From an anonymous "Poem Written during the Last German War," published in the *Edinburgh Bee*, 12 October 1791, and used by Scott as an epigraph to ch. 34 of *Old Mortality*.

7. Ernst Heinrich Haeckel, *Natürliche Schöpfungsgeschichte*, Jena, 1868. GHL's copy is at Dr. Williams's Library.

[*17 November 1868*] 437

early a call, I will come on to you, and so shall be there at 10½—to 11. But I must just add that my movements are always doubtful and if I do not appear by 11. you will understand that my tiresome head has failed me.—

I am engaged on Sunday morning, otherwise I would not have proposed to call at such a time, and we go home quite early on Monday: almost every afternoon I am good for nothing in this world.

Forgive these tedious particulars—

Yours very sincerely
C. Darwin.

I hope this note will reach you before I call.

IV, 488:16 GHL TO CHARLES ROBERT DARWIN, LONDON, [17 NOVEMBER 1868]

MS: Cambridge University Library.

The Priory, | 21. North Bank, | Regents Park.
Tuesday.

Dear Mr. Darwin

I wish very much to belong to the 'Linnæan Society' for the sake of its Library; and under the august shadow of your name I should perhaps not be objected to. If you have no objection to propose me, Busk offers to second the proposal.

My disreputable German was better than I feared and not only has he failed to 'shoot my duck' he has failed even to see it flying; so I am at ease on that score, and the labor of years is not yet proved to have been misdirected.

By the way, do you think Sir Charles Lyell would mind setting forth his objections to my papers in the shape of Notes? When I recast the papers into a book I should be glad to have everything that tells against them distinctly before me. That indeed was one of my objects in publishing the papers which were only intended as a sort of nucleus for the future book.

You made Mrs. Lewes and myself very happy by your visit[8] and we only hope your head was none the worse for it. Believe me,

Faithfully yours
G. H. Lewes.

8. Darwin's call, 14 November, is not noted in GE's or GHL's Journal.

IV, 488:16 CHARLES ROBERT DARWIN TO GHL,
DOWNE, 18 NOVEMBER 1868

MS: Cambridge University Library. Only signature and postscript are in Darwin's hand.

Down. | Bromley. | Kent. S.E.
November 18 1868.

My dear Mr. Lewes

I shall be delighted to propose you for the Linn[ean] Soc[iety]. As Mr. Busk[9] is familiar with what is usually done will you ask him to fill up the printed form with your claims for admission, and second it, and be so kind as to forward it to me. I will then return it to the Society or to you as I may be directed. I think you will not repent of joining the Society which deserves patronage.

As Sir C. Lyell[1] is very much engaged, not to mention his advanced years, I am very doubtful whether he will feel inclined to put his remarks on paper, though he was certainly very much interested by your articles. I will however write to him by today's post and hint your request, leaving it quite open to him to comply or not.

As for my own opinion I have no objection to your "Germinal membrane" developing 1000 forms of life, if you will allow me to kill all in the course of time except as many as there are leading types.[2] I do not think I shall ever be convinced that organisms belonging to the same type, having a similar embryological development or homological structure, and graduating into each other with no very wide intervals, are the offspring of primordially distinct so-called creations. ⟨After the most careful study⟩ All the arguments from Geographical Distribution, Geological Successions or mutual affinities, which arguments appear now to be fairly harmonious, would be greatly invalidated, as it appears to me, if your views were admitted.[3] This I think is Lyell's main objection.

9. George Busk (1807–86) became a Fellow of the Linnean Society in 1846 and Under-(Zoological) Secretary in 1857.

1. Sir Charles Lyell (1797–1875), the founder of modern geology.

2. GHL wrote: "May we not rather assume that the earth at the dawn of Life was like a vast germinal membrane, every slightly diversified point producing its own vital form.... The point raised is the immense improbability of organic substance having been evolved only in one microscopic spot; if it were evolved at more than one spot, and under slightly varying conditions, there would necessarily have arisen in these earliest formations the *initial* diversities which afterwards determined the essential independence and difference of organisms." (*Fortnightly*, 10 [1 November 1868], 494.)

3. Cf. *The Physical Basis of Mind*, 1877, pp. 111–113.

[*November? 1868*]

I *thoroughly* enjoyed my hour's talk with you and Mrs. Lewes—and I remain

Yours very sincerely
Ch. Darwin.

P.S. There is much truth in what Professor Weismann writes me, that the nature of the organism which is acted on is as important as, or more important a factor in the resultant variability, than the conditions of life. —This I have also insisted on in very strong language and shown to be the case in my last book.—Now if two distinct independently ⟨created⟩ produced primordial organisms, were exposed to precisely similar conditions, they would vary differently, besides inheriting differently, and therefore I cannot believe that they would be developed to form members of the same type or group.—All the curious cases insisted on by Fritz Müller of the same end being generally analogous and not strictly homologous structures, seem to me to point to a similar conclusion.

IV, 491:17 GHL TO GEORGE BUSK, LONDON, [NOVEMBER? 1868]

MS: Yale. *Endorsed:* Nov. 1868.

The Priory, | 21. North Bank, | Regents Park.

My dear Sir

Mr. Darwin says if you will be good enough to fill up the paper for my nomination he will sign the proposal and return it to you or to whom ever it may concern. Will you kindly take this trouble?

Yours faithfully
G. H. Lewes.

I remember your offer to second the proposal.

IV, 491:17 GHL TO HENRY CHARLTON BASTIAN, LONDON, [NOVEMBER? 1868]

MS: Nuneaton Public Library.

The Priory, | 21. North Bank, | Regents Park.
Saturday.

My dear Bastian

Your paper seems to me not only valuable in itself but one eminently adapted to the 'Fortnightly' were it not that both editor and readers might be repelled by the too technical nature of the introduction; my advice is either that you rewrite the first eight pages with a view to an ignorant audience—or perhaps safer still—omit this introduction and begin at once with the question of language.⁵ I send you back the paper for your decision on this point, and will gladly forward it when revised to Morley.

Shall I write to him at once saying there is such a paper to be had if he has room for it? In case he says 'yes' you could send it him direct when finished. In case he says 'no' you can try elsewhere. I would send it to Trollope for you if you liked.

Ever yours truly
G. H. Lewes.

IV, 500:22 GE TO EMILY DAVIES, LONDON, 30 DECEMBER 1868

MS: Girton College. *Envelope:* Miss Davies | 17 Cunningham Place N.W.

The Priory, | 21. North Bank, | Regents Park.
December 30. 68.

My dear Miss Davies

It was a very unpleasant chance to me that I missed you a second time when you were so good as to come to me. Pray do not be discouraged from another kind effort: it remains true that I am hardly ever away from home *after* 4 o'clock.

Next Wednesday, indeed, we are going to take a little boy to see a Pantomime,⁶ and that dissipation will make us late in our afternoon absence.

I was not able to get to Suffolk Street⁷ as I should have liked to do, for during half that week I was not well enough to look and listen. Always

Yours most sincerely
M. E. Lewes.

Miss Davies

5. "The Physiology of Thinking," *Fortnightly,* 11 (1 January 1869), 57–71, begins with the question of language.

6. GE and GHL took Mrs. Burne-Jones and her son Philip to the pantomime Wednesday, 13 January 1869. (GHL Diary.)

7. The United University Club, 1 Suffolk Street, Pall Mall.

IV, 502:7 GHL TO JAMES REDPATH,[8] LONDON [1868?]

MS: Huntington Library.

The Priory, | 21. North Bank, | Regents Park.
Wednesday.

My dear Sir

Mrs. Lewes begs me to thank you for the kind expression of your letter of the 7th and to say that the rumour of her intended visit to America is entirely without foundation. She could not be induced to give readings anywhere.

Yours truly
G. H. Lewes.

James Redpath, Esq.

8. James Redpath (1833–91) established the Boston Lyceum Bureau in 1868. (C. F. Homer, *Life of James Redpath*, 1926.)

Thornie's Death

1869 January	GHL working at *Problems of Life and Mind*.
1869 Feb. 19	GE begins to plan *Middlemach*.
1869 March–May	GE and GHL in Italy.
1869 March 20–25	Visit the Tom Trollopes in Florence.
1869 May 5	Return to the Priory.
1869 May 8	Thornie arrives from Natal, seriously ill.
1869 May 19	GE sells American rights of works to Fields.
1869 August 2	GE begins Vincy-Featherstone part of *Middlemarch*.
1869 August 21	Discusses *The Mill on the Floss* with Emily Davies.
1869 October 19	Thornie dies.
1869 Oct. 23—Nov. 13	GE and GHL at Limpsfield.
1869 Nov. 19	GE and GHL give their books to Girton College.
1870 March 7	*Middlemarch* "creeps on."
1870 April	GE and GHL visit the Lyttons in Vienna.
1870 May–July	GHL advises Lytton about his poems.
1870 June–July	GE and GHL at Cromer, Harrogate, and Whitby.
1870 July	Mrs. Burne-Jones and children join them at Whitby.
1870 August 21	GE declines to write for Scribner's.
1870 December 2	GE experimenting with "Miss Brooke."
1870 December 10	GHL's mother, Mrs. Willim, dies.
1870 Dec. 20–28	GE and GHL visit Mme Bodichon at Ryde.

V, 5:1 GHL TO THOMAS ADOLPHUS TROLLOPE, LONDON, 14 JANUARY 1869

Text: T.A. Trollope, *What I Remember*, 2d ed., 2 vols., 1887, II, 317–318.

The Priory, | 21. North Bank, | Regents Park.
January 14. 1869.

Dear T. T.

We did not meet in Germany because our plans were altogether changed. We passed all the time in the Black Forest, and came home through the Oberland. I did write to Salzburg however, and perhaps the letter is still there; but there was nothing in it.

You know how fond we are of you, and the pleasure it always gives us to get a glimpse of you. (Not that we have not also very pleasant associations with your wife,[9] but she is as yet stranger to us of course.) But we went away in search of complete repose. And in the Black Forest there was not a soul to speak to, and we liked it so much as to stay on there.

We contemplate moving southwards in the spring, and if we go to Italy and come *near* Florence, we shall assuredly make a *détour* and come and see you. Polly wants to see Arezzo and Perugia. And I suppose we can still get a *vetturino* to take us that way to Rome? Don't want railways, if to be avoided. I don't think we can get away before March, for my researches are so absorbing, that, if health holds out, I must go on, if not, we shall pack up earlier. The worst of Lent is that one gets no theatres, and precisely because we never go to the theatre in London, we hugely enjoy it abroad. Yesterday we took the child of a friend of ours[10] to a morning performance of the pantomime, and are utterly knocked up in consequence. Somehow or other abroad the theatre agrees with us. Polly sends the kindest remembrances to you and your wife. Whenever you want anything done in London, consider me an idle man.

Ever yours faithfully
G. H. Lewes.

9. Trollope married his second wife Frances Eleanor Ternan 29 October 1866.

10. "Mrs. Burne-Jones and her son Philip (1861–1926) lunched with us and went to morning performance of *Pantomime*." (GHL Diary, 13 January 1869.)

V, 11:30 GHL TO MRS. SHIRLEY BROOKS, LONDON, [FEBRUARY 1869]

MS: Berg Collection, New York Public Library.

The Priory, | 21. North Bank, | Regents Park.

Dear Mrs. Brooks

I wrote no pamphlet about Hofwyl, only a letter in the Pall Mall saying what I may say to you, that had I fifty sons, I would send them all there. My youngest boy was very delicate when he went and came away as strong as a ploughboy. The physical advantages of Hofwyl are great, but I regard the moral advantages as still greater.

Enclosed is a prospectus. I would call at once, but my mother's illness[11] absorbs me just now. I will however seize an early opportunity of calling,[1] though indeed all is said in the two words above. Believe me

Yours faithfully
G. H. Lewes.

V, 17:6 GHL TO WILLIAM BELL SCOTT, LONDON, [20 FEBRUARY 1869]

MS: Princeton. *Endorsed:* 1869.

The Priory, | 21. North Bank, | Regents Park.

Saturday.

My dear Scott

Ever since we came to live in London Mrs. Lewes has been forced to adopt the rigorous rule of not going out, nor returning calls, except to friends living out of town. On no other condition would life have been practicable, (that is peaceful and workful) for us. This has also made me adopt the same rule, though less absolutely, and as I do *some*times make exceptions I cannot refuse an old friend like you, so I shall gladly come to you on the 25th.

Yours faithfully
G. H. Lewes.

---

11. Mrs. Willim fell ill near the end of January, and GHL went to see her every day.

1. "Went to Mother. Called on Mrs. Brooks about Hofwyl." (GHL Diary, 15 February 1869.)

V, 20:25 GHL TO THOMAS ADOLPHUS TROLLOPE,
LONDON, 28 FEBRUARY 1869

MS: Princeton.

The Priory, | 21. North Bank, | Regents Park.
28 February 69.

Dear Trollope

Blackwood is in Edinburgh but I have written him a letter which must bring him to book.[2] He's a dreadful correspondent because he will do everything himself and has more than one man can get through.

Touching our visit to Florence you may be sure we should not lightly forego such a pleasure. We start tomorrow[3] and unless we are recalled by my mother's health we calculate being with you about the end of March, but we shall give due warning of our arrival. Pigott was with us when your letter came and his kind eyes look[ed] kinder when I read the pleasant sentence about Bice's[4] improvement.

We both look forward to this holiday and 'languish for the purple seas.'[5] Though the high winds now howl a threat of anything but pleasant crossing to Calais. Che! Che! One must pay for one's pleasure.

With both of our warmest salutations to you and yours, | Believe me
Ever faithfully
G. H. Lewes.

V, 20:25 GHL TO THOMAS ADOLPHUS TROLLOPE,
GENOA, 17 MARCH [1869]

MS: University of California Los Angeles.

Hotel del'Italie Genoa Wednesday | 17 March.

Dear Trollope

Thus far on our most unsuccessful journey have we reached, seeking warmth and sunshine everywhere and finding ⟨not⟩ little but rain and

2. Trollope wrote to William Blackwood 15 October 1868, recalling their conversation in London when Blackwood said that a novel would not suit *Maga,* but that short stories might. Accordingly he sent a story ["Plagassian"] of about 130 pp. in 3 parts; if unsuitable, it could be returned, c/o Mrs. Ternan, 32 Harrington Square, Hampstead Road. (NLS.) No contributions by T. A. Trollope appeared in *Blackwood's.*

3. Raging wind postponed their departure till 3 March.

4. Beatrice Trollope (1852–81).

5. Tennyson, "You Ask Me, Why," line 4.

mistral which your *lumbagious* friend thinks less agreeable even than British East wind! At Avignon it was frightful and after giving us both a congested liver and me a touch of sciatica, it drove us from the place before we had stayed more than one day. At Nice we waited for fine weather. Along the Corniche we had one day fine and another half day sunny but bitter. Here it has poured almost all day, and tomorrow we start for Sestri, on Friday get to Spezia, and on Saturday (E.O.W.†) we shall reach Florence by the 4.40 train; so that by 5 we may hope to bask at least in the sunshine of friendship if not of that grim impostor "sunny Italy." We propose to trespass on that friendship till Tuesday when (again E.O.W.) we wend towards Naples in the romantic belief that sunlight and warmth will be something more than mythical *there*.

Polly bids me add her kindest regards to both.

Ever yours faithfully
G. H. Lewes.

†A better Briton would say D.V. But our providence is the External Order, and we find it somewhat of the unmodifiable type!

V, 33:23 GHL TO ROBERT LYTTON, LONDON, 8 MAY 1869

MS: Lady Hermione Cobbold.

21 North Bank, 8 May 1869.

My dear Lytton

On my return from Italy two days ago I found your letter and the Jahrbücher with Meynert's paper,[6] which was very welcome as everything on that subject is just now. I know his name well, and believe I have read some previous memoir of his; but I have read so many! There are several points in this paper which seem all the more important to me that I hold similar views; but I could wish so distinguished an inquirer had not fallen into what I regard as a pitfall to so many—viz. the belief that differences in the form and size of nerve-cells have any reference whatever to differences of function.—When next you write I should be glad if you could send me the titles of other papers or works by Meynert on the anat[omy] or phys[iology] of the brain.

Had I known of your removal to Vienna[7] it would have been a strong

---

6. Theodor Hermann Meynert (1833–92).

7. Lytton was Secretary in Vienna 1869–72.

11 May 1869   449

temptation to us to come home from Inspruck that way instead of by Munich. Some day or other we shall go to Constantinople and then we shall take Vienna en route, but I cannot be away from home now for many weeks because my mother who is 82 and lives mainly in the pleasure of seeing me twice or thrice a week, must not be deprived of her comfort many weeks in succession.

Had you been in London or otherwise amenable to viva voce lecturing I should have inveighed against the prodigal waste of power on such a subject as 'Orval.'[8] Of course you would not have been convinced; for since the subject had fascinated you, you could not see its radical defects, but would have contended for your bantling, as in duty bound. I should not the less have been peremptory, and we should both have 'marvelled' at each other. But one can't *write* such lectures.

Say all kind and pretty things for me to your sweet wife and believe me
Ever faithfully yours
G. H. Lewes.

V, 35:25   GE TO JAMES HOLDEN, LONDON, 11 MAY 1869

MS: University of California Los Angeles.

The Priory, | 21. North Bank, | Regents Park.
May 11. 1869.

Dear Sir

I am very much obliged to you for the kind feeling expressed in your letter forwarded to me by Messrs. Blackwood, and for your wish to give me a token of that feeling by the gift of your poems.[9]

Very heavy domestic trouble, owing to the illness of a son who has just returned to us from Africa,[1] will prevent me for some time to come from giving more attention to the present than a grateful acceptance.

I remain, dear Sir

Yours faithfully,
M. E. Lewes.

James Holden, Esq.

8. *Orval or the Fool of Time; and Other Imitations and Paraphrases*, Chapman & Hall, 1869.
9. *Poetic Zephyrs*, privately printed, Bury, 1866.

1. For an account of Thornton Lewes just after his return see *The Letters of Henry James*, ed. Leon Edel, 2 vols., New York, 1975, I, 116–117, and Haight, *George Eliot*, 416–417.

V, 36:1 GHL TO WILLIAM BELL SCOTT, LONDON, 12 MAY [1869]

MS: Princeton. *Endorsed:* 1869.

The Priory, | 21. North Bank, | Regent Park.
12 May.

Dear Scott

It was very kind of you to send us that spirited sketch[2]—though the 'old times' remain indelible and need no souvenir. I am often in that study of yours in Edwards Street[3] where we passed the night "talking of lovely things that conquer death." If I don't find time in the hurry of our last three weeks to come and see you, I will come in the Autumn. Meanwhile we both hope to see you again.

Ever yours
G. H. Lewes.

V, 36:15 GE TO MRS. EDWARD LEWES, LONDON, [MAY 1869]

MS: Morgan Library.

My dear Susanna[4]

With my usual imperfection in such matters, I forgot the pocket of the dress. Eccola! Treat my work just as it suits you with regard to time.

Yours affectionately
Marian.

---

2. About 1840 Scott made a sketch of Leigh Hunt, Vincent Leigh Hunt (1823–52), GHL, and himself sitting before Hunt's fire at 4 Upper Cheyne Row, Chelsea. His etching of it was published in *Autobiographic Notes*, I, 130.

3. Now Varndell St., at the end of Harrington St., Hampstead Road, where GHL lived with his mother in 1838.

4. Susannah Pittock Lewes, widow of GHL's brother Edward, who died at sea in 1855, leaving her with an infant son Vivian Byam Lewes (1852–1915) and a daughter Florence.

V, 36:15   GHL TO MR. AND MRS. CHARLES LEWES, LONDON, [19 MAY 1869]

MS: Yale. *Endorsed:* 19 May 1869. *Extracts published:* v, 36–37.

The Priory Wednesday.

Dearest Children
   Your pleasant letter was very welcome, especially the intimation of the fine weather you have had. Here it has been uniformly bad. We got home on the 5th after a journey to Ravenna, Verona, Brenner Pass, Munich, Paris. Knocked up we were, and have not found London conducive to health; but there is nothing specially to complain of—only we don't seem to have had a holiday. Grandmamma is amazingly recovered.
   Normandy struck us with its English aspect as it strikes you. But Rouen we were delighted with (not having contemplated it from under an umbrella) so much so that we went back to it. At Avranches we were in your hotel, possibly your room, but the weeping mists greatly obscured the landscape and we did not much enjoy it.
   Hints about Paris seem difficult to give. Yes—here is something, when you want a good and *cheap* luncheon try one of the many Etablisements *Bouillon*—some are much better than others—but all are conducted on an excellent plan and as you won't miss the want of *elegance* for the sake of good food at a third of the ordinary price—tu m'en diras les nouvelles! *Passage Jouffroy* has a restaurant where (I'm told) good dinners and dejeuners are to be had reasonably. *Don't* dine at the *Diner Européen*—no longer good. If you go the Hotel Choiseul tell Mr. Demelette that I wrote to him from Munich to secure rooms but arriving at 5 in the morning instead of 8 at night I found he had no rooms vacant and was forced to go to the Louvre.
   A fine day should tempt you to take the *omnibus rail* to St. Cloud—dine there at the restaurant on the water at the entrance of the Park and order a *matellotte*[5] (I really don't know how to spell it!) but spell it how you will the taste is the same. About theatres I can say nothing—we did not try one of them. The *Gobelins* is well worth a visit.
   Fields of Ticknor and Fields has just been with us offering half share in a uniform edition of the Mutter's works in America—but as they will certainly be reprinted by Harpers at a very low figure, the price must be so low as not to make a half share much of a *pecuniary* benefit. He has offered 300£ for the right of printing 'Agatha' in the Atlantic Monthly and the

5. Matelote, a dish of fish, especially eel, prepared with wine and onions.

Mutter inclines to accept, only demurring to the greatness of the sum. Don't mention this to any one. He says the Spanish Gypsy grows and grows in America—Longfellow, Lowell, and the Boston set know the lyrics by heart, and are in a high state of enthusiasm.

When we were at Florence on our return the American Ambassador[6] induced us to dine with him as Mrs. Marsh is an invalid and couldn't come out; they promised that no one should be asked. Longfellow called that afternoon on them and begged hard to be invited, he wanted so much to see the Mutter, but Mrs. Marsh was inexorable, she had pledged her word. When we learnt this we were sorry and then Mrs. Marsh sent a note to Longfellow to ask him to come in the evening but he was out, and the next morning we were off for Ravenna!

I have a heap of things to do and can't stop to say more than that we both send our dearest love to you both.

Pater.

V, 38:1 GHL TO JAMES THOMAS FIELDS, LONDON, [19 MAY 1869]

MS: Historical Society of Pennsylvania.

The Priory, | 21. North Bank, | Regents Park.
Wednesday.

My dear Sir

On returning home from a most pleasant visit to Mrs. Fields I find your note. Mrs. Lewes is quite willing to let 'Agatha' be published in the A. M.[7]; and we will concoct a Letter or Prefatory Note which we will submit to you when ready.

In case you should contemplate calling this week I may as well say that on each day there is danger of our not being alone—Saturday certainly not alone. Perhaps Monday[8] would be the safest.

Ever yours truly
G. H. Lewes.

---

6. See v, 37, n. 4.

7. *Atlantic Monthly*, 24 (August 1869), 199–207. It was published without a prefatory note. See v, 36, n. 2. For GE's letter to Fields, Osgood & Co., 20 May 1869, see facsimile in each volume of GE's novels in their Library edition and V, 38.

8. "Fields called and carried off 'Agatha' (£300)." (GHL Diary, Monday, 24 May 1869.)

V, 40:7 GHL TO ROBERT LYTTON, LONDON, 25 MAY 1869

MS: Lady Hermione Cobbold.

The Priory 21 North Bank N.W. | 25 May 1869.

My dear Lytton

I should have replied at once to the long and very interesting letter you took the trouble of writing, but alas! my time has been occupied in a melancholy manner. My second son has just returned from Africa with a disease of the spinal cord, and although we are not without hopes of a recovery, since he is young and vigorous, yet under the most favorable circumstances it will be a long time before he will get about. Paget thought very seriously of the case at first; but the rapid improvement which has followed complete rest and careful treatment has given more hope. It has been a serious affliction to us to witness his pain—when the attacks come on he yells with agony. Mrs. Lewes, always of an apprehensive and easily agitated nature, is of course much tried by this; and our time is mainly devoted to amusing and watching him.

You will see from this that there is no chance of our invading you at Vienna this year; though some time or other I certainly mean my wife to get a fuller knowledge of that attractive city. I was there 30 years ago for some months, and we were both there for a few days in 1859, leaving it with the intention of speedily revisiting it! The presence of you and your wife will be an extra attraction, but you must not think us too 'sauvage' if we go to an hotel in lieu of accepting your most friendly invitation. The fact is we resist all such friendly attentions whenever it can be done without offence, and I am sure *you* won't be offended. The more we can see of you the pleasanter, but let the hedgehogs roll themselves up in their own nests!

Apropos of Meynert,[9] I should indeed be glad to see him and discuss many points with him. Respecting the functions of nerve cells however I cannot help the conviction that he is altogether on a *wrong tack*. Ever since Owjanniskow[1] and Jacubowitch[2] started the idea of motory and sensory cells, I have seen both anatomical and physiological grounds for discrediting the notion. Anatomical, because cells answering to these types are found in places where they should *not* be—e.g. in the retina or posterior

---

9. See v, 88, n. 1.

1. Filipp Ovsyannikov, *Disquisitiones microscopiae de medulla spinalis textura,* Dorpati Livororum, 1854.

2. Nicolaus Martin Jacubowitsch, See II, 470, n. 9.

cornea—and because it is very far from clear that the specified differences always relate to *nerve* cells; and finally because in the invertebrate I find the cells of the ventral ganglia of *all sizes and shapes*. But the main objection is physiological. *Functions* do not depend on nerve cells but on the organs innervated—the motor function (contraction) depends on the muscle, the secretory function on the gland, the sensory function on the ganglion. The *property* of the nerve cell is the same throughout; and although differences in form and size may, and most probably do, imply differences in the modality of this property—as a hempen twist may be a strong cable or a slight string—whenever the cell is a *nerve* cell it will have the common property of nerve cells. I have argued this point at some length both in papers read before the British Association and in the 2nd volume of the 'Physiology of Common Life' (which has been translated into German by Carus,[3] if Meynert cares to look at it). That is a very interesting fact about the frontal region of the brain losing more weight in paralysis. It is to be observed however that paralysis is almost always a sensory not a motor affection; and it is the posterior columns of the cord which usually degenerate in ataxy and paralysis. When a limb has been amputated, the post. cols. show a slight decrease in size after some years; the anterior cols. remaining unaffected.

About the olfactorius what you say is well known. By the way Schiff[4] made a curious observation on this point. He destroyed the lobe in a puppy —and found that with the absence of smell there was an entire absence of *attachment* to one person more than another. The dog would follow and play with any one quite as readily as with Schiff, who had always fed him and petted him. I remember some physiologist had a theory that the sexual instinct was wholly prompted by smell—so I suppose the reason we like some women (and men) and dislike others is that they are "in good odour." (You remember the Frenchman's surprise at finding the Bishop of Oxford[5] "in a verry bad smell"?)

My paper is run out and perhaps your patience. Kindest regards to your wife from

Yours truly
G. H. L.

3. See II, 476, n. 6.
4. See v, 21, n. 6.
5. Samuel Wilberforce (1805–73), whose sarcastic attack on the theory of evolution gave Huxley the opportunity for his brilliant defence of Darwin at Oxford in 1860.

V, 42:1 GHL TO JAMES HOLDEN, LONDON, [JUNE 1869]

MS: Yale.

The Priory, | 21. North Bank, | Regents Park.

Sir
  Mrs. Lewes answered your note immediately on our return from Italy. Her answer appears to have missed. She begs me to say that it will give her much pleasure to receive your volume of poems.

                                    Yours truly
                                    G. H. Lewes.

V, 42:1 EMILY DAVIES TO ANNA RICHARDSON[6], LONDON, 4 JUNE [1869]

MS: Girton College.

                                    June 4th.
My dear Anna
  I have been seeing Mrs. Lewes today. They are in great trouble about a son of Mr. Lewes's, who is come home from Natal with serious spinal illness. His recovery is very doubtful, and in the meantime, he is almost helpless and requires a great deal of nursing. Mr. Lewes is quite knocked down by it. Mrs. Lewes says that only people who have had some similar experience, realize what it means to have a sick person in your house, and how completely it puts an end to happiness "if we thought about that." She said humbly that as one got older one ought to be less easily excited and more able to make use of moments, and that she was better than she used to be at it.
  She talked a great deal about Italy. They seem to have been very much on your track. She has seen *now*, the frescoes at San Marco. She began talking about them before I had time to ask her, and in very much your tone. She has come to the conclusion that the Pre-Rafaelites are right, and that the time of really high, noble art, was before Rafael. She thinks his great picture of the Transfiguration detestable and went from it with delight to Fra Angelico; and to Ghirlandajo, whom she seemed to care for almost as much. It is Rafael's academical-ness that she dislikes so much; the want of

---

6. Anna Richardson, eldest daughter of Edward Richardson of Newcastle.

effort after noble Nature. On the whole, her impressions of Italy were sadder this visit than before. She thought the voices of the people harsh and that they seemed ill-tempered in their intercourse with each other, but the North she thought (partly from what she heard) more hopeful than the South. She thinks the dissolution of the monasteries right, but that the *present* monks ought not to have been expelled and that the confiscation is an example of the mean things governments, like private people, will do when they are pressed for money. She spoke with great admiration of Giotto's frescoes at Assisi, and she went besides to the little church built on the spot where St. Francis is said to have been born, and had a long talk with an old monk. "As I listened with reverence, he quite understood that I believed all he said." She saw that he watched to see whether she crossed herself with holy water and would not pain him by not doing it, so he went on to give her a little book containing a life of St. Francis.[7] She thought he seemed to have seldom had such a reverent listener and that it had been "quite a rich morning" to him. She admires the country very much and mentioned the Campagna as being to her peculiarly impressive, but she says the scenery is so different from that of England that you must tune your mind into quite a different key, to appreciate it. She has been to the English Lakes twice. Once, about 20 years ago, she staid ten days with Harriet Martineau[8] and they made a delightful excursion to Derwentwater.

I did not pay a very long visit today. As usual, she desired me to come again. Mrs. Bodichon is sure she is writing something, as she is always at work, but evidently this illness of "Thorny's" has upset her very much. She is so bound up with Mr. Lewes that if one asks how *she* is, she answers by telling one how *he* is. I don't tell you quite all that she says, because some things I fancy she might not like repeated, and she is so good in talking frankly that I feel bound to keep on the safe side....

V, 45:9   GHL TO MME EUGÈNE BODICHON, LONDON, [16 JUNE 1869]

MS: Yale.

The Priory, | 21. North Bank, | Regents Park.

Dear Barbara

By all means bring Mr. A.[9] Polly would like to see Julia W.[1] but will speak to you about it. Thornie so much worse that Paget has suggested

---

7. A copy of the *Manual of the Third Order of St. Francis*, 1855, is among GE's books at Dr. William's Library.

8. GE stayed at Ambleside 20–26 October 1852.

9. William Allingham, an old friend of Mme Bodichon.

1. Julia Wedgwood. See v, 41.

calling in Dr. Reynolds to consult with. He comes to-night. We are very miserable and it's too much for Polly.

Ever yours affectionately
G. H. L.

That Mr. Webster[2] has written to me!

V, 46:1   GE TO MRS. MARK PATTISON, LONDON, 23 JUNE 1869

MS: British Museum.

June 23. 69.

My dear Mrs. Pattison

If it were not that, in addition to our other troubles, we have a valuable [*the rest of the page torn away*] on Sunday?[3]

Always yours affectionately
M. E. Lewes.

V, 46:1   GE TO MME EUGÈNE BODICHON, LONDON, 2 JULY [1869]

MS: Berg Collection, New York Public Library.

The Priory, | North Bank, | Regents Park.
Friday July 2.

Dearest Barbara

It is difficult to say how Thornie is. He varies greatly, sometimes remaining a day or two without pain, and then having severe returns and taking more and more morphia;[4] sometimes seeming torpid and full of indescribable uneasiness, and at other times looking bright and showing his old spirits. The doctors seem to be as much in the dark as we are, but they all—Dr. Bastian, in addition to the others—concur in saying that the glandular disorder is more serious than the spinal. My chief anxiety now

---

2. An acquaintance of Mme Bodichon in Algiers.

3. This mutilated MS is a typical example of Dilke's treatment of GE's letters. Among the guests Sunday, 27 June 1869, GHL lists Mr. and Mrs. Pattison, Burton, Deutsch, Mr. Leighton, Mrs. Orr, Dr. and Mrs. Bastian, Woolner, W. G. Clark, G. Smith. "Dr. B. saw Thornie and Mrs. P. sat with him." (GHL Diary.)

4. On 28 June GHL gave Thornton "110 drops of morphia and much methylene." The next day he felt "better than he has felt since his return." But on 1 July he had a bad night with more morphia. (GHL Diary, 1869.)

is that Mr. Lewes should get into a calm and ordered way of life, such as will make the least evil for him of this long trouble. His health was so wretched last week that Paget said to him "You must go away." So Gertrude and Charlie took our places on Monday, and we went to Sevenoaks, hoping to stay the whole week. But the gloomy sky and cold wind drove us back yesterday. However, George is better, and I hope has recovered from the bodily disturbance which he needlessly brought on by taking a too large dose of podophillin[5]—if you know that important-sounding name.

I felt sure you would like to know how the boy was going on, and so I determined to overcome the obstacle of having nothing new or definite to say about him. I feel hopeful as to his ultimate recovery because he shows surprizing revivals of force and spirits.

I fear that your country pleasures are diminished by the cold winds and cloudy skies.

Always yours lovingly
Marian.

I have read Mill's Book,[6] and think the second chapter excellent; the 3d and 4th not so strong and well argued as they ought to have been coming from him.

V, 46:24 GE TO MRS. CHARLES BRAY, LONDON, [8 JULY 1869]

MS: Princeton.

The Priory, 21. North Bank, | Regents Park.
Thursday.

My dear Cara

Either on Friday or on Saturday evening, I shall be delighted to see you.[7] Friday, if you can come with equal convenience on either day; if there is any appreciable difference to you, Saturday will do well for me.

Thornie has had better medical reports, but is sadly fluctuating in his state. The prospect of recovery is very far off. This is a time of trouble, but we have alleviations that might easily be missing in this world.

We dine at six now. I shall be ready to see you any time after 7.

Ever your affectionate
Marian.

5. A resin extracted from the May apple, formerly used as a cathartic.
6. John Stuart Mill, *On the Subjection of Women,* 1869.
7. Mrs. Bray came after dinner Friday, 9 July. (GHL Diary.)

V, 46:24   GE TO MME EUGÈNE BODICHON, LONDON, 11 JULY 1869

MS: Berg Collection, New York Public Library.

The Priory, | 21. North Bank, | Regents Park.
July 11. 69.

Dearest Barbara

Mr. Lewes would delight in the vipers, but alas! he says he could not give the proper attention to them now. He thanks you for the kind thought. Dearest, don't get bitten in the heel.

On Saturday last, I received a letter from Madame Mohl saying that she was going to leave town on the following Friday, but did not like to go without asking me whether I could see her. I wrote immediately addressing to the Deanery, Westminster,[8] from which she dated her letter, and assured her that I should be very sorry not to see her, begging her, if she could, to come to me either on Tuesday or Wednesday at 4 o'clock. She did not come, and I have not heard from her. I wished very much to see her, and I cannot help being uneasy lest my letter should have missed her. She is one of the people whom I should most bitterly regret to have treated with apparent neglect. Will you try and ascertain the truth for me? I would not trouble you, but that I am ignorant of her present address.

I cannot write very cheerfully about the Boy. He gets no strength—on the contrary, appears to lose some of his reduced store, and he has frequent attacks of pain. The alternations from discomfort to ease and brightness are as frequent as ever, but his spirits, though not depressed, seem to share in the increased feebleness. But one is so utterly in the dark, that it seems irrational either to be hopeful or fearful.

I will write in answer to your ⟨other⟩ letter, on the next sheet.

Yours lovingly
M. E. L.

We think of going to St. Alban's next week, Charlie and Gertrude taking our place again.

I have just re-read your letter and see that the nest is a wren's—not formidable. I will not forget to write to you when we come back. Kind regards to Miss Edwards.

Ever thine lovingly
Marian.

---

8. Mme Mohl was visiting the Dean of Westminster, Arthur Penrhyn Stanley, and his wife Lady Augusta.

V, 50:1 GE TO MRS. FRANK RODBARD MALLESON, LONDON, [20? JULY 1869]

MS: University of Minnesota.

The Priory, | North Bank, | Regents Park.

Dear Mrs. Malleson

I feel painful doubts and difficulties about your undertaking, but I am never confident in my own opinions positive or negative on practical matters, so that I am hardly hopeful about the value any questioning of mine could have. But if you *have* half an hour to spare for a call on me I should like very much to inform myself further about the views on which the Prospectus is based.[9]

The instruction of Working Women on so high and difficult a scale seems to me unpracticable, nay, not desirable.

But I feel sure that you have weighed the matter more than I have, and that your plan includes conditions, and perhaps embraces a class, other than I had contemplated.

I am very ignorant of London life.

Ever yours faithfully
M. E. Lewes.

Mrs. F. Malleson

V, 50:19 GE TO OSCAR BROWNING, LONDON, 22 JULY 1869

MS: Nuneaton Public Library.

The Priory, | 21. North Bank, | Regents Park.
July 22. 69.

Dear Mr. Browning

We are a little more at ease now, our son being on the way towards recovery. Is it too late for me to ask you to fulfil your kind promise of sending me the Sicilian photographs?[1] If not, and if you will kindly trust me with them, you will do a valued service to

Yours always truly
M. E. Lewes.

Oscar Browning Esq.

---

9. Elizabeth Whitehead Malleson was interested in establishing the College for Working Women in Queen Square. She called on GE 23 July 1869. GE contributed £2.2 to the College annually 1872–80.

1. Browning called at the Priory Sunday, 20 June 1869. (GHL Diary.)

V, 50:19 GE TO OSCAR BROWNING, LONDON, 28 JULY 1869

MS: Yale.

The Priory, | 21. North Bank, | Regents Park.
July 28. 69.

Dear Mr. Browning

A thousand thanks! The photos have arrived safely, and shall be safely guarded, until your return from your holiday journeyings, which I hope the sun will smile on mildly. I should think it is wise of you to give up Russia. It is good to be saved from too much of that hurry which is the "Occidental" disease.

You probably know the volume of Lowell's poems[2] published a few months ago. There is a fine heroic spirit in them, especially in the Commemoration Ode[3]—and they are lighter reading than the "Hymns to the Maruts."[4]

I am interested in the Fragments you have sent me: there is a touch of originality in them.

Yours always sincerely
M. E. Lewes.

Oscar Browning Esq.

V, 51:1 MRS. CHARLES SANDERS PEIRCE TO GE, CAMBRIDGE, MASSACHUSETTS, 2 AUGUST 1869

MS: Yale. *Extracts published:* McKenzie, p. xiv.

Cambridge, Mass. August 2nd/69.

Dearest—

You will not be bored by another love-letter—a little one? It is three whole years since I wrote to you before, and you sent me such a grave, kind, precious little answer. O how wise thou art! Where didst thou learn it all?

---

2. James Russell Lowell, *Under the Willows*, Boston, 1869, now in my collection, was given to GE by its publisher, J. T. Fields. The poet's daughter Mabel Lowell called at the Priory with Mrs. Fields several times in May 1869 (GHL Diary.)

3. "Ode Recited at the Harvard Commemoration, July 21, 1865." pp. 254–275.

4. The Maruts are the storm gods of Hindu mythology, prominent in the Rig-Veda. GE was reading Max Müller's *A History of Ancient Sanscrit Literature*, 1859, which she finished 13 October 1869.

Some one sent me to-day the "Weekly American Workman," and the first thing in it was this heading [*cutting pasted on*]:

OUR STORY.
This story cost the Original English Publishers
twelve hundred and fifty dollars in gold.[5]
SILAS MARNER:
THE WEAVER OF RAVELOE.
XI.

Though it is horrid to have you so preyed upon, yet I was surprised and gratified that the "intelligent American mechanic should know enough" as he says, to select a classic for his fellow workmen to read and call it "Our Story." I read the chapter—that immortal one where that blessed Dolly took her little Aaron to see the poor robbed Silas—and it was such a sweet and unexpected breath of *thee*—that—here I am writing this note.

I meant ere now to have sent you my one small published labour, a little book called *Cooperative Housekeeping*,[6] but I have not yet found a publisher. It came out last winter as articles in the *Atlantic* under promise of Mr. Fields that if it were a success he would publish it as a book. His assistant-editor[7] assured me it was a "great success" in the magazine, but Mr. Fields found it convenient to take a different view, and so left me in the lurch. I don't suppose in itself it would interest you much, it is so revolutionary. Still I wanted you to see it, for your letter helped me so much to write it. Writing is such an intense and hateful labour to me that I need all the outside pressure I can get to enable me to finish anything, and countless times has it strengthened me. 'The only problem for us, the only hope, is to try and unite the utmost activity with the utmost resignation.'[8]

You wrote it for me, dearest, and often it has shamed me and spurred me on. Yet I wish I were as faithful as you. I might have done much by this time, and be more worthy to be your little sister. That small book was finished more than a year ago, and I have hardly touched the pen since. I am always waiting for a more convenient season. My sisters are flitting from me now, sweet things; one is going to Berlin to study the piano, another elsewhere, so that I might have long stretches of time; but the ladies here are organizing a cooperative housekeeping society, and as

---

5. For the terms of payment for *Silas Marner* see III, 383.

6. *Cooperative Housekeeping* was not published until 1884.

7. William Dean Howells (1837–1920) was assistant editor to James Thomas Fields 1866–71, when he became editor-in-chief of the *Atlantic Monthly*.

8. Quoted from GE's letter to her, 14 September 1866.

2 August 1869

I originated the idea, they look to me to function through. So study and writing must again go to the wall for an indefinite period, and I am getting very tired or very lazy or both. Such is the disorganization of the old relation of mistress and servant in this country that there are already eight towns where women are waiting only to see us get fairly started here to attempt the same thing themselves.

I wish you would come over here. The student of mankind ought to see this young, generous, reckless nation. The times are great if one can only live worthily up to them. It vexes me to think of my townspeople[9] who have met you, know you, and I do not. The Nortons, Harry James Jr—sentimentalist and transcendentalist Harry James' efforts to take you in amuse me.[1]

Darling, The Spanish Gypsy made me sad, it was so noble: the poetry was so beautiful, but must noble women always fail? Is there no sumptious flower of happiness for us? And then you made all the people in the book faithful but the Christian! Is that indeed the shallowest of all human allegiances? Nay. By Him who hung on the Cross, if I could not die with joy at the foot of it if he called me, I would choose to die now. Life else would have no value equal to the burden. The world would shrink into blackness like a scroll. And how many thousand felt and have felt the same in every age. Forgive me if I am stupid. I know the consummate artist makes characters as they are, not as he would like to have them. But when I grope after you, I can't *help* wishing I could find you.

Don't answer this, dearest. I don't require you to think of me as anything more than the evening breeze that sometimes kisses your cheek. I *love* to love you, you are so love-worthy. And once in a long time I *love* to say so to you. But I would not have it burden you with the weight of a rose leaf.

[*No signature.*]

9. Mr. and Mrs. J. T. Fields, Mr. and Mrs. Charles Eliot Norton, Grace Norton, Sara Sedgwick, and Henry James had met GE at various times.

1. James had written articles on GE in the *Atlantic*, the *Nation*, and the *North American Review*, and in letters to his family described his unfortunate call at the Priory 9 May 1869, the day after Thornton Lewes returned gravely ill from Africa. Mrs. Peirce is probably referring to James's review of *The Spanish Gypsy* in the *North American Review*, 107 (October 1868), 620–635.

V, 52:28 ANTHONY TROLLOPE TO GHL,
WALTHAM CROSS, 13 AUGUST 1869

MS: Yale. *Published: The Letters of Anthony Trollope,* ed. B.A. Booth, 1951, p. 245.

Waltham House, | Waltham Cross.
August 13. 1869.

My dear Lewes.

Your news about your boy is very bad. I can only tell you how strongly I feel for you.

I do admire Horne[2] as a poet,—that is I think highly of his Orion;—but I do not know of what nature is his prose, or how the man who wrote Orion in 1839 (or thereabouts) would write now in 1869. Nor am I specially wedded to serial articles (to use an abominable word). Readers of magazines skip them when on dry subjects. Seebohm[3] did answer with you,—but then they were very good. Bell's did not.[4] But they were very bad. If he has ought written and will send it to me I will read it;—but I will not pledge myself.

And now I have a bit of news for you of the domestic kind which will surprise you. My eldest boy Harry has gone into partnership with Chapman. I pay £10000—(of course this is private)—and he has a third of the business. I have had an immense deal of trouble in arranging it, and will tell you details when we meet. It is a fine business which has been awfully ill used by want of sufficient work and sufficient capital.

Do not let me intrude on you;—but if you are disengaged and Thornie is not too ill, I will come up to you next week some evening. My wife is away,—in Paris,—or rather goes tonight. I go with her, but return. Address Athenæum Club.

Yours always affectionately
A. T.

2. Richard Hengist Horne returned to London in July 1869 after 17 years in Australia and bombarded his old friends with articles, few of which were published. GHL apparently suggested that Trollope might take a series of them for the *St. Paul's*. For an account of *Orion* (1843) see Ann Blainey, *The Farthing Poet. A Biography of Richard Hengist Horne 1802–84,* 1968, pp. 130–140.

3. GHL published a series of 4 articles by Frederic Seebohm, (1833–1912), "The Oxford Reformers of 1498," in the *Fortnightly,* May–September 1866.

4. Robert Bell (1800–67), "Social Amusements under the Restoration," a series of 3 articles, September–October 1865 in the *Fortnightly.*

21 August [1869]

V, 54:1 EMILY DAVIES TO JANE CROW,⁵
LONDON, 21 AUGUST [1869]

MS: Girton College. *Published:* Barbara Stephen, *Emily Davies and Girton College*, 1927, pp. 182–184.

17 Cunningham Place. | August 21st.

My dear Jane

I went to see Mrs. Lewes this afternoon, and though I did not stay very long, she said a great deal. We spoke of her health, which is such that she has scarcely ever had the feeling of being really well or can work without a sense of drag, but it does not come to an illness, and she is afraid she inherits from her father, longevity. The anxiety about Mr. Lewes's son upsets her a good deal, "but one hates oneself for being perturbed." Then she remarked how easily one fell both into any little vice that belongs to us, after being disturbed in it, and spoke of the state of perturbation as entirely caused by not being sufficiently occupied with large interests. I referred to something in Felix Holt about Mr. Lyon's preoccupation which set him above small cares,⁶ and said what an enviable state it must be. She said Yes, one only knew it by contrast, by the sense of the want of it.

Somehow we got to talk of the Mill on the Floss. She said her sole purpose in writing it was to show the conflict which is going on everywhere when the younger generation with its higher culture comes into collision with the older, and in which, she said, so many young hearts make shipwreck far worse than Maggie. I asked if she had known actual people like the Dodsons, and she said "Oh, so much worse." She thought those Dodsons very nice people and that we owe much to them for keeping up the sense of respectability, which was the only religion possible to the mass of the English people. Their want of education made a theoretic or dogmatic religion impossible, and since the Reformation, an imaginative religion had not been possible. It had all been drained away. She considers that in the Mill on the Floss, everything is softened, as compared with real life. Her own experience she said was worse. It was impossible for her to write an autobiography, but she wished that somebody else could do it, it might be useful—or, that she could do it herself. She could do it better than any one else, because she could do it impartially, judging herself, and showing how wrong *she* was. She spoke of having come into

---

5. Jane Crow, a childhood friend of Emily Davies at Gatehead, Yorkshire, was Secretary of the Society for Promoting the Employment of Women, Langham Place.
6. See *Felix Holt*, ch. 4.

collision with her father and being on the brink of being turned out of his house. And she dwelt a little on how much fault there is on the side of the young in such cases, of their ignorance of life, and the narrowness of their intellectual superiority.

Then we got to talk of fiction, and she was eager to explain the difference between prosaic and poetical fiction—that what is prosaic in ordinary novels is not the presence of the realistic element, without which the tragedy cannot be given ⟨shown⟩—she herself is obliged to see and feel every minutest detail—but in the absence of anything suggesting the ideal, the higher life. She seems quite oppressed with the quantity of second rate art everywhere about. It gives her such a sense of nausea that it makes it almost impossible to her to write—"such a quantity of dialogue about everything, every hole and corner being ransacked, every possible incident seized upon," not *well* done, but done in such abundance that good art is discouraged and the higher standard works are thrust aside. She was anxious to impress upon me what she felt about the difference between prosaic and poetical work, because she thought I might disseminate it. She said in an appealing tone "Then when you talk to young people and teachers, you *will* advise against indiscriminate reading?"

She thinks she has done very little, in quantity. She cannot write what she does not care about. She has not that kind of ability. Whatever she has done, she has studied for. Before she began to write the Mill on the Floss, she had it all in her mind, and read about the Trent to make sure that the physical conditions of some English river were such as to make the inundation possible, and assured herself that the population in its neighbourhood was such as to justify her picture. It is still amazing to me, though she seemed only to feel how *little* she had done, how she has managed to get through so much work, actual hard labour, in the time. A great deal of it must have been very rapidly done.

Mrs. Lewes said a good deal besides what I have put down. She thinks people who write regularly for the Press are almost sure to be spoiled by it. There is so much dishonesty, people's work being praised because they belong to the confederacy. She spoke very strongly about the wickedness of not paying one's debts. She thinks it worse than drunkenness, not in its consequences, but in the character itself. . . .

V, 55:8 GE TO MME EUGÈNE BODICHON,
LONDON, 30 AUGUST 1869

MS: Berg Collection, New York Public Library. *Envelope:* Madame Bodichon | 5 Blandford Square. *Endorsed:* Aug. 1869.

The Priory, | 21. North Bank, | Regents Park.
August 30. 69.

Dearest Barbara

I think no one but you could be the kind donor of the beautiful flowers and the bulrushes which were addressed to Thornie the other day. I delighted in them, but Thornie seemed to be grateful for the kindness only and not for the material signs of it. He is fond of flowers in the field and on the mountains, and, you know, was a great collector of them, but he says they do not affect him agreeably in a room. Du reste, he is strangly indifferent about everything now, in contrast with his former vivacity. I tell you the truth about the flowers, because I value the time and trouble and pretty thoughts you give to such efforts for others' pleasure, far too highly to be willing that you should bestow them—if not in vain, at least with rather a different result from the one you contemplated.

Physically, Thornie has gone on suffering less and less pain, and acquiring comparatively good looks in the face. He moves himself better in the bed, but he has not quite recovered the power of standing, ⟨still less⟩ not to speak of walking. Usually he has ceased to care about conversation, unless it is with some male friend who is a rare or a new visitor. He eats fruit, and drinks milk chiefly, and seems to flourish on this diet.

I hope you are still thoroughly enjoying your country life. I am rather hungry to have a word from you that will give me some assurance of your being well and happy.

Ever your loving
Marian.

V, 60:27 GE TO MRS. JOHN CASH,
LONDON, 20 OCTOBER 1869

MS: Nuneaton Public Library.

The Priory, | 21. North Bank, | Regents Park.
October 20. 69.

My dear Mrs. Cash

This is a house of mourning. Last night our dear son died.

You will not distrust my friendship or my wish to see you another time. This time death has come between us. [*Signature cut away.*]

V, 68:19 GE TO EMILY DAVIES,
LONDON, 18 NOVEMBER 1869

MS: Girton College. *Envelope:* Miss Emily Davies | The College | Hitchin. *Postmark:* LONDON-N.W | 5 | NO 18 | 69. *Brief extract published:* Barbara Stephen, *Emily Davies and Girton College*, 1927, p. 227.

The Priory | 21 North Bank | November 18. 69.

My dear Miss Davies

Thanks for your kind remembrance of me. We have been in the quiet country, in our dear dual solitude among the autumn woods and fields, and we have returned much restored.

I am cheered by hearing that the beginning at Hitchin[7] looks so happy and promising. I care so much about individual happiness, that I think it a great thing to work for, only to make half a dozen lives rather better than they might otherwise be.

Of course you are only paying a visit to the College? I ask rather selfishly, in the hope that you will answer me some day in person, and let me feel that you are still a neighbour.

About giving our books to the College Library. We don't own our copyrights, so that our books belong to our publishers, and we are not therefore fond of giving them away, since the generosity must be exercised by our publishers and not by us. I mention this that you may understand how Mr. Lewes is only able to send three or four of his books. He would not like to ask Longmans for a copy of the History of Philosophy. I can ask Blackwood to send the cheap edition of my books and we will get Romola and the Life of Goethe from Smith & Elder.

We have told friends that we shall be glad to see them at the end of this month, and until then we are inclined to remain alone, accustoming ourselves to an undisturbed home life which has been made strange to us.[8]

Always, My dear Miss Davies

Yours most sincerely
M. E. Lewes.

7. The opening of Girton College at Hitchin, Herts., in October 1869, with five students.

8. By the illness and death of Thornton Lewes.

**V, 71:1 GE TO EMILY DAVIES,
LONDON, 7 DECEMBER 1869**

MS: Girton College. *Envelope:* Miss Davies | The College | Hitchin. *Postmark:* LONDON-N.W | 4 | DE 7 | 69; HITCHIN | DE 8 | 69.

21 North Bank | December 7. 69.

My dear Miss Davies

My friend Mrs. Nassau Senior,[9] whose name must be well known to you, is anxious to learn all about the College. She expects to be on a visit to her brother Mr. Hughes at or about Christmas and wishes to take that opportunity of calling on Mrs. Manning[10]—or on you, if you were there.

It has occurred to me that the family at the College may be dispersed by that time, so, before writing to Mrs. Senior, I think it better to trouble you with this note.

Is it of any use for Mrs. Senior to call at the College about Christmas? If you can say "Yes," I am sure you will oblige me by doing all you can to prepare a pleasant reception for her, since you are the only lady connected with the College to whom I am personally known. I have a high esteem for Mrs. Senior. She is a woman who tries to put her beliefs into action, and after having been prejudiced by others against the College, she is anxious to found her judgment on fuller knowledge.

I hope that the books were duly sent by Blackwood. We have been informed that Smith & Elder sent theirs.

You see, I imagine that you are still at the College, since you have not shone on me here.

Ever yours sincerely
M. E. Lewes.

9. See IV, 317, n. 2. Mrs. Senior was a sister of Thomas Hughes, author of *Tom Brown's School Days*.

10. Charlotte Solly Manning (1803–71), widow of James Manning, was Mistress of the College for the first term.

V, 72:19 ANTHONY TROLLOPE TO GHL, WALTHAM CROSS, 13 DECEMBER 1869

MS: Yale. *Published: The Letters of Anthony Trollope*, ed. B.A. Booth, 1951, pp. 252–253.

Waltham House, | Waltham Cross.
December 13. 1869.

My dear Lewes.

What can I do for you about cigars? If you liked that one I left with you, (which I think very mild though perhaps a little large,) I can send you a hundred of them,—strictly commercial—4d apiece. I have a large parcel of unopened cigars,—12 hundred,—of which you shall have a box on trial instead if you prefer them. They are of course 12 months younger. I think they are probably quite as good a cigar, but a little stronger. Would you like a box of each? I write as I was led to believe you were getting short of baccy.

Yours always
Anthony Trollope.

You said a word as to the impossibility of inferring God's intentions with created things, from the observed habits of the creatures. Is this not a fair mode of argument for our own guidance. We know that there have been men who think it wrong to eat flesh; but may we not argue that we are intended to eat flesh, by seeing that certain animals do so, who from their nature cannot act against the Creators intentions?

But you may have cigars without answering all this.

V, 74:15 GE TO JULIA WEDGWOOD, LONDON, 21 DECEMBER 1869

MS: Nuneaton Public Library.

21 North Bank | December 21. 69.

My dear Miss Wedgwood

It happens that for next Thursday we have made an engagement with some friends[1] in the country. I am sorry for this little perversity in things. But I hope you may not find it difficult to fix on another day when I may have the pleasure of seeing you. On Monday, Tuesday and Wednesday in next week I expect to be quite at liberty, and if you will kindly send me

1. The Richard Congreves. (GHL Diary.)

[*16 February 1870*] 471

word whether you can give me a little of your time on either of those days, I shall feel it a gain to keep the afternoon clear of other engagements. Believe me

Sincerely yours,
M. E. Lewes.

V, 75:13 GE TO MME EUGÈNE BODICHON, LONDON, [10 JANUARY 1870]

MS: Berg Collection, New York Public Library.

Monday Morning.

Dearest Barbara

Now you *are* getting morbid and remorseful! I saw nothing on your part but the most perfectly graceful behaviour—indeed I was struck with your immediate thoughtfulness on behalf of Rosetti,[2] that he should not be robbed of too much time by visitors. My own immediate feeling (knowing your old acquaintance with him) was that we should be interfering with both the artistic and friendly chat that would naturally occur between you. On all other grounds I was glad that we should all go together.

I am tormented with my teeth—a depressing condition even for brave cheerful people, and I am not queen of them. So I can hardly bear seeing anybody. I hope to be better before Thursday.[3]

Ever your loving
Marian.

V, 77:18 GE TO MME EUGÈNE BODICHON, LONDON, [16 FEBRUARY 1870]

MS: Berg Collection, New York Public Library.

The Priory, | 21. North Bank, | Regents Park.
Thursday.

Dear B.

With my usual felicity, I yesterday[4] forgot your photograph and brought away your mouchoir, which I must have been embezzling in my muff at

---

2. D. G. Rossetti and Burne-Jones lunched at the Priory, Sunday, 9 January 1870; Barbara was among the visitors in the afternoon.

3. On Thursday, 13 January 1870, GE and GHL went to Rossetti's to see his pictures; on Friday the 14th to John Tomes the dentist. (GHL Diary.)

4. GE and GHL went to Barbara's, 15 February 1870, to see her drawings. (GHL Diary.)

the very time you were hunting for it. When you come to lunch bring the photo. and help me to remember the other article.

Yours always
M. E. L.

On Saturday we go to the concert, so come on Sunday, if you can.

V, 77:18 GE TO WILLIAM MORRIS, LONDON, 17 FEBRUARY 1870

Text: Maggs Bros. Catalogue 934 (1971), item 79.

The Priory | 21 North Bank. | February 17. 70.

Dear Sir

I am delighted with your handsome present[5] and sincerely obliged to you for it.

I like a great margin to a good book—a great margin, when there is such a rivulet flowing down by it as that of the Earthly Paradise.

Yours sincerely
M. E. Lewes.

V, 86:3 GHL TO ROBERT LYTTON, BERLIN, 30 [MARCH 1870]

MS: Lady Hermione Cobbold.

British Hotel, Berlin, Wednesday 30th.

My dear Lytton

We have been here ten days almost torn to pieces by the kind people and propose transferring les restes to Vienna on the 5th where we hope for more quiet and a better hotel. This hotel is aristocratic in the worst sense. On every staircase you rub coats with an Excellency and no other excellences can you by the best efforts of imagination discover. It is dirty, ill waited, and the food indifferent. But we can't move partly because all our friends would have to be informed and partly because the Berlin hotels have a bad reputation and we might fare no better. To avoid if possible a similar mistake in choice at Vienna, I write to you to ask if you know of a quiet, good hotel,—where English and Americans are scarce would be

---

5. *The Earthly Paradise,* large paper edition, 6 vols., 1868–70, presentation copy from the publisher with autograph inscription to GE, original boards, uncut, was sold at Sotheby's, 27 June 1923, item 550, and bought by Dobell for £2.

preferred, but as we take our meals in our own rooms *that* is of less consequence than if we were liable to meet them at dinner. You may not have had any experience of Vienna hotels but if you have give us the benefit. Address poste restante, Prague (where we shall *probably* be on the 6th) unless your letter would reach us here by the morning of the 5th.[6]

One great object in coming to Vienna is to see your friend Meynert and discuss gehirnbau with him. Another is to enjoy a little repose and see what is to be seen without fatigue.

I say nothing about seeing more of Mrs. Lytton and making my wife acquainted with her—*that* you will need no mention of.

Ever yours faithfully
G. H. Lewes.

V, 92:1 GE TO LORD HOUGHTON, LONDON, 7 MAY [1870]

MS: Trinity College, Cambridge.

The Priory, | 21. North Bank, | Regents Park.
May 7.

My dear Lord Houghton

I read your kind letter only last night, on our return from a long journey which took us as far as Vienna.

We shall be very happy to accept Lady Houghton's kind invitation for the 15th.[7] I am rejoiced to hear that her health has improved.

In our rambles we saw more than one person who spoke to us about you—the Lyttons, for example, who were very good to us at Vienna.

Yours very truly
M. E. Lewes.

---

6. Lytton wrote to John Forster, 5 April 1870: "I should already have been on the road to Carlsbad, but for a letter I have received from Lewes telling me he, and Mrs. Adam Bede, will be here on the 7th. I have put off my departure for a few days in order to see them." (*MS:* Lady Hermione Cobbold.)

7. "Dined at Lord Houghton's— (Polly also). Annie Thackeray, Mrs. Procter, Mrs. St. Ives, Rossetti, Butler-Johnstone, Gaskell, Locker, Arthur Russell, Kinglake, Lecky." (GHL Diary, Sunday 15 May 1870.)

V, 92:19 GE TO MME EUGÈNE BODICHON, LONDON, [8 MAY 1870]

MS: Berg Collection, New York Public Library.

My dear Barbara

Tomorrow will be equally pleasant to us. Our hour is $\frac{1}{2}$ past six.[8]

I am a little rested this morning but not well. The voyage disturbs one's liver, and makes one half jaundiced.

Ever your
M. E. L.

V, 95:1 GHL TO [?], LONDON, 9 MAY 1870

MS: University of Minnesota.

The Priory, | 21 North Bank, | Regents Park.
9 May 1870.

Madam

In returning to England after some weeks absence I find your note requesting my autograph which I gladly send on the other page, begging you to accept the apology for its delay.

I remain, Madam

Yours truly
G. H. Lewes.

V, 95:1 GHL TO ROBERT LYTTON, LONDON, 9 MAY 1870

MS: Lady Hermione Cobbold.

The Priory, | 21. North Bank, | Regents Park.
9 May 1870.

My dear Lytton

We reached home on the night of the 6th and found your two letters with enclosures. I like the 'Arrogant'[9] very much and think it a good vanity

---

8. "Barbara dined with us." (GHL Diary, 9 May 1870.)

9. "The Last Cruise of the Arrogant; or No Compromise," finally published in *Fables in Song*, 2 vols., 1874, I, 153–160.

to send a 'specimen brick': all three are dispatched to Fields and I have good hopes of a proposition from him which will meet your views. Smith I shall see tomorrow, if possible, and sound him. It has occurred to me that Fields would not very well be able to print *all* the Fables in the Atlantic—if for no other reason than that they would occupy 20 months. Therefore when we have heard from him how many of them he is likely to want, Smith might have some of the others for the 'Cornhill.' I shall, therefore, in speaking to him, only mention your intention of leaving Piccadilly,[1] and your desire to arrange about the new volume *when ready*. By the time you come to London I hope to have both American and Smithian answers.

We stayed a whole week at Salzburg in delicious weather, and in much wished-for peace. There Mrs. Lewes finally got rid of her sore throat; but was too feeble to write to your sweet little wife (je maintiens mon dire: *little* c'est le mot!) although every day she vowed she *would* do so. She now sends 'Jubal'[2] with her affectionate regards, and reserves for the Priory or Watford all effusive expressions.

From Salzburg, after a visit to Berchtesgaden and Königsee we went to Munich and stayed there two days, only seeing our old friends the von Siebolds and Baron Schack.[3] Thence to Nürnberg, where she was too ill to enjoy the dear old place. Thence to Würtzburg where I saw Kölliker, Fick, and von Recklinghausen.[4] Thence to Heidelberg where we saw no one—to Strasburg—and finally Paris.

A heap of some 60 letters awaited me and I am toiling through them slowly. Somebody I have heard of used only to answer his letters once a fortnight on the ground that in the interim the majority answered themselves. *Mine* don't—d——n their souls!—My plan is to make literary sandwiches, namely between two tiresome or uninteresting letters to insert one which has either friendship or interest to give it flavour—(*this* letter is a slice of ham, with mustard).

Give my love to your wife and send a *bite* to Baia.[5] London looks horrible. Glad to have such good news of Karlsbad.

Ever yours affectionately
G. H. Lewes.

1. Lytton had grown dissatisfied with his old publishers Chapman and Hall, 193 Piccadilly. *Fables in Song* was published by Blackwood in Edinburgh and by Fields in Boston; none of them appeared in the *Atlantic Monthly*.
2. "The Legend of Jubal," *Macmillan's*, 22 (May 1870), 1–18. GE perhaps sent a proof or offprint.
3. Count Adolf Friedrich von Schack (1814–94), poet and literary historian, established the Schack Art Gallery at Munich.
4. Rudolf Albert Kölliker (1817–1905) and Adolf Eugen Fick (1821–1901), physiologists, and Friedrich Daniel von Rechlinghausen (1833–1910), pathologist.
5. Lytton's daughter Elizabeth Edith Lytton, Countess of Balfour (1867–1942).

Will you address the enclosed to Fürstenberg?[6]

Mrs. Lewes not content with the idleness of a message has just brought in the enclosed note.[7] Oh! les femmes! La donna e mobile come fiumo al vento![8]

V, 98:26 GHL TO MME EUGÈNE BODICHON, LONDON, [21 MAY 1870]

MS: Yale.

Saturday.

Dear Barbara

I have not a copy of Seaside Studies or you should have received one by return of post. However I wrote to Blackwood to send you one which will reach you as soon as this. You will find a great deal about Anemones in it—and more in the chapter on Parthenogenesis[9] if I remember aright.

You seem to be thoroughly enjoying your new place but say nothing of your sketching. I hope we shall see good results!

Glad you like 'Jubal.' There are divine things in it—but isn't she a divinity clothed in petticoats and flesh of an imperfect kind?

We are going to the Pattison's on Tuesday but only for three days. Polly would send her love if she knew I were writing. I send it for her.

Ever yours faithfully
G. H. L.

V, 101:3 GE TO CHARLES V. STANFORD,[1] LONDON, 29 MAY 1870

MS: Royal College of Music.

The Priory, | 21. North Bank, | Regents Park.
May 29. 70.

Mrs. G. H. Lewes (George Eliot) presents her compliments to Mr. C. V. Stanford and begs to say that she has no objection to the publication

---

6. Moritz Fürstenberg (1818–72), professor of medicine, who treated GE at Vienna.

7. Probably to Mrs. Lytton, not found.

8. The Duke's song in Verdi's *Rigoletto*, Act I.

9. *Sea-side Studies*, 1858, pp. 115–143 and 287–322.

1. Charles Villiers Stanford (1852–1924), born in Dublin, went up to Queens' College, Cambridge as a choral scholar in 1870.

of the music which he has written or may write to the songs in "The Spanish Gypsy."

V, 101:3 GE TO LADY AMBERLEY, LONDON, 2 JUNE 1870

MS: The Bertrand Russell Archives, McMaster University.

The Priory, | 21. North Bank, | Regents Park.
June 2. 70.

Dear Lady Amberley

I am very glad to have had an opportunity of reading your lecture in a more complete form than the report in the Times.[2]

Now that I have read it at length I find little of which I cannot say that I both agree and keenly sympathize with it. I am glad to see your energetic protest in the beginning against that common position—"*I* see nothing amiss in the world: *I* am very comfortable in it."

I have addressed the newspaper to Miss Octavia Hill. Her home is 14 Nottingham Place, N.W.

Mr. Spencer mentioned to us last Sunday that he was intending to go to Standish.[3]

If we were seated quietly together this morning, I should say many things which a letter could not easily convey, even if one were industrious enough to write lengthily. There are "nuances" which require the eyes and voice.

Yours always truly
M. E. Lewes.

V, 101:3 GHL TO ROBERT LYTTON, LONDON, [12 JUNE 1870]

MS: Lady Hermione Cobbold.

The Priory, | 21. North Bank, | Regents Park.
Sunday.

My dear Lytton

We must postpone our visit to Wales. I am under doctor's orders to leave London at once for the seaside. I go on Wednesday to Cromer to see

---

2. Lady Amberley read a lecture at the Stroud Institute, 25 May 1870, on "The Claims of Women," advocating suffrage, equal rights for education, professions, employment and wages, and property rights for married women. (*The Times*, 27 May 1870, p. 5e.) The Amberleys called at the Priory 15 May 1870.

3. Spencer often visited the Richard

if that will suit us, return on Sunday and take my wife there—or somewhere else—on the following Tuesday.[4]

I will duly report myself on returning from the coast and write to you as soon as I hear from Fields.

Ever yours
G. H. L.

V, 106:18 GHL TO ROBERT LYTTON, CROMER, [26 JUNE 1870]

MS: Lady Hermione Cobbold.

Albert House, Cromer | Sunday.

My dear Lytton

Feeling very disappointed at not hearing from Fields, I again wrote to him last week saying you were now in town and asking if any letter had reached. With regard to telegraphing I should counsel *not*—in the first place it wouldn't do for you to appear too anxious, in the next you cannot expect him to telegraph a full proposition to you and my letter (the last) having been addressed to the *firm* will be certain of a reply by return and you shall have it as soon as possible after I get it. If you like to telegraph merely to ask Fields to address the letter to you direct—saying that I am out of town—that might hasten the receipt of the answer by two or three days. His address is—or rather the firm—Fields Osgood and Co. | Boston U.S. | I would just say, "Please address your answer to Mr. Lewes on my affair to R. L. at —"

My advice is to *see* Smith rather than write to him. But not till after hearing from Fields.

We shall be here till the 30th and then go on to *Whitby*. Let me hear of your whereabouts as you move that I may communicate when necessary.

Our love to your wife and kisses to the children.

Ever yours affectionately
G. H. L.

Potter family at Standish House, about 14 miles from Gloucester.

4. GHL and GE left London together on Wednesday, 15 June, lunched at Norwich, and went by coach to Cromer. After staying at Tucker's Hotel overnight, they took the drawing-room floor of Miss Stephens's Albert House at 2 guineas a week. They rambled on the cliff, and sat on the pier. GHL read Trollope's *Vicar of Bullhampton*; GE read Mendelssohn's *Letters*, Taine's *De l' Intelligence*, and Morris's *Earthly Paradise* aloud. (GHL Diary, 15–19 June 1870.)

V, 106:18 GHL TO ROBERT LYTTON, HARROGATE, 5 JULY [1870]

MS: Lady Hermione Cobbold.

27 Brunswick Terrace, | Harrogate | Tuesday 5 July.

My dear Lytton

It is only your affectionate and grateful nature that could conceive a debt of thanks for the very very small efforts I have yet been able to make for you. Would they had been greater and more successful!

Macmillan was in my eye in case you should not come to terms with Smith. But the matter is so far propounded to Smith that on this ground, as well as on others, I think he ought to have the first refusal. Were I in town I would see him about it; but if Forster could do so he would be even more influential with Smith; and should Smith object to the terms (which I do not think—having an eye to Cornhill publication) then Macmillan might fairly be approached. You will understand that in no sense are you bound to make any mention of the subject to Smith. I kept you entirely out of the matter, acting as if only on my own wish to bring you both together in business relations. Still if you did not offer him the book there would be so much of an implied slight. I think you would like to have him to deal with; and moreover if he does not come to terms you have done all "that could be expected." I don't think better terms could be got—the volume being necessarily a small one and it would take 5,000 to pay, were there no publication in magazine.

I am sorry to hear of Forster's health, and the unfortunate accident. At such a time too!

Cromer did me no good, so we came here in the hopes of the bracing air (quite Bergluft) and the chalybeate water giving some strength to this much needing party. My pulse is better and my appetite begins to show more vigour, but I can't read long and writing is so entirely out of the question that I don't even write notes unless forced. Mrs. Lewes will now write to Mrs. Lytton, to whom give my love. We shall remain here some days yet.

Ever yours faithfully,
G. H. Lewes.

V, 106:18 GE TO FREDERIC WILLIAM BURTON, HARROGATE, 6 JULY 1870

MS: Yale.

27 Brunswick Terrace | Harrogate | July 6. 70.

My dear Maestro

The sight of your card with its pencilled greeting was so fresh a pleasure that it seemed for a moment like your actual presence. But it could answer no questions and soon sank into a mere reason for wishing that we had been at home to prevent any need of a pasteboard representative being sent to us.

I long to have a full assurance that your absence has been too great a gain to you for your friends at home to feel that it has been a loss to them. I heard with satisfaction that you had settled for a little in Rome, taking that as a proof of your delight in the place; but the satisfaction was somewhat checked when Mrs. Martin told me that you had had rather a sharp attack of illness. By this time, I trust, the illness seems only a dark streak in the midst of fire—giving and following brightness. It was too hard that you should be ill again, for you had been severely tried in that way before setting out, though when you came to us you always looked courageous and cheerful.

According to our present plans we shall remain in these northerly regions till the end of July, and after that we have arranged to go to our old quiet nest in Surrey. George likes the place and seems to be getting benefit from it. He collapsed sadly after our return from Germany, but Dr. Reynolds said that there was no other name for his ailments than feebleness, and that he must simply be idle and get into fresh air. The chalybeate waters are an additional chance of good here, and I think he is really prospering.

George is out walking, else he would send an affectionate welcome to you in your more accessible personal nearness. In thought you have never been very far away. All best wishes from

Yours ever affectionately
M. E. Lewes.

15 July 1870

V, 106:18 GHL TO ROBERT LYTTON, HARROGATE, 7 JULY [1870]

MS: Lady Hermione Cobbold.

27 Brunswick Terrace, | Harrogate | 7 July.

My dear Lytton

I have written to Smith by tonight's post. Had I been in town I should have said viva voce to him what you wish and so I have said it by letter and told him why I didn't mention names—only the sum. It will be a fact for his guidance; and there is nothing like a publisher for a dog in the manger.

Ever yours affectionately
G. H. L.

V, 110:1 GHL TO ROBERT LYTTON, HARROGATE, 15 JULY 1870

MS: Lady Hermione Cobbold.

Harrogate Friday July 15th 70.

My dear Lytton

I shall be truly glad to hear that you have made a satisfactory arrangement with S.[5] on all accounts. I am sure you will be pleased with him and it is of eminent importance to us authors to have a gentleman to deal with. I put on the screw to him, but he intimated that he thought the sum a large one. So it is. Yet I have good hopes.

We leave this on Monday for Whitby—(whither please address till you hear from me—post office). We only leave because our delightful lodgings are let on that day, and we shall quit with regret, for the place has been of very decided benefit to your dilapidated friend, and is moreover pleasant enough. We drink the waters and walk before breakfast. After the matutinal cigar, if I cannot seduce Polly from her beloved Theocritus,[6] I ramble among the fields, glens, or over the moors musing "on lovely things that conquer death." If I can seduce her we both ramble and talk of the said

---

5. George Smith did not publish the Fables in the *Cornhill* or as a book.

6. GHL seems to be putting it on here. There is no other reference at this time to GE's reading Theocritus, which she often noted in the 1860s. She was reading a life of Keats, *Edwin Drood*, Rossetti's *Poems*, Lockhart's *Scott*, and Milton's poems.

lovely things. To be with her is a perpetual Banquet to which that of Plato would present but a flat rival. Then we drink again and listen to some not very thrilling music in the Spa Gardens, where there are pretty children, high cheekboned women and a few swells from Leeds. But no fashion, not much costume, and above all no one who knows us! At 2 we dine copieusement, then a nap, and Polly reads to me for a couple of hours, when again we ramble, and go to the evening concert. Supper at nine, a french novel, and bed at 10 or $\frac{1}{2}$ past. 'So runs the round of life from day to day.'[6a]

I hope the sea at Whitby may be as strengthening as this bracing air. We shall not stay there long and then we go to our Farm in Surrey but shall certainly be at the Priory again in the first week of September and hope to see as much of you and 'Edith'—(to whom our love) as you can honestly spare us.

Ever yours faithfully
G. H. Lewes.

V, 111:6 MRS. EDWARD BURNE-JONES TO GE, WHITBY, 2 AUGUST [1870]

MS: Yale. *Extracts published:* Haight, *George Eliot,* p. 429.

1 East Terrace. | Tuesday. | August 2nd.

Dearest Mrs. Lewes,

Don't laugh if I say that my impulse is to address you as "Honoured Madam"—I wish you wouldn't think it ludicrous and would allow me to do so—it so exactly says what I mean. I miss your kind selves very much—and am only reconciled to your having gone by the hope that you will be the better for it. The mist has more than fulfilled your prediction, for here it is still, in spite of warmth and a ghastly effort at sunshine—indeed I'm almost used to it now, and feel quite grateful if it rises for a few minutes so far as to give me a glimpse of the red roofs beyond the river—I don't expect the church or Abbey. Do you think I shall get to *like* it?

I think much of you, and of your kindness to me during this past fortnight, and my heart smites me that I have somewhat resembled those friends who talk only of themselves to you. I thought so on Sunday evening, but would not do so embarrassing a thing as to fit on to my head a cap which I am sure your kindness did not mean for me, however I might see its suitability. Forgive me if it has been so, and reflect upon what a

---

6a. Tennyson, "Circumstance," line 9.

trap for egotism your unselfishness and tender thought for others is. The
only atonement I can make is a resolve that what you have said to me
in advice and warning shall not be lost. Give me also, please, a little credit
for bashfulness before you, and a fear of appearing inquisitive, and then
I think I need spend no more time in this looking back—the balance of
everything is that you have won my grateful affection, and I hope you
will accept it.

There was mention of books which you would lend me—Balzac, and
some milk for babes, about great things, which you mentioned. Will it be
too much to ask you to leave them for me at the Priory, that I may have
them for the fetching? I have not ventured on a line of Faust by myself,
and know well that I shall meet with no other helper and expounder of
it like you—but I think you have launched me safely into its spirit and
atmosphere, and that is a great thing with regard to a great work. I might
have been helped by some kind, prosaic friend to a literal, but comparatively dead translation, mightn't I? It is sad to think how the best things
may be regarded, as our dear Dickens says "in a *boney* light."[7]

I do hope you were neither of you quite knocked up with the long
journey—we followed you on it with our thoughts. And I trust you found
Ben[8] well and happy, with a good account of how he has spent the quiet time
your absence gave him? I suppose he will go with you into Surrey—at
least I hope so for his sake. The children are out or would join me in much
love to you both. Please not to look on this as something which must be
answered—a line from you at your leisure is what I venture to hope for.

Believe me in truth, Your loving

Georgie.

V, 111:6 GHL TO LORD AMBERLEY, LONDON, 4 AUGUST 1870

MS: The Bertrand Russell Archives, McMaster University.

The Priory, | 21. North Bank, | Regents Park.
4 August 1870.

My dear Lord

I cannot say that I shall not regret your decision if you stick to it,
since I should like to see those very suggestive papers republished. At the
same time I thoroughly sympathize with every author's disinclination to

---

7. Mr. Venus in *Our Mutual Friend*, Book I, ch. 7.

8. Ben, a bull terrier, given to GHL by his friend S. D. Williams, Jr., in 1864.

go back upon his work and 'uncrop the cask.' It is a wearisome and distasteful business—especially when fresh work ⟨falling to⟩ claims attention. (I am groaning under that task just now with the 4th edition of the Hist[ory] of Phil[osophy] thrusting itself between me and pleasanter work.) But your lordship may decide to republish, or to leave the matter as it stands, without further reference to Chapman.⁹ My arrangement with him, on your lordship's behalf, was simply that *if* you chose to republish the essays, he was to bear the expence and pay you half the profits. If you never stir a step in the matter he is under no disadvantage beyond that of not* having you among his authors. And as you *may* perhaps at some future time like to republish them, I should suggest that the matter be left precisely as it now stands. Should this suggestion not meet your views I will at once communicate your decision to Chapman and put an end to all expectation on his side.

I cannot understand Morley's cavalier disregard of the well merited honorarium.¹ If he could not afford to pay for articles he should at least have stated as much before printing them.

We envy you your purchase² in that charming district and doubt not that the two great points of health and study will be all the better, though your friends will be all the poorer for your absence from this horrible London. We have been away five months out of this year and are off again on Monday to a little Farm in Surrey where we shall rusticate till September.

Mrs. Lewes begs me to offer her kind remembrances to Lady Amberley and yourself, and I remain My dear Lord

Your lordship's faithful Servant
G. H. Lewes.

*What an omission!

9. Frederic Chapman of Chapman & Hall. But Lord Amberley's only book, *An Analysis of Religious Belief*, was published by Trübner, 1876.

1. John Morley succeeded GHL as editor of the *Fortnightly* in January 1867. Amberley contributed two more articles to the *Fortnightly*: "Can War Be Avoided?," 15 (May 1871), 614–633, and "Experiences of Spiritualism," 21 (January 1874), 82–91.

2. In 1870 the Amberleys purchased Ravenscroft, an 18th-century house with 40 acres of land at Trelleck, Monmouthshire, near the Wye. See Ronald W. Clark, *The Life of Bertrand Russell*, New York, 1976, p. 22.

V, 113:6 GHL TO ROBERT LYTTON, LIMPSFIELD, [12] AUGUST [1870]

MS: Lady Hermione Cobbold.

Park Farm, Limpsfield, Red Hill | Friday 10³ August.

My dear Lytton

How could a diplomat be so oblivious of written instructions as to send a dispatch to Harrogate after I had left that for Whitby, stayed there a fortnight, left for London, stayed there a week, and again left for Surrey? All my campaign had been laid out before you with the precision of a Moltke, executed with the same, and you went on the hypothesis that I was a Nap[oleon] III.⁴

We had been marvelling at not hearing from you and considered that the war had forced you back to Vienna. Glad we are to hear that such is not the case and that we shall see you in London, where we shall return by the beginning of September (say the 8th) at latest.

I am sorry about Smith's decision. He evidently does not see a *large* sale in the Fables, and only on the hope of a very large sale could he afford to give £500 (which sum I had named to him as what ought to be offered). Just now indeed Fables would have *no* chance; and on all accounts it is well that you keep them back.

We are here in the prettiest and peacefullest village I know in England —seven miles from the railway whistle—and unable to get The Times until the following day—which is primitive but irritating in such times as these. It seems like Sadowa⁵ over again, and all that appeal ad misericordiam of the official journal to Prague to protect France against the rapacity of invading Prussia!

I am slowly going on with the preparation of my 4th ed.⁶ glad to be at work again; and Polly is at work in her own den. We both count upon seeing you and Edith in town.

Give her our love and *bite* bambine for us.

Ever yours affectionately
G. H. Lewes.

3. Friday was 12 August 1870.
4. The Prussians under Bernhard von Moltke defeated the French commanded by Napoleon III at Wissembourg 6 August and pushed on to Châlons-sur-Marne as they began their march on Paris.
5. The Prussian army crushed the Austrians at Sadowa, 3 July 1866.
6. *History of Philosophy*, 4th ed., appeared in April 1871.

V, 113:6 GHL TO MESSRS SCRIBNER & CO., LIMPSFIELD, 21 AUGUST [1870]

MS: Yale.

21 North Bank | Regent's Park | August 21st.

Gentlemen

Mrs. Lewes begs me to thank you for the kind expressions of your letter of the 7th and to say that it is entirely out of her way to write short stories— she has no impulse in that direction.[7]

I may also add that were she so disposed the terms you offer are totally inadequate; ten times that sum would not be equivalent to the prices she is accustomed to receive.

Believe me, Gentlemen

Yours truly
G. H. Lewes.

Messrs Scribner & Co.

V, 114:1 GHL TO ADOLF AND FANNY STAHR, [LONDON], 1 SEPTEMBER 1870

Text: Aus Adolf Stahrs Nachlass, ed. Ludwig Geiger, Oldenburg, 1903, pp. 314–315.

1 September 1870.

Dear Friends

Stahr's Sturmglockenrufe[1] awoke response in the peaceful Priory, as you can well believe. The translation of Prestige should be painted in letters of gold!

This morning I read Frau Fanny's well-timed protest against the favouritism shown to French prisoners by those who wish to give their French an airing and although we do not refuse our sympathy with suffering French still on all accounts the Germans must have the first place—and

---

7. "Mr. Edward Seymour (Scribner & Co.) wrote desirous of purchasing Polly's early sheets or engaging her to write a story independently." (GHL Diary, 21 August 1870). Seymour "called to ask about Polly giving them 'advanced sheets' or writing a story. Nothing concluded." (GHL Diary, 2 September 1870. *Scribner's Magazine* was founded in 1870.)

1. "*Er muss nieder!* Sturmglockenrufe wider den Einbrecher," first published in the *National Zeitung,* 22 (30 July 1870), is quoted by Stahr in the Nachwort dated 20 September 1870 to his *Lebenserinnerungen,* Leipzig, 1870, pp. 227–228, a strident patriotic appeal for German unity against Napoleon III, the "meineidigen blutigen Macbeth auf Frankreichs Throne."

26 September 1870 487

this would be so even were my wife and I not specially bound by many a grateful thought to German friends and to the German people. It is the memory of the many kindnesses we have received at German hands, especially in dear Berlin, that prompts us to send the accompanying trifle towards the relief of German sufferers—wounded or orphans—to be applied as you will best know how to apply it, either in private aid, or to merge in public efforts. Any banker will cash the checque for you, but you must first write your name on the back. As we are certain that Frau Fanny will be active in many good works, we feel that she can best decide in what direction our small contribution can be best applied. The English subscription is already over 50000£ and goes on vigorously. But it is for French and German alike.

V, 117:24 GE TO MRS. ERNST LEOPOLD BENZON, LONDON, [26 SEPTEMBER 1870]

MS: Knox College, Galesburg, Illinois.

The Priory, | 21. North Bank, | Regents Park.
Monday.

My dear Mrs. Benzon
 I am an unfortunate person. Yesterday I was attacked with an aching in the gums, from cold or some other disturbance. It increased during the night, and now I am not well enough to dare the journey which would take me to you. Happily, I know Tunbridge Wells and many of its pretty drives and walks, so that I shall be able to imagine my husband's enjoyment in walking and driving with you.
 I shall trust to your coming to smile on me when you are once more in town. With best regards

Ever yours affectionately
M. E. Lewes.

V, 117:24 GE TO ROBERT LYTTON, LONDON, 26 SEPTEMBER 1870

MS: Lady Hermione Cobbold.

The Priory, | 21. North Bank, | Regents Park.
September 26. 70.

Dear Mr. Lytton
 The photographs are lovely, and I am grateful. But my gratitude includes some anticipation. I think Mrs. Lytton promised me the complete

group—parents as well as children. Still I should not like to be troublesome, so you must let the fulfilment of the pretty promise depend on your convenience.

I am getting more and more gloomy about the War. It seems as if every one were getting the worse for it (I mean morally worse), spectators as well as agents. In my intense dislike of vague blame, it is always a satisfaction to me when any one will speak who (like Sir Henry Bulwer)[2] is practically acquainted with affairs. If you were here I should ask you whether there is any real authority, any evidence beyond Parisian conceptions for the statement that the other neutral Powers hold back from recognition of the French Republic because they wait for England to take the initiative. I find excellent people, in talking of such matters, as free as savages from the need of any evidence for a statement which falls in with their dominant mood. Those who sympathize with the French believe what is discreditable to the Germans, and vice versa. This is to me the most pitiable weakness, and precisely that slavery of the judgment which it is one end of life-discipline to get rid of. To keep the temper also is an accomplishment which people are fast letting slip in this War discussion. Perhaps the aristocratic regions are more serious than the mid-air we are breathing. After all, one is glad that any public question should be a matter of general interest, and hot temper about them is better than the indifference of philistinism.

Mr. Lewes is going to Tunbridge Wells on this beautiful day to visit some friends[3] of ours who have a country paradise there. I was to have gone with him, but have been entered by a demon of tooth-ache and general misery, and am glad to hide myself from the world like a sick crab. This demon, of course, has written a muddled letter, and not allowed me to guide my own pen.

Mrs. Congreve sent me a note the day you were with us,[4] hoping that it would reach us in time for us to convey her thanks to you for the note you had sent to her.

2. Sir Henry Bulwer (1801–72), Robert Lytton's uncle, had long served as ambassador at Washington and most of the European capitals. He retired from the diplomatic service in 1865 and was elected to Parliament 17 November 1868.

3. GHL wrote in his Diary, 26 September 1870: "Polly too unwell to accompany me to the Benzons' at Tunbridge Wells. Perfect weather; delightful place. Benzon full of details of his visit to the wounded at Metz." The next day they drove to Penshurst to visit James Nasmyth, inventor of the steam hammer. "Much talk about War and wounded." Returning to London 28 September, GHL "Found Polly in bed, abcess in her gum! Strasburg surrendered."

4. Mr. and Mrs. Lytton lunched at the Priory 16 September 1870 and stayed till 4. (GHL Diary.)

12 December 1870

The demon allows me to feel lovingly, though not to write clearly, and much of that lovingness goes out towards Mrs. Lytton. To her other self also I am always

His affectionately
M. E. Lewes.

V, 125:18 GE TO MME EUGÉNE BODICHON, LONDON, 12 DECEMBER 1870

MS: Berg Collection, New York Public Library.

The Priory, | 21. North Bank, | Regents Park.
December 12. 70.

Dearest Barbara

Mr. Lewes's Mother died on Saturday and her funeral is to take place on Wednesday. There will be many things, of course, for him to attend to after Wednesday, so that it will be impossible for him to leave.

We should both of us have liked to go to you, and we cannot help longing to manage it, if you can still put up with us a little later on. If you had no other visitors in prospect for the next week or for Christmas week we could perhaps leave for a few days either in the one or the other. Will you let me know?

George is writing to Mr. Bullock[5] and forwarding your letter.

The weather has been indescribably oppressive, and we have both had colds. We seem to be groping about in a limbo, not in a world of the living. George has just finished the revision of his History. I am working at something[6] I want to go on with, but I could carry my pen and paper with me.

Ever thine lovingly
M. E. Lewes.

Between you and me, I am very sorry the French have not had better success.

5. William Henry Bullock (later Hall). See v, 134, n. 2.

6. "Miss Brooke," later combined with *Middlemarch*.

V, 125:18 GE TO MME EUGÈNE BODICHON, LONDON, [15 DECEMBER 1870]

MS: Berg Collection, New York Public Library.

Dearest Barbara

Unhappily I can't travel alone, being a disgrace to my sex for helplessness (or idleness). But we are longing to get to you and as soon as George's business will allow him to leave, I shall write to you and announce our coming. He hopes this will be next week.

The weather here is muggy.

Ever thine
Marian.

Thursday

V, 125:18 GHL TO MME EUGÈNE BODICHON, LONDON, [19 DECEMBER 1870]

MS: Yale.

21 North Bank | Monday.

Dear Barbara

Unless the Gods or the Lawyers interfere we shall present ourselves at the parsonage[7] tomorrow (Tuesday) about three. If not Tuesday then Wednesday. We hope to be able to stay over Christmas day, but may be called up to town suddenly, which would be odious.

We both need a holiday, but as you can give us our mornings we can do a little work, and so make the rest of the day more enjoyable because *earned*. At our age a day *lost* is a serious loss!

Ever yours faithfully
G. H. Lewes.

7. Swanmore Parsonage, Ryde, Isle of Wight, which Mme Bodichon had taken for two months.

V, 126:6 HERBERT ARTHUR LEWES TO GE, WAKKERSTROOM, 23 DECEMBER 1870

MS: Nuneaton Public Library.

Falls of the Assagai, 23 December 1870.

Dear Mutter,

Many thanks for your kind letter. I am very sorry to hear Pater has been so ill. I hope by the time this reaches England, he will be strong again.

I gave Mr. Harrison[8] Paters letter. He told me when I engaged myself to Eliza that he had nothing to give her. He has just enough to live on.

I have just sold my Farm for a new wagon complete worth £100, one span of 12 oxen, 5 cows, 2 mares and a riding horse. The bargain is not yet closed, I have not yet taken over the cattle. Albert Harrison (Mr. H. eldest son) is going to get me a place (1000 acres) close to him in Natal, not far from Newcastle. He is a wagon builder; and wants me to be close to him, so that we can help each other. He is engaged to be married, and as soon as he has his things put to rights he will get married. I would sooner live in Natal than here, there is more societie. I shall not be quite buried alive as I am here. Mr. and Mrs. Harrison are very glad I have sold the farm. I think it is done for the best.

I am going to spend Christmas with Eliza. I hope you and Pater will spend a pleasant Christmas. Eliza can play the piano, a little. I still keep up my music, I don't do much singing, because my voice has got very rough. I suppose it is from shouting to oxen, when I am wagon driving. I will let you know when I have got another farm. I don't suppose it will be very long. I have plenty to do for the next few months, riding timber etc. Jacob is still with me. I don't suppose he will ever leave me. He is so useful I could not very well do without him, he is cook, washer woman, laundress, Tailor, mason etc. all in one.

I have no news to tell except, that everybody is diamond mad. You must excuse me writing any more for I am getting sleepy, and the candle is going out. Love and kisses to Pater etc. I remain

your affectionate son
H. A. Lewes.

P. S. Still address my letters to Wakkerstroom.

8. C. I. Harrison of Coldstream, Newcastle, Natal, father of Herbert's fiancée Eliza Stevenson Harrison.